The American
Northern Theater
Army in 1776

The American Northern Theater Army in 1776

The Ruin and Reconstruction of the Continental Force

Douglas R. Cubbison

McFarland & Company, Inc., Publishers
Jefferson, North Carolina, and London

LIBRARY OF CONGRESS CATALOGUING-IN-PUBLICATION DATA

Cubbison, Douglas.
The American northern theater army in 1776 : the ruin and reconstruction of the Continental force / by Douglas R. Cubbison.
p.   cm.
Includes bibliographical references and index.

ISBN 978-0-7864-4564-6
illustrated case binding : 50# alkaline paper

1. Canadian Invasion, 1775–1776.
2. Québec (Québec) — History — Siege, 1775–1776.
3. United States. Continental Army — History.
4. United States — History — Revolution, 1775–1783 — Campaigns.
I. Title.
E231.C83   2010   973.3 — dc22   2009046698

British Library cataloguing data are available

©2010 Douglas R. Cubbison. All rights reserved

No part of this book may be reproduced or transmitted in any form or by any means, electronic or mechanical, including photocopying or recording, or by any information storage and retrieval system, without permission in writing from the publisher.

On the cover: "Cannon Exploding on the Gunboat New York off Valcour Island, October 11, 1776" by Ernie Haas (collection of the Lake Champlain Maritime Museum)

Manufactured in the United States of America

*McFarland & Company, Inc., Publishers
Box 611, Jefferson, North Carolina 28640
www.mcfarlandpub.com*

To the American soldier. Climb to glory.

"I am heartily tired of this Retreating, Ragged, Starved, lousey, thevish, pockey army in this unhealthy Country."
— Colonel Jeduthan Baldwin, Fort Ticonderoga, July 17, 1776*

*Colonel Jeduthan Baldwin, "Extracts from the Diary of Colonel Jeduthan Baldwin, Chief Engineer of the Northern Army, July 6 1776 to July 5 1777."
In Bulletin of the Fort Ticonderoga Museum *IV,* No. 6 *(January 1938),* 12.

Acknowledgments

I wish to acknowledge the assistance of Deborah DeSilvo, Heather Bischoff, Sharon Gillespie, and the other members of the Inter-Library Loan Department of the U.S. Military Academy Library, West Point, New York; and Wendy Newell and other members of the Fort Drum Library, Fort Drum, New York, who located numerous references and sources for me that would have otherwise been unobtainable. This book could not have been prepared without their generous and always uncomplaining assistance.

Katherine Ludwig, librarian, Greg Johnson, and the other members of the David Library of the American Revolution, Washington's Crossing, Pennsylvania, provided me with considerable assistance on numerous occasions, and I deeply appreciate their always friendly aid.

I wish to acknowledge the considerable assistance of my brother, the Reverend Robert Kaylor, an elder in the United Methodist Church, who generously helped by providing interpretation of the various sermons presented by American chaplains during this campaign.

My very close friend of four decades, practically my entire life, Dr. Walter L. Powell of Gettysburg, Pennsylvania, and another close friend, Christian Cameron of Toronto, Canada, both formidable historians in their own rights, shared hundreds of beers and cigars and cups of coffee with me in lengthy, detailed discussions of the campaign that I always found insightful and that greatly facilitated my comprehension and interpretation of the events of 1776.

Walt and his son, Nathaniel Powell, also assisted me with translating the letters of General Baron de Woedtke to Benjamin Franklin. The Horse Soldier Relic Shop, Gettysburg, Pennsylvania, and Walt generously provided access to Lorenzo Hagglund's original scrapbook that he maintained during his 1934 salvage of the *Royal Savage*.

Others who demand recognition include my good friend, Alan Aimone, reference librarian, U.S. Military Academy Library, who regularly assisted me throughout this entire project. In particular, Alan frequently verified sources and reviewed working portions of the manuscript for accuracy.

I significantly benefited from participating in a staff ride conducted by the leadership of the 3rd Brigade Combat Team, 10th Mountain Division, U.S. Army, to the Saratoga Campaign for three days during a snowy, cold December 2007. I ostensibly served this staff ride as facilitator and tour guide. In fact, it was I who gained considerable insights into the campaign from extended conversations with the leadership of the Brigade, entirely composed of combat veterans of the U.S. Army from recent campaigns in Afghanistan and Iraq. I deeply appreciate all of the comradeship and contributions that I received from these superlative officers and senior NCOs and thank Colonel David Haight and Lieutenant Colonel Mike Forsyth, the 3rd BCT Commanding Officer and the Executive Officer, for providing me with that great opportunity.

My very good friend Dave Austin provided his hand-built 20-foot wooden canoe and participated with me in a long weekend excursion to the Ticonderoga vicinity, to include exploring the La Chute River and portions of Lake Champlain by canoe. Another of our mutual friends, Dave Rickard, accompanied us to assist with the paddling. I appreciate these two gentlemen's companionship and contributions on this terrain reconnaissance. I am deeply appreciative of the nautical abilities, knowledge and contributions of my friend Bob Frederick, who provided and captained his ship, *Double Trouble*, for an extremely enjoyable and educational four days on Lake Champlain.

My wife, Rebecca Jordan, transcribed several of the orderly books of the Continental Army, at considerable effort. In addition to her professional assistance, the number of cups of coffee and meals that she carried to me in my office are inestimable. Without them, I would doubtless have expired of starvation and exhaustion long before this manuscript was completed.

Table of Contents

Acknowledgments	vii
Preface. *"A Desperate Rush Which Cost Too Many Brave Men"*: Assault on Quebec, December 30, 1775	1
1. *"Scarcely Anything to Support Nature"*: Invasion of Canada to December 30, 1775	5
2. *"A Mere Ghost of an Army"*: Winter Before the Lady of the Snows, January–May 1776	25
3. *"His Majesty's Deluded Subjects"*: British Arrival, May 6, 1776	81
4. *"Enough to Make Anybody's Blood Crawl"*: Failure of American Leadership at the Affair at the Cedars, May 18 to 30, 1776	92
5. *"Founded in Rashness and Executed with Timidity"*: The American Attack on Three Rivers, June 7 to 11, 1776	100
6. *"I Can Scarcely Imagine Any More Disastrous Scene"*: The Destruction and Death of an American Army, June 1776	120
7. *"General Gates Is Putting the Most Disordered Army That Ever Bore the Name into a State of Regularity and Defense"*: Reconstitution at Ticonderoga, July to October 1776	150
8. *"I Think We Shall Be Very Well Prepared for the British Army"*: Gates Establishes a Fortified Position at Ticonderoga	180
9. *"We Build a Thing Called a Gondola"*: Creation of the American Advanced Guard, Skenesboro, July to September 1776	200
10. *"The Enemys Fleet Attacked Ours with Great Fury"*: Destruction of the American Advanced Guard on Lake Champlain, October 1776	228
11. *"Our Appearance Was Indeed So Formidable"*: British Advance and Withdrawal Before Ticonderoga, October 1776	250
12. *"As Great Consequence as If They Had Been Defeated"*: The Campaign Ends; Analysis and Conclusions	267
Chapter Notes	277
Bibliography	294
Index	311

Preface

"*A Desperate Rush Which Cost Too Many Brave Men*"
Assault on Quebec, December 30, 1775

The snow began falling in the late afternoon on December 30, 1775. The flakes were thick and heavy, dense and clinging, obscuring details of the snow-shrouded landscape. The assault columns went in under their cover, in the early morning hours of New Year's Eve. Shortly the fog and night were briefly lit by brilliant red flashes of gunfire, sounds muffled by the swirling cotton balls of the snowstorm, and then the first casualties began to drift back, slowly and painfully. Ominously, among the first to return was Colonel Benedict Arnold of Connecticut, cursing through the agony of a ghastly leg wound. Then a torrent of confusion as the shattered remnants of the Cape Diamond force fled back in panic and disarray, led by Lieutenant Colonel Donald Campbell of the rebellious New York colony. They bore the crushing news that Brigadier General Richard Montgomery, desperately leading the forlorn hope of his contingent to stiffen its questionable resolve, had fallen with most of his senior staff in the first contact. Upon Montgomery's death his surviving men and officers had ignominiously fled. From Arnold's column there was a trickle of wounded, then silence. The New Year's Eve dawn slowly rose and the quiet, heavy snow continued, and not a word was received from the stalwart men that had trekked through a forlorn wilderness to reach out for the walls of Quebec. The feeble pink glow of dawn illuminated the stalwart masonry walls of the great citadel, with the flag of the English crown still proudly displayed. To the American observers it was obvious that the assault column had vanished within the confines of the city's stone walls, for they would have been loath to leave such a prize unclaimed. The American attempt to seize Quebec by storm, the last military action of the year, had failed.[1] And with that failure, the destruction of an American army, chronicled today only through a single work of fiction, began.

When I was thirteen years old, my father suggested that I might enjoy reading the historic novel *Rabble in Arms* by Kenneth Roberts over my summer vacation.[2] I was absolutely entranced and enthralled with the book, and shortly thereafter read his other novels. In the ensuing years, I am quite certain that I have read *Rabble in Arms* no fewer than ninety times. This book, quite possibly Roberts' best effort in a lengthy career of superb writing, recounted the experience of the American Northern Theater Army in the 1776 and 1777 campaigns. In the ensuing forty years, I have looked in vain for a history that adequately does credit to the accomplishments of the American Northern Theater Army in overcoming every possible obstacle, shortage and disadvantage to gain the first significant victory of the War of American Independence. Regrettably, historians have failed to produce such a volume. Finally, I have determined to produce this desperately needed history myself.

I feel compelled to note that this is intended to be what the modern U.S. Army would refer to as an operational or campaign level history of the operations performed by the American Northern Theater Army in 1776. This book is not intended to be a detailed tactical rendition of every military operation or incident that occurred throughout Canada and upper New York State in 1776. Additionally, this is also a military history. Predominantly political activities and events, such as those performed by Major General Phillip Schuyler to retain the Mohawk Valley, a stronghold of British loyalist sympathies, under American patriotic control, or his negotiations with the Iroquois Indians to maintain their neutrality, are not recounted in this history. For readers interested in these endeavors, I would refer them to the superb biographical works on Schuyler prepared by New York State Historian Don R. Gerlach. Finally, this is the story of the American Northern Theater Army, and not the British army in Canada in 1776. The British Army's efforts and accomplishments are addressed only as they impacted or affected the American army. The most important and impressive story of the British Army during this campaign, simply the organization and dispatching of a powerful British force to Canada from England and Ireland in the spring of 1776, unfortunately remains un-recounted by historians. I fear that this will bitterly disappoint my many close friends within the British living history community. However, in my estimation, the most significant story of this campaign is the tale of the American army's fortunes and misfortunes in Canada.

For, in the first six months of 1776, an American army was destroyed in Canada. One contemporary officer of the Continental Army estimated that several thousand men had simply vanished from the rolls, either dead or deserted. When the American Northern Theater Army finally stumbled ashore at Crown Point in the early days of July 1776, the army was no longer combat-effective. Thousands of men were sick with various diseases, smallpox being the most debilitating. The men who were present for duty lacked everything. They found themselves without weapons, ammunition, clothing, artillery, equipment, rations, accouterments, shoes, surgeons and medicines. No fortifications had been constructed for them to occupy; in fact, no provisions whatsoever had been made for their defense. The army lacked leadership, discipline, cohesiveness and morale. In short, it was no army, merely a military mob, a "Rabble in Arms" as British General Jonathan Burgoyne so astutely described it.

Yet, by October, that feeble vestige of a military force had been reconstructed, re-armed, re-equipped, re-organized and re-trained. It was emboldened by new leadership. When the British army and navy finally ventured south on Lake Champlain in mid–October 1776, they found a grimly determined naval advance guard that contested every foot of their movement forward, and an even more formidable main defensive complex established at Fort Ticonderoga, garrisoned by an alert, disciplined force. The British gingerly probed the American defensive complex and found it to be far too tough a nut to crack so late in the campaigning season, and withdrew. Thus the stage was set for the ultimate defeat of the British army at Saratoga the next year, in 1777, the year of the hangman.

This history relates how an American army was first destroyed in Canada, and was then reconstructed at Ticonderoga, within less than a single year. This story, although it occurred over 225 years ago, remains highly relevant today, for modern American soldiers are engaged in reconstructing armies in Iraq, Afghanistan, Somalia, and other nations throughout the globe. It is also a story that describes much of the War for American Independence, and sadly enough much of American military history. This is a story of how an inadequately trained, equipped, organized and led American army was given an impossible mission that would eventually defeat and destroy it. This American army did not simply arise like the mythological phoenix from the ashes, for it was re-established at great effort, literally underneath the very guns of the enemy, and in a desperate urgency. This is that army's story.

1

"Scarcely Anything to Support Nature"
Invasion of Canada to December 31, 1775

For nearly all of the 18th century, conflicts raged between New France, nestled in the St. Lawrence River valley, and the English colonies of New England and New York on the Atlantic coastal plain. Sometimes these conflicts burned hot, sometimes they cooled down, but they were always there. Finally they had been blown into open flames, and when the Seven Years' War was concluded, New France had become the English colony of Canada. The British crown and parliament had puzzled over what to do with the prize, a question that was finally answered by the governor of Canada, Guy Carleton, when he managed to have the Quebec Act passed in 1774.

To the American colonists, already furious over a decade's succession of poorly considered legislation, the Quebec Act when combined with the other four Intolerable Acts was the last straw, and led directly to rebellion.[1] The Quebec Act's salient points were that the Catholic religion would be permitted in Canada; the British Oath of Allegiance was replaced in Canada with a modified oath that swore loyalty to King George III but made no mention of Protestantism; French civil law was maintained in Canada; a legislative system was established in Canada that was appointed by the Crown and not through popular referendum; and the boundaries of Canada were extended so that nearly all of the western lands were now in Canada, and not in the other colonies. Suddenly, with one grandiose action, the future expansion of every other colony in North America was brought to a cessation. The uproar was immediate, and angry. Reaction in the American newspapers alone was virulent.[2]

Anti-Catholic sentiment was strong in North America at the time, in large part because of the Puritan background of the Massachusetts Colony that had been aligned against the Catholic Cavaliers of the Stuart Crown, and the Jacobite Rebellion that had occurred in 1745 and 1746. When Merchant John Jenks visited Montreal in late March 1776 he went to a Catholic Chapel on the Sabbath and observed, "We all went to the Romish Church I was much surprised to see the ignorance & superstition of the laity & the absurdities that the Priests practice."[3] November 5 annually was Guy Fawkes Day, or as it was known in New England, either "Gun Powder Treason Day" or "Pope's Night." The celebration of victory over the Jacobite Catholic Pretender was celebrated with fireworks, gun firing, bonfires, parades, broadsides, and torch-lit processions. Soldiers at Fort Crown Point in 1760 reported, "Last evening the provincials, as it was Pope Night, kept firing all over the camps. Altho all possible care was taken to detect them & suppress the fire, yet they kept a constant firing & squibbing in different parts of the incampments till bed time."[4]

Although the Quebec Act touched an emotional response with its legitimization of Roman Catholicism, it was the expansion of Canada and the curtailment of western expansion that had the greatest effect. Historian John Miller, whose 1943 *Origins of the American Revolution* remains the premier study of the outbreak of the War of American Independence, stated:

> The Quebec Act, by extending the southern boundaries of Quebec to the Ohio River, ruined the prospects of many Western land speculators. Schemes such as the Vandalia colony in which Washington, Patrick Henry, and a group of Philadelphia merchants had invested were crippled and the stock rendered worthless. Moreover, by establishing metes and bounds to the westward progress of the colonists the act indicated that the British government was resolved to stand upon the policy of the Proclamation of 1763, at least as regards the region north of the Ohio. It was Great Britain itself which now was seen to be preventing the spread of Englishmen and English liberties over the American continent, thus denying the "manifest destiny" of Americans to expand the frontiers of freedom. "The finger of God," the colonists were told, "points out a mighty Empire to your sons: the Savages of the wilderness were never expelled to make room in this, the best part of the Continent, for idolators and slaves."[5]

The colonists feared that the specter of a royally appointed legislature was their own future. Additionally, the colonists had been attacked from Canada for over a century, and greatly feared a British column marching south along the same lines that so many French raiding parties and attacking battalions had followed against their homes. The American colonies viewed the Quebec Act with nothing short of abject consternation. It was inevitable that among the first military endeavors of their rebellion they would attempt to conquer Canada, thus eliminating a grave danger to their northern flank, while at the same time removing the constraints to western expansion engendered by the Quebec Act.

In 1775 they had dispatched two columns against Canada, one commanded by an experienced English officer commissioned as a Brigadier General. Richard Montgomery of the Continental Army had led the American column that traveled the traditional invasion route of Canada, north up Lake Champlain, still north along the Richelieu River, and then ascending the St. Lawrence River. A smaller column had taken a different route that surprised the British, for it had traveled a hitherto unknown route across the mountains of Massachusetts to follow the Kennebec and Chaudiére Rivers directly to Quebec. This force was under the command of an aggressive, naturally talented Connecticut militia officer who had been commissioned Colonel, Benedict Arnold of the Continental Army. It was these combined forces that had launched the unsuccessful New Year's Assault on Quebec.

The city that on the morning of New Year's Eve stood imperious and haughty was a formidable citadel. Francis Grant, a British visitor in 1767, recalled:

> Quebec is situated on a point formed by the river St. Lawrence and the River St. Charles, running from the Northwest into the River St. Lawrence, nearly at right angles. It is surrounded by a regularly fortified wall on the landside, to the North,

with bastions etc. but no out fortifications. This wall is of a considerable height, and commands the plain immediately behind it, as far as gun shot. The town is divided into the upper and lower; the upper is considerably the most extensive and is built on the hill. The streets are very irregular, and the French buildings left standing after the siege but indifferent, and entirely in the French taste. The lower town is situated to the east, between the foot of the hill and the river, some part of it winds towards the north. It consists of one long street from end to end with seven cross streets.[6]

New Year's Day of 1776, the year before the hangman, found the American forces shattered, defeated, demoralized and disorganized in the suburbs west of Quebec. Arnold remained in command, but with a life-threatening wound in his leg he could in no ways be considered to be combat effective. His own force that he had led through the brutal wilderness path of the Kennebec River had largely been killed or captured. A few score wounded men had, like Arnold himself, safely made it out of the city. Montgomery's column, made up of considerably less sturdy material than that Arnold had forged, had been stunned and badly shaken with the demise of its commander. With the losses of the night's assault, Arnold had only seven hundred soldiers remaining under his command, and many of those were sick.[7] Any other officer would have immediately abandoned the siege of Quebec, and withdrawn to combine the army at Montreal. Arnold was made of sterner stuff, and he espoused no such plans. Dr. Isaac Senter, the American surgeon who had accompanied Arnold up the Kennebec River earlier that fall, recalled in stunned admiration:

> We were momentarily expecting them [the British] out upon us, as we concluded Arnold's division ... were all killed, captured &c. Under these circumstances we entreated Colonel Arnold for his own safety to be carried back into the country where they would not readily find him when out, but to no purpose. He would neither be removed, nor suffer a man from the Hospital to retreat. He ordered his pistols loaded, with a sword on his bed, &c. adding that he was determined to kill as many as possible if they came into the room. We were now all soldiers, even to the wounded in the beds were ordered a gun by their side. That if they did attack the Hospital to make the most vigorous defense possible.[8]

With Arnold grimly resolute, the Americans would stay, and their blockade of Quebec would continue. But as Doctor Senter recorded, "The storm still continued tremendously. The prospect was gloomy on every side. The loss of the bravest of Generals...."

On January 14, 1776 Benedict Arnold would turn 35 years of age.[9] It is doubtful that he did much celebrating, given the circumstances of this birthday in front of Quebec. Still, if any officer in the American army was resolute, it was Arnold. He was named for his great-grandfather, who had served as an early governor of the colony of Rhode Island. The Arnold family was a prominent one in Connecticut, but Arnold's father was an alcoholic and had caused the family to lose considerable respect in the community. As a teenager, Benedict Arnold served at least one brief term of service with the Connecticut Provincials, marching in 1757 for Fort William Henry on Lake George.[10]

He was apprenticed to Daniel and Joshua Lathrop, who were wealthy apothecaries and successful merchants in Norwich, Connecticut. Having completed his apprenticeship, in 1762 Arnold, with the willing assistance of the Lathrop brothers, established himself in business as a pharmacist and bookseller in New Haven, Connecticut. Arnold shortly proved himself to be an extremely astute businessman. Essentially a junior partner of the Lathrops, Arnold took for himself the business motto "for himself and for all." Arnold was a congenial businessman who stocked a popular assortment of goods. By 1764 he entered into a partnership to operate a sailing shop, and by 1765 he owned two small ships of his own. He rapidly established a successful trading business, sailing to the West Indies to obtain cheap molasses, carrying it to New England to make rum, and frequently visiting Canada and Great Britain to expand his trading ventures. Within a few years Arnold was a wealthy man, and he had restored his family name.

As with many American businessmen, British efforts to impose new commercial taxes and regulations seriously endangered his prosperity. Shortly, he became one of the leading patriots in New Haven, at one point even being arrested and fined for the fervor of his passion. When the news of the engagements at Lexington and Concord reached New Haven, Arnold marched immediately to Boston. He had, quite literally, been in the War for American Independence from the beginning.

Arnold's determination and valor in leading his small army up the Kennebec River remains one of the most compelling and incredible accomplishments in American military history. He possessed limited military knowledge, training or experience. However, there is compelling evidence that he was quite well read on military matters, and it is apparent that he was gifted with natural leadership qualities. Arnold was fiery and aggressive, and less than tactful, traits that earned him enmity from lesser men or those he crossed. He had little patience for incompetence, inactivity, complaints, or weakness. Still, Arnold worked exceptionally well with officers that he respected and admired, and he had an extremely positive relationship with such men as George Washington and Philip Schuyler. When Charles Carroll of Carrollton first met him in April 1776 in Montreal, he would record his impressions of Arnold:

> If this war continues, and Arnold should not be taken off pretty early, he will turn out a great man: he has great vivacity, perseverance, resources & intrepidity, and a cool judgment: he has truly, what was said about Marlborough, a cool head & warm heart — he is still lame, but his lameness does not prevent him from stirring about, and he may in time get the better of it entirely — what think you of a man, who with 500 beaten & dispirited troops confined a victorious garrison consisting of 1500 men & to confine them was obliged to divide his small body over a circuit of 15 miles.[11]

In short, Arnold had already proven himself to be an accomplished and skillful commander.

Given the situation that the American Army faced in front of Quebec in the winter of 1776, Arnold may well have been the only officer in the American Northern Theater Army that had the strength, will and commitment to the patriot cause to maintain the blockade of the citadel city. He was a military commander of the first magnitude, his leadership skills were unsurpassed, and he was perfectly suited for the task at hand. In Arnold, the British garrison faced a truly formidable opponent.

Following the defeat of Arnold's and Montgomery's assault upon Quebec, the American army that Arnold assumed command of was little more than a confused rabble. On paper, it consisted of the following commands:

- 1st, 2nd, 3rd and 4th New York Regiments (remains of Montgomery's force, effectively fragmented outside of Quebec), commanded by Colonel James Clinton;
- Colonel James Livingston's 1st Canadian Regiment (still forming, and of dubious reliability once it was formed);
- Brigadier General David Wooster's Provisional Connecticut Regiment (at Montreal with Brigadier General David Wooster);
- Major John Brown's Detachment (at Montreal, and because of animosity between Arnold and Brown this battalion would not accept orders from Arnold);
- Colonel Benedict Arnold's Detachment (remnants of his column, at Quebec);
- Colonel Seth Warner's New York (New Hampshire) Regiment (still being recruited and moving to Canada);
- Colonel John Fellow's Massachusetts Regiment (in two sections, still being recruited and moving to Canada);
- Lt. Colonel Jeremiah Duggan's Battalion of Canadian Rangers (still forming, and of dubious reliability in any event); and
- Captain Isaiah Wool's Artillery Company (In front of Quebec).[12]

It was a motley assemblage, and its precise strength and organization can only be guessed at.[13] Not until February are regular returns available for the army. By late January Arnold probably commanded approximately eight hundred men, consisting primarily of those New Yorkers remaining from Montgomery's column and the survivors of his own column. Brigadier General David Wooster of Connecticut commanded a detachment of similar strength in Montreal, and being senior to Arnold ostensibly commanded the American Army in Canada. However, Wooster took no active interest in events outside of Montreal.

The Americans faced a grim prospect. Even with Montgomery's and Arnold's men combined, they had not really been able to effectively besiege the city of Quebec. In fact, they lacked sufficient manpower to even successfully blockade the city. They had been able to interdict the most obvious routes of supply into the town, and were able to maintain a close watch upon the garrison's activities. But now, with the loss of Arnold's column, the Americans could do little except try to keep from freezing outside the walls of Quebec, while maintaining a presence, concealing their weakness from the British, and launching various stratagems that would accomplish little except for keeping the soldiers gainfully employed.

Even more ominous, only a single surgeon, Dr. Isaac Senter of Rhode Island, was with the army in front of Quebec. He lacked many essentials, particularly including medicine:

> Medicines are much wanted here, and I am told that Dr. Beaumont [in Montreal] has claimed a chest worth fifty pounds, which was the property of the Crown and ought to belong to Congress.... I hope you will not forget to remind the Congress of the necessity of furnishing a suitable chest for the Army that may be ordered here, a thing much neglected this campaign for our army.[14]

American accounts of the long winter's blockade before Quebec are relatively scarce, which is to be expected given the small size of the force huddled outside of the city, and the conditions in which they existed. One comprehensive diary survives from the young Musketman Caleb Haskell, a Newburyport, Massachusetts, volunteer who had marched with Arnold up the Kennebec River, only to be stricken with smallpox and thus rendered incapable of joining the New Year's Eve assault. Although Haskell found himself "weak and feeble" he re-joined the camp on New Year's Day upon hearing that the assault had been launched, only to find "almost all the company taken or killed, and the rest in great confusion."[15] A second valuable source is marked as the Orderly Book of the 3rd New York Continental Regiment, commanded by Colonel James Clinton, one of Montgomery's original column. Most likely, this is actually the Orderly Book of the combined New York Regiment, and thus is the Headquarters Orderly Book of Arnold. Dr. Senter also maintained a journal of this period, but he was clearly heavily engaged in his own arduous duties, as he was the single surgeon with the Army, and his entries were accordingly brief and irregular. Arnold maintained a regular and exhaustive correspondence.

James Knowles, another survivor of Arnold's column, wrote his "Dear Wife" on January 15, "Thank God I am in very good quarters have very good living and am very well cloathed would have you give yourself no trouble about my circumstances, I am well provided for, as to food and rainment."[16] Given the desperate circumstances that the Americans were then in, Knowles had told his wife one monstrous lie, but Knowles must be excused, for if he had told her the truth it would doubtless have shattered the poor woman's constitution. The American Army was short of everything, it was lacking officers, soldiers, weapons, ammunition, food, clothing, and in fact every vestige of military equipment. The solitary exception was their quarters, however, which were generally good as they had established themselves in the residences and buildings of the Canadian habitants, where they had large fireplaces and stockpiles of firewood to keep warm. Yet, as Caleb Haskell noted, "Most of our men fit for duty are on guard" and regular tours of duty kept most of the soldiers outside and exposed to the frigid cold temperatures, bone cutting wind, and incessant wet snow rather than warming themselves over a roaring Canadian fire.

In contrast to the American army, the British army enjoyed considerable advantages. They had established fortifications to protect them, and warm, comfortable homes and barracks to shelter in. They had more than ample supplies of provisions and medicines, and had sufficient quantities of heavy winter clothing. Hospitals were established and manned by nuns and surgeons. Quebec's magazines were bulging with cannon, gunpowder, shot and shell, military stores of all kinds. A full military chest provided necessary silver and gold, should its expenditure be called for.

But perhaps the greatest advantage that the British garrison possessed was its commanding officer, governor of Quebec and Colonel in the British Army, Guy Carleton. Carleton was 52 years old, having been born of Scotch-Irish stock in Ireland in 1724.[17] His military service had begun in 1742, when he was commissioned an Ensign at seventeen years of age. Carleton was a close personal friend of James Wolfe, and they served together in Holland. During the Seven Years' War Carleton had gained considerable military experience. He served with his friend Wolfe at the Siege of Quebec in 1759, and was wounded commanding the 2nd Battalion of the 60th Foot on the left flank of the British battle line at the Plains of Abraham. An indication of the esteem that Wolfe and

Carleton had for each other is that Wolfe left his professional library to Carleton in his will.[18] Carleton was seriously wounded in an amphibious assault on the shores of France in 1761, and was again wounded at the Siege of Havana, Cuba, in 1762.

Carleton was appointed lieutenant governor and administrator of Quebec in 1766, and he had spent almost ten years administering the colony of Canada for King George III before the War for American Independence broke out. He was fanatically loyal to the English Crown. The Quebec Act was his brainchild, and he knew Canada, its weather, its geography, its commerce, and its inhabitants intimately. He was a skilled and experienced military officer.

Governor Carleton had no intention of launching a sortie beyond the stalwart ramparts of Quebec. He had weathered numerous St. Lawrence winters as governor, and he well knew the power of the biting cold and drifting snow. He would not endanger his soldiers by exposing them to the elements. Quebec had cannon, plenty of ammunition, ample quantities of food, and warm dwelling places. If the Americans wanted to freeze and starve outside of the city, they were more than welcome to do so. Carleton would let the elements of the frosty Canadian winter take their toll on the Americans, while he planned for a movement upon them in the spring. Carleton's only shortfall was firewood, and he was compelled to launch regular raids outside of the walls of the citadel to secure additional supplies of wood.

Carleton's garrison was also relatively small, although considerably larger than Arnold's force. On November 14, 1775, the garrison's strength was recorded as:

British Militia	300
Canadian Militia	480
Colonel McLean had arrived from above on the 12th, with Royal Fusileers and Emigrants	200
Seamen on shore	24
Artificers from Newfoundland	32
Colonel McLean's recruits, from Newfoundland and St. John's Island, by Captains Campbell and Fraser	90
Total	1,126[19]

This garrison would later be strengthened with 37 Royal Marines, 271 Royal Navy sailors, and 74 civilian sailors from ships that were retained at Quebec over the winter. There were also a handful of Royal Artillery gunners. Of the garrison, Colonel McLean's detachment was loyal, dependable and experienced, as many men had been discharged and provided with land grants following years of service in the British Army during the Seven Years' War. The British seamen and marines were well drilled and superbly disciplined, and they provided excellent service as impromptu infantrymen and gunners throughout the winter. These two detachments were the core of Carleton's garrison. The British Militia was considered to be reliable and loyal, if relatively untrained.[20] The Canadian militia's resolution was considered to be suspect, the officers and men were quite poorly trained, and the British generally looked down upon them.[21] Eventually, Carleton would have approximately 1,500 men at his disposal throughout the winter. This may have seemed like a large force, but only a portion of it was both trained and reliable, and it had to defend a large city with several miles of walls.

Major Henry Caldwell, who had served as Assistant Quarter Master General under British General James Wolfe in 1759, was active with the British garrison, and recalled of the strength of the citadel of Quebec:

> We were not idle ... we got the merlons and embrasures repaired, platforms laid, guns mounted, the picketing at Cape Diamond and behind the Hotel Dieu repaired, barriers were made between the upper and lower town, and at the extremities of the lower town ... these posts were strengthened with cannon.

Caldwell went on to remark:

> We made ourselves very strong ... in every accessible place. We kept the ditches clear of snow, every man without distinction taking a shovel on that occasion, we got at length about 140 pieces of cannon mounted in different parts about the town, we had not originally above 30 carriages made from the King's ships, and the carriages made during the winter, the rest were completed ... plenty of provisions in the garrison, and everybody in good spirits.[22]

Captain Thomas Jones, Commander, No. 3 Company, 4th Battalion of the Royal Artillery recorded in his journal that he mounted a large number of artillery pieces on a regular basis throughout the entire siege.[23] All in all, the Canadian lady of the snows had a thinly stretched, but extremely well disciplined, determined and formidable garrison that had successfully repulsed the American forces already. Their morale was high, and both officers and men were supremely confident in their commander, and in themselves.

This small garrison had nobody to dispatch correspondence to, for the Americans had blockaded the lines of communication out of the city, and the St. Lawrence River was frozen solid. As a result no letters survive from the garrison until after the end of the blockade in May. A number of journals exist, which collectively provide a fine impression of the garrison's activities, which were principally standing guard duties in case the Americans were so foolish as to launch another attack, and dispatching regular forays after firewood when the weather permitted.

The winter's activities were monotonous. Both British and American soldiers were more concerned with avoiding freezing to death than they were with offensive actions. But it was in this frigid winter that the seeds of the ensuing destruction of an American army were planted, and without comprehending the winter conditions that the soldiers labored under, an understanding of precisely how an army disintegrated cannot be achieved.

New Year's Eve was a sad day in the American camp. Once the trickle of wounded, including Arnold, that had emerged from the city had been treated, it was a waiting game, hoping first for victory to be achieved behind the stone walls of the citadel, then praying that Arnold's column would return. By midmorning, all of those hopes had been dashed.

Almost immediately thereafter, remarkable in that he had been severely wounded in the leg and had lost considerable blood, Arnold wrote the senior American general then serving in Canada, Brigadier General David Wooster, advising him of the defeat. Arnold followed up this brief initial letter with a more detailed letter on January 2, pleading with Wooster:

for God's sake order as many men down as you can possibly spare consistent with the safety of Montreal, and all the Mortars, Howitzers and Shells that you can possibly bring. I am in such excessive pain from my wound as the bones of my leg are effected.[24]

Given a defeat of such monumental proportions, any mildly aggressive, professional military officer possessed of even marginal leadership qualities would be expected to immediately move forward to Quebec to take charge of the shattered army and reconstruct the morale and organization of American forces. This was particularly true as the only location in the province of Canada where there were still any British soldiers or opposition was Quebec. Governor Carleton was also ensconced in Quebec, and the center of the struggle in the Northern Theater was clearly to be found at that post. General Wooster, however, was comprised of different qualities. Wooster, inexplicably, remained rooted in Montreal. He would not move to Quebec until early in April.

Continental Army Brigadier General David Wooster had been born in 1710 in Derby, Connecticut. He had served as a Captain in the predominantly Massachusetts expedition to Louisburg, Nova Scotia, in 1745, and had served as a Colonel commanding a regiment of Connecticut Provincials during the Seven Years' War. Wooster possessed considerable military experience, but his finest years were now far behind him. At sixty-six years of age Wooster cherished his comforts, was not particularly active, and he had numerous other faults that would substantially harm the efforts of the independent colonies in Canada. Wooster had at first proven to be a less than a fervent supporter of the cause of liberty. Employed by the British government as the customs commissioner for the port of New Haven, Connecticut, he had in fact prosecuted Arnold for early patriotic activity in 1766. On the morning of April 21, 1775, upon the arrival of the news of Lexington and Concord at New Haven, Arnold had determined to lead a group of Connecticut Militia immediately to Boston. When the militiamen attempted to obtain badly needed gunpowder from the magazine in New Haven, Wooster refused to unlock the doors and issue it, until Arnold and the strength of patriotic fervor in the community forced him to yield.[25] Once Wooster perceived what direction the wind was blowing, he transformed into an ardent patriot.

Wooster's selection for an independent command in Canada was a poor one. Vigor and energy were needed for the command along the St. Lawrence River, and the elderly Wooster possessed neither of these virtues. Additionally, tact and circumspection were necessary for negotiations and consensus with the Canadian inhabitants, and Wooster also lacked these virtues. Historians have intimated that Wooster was overweight, and overly fond of various popular beverages that prominently included rum as their principal ingredient.[26] Whether or not these allegations were true, Wooster was not a particularly effective commander. Wooster's first communication to Major General Philip Schuyler, the American Northern Theater Commander, following the defeat on January 5 reveals Wooster's resolve (or lack thereof): "I shall not be able to spare any men to reinforce Colonel Arnold. This place must be secured for a retreat."[27] Continental Army Commander General George Washington observed discreetly of him, "General Wooster, I am informed, is not of such activity as to press through difficulties."[28] When a congressional delegation arrived in Canada in April 1776 to inspect the situation there, they reported back to Congress that "General Wooster is, in our opinion, unfit, totally unfit, to command your army, and conduct the war. We have hitherto prevailed on him to remain in Montreal. His stay in this Colony is unnecessary, and even prejudicial to our affairs. We would therefore humbly advise his recall."[29]

Whether Wooster drank to excess or not, what is known is that he, like many New Englanders, was strongly anti–Catholic. He was also short-tempered, irritable, and slightly paranoid. A full rendition of Wooster's errors in judgment at Montreal this winter would require a monograph in their own right. Suffice to say that he arrested priests and merchants, took the unprecedented action of closing Catholic chapels, confiscated personal weapons, and antagonized nearly every citizen that he came into contact with.[30] In an interview with leading civil leaders of Montreal he stated, "I regard the whole of you as enemies and rascals," as recorded by one of the citizens in his journal.[31] He held the habitants in little regard, writing of them, "They are not to be depended upon, but like the savages are extremely fond of choosing the strongest part, and add to this, the enemies in the country, of which there are many."[32] In a letter dated April 23, Wooster demonstrated his paranoia: "Almost every day discovers new traitors even in our bosoms who endeavor to frustrate all our designs."[33] At this critical juncture, American success depended upon support from the people of the colony of Quebec for a wide and important range of services. The American Army needed the Canadians to provide provisions, to accept their currency and provide credit, to nurse the sick and wounded back to health, to enlist in their army, and to guide their marching columns across the Canadian roads and swamps. Wooster's actions ensured that none of this support would be proffered to the American army. Charles Carroll of Carrollton neatly summarized Wooster's performance in a private letter to his father written in late May, 1776:

> General Wooster has been the ruin of our affairs in this country: he is now shamefully flying out of it: I wish he was gone. One Nicholson, who lived in Annapolis, Mr. Deards knows him, was made Town Major by Wooster. This low life scoundrel had done nothing but pillage & commit outrages on the inhabitants of this city during the whole winter.... Everything here is confusion for want of management & proper departments.[34]

Arnold was flat on his back and in severe pain with his wound when he mustered enough strength to write to Wooster on January 2. In this missive Arnold advised Wooster of what would become two of the greatest challenges that the American army would face in Canada, those of proper funding and adequate food. "We are short of cash not more than 4 or 500 pounds and only twenty Barrels of salt pork. If any cash can be spared from Montreal I think best to bring it down and all the Butter."[35] The shortage of hard cash should not in itself have been surprising. The North American colonies were always limited in their stocks of hard money of copper, silver or gold, then referred to as specie. The traditional colonial approach to the problem was to print paper money as legal tender, which would then be paid off at a future date. It was a system that had been used at one time or another by every colony, and it had worked relatively well, so long as the issue and management of the paper currency was closely monitored and controlled.[36] Recognizing that they would have to send their army into Canada without a sufficient war chest of silver and gold, the Continental Congress had clearly been hopeful that they could induce the Canadian citizens and merchants to accept Continental paper currency.

Unfortunately for their carefully laid plans, the Canadians had a long, and most unpleasant, experience with paper money.

While Canada had been New France, there had also been shortages of hard species. As a fledgling colony, New France typically imported more than it exported, such that silver and gold coin tended to flow back to France, instead of remaining in Canada. Cash shipments from France were few and far between. As a result, in 1685 paper money was officially issued for the first time in New France, and was intermittently used thereafter. On several occasions, playing cards that were stamped and countersigned were actually pressed into service, for even paper was short in the colony. The king, when he discovered this use of such an impromptu paper money, expressed his "strong disapproval." The card money served to generate inflation, and the paper currency was generally viewed without trust. During the Seven Years' War the problem became epidemic, and at the end of the war the playing card money was no longer accepted as currency, and had become valueless.[37] Those French Canadian habitants that remembered the playing card money fiasco had been burned once by paper currency, and they did not intend to be fooled a second time. A letter published in the October 5, 1775, *Quebec Gazette* revealed the Canadian's concern with American paper money: "They will pay you with notes, which they call Province Bills, or Bills of Credit, what will you do with such money? Nothing." If the Americans wanted to buy something, the French Canadian habitants were more than willing to sell. As a British investigation in the summer of 1776 revealed, the habitants of Cap Santé Parish "willingly delivered provisions to the rebels camp as long as they were paid in money."[38] But the habitants were not interested in any of that paper nonsense. The habitants dealt only for copper, silver or gold.

Interestingly enough, although British Army counterfeiting of Continental paper currency was rampant during the War for American Independence, there is no evidence that the British in Quebec made any effort to counterfeit the American money during the 1776 campaign. Possibly, the bills were too new, and the British had not obtained sufficient examples this early in the war for them to launch a counterfeiting effort. Additionally, there was extremely limited communications between the British and American armies at Quebec in the winter of 1775 and 1776. Thus, there were few opportunities for the British to have first obtained examples of the paper money, and then passed counterfeited currency into circulation even if they had manufactured any.[39]

The Canadians had also had a bad experience with credit. In any economy where there is a shortage of specie, credit has to be employed. But the Seven Years' War had caused rampant inflation in New France, and the inevitable result was a loss of trust in credit, for it could not keep pace with inflation. Exacerbating the problem was that when the French king's debt to Canada was paid off following the Seven Years' War, many notes were reduced to half or a quarter of their face value. The result was all too frequently bankruptcy on the part of merchants and other businessmen.[40] The habitants mistrusted paper money, but they distrusted credit even more, and the Americans were hard pressed to make purchases based on the good faith and confidence of the Continental Congress. When the opportunity presented itself, the American Army borrowed tens of thousands of pounds in credit from the Canadians, until there was no longer any good faith and confidence remaining in the Continental Congress.

Paper money was certainly unpopular in Canada, as merchant John Jenks discovered when he tried to make a purchase near Isle Aux Noix in mid–March: "Bought a loaf of bread at a house that we stopped ... at, where paper money was refused as payment until they saw that we would not pay any thing if they did not take that."[41] Simeon Bloodgood, carrying supplies by sleigh to the Continental Army, had a similar experience in Montreal, at about the same time: "Our Continental Money required a good deal of gesticulation to make it go. It was not much relished by our Canadian friends, at its par value."[42] Merchant John Blake of Albany complained to the Albany Committee of Correspondence in June 1776 that "he owed money in Canada where nothing passed but hard money."[43] In response to the desperate shortage of specie in Canada, various governments in the colonies attempted to encourage contributions of silver and gold to support the war effort to the north. Two of these early specie drives of the War of American Independence are documented, both occurring in Massachusetts.

> Massachusetts House of Representatives, February 14, 1776
>
> Whereas the Honorable the Continental Congress have desired this court to make application to the several towns in this colony to know what quantity of silver and gold can be procured in exchange for the Continental bills, as that sort of money is greatly wanted to support that part of the Army gone against Quebec. Resolved that the persons hereafter named in each county of the colony, be a committee to make inquiry what money in silver and gold can be procured in exchange for Continental bills, and the same Committee are required to obtain subscriptions in their several counties, of all persons that are willing in this time of danger and distress to exchange hard money for said bills.
>
> [Committee members are listed by name for each county]
>
> Massachusetts House of Representatives, June 26, 1776
>
> Whereas repeated applications have been made by the Honorable Congress to this court, to procure a sum of hard money to be forthwith sent into Canada for the support of our Army in that quarter, and have sent us Continental bills to be exchanged for said hard money, but this court have not been able, as yet, to procure more than 2,000 pounds of the 30,000 required by Congress, and whereas it appears to this court necessary to carry on the Canada expedition with success, that our Army in that quarter be supplied with hard money without delay, it is therefore resolved, that it be and hereby is recommended to the Friends of America in the several towns in this Colony, that they sign subscription papers purporting what sum in hard money each man is willing to exchange for Continental bills, and the Committees of Correspondence in the several towns are hereby further called upon to procure subscriptions as aforesaid.[44]

Given the fact that the colonies were engaged in open warfare, and that valuable metals and hard cash tend to be hoarded in times of conflict, it is unlikely that these efforts met with much success. The need for a second specie raising effort in Massachusetts, only four months after the first endeavor, tends to support this premise. Still, apparently some quantity of specie was successfully obtained. The Continental Congress resolved on December 30, 1775:

> *Ordered,* That the Delegates of Pennsylvania do immediately count the Silver and Gold in the Treasury, and forward the same with all convenient speed, under a guard of five men, to General Schuyler, and that the persons to be sent by the above Committee accompany said guard; and
>
> *Resolved,* That the Treasurers be empowered to employ a Broker to collect Gold and Silver, in exchange for Continental Bills of Credit.[45]

The American Northern Theater Commander that this money was destined for was 42-year-old Major General Philip Schuyler.[46] He had been born in Albany, New York, into the distinguished Schuyler family of the Hudson River Valley, which had been among the earliest settlers, and owned impressive quantities of land along the Hudson River. The family was politically active, socially prominent, and wealthy. The family also owned a large mansion in Albany, and a substantial undeveloped estate in Saratoga (now Schuylerville), 35 miles north of Albany. As a youth, Schuyler learned to speak French and Mohawk, and was a gifted mathematician. Schuyler was tall and slender, and prone to attacks of rheumatic gout that caused him considerable problems throughout his entire life. Schuyler was married to Catherine Van Rensselaer during the Seven Years' War. The bride was the daughter of Colonel Johannes Van Rensselaer, patroon of another prominent Hudson River family. This marriage linked two of New York's great landholding entities.

Schuyler had served with distinction as a provincial officer during the Seven Years' War. He had raised a company of New York Provincials at the age of twenty, and fought with William Johnson against the French at Lake George in September 1755. He served in the campaign of 1756 with Colonel John Bradstreet, carrying supplies to the threatened Fort Oswego on Lake Ontario. Here he gained his first experience with bateaux transportation and military logistics. Schuyler returned to military life in 1758 as Deputy Commissary to General James Abercromby in his ill-fated attempt on Fort Carillon at Ticonderoga. Schuyler continued to serve under Bradstreet as Commissary to Bradstreet's capture of Fort Frontenac later in the summer of 1758. In the Campaign of 1759 Schuyler again served as Deputy Commissary to British General Jeffery Amherst, who successfully seized Fort Carillon this time. Schuyler thus had considerable and extensive experience with military logistics and transportation, experience that no other American officer possessed.

In 1761 through 1762 Schuyler had constructed his own prominent brick Georgian style mansion immediately south of Albany, and he worked to develop his estate at Saratoga into a financial success. In short order, he became one of the most prominent and wealthy landowners in the upper Hudson Valley. He served as a delegate from the colony of New York to the Second Continental Congress, and was appointed one of three Major Generals of the Continental Army on June 19, 1775.

Schuyler was an excellent selection for Commander of the American Northern Theater, and he performed in this capacity for over two years with skill and aplomb. His previous experience with military logistics and transportation over this very route for the British Army would prove invaluable. He knew the terrain from years of habitation and travel. Schuyler, as a prominent businessman and member of the community, had numerous business and commercial contacts throughout the colony of New York. Schuyler operated a number of sailing vessels on the Hudson River, so he also had relations with the nautical and shipbuilding community. He had a large personal fortune, and possessed considerable credit should it prove necessary. He understood the world of banking and finances. Schuyler operated a sawmill on his estate at Saratoga, and had supervised every detail of the construction of two homes (his Albany mansion and a large summer estate at Saratoga), so that he had architectural and building materials knowledge. Schuyler also had considerable management experience, as he administered his large estate located at various points throughout the Hudson Valley. He had a reputation as a reliable, honorable, courteous man in all of his dealings, albeit having a somewhat aloof personality. Schuyler had a solid reputation as a deeply committed, passionate patriot. Among his closest friends was George Washington, a man well known to be an exemplary judge of character.

Schuyler's sole fault was his sometimes distant and cool personality. Contemporaries, particularly egalitarian-minded New Englanders, accused him of being both haughty and aristocratic. Most likely, this antipathy was more a result of Schuyler's partisan efforts on behalf of New York colony in boundary disputes with Massachusetts and New Hampshire in the pre-war years. He was extremely well regarded in New York, as a young man, Simeon DeWitt Bloodgood, would later record, "We looked up to him with a feeling of respect and affection. His popularity was unbounded, his views upon all subjects were considered sound, and his anticipations almost prophetic."[47]

Schuyler, serving as what the modern US armed forces would refer to as a theater commander, has been criticized by historians for not assuming direct command of the American Army in Canada. But as a theater commander, Schuyler was not only concerned with the American Army in Canada. Schuyler was also charged with conducting negotiations with Native Americans, particularly the Iroquois Confederation of western New York State; maintaining the security of the Mohawk Valley which had strong loyalist tendencies as the result of the influence of the recently deceased Sir William Johnson; and obtaining necessary supplies and transportation from the Hudson River region for not only the American Army in Canada, but also the main American Continental Army in first Boston and then New York City. Under Schuyler's leadership, he gathered a considerable quantity of artillery pieces at Forts Crown Point and Ticonderoga; and then provided American Artillery Commander Henry Knox with the necessary transportation and draft animals to move this impressive train of artillery from the forts to Boston. This artillery train would comprise the core of the Continental Army's artillery corps throughout the American Revolution, and result in the expulsion of the British Army from Boston in March 1776. Schuyler had considerable responsibilities. Without Schuyler's considerable and exhaustive efforts, New York colony would have faced an early Native American uprising, would have been endangered by strong Loyalist sympathies in the Mohawk Valley, the main Continental Army of Washington would have been short of both artillery and provisions, and the American Army in Canada would have starved and dissolved.

Schuyler was also sensitive to the need to maintain positive relationships with the Canadian habitants, and stressed to commanders that they were to have their soldiers respect the local civilians who would have to be depended upon for provisions, information, and other support in Canada. An example is provided in a letter written from Schuyler to Lt. Colonel Israel Shreve of Maxwell's New Jersey Regiment on April 5, 1776. During that regiment's movement north to Canada, Schuyler counseled, "Be particularly careful that no depredations on the inhabitants are committed by the troops under your command on their march, as such practices will be punished with unremitting severity."[48] Unfortunately, not all of the American officers were as adroit as Schuyler was to the need to keep the Canadians as friends. Wooster certainly was not.

The soldier chosen to carry the desperately needed specie to General Schuyler was a 23-year-old Pennsylvania legal student recently commissioned as a Captain in the Continental Army, Alexander Graydon. It was his first military assignment. Accompanied by another young Ensign, Graydon noted that they carried the money on a chair, "that being thought the most convenient mode of carrying the money, which was enclosed in two or three sealed bags. One soldier mounted and armed in addition, constituted the escort." Graydon noted, "We did not like the responsibility of our charge. It is obvious that it might have been wrested from us, without great difficulty, even though each one of the triumvirate had possessed the bravery of Caesar." At Albany Graydon and his two companions encountered Colonel Rudolphus Ritzema, a New York Colonel who had accompanied General Montgomery in the invasion of Canada, and had been stationed in Montreal during the New Year's Eve assault on Quebec. Wooster had dispatched Ritzema on January 29 to consult with General Schuyler "about the best Means to be put in practice for a speedy reduction of Quebec and for establishing the York battalions on a permanent footing."[49] Colonel Ritzema did not exactly exude a spirit of optimism and devotion to the cause. Graydon remembered, "He had just returned from Canada, and drew a most lamentable picture of our affairs in that country, explaining to the young officers, '...in short, gentlemen, we have commissaries there without provisions, quarter masters without stores, generals without troops, and troops without discipline, by God.'"

At length, as Graydon noted "after a journey of three hundred and thirty miles" he located General Schuyler "on the border of the Lake" [at Fort George on the southern end of Lake George] and delivered the bags of silver and gold safely to him. Graydon noted that

> though General Schuyler has been charged with such haughtiness of demeanor as to have inducted the troops of New England to decline serving under his command, the reception we met with was not merely courteous but kind ... we experienced civilities that were flattering from an officer of his high rank.[50]

The hard money was certainly a welcome addition to Schuyler's sadly depleted war chest, but two or three bags of gold and silver were unlikely to make a significant alteration to the situation in Canada. In fact, the Continental Army in Canada was always short of specie, and that in turn meant that they were always short of provisions, clothing, and most importantly, the good will of the Canadian habitants and merchants. One impact of the chronic shortage of specie was that the ability of the American army to purchase provisions within Canada was seriously curtailed. It seemed that the suspicious habitants were unwilling to part with valuable food for paper of highly questionable provenance, and that in fact had had its value as good paper depreciated by smearing ink all over it. Once their supplies of silver and gold were drained, the American Army's stockpiles of rations also ran short.

To comprehensively examine the topic of provisions, the first question that must be resolved is what the daily ration of the army was supposed to be. In military terms, one ration was defined as one day's food for one soldier. The American Army ration, in turn, was very closely based upon the British Army ration of the timeframe. There are a number of period military manuals that clearly articulate the standard British Army ration. Williamson's 1782 *Treatise on Military Finance* stated:

> The complete ration in every specie is, of flour or bread 1½ lb. [;] beef 1 lb. [;] or pork ½ lb. [;] pease [peas] ¼ pint [;] butter or cheese 1 oz. [;] rice 1 oz. But when the small species are not issued, 1½ lb. of bread or flour, and 1½ lb. of beef, or 10 oz. of pork make a complete ration: when nothing but flour or bread can be distributed, 1 lb. of flour or bread is a ration, as are also 3 lb. of beef, 2 lb. of cheese, or 1½ lb. of rice. Only one ration is issued for each effective officer and soldier, for which they pay 2½ d. [pence]. On board of transports, the ration is two-thirds of a seaman's allowance, for which, each officer and soldier pays 3d. per diem. Exclusive of the ration, the officers and soldiers are commonly supplied, in North America, with three pints of spruce beer each per diem, gratis.[51]

Thomas Sullivan, a Private with the 49th Foot of the British Army, confirmed that these rations were the standard in garrison. Stationed in Boston early in the war, Sullivan reported:

> Of the Provision the Troops Received in Boston. The Provisions were Issued out of the King's Stores, as follows. The Bakers always received 7 Pounds of Flour, for every man in the Regiment or Company, for whom they baked: Out of the 7 lb. of Flour the Baker gave two loaves, weighing 4½ lb. each, which were served twice a week to the troops. Once a week we received 4 lb. of Pork or 7 lb. of Beef; 6 ounces of Butter; 3 pints of Pease or Oatmeal; and ½ lb. of Rice per man. Every Woman had ½ a man's share, and every Child ¼ Rations.[52]

On November 4, 1775 the standard American Army ration was established as follows:

> 1 lb. of beef, or ¾ lb. pork, or 1 lb. salt fish, per day.
> 1 lb. of bread or flour per day.
> 3 pints of pease, or beans per week, or vegitables equivalent, at one dollar per bushel for pease or beans.
> 1 pint of milk per man per day, or at the rate of 1/72 of a dollar.
> 1 half pint of Rice, or 1 pint of indian meal per man per week.
> 1 quart of spruce beer or cyder per man per day, or nine gallons of Molasses per company of 100 men per week.
> 3 lb. candles to 100 Men per week for guards.
> 24 lb. of soft or 8 lb. of hard soap for 100 men per week.[53]

The standard for the Army, as further delineated in December 1775, was that salt beef or pork was to be issued four days a week, salt fish one day a week, and fresh beef for two days. When milk could not be obtained, each man was to receive 1½ pounds of beef or 1¼ pounds of pork. This ration was accepted as the standard for the American Army at Quebec as published in General Orders on February 8, 1776.

Spruce beer was intended as an anti-scorbutic. Spruce beer was made by boiling molasses (substituted for the traditional malt used in regular beers) with tips cut from spruce trees, and then fermented with yeast. It created a mildly alcoholic beer, similar to modern 3.2 percent beer. When available, hops might be incorporated into the recipe to help preserve the spruce beer if it was not going to be immediately consumed, and this also increased the alcoholic content of the brew. Because of the fact that the wort would have to boil for about an hour, any nutritional benefits from the spruce tips would probably have been lost. However, given the fact that the beer was boiled for an extensive period of time, the spruce beer would have been sterilized and thus was considerably safer to drink than water or similar beverages. Spruce beer has a distinctive taste, somewhat like modern horehound cough drops or candy, and it appears to have been popular with the soldiers. Both the Continental army and British army regularly issued it throughout this timeframe.[54]

Modern historians have noted that "Massachusetts soldiers in the Seven Years' War living on British army rations received about 2,400 to 3,100 calories per day, depending on whether the meat was beef or pork, salt or fresh."[55] This compares favorably with modern dietary requirements, although if the soldiers were spending most of their day outdoors and at heavy labor, young soldiers would require closer to 4,000 calories daily to maintain health. If all of the specified articles could be provided, the diet was more than adequate to fulfill all necessary nutritional requirements.[56] Although a modern palate would find such food to be extremely bland and repetitious, colonial soldiers would have been familiar with such a diet, and of course they had the ubiquitous spruce beer to flavor it. It was an adequate ration to keep the soldiers acceptably fed and nourished. If, of course, these specified rations could actually be obtained. And, within the frozen winter confines of Canada, that was the rub.

Attempting to ascertain actual quantities of provisions in Canada available for issue at any given time is quite problematic. Arnold wrote that he had "twenty barrels of salt pork" available on January 2. A barrel was supposed to contain 200 pounds, but most of the barrels of pork received by Schuyler only contained about 170 pounds of meat; thus if Arnold had twenty barrels of salt pork at Quebec he had approximately 3,400 total pounds.[57] Given slightly reduced rations of ½ pound of pork per day, his army of eight hundred men only had enough meat for eight days, with a ninth day at half rations.

This would have been a critical time for rations. All of the army's rations not purchased locally would have to be obtained in Connecticut or New York colonies, then shipped up the Hudson River to Albany. From Albany, the rations would be transferred to bateaux and wagons for the journey up to Fort Edward, as rapids north of Albany required several portages and precluded the use of the larger sailing vessels. Once at Fort Edward, two routes were available. A poor road was available to Fort Anne, approximately a one to two day trip, at which point supplies could be loaded into a bateaux for transportation in high water down Wood Creek, then down Lake Champlain to St. Jean. At periods of low water, the goods would have to be transferred all the way to Skenesboro at the southern end of Lake Champlain by this poor road, which traversed extremely difficult terrain consisting of numerous hills interspersed with even more numerous small rivulets and swamps. When Captain Thomas Bloomfield, from the comparatively civilized colony of New Jersey, traveled this road in October 1776 he found it to be "the meanest, worst & most desolate road I ever traveled."[58] The Fort Anne route was not preferred.

A much better trail, a two-day trip for a laden wagon or cart, led from Fort Edward to Fort George at the southern point of Lake George. Here the provisions would be loaded into bateaux for the trip north on Lake George. At the Ticonderoga portage they would be unloaded again, taken across the portage road past the Carillon Falls, and then placed aboard bateaux or sailing ships again for transportation north on Lake Champlain to St. Jean. Apparently this was the most typical route used.

The Fort Ticonderoga portage extended from the landing on the east side of Lake George, across a 1½ mile road originally constructed by the British army as a straighter, more direct route than the convoluted French portage road had been. The British portage road led approximately due north to the bateaux landing, just east of the sawmill and last falls of the La Chute River. The portage is not long, and from Lake George it drops approximately 261 feet. From Lake George, the portage road is a relatively easy traverse, although at the very end towards the landing the incline becomes more steep and treacherous, and when wet weather arrives the soils around Ticonderoga turn into a thick clay mess that is extremely slippery and difficult to traverse. From the landing, it was a smooth, relatively easy two-mile paddle or row to Fort Ticonderoga. The prevailing current, leading from Lake George into Lake Champlain, greatly facilitated the short trip from the landing to Ticonderoga.

Once at St. Jean the provisions would again have to be unloaded, portaged around the rapids between Chambly and St. Jean, and then loaded onboard bateaux or larger sailing ships for the remainder of the trip north down the Richelieu River and then down the St. Lawrence River to Quebec. During the winter, sleighs would be substituted for bateaux, and transportation was actually easier because the rapids froze over and the waterways became smooth trails. It wasn't an accident that Henry Knox determined to move the heavy train of artillery from Forts Ticonderoga and Crown Point to Boston during the depths of an Adirondacks winter.

This route was easily interrupted. Adverse winds were the greatest culprit, and they would temporarily stop all waterborne transportation until they shifted or ceased. In the fall, the lakes and rivers would be closed from the first appearance of ice (usually in November) until they froze completely over (usually in late December or early January). Once they were frozen over sleighs could be used with great success, but partially frozen waterways could not be traversed. So at Quebec, early January was one of the most difficult times, because the bateaux had been shut down for four to six weeks, and no appreciable supplies could be delivered until the sleighs could again be utilized. When the ice started to break up, usually in April, the waterways would again be interrupted until the watercourses cleared and the bateaux could again be used safely.

It was a lengthy supply route, and the importance, indeed the utter necessity of being able to purchase provisions in the country in which an army is operating is obvious. Simply put, without being able to make regular local purchases of large quantities of provisions, the American army in Canada could not subsist. Records of such purchases are extremely scarce, and obviously incomplete. One rare source is the Expense Book of John Halsted, who was commissary for Arnold. It is a slender volume that succinctly records payments to and receipts for cash from Arnold (regrettably, whether or not the payments are in paper Continental dollars or specie is not indicated). However, it does contain a glimpse into the frequency and amount of provisions that Halsted as commissary was able to purchase from local vendors for the army:

> February 26, 1776 — 27 cattle bought;
> March 27, 1776 —
>   Bought flour, 11,3,14 (1,330 pounds) flour @ 10, total 5 pounds/18 shillings/9 pence;
>   Bought 15 bushels peas @5, total 3 pounds, 15 shillings, 0 pence;
> April 1, 1776 — Bought 319 pounds beef, 185 pounds pork, 20 ct. (hundredweight, or 2,240 pounds) flour;
> April 1, 1776 — Bought 300 bushels wheat, 50 bushels wheat, 1,546 bushels wheat, 396 bushels wheat from different vendors, no prices specified;
> April 20, 1776 — Bought 8 cords of wood for the bake house;
> April 26, 1776 — Bought 550 bushels wheat; and
> April 26, 1776 — bought 18 bushels wheat.[59]

These are, in fact, extremely minimal purchases of food for an entire army. At the end of March, Arnold had 1,688 soldiers under his command. Thus, the purchases recorded between March 27 and April 1 were enough for one day's half meat ration for his entire army, less than a pint of peas per soldier for a week's rations (⅓ rations), and just over two days' full flour rations.[60] Without question, the army before Quebec was facing a shortage of provisions throughout the entire siege. Jonathan Hill, a soldier who marched in the spring of 1776 for Quebec and only reached the Richelieu River before he was turned around, wrote on May 13, 1776, from the vicinity of St. Jean: "At this time there seems to be a general complaint for want of provisions, scarcely anything to support nature."[61]

By the end of May, both Major General John Thomas and the Continental Congress commissioners recorded nearly identical tales of privation and desperation. Thomas would write on May 20 from Sorrel:

> I am unfortunately obliged to inform you that the army have now for two days been entirely destitute of meat, that no flour is provided, nor have any money to purchase provisions were they to be procured in the country, that in addition to this great part of the army are or very speedily will be not withstanding everything I can do to the contrary unfit for duty by means of inoculation, that in consequence of the unhappy intelligence received this day of the situation of the troops under the command of Captain [Colonel] Bedel. I have thought it prudent to detach two regiments, the one to Montreal, the other to Chamblee & Saint Johns. The want of provisions has made it absolutely necessary for me to order Colonel Maxwell with the troops under his command to join me here, in order truly to judge of my situation you will be pleased to figure to yourselves a retreating army disheartened by unavoidable misfortunes, destitute of almost every necessary to render their lives comfortable or even bearable, sick & as they think wholly neglected, no probable prospects of a speedy relief.[62]

The commissioners would write the Continental Congress on May 27 in distress:

> We cannot find words strong enough, to describe our miserable situation. You will have a faint idea of it, if you figure to yourself an army broken and disheartened, half of it under inoculation, or under other diseases; soldiers without pay, without disci-

pline, and altogether reduced to live from hand to mouth, depending on the scanty and precarious supplies of a few half-starved cattle, and trifling quantities of flour which have hitherto been picked up in different parts of the country.[63]

Arnold's army was unquestionably malnourished at Quebec. Insufficient rations were available. Besides weakening the soldiers, this made them vulnerable to a host of other ailments including but certainly not limited to the dreaded smallpox. It was quite literally a deadly combination for this or any other army.

2

"A Mere Ghost of an Army"
Winter Before the Lady of the Snows, January–May 1776[1]

By January 3, Arnold had begun to achieve order out of the post-assault chaos. On that date, regular Orderly Book entries began to be recorded ostensibly for Clinton's 3rd New York Regiment, but actually for Arnold's headquarters. They were diligently documented by Frederick Wesson, Major of Brigade for the American Army in front of Quebec. Arnold's headquarters, and the headquarters for what was left of Montgomery's Yorkers, was established at Hollands House (also known as the White House) in Saint Foyes, about a mile outside the city's walls.

> Head Quarters   Saint Foyes, Hollands House   January 3, 1776
>
> Parole Montreal   Countersign Campbell
>
> Colonel Arnold is by the unanimous voice of the Field officers and Captains of the Different Corps assembled in Council, judged to be commander of the troops now before Quebec. The guard for the advanced post is to remove to the house which Colonel Nicholson formerly occupied, and from thence the captains is to detach one Sergeant twelve men to the advance guard and 1 Sergeant and twelve men to the house upon the hill which was occupied by Captain Dubois. Tomorrow a party of 1 captain 1 Subaltern 1 Corporal 40 Privates is to be a patrol through the night who are all to be supplied with snowshoes. Colonel Livingston's Regiment is to be employed for that service, and is to send every day to Head Quarters for orders concerning that service.
>
> Mr. Tetardis is to translate such bills of war of the Continental Army in French as may be judged necessary for the better disciplines of the Canadians who may be engaged in the Continental Service.
>
> Captain Babcock of Major Brown's Detachment is appointed Assistant Engineer in the room of Captain Lickwood until further orders.
>
> An officer is to be appointed every day to visit the sick at the hospital and other places to see that they are well supplied and taken care of.[2]

Still, the American army remained jittery, for as Musketman Haskell reported: "About twelve o'clock last night were alarmed by a report that the enemy had come out upon us. Marched to headquarters and found the alarm false." Doctor Senter confirmed for January 3, "No movements of the enemy this day."

Almost immediately, Arnold began formally implementing decisions made the previous day, as an officer was ordered from a specified regiment to visit the sick and wounded at the hospital every day.

> Head Quarters Saint Foyes[,] Hollands House January 4, 1776
> Parole York Countersign Montreal
>
> Colonel Arnold recommends that under the direction of Colonel Livingston & Major Dubois, places be provided for the parading of the different companies as a rendezvous. Captain Vyshor & Captain Genshortes Company with Captain Grahams & Brown are to march immediately to head quarters. Major Dubois detachment is to join the different companies as soon as possible to each other that in case of an attack they may be able to defend themselves the better. Field officer for the day is Major Zewicks. The officer for visiting the hospital is to be given by the First Regiment of Yorkers.

Haskell reflected the common soldier's interests and hopes, and the inevitable army rumor mill, for he noted on January 4: "The most of our men fit for duty are on guard. We hear that provisions and wood are scarce in the city." Doctor Senter discussed the British activity (or lack thereof) and weather: "The enemy very still — nothing of moment transpiring relative to the troops on either side. Had a heavy rain, unknown almost to the country at this season."

Although he was "obliged to write lying on my back," on this date Arnold again dispatched a letter to Wooster, imploring him to send "all you possibly can with three or four hundred pairs of snow shoes, a few barrels of sugar for the hospital and fifty light shovels, our cash is nearly expended."[3]

The complete Orderly Book order for January 5 was not documented, but apparently Arnold was attempting to ensure that the notoriously independent minded American soldiers were beginning to be placed under somewhat tighter discipline.

> Head Quarters Saint Foyes Hollands House January 5, 1776
> Parole Point Levy Countersign Master
>
> The officers in general are very strictly engaged to prevent the private men strolling from their quarters at a time when the greatest [entry ends here, the full order was omitted in the Orderly Book].

Haskell again reported the activities of the army's rumor mill: "We are in expectation every night that the enemy will come out upon us. We took two spies who came out last night." Doctor Senter remained focused on the British and the weather: "Thaw continuing. Snow six feet deep. No occurrences of moment." Arnold again wrote to Wooster, doubtless wondering just what was keeping his superior, but still he remained steadfast in front of Quebec. "We have brought three pieces of cannon from our battery ... for defending our magazine. We are entirely out of lead, inclosed is a list of sundry articles, much wanted which with such as have been wrote for before, I make no doubt you will order as soon as may be — I am very anxious to see you here. The burthen lies very heavy on me considering my present circumstances."[4]

January 6 must have been a quiet time in camp, for the Orderly Book only contained routine orders.

> Head Quarters Saint Foyes, Hollands House January 6, 1776
> Parole [blank] Countersign [blank]
>
> A guard to mount this evening consisting of 1 Captain 1 Subaltern 2 Sergeants 2 Corporals & 50 men. This guard to be furnished by the 1st regiment of Yorkers. Field

Officer for this day is Major Brown. The officer for visiting the hospital is to be given by the 4th Regiment Yorkers.

Probably because it was a calm day at headquarters, Arnold finally had the opportunity to write his sister, Hannah Arnold, back home in New Haven taking care of his young sons.[5] As he explained to her, "I should have wrote you before, but a continual hurry of business prevented me." He then took the time to update her on the situation in which he found himself, "The command of the Army, by the death of my truly great and good friend, General Montgomery, devolved on me; a task, I find too heavy under my present circumstances.... Though the enemy are now double our number, they have made no attempt to come out. We are as well prepared to receive them as we can possibly be in our present situation, divided at a distance of two miles. I expect General Wooster from Montreal in a few days with a reinforcement. I hope we shall be properly supported with troops by the Congress." He ended his missive with the determination of a lion, as he remonstrated, "I have no thoughts of leaving this proud town, until I first enter it in triumph.... I know that you will be anxious for me. That Providence which has carried me through so many dangers, is still my protection. I am in the way of my duty, and know no fear."

Musketman Haskell, on the other hand, was busily engaged, for he wrote, "At night we began to build a breastwork with snow to secure us from musket balls if the enemy should come out against us." Here, we doubtless see Arnold's hand at work, as he was attempting to keep his soldiers gainfully employed so that they had little time or energy to "stroll from their quarters." Certainly, constructing a snow breastwork was of limited utility, for it would provide feeble protection at best against a musket ball!

On Saturday, January 6 the good Doctor Senter recorded a particularly long journal entry:

> The troops were stationed in the most advantageous position for preventing the enemy making any descent upon us. The number I cannot exactly ascertain, but imagine them to be about 400. We had now relinquished the idea of taking the city by force till a reinforcement should arrive. Contented ourselves with barely keeping up the blockade, and found ourselves very happy and undisturbed. We were, however, alarmed often by their coming out into the suburbs, pillaging after fire-wood, etc. They took down any building they could come at for that purpose. This occasioned the Colonel to give orders to our troops to turn and destroy as many of the houses as they would be likely to obtain, in order to distress them, in hopes they would be obliged to capitulate for want of fire-wood, etc. We, however, came short in our expectations to reduce them in this way, notwithstanding every house burnt in the city suburbs where our troops could come nigh enough.

The demoralized conditions prevailing in the army were apparent, as the Orderly Book attempted to impose discipline upon the unruly band that squatted outside of the great frozen city.

Head Quarters   Saint Foyes[,] Hollands House   [Sunday] January 7, 1776

Parole Norwich   Countersign [faded out illegible]

The neglect which some persons and soldiers are guilty of in not strictly observing the orders is so notorious that it is impossible to pass by reprimanding them. How inconsistent it is with their duty and of dangerous consequences to the whole army. It is therefore once more notified that all orders of a public value must strictly be observed in whatever officer or soldier for the future are found negligent they must expect to be dealt with according to the strictest sense of the articles of War. Tomorrow morning a party of 20 men and 1 Subaltern and 1 Sergeant 1 Corporal is to attend Engineer to mount the cannon at Head Quarters. This party Captain Fisher's party is to furnish.

Haskell must have had an easy day of it, for his only record was, "Today had orders to carry the packs and clothing belonging to our messmates prisoners to headquarters to be sent to them." From this date, Doctor Senter ceased to make regular journal entries, covering a six weeks' period with a single terse entry: "From this to the 18th of March nothing extraordinary happening. Burning the houses to prevent the enemy's getting them often occasioned slight skirmishing, with various success, but nothing capital."

On Monday, January 8, the prevailing interest in the Orderly Book remained attempts to impose some level of discipline upon the army.

Saint Foyes Near Quebec

Head Quarters   Hollands House   January 8, 1776

Parole [ink blotted—illegible]   Countersign Livingston

The uneasiness which prevails in Captain Visshier's Company of 2nd Regiment of Yorkers is to be feared will be of bad consequence if not speedily removed. Captain Visshier is therefore desired to make a settlement with his officers and men that the commander in chief may be satisfied and his company be under his command as heretofore. It is often observed that rum has been sold in different houses to the soldiers. The barracks master is hereby ordered to go his rounds every evening to houses supposed places who sell to the soldier. The officer of the advanced guard is to be furnished every evening by the Canadians with snow shoes who are to be sent 3 men at a time to patrol between the guards. Captain [entry ends here, the full order was omitted in the Orderly Book].

Haskell again must have had a relaxed day, for he simply noted, "This morning we carried the prisoners' packs to headquarters."

January 9 was also a quiet day in camp, for the Orderly Book entry was mundane.

Saint Foyes Near Quebec   January 9, 1776

Head Quarters   Hollands House

Parole [omitted]   Countersign [omitted]

A guard to mount this evening consisting of 1 Captain 1 Subaltern 2 Sergeants 2 Corporals and fifty privates. The above guard to be furnished by Major Brown's party. Field officer this day is Major Sedwicks. The officer for visiting the hospital is to be given by Captain Vishor is to appoint Sergeant major who is to stay by to receive orders at Head Quarters.

The army rumor mill, which had apparently been quiet for several days, was back in operation on this date, as Haskell documented, "Heard that General Worcester [Wooster] was on his way from Montreal. A bad snow storm today."

The next day must also have been a routine, and doubtless boring, day in the soldiers' lives.

## 2. "A Mere Ghost of an Army"	29

> Saint Foyes   Head Quarters   Hollands House   January 10, 1776
>
> Parole Effingham   Countersign Chatham
>
> A guard to be furnished by this battalion the 1st Regiment of Yorkers consisting of 1 Captain 1 Subaltern 3 Sergeants 2 Corporals & 50 Privates. A Quarter Guard at Head Quarters to consist of one Sergeant one Corporal and 15 Privates this guard to be given by Captain Vyshires Detachment. Field Officer for this day [line omitted] Officer for visiting the hospital is given by the First Regiment of Yorkers.

Haskell recorded a succinct entry, "Severely cold and uncomfortable." Clearly, Haskell's primary emphasis on this date was keeping warm!

Possibly because of the severe weather, the next day's Orderly Book entry was also succinct.

> Saint Foyes Near Quebec   Head Quarters   Hollands House   January 11, 1776
>
> Parole Clinton   Countersign Price
>
> A guard to mount this evening consisting of one Captain one subaltern 3 Sergeants 3 Corporals & 50 Privates this guard to be given by Major Brown's Detachment. Officer for this day Major Livingston.

Haskell discussed the miserable weather and the effects that it had upon the soldiers: "Continues cold. In the afternoon we went to the hospital to bury one of our company who died of a wound. At night a bad snow storm."

Arnold took advantage of the heavy snow to catch up on his correspondence, writing to the Continental Congress on this date.[6] He began, "I take the liberty, most heartily, to condole with you the loss of great, amiable, and brave General Montgomery ... by his death, the command of the Army devolves on me." After informing the Congress of the situation on the ground, Arnold then analyzed the possibilities of successfully wresting Quebec from British control:

> What is to be done? A sufficient force employed to reduce it, by a regular siege, or assault? If the first is attempted, an addition of three thousand men to our present force will, I make no doubt, be thought necessary; if the latter, at least five thousand. The former, with a vast expense and great waste of ammunition, may prove unsuccessful; the latter, from the extensiveness of their works, I think cannot; and five thousand men will hardly be a sufficient garrison, if the place is taken. I beg leave to recommend the sending a body of at least five thousand men, with an experienced General, into Canada, as early as possible; and, in the mean time, that every possible preparation, of mortars, howitzers and some heavy cannon, should be made.

Characteristically, Arnold concluded with concerns regarding his soldiers: "The men are obliged to lay on their arms constantly, and to mount guard every other night. Their duty is exceedingly hard; however, the men appear alert and cheerful, though wanting many necessaries, which cannot be procured here." Obviously, Arnold trusted that Congress would read between his lines, and forward the "many necessaries" which his soldiers wanted. He was to be disappointed.

The winter storm continued the next day, resulting in another brief Orderly Book entry.

Saint Foyes Near Quebec   January 12, 1776
Head Quarters   Hollands House
Parole Wilhis [Willis]   Countersign Moreland

As Colonel Arnold finds himself indisposed and Colonel Clinton's arriving at Head Quarters[,] by order of General Wooster his desire is to promote the good of the service by all the means in his power it is hereby ordered that Colonel Clinton will take the command of the troops now before Quebec until the health of Colonel Arnold will permit to resume the same again or orders from General Wooster to the contrary, and the troops are ordered to obey accordingly. A Quarter Guard to mount this evening consisting of 1 Captain 1 Subaltern 3 Sergeants 3 Corporals & 50 Privates this guard to be given by Captain Vishier Detachment.

On this date, Arnold was informed by Colonel Clinton that Wooster was not going to depart Montreal, for Clinton had come down from that city bearing this news, and with orders to assist Arnold with the field command until his leg could heal.[7] Arnold informed the Continental Congress, without comment, "Colonel Clinton acquaints me, we cannot expect more than two hundred men from Montreal." Arnold doubtless figured that the Continental Congress was astute enough to draw their own conclusions. Haskell's diary entries continued in the same vein, as he dealt with the miserable weather: "Cold, uncomfortable weather. The snow deep and bad storming. One of our company died with the small pox today."

Its clinical name is *variola*. It is a virus. It had devastated mankind for thousands of years. Intermittently, it would sweep through a population as an epidemic, emptying homes with ruthless efficiency. It was terribly feared, for it could easily leave a person scarred, if not crippled, for life. Like all viruses, its source is unknown. Smallpox thrives on conditions where humans cannot keep clean, and where their bodies are being stressed by difficult living conditions. Smallpox spreads with devastating efficiency in circumstances where people are kept in close quarters. Arnold's army outside of Quebec achieved all these conditions. Dr. Senter recorded the ominous event in his journal for December 17: "Smallpox broke out in the army." More horrific news could not possibly be imagined.[8]

The smallpox was a savage and horrendous disease, which in short order absolutely devastated the army squatting outside of Quebec. Uriah Cross, a Vermont soldier who was serving with the American army at Quebec, was detailed to assist one of the officers of his regiment who was gravely ill. His brief reminiscences provide a glimpse into the horrors of the disease:

> Our army was a number taken sick with the small Pox. A Hospital was prepared at Wolfs Cove. I had gone thru it, almost the only one in the army. Adjutant Green had the small Pox harder than usual ... he was in poor health. I was sent as nurse & watcher to take care of him six miles back in the country. He was almost covered with sores caused by small pox. If I should at the time relate the distress sickness & numerous deaths in the hospital you would hardly believe it. Rising one hundred died of the small pox at Wolfs Cove in the course of the winter.[9]

After the initial infection, the virus incubates in its host (a tired, cold, hungry American soldier exhausted from constant fatigue parties and guard details in ragged, filthy, and torn clothing) for seven to seventeen days, although most frequently twelve to fourteen days. During this time the young soldier would feel fine, and was not contagious.

At some point, the soldier would be struck with the initial symptoms of smallpox, generally involving fever, malaise, and severe body aches and pains (often in the back and shoulders). Sometimes the victim vomited. These symptoms are vague enough that the soldier and his compatriots, crowded into a small French Canadian house for warmth, would not know that he had smallpox. Any number of illnesses common to armies could account for these symptoms, such as bad or poorly cooked food, overwork, influenza, or even the common cold. These symptoms would continue for two to four days. At this time, the soldier may or may not have been contagious.

But shortly thereafter, the rash would begin to develop. At this point, the soldier and his comrades would know that he had the smallpox. The rash would begin at the mouth and throat, and then spread throughout his entire body. It would start as red bumps, which would swell and fill with liquid. The soldier is incapacitated by this time, having an exceptionally high fever. Now the virus is most contagious. Given the close living conditions that the severe Canadian climate forced upon the army, the soldier would almost immediately infect all of his fellow soldiers. This condition would last approximately four days. Given the medical knowledge of the time, all that the soldier's friends could do for him was to carry him to a designated smallpox hospital, usually isolated and a considerable distance away from the camp. Here, the soldier would suffer by himself, with only a couple of nurses or surgeons to assist him. His friends and relatives, not knowing that they had already been infected, would not dare to visit him for fear of catching the smallpox themselves. The soldier's breath, his clothing, his bedding, his bodily fluids would all be contaminated with the virus. It would almost be impossible to escape *variola*, so powerful and encompassing had it become. The soldier would suffer in solitary misery, living and dying depending upon the severity of the smallpox, his own physical strength, and his will to live.

By the end of four days, the red bumps would become the infamous pustules, the characteristic of the disease. The itching would become terrible, yet if the victim scratched, rubbed, irritated or opened a pustule the result would be a scar or pit in the skin for life. In severe cases, the pustules would overwhelm the victim's throat and mouth, and prevent him from breathing. A slow, tortured death would be the inevitable result if the malady became this serious. If the smallpox attacked the soldier's eyes, he would be blinded. The high fever would continue, and the victim would remain incapacitated and desperately thirsty. The fever alone could kill him. After another five days the pustules would finally begin to form a wet crust as they opened, and then the pustules would slowly scab over. As the pustules opened up they would have a sickeningly sweet odor that was apparently unmistakable. Scabs would replace nearly all of the pustules within about two weeks of the onset of fever. Finally, with the arrival of the scabs, the fever would relent, assuming that the patient had lived this long.

After another week, the scabs would finally fall off. Only now, after the last of the scabs had departed, and approximately three weeks after the rash had first appeared, would the patient no longer be contagious. The soldier could safely rejoin his comrades. Mercifully, he would now be immune from the disease for the rest of his life. In many cases, he would also be scarred or pitted for life, bearing the marks of the disease prominently. In severe cases, where the pustules had attacked the reproductive organs, the sufferer might be rendered impotent. If the pustules had assailed the soldier's eyes, he could be blinded for life.

It was a terrible, horrible disease and it was desperately feared and dreaded.

One of the characteristics of the virus is that it is considerably worse if it infects a person with a similar genetic make-up. Thus, if a member of the family infects his relatives, smallpox will be considerably more severe. In a Native American population, or small towns where the genetic pool was limited, the smallpox would be incredibly violent. Arnold's Provincials had been enlisted from just such communities in New England, and many companies contained brothers, even twins, and cousins. If these soldiers were lucky, if that word could be used in conjunction with the *variola* virus, they would be infected by complete strangers.[10]

Once exposed to *variola*, there was a near certainty that the soldier would come down with smallpox. In about a third of the cases, the pustules or fever would prove fatal. Medical professionals of the 18th century knew that smallpox was spread through contact, but they had no knowledge of germs (a microscope did not even exist in the colonies), and what smallpox was and the mechanism that spread it was obviously a mystery.

In 1776, there was no way to avoid it, and the odds were all against the young soldier. But there was a method to mitigate it. It was called inoculation. Vaccination prevents the patient from ever getting the malady, but it would not exist for two more decades. Inoculation, on the other hand, consists of deliberately giving the patient the disease. As with all diseases, the intensity of smallpox cases tends to vary, such that some cases are relatively mild. As noted, smallpox is always less violent if caught from a stranger rather than somebody with a similar genetic makeup. For these reasons, a patient could be deliberately infected with a relatively mild case from a stranger. Inoculation had been practiced in the historic Ottoman Empire, Africa and China for centuries, and inoculation was introduced to England in 1721. It was first utilized in Boston, Massachusetts Colony, as a result of a smallpox outbreak in 1721, when Cotton Mather had the audacity to inoculate his children to protect them.[11] One great obstacle to inoculation, however, is that the patient is still contagious. Thus, if not carefully controlled, and the patient or patients not faithfully isolated, inoculation can obviously spread the disease. Inoculation was strongly resisted. First, because it could still disseminate the disease; also because it was artificially and deliberately infecting a person with a potentially lethal malady; and most importantly on religious grounds because it violated the will of God.

During the severe smallpox outbreak of 1721 to 1722, 242 persons were inoculated in Boston, with only six deaths resulting. This was slightly greater than the two percent death rate that experience with inoculation had achieved by 1776. For whatever reason, inoculated smallpox lasted approximately two weeks rather than the four weeks of illness caused by a natural outbreak. By the time of the American Revolution, the British Army routinely performed inoculation for smallpox. It is known to have practiced it in Quebec, which may possibly have been the cause of it within the American army.

From a military standpoint a soldier, even if inoculated, can still not perform his duties for the two-week period when he actually has smallpox. For this reason, some officers objected to the practice, as the soldier's services would be lost to the army during this time. Still, although considerable resistance to its use remained even as late as 1775 in Massachusetts, it was proven to be considerably safer than catching smallpox in the natural manner, and medical professionals were beginning to regularly practice inoculation. George Washington, who had suffered through smallpox as a young man, was a great proponent of inoculation, and in the later years of the American War for Independence it would be routinely practiced in the Continental army. But that time had not yet come for Arnold's soldiers suffering in squalid conditions outside of Quebec, and most soldiers caught smallpox the natural way.

What occurred in Arnold's army was the medical and military equivalent of a panic. The source of the disease cannot now be determined. Given the weakened condition of his army and the poor hygienic conditions in which they were squatting, and their proximity to Quebec where the disease was known to exist, the appearance of smallpox was almost inevitable. The poor soldiers, desperately fearing the disease, determined to inoculate themselves. The army then issued positive orders against the practice of inoculation, as it removed so many soldiers from the duty rolls and the army was already sorely under strength. Being absolutely terrified of the disease, the soldiers continued the practice in secret. Isolation was not enforced, and thus the obedient soldiers that had followed orders were in short order infected by the soldiers that had inoculated themselves. Still more soldiers fell sick, and more positive orders were issued against inoculation while there was still an army available to maintain the blockade of the city. Smallpox swept through the ranks of Arnold's force, either through inoculation or the more virulent natural strain. Those men fortunate enough to have had the disease previously now found themselves pulling an inordinate amount of guard details and fatigue duty, while their comrades sickened and either healed or died. The smallpox resistant men, who had purchased their immunity at a terrible price and great risk, were now being overworked and exhausted, and they in turn fell ill with other maladies. The army was shattered. Arnold wrote of this disintegration, "From the 1st of January to the 1st of March, we have never had more than seven hundred effective men on the ground, and frequently not more than five hundred." When reinforcements arrived, if they had not been inoculated or were already immune, within two weeks they were inevitably on the sick rolls, from either smallpox, from exposure and overwork, or both. General Wooster would relate to Congress on April 27 that as soon as reinforcements arrived at Quebec they "took the smallpox as they arrived, either by inoculation or the natural way, and for want of physic to purge them properly after the distemper, we have had little assistance from them yet."[12]

Doctor Senter would record in despair regarding the ravages that the smallpox inflicted upon the American army throughout the long winter in front of the Lady of the Snows, "The small pox still continued in the army. Numbers of the soldiers inoculated themselves, and indeed several officers, tho' contrary to orders at this time. Scarce any of the New England recruits had ever had the disorder, and coming into the army when it was very brief, gave apprehensions of taking it in the natural way, which many did."

Haskell's fellow soldier had most certainly not been the first to die of smallpox in Arnold's army, and tragically he would not be the last. Smallpox, more than any other single factor, would quite literally destroy the American army in Canada. When initial reports reached Washington's chief surgeon, Dr. John Morgan, they were so alarming that he found them "scarcely credible."[13] Sadly enough, the smallpox epidemic was more than credible. When he received a full reporting, member of the Continental Congress John Adams would write, "Our misfortunes in Canada are enough to melt the heart of a stone, the small-pox is ten times more terrible than Britons, Canadians and Indians together. This was the cause of our precipitate retreat from Quebec."[14]

The winter storm continued unabated the next day, again limiting activities.

> Saint Foyes Near Quebec   January 13, 1776
>
> Head Quarters   Hollands House
>
> Morning Orders   Parole Johns   Countersign Point Levis
>
> A court of inquiry to sit on the conduct of Captain Lanie Of Colonel Livingston's Regiment. President Major Dubois of 3rd Regiment of Yorkers. Members. Captain Vishers, 2nd Regiment of Yorkers, Captain Leviston of Colonel Dubois Detachment, Captain Cochran Major Brown's Detachment, Captain Mott the 1st Regiment of Yorkers.
>
> A guard to mount this evening consisting of 1 Captain, 1 Subaltern, 3 Sergeants, 3 Corporals & 50 Privates, this guard to be furnished by the First Regiment of Yorkers. Field Officer for Major Dubois. For guard Major [blank] detachment is to send 10 men & 1 Corporal to Head Quarters.

Haskell had little interest in the upcoming court-martial, as he was apparently bored and cold: "Cold and squally. Little stirring. Nothing new." On this date General Wooster wrote General Schuyler from Montreal, updating him on the continued deterioration of the situation in front of Quebec:

> I have just received intelligence from our Army before Quebec, they still keep up the blockade with spirit; yet are greatly distressed for want of men, being alarmed almost every night, and having so few men, if not assisted in a little time, good as they are (and men never behaved better), they must be worn out. I have sent them a reinforcement of a hundred and twenty, who I suppose will arrive there tomorrow, and another party of seventy will set off from this place tomorrow. What they will do at Quebec or what any of us can do for want of money, God only knows. Money we must have, or give up everything. Our friends are drained already. I hope the Paymaster is on the way. All that can be done will be done to preserve it, but it is impossible to exist as an army much longer without it.[15]

For Sunday, January 14, the weather continued awful, and apparently both soldiers and officers were focused upon creature comforts and not military duties. The officer or NCO responsible for the Orderly Book even failed to properly record the date!

> Saint Foyes Near Quebec   January the [blank] 1776
>
> Head Quarters   Hollands House
>
> Parole [blank]   Countersign [blank]
>
> Field officer for this day Major Brown. Officer for visiting the hospital is to be given by Major Brown's Detachment.

Haskell was similarly brief for this date, complaining, "Continues cold and uncomfortable. No remarks." As was apparently typical for Arnold, when the weather was severe, he used the opportunity to catch up on his correspondence, writing this date to General George Washington in Boston.[16]

The next day, surprisingly absolutely nobody, a heavy snowstorm accompanied by severely cold temperatures struck the Quebec area. The miserable weather continued causing problems in the American camp.

> Saint Foyes Near Quebec   January the [blank] 1776
>
> Head Quarters   Hollands House
>
> Parole Lee   Countersign Philadelphia
>
> 22 men of Captain Vyshir's Company who have promised to separate themselves from it are ordered to join their said company, and in failing thereof must expect to be punished according to the articles of war as being guilty of mutinying. The troops which are before Quebec under the command of Colonel Arnold are ordered in case of an attack as follows. The troops at head Quarters to turn out & arrange themselves around the house by their respective companies as they shall be directed. Field Officer Major Dubois. Provided that Head Quarters is attacked he is to send by the road leading to Major Brayern's Quarters such assistance as he consistent with his own spare. Major Brown as in that circumstance renders his men gives to the assistance of head Quarters in such manner that the guard of 50 men is allowed to defend the cannon. Captain Fisher's Detachment is on the first alarm to repair to Head Quarters and put themselves the command of the commanding officer appointed to the defense of the post. The artillery is to [blotted] so that two men may be by each cannon. A guard to mount this evening consisting of one Captain, one Subaltern, 2 Sergeants 2 corporals & 50 Privates, this guard to be furnished by Captain Fisher's Party. Field Officer is Major Brown.

Haskell was apparently fortunate that he could keep his ink from turning to ice upon this date: "A bad snowstorm, and so cold that a man can scarce get out without freezing."

More unrest, and disciplinary problems among the soldiers, occupied the Orderly Book entry for January 16.

> Saint Foyes Near Quebec   January the [blank] 1776
>
> Head Quarters   Hollands House
>
> Parole Bristol   Countersign Elizabethtown
>
> A guard to mount this evening consisting of 1 Captain, 1 Subaltern, 3 Sergeants, 3 Corporals & 50 Privates, this guard to be furnished by the first regiment of Yorkers. Field Officer for this day is Major Brown. Officer for visiting the hospital is to be given by the First R. of Yorkers.
>
> Captain Vishers Detachment is to furnish the guard at Head Quarters with 6 Privates. The officer who mounts the advanced guard to be again told that complaints has [sic] been made that they and their guard encroaches upon the people who dwell in the house, and those who are quartered there it is hoped that the offices will oblige this guard to remain in the guard house.

Haskell's only commentary on the day was that letters were received from the prisoners inside the city.

The Orderly Book entry for January 17 suggests that the letters that Haskell perused may have been received in a somewhat irregular manner.

Saint Foyes Near Quebec   January 17, 1776

Headquarters   Hollands House

Parole Williamsburg   Countersign Clinton

The officer of the guard is ordered that in case any person whosoever which may come out of town except with a flag are to be fired upon in order to cause them to return again from whence they came.

 A guard to mount this evening consisting of 1 Captain 1 Subaltern 3 Sergeants 3 Corporals 50 Privates this guard to be furnished by Major Browns Detachment. Field Officer for this day Major Leviston. Officer for visiting the hospital to be given by Captain Viskin's Detachment.

Haskell's principal concern, not surprisingly, remained with the state of the weather. Which was, in a word, abysmal. "A cold snowstorm, the snow deep."

A break in the weather finally came on January 18.

Saint Foyes Near Quebec   January 18, 1776

Parole Wick   Countersign Eaton

The necessaries sent for by the prisoners in Quebec will be admitted on Friday next [January 19] between the hours of 12 & 2, it is therefore ordered that all the above mentioned baggage or any letters who may be sent into town be tendered tomorrow morning at 10 O'clock of the 1st Regiment of Yorkers. The Officer of the Day at Head Quarters is to make a report to the Brigade major every day of the number of person their crimes & names, this is to be punctually observed. Mr. Shedon Is appointed Sub Commissary under Mr. Hatstead [Halstead] To provide necessary provisions for the troops which are quartered at Saint Foyes until further orders.

 A guard to mount this evening consisting of 1 Captain 1 Subaltern 3 Sergeants 3 Corporals 50 Privates this guard to be furnished by Captain Viskin's? Detachment. Captain Viskin gives 1 Captain 1 Sergeant 1 Corporal & 30 Privates, Captain Leviston gives 1 Subaltern, 1 Sergeant, 1 Corporal & 20 Privates. Field Officer for this day Major Leviston. The Officer for visiting the hospital is to be given by Major Brown's Detachment.

Haskell noted the improvement in the weather, "Clears off pleasant in the afternoon. I went on guard down to St. Roche's." On this date, Arnold had received good news from a supporter at Point aux Trembles: "I am ... most obliged to you, for your kind offer of Cash, which I accept with thanks, as we are really distressed for that Article."[17] This letter, obviously written on his back as he slowly recovered from the gunshot wound in his leg, displays strange and excessive punctuation. The explanation, as revealed by historian and author Kenneth Roberts, is that every time Arnold shifted position in his sickbed to continue writing the letter, he had to stab the point of the pen into the paper to hold it in place. This simple fact, in and of itself, reveals much of the severity of the wound that Arnold had sustained, and reveals much more regarding the timber of the man who had sustained it.

Although the warmer and clearer weather was certainly appreciated, the American officers understood that the British would employ the respite by marching out of their works to obtain more firewood, and issued appropriate instructions.

Head Quarters   Before Quebec   January 19, 1776

Parole London   Countersign Lee

A guard to mount this evening consisting of 1 Captain 1 Subaltern 3 Sergeants 3 Corporals 50 Privates. Major Brown's Detachment is to give a Captain, the rest are furnished by the 1st Regiment of Yorkers. Field Officer for this day is Major Dubois. The Officer for visiting the hospital is to be given by Captain Viskin's Detachment. Major Brown's detachment gives 6 men for the guard at Head Quarters.

Haskell noted of the officers' concerns, "At night was relieved from guard. This evening some of our guards at St. Roche set fire to some buildings there that the enemy were going to make use of for firewood."

The next day the Orderly Book concerned itself with permitting the local habitants to bring provisions to sell to the army, without being disturbed (or, presumably, looted) in the process. Clearly, Arnold was focused upon rations for the small army.

Head Quarters Holland House January 20, 1776

Parole Lisbon Countersign New Haven

The officers on all the guards are desired to suffer the inhabitants who brings provisions to head quarters or the commissary to pass unmolested as it is the intention of the commanding officer to encourage the country people to provide the army with eatables.

The guard to mount this evening consisting of 1 Captain 1 Subaltern 3 Sergeants 3 Corporals & 50 Privates. This guard to be furnished by Major Brown's Detachment. Field Officer for this day is Major Brown. The officer for visiting the hospital is to be given by the First regiment of Yorkers.

Haskell, on guard duty, had other concerns: "Moderate, but some snow. The enemy were firing some part of the day from the city."

Arnold was clearly still concerned with his soldiers' morale on January 21, and he attempted to raise their spirits by promising relief.

Saint Foyes Head Quarters Hollands House January 21, 1776

Parole Lewisburgh [Louisburg] Countersign Price

The subaltern officers who formerly was appointed officer of the day at Head Quarters is ordered for the future to mount his guard at that place in his tower and to be accountable for his guard in all respects. The officers in their different quarters are reminded to in respect to former orders that they may be absolved with as if there was no such orders has been given to prevent the same. It is also necessary to acquaint the troops that the large reinforcements which are on their march for this place and their arrival is daily expected.

The guard to mount this evening consisting of 1 Captain 1 Subaltern 3 Sergeants 3 Corporals & 50 Privates, this guard to be furnished by Captain Visken's Detachment. Captain Visker is to give 1 Captain 1 Sergeant 2 Corporals & 25 Privates. Captain Lewiston gives 1 Subaltern 2 Sergeants 1 Corporal & 50 Privates. Mr. Silas Gray Sergeant in Captain Raymond's Company of the 2nd Regiment of Yorkers is appointed Second Lieutenant in said company, until the pleasure of the congress be known. Field Officer for this day Colonel Leviston. The officer for visiting the hospital is to be given by Major Brown's Detachment.

Haskell, as usual, was more interested in the weather and army rumors: "A pleasant day. This morning three of our prisoners made their escape from the city."

Arnold specified improvements to the army's security on January 22.

> Saint Foyes   Head Quarters   Holland House   January 22, 1776
>
> Parole Hancock   Countersign Adams
>
> A general court martial is to be held at Head Quarters at 12 o'clock this day of the trial of such persons as may be brought before them. Colonel Livingston President. Major Brown, Major Dubois, Major Leviston Members. The 1 Regiment of Yorkers gives 1 Captain 3 Lieutenants. 2nd Regiment Yorkers gives 2 Captains & 3rd Regiment of Yorkers gives 2 Captains. Colonel Livingston's regiment gives 1 Captain. Lieutenant Platt Judge Advocate. The officer of the guard is to sign a provision return every day for the prisoners which are in the guard house. He is also to be sure that every night at 2 O'clock there must be performed by himself taking in his turn the guard on the hill and to return by the Sillery Road.

Haskell, on guard duty, recorded, "Last night some of our guards at St. Roche's set a number of vessels on fire that lay against the village. In the evening I was on guard at St. Roche's."

Arnold's General Orders of January 23 clearly indicated that his soldiers were still unhappy, even with the promised reinforcements.

> Head Quarters   January 23, 1776
>
> Parole Brewster   Countersign Clinton
>
> Captain Brayn of Colonel Clinton's Regiment is to remove his Quarters with his company & join his Regiment. The officer Commanding Detachments & those who Command companies are desired strictly to [illegible word] the conduct of their men that all mutining [sic] & disorders may be suppressed as it were in the very bad, for it is notorious that disorders of this kind have been productive [word omitted in original document] dangerous consequences almost to the disturbing of the whole army.
>
> The guard to mount this evening consisting of 1 Captain 1 Subaltern 3 Sergeants 3 Corporals & 50 Privates. This guard to be furnished by Major Brown's detachment. Officer for visiting the hospital is to be given by the 4th Regiment of Yorkers.

Poor Musketman Haskell remained on guard. "A pleasant day. We had several shot thrown at our guard house; in the afternoon we took three prisoners — merchants belonging to the city; carried them to headquarters. In the evening I was relieved from guard."

January 24 was apparently a quiet day at headquarters, for only routine assignments were published.

> Head Quarters   Holland House   January 24, 1776
>
> Parole Montreal   Countersign Saint Johns
>
> A guard to mount this evening consisting of a Captain a Subaltern 3 Sergeants 3 Corporals & 60 Privates this guard to be furnished by Captain Vyphers Detachment. Captain Vither Detachment gives one Captain one Subaltern 3 Sergeants 2 Corporals & 38 Privates. Captain Lewiston gives 1 Captain [probably should be Corporal] & 12 Privates.
>
> Field Officer for this day is Major Dubois. Officer for visiting the hospital is to be given by Captain Vither Detachment. Captain Lewiston is to remove tomorrow morning to join his regiment. Doctor Mr. Peck Is to attend the small pox hospital until further orders.

Haskell also had a quiet day, doubtless resting from his long tour of duty on guard, "Moderate weather. One hundred and forty men arrived from Montreal. At night some of our guards set some houses on fire in St. Roche's suburbs." Arnold followed up his earlier communiqué to the Continental Congress on this date, providing them with a very detailed list of his requirements for artillery and ammunition to prosecute a full blown siege of the city of the snows. He also mentioned that he had "encouragement" from a Monsieur Pelissier, who operated a foundry at Three Rivers. Pelissier had the capability of casting cannonballs and shells, and could provide them for the army (presumably, for hard cash, and at a considerable profit). He ended by pleading for additional specie: "our finances are low; we have been obliged to beg, borrow and squeeze, to get money for our subsistence."[18]

January 25 was also a quiet day at headquarters.

> Head Quarters   Holland House   January 25, 1776
>
> Parole Campbell   Countersign Adams
>
> A guard to mount this evening consisting of 1 Captain 1 Subaltern 3 Sergeants 3 Corporals & 60 Privates. The 4th Battalion of Yorkers gives 1 Captain 1 Subaltern 1 Sergeant & 15 Privates. The 1st of Yorkers gives 1 Subaltern 2 Sergeants 3 Corporals & 35 Privates.
>
>   Field Officer for this day is Major Gansevoort. Officer for visiting the hospital is given by Major Brown's Detachment.

Haskell reported a sortie by the British, doubtless encouraged by the moderate weather, and probably intended to cover a party to obtain lumber. "This day, about noon, 500 of the enemy came out at Palace Gate. About 200 advanced almost to our guard house. As soon as we were mustered they retreated in again."

Arnold's headquarters continued to issue relatively uninspiring orders on January 26.

> St Foyes Near Quebec   January the [26] 1776
>
> Head Quarters   Hollands House
>
> Parole London   Countersign Liberty
>
> A guard to mount this evening consisting of 1 Captain, 1 Subaltern, 3 Sergeants, 3 Corporals & 50 Privates. Captain Visschers gives 1 Subaltern, 2 Sergeants, 1 Corporal, 30 Privates. Captain Livingston gives 1 Captain, 1 Sergeant, 2 Corporals & 20 Privates. Field Officer for this day Major Livingston. The officer for visiting the hospital is given by Major Brown's Detachment.

Haskell, however, reported that Arnold initiated measures to prevent the British from obtaining firewood, probably inspired by the British sortie the day before: "This day we had orders for all of Col. Arnold's detachment to go down to Bon Poor passage to keep a stationed guard, to prevent the Tories from carrying wood and provisions into the city that way."

Saturday, January 27, featured General Orders issued for divine services the next day. Obviously, Arnold was still attempting to improve the morale of his command.

> Head Quarters   January 27, 1776
>
> Parole Falmouth   Countersign Victory
>
> Divine worship will begin tomorrow morning at Eleven O'clock at Count Dupress House. The officers are desired to bring as many men to that place as conveniently

can be spared from their quarters, complete by arms [this means that the men are supposed to carry their arms to services]. Observing at the same time that the inclemency of the season will not suffer the men to stand outdoors during the service, neither will the different quarters be left empty. The soldiers who did not formerly belong to Colonel's [illegible] Detachment are ordered to give in their names to Lieutenant Bailey in order to receive their clothes and those companies to which they now belong are to leave them out of their returns for clothing.

 A guard to mount this evening consisting of 1 captain 1 Subaltern 3 Sergeants 3 Corporals & 50 Privates. This guard to be furnished by Major Gansevoort's Detachment of the 2nd regiment of Yorkers. Field Officer for this day is Major Gansevoort & the officer for visiting this hospital is to be given by Major DuBoise's Detachment. The officer of the different guards are to instruct their sentries that when they see any rockets thrown from the guards at the hospital or the advanced guard at Major Brown's Quarters it is to be taken as a signal of alarm.

Haskell had other problems on his mind: "Exceeding cold weather."

January 28 was Sunday, and although the General Orders did not note it, religious services were conducted for the army.

Head Quarters January 28, 1776

Parole Arnold Countersign Campbell

The officers commanding detachments are desired to prepare their monthly returns to be delivered by the first day of February next to the Commander In Chief. It has been frequently ordered that when there is no Adjutant appointed in any troop or detachment a commissioned officer should be sent to received orders which order has neglected, the officers commanding detachments are desired again to see their orders punctually obeyed as no orders for the future will be given to a non commissioned officer.

 A guard to mount this evening consisting of 1 captain 1 Subaltern 3 Sergeants 3 Corporals and 50 Privates this guard to be furnished by the 1st regiment of Yorkers. 1 Subaltern 1 Sergeant 1 Corporal & 15 Privates for a quarter guard at Head Quarters is to be given by Major Brown's Detachment. Field Officer for this day is Major Brown, officer for visiting the hospital is given by the 2 Regt of Yorkers.

Haskell was among those men who attended church, presumably armed in the event that the dastardly British were to attack on a Sunday. "Mr. Spring, our chaplain, preached."

Apparently the General Orders were not being regularly adhered to, as the Orders for January 29 addressed a previous failure to comply with the January 17 Order to fire upon any member of the British garrison leaving Quebec without a flag of truce.

Head Quarters January 29, 1776

Parole Senegal Countersign Bristol

At a Court of Inquiry held the 28 instant, Captain Loinden Of Colonel Livingston's Regiment being called, pleaded not guilty as he had no orders commissioned to him of the charge laid to said Captain for not obeying the said orders of the 17th instant. Sergeant Manager of Colonel Lewiston Regiment being called the evidence declaring that said Leftenant did not judge it prudent to fire on the enemy upon uncertainty. Resolved that said officer be the command to the commander in chief for discharge of their confinement and are that they be discharged but that for the future ignorance of orders may be pleaded. It is recommended that orderly books are provided by every commanding officer of detachments when the adjutant received orders from Head Quarters they are immediately to deliver them to all officers.

A guard to mount this evening consisting of 1 Captain 1 Subaltern 3 Sergeants 3 Corporals & 50 Privates this guard to be furnished by Major Brown's Detachment. The guard at the hospital to be mounted as usual. 1 Subaltern 1 Sergeant 1 Corporal 15 Privates as a Quarter Guard at headquarters to mount this evening at 5 O'clock and is to be given by the 2nd Regiment of Yorkers & Field Officer for this day.

Haskell was apparently uninterested in the activities (or lack thereof) in the officers. He was trying to keep warm: "Continues cold, but something more moderate in the evening." This day, an incident happened on the walls of Quebec that indicated just how frigid cold the temperatures really were. Captain Jones recorded in his journal for the day:

> Clear cold weather. It is worth remarking that this morning about 5 o'clock when the Field Officer of the Day was going his rounds, he hailed a sentry who had not challenged him & was very angry for the sentry's negligence. "God Bliss Your Honor" replied the sentry, "I am glad you are come for I am blind." On the Officers examining him he found the mans eyes had watered with the severity of the cold & that his eye lids were froze together — his face was tender he durst not rub them & the officer was obliged to carry him to the guard to be thawed.[19]

Arnold, apparently desperately attempting to infuse discipline into his unruly army, continued to order court-martials on January 30.

Head Quarters   Holland House   January 30, 1776

Parole London   Countersign Schuyler

A court martial of the line to be held at Head Quarters in Doelin's Room at Eleven O'clock for the trial of all such persons as may be brought before them. The President a Captain of the 2nd Regiment of Yorkers 2 Lieutenants of the 2nd Detachment, 2 Lieutenants of the 1st Detachment members.

This detachment who are in want of leggings, socks, mittens & caps are desired to apply to Colonel Campbell for the same.

A guard to mount this evening consisting of 1 Captain 1 Subaltern 3 Sergeants 3 Corporals & 50 Privates. This guard to be furnished by 4 Regiment of Yorkers. A Quarter guard at Head Quarters of 1 Sergeant 1 Corporal & 15 Privates, this guard to be given by the first Regiment of Yorkers. A Captain of the First Regiment of Yorkers is to go the rounds at 12 O'Clock this night.

Haskell recorded a particularly lengthy entry for January 30, occasioned by his company refusing to following orders: "This day we had to go down the Bon Poir Ferry and join Captain Smith, which was not agreeable to our company, we looking upon ourselves as freemen, and have been so since the first of January, refused to go. Our company consisting of fourteen men fit for duty enlisted for two months under Captain Newhall in Colonel Livingston's regiment. In the afternoon were put under guard at head quarters for disobedience of orders."

Conveniently, Arnold had ordered a court-martial for January 31, which quickly dealt with Haskell and his fellow malcreants.

Head Quarters   January 31, 1776

Parole Wooster   Countersign Putnam

A guard to mount this evening consisting of 1 Captain 1 Subaltern 3 Sergeants 3 Corporals & 50 Privates this guard to be furnished by the 2nd Regiment of Yorkers. 1 Subaltern, 1 Sergeant, 1 Corporal & 20 Privates for a Quarter Guard at Head Quarters, it is to be given by Major Brown's Detachment. Field Officer for this detachment be from Major Livingston. Field Officer for the Advanced Guard at head Quarters Major Gansevoort. Officer for visiting the hospital is to be given by the 2nd Regiment of Yorkers.

Haskell recorded the success of their attempted labor strike: "To day we were tried by a Court Martial, and fined one months pay, and ordered to join Captain Smith immediately, or be again confined and receive thirty-nine stripes, two minutes allowed to answer in. We finding that arbitrary rule prevailed, concluded to go with Captain Smith. Then we were released and sent to our quarters."

The new month opened with the announcement of the court-martial results of Haskell's compatriots.

Head Quarters   Holland House   February 1, 1776

Parole Point Lewis   Countersign Wren

A court martial of the line to be held at Point Levy of all such persons as may be brought before it. Captain Ben Schoter? President, Lieutenant Hutson, Lieutenant Shelton of the 1st Regiment of Yorkers, Detachment of the Yorkers, Lieutenant Vandeburgh of 3rd Regiment members.

At the court martial of the line held at head Quarters January the 30 resolved that Daniel Connor & Samuel Rotch For absenting themselves from their quarters & engaging in another company after they enlisted with Captain Craighorn of the 2nd regiment of Yorkers & had received money & clothing from said Captain, received 39 lashes on their backs & that they return to the said Company. The Court Martial according to adjournment the 31st of January

Calib Horsehale [Caleb Haskell ... and thirty other names] refusing to obay Coll. Arnild's orders ordered that they 2 Sergeants be reduced to the ranks of privets and that they with the above mentioned be fined a month pay each & that they ameadiately join Captain Smiths Company according to Coll Arnilds orders

John Waning of the 1st Regt of Yorkers confined on suspicion of having stoling som shirts from the bails committed to his charge when on sentry & being privy to the theft committed by others & having sold som Ridgemental shirts to a French man ordered that he receive 39 lashes on his bair back & that he return to the French man the sum he received for the blankets & shirts be restored to Coll Arnild.

The officers commanding detachments are to apply to Colonel Campbell 2 axes to each detachment and one for each hospital for which the Doctor must apply for to Colonel Campbell. A guard to mount this evening consisting of 1 Captain 1 Subaltern 3 Sergeants 3 Corporals & 50 Privates this guard to be given by the 1st Regiment of Yorkers. 1 Subaltern 1 Sergeant 1 Corporal & 15 Privates for a guard at Head Quarters is to be given by the 5th Regiment of Yorkers. Field Officer for this day below Major Dubois. Field officer for this day for the guard at Head Quarters is Major Brown.

Haskell was still nursing a grudge this day, but he performed his duties. "This morning we marched down to Bon Poir Ferry and joined Capt. Smith's guard, much against our will. Last night some of our guards at St. Roche's set some of the buildings on fire.

The enemy firing upon them with canon and small arms, killed one and wounded two men. We were alarmed, went to our rendezvous. When all was still again went back to our quarters." Arnold, who must have regularly worn out pens, continued his bombardment of the Continental Congress with another note on this day. The major topic of this letter regarded the promotion of Major John Brown, who apparently was taking advantage of the recent demise of General Montgomery to claim a promotion that Montgomery had allegedly promised him. Arnold had other information regarding this alleged promotion which rather suggested that a court-martial was in order for Brown, and he wished to advise the Continental Congress of Brown's nefarious conduct.[20]

The next day, February 2, must have been a quiet day in camp based upon the brief Orderly Book entry.

Head Quarters   Before Quebec   February 2, 1776

Parole Halifax   Countersign Lisbon

A guard to mount this evening consisting of 1 Captain 1 Subaltern 3 Sergeants 3 Corporals & 50 Privates to be given by the 1st regiment of Yorkers. Field Officer for the guards below is Major Leviston. Captain Palmer of the Fourth Regiment of Yorkers goes the rounds at 12 o'clock by the different guards and headquarters.

Haskell returned to his most common commentary, that of the frigid weather: "Exceeding cold. A number of the enemy out in St. Roche's gathering up the ruins of burned buildings for fire wood."

February 3 saw Colonel Arnold issuing extremely lengthy Orderly Book instructions, as he continued to attempt to maintain some control over his unruly subjects, even summoning the chaplain to assist him.

Head Quarters   Before Quebec   February 3, 1776

Parole Wardchester   Countersign London

A Court martial of the line held at Head Quarters this day at 10 O'clock in Datererplines Room for the trial of such persons as shall be brought before them. Captain Mott President, one Lieutenant of the 1st Regiment of Yorkers, one of the 4th regiment of Yorkers, two of the 3rd Regiment of Yorkers. It has been observed that the orders of the 17th of January to which every officer is reserved for inspection is not well understood & a flag has been sent back 1st Instant contrary to orders and has been public declaration sent for the purpose into town by Captain Mott. It is therefore information to the officers of the guard thus explained that any person shall they man woman or child should appear in sight of our guards with a flag upon a staff or in the hand must be suffered to approach for our guards & from then be conducted under a proper guard for [information lined out] accommodation. It is also observed that the orders respecting the Doctors of the 22nd of January is not put into execution it will be necessary then for that the Adjutants of the different corps inform the Doctors of the same for it is apprehended that the Adjutants never have produced these orders to the Doctors so the after orders of January the 25th are to be repeated to all the officers that they may be put in execution excepting the last clause which is not General. The Quartermasters & Commissary complain that a practice is made by some officers to draw rum under the notion of fatigue. It is therefore ordered that henceforth no such order be given but by a special order from the Commander In Chief as also no orders must be given from an officer of the Guard for any rum but they must go to their respective companies for their allowances & the Commissary & his Deputy is ordered not to allow such orders but by a Special Command as aforementioned as this campaign is full of inconveniences, dangers, hardships.

It will not be judged by the gentleman officers when they are reminded that their absence from their quarters both by day & night is extremely dangerous if an attack should be made therefore they are desired to remain at their respective quarters especially in the evening & in the night. The officers of the different guards excepting the Quarter Guard at Headquarters are desired to make a report every day when relieved to the Field Officer of the Day or the captain which goes the rounds that he may be enabled to make his report to the Commander In Chief. It is very certain that the orders are not published at roll calling because officers & men plead ignorance when any fault is committed against orders. Therefore Commanding Officers of Corps or Detachments are desired to have the laudable rule of roll calling put in execution. The officers commanding companies are earnestly desired to inspect into provision returns delivered to them by their Sergeants that mistakes may be prevented and they themselves clear from any censure of that kind.

A sermon will be preached at Head Quarters tomorrow morning at 11 O'clock.

A guard to mount this evening consisting of 1 captain 1 Subaltern 3 Sergeants 3 Corporals & 50 Privates this guard to be furnished by the 4th Regiment of Yorkers. A Quarter Guard at Head Quarters is given the by the 1st Regiment of Yorkers. Field Officer for this day below is Major Leviston. The Brigade major goes the rounds by the guards at Head Quarters. It is Colonel Orders that any person who comes out of Quebec must be stopped at the guards until Head Quarters is acquainted thereof & an Officer sent down for examination consequently the clause [of the previous General Orders] conducted under proper guard to Head Quarters for examination is no notice to be taken of but the [one word blotted out] of the flag stands in full force.

Haskell had other concerns on his mind: "The weather almost unendurable by reason of the cold."

Apparently having exhausted himself, Arnold returned on February 4 to only issuing succinct orders. Possibly his ink was frozen.

Head Quarters   Before Quebec   February 4, 1776

Parole Amsterdam   Countersign New York

A Court martial of the Line held at Head Quarters the 3rd Instant [long list of Court Martial findings omitted]. A guard to mount this evening consisting of 1 Captain 1 Subaltern 3 Sergeants 3 Corporals & 50 Privates this guard to be furnished by the Second regiment of Yorkers. A Quarter Guard at Head Quarters of 1 Lieutenant 1 Sergeant 1 Corporal & 15 Privates to be given by Major Brown's Detachment. Field Officer for this day below is Major Dubois. Field Officer for the guard at Head Quarters is Major Gansevoort. Lieutenant Felton of the1st Regiment of Yorkers is appointed Barracks master until orders. Sergeant Brown is to act under him.

Haskell noted that the army was actually being augmented. "Reinforcements are daily coming in. Twenty-five men arrived from New England."

These reinforcements, most of them arriving fresh from New England as Haskell observed, apparently had a rough time of it. A typical soldier was John Spafford, assigned to Colonel Bellows' Massachusetts Regiment. Spafford left the Continental Army encampment at Cambridge, Massachusetts, on February 1. After what must have been a grueling winter march of what he recorded to be four hundred miles, Spafford arrived at Quebec on February 24. Probably within hours of his arrival he was exposed to and contracted the smallpox. After only twelve days at Quebec, "I was taken sick 14 day broke out with the small pox Simon Howard broke out with the small pox 12 March and the 23d of March he died." Spafford was not able to rejoin his company until April 4.[21] Thus, Spafford had barely served in front of Quebec until he was on the sick rolls for nearly six weeks.

Succinct orders continued on February 5. Again, Haskell commented upon the weather, and it appears that nobody at headquarters had an inclination to write any more than necessary.

Head Quarters   Before Quebec   February 5, 1776

Parole Bristo   Countersign Lee

A guard to mount this evening consisting of 1 Captain 1 Subaltern 3 Sergeants 3 Corporals & 50 Privates[.] This guard to be furnished by the 1st Regiment of Yorkers. Quarter Guard at Head Quarters is to be given by the 4th Regiment of Yorkers. Field Officer for this day below is Major Livingston, Field Officer for the guard at Head Quarters is Major Brown.

Haskell grumbled, "The weather continues extremely cold, it has been so for three days past. At night three of our prisoners made their escape from the city. They brought news of our friends, prisoners in the city, that provision is scarce, that the enemy intends to come out upon us soon, and take our stores."

The cold weather continued unabated on February 6.

Head Quarters   February 6, 1776

Parole Londonderry   Countersign Property

A guard to mount this evening[,] consisting of 1 Captain, 1 Subaltern, 3 Sergeants, 3 Corporals & 50 Privates this guard to be furnished by Major Brown's Detachment. A Quarter Guard at Head Quarters to be furnished by the 2nd Regiment of Yorkers, 1 Subaltern, 1 Sergeant, 1 Corporal & 15 privates. Field officer for this day is Major Livingston. Captain Sackett of the 4th regiment of Yorkers is to go the rounds by the advanced guard and Quarters Guards at Head Quarters. Officer for visiting the hospital is given by Colonel Clinton's Regiment.

Haskell's shivering was relieved by some excitement this evening. "It continues as cold as ever. There is a little stirring by reason of the cold. In the evening we espied a bright light in the city, and another on Bonpoir village. Supposed to be a signal made by some Tory in order to carry some provisions in across the river. A party was sent out from our guard to Bonpoir to find out the occasion of the light. Before we had gone far the light was gone. We marched down to a Tories house where we supposed the light was made and set a guard this night. In the morning we returned back to our quarters."

February 7 continued just as cold, and Arnold finally relented and issued his working parties rum to warm their spirits. This measure had not been executed earlier due to a ghastly shortage of that essential store.

Head Quarters   February 7, 1776

Parole Sicily   Countersign Whales

Every detachment which has any soldier of Colonel Arnold's Regiment in their different companies are desired to give a list of their names in what companies they did belong.

A court martial is to set this day at Mineus Tavern at Ten O'clock on the trial of two officers of Colonel Livingston's Regiment. Colonel Clinton President. Major Gansevoort, Major Dubois, Captain Teneyek, Captain Vipher, Captain Johnston, Captain Sackett, Captain Dewitt, one Captain of Lewistons's, one Lieutenant of the 1st Regiment of Yorkers, one Lieutenant of the 2nd Regiment of Yorkers, one Lieutenant of Major Brown's, one Lieutenant of Colonel Livingston's, Members. Aaron Brown Judge Advocate. Reverend Mr. Detard Interpreter.

A guard to mount this evening[,] consisting of 1 Captain, 1 Subaltern, 3 Sergeants, 3 Corporals & 50 Privates. This guard to be furnished by the 4th regiment of Yorkers. A Quarter Guard at Head Quarters of 1 Subaltern 1 Sergeant 1 Corporal & 15 Privates. Field Officer for this day below is Major Livingston. Field Officer for this day to visit the Advance Guards & Quarter Guard is Major Gansevoort. A Lieutenant & 1 Sergeant & 1 Corporal & 40 Privates of Major Brown's Detachment are to be employed to bring away all the remaining part of the carrying & entrenching tools from the battery they shall be exempted from all other duty of mounting guards until all is carried away. A captain of that detachment is to superintend this work in the room of Captain Babbock until he returns. This party when at work shall be entitled to a gill of rum extraordinary.

Haskell was particularly succinct this day; clearly he was not enjoying the weather, and most likely he was not among those offered a rum ration. "Continues as cold as ever."

On this date Philip Schuyler, at his headquarters in Albany, wrote to the Continental Congress relaying the desperate straits that the army in Canada was in for supplies. Schuyler stated:

Mr. [Joseph] Trumbull's Deputy goes to Canada with what little Money there is in the chest.... The Captains of the two Pennsylvania Companies [moving up to Canada] have this moment informed me that their men are without mittins and mockasins, of the latter I have only been able to procure about 120 pair, of the former I have none.... The troops in Canada will be in great want of shoes, Major Ogden informs me that none are to be had there, nor can I get any here.[22]

Perhaps recognizing the difficulties of the nearly continuous duty that the men had to perform, and the arduous physical demands that were required to work under the frigid temperatures, Arnold ordered the men to be paid on February 8.

Head Quarters   February 8, 1776

Parole Schuyler   Countersign Howe

The honorable Continental Congress have been pleased to appoint Colonel Benedict Arnold a Brigadier General in the Continental Army. The troops are hereby ordered to take notice & pay obedience. Captain Rawlin [blotted, hard to discern] is appointed Muster Master for the time being. The Captains and Officers commanding companies are desired to prepare muster rolls to be prepared next morning where an order will be given at what time. The different regiments shall pass muster in order to receive one month pay for the troops who have pay due to them are to be paid at another time.

A guard to mount this evening consisting of 1 Captain 1 Subaltern 3 Sergeants 3

Corporals & 50 Privates this guard to be furnished by the 2nd Regiment of Yorkers. Quarter guard at Head Quarters is to be given by Major Brown's Detachment. Field Officer for this day is Major Dubois below & Major Brown at Head Quarters.

The prospect of receiving pay apparently mellowed Haskell's perception of the weather: "A pleasant day. A large number of the enemy are out in St. Roches picking up the ruins of burnt buildings for fuel. We had several shells thrown at our guard house, but they did no damage."

Arnold's General Orders of February 9 dealt with two subjects near and dear to any soldier's heart: rations and pay.

Head Quarters   February 9, 1776

Parole Philadelphia   Countersign Orleans

At a General Court martial held the 2nd Instant in the trial of Captain Livingston Quartermaster batman of Colonel Livingston Regiment for threatening to burn the hospital & abusing the priests and superior of the nunnery and threatening the doctors & attendants on the sick and behaving in riotous, disorderly & inhuman like manner, resolved that it is the opinion of this court that Captain Livingston Quartermaster Batman are not guilty of the charges but that they ought to receive a reprimand from the General for [illegible word] as they did. James Clinton President, approved by the General.

The Deputy Quartermaster General, Commissary, Barracks Master & Officers Detached Parties and others who pay any public money to the inhabitants who cannot read nor write are desired to have their receipts witnessed by an American Commissioned Officer for proper voucher for the payment.

Resolved of the Continental Congress that a return consisting of the following kind and quantity of provisions 1 pound of Beef or Pork, ¾ Pound of Salt fish per day, [illegible] Soft Bread of flour per day, 3 pints of peas or beans per day, 1 pint of milk per man per day or the rate ½ part of a dollar, ½ half pint of rice, 1 pint of Indian meal per man per week & quart of spruce beer or cider per man per day, or nine gallons of molasses per company of 100 per week, 3 pounds candles for 100 men per week. For guards [sic] 24 pounds of hard soap per week. Whereas many of the articles vested to a return cannot be provided in this country the bread and meat is augmented to 1 pound ¼ to a ration and in the lieu of beer of cider, Roman Wine is issued. If this shall hereafter appear deficient in the rations as stated by the Congress the General engaged for them that so deficiencies shall be paid to the soldier in consequence. January 8, 1776, resolved that the officers of the Northern Army be accountable for such public stores issued to them, as may be lost through carelessness by their respective corps & that [blotted out word] future there of be deducted out of the pay of those who have embezzled or wasted the same. Resolved that the Congress doth [sic] approve of the raising of a Battalion of Canadians & of the appointment of James Livingston, Esquire Colonel. Resolved that Captain Lamb be appointed commander of the Artillery of the Northern Detachment with the rank of Major. Resolved that no postage shall be paid for any letters to or from any private soldiers while engaged in the Continental Service in defense of the United Colonies & that such letters be forwarded? By some person [illegible word] raised for that purpose by the Commanding officer for the Detachment. Resolved that all the officers & soldiers in the Northern Detachment be paid in person by the Deputy Paymaster General or their assistant to be appointed by him in consequence of their foregoing resolutions.

A guard to mount this evening consisting of 1 Captain 1 Subaltern 3 Sergeants 3 Corporals & 50 Privates this guard to be furnished by the 1st Regiment of Yorkers. A Quarter Guard at head Quarters consisting of 1 Subaltern 1 Sergeant 1 Corporal & 15 Privates to be given by the 4th Regiment of Yorkers. Field Officer for this day below Lieutenant Colonel John Nielson. For the guard at head Quarters Colonel Clinton.

Even with rations and pay the true passwords of the day, February 9 again featured miserable weather, as Haskell related: "A severe snow storm came on this afternoon, increasing this evening." The British garrison in the city was amazed at the vehemence of the storm. One anonymous journal recorded, "A heavy wind at NE with thick snow, the storm encreas'd until evening when it blew a mene [mean] hurricane — it was impossible to face it ... in some places the snow is driven by the wind to twenty foot deep."[23] Lieutenant Patrick Daly, of Colonel Allen MacLean's Royal Highland Emigrant Regiment, echoed, "blowing very hard. Occasioned a great drift of the snow, making it 9 or ten feet in some places on the ramparts, and in different places of the town. From the excessive cold, the sentries obliged to be relieved every half hour."[24]

Facing a snowstorm of monumental proportions, Arnold's topic of conversation on February 10 was snowshoes.

Head Quarters   February 10, 1776

Parole Manly   Countersign Lee

A guard to mount this evening consisting of 1 Captain 1 Subaltern 3 Sergeants 3 Corporals & 50 Privates this guard to be furnished by Major Brown's Detachment & the 4th Regiment of Yorkers gives 1 Subaltern, 2 Sergeants, 2 Corporals & 20 Privates, the 1st Yorkers gives 1 Captain 1 Sergeant 1 Corporal & 30 Privates to a Quarters Guard at Head Quarters, 1 Subaltern, 1 Sergeant, 1 Corporal & 15 Privates to be given by the 2nd Regiment of Yorkers. Field Officer for this day below is Colonel Livingston. For the guard at Head Quarters major Gansevoort.

All the snow shoes among the different detachments which are not fit for use are ordered to be brought to head quarters to have them mended.

Haskell lamented, "The storm continues. Such a storm, I believe, never was known in New England. Two of our men nearly perished going after provisions." Captain Thomas Jones, a British artillery officer in the city, remarked, "It was the greatest fall of snow this year."[25] An anonymous British soldier was stunned to find, "It was impossible to walk in many parts of the Town without snow shoes, the first stories of many houses are under the snow, the windows of the second level with it, and serve as doors."[26]

The snow finally abated late in the afternoon of February 10. Both British and Americans spent the next day in digging themselves out. Possibly because of the fact that the American army was confined to quarters because of the blizzard, smallpox became an even greater problem for Arnold.

Head Quarters   February 11, 1776

Parole Hartford   Countersign New Haven

A guard at Head Quarters consisting of 1 Captain, 1 Subaltern, 3 Sergeants, 3 Corporals & 50 Privates, this guard to be given by the 2nd Regiment of Yorkers. Quarter Guard at Head Quarters to be given the 1st Regiment of Yorkers. Field officer for this day below is Major Livingston, For the guard at Head Quarters Major Brown.

> Whereas repeated orders [have been] given to prevent the scattering [of] the fatal disorder [of] the smallpox has been in a great measure disregarded it is ordered that the commanding officer of every company immediately send such of his company as are vexed with it to the hospital. All officers and soldiers who shall know of any person sick with that disorder in their private quarters & cannot make a immediate compliance thereof shall be treated as neglecting their duty and guilty of a breach of orders.

Haskell barely noted that it was a Sunday. "It clears off pleasant. Our commander sent a flag to the city today. The enemy did not fire upon him, but gave him ill treatment and refused to receive any letters from him."

Monday, February 12, returned to normal, as Arnold again ordered court-martials to attempt to instill discipline into his soldiers.

> Head Quarters   Saint Rocks   February 12, 1776
>
> Parole Hamden   Countersign Sidney
>
> A guard to mount this evening[,] consisting of 1 Captain, 1 Subaltern, 3 Sergeants, 3 Corporals & 50 Privates this guard to be furnished by the First of Yorkers. Quarter Guard at head Quarters 1 Subaltern 1 Sergeant 1 Corporal & 15 privates to be given by Major Brown's Detachment. Field Officer for this day below Major Dubois. For the guard at Head Quarters Colonel Clinton.
>
> A General Court martial to be held at head Quarters tomorrow morning at 10 O'clock on the trial of Lieutenant Dominy arrested by order of the General for disobedience of orders & all such persons as shall be brought before them. Lieutenant Colonel Nielson President. Major Gansevoort, Major Dubois, Major Livingston, 2 Captains of the 1st regiment, 2 Captains of the 3rd Regiment, 1 Captain of the 4th Regiment, 1 Captain of Livingston's regiment, 1 Lieutenant of the 1st Yorkers, 1[Lieutenant] of Major Brown's Detachment [members]. Lieutenant Cross of General Arnold's Regiment is to appear as an evidence. Lieutenant Capp of the 1st Regiment of Yorkers to be Judge Advocate. Reverend Mr. Tetor interpreter.

Haskell was still impressed by the Canadian weather, "Pleasant sun, but cold, which is nothing strange in this country." On February 12 Arnold wrote to the Continental Congress regarding the strength of his force. "We have been reinforced with only one hundred & seventy five men, our whole force is about eight hundred effective men, we have about two hundred, sick & unfit for duty, near fifty of them with the small pox." More ominously, he noted, "The Canadians, in most of the Parishes, inoculate for their own safety."[27]

February 13 appears to have been a quiet day outside of the snow covered ramparts of Quebec.

> Head Quarters   February 13, 1776
>
> Parole Effingham   Countersign Randolph
>
> A guard to mount this evening consisting of 1 Captain, 1 Subaltern, 3 Sergeants, 3 Corporals & 50 Privates this guard to be furnished by the 4th regiment of Yorkers. The Quarter Guard at head Quarters 1 Subaltern 1 Sergeant 1 Corporal & 15 privates this guard to be given by the 2nd of Yorkers. Field Officer for this day below Colonel Nicholson. For the guard at Head Quarters Major Gansevoort.
>
> [written below without explanation, possibly the parole and countersign was changed during the day]
>
> Parole Saint Foys   Countersign Saint Johns.

Haskell managed to record a particularly juicy piece of rumor in his diary. "This morning one of our prisoners made his escape from the city. Two British soldiers deserted and came with him." In Montreal on February 13, the paymaster arrived. Certainly, this would normally be greeted with joy and approbation. Instead, it was shortly revealed that the paymaster had only brought Continental paper money. Wooster reported sorrowfully to Schuyler:

> The Paymaster has arrived, but has brought no hard cash with him. We can buy no provisions or wood with continental currency. Yet they must be had, and that before the middle of March; after that time, there will be no passing up and down this river, for three or four weeks. Perhaps the expedition may fail for want of supplies.... Meat we have will soon be gone.[28]

February 14, St. Valentine's Day, passed uneventfully outside of Quebec.

> Head Quarters   February 14, 1776
>
> Parole Chatham   Countersign Wilkes
>
> A guard to mount this evening consisting of 1 Captain, 1 Subaltern, 3 Sergeants, 3 Corporals & 50 Privates this guard to be furnished by the 2nd regiment of Yorkers. The Quarter Guard at head Quarters 1 Subaltern 1 Sergeant 1 Corporal & 15 privates to be given by the 1st Regiment of Yorkers. Field Officer for this day below Colonel Livingston. For the guard at Head Quarters Major Brown.

Haskell saw an uncommon sight above the city: "A pleasant day, and the sun is so warm that snow gives a little on the roofs of the houses, which is something remarkable. We had a number of shots fired at our guardhouse, but did no damage. Some troops arrived from New England."

The Orderly Book entry for February 15 was badly confused, and made little sense in the journal. One suspects that some of the excess rum was eliminated at headquarters on this date, if the Orderly Book entry is any evidence.

> Head Quarters   February 15, 1776
>
> A guard to mount this evening[,] consisting of 1 Captain, 1 Subaltern, 3 Sergeants, 3 Corporals & 50 Privates this guard to be furnished by the 1st regiment of Yorkers. The Quarter Guard at head Quarters 1 Subaltern 1 Sergeant 1 Corporal & 15 privates to be furnished by Major Brown's Detachment. Field Officer for this day below is Major Brown. For the guard at Head Quarters Colonel Clinton.
>
> [note: List of names written below without explanation, names are not transcribed]
>
> [note: two confused and befuddled paragraphs that make no sense and are not transcribed as they are perfect nonsense]
>
> Thomas Lenington His Hand Received of Captain Dubois 1 cap, 1 pair of mittens, 1 pair of stockings, 1 pair of shoes, 1 pair of leggings, 1 shirt, 1 pair of breeches [what this is doing in the Orderly Book cannot now be ascertained; it certainly does not belong!].

Haskell apparently was not invited to partake of the now unknown festivities at headquarters, but fortunately the British artillerymen managed to liven up the day for him: "Raw, cold weather. Today we had a number of shots fired at our guardhouse, but received no damage. This evening six of our prisoners made their escape from the city, and brought one deserter with them. In the evening we had some shells thrown at our guardhouse, but received no damage."

Apparently the merriment was terminated at headquarters by February 16, for this day's Orderly Book entry was all business, although it was misdated, suggesting that some evidence of the previous day's merriment still hung over.

> Head Quarters   February 17[16], 1776
>
> Parole Effingham   Countersign Hampdon
>
> At a court martial held the 13th instant resolved [long list of findings and punishments not transcribed]. Daniel McCarty confined by Lieutenant Cross for having feloniously detained a shirt & stock of his the court is of opinion that said Daniel McCarty is guilty, ordered that he receive 20 lashes on his bare back.
>
> General Arnold approving of all the sentences except that of Daniel McCarty as it appears to him that it is difficult to reconcile a person's feloniously taking or detaining anything through ignorance. Orders that said McCarty be discharged.
>
> A guard to mount this evening consisting of 1 Captain 1 Subaltern 3 Sergeants 3 Corporals & 50 Privates, this guard to be furnished by the 4th of Yorkers. A Quarter Guard at Head Quarters of 1 Subaltern 1 Sergeant 1 Corporal & 15 Privates by the 2nd Regiment of Yorkers. Field officer for this day below Major Dubois. For the guard at Head Quarters Major Brown.
>
> A general court martial to set on Monday the 19th instant on the trial of all such prisoners as may be brought before them. Colonel Clinton President. Colonel Campbell, Major Dubois, Major Gansevoort, Captain Teneyck, Captain Sacket, Captain Wright, Captain Brown, Lieutenant Pratt, Lieutenant Gano, Lieutenant Dow, Lieutenant Gregg members.
>
> The adjutant of the different regiments & detachments are desired to give in their names & the ranks of all their commissioned officers to the Brigade Major tomorrow morning. The officers who muster the quarter guard is every day to visit the armor & black smith shop and see that the smiths employ in their work & report them whom they find negligent to the Brigade Major. He is also at the bottom of his days report to mention the number of watch coats & blankets delivered to the guard house.

Haskell stayed hunkered down. "We had a number more shot fired at our guardhouse today, but none have done us any damage yet."

The cold weather returned on February 17, and as a result the Orderly Book entry was accordingly limited.

> Head Quarters   February 17, 1776
>
> Parole Burk   Countersign Barry
>
> A guard to mount this evening consisting of 1 Captain, 1 Subaltern, 3 Sergeants, 3 Corporals & 50 Privates this guard to be furnished by Major Brown's Detachment. A Quarter guard at Head Quarters of 1 Subaltern 1 Sergeant 1 Corporal & 15 Privates to be given by the 4th of Yorkers. Field officer for this day below Colonel Nicholson. For Head Quarters Major Gansevoort. Divine services at Count Dupree's House tomorrow morning at 11 o'clock.

The British gunners tried again today to adjust Haskell's rebel attitude: "A cold, sharp air. We have shot flying around our guardhouse every day from the enemy, but have received no damage yet."

The return of the cold weather apparently resulted in some officers and soldiers "slacking off," which did not pass without Arnold taking notice.

> Saint Rocks   Head Quarters   February 18, 1776
>
> Parole Honor   Countersign Woolford
>
> A guard to mount this evening consisting of 1 Captain 1 Subaltern 3 Sergeants 3 Corporals & 50 Privates, this guard to be furnished by the 1st of Yorkers. Quarter guard at Head Quarters consisting of 1 Subaltern, 1 Sergeant, 1 Corporal & 15 Privates. Field Officer for this day below Colonel Livingston. At Head Quarters Brigade Major.
>
> The officer of the quarter guard is to be constantly with this guard especially in the night it would have been needless to repeat this order but it has been observed that unpardonable neglect have been committed, it is judged necessary to warn every officer that mounts any guard whatsoever to be circumspect in their duty to prevent the common soldier taking notice of their conduct & putting out of theirs to excuse authority [sic]. The court martial ordered the 16th instant is postponed to Thursday the 22nd.

Haskell must not have been pleased on this Sabbath, for although the British guns cut him a break this date, the weather did not: "We had a severe cold night and it continues cold today."

Monday, February 19, must have been a quiet day in camp, for the General Orders were nothing except routine.

> Head Quarters   February 19, 1776
>
> Parole Saint [Illegible]   Countersign Arnold
>
> A guard to mount this evening consisting of 1 Captain 1 Subaltern 3 Sergeants 3 Corporals & 50 Privates. This guard to be furnished by the 1st of Yorkers. Quarter Guard at head Quarters of 1 Subaltern 1 Sergeant 1 Corporal & 15 Privates to be given by Major Brown. Field officer for this day below Major Livingston. For the guard at Head Quarters Colonel Clinton.
>
> The Commissary of Provisions is required to make a return at Head Quarters every morning of the different articles supplied the hospital of the army specifying the Doctors names who draw the same.

Haskell had other concerns: "Clear, cold weather. All still."

Wooster wrote to Schuyler on February 19 with the standard concerns: no money, no provisions, and no ammunition:

> Flour may be purchased ... we ought to purchase a quantity of beef also — what we have now will soon be gone — I understand there is a quantity at Ticonderoga — I think it very necessary that it should be pushed over the Lake immediately — I need say nothing more than inform you, that there is not one thousand left of the money which you sent us, and that will be gone in a very few days.... I shall be obliged to you, if you will be good enough to inform me whether there are not any twelve or twenty four pound shot, or 8 inch shells at Ticonderoga or Crown Point. If there is we shall be very glad to have them sent us, they will be much wanted. We have at St. John's a 24 lb and several 12 lb cannon and an 8 inch howitzer — it will not be worth while to take them to Quebec unless we have shot & shells for them.[29]

Unaccountably, no Orderly Book entry was recorded for February 20. Haskell enjoyed a break from the weather, but unfortunately the British gunners did not. "A moderately pleasant day. We had a number of shot fired at us today. Not a shot has struck our house yet."

An honest soldier located a silver pocket watch on February 21. Either the soldier must have been uncommonly honest, or it must not have been a very good watch.

> Head Quarters   February 21, 1776
>
> Parole Arnold   Countersign Shirley
>
> A guard to mount this evening consisting of 1 Captain 1 Subaltern 3 Sergeants 3 Corporals & 50 Privates this guard to be given by the 4th of Yorkers. Quarter Guard at head Quarters is to be given by Major brown's Detachment. It is ordered by the General that every house where the smallpox are shall have a flag that every soldier may avoid running into danger. Whereas little attention has been paid to the observation of the 16th and 17th articles of War requiring all Non Commissioned Officers & Soldiers not to go out of their quarters without leave & commissioned officers to lodge in their Quarters the General desires & hopes that officers & soldiers will be more attentive or expect the consequences arriving from their neglect. Found by one of Captain Johnston's soldiers a silver watch, any person or persons proving it to be their property may have it again by applying to Captain Johnston.

Haskell and the British artillerymen enjoyed the weather on the same day: "Continues pleasant. This morning a hot cannonading began on both sides, which lasted some hours; we received no damage." From Montreal on February 21, Wooster again begged Schuyler for hard money, as the situation was clearly becoming desperate:

> Our distressing circumstances, together with the fatal consequences we have reason to apprehend, for want of hard money, have induced me to send my secretary, Mr. Cole, to you, to bring forward what can be procured. Provisions and wood can not be obtained, nor can we pay for the transporting of anything but with hard cash, which, if we are not immediately supplied with, we must either starve, quit the country, or disgrace our Army and the American cause by laying the country under contribution; there is no other alternative. We have not by us half money enough to answer the demands of the country people to whom we are indebted. By the middle of March, or a little later, we shall not be able to pass with anything up or down this country; our flour is already in a manner gone, and every other kind of provision soon will be, yet a large supply must be sent to the camp before the roads are impassable. Our friends here can supply us with specie no longer, our credit sinks with the inhabitants.[30]

February 22 was another quiet day at American headquarters. No watches, be they wooden, tin, silver or gold, were discovered on this date.

> Head Quarters   February 22, 1776
>
> Parole Norwich   Countersign Jersey
>
> A guard to mount this evening consisting of 1 Captain 1 Subaltern 3 Sergeants 3 Corporals & 50 Privates. This guard to be given by the 2nd of Yorkers. Quarter Guard at Head Quarters of 1 Subaltern 1 Sergeant 1 Corporal & 15 Privates to be given by the 1st of Yorkers. Field officer for this day below Major Livingston. For the guard at Head Quarters Colonel Clinton.

The cold returned again. By now Haskell must have figured out that it was either cold and snowing, or it was pleasant weather and deluging cannonballs. "A cold day. Our guard divided into two companies. Set another guard below us, one mile's distance."

February 23 saw a return to more lengthy General Orders. Unfortunately, they are not particularly interesting lengthy General Orders.

> Head Quarters   February 23, 1776
>
> Parole Grafton   Countersign Battalion??? Littleton??? [illegible]
>
> A guard to mount this evening as usual to be given by 1st of Yorkers. The captain mounting this guard on account of Captain Motts indisposition is Captain Brown of Major Brown's Detachment. At Quarter Guard at Head Quarters of 1 Subaltern 1 Sergeant 1 Corporal & 15 Privates this guard to be given by the 4th of Yorkers. The guards below as usual. Field officer for this day below is Lieutenant Colonel [name smudged and illegible]. For Head Quarters is Major Gansevoort.
>
> Common Orders.
>
> Every officer or non commissioned officer going with corps or with a party from one post or place to another is to call upon the Commissary of Provisions for a certificate mentioning to what day such party is victualed [*sic*]; Any officer coming to a post without such certificate and drawing provisions there will be charged for the same. Which charge the Commissary is hereby ordered to make & transmit monthly accounts of the same to the Deputy Commissary General that the pay of such officers or non commissioned officers so neglecting may be stopped for the same. Every commissary in the Northern Department is strictly enjoined to keep a copy of these orders constantly posted up in his office that none may plead ignorance.
>
> All officers & non commissioned officers who commit any soldiers to the guard house are to acquaint the officers to which company such soldiers belong that they may have their provisions sent there.

Haskell was apparently out in the weather on this date, but he didn't enjoy the scenery: "Cold, uncomfortable weather."

February 24 was a common day, much like every other day outside the citadel of Quebec.

> Head Quarters   before Quebec   February 24, 1776
>
> Parole Connecticut   Countersign Hampshire
>
> A guard to mount this evening consisting as usual. This guard to be furnished by General Wooster Detachment. Captain Woodbridge gives 1 Sergeant 2 Corporals & 20 Privates. Captain Chapman gives 1 Captain 1 Subaltern 2 Sergeants 2 Corporals & 30 Privates. Colonel Warner gives the Quarter Guard. Lieutenant Patterbrun gives 1 Sergeant & 4 Privates. Lieutenant Munson gives 1 Sergeant 1 Corporal & 7 Privates. Captain Woodbridge gives for the Quarter Guard 4 Privates. Captain Chapman mounts the main guard. Lieutenant [name illegible] the Quarter Guard. Field Officer for this day below Major Dubois. Field Officer at Head Quarters Major Brown.

Haskell kept a close watch upon the British on this date, for their foraging lumber parties were again active. "A number of the enemy are out in St. John's suburbs, taking down the buildings for fire wood."

As seen by American Continental Army Headquarters, Sunday February 25, was spent in attempting to locate the various entrenching tools belonging to the army, and apparently promiscuously scattered about.

Head Quarters   before Quebec   February 25, 1776

Parole Albany   Countersign Boston

A guard to mount this evening consisting as usual. This guard to be given by Major Brown's Detachment. Quarters guard likewise as usual. This guard to be given by the 2nd of Yorkers. Field Officer for this day below Colonel Livingston, at Head Quarters Colonel Clinton.

The Conductor of Stores is orders to collect all the [illegible-probably tools] & put them in a safe place as also to examine the different quarters for the entrenching tools which has been scattered throughout the whole camp. He will be furnished with a party of men to search the battery, what tools may be found & when they are all gathered he must deliver an account to the General.

Haskell was not seeking spades or shovels, for he had bigger fish to fry. "About nine o'clock last evening had orders to lay on our arms and double our guards, as there is a movement among the enemy. We kept a good lookout, but all still."

Arnold apparently decided on a little bit of housekeeping on Monday, February 26, to liven up the mundane monotony of camp life.

Head Quarters   February 26, 1776

Parole Dean   Countersign Sears

A guard to mount this evening consisting as usual. This guard is to be given by the 2nd of Yorkers. Quarter guard by the 1st of Yorkers. Field Officer for this day below Major Livingston. Field officer for this day at Head Quarters Major Gansevoort.
The artillery men who are quarters at Major Brown's Quarters are to move their quarters into a house prepared for them by the Barracks Master Lieutenant Pelton to whom they must apply the monthly returns for the first of March to be prepared to be given in time the officers in general are ordered to see that their quarters are kept clean as much as the nature of the cantonment will admit of and that the filth and snow is cleared away from the doors by the camp color men for which purpose each company is to choose one man who shall be freed from all other duty.

Haskell was again too busy to be shoveling snow on this date: "There is a brisk firing in the city with small arms."

Monotony apparently returned to headquarters on February 27.

Head Quarters   February 27, 1776

Parole Handenhall   Countersign Norwich

A guard to mount this evening[,] consisting as usual, this guard to be given by the 1st of Yorkers. Quarter Guard at Head Quarters to be given by the 2nd of Yorkers. Field Officer for this day below Colonel Nicholson. Field officer for Head Quarters Major Brown.

Haskell reported, almost with glee, an improvement in the weather: "A warm, pleasant day; the snow beginning to thaw, at night we had some rain." Arnold apparently had fallen into the habit of writing the Continental Congress about every two weeks, and was due for another letter. Even though he began by declaring "nothing of consequence has occurred here," he wrote a fairly lengthy communications, and provided the Continental Congress in Philadelphia with considerable information regarding his own morale and belief in the cause, and the conditions that his army labored under:

> Sensible of the vast importance of this country, you may be assured my utmost exertions will not be wanting to effect your wishes, in adding it to the United Colonies. I am fully of your opinion, that the balance will turn in whose favour it belongs. The repeated successes of our raw, undisciplined troops, over the flower of the British army; the many unexpected and remarkable occurrences in our favour, are plain proofs of the overruling hand of Providence, and justly demands our warmest gratitude to Heaven, which I make no doubt will crown our virtuous efforts with success.
>
> I am sorry to inform you, notwithstanding every precaution that could be used, the small-pox has crept in among the troops; we have near one hundred men in the Hospital; in general it is favourable, very few have died. I have moved the inhabitants of the vicinity of Quebeck into the country, and hope to prevent its spreading any further. The severity of the climate, the troops very illy clad, and worse paid; the trouble of reconciling matters among the inhabitants, and lately an uneasiness among some of the New York and other officers, who think themselves neglected in the new arrangement; while those who deserted the cause and went home last fall have been promoted; in short, the choice of difficulties I have had to encounter, has rendered it so very perplexing, that I have often been at a loss how to conduct matters.
>
> As General Schuyler's ill state of health will not permit his coming this way, I was in hopes General Lee, or some experienced officer, would have been sent to take the command here. The service requires a person of greater abilities and experience than I can pretend to. General Wooster writes me his intention of coming down here; I am afraid he will not be able to leave Montreal.

Arnold was mostly correct, as it would be another month before Wooster managed to bestir himself from Montreal. Arnold concluded by updating Congress on his health, as he continued to heal, albeit slowly, from his severe wound received in the abortive assault on New Year's Eve. "I have the pleasure to inform you my wound is entirely healed, and I am able to hobble about my room, though my leg is a little contracted and weak. I hope soon to be fit for action."[31] In just two sentences, Arnold reveals much about his determination and leadership. In the middle of a Canadian winter, with an army of about 1,300 men of which one-quarter was sick; the men on short rations, without proper winter clothing, and receiving no pay; fearful of falling sick with smallpox, one of the most feared and contagious diseases known to mankind and that was raging in the army; serving guard duty every other night; and with a severe wound that had kept him confined to his quarters for two months, Arnold still had the considerably larger, spectacularly equipped British army bottled up inside the city. It was one of the most impressive feats in American military history.

On this date General Schuyler wrote to the Continental Congress, with a detailed discussion of the provisions situation:

> There is scarcely pork sufficient to be got on the East side of Hudson's River to supply the small quantities intended to be stored near that river — What is gone to Canada and remains at the posts above, will serve the army but a very short time, and no supplies of the meat kind can be had even with hard Cash in Canada from the beginning of April until the middle or latter end of September; hence a very considerable quantity of provisions will be wanted — I shall therefore order the Commissary General to send for 1,000 barrels of pork to New Jersey; but being apprehensive that the Men of War will not suffer any vessels to pass, I have directed that it should be sent by water to Hackinsack, from whence I believe the traverse to Hudson's River is short and

sloops may be sent down to transport it to this place, but as this will be far from being a sufficiency, I propose if agreeable to Congress, and that they judge fresh meat cheaper than salt pork which is very doubtful with me on account of the numbers lost in driving, extra waste in issuing etc. and that a supply of cattle should be sent to Onion River to be from thence conveyed in our vessels and row gallies to St. Johns but not to be put on board at Onion River until there is a fair wind lest they should suffer in their passage — I do not mean that the cattle should be sent before there is grass sufficient for their subsistence on the road.... If the lakes should open before I can hear from Congress, I will venture to raise a Company of one hundred batteaumen for foresee that great quantities of provisions must be sent into Canada.[32]

Since General Wooster had finally seen fit to dispatch some reinforcements to Quebec, the General Orders had to be somewhat more detailed than normal on Wednesday, February 28, to ensure that the new arrivals understood their responsibilities.

Head Quarters   February 28, 1776

Parole Levery   Countersign Ward

Lieutenant Bailey is ordered with his party to join a party of Captain Smith's & Lieutenant Baly and to march to Bowport to relieve the French guard there. Mr. Aaron Bower is appointed to rank in the Northern department according to the Directions of Congress. A guard to mount at 5 O'clock as usual & to be furnished by General Wooster's Detachment. Quarter Guard by Colonel Warner.

   Captain Woodbridge gives 1 Lieutenant, 2 Sergeants, 2 Corporals & 30 Privates
   Captain Chapman gives 1 Sergeant, 1 Corporal & 20 Privates
   Lieutenant Pittebore gives 1 Corporal & 4 Privates
   Manson gives 1 Sergeant, 1 Corporal & 7 Privates
   The volunteers at Major Brown's gives 7 Privates.
   Captain Woodbridge mounts the main guard, Lieutenant Munson the Quarter Guard.
Field Officer for this day below Colonel Nicholson, At Head Quarters Colonel Clinton.

Haskell made what must have been a dispiriting discovery this day: when the snow finally does melt in Canada, it creates one unholy terror of a mess. "Continues rainy, the going is exceeding bad."

Seventeen-seventy-six was a leap year. Some of the soldiers apparently took it upon themselves to celebrate this magnificent holiday.

Head Quarters   February 29, 1776

Parole London   Countersign Bristol

Any person who sells spirituous liquors to the soldiers without license from the general and an order from a commissioned officer to which said soldier belongs shall forfeit the liquor found in his possession & the penalty of 10 pound currency, one half to the informer & the other half to the wounded & sick soldiers of the army. Lieutenant Baly & Quickly is ordered to leave the place at Bayport to Mr. Derousey & occupy all the convenient places from thence to Captain Smith's Quarters & place guards in those places. A guard mount this evening consisting as usual. This guard to be given by Major Brown's Detachment. Quarter guard by 2nd of Yorkers. Field officer for this day below Major Dubois. For the guard at head quarters Major Gansevoort.

Haskell was marching about through the mud and slush, and probably to his regret, he did not partake of the leap year festivities. "This morning our company had orders to go to Bonpour village to join a guard with Captain Bailly and relieve a French guard. We went down and took our quarters in a house by the river side."

At the end of February the American army in Canada was finally well enough organized to begin to submit monthly reports. The first report indicated that Arnold had 1,290 soldiers in his army before Quebec, if so few men could be referred to as an army. Of this pitifully small force 326 men were unfit for duty, presumably sick, leaving him under one thousand soldiers to prosecute the blockade of the city.[33]

The first day of March saw a very succinct order.

> Head Quarters   March 1, 1776
>
> Parole Philadelphia   Countersign Jersey
>
> A guard to mount this evening consisting as usual. This guard to be furnished by 4th of Yorkers. Quarter Guard at head Quarters by the 1st of Yorkers. Field officer for the day below Colonel Livingston, at Head Quarters Major Brown.

It was also a routine day for Haskell: "Extremely cold. In the afternoon we had a number of shot fired at our guard house, did no damage."

The second day of March saw snow, apparently heavy at times. As was typical for days with considerable snow or extreme cold, the Orderly Book entries were distinctly limited.

> Head Quarters   March 2, 1776
>
> Parole Charlestown   Countersign Sterling
>
> A guard to mount this evening at 5 O'clock consisting as usual. This guard to be furnished by the 2nd of Yorkers. Quarter guard by Major Brown's Detachment. Field Officer for this day below Major Livingston. At Head Quarters Colonel Clinton. The guard below as usual.

Haskell, as for most days with heavy snow or extreme cold, remained focused on the weather: "Thick weather, and some snow, clears off pleasant in afternoon."

On March 3 Arnold decided to implement an interesting innovation to replenish his artillery supplies, which were distinctly limited. He offered rewards for soldiers who retrieved shot that had been fired by the enemy. This was not a new scheme, as Washington had previously employed a similar approach at the Siege of Boston.

> Head Quarters   March 3, 1776
>
> Parole Newport   Countersign Providence
>
> A guard to mount this evening consisting as usual. This guard to be given by the 1st of Yorkers. Quarter Guard by Colonel Livingston's detachment. Lieutenant Walker of that detachment mounts the Quarter Guard. The Adjutant of the 1st, 2nd, 3rd 7 4th of Yorkers, the adjutant of Major Brown's, the Sergeants of general Wooster's, the Sergeants of Lieutenant Pettbone & Munson & the Adjutant of Colonel Livingston, a Sergeant of Captain Neverly, A Sergeant of Lieutenant Sufferly [this name blotted], Sergeant of Jenkins are every day at Nine O'clock in the morning to bring in a report to the Brigade Major of their effectives both officers & men. This order to be strictly observed. The General will give a reward to every one who brings in either balls or shells for every ball under 12 pounds four pence & about that size six pence & for every shell of a large dimension 1 shilling. Field Officer for this day below Major Dubois, at Head Quarters Major Gansevoort.

The word about the possibility for rewards apparently did not reach Haskell, and in any event he remained focused upon the inclement weather of Canada, "Severe cold. In the evening we took three prisoners who came out of the city."

On Monday, March 4, the Orderly Book stipulated the formation of a working party. Arnold apparently believed that constructing new firing positions, presumably to return the retrieved solid shot at the citadel, would keep his soldiers more gainfully employed and out of trouble.

> Head Quarters   March 4, 1776
>
> Parole Wilkes   Countersign Liberty
>
> A guard to mount this evening consisting as usual. This guard to be furnished by General Wooster's Regiment. Captain Chapman for this guard. Quarter guard by Colonel Warners, in Captain Himan's [faded out] Company. Captain Woodbridge gives for the main guard 1 Sergeant, 1 Corporal & 29 Privates. Captain Chapman gives 1 Lieutenant, 2 Sergeants, 2 Corporals & 30 Privates. For the Quarter Guard Lieutenant Munson his party gives 1 Corporal & 4 men. Lieutenant Pettibone gives 4 men & 1 Sergeant. Captain Himan gives 1 man. A work party to be issued immediately consisting of 1 Subaltern, 1 Sergeant, 1 Corporal & 30 privates. The half of them to be without arms. This party to be furnished by Major Brown's Detachment. Captain Ayres will direct this party. Field Officer for this day below Colonel Livingston, at Head Quarters Major Brown.

Haskell apparently avoided this onerous duty, and could stay concerned with the miserable weather: "Uncomfortable weather, in the evening we had a heavy rain."

The Orderly Book entry for March 5 was committed to keeping the various guard detachments and working parties straight. Apparently this was a challenging feat.

> Head Quarters   Before Quebec   March 5, 1776
>
> Parole Lisbon   Countersign Hopkins
>
> A guard to mount his evening consisting as usual. This guard to be given by Major Brown's Detachment. Quarter Guard by the 2nd of Yorkers. Field officer for this day below Major Livingston, at Headquarters Colonel Clinton. The guard below mount as usual. Lieutenant Doling of the 3rd of Yorkers is to direct the different detachments below how to furnish their quota for the different guards & working parties as occasions may require. For this purpose all the Adjutants & Orderly Sergeants of the different detachments in these quarters are to give to said Lieutenant returns of their strength, and he is to make a daily report of the whole to the Brigade Major instead of the Adjutant & Sergeants as ordered the 3rd instant. Lieutenant Pawling is also to receive from the Brigade Major every day at 10 O'clock general Orders which he is to communicate to the detachments below at 12 O'clock when the Adjutants & Sergeants is to wait upon him for that purpose in such place as he shall direct. It is to be observed that all the troops about headquarters are to make their returns to the Brigade major as ordered.

Haskell was fortunate enough to continue evading these various working parties. "Continues rainy. This morning we hoisted a red flag before the city. At night a bad storm of snow, with a hard gale of wind at northeast."

The red flag was a morale building effort by Arnold to commemorate the anniversary of the famous Boston Massacre. It was intended to be a red or bloody flag to mark the vicious murder of the allegedly peaceable Boston citizens by the brutal British soldiery. The point was not lost on the British garrison, for Captain Jones reported, "This morning the Rebels hoisted a red flag at the ferry Guard house, supposed to be in commemoration of the attempt made by the mob at Boston on the Custom House, when five of the rioters were killed by the troops."[34]

Discerning the Orderly Book entry for March 6 is somewhat challenging. Apparently Arnold had some scheme afoot, for he put a number of blacksmiths to work on this date.

> Head Quarters   March 6, 1776
>
> Parole Saint Vincent   Countersign Washington
>
> A guard to mount this evening at 5 O'clock consisting as usual. This guard to be furnished by the 4th of Yorkers. Quarter Guard by the 1st of Yorkers. Field Officer for this below Colonel Nicholson, at Head Quarters Major Gansevoort.
>
> Lieutenant Conklin of the 3rd Regiment of Yorkers is to oversee the blacksmiths employed in the service & he is to choose 5 or 6 Blacksmiths out of Colonel Clinton's Regiment to be immediately set to work. The bakers out of the 2nd Regiment of Yorkers who are to go Sillery are to give in their names to the Commissary. The troops who are now or may hereafter be quarters the other side of the hospital except the Canadians under Colonel DuGugary are to bring their morning reports to Lieutenant Pawling.

Haskell had much to celebrate on this Wednesday: "We had some rain this morning, but cold. We received our pay of Captain Smith for one month."

By March 6 the ice on the Hudson River and Lakes George and Champlain was beginning to break up, completely interrupting the American supply lines of communication as Schuyler ruefully informed the Continental Congress from Albany:

> The winter here is entirely broken up, and I believe Hudson's River will be clear of ice in a few days. It may be best therefore that the remainder of the troops from New Jersey and Pennsylvania should embark at New Windsor or still lower down, if craft can be procured. Only one company of Colonel [Charles] Burrell's Regiment is gone past here, I greatly fear that the remainder will not be able to pass the Lakes on ice unless a sudden change in the weather takes place, some horses and one man have already been drowned on Lake George and Lake Champlain. It would be happy for us if the Lakes immediately opened, as I have got matters in such a way that I can immediately send on the troops by water but should the Lakes become impassable in any way, I must of necessity detain the troops at this place until they open, as well to save the expenditures of what pork we have at Fort George as that they cannot be quartered there. The sleds that left this, with the last Pennsylvania Company I am this moment informed are returned not being able to proceed further than twenty miles from this, Hudson River being broken up there but as yet impassable. On the 28th February I sent General Wooster something above 2,000 pounds in Specie, which I have collected.... We are greatly distressed for money for the current expenses of the day.[35]

The weather finally improved at Quebec on March 7, although the Orderly Book failed to notice this fact.

> Head Quarters   March 7, 1776
>
> Parole Northhampton   Countersign Bristol

A guard to mount this evening at 5 O'clock consisting as usual. This guard to be furnished by the 1st & 2nd of Yorkers. The 1st regiment gives 1 Lieutenant, 1 Corporal & 25 Privates. The 2nd Regiment gives 1 Captain, 2 Sergeants, 2 Corporals & 25 Privates. The Quarter Guard to be given by General Wooster's 1 Subaltern, 1 Sergeant, 1 Corporal & 15 Privates. Field officer for this day below Major Dubois, at Head Quarters Major Brown.

A Quarter Guard is to mount in a convenient place at Major Dubois Quarters consisting of 1 Sergeant, 1 Corporal & 12 Privates, for the reception of all prisoners which may be confined by the troops below the hill.

Haskell enjoyed two excellent days in a row, for on this Thursday he reported, "Pleasant weather." He must have been appreciating the improvement too much to spend time writing in his journal.

The crafty Arnold took advantage of the good weather to order another heavy working party on Friday, March 8.

Head Quarters   March 8, 1776

Parole Saint Anne   Countersign Amsterdam

A working party to be at Head Quarters at 7 O'clock this evening consisting of 1 Subaltern 1 Sergeant 1 Corporal & 30 Privates. This party to be furnished by the troops below. Lieutenant Barnes of General Wooster's detachment is appointed Adjutant pro tempora [temporarily]. A guard to mount this evening consisting of 1 Captain 1 Subaltern 3 Sergeants 3 Corporals & 50 Privates. Major Brown gives for this guard 1 Subaltern, 2 Sergeants 2 Corporals & 35 men. Captain Herman gives 1 captain, 2 Sergeants, 1 Corporal & 10 Privates. Captain Smith gives 5 Privates. For Quarter Guard Lieutenant Walker. The 4th of Yorkers gives for this guard 1 Sergeant and 9 Privates. Lieutenant Munson gives 1 Corporal & 6 Privates. Field Officer for this day below Major Cady. At Head Quarters Colonel Clinton.

Haskell again wrote succinctly, "Some troops arrived from Philadelphia." Apparently the young Musketman was growing weary of even keeping a journal of a winter in Canada. What he felt of winter and Canada must, of course, be conjectured at. This is probably fortuitous, as one suspects that profanity would somehow have been involved.

The General Orders book for Saturday, March 9, concerned itself again with the liberal use of spirituous beverages in the American camp, and directed measures that the army was to take in case of British attack. Apparently Arnold was concerned that the British might attempt to take advantage of the slight improvement in weather.

Head Quarters   March 9, 1776

Parole Cody   Countersign Dorsey

Whereas in the order of the 28th of February every sutler convicted of selling spirituous liquor to any soldier without an order from a commissioned officer of the company to which said soldier belongs is subject to a penalty of 10 pounds. And whereas Hareman proves evidences verified that he did buy spirituous liquors of Mr. Broth without any such orders the general concludes the court have rather mistaken the orders evidence & orders that they set again at 10 O'clock this evening to reexamine said orders and sentence.

A guard to mount this evening at 5 O'clock consisting as usual. This guard to be given by the 1st of Yorkers. Quarter Guard by 4th or Yorkers. A working party, this evening to be at head Quarters at 6 O'clock consisting of 2 Subalterns, 2 Sergeants, 2 Corporals & 40 Privates. The 2nd of Yorkers gives 1 Subaltern, 1 Sergeant, 1 Corporal & 20 Privates. The 4th of Yorkers gives 1 Subaltern, 1 Sergeant, 1 Corporal & 20 Privates. Field officer for this day below Colonel Nicholson. At Head Quarters Major Gansevoort.

When at any time an alarm happens in the camp at night the officers are to observe that the beating to arms is allowed only but no drum is to beat nor fife to play any march nor troop, and all maneuvers are to be performed as silent as possible.

Haskell observed the British at work, so Arnold's General Orders were not directed against a ghost. "The enemy are busy cutting a channel in the ice to make a passage into the lower town."

The General Orders of March 10 were routine; the major event was that some of the guards were apparently re-shuffled.

Head Quarters   March 10, 1776

Parole Soilly [Sillery]   Countersign Liberty

A guard to mount this evening at 5 O'clock consisting as usual. This guard to be furnished by General Wooster's Regiment & gives 1 Captain, 1 Subaltern, 1 Sergeant, 2 Corporals & 40 Privates. The 1st of Yorkers gives 1 Sergeant, 1 Corporal & 10 Privates. Quarter Guard likewise as usual to be given by the 2nd of Yorkers. Field officer for this day below Major Dubois. At head Quarters Major Brown.

A Court martial of the line to be held tomorrow morning in Dejardins Room for the trial of such persons as may be brought before them. Captain Palmer President. Lieutenant Austin, Lieutenant Gray, Lieutenant Vavarst, Lieutenant Waterbury Members.

A Sergeant, 1 Corporal & 12 Privates from the 1st of Yorkers will hold themselves in readiness at a moments warning to march with the artillery to Sillery there to remain as a guard till further orders.

Haskell's thoughts returned to the weather: "Cold, uncomfortable weather."

Sadly enough, the Orderly Book for Clinton's 3rd New York Regiment came to an abrupt cessation on March 11, and although it was certainly resumed, the original may not have survived the years, and its whereabouts are now unknown.

Head Quarters   March 11, 1776

Parole Warner   Countersign Williams

A guard to mount this evening at 5 O'clock consisting as usual. This guard to be furnished by Major Brown's Detachment. Quarter guard to be given by Captain Sain, 1 Lieutenant, 1 Sergeant & 7 Privates. Captain Hinman gives 1 Corporal & 8 Privates. Field officer for this day below Colonel Livingston. At Head Quarters Major Gansevoort.

The reveille is to beat every morning at daybreak through the whole camp. The commanding officers of regiments & detachments are to observe that the stated [Orderly Book abruptly ends].

Haskell briefly recorded what must have been an extremely exciting day: "A pleasant morning. This afternoon our house took fire on the roof; with much difficulty we put it out."

With the termination of the Orderly Book, we are left with Haskell's Journal for a daily record of the American army's activities outside of Quebec. On Tuesday, March 12, Haskell, as many of his journal entries have validated, remained focused upon the weather: "A cold snowstorm and hard gale of wind, it clears off this morning."

Haskell recorded the first significant combat action since the American assault on March 13: "This afternoon a party of the enemy came out of the city on a party of our men at Wolfe's Cove, on fatigue. After a small skirmish the enemy went in again." The next day Haskell recounted a particularly interesting bit of army rumor: "This afternoon our General sent a flag to the city. The enemy would take no letters from him, and ordered him back again, or they would fire on him immediately."

On March 15 Musketman Haskell again stayed focused on the weather: "A pleasant day." On this date Adjutant Russell Dewey also arrived at Quebec, having completed a long and arduous march from his home at Chester, Massachusetts. Adjutant Dewey's arrival provides us another glimpse into life in the American army outside of Quebec in the raw, cold spring of 1776.[36]

March 16 was a Saturday, and the pleasant weather of the day before inspired Arnold to begin planning a serious attack upon the citadel, "We are making preparations for another attack on the city, collecting fascines and other materials to build batteries as soon as the weather will permit." Adjutant Dewey was not impressed with his new quarters at Quebec that he moved into on this date. "Nothing remarkable happened except a smokehouse which our Company was put into and almost smoked my eyes out; three company is march in this day."

Haskell had a particularly interesting Sunday, March 17. "It being St. Patrick's Day we had the curiosity to go to Mass in Bonpoir." Adjutant Dewey saw his first gunfire on this date: "They fired from the walls of Quebec considerable."

On March 18 things started to heat up across the stark stone walls that encircled the city of Quebec. "A brisk firing with cannon and small arms in the city." Dewey also reported, "I viewed the wall of Quebec; they fired at me 2 or 3 times without danger." The hard working Doctor Senter made a brief entry for this date: "About this time arrived troops from Montreal to our assistance. Several deserters coming out, but never able to obtain a true state of their army. From this to April the 3d, no occurrences of moment. Troops coming up to our relief."

Things continued to look up for the American Army in mid–March, as Haskell reported for March 19 and 20. "To day we had one piece of cannon and two howitzers come into camp" and "Troops are daily coming in to our assistance from various parts. One large company came in today." Adjutant Dewey, who had provided little service in his brief stay at Quebec, would now begin preparing for the smallpox inoculation, "Nothing remarkable happened except the infection of the small pox, which we began to prepare for." From this date forward, Dewey was confined to quarters with the small pox.

On Thursday, March 21, the Canadian winter demonstrated its resolution not to depart without a struggle, as Haskell had to document: "Cold uncomfortable weather. Our battery at Point Levi is almost completed." The British were not about to let the Americans open a battery without taking action, and on Friday, March 22, Haskell recorded the British response, "A hot firing began this morning in the city upon our men at Point Levi, at work on the battery and continued all the forenoon. Three companies more are ordered on to Point Levi."

The British were beginning to stir, and the Americans were acting to counter them. "March 23ᵈ Saturday, We had information this morning that a party of the enemy had gone down the river by water after provision. About one hundred and fifty men were sent down to obstruct them and three companies of Canadians were sent to Orleans to strengthen our guards there." The brief flurry of activity was interrupted by inclement weather on Sunday, March 24, "a cold stormy day. One of our prisoners belonging to Captain Lane's artillery made his escape from the city." Dewey, confined to quarters and fasting while waiting for the small pox to erupt, reported this day, "It was a cold windy day and the snow flew and the winds was so high that we was afraid to go out a door for fear we should be blowed away for our preparation [for the smallpox] brought us so low that we were almost as light as eagles."

At the end of March, another ominous event occurred, as a number of French Canadian habitants organized against the Americans. It was a relatively insignificant affair. One Monsieur Beaujeu, the French seigneur of Crane Island, formed a small force about thirty miles down the St. Lawrence River, with the intent of cutting off American supplies, organizing a force of opposition to operate between the American garrisons of Montreal and Quebec, and possibly even attacking the Americans before Quebec from their rear. Dr. Senter reported, "About this time an insurrection happened down the river St. Lawrence, about six leagues from Quebec, in consequence of some of the enemy's emissaries, joined to the envious instigations of some of their priests. They collected a number of Canadians, and were marching up in form to take possession of our troops at Point Levi."[37] It was an ambitious undertaking, and sufficient habitants still favored the American cause that the Americans shortly received word of Beaujeu's efforts.[38] As Haskell and Arnold's Orderly Book recorded, the garrison at Point Levi (the closest American force at Quebec to the uprising) was reinforced; an American battalion was dispatched to deal directly with the problem while Canadians loyal to the American cause were sent to the St. Lawrence River to strengthen American posts along their lines of communication. A brief but brutal skirmish at the house of Michel Blay on the Riviére de Sud on March 24 killed seven and wounded two of Beaujeu's men and captured thirty-eight more.[39] This aggressive action on Arnold's part terminated Beaujeu's efforts on behalf of the Crown. This rebellion had been quickly controlled, but simply the fact that it had taken place at all suggested that the Canadians were losing interest in the American cause and presence. A French Canadian leader of another century summarized the state of affairs quite nicely: "It was all very simple. We had to choose between the English of Boston and the English of London. The English of London were further away and we hated them less."[40]

Things were heating up, as Haskell documented for the next several days. "March 25th, Monday. We had a number of shot fired from the city at our battery at Point Levi. One company arrived in camp from the Jerseys. March 26th. Tuesday. We heard from the party down the river. They had a skirmish with the enemy and have taken a party of thirty men without any loss on our side, only three men wounded. About two hundred more were sent to reinforce our party down the river. Upwards of one hundred cannon were discharged within a few minutes in the city and some shells thrown at our troops at Point Levi."

Haskell's interest in the machinations of the British Royal Artillery were interrupted the next day with a repeat of the earlier excitement. "March 27th, Wednesday. This morning about 11 o'clock our house took fire on the roof the wind blowing fresh at North West, the fire spread fast, we saw no possibility of saving the house, and went to clearing it as fast as possible. It was soon after burned down. We moved up to Bonpoir village. This afternoon some prisoners taken down the river were brought to headquarters."

From Albany on March 27, Schuyler kept George Washington appraised of the current ice conditions, for much depended upon the lakes and rivers opening up as soon as possible, to permit reinforcements to begin flowing to Quebec. Since New York, the source of all the replacement soldiers and supplies for Arnold's army, was to the south of Canada, the hope was that the American reinforcements would reach Quebec before the British reinforcements could. If so, the Americans could realistically hope to conquer a weakened, winter-weary Quebec. If not, and the British reinforcements arrived first, Arnold's small army would be swept away. Schuyler reported:

> The north end of Lake Champlain is open, and I hope a few warm days will open the remainder of that, and also Lake George — we have here now about six hundred men, who will move as soon as there is a prospect of conveying them across the lakes. On the 22nd instant, one hundred new batteaus were finished at Fort George, as far as they can without pitch & oakum, which is not yet arrived from New York, Thirty five are however completely finished — I am of opinion that a much greater number are necessary to pour troops into Canada ... but Congress has stinted me to the number I have built.[41]

In his new quarters on March 28, which must not have been as comfortable as the house that had just been converted to ashes, Haskell again grumbled about the weather: "Uncomfortable weather. Raw cold wind for several days."

Haskell, on March 29, recorded some more skirmishing as the British began to stir outside of the citadel city. "Some firing at our troops at Point Levi from the city." The next day, Saturday, March 30, the British finally got lucky. "One of the guard at the lower guard house was killed by a cannon ball from the city. A number of the enemy came out on St. John's. We went down to them, after a short skirmish with them they went in again. We received no damage." Dewey, barely recovering from the smallpox (he must have had a mild case), reported of this event, "The Regulars hawled a gun out of the city and fired at our main guard and just at night they killed one of our men."

March 31 was the Sabbath, and for only the second time in the winter Haskell reported a sermon being preached to the soldiers (attending Catholic mass "for curiosity" on St. Patrick's Day not being counted). "Reverend Mr. Briggs came to our quarters and gave us a discourse from 36th Psalms and 7th verse." The first four verses on 36th Psalms are about the wicked and how they do not fear God (verse 1), they flatter themselves that their sin won't be found out (verse 2), they are deceitful and don't reject evil. An implied "but" then comprises verses 5–6, in that God's "steadfast love" rules the whole creation. The Reverend Briggs may have used these verses to say that despite present circumstances,

God was still in charge. Verse 7, then, reveals God's steadfast love as being a place of refuge. "Under the shadow of your wings" is a metaphor for God's providence (like seeking asylum in the Temple). Verses 10–12 then contain an entreaty for God to continue his steadfast love for the faithful, while saying, "Do not let the foot of the arrogant tread on me" and the evildoers are "thrust down, unable to rise." Thus, the good Reverend Briggs was exhorting the American troops that God's steadfast love was with them despite all the hardship and that the evil ones (the enemy) would get theirs in the end. It must have been a particularly poignant and meaningful sermon for the tired, sick, cold, and hungry soldiers that comprised Arnold's tiny army.[42]

Wooster finally stirred himself from Montreal. John Jenks, a New England merchant transacting business in the small community of Three Rivers, reported seeing him on his way down the St. Lawrence:

> [March] 29 — Pleasant weather. General Wooster arrived here on his way to Quebec with a number of gentlemen. Who [blotted — accompanied or assisted] him.
>   30 — Pleasant. The General set off about 11 O'clock.[43]

By the end of March Arnold's army had increased to 2,505 soldiers, indicating that reinforcements had been reaching him. However, many of these new soldiers had fallen ill immediately or shortly after arriving at Quebec, such that no less than 786 (over 31 percent) of these soldiers were sick, leaving Arnold just over 1,700 soldiers present for duty.[44]

Halkett apparently did not get fooled on April 1. However, the British gunnery remained deadly, while Halkett also recorded a significant change in the American command structure. "General Worcester [Wooster] arrived at camp; we lost one man, killed at Point Levi with a cannon ball from the city." Wooster had finally made it to Quebec. It was over three months after the failed assault on the Lower Town, and three months to the day after Arnold, still bleeding from his wound, implored Wooster to stir from his warm and comfortable quarters in Montreal and assume command.

On Tuesday, April 2, Haskell was assigned to a work party. "We are at work building batteries at different places." Dewey, still recovering, reported some firing on this date: "They wounded 2 of our men at the alarm post." By April 2 the Hudson River, Lake George and Lake Champlain had all become free of ice, and American reinforcements were starting to flow to the north. Among the most valuable of those soldiers was Major General John Thomas, who leadership had just been responsible for the evacuation of Boston.

Thomas was a 53-year-old surgeon from Marshfield, Massachusetts.[45] He had studied under Dr. Cotton Tufts, a distinguished physician. Following his apprenticeship he moved to Kingston, Massachusetts, where he practiced medicine and was active in community politics and leadership. His first military experience was as a surgeon for a Massachusetts provincial regiment during King George's War in 1746. He was also appointed as a surgeon for Shirley's regiment at the commencement of the Seven Years' War, but shortly transitioned to a more martial post. By 1759 he commanded a regiment of Massachusetts provincials in Nova Scotia, and served with the main British army under General Jeffery Amherst in the 1760 campaign that captured Montreal and finally defeated

New France. Thus, Thomas was one of the few American officers who had served in a high-ranking command position in the British army in Canada.

Appointed one of the first eight Brigadier Generals by the Continental Congress in 1775, Thomas had earned his reputation by leading the occupation of Dorchester Heights above Boston on March 4, 1776. Thomas' efforts were in large part responsible for the subsequent British abandonment of Boston on Saint Patrick's Day, and given this recent accomplishment he was a natural selection to assume command of the army in Canada. Promoted to Major General, Thomas almost immediately turned his face for Quebec, and had arrived at Albany on his way north by March 29, 1776.[46]

Thomas had a reputation as a capable, energetic officer.[47] Washington praised him as a "brave and good officer." Lieutenant Colonel Israel Shreve of New Jersey, who traveled with Thomas up the Lake Champlain route to Canada, recorded his impressions: "General Thomas is here from the camp at Boston. He is going to Canada to take the command there — he is a plain, sociable, sensible, good old man, about 60 to apperance."[48] One historian has described him thus: "Six feet in height, erect and well proportioned, he looked the soldier that he was."[49] His biographer has noted that "his appearance was commanding. In his manners, affable, gentlemanly and of unaffected sincerity. He never lessened his character or martial fame by arrogance or ostentation. He was cool and self-possessed in every emergency."[50]

Schuyler advised the Continental Congress:

> General [John] Thomas arrived here on Thursday [March 28] and will move in a very few days — as the season is so far advanced that it might be possible for the enemy to reinforce Quebec before he could reach it, unless he goes by water, we have both concluded that it will be most prudent to take as many bateaux as may be necessary to convey the troops, baggage, artillery and stores down the Sorel and St. Lawrence. Besides, the dispatch which this will give, it will relieve the men from the almost insuperable fatigue of a march of two hundred miles, in roads that will be extremely deep [in mud and spring freshets] and also save the heavy expense of the land transportation, nor can he do without a number of bateaux in the St. Lawrence to bring provisions from [Fort] Chambly. For all this service about seventy bateaux may suffice, and we shall have then about an equal number left in the lakes, a number

Major General John Thomas. A Massachusetts physician who had served as a Regimental Commander of Massachusetts Provincials during the Seven Years' War, and had led his regiment to Montreal in 1760, Thomas was one of the most experienced military men in the colonies in 1775. His service in Canada was tragically short, as he died of smallpox shortly after arriving to take command of the American Northern Theater Army (author's collection).

much too small, under the situation that our affairs will in all probability soon be in, in Canada.[51]

April 3 saw heavy firing, as the Americans placed their artillery battery on Point Levi into action. "This morning we opened our battery at Point Levi; there was a hot cannonading on both sides all day; we received no damage; we had some rain in the evening; the snow is now five feet deep on a level." As this battery opened fire with a roar, it occasioned Dr. Senter to return to his journal. "A battery opened from Point Levi upon the city, but being scanty of ammunition were allowed only a few round per day, just to keep the enemy in a continual alarm." Dewey also reported, "Our men opened a battery from Point Levi upon the town, 3 companies marched in this day belonging to Colonel Poor."

The firing continued on the next day. "We had cannonading on both sides to-day." Haskell was apparently placed on another work party on April 5, suggesting how frequently this and guard duty was assigned. In point of fact, the American army was working themselves to exhaustion, particularly when the brutal winter weather and limited rations were taken into account. Their labors doubtless kept them tired enough that their propensity for mischief was distinctly limited, but their weakness exposed them to smallpox and other diseases. Haskell's account for April 5 read, "We began to work on the battery at Bonpoir ferry. The enemy discovered us and fired on us but did no damage." Haskell's labors continued the next day: "This night all our company was on fatigue at the passage battery, two twelve-pound cannons were brought to the battery." Dewey wrote on April 6, "Gunpowder, smoke, fire and balls about these days."

On April 6 Daniel Kimball, the young soldier from New Hampshire, was finally able to rejoin his company for duty in front of Quebec.[52] He had actually arrived at Quebec on March 19, but had inoculated for smallpox the next day and performed no further service until this date.

Eventually Halkett had a respite on Sunday, April 7. Not because it was the Sabbath, but because a wintry mix of weather returned: "A bad storm of hail and rain; no stirring today." Kimball recorded about the same entry: "A very stormy tedious day for guard none mounted guard." Dewey recalled on this date, "Ball flying in the air." Monday morning saw a return to the exchange of cannonballs. "We fired several shot from our battery at Point Levi." Dewey wrote for April 8, "Some firing." The next day, Tuesday, April 9, saw Haskell again assigned to a work party. "At work on the passage battery hauling fascines and plank for platforms." Dewey continued to note, "Continual firing from Point Levi and from town." Kimball also noted the heavy firing. "They kept a heavy fire all day Point Levy battery." Finally, Halkett was able to record good news on Wednesday, April 10, in gleeful merriment: "A pleasant warm day!!"

However, Halkett now made the discovery that when spring comes to the north country and the snow pack melts, that it becomes unbelievably wet and sloppy, as he mentioned on April 11: "Bad stirring! The snow goes away fast; the ground overflowed with water." The weather continued to improve on Friday, April 12: "We have an easterly wind that carries off the snow and ice fast." Dewey, relatively new to the camp and apparently still susceptible to camp rumor, reported one whopper of a tale this day. Apparently, for newcomer Dewey, April Fools Day had come late:

> There was a report in the camp that a woman came out of the city this night and brought out this news, that there was a mutiny in the City and that General Carlton was for giving up the City and Colonel Macklen [McLean] was for keeping it. Macklen had the stronger party and over came Carlton and confined him.

Schuyler, having now moved forward to Fort George, complained to the Continental Congress that the lakes had not cleared of ice as rapidly as he had anticipated:

> The troops that arrived too late at Albany to cross the lakes on the ice are now at this post and Fort Edward impatiently waiting for the lakes to become navigable. I hope a day or two will effect it. All is in readiness to move immediately. The cannon are embarked and all such stores as are not perishable. General Thomas is seven miles from this place where I have advised him to remain until the Lake [Lake George] opens as we have scarcely room to lay down at this place. The Gentlemen Committee remain at Saratoga for the same reason.[53]

The "Gentlemen Committee" that Schuyler alluded to was actually a four member committee of the Continental Congress, dispatched to Canada to investigate the fiasco that the invasion had become, to attempt to reverse its disastrous course if feasible, and if not feasible to issue revised directions to the military leaders. The Continental Congress had spent the winter safely and comfortably ensconced in the largest commercial center and harbor of North America, Philadelphia. However, unlike other Congresses which have traditionally managed to evade or ignore bad news at will, the 2nd Continental Congress was extremely alarmed at reports that reached it from Arnold, Wooster, Schuyler and other parties in Canada. Accordingly, the Continental Congress assembled a committee to be dispatched to Canada. This committee had been carefully composed of some of its finest members, and in fact no better selection could possibly have been made. On Thursday, February 17, 1776, it was "Resolved, That a Committee of Three (two of whom to be Members of Congress) be appointed to proceed to Canada, there to pursue such instructions as shall be given by Congress." The two members of Congress selected were Benjamin Franklin and Samuel Chase, and Charles Carroll was selected as the third member.

The leader of the committee was Benjamin Franklin, senior delegate to the Continental Congress from Pennsylvania. Franklin was 70 years old in the spring of 1776. He was well respected, intelligent, articulate, amiable, and persuasive. His scientific efforts were well known, and internationally recognized. He had spent considerable time in Great Britain, and as a result was more cosmopolitan than many Americans who had never left the North American continent. He was fluent in six languages, including French. His traveling companion on this journey, Charles Carroll of Carrollton, would record of Franklin:

> Doctor Franklin is a most engaging & entertaining companion of a sweet, even and lively temper full of facetious stories & always applied with judgement & introduced apropos — he is a man of extensive reading, deep thought & curious in all his enquiries. His political knowledge is not inferior to his literary & philosophical. In short I am quite charmed with him: even his age makes all these happy endowments more interesting, uncommon & captivating.[54]

His seniority and well-deserved reputation were likely to be highly respected in Canada. Franklin was extremely concerned with the rigors of the winter journey to Canada, and feared that he would not be able to withstand the severe weather. In fact, as he departed on this journey he wrote farewell letters to family and friends.[55] But clearly Franklin also felt that the Continental Congress' efforts in Canada were critically important to the cause of the United Colonies, and were worth risking his life to salvage.

Thirty-five-year-old Samuel Chase was a prominent Annapolis, Maryland, attorney and member of the Maryland legislature. He was also literate in the French language. Chase was known to have an active mind, was well educated, highly intelligent, and was relatively young and vigorous. Throughout his life he had been a strong proponent of American liberty, and was a steadfast denouncer of British interference in American activities. Not as well known as Franklin, he was an excellent choice for a journey of this length and difficulty, and if any two men could convince the Canadians to continue supporting the cause of liberty it would be the fervent, young and aggressive Chase and the distinguished, highly-respected Franklin.

Charles Carroll of Carrollton (to distinguish him from his father) was 39 years of age in 1776. At the time he was not a member of the Second Continental Congress, he would become a member of Congress later in 1776, and go on to sign the Declaration of Independence. Although he was one of the wealthiest men in North America, he was a fervent patriot. John Adams would justify his selection as the third member of the committee to Canada:

> He is a native of Maryland ... he had a liberal education in France and is well acquainted with the French Nation. He speaks their language as easily as ours, and what is perhaps of more consequence than all the rest, he was educated in the Roman Catholic Religion and still continues to worship his maker according to the rights of that church. In the cause of American Liberty his zeal, fortitude and perseverance have been so conspicuous that he is said to be marked out for peculiar vengeance by the friends of Administration. But he continues to hazard his all, his immense fortune, the largest in America, and his life. This gentleman's character, if I foresee right, will hereafter make a greater figure in America.[56]

Carroll had apparently been suggested for the committee by Samuel Chase, who had worked closely with him in the Maryland legislature, and knew well his worth and sterling patriotism.[57]

The Continental Congress further went on to resolve "that Mr. Carroll be requested to prevail on Mr. John Carroll to accompany the Committee to Canada to assist them in such matters as they shall think useful." Father John Caroll was a Catholic priest, educated in France, and a cousin of Charles Carroll. Educated as a Jesuit, he spoke French fluently. Charles Lee had suggested to the Continental Congress that Carroll be included as a member of the committee to Canada:

> I should think that if some Jesuit or Religieuse of any other order (but he must be a man of liberal sentiments, enlarged mind and a manifest friend to Civil Liberty) could be found out and sent to Canada, he would be worth battalions to us.... Mr. Carroll has a relative who exactly answers the description.

Father Carroll was known as a "gentleman of learning and abilities."[58]

Besides these four distinguished Americans, the committee also took with them a French printer and printing press to conduct what would today be known as information operations in Canada, and a war chest. Although this war chest contained no less than 20,000 pounds in currency, it was all paper Continental currency, and contained no silver or gold specie. Accordingly, it was all but useless in Canada.

The committee left New York City on April 2, and would require most of the month to travel to Montreal, not arriving there until April 29. The melting ice on Lake George and Lake Champlain would considerably slow their passage. While the four members of the congressional committee slowly struggled across the lakes on the long way north, it was now time for the spring freshets. On April 13, Halkett grumbled, "It is bad travelling, by reason of the water being in many places in the road three feet deep; the ground begins to appear on the top of some of the hills."

April 13 was significant from a command standpoint in that Arnold left the city of Quebec, or more properly he was driven out of it by Wooster's sanctimonious and aloof nature. Wooster, having accomplished nothing except to antagonize the French Canadian inhabitants of Montreal during his three months of inactivity in that city, would require less than two weeks to similarly antagonize Arnold. Wooster determined that his own military genius was equal to the task, and deemed Arnold unworthy and unqualified for him to consult with. This although Arnold by now had been in front of Quebec for five long months, with Montgomery had planned and initiated an assault upon the city, and then successfully pursued a surprisingly effective blockade of the powerful city and garrison that drastically outnumbered him. He was intimately familiar with his army, its officers, its men, its weapons and equipment. He was intimately familiar with the terrain in front of and around the city. Wooster did not even see fit to consult with Arnold regarding his future plans and intentions. To add injury to insult, Arnold's horse had thrown him, and severely battered his just barely healing leg. Arnold himself stated, "Had I been able to take an active part, I should by no means have left the camp, but as General Wooster did not think proper to consult me in any of his matters, I was convinced I should be of more service here than in the camp, and he very readily granted me leave of absence until I recovered of my lameness."[59] With this, Arnold transferred his flag to Montreal, where he assumed command of that city while Wooster now commanded at Quebec. Merchant Jenks, still conducting business in the Town of Three Rivers on the St. Lawrence River, recorded:

> [April] 14 — General Arnold came to town from Quebec.
> 16 — General Arnold set out from here for Montreal in a canoe.[60]

April 14th was still extremely bad, as the snow and ice continued to depart, "but little done on our battery on account of the badness of the road."

With considerable pleasure Halkett wrote in his journal for Monday, April 15, "The time of our last engagement has expired; we intend to set out for New England soon." Halkett enjoyed what must have been a pleasurable experience the next day: "We had an invitation today from the officers of Col. Livingston's regiment to go to Bonpoir; they treated us handsomely, after going through the manual exercise we returned to our quarters." Still, the Americans were desperately short on manpower, and attempts were made on Wednesday, April 17, to convince Halkett and his compatriots to stay longer, "The general desires that we would stay a few days more in camp."

Apparently Wooster's entreaties were not particularly successful, for as Halkett wrote on Thursday, April 18, "Our company went to headquarters to get a pass to go home. By the general's desire we concluded to stay a few days longer; we have two fire ships at Orleans with which at a convenient time we intend to burn shipping in the lower town; a woman belonging to the Pennsylvania troops was killed to-day by accident — a soldier carelessly snapping his musket which proved to be loaded." Kimball, who had had a rather mundane week, recorded on April 18 "General orders for every man to be ready at a moments warning."

Winter expressed its reluctance to abandon the St. Lawrence River valley on April 19: "Cold, uncomfortable weather! The enemy fired several shots at our guard house at Bonpoir ferry and struck the house two or three times." Kimball recorded an accident in his billets, which suggested a deplorable lack of discipline among the soldiers: "Ensign Webster hung up his gun and it went of on the half bent [or half cock] and shot one mans hair of as he lay in bed." The next several days the British gunners proved their superiority over the American artillerymen and breastworks, on April 20. "I received four pounds [probably Continental paper money] of Captain Smith; the enemy began a brisk fire upon our guard house at the ferry at different parts of the city; damaged the house much; drove us out of it into the battery but hurt no man." And then on Sunday, April 21, "The enemy have almost beat our guard house down at the ferry, although it is very strong, nearly three feet thick through with stone, we heard the Americans had taken Boston." Adjutant Dewey made a brief entry, noting, "This day 1 man died out of the Company it being the first man we lost since we left home." Kimball recorded another deplorable break in discipline in the barracks on April 21: "Last night Uriah Curtis was put on arrest for gitting drunk and firing off his gun in the house. And we had 21 Yorkers under guard for trying to desert the camp and the worst men that ever I saw."

Poor weather apparently put a cessation to inhospitable tendencies on Monday afternoon, April 22, as recorded by Halkett. "This morning we opened our battery at Bonpoir Ferry, fired a number of shot into the city and received some from it, being stormy in the afternoon the firing ceased on both sides, 150 men arrived from Montreal on batteaux." The arrival by these soldiers on bateaux was significant, for it meant that the ice was clear from the rivers and lakes, and that reinforcements and supplies could soon be expected. Now the question was whether the American or British reinforcements would arrive first, and decide the fate of Quebec.

Doctor Senter also noted the battery's activities on April 22: "The 22d of this month a battery opened from the bank of Charles River, by the name of Smith's battery. From this was discharged red hot shot, in hopes of firing the town. They returned the fire exceeding heavy, but no considerable harm from either side." The battery clearly made a big impression, for Dewey also wrote, "Our men opened a battery down by the nunnery upon the town and there was a continual fire from the battery and town all the A.M. our men fire 40 shot from the battery that day and they plumpt 39 of them into the thicket of the city." Kimball recorded that "battery was opened" but other concerns were more important, "to day we had no bread and very hungry."

With weather clearing on Tuesday, April 23, hostilities resumed, as documented by Halkett. "A hot cannonading began on both sides this morning, we opened a bomb battery in the evening and threw a number of shells into the city." Dewey also noted on this date, "They fire from the town dismounted the Bellows with their balls but hurt nobody."

Halkett continued the next day, "This morning we began to fire hot shot from the ferry battery, as one of our men was ramming home a cartridge in one of the guns — we had fired hot shot out of it — the piece not being well sponged — the cartridge took fire and mortally wounded the man." Dewey succinctly recalled, "One our men was a raming down a hot ball and not having sufficient wading the gun went off and burned the man badly." Doctor Senter, who presumably treated the wounded soldier, elaborated on the incident: "Two of our artillery men were wounded very much, by the cartridges taking fire while ramming them home, but recovered again."

The cannon of the time fired a pre-measured cartridge consisting of black gunpowder (a substantial amount) wrapped in paper or flannel. These cannon were all muzzle loaders. As the gunpowder cartridge was being rammed down the cannon's barrel, if any spark or burning debris remained inside the cannon it could detonate the cartridge. To avoid this, the cannon was carefully searched to remove all debris, then sponged with water twice while creating a tight seal at the vent to produce a vacuum to further extinguish any sparks. The fact that this cannon had prematurely ignited as the cartridge was being rammed was most likely due to the inexperience and poor training of the American gunners. Interestingly enough, the more seasoned British artillerymen fired considerably more and larger cannon throughout the siege, without a single documented case of this type of problem occurring.

The hearty Americans were apparently not demoralized, and maintained a heavy rate of fire the next few days. Thursday, April 25, Halkett wrote, "We have kept a steady cannonading from the batteries for three days past." Doctor Senter noted the heavy firing: "The enemy continued their cannonade and bombardment excessive heavy, while we were restricted to a certain number per day, in consequence of very little ammunition. There was very little damage from either cannon or bombs. Some wounded, but very few of our men killed." Dewey was called out for service on the evening of April 25, but it came to nought:

> We was alarmed in the night and ordered to be upon Abraham Plains immediately for what we knew not, but it was supposed that our men was a going to send a fire ship in among their shipping that lay hawled up close into the town in order to burn them but it being a rainy night our men had but just turned out before we was dismist and there was nothing done that night.

And then on Friday, April 26, more bad luck struck the Americans, as Haskell discussed: "A storm of rain; but little firing on either side today; we split a twelve-pounder in our battery at the ferry which wounded a number, but none mortally." Dewey also noted, "There was such a firing that the air was full of balls some of them flying one way and some the other, our men being so engaged afiring that they split one of their cannon and hurt 1 man very bad so that he died." Kimball briefly noted on April 27, "Yesterday we bust one of our 12 pounders." Most likely, this was an iron cannon, which were prone to shatter when fired. Unlike the earlier accident, this was an occupational hazard of firing iron cannon, and could not be credited to inexperience or lack of training. For this very reason, the British Royal Artillery by this time favored the use of bronze (often called brass) cannon, which were more expensive and considerably more difficult to produce, but were substantially more reliable.

The next day, Saturday April 27, the Americans' woes continued, as Haskell observed: "This morning we mounted a brass twenty-four pound cannon in the ferry battery — discharged her once and broke the axle tree, which was all we fired to-day." The axle tree was the central portion of the gun's carriage. It is also the strongest and most substantial portion of a gun's carriage. For it to break, the Americans must have done something rather incredibly wrong, in conjunction with a badly flawed carriage in the first place. The author suspects that the carriage was either badly constructed, old and fragile, or green and unseasoned, and thus vulnerable to disintegration.

The Sabbath was not celebrated on April 28. "Fine pleasant weather, a number of troops arrived in camp from New England, we have a steady cannonading on both sides today." That Monday they re-mounted the heavy cannon, and got back to work. "A number of the New York troops are discharged and are to set off for home up the river by water tomorrow morning. This morning we mounted our Brass piece again and got in readiness for a warm fire in the morning."

Halkett received very welcome news on that Tuesday, April 30: "Thick, rainy weather. No firing today on either side. General Thomas is expected in camp with a large reinforcement, when he arrives we that are left of Col. Arnold's detachment are to be discharged." For whatever reason, no returns for the month of April for the Quebec army were prepared. One suspects that the stellar leadership of Wooster was somehow directly responsible for this absence.

On Wednesday, May 1, the fickle Canadian weather gave a farewell caress to poor Haskell. "We had snow last night. A raw cold day. But little firing on either side for some days past." Two important events took place in Canada this week: the arrival of the congressional commissioners in Montreal on Monday, April 29, and the arrival of Major General John Thomas at Quebec on May 2. Kimball, who had made no entries in his journal for several days, recorded on May 2, "Ginneral Thomas arrived at head quarters with great joy."

Having survived their tedious and miserable trip up the Hudson River, Lake George and Lake Champlain, then across country from St. Jean to Montreal, the four commissioners must have been ecstatic to finally reach Montreal on April 29. Brigadier General Arnold welcomed them with appropriate honors, courtesy and ceremony. Arnold had in short order ingratiated himself with the French Canadian leadership and elite of the city. This, in and of itself, was probably not a particularly difficult challenge, given that he was succeeding the miserable David Wooster. Charles Carroll recalled Arnold's treatment of the commissioners in glowing terms:

> We were received by General Arnold, on our landing in the most polite and friendly manner; conducted to headquarters, where a genteel company of ladies and gentlemen had assembled to welcome our arrival. As we went from the landing place to the general's house, the cannon of the citadel fired in compliment to us as the commissioners of congress. We supped at that general's, and after supper were conducted, by the general and other gentlemen, to our lodgings — the house of Mr. Thomas Walker, the best built, and perhaps the best furnished in this town.[61]

Headquarters was the Château Ramezay, located just off Montreal's major square and market. Constructed in 1705, its first service was as the residence of the French governor of Montréal, Claude de Ramezay. A stunningly attractive stone building, it featured well-laid-out formal gardens in the rear, spectacular woodwork inside, and an ornate iron fence surrounding it. Given the ragged and threadbare appearance of much of the Continental army, the chateau was perhaps the only picturesque part of the city's American garrison. The Walkers were the social and economic upper crust of the city, and also fervent patriots who had done much to facilitate the American successes in the province. The elite of the community had come out to welcome the commissioners, for Franklin in particular was internationally famous and renowned. It was to prove an enjoyable and gracious evening, but once the commissioners went to work and began to delve into the fortunes of the American cause, it was to be their sole pleasurable moment during their stay in Canada.[62]

At Quebec, among his first actions Thomas ordered a general muster of the army. What he discovered appalled him. The army consisted of only 1,900 men, with only 1,000

Chateau Ramezay, Wooster's and Arnold's headquarters in Montreal. One of the oldest surviving structures in Montreal, the Chateau Ramezay served as the American army's headquarters in Montreal from the fall of 1775 until the American retreat in May 1776. It hosted the visit by the committee from the Continental Congress, and such men as Benjamin Franklin, Charles Carroll of Carollton, Richard Montgomery, and Benedict Arnold. David Wooster spent the winter of 1775 and 1776 enjoying its comforts, rather than joining the American army shivering outside of Quebec. It is today operated as a museum, and retains much of the charm that it presented in the eighteenth century (author's collection).

of them deemed effective. Among these effectives were three hundred men like Haskell, who had served past their enlistment, and were promised their discharge as soon as reinforcements arrived for the army, an event which had obviously just occurred. For every well man, one man was sick in the hospital. Most of these sick men were victims of the feared and deadly smallpox.[63] Dr. Senter recorded of Thomas' arrival before Quebec: "General Wooster being superseded gave him great distress, and General Thomas being an utter stranger in the country, and much terrified with the small pox."[64]

On May 1 the commissioners wrote a lengthy missive to Congress. Since they had only been in Montreal two days, it is remarkable that they had captured the plight of the army so rapidly and accurately. The excellence of its members was clearly demonstrated by this astute analysis.

> It is impossible to give you a just idea, of the lowness of the Continental credit here, from the want of hard money and the prejudice it is to our affairs. Not the most trifling service can be procured without an assurance of instant pay in silver or gold.... Therefore the utmost dispatch should be used in forwarding a large sum hither (we believe 20,000 pounds will be necessary), otherwise it will be impossible to continue the war in this country, or to expect the continuance of our interest with the people here, who begin to consider the Congress as bankrupt and their cause as desperate. Therefore till the arrival of money, it seems improper to propose the federal union of this province with the others, as the few friends we have here, will scarce venture to exert themselves in promoting it, till they see our credit recovered, and a sufficient army arrived to secure the possession of the country.... We understand that the troops before Quebec have not now ten days provisions, but hope, as the lakes are now open, supplies will soon reach them.

Ominously, the commissioners concluded with a dreadful note: "The small pox is in the army & Genl Thomas has unfortunately never had it."[65]

Arnold, finally bowing to the inevitable, implemented a program of inoculation for the army on May 15.[66] However, this measure would obviously remove a large number of men from the army as they healed from the inoculation at precisely the moment when they were desperately needed to fight the British. Thomas, almost immediately, rescinded the order. Thomas was a physician, and he must have been aware that once exposed, the soldiers were almost certain to get the smallpox in the natural way. And that incurring the disease naturally would not only result in a longer sickness (four weeks to recover, versus two weeks for inoculation), but would result in a 30 percent fatality rate. But Thomas apparently feared to weaken his army. It was a fatal error.

Although temperatures remained cold, the arrival of General Thomas on May 2 must have warmed Musketman Halkett: "General Thomas arrived in camp with five hundred men. We had a report that there is a British fleet in the river." Since Thomas had arrived, Halkett's company could now begin their return home, as he noted in his journal for Friday, May 3: "Our Captain went to headquarters to get a pass for us to go home, he got a promise of one. In the evening we brought up some of our fireships against the city, and set them on fire, but being too late in the tide did no execution." Doctor Senter reported of the arrival of Thomas: "The reign of Wooster was but short, and about the 5th of May he was superseded by General Thomas." Kimball did not document the activities of the General Officers at headquarters, for he was involved with much more pressing interests: "To day we drawed some very poor beef but carried it back again and got pork."

In fact, during the month long period that Wooster commanded at Quebec, he implemented only a single meaningful operation. As member of the Continental Congress John Jay would relate later in the summer of 1776 in an obviously sarcastic letter to one of his many correspondents:

> I'll tell you a pretty story of Wooster. While he was smoking his pipe in the suburbs of Quebec, he took it into his head that he might do wonders with a fire-ship; and with an imagination warmed by the blaze of the enemy's vessels, sent for a New York captain, who, it seems, understood the business of fire-ship building. Under the strongest injunction of secrecy, he communicated to him the important plan, and ordered him to get the ship in readiness with all the dispatch and privacy in his power, wisely observing that if the enemy should get any intelligence of his design, they would carry their vessels out of the way of his fire-ship. The captain accordingly set about preparing the material, etc. necessary for the exploit which was to heroize the General.[67]

The truth is that, as Halkett related, on May 3 Wooster had launched what had to be the single most visually spectacular American attempt on Quebec. It had been in preparation by Wooster throughout April, and rumors of the impending arrival of the British relief fleet spurred the attack on early in the night of May 3. Wooster determined to launch a fireship attack upon the marooned British shipping tied up at Quebec, with the hope that the ships would catch fire, communicate the conflagration to the city, and so damage the city or its defenses that its capitulation would be ordained. In the meantime, the army would be drawn up with scaling ladders so that they could exploit any confusion in the city's defenses. The fireship was cleverly constructed to the east of the city, so that the British would presumably mistake it for one of their relief vessels, and hopefully would be deceived long enough for the fireship to sail into the Cul-de-Sac Harbor. The British had received intelligence that the Americans were building a fireship as early as April 10, but they apparently had only limited information on the Americans' intentions.[68]

The British ships deliberately marooned for the winter at Quebec so that their sailors and marines could contribute to the garrison of the city were drawn up in Cul-de-Sac Harbor at the Lower Town of Quebec, well protected under the city's guns. This was necessary because they were either very lightly manned, or completely un-manned. Henry Caldwell with the British militia noted "a 28-gun frigate, a King's sloop and 30 merchant men and transports."[69] Obviously, if this collection of ships could be ignited, the flaming rigging and masts would constitute a bonfire of biblical proportions, and would almost certainly cause consternation and panic among the population and the garrison. Realistically, such a fire at Cul-de-Sac Harbor would also inevitably transmit itself to the Cul-de-Sac Wharf and in turn the Lower Town.

As with all of the Americans' efforts in front of Quebec, almost nothing went right. The timing of the attack was all wrong, for it had to be carried on underneath the moon, which was at first quarter on May 3, 1776, and would have shone for the nearly the entire night. Unfortunately, because of the anticipated arrival of the British fleet, the Americans could not wait for the moon to set or change, or for cloudy weather or a fog to set in. The attack had to be launched early in the evening to take advantage of the tide, at an hour when the garrison was certain to still be quite alert. Captain Thomas Ainslee with the British Militia had a front row seat for the ensuing festivities:

> On the top of the tide between 9 & 10 o'clock at night (the moon shone very bright) a vessel was descried full sail, coming up to Town before the wind, those who saw here wish'd one another joy of the 1st ship from England. A messenger was sent to inform the General [Carlton] that the first of the fleet was in sight—he order'd the artillerymen to their guns—when she came within hail, it was ask'd from whence she came—no answer—hail'd again—still silent—the third hail was attended with a threat to sink her if no answer was made—she then gave a sheer on shore & at that instant the batteries play'd briskly on her—in a moment she was all in a blaze, very near the beach & about 200 yards from the shipping in Cul de Sac. She was well garnish'd in all parts with shells, grenades, petards, pots a feu [fire pots], etc. they spent themselves very regularly—she seem'd to have been well prepar'd; she must have done very great mischief if she had been steer'd into the Cul de Sac. The instant that she steer'd on shore a boat row'd from her with amazing speed. It is surprising that they chose to send her up in such clear weather.[70]

Why the fireship was ignited too early is speculation. Either the thundering British artillery fire panicked the American crew (which was completely understandable, given that they were manning what was for all practical purposes a floating bomb), or a well-aimed British cannon shot had ignited the incendiaries aboard the fireship. The result was the same in either case, and the fireship failed to accomplish its intended purpose. In the ensuing debacle, Captain Anderson commanding the fireship "was considerably burnt" and had to be subsequently be evacuated to New York City to recover.[71]

Carleton had not been fooled, for as Ainslee noted, "The whole city was under arms in a moment, no confusion apear'd, every body was cool & wishing that the Rebels might attack." American Captain Henry Dearborn in prison in the city heard alarm bells ringing.[72] Senter noted of the attack, "A plot was formed to burn the shipping in the harbor. A fire ship was completed in charge of Adjutant Anderson, a very brave officer, but proved abortive, by reason of the tide ebbing before he could get up to the shipping. The combustibles took fire before he intended, by which accident he was much burnt. He was, however, got on shore and no lives lost."[73]

An anonymous British observer recalled, "'Twas a noble sight."[74] Captain Jones with the Royal Artillery detachment was particularly impressed by the sight:

> She instantly broke out in a prodigious smoke, followed by a great flame, on which all her rigging & sails catched fire & she afford'd a very pretty prospect while she was floating down the River, every now & then sending up sky rockets, firing cannon or bursting of shells & so continued till she disappear'd in the channel.[75]

It must have been an incredible vision, with the fireship illuminating the entire valley of the Saint Lawrence River, throwing red and yellow light into every corner of the Lower Town of Quebec City. Interspersed throughout the lurid spectacle was the frequent flaring up of hand grenades and shells bursting in the air and detonating onboard the ship. It was an impressive pyrotechnics display of the greatest magnitude, but it had accomplished absolutely nothing except for amusing the American and British armies and citizens alike. It was Wooster's solitary accomplishment in his month's leadership in front of Quebec. Kimball had a succinct journal entry that perhaps summarized the night's festivities best: "Last night the fire ship was fixed out ... but to no effect for the ship did not get into the harbor."

The next day the Americans again pressed the siege, even though Wooster's grand fireship attack had failed. Halkett was not particularly interested in tactical developments, for he had a considerably more important movement holding his attention, "The Canadian troops are all called into headquarters. It is supposed that there will be another attack on the city soon. Our Captain got our discharge and a pass for us to march home." Lieutenant Colonel Israel Shreve, assigned to the New Jersey Regiment commanded by Colonel William Maxwell, arrived at Quebec on May 3. Colonel Shreve's impressions of Wooster's army were grim: "I found the Army very weak, and in want of almost everything."[76] Another young American soldier, Sergeant Samuel Hodgkinson with the 1st Pennsylvania Battalion, wrote a lengthy letter from before Quebec at the end of April. In it he described how widely dispersed the American positions were:

> I think it is now time for me to give you a description of our camp. It is nigh four miles in length, and better than two in width. It is pretty thick with houses, and the troops have all the houses to live in. There are two divisions — the Upper Division and the Lower Division. The First Pennsylvania Battalion, that is our Battalion, and some of the New England Troops, with a party of hearty riflemen command the Lower Division. The Lower Division lays at the bottom of a very great hill upon a clever level. The house our company is in is called the White House. It is a very large one.... Our house lays about one miles and a half from Quebec. We have a very clever prospect of Upper Town. The house we live in is called Head Quarters, that is the house the General lives in. The Upper Division is upon a large hill. Necessaries in the camp are very dear. Rum four shillings a quart, and that the worst of Yankee. Chocolate three and nine pence per pound. Brown sugar two and sixpence, and everything else in proportion. I have been four or five days writing this letter as I can't stick to it but a little while at a time, for I am called away for something or another, either guard, fatigue, or working party, or exercising the men.[77]

In the event of a British irruption from the city, which was certain to occur as soon as reinforcements arrived, the Americans would be hard pressed to concentrate in time to repulse the onslaught.

Thomas apparently saw the same thing as Shreve and Hodgkinson. Aghast at the circumstances and condition of the army Thomas called a council of war for May 5. As Thomas reported to the commissioners of the Continental Congress:

> In all our magazines there were but about one hundred & fifty pounds of powder & six days provision.... Considering these and many other disagreeable circumstances, I thought it expedient to call a council of war; and the Council consisting of Brigadier General Wooster and all the field Officers in camp, after mature deliberation, were unanimously of opinion, that as upon the first arrival of any reinforcement to the enemy, all communication by the River would inevitably be cut off by their armed vessels, it was absolutely necessary for the sake of the invalids, immediately to remove them in bateaux to the Three Rivers & to collect the artillery and other stores, in order

to remove them and the army farther up the River, as soon as it could conveniently be done, for the purpose of securing some important posts, where there would be a prospect of resisting with success.[78]

It is hard to see what other options Thomas had. As renowned military historian Christopher Ward evaluated the situation, "A mere ghost of an army was besieging a strongly fortified town of 5,000 inhabitants, mounting 148 cannon, with a garrison of 1,600 fit to fight, besides a frigate, a sloop of war, and several smaller armed vessels as auxiliaries. It was an absurd situation."[79] Thomas carefully evaluated this "absurd situation" and determined to withdraw the army from in front of Quebec while there was still something left to salvage. He would have to move fast, for as the false alarm that had instigated the fire ship attack two days earlier had suggested, British reinforcements aboard a strong fleet were momentarily anticipated to appear in the St. Lawrence River. Wooster, who had required three full months to execute the movement from Montreal to Quebec, immediately gathered up the baggage, and began moving it down the St. Lawrence River to safety the next day.[80] Wooster might have been slow and deliberate in his maneuvers forward, but he was certainly aggressive and rapid in his movements away from the enemy.

The Sabbath, May 5, and Monday, May 6, must have been big days for Halkett. "We marched to Head Quarters to get in readiness to march home," and "This morning three frigates came up the river, anchored before the city. We drew four days provisions. At three o'clock marched for home. The frigates fired a parting salute. We marched up as far as Point aux Tremble. An express overtook us and told us that the whole army was on the retreat. That the enemy came out and drove all our army off the ground, took our cannon and a number of our sick. We marched on five miles farther and put up being much fatigued."

3

"His Majesty's Deluded Subjects"
British Arrival, May 6, 1776

On May 6 in Montreal, the Congressional Commissioners still struggled with finances, and bowing to the inevitable wrote the following brutally direct letter to Congress:

> If hard money cannot be procured and forwarded with dispatch to Canada, it would be advisable, in our opinion, to withdraw the army & fortify the passes on the lakes to prevent the enemy & the Canadians, if inclined, from making irruptions into & depredations on our frontiers.[1]

Thomas and the commissioners were already too late. On the morning of May 6 it all came to an end. The British were no longer coming, rather they had arrived at Quebec. And they had arrived in overwhelming force.

Thomas had received some intimation that British warships had been spotted upstream in the St. Lawrence River. However, it was relatively early in the year for the river and North Atlantic to be free of ice, and Thomas hoped that the reports were exaggerated or incorrect. He had made the fateful decision to retreat from in front of Quebec, but he needed additional time to ensure that the army withdrew in good order, that all the sick were evacuated, and that what little artillery he did have at Quebec along with the precious provisions and military stores were all removed. And at the same time he needed to keep the British deceived of his intentions, so that they would not sortie from the Citadel and disrupt his orderly withdrawal. Thomas would not get the time that he so desperately needed. Doctor Senter left a clear account of the ensuing debacle:

> [We received] a report from down to river, brought to us by some of the honest peasants, that a fleet was coming up. To this there was not sufficient credit given, imaging it impossible for any arrival so early in the spring. General Wooster being superseded gave him great distress, and General Thomas being an utter stranger in the country, and much terrified with the small pox. Strongly neglecting the reports of the approach of the enemy's fleet, tho' repeatedly attested to by several of the good inhabitants, till the morning of the sixth, when we were alarmed by the discharge of cannon down the river. These were immediately answered from the city, and at half an hour by sun, four ships arrived in the harbour. Immediately upon landing their marines, soldiers, etc. they rushed out in parties, the one for Head Quarters upon the plains of Abraham, and the other for the Hospital General. The army was in such a scattered condition as rendered it impossible to collect them either for a regular retreat, or to bring them into action. In this dilemma, orders were given to as many of the

troops to retreat as the time would permit, and in the most irregular, helter skelter manner we raised the siege, leaving every thing. All the camp equipage, ammunition, and even our clothing except what little we happened to have on.[2]

The British warships were HM sloop *Surprise* and HM sloop *Martin*, followed by the HM frigate *Isis*, carrying a battalion of the 29th Regiment of Foot. At 5:00 A.M. the ships fired cannon and displayed flags in a pre-arranged recognition signal, and docked at the Lower City. By 8:00 A.M. the three ships had disgorged their infantrymen.[3] Incredibly, for five hours Thomas took no action. He stared at the Citadel of Quebec, he deliberately continued to arrange his withdrawal, he made no plans, he issued no commands to his leaders or soldiers, and he failed to take even the elementary precaution of concentrating his forces. Carleton, within the city, was conversely extremely busy. He provided the 29th Foot and marines a brief opportunity to rest their sea legs while he organized his garrison's indigenous forces. About 1:00 P.M. Carleton formed his army, new and old, into two columns. He then had St. Johns and St. Louis gates opened, and placing himself at the head of his soldiers and sailors and marines, his powerful army poured forth onto the Plains of Abraham, free of the bondage of their long winter for the first time.[4] Thomas stared in indecision and dismay as his worst nightmare played itself out:

> About one oClock a considerable body of the enemy attacked our sentinels & main guard; in consequence of which I instantly ordered the Troops under arms & detachd a party to support the main guard, which was now coming off in good order. By the best judgement I could make, the enemy were one thousand strong, formed into two divisions, in columns six deep supported with a train of six pieces of cannon. The most that we could collect at this time, on the plains, to oppose them did not exceed one quarter of that number, with only one field piece.[5]

This perhaps sounds well organized and well disciplined. It was nothing like that. Thomas had failed to take advantage of the five hours' respite that he had been provided, and now the campsite established over several miles betrayed him and the American cause. The American army could not be gathered in time to resist the well-ordered, well-disciplined, British advance. In short order, scattered and outnumbered, the Americans panicked and fled in utter pandemonium and chaos. The British accounts consistently relate the same tale. Captain Thomas Jones, commanding the four bronze 6-pounders that accompanied Carleton's sortie, recalled in glee:

> [We] marched out to engage them, with a strong party, from the Gates of St. Louis and St. John. The enemy were found busied in making preparations for a rapid retreat, and after exchanging a few shots, fled in the utmost confusion. The alarm being given, the plains, as well as the adjacent wood, were soon completely cleared of the marauders. Several stragglers were made prisoners, and the dastardly villains, after in vain attempting to rally and charge our troops, scampered off, having abandoned fifteen pieces of cannon, with all their military stores, petards, scaling ladders, and baggage. The parties on each side of the river were prevented from joining in their flight towards Montreal by two armed vessels ... in the hope of annoying them in their retreat, which was so precipitate, that most of their cannon were left ready loaded, and their ammunition, provisions, entrenching tools, and even muskets, in many cases abandoned.[6]

Ainslee, with the British Militia, echoed Jones' account:

> About 6 o clock a vessel appear'd turning Point Levy to the inconceivable joy of all who saw her; the news soon reached every pillow in town, people half dress'd ran down to the Grand Battery to feast their eyes with the sight of a ship of war displaying the Union flag.... The drums beat to arms; the different corps assembled on the Parade. It was there propos'd that the volunteers of the British & Canadian Militia shou'd join the troops & sailors to engage the rebels on the plains; to their credit be it said that almost to a man both corps were anxious to be led to action. The General at the head of about 800 men march'd out ... the little army extended itself quite across the plains making a fine appearance. The Rebels saw us very formidable. A few shots were exchang'd by our advanc'd party & the rear guard of the enemy, their balls whistled over us without hurting a man — they fled most preciptately as soon as our field pieces began to play on their guard houses & advanc'd posts, they left cannon, mortars, field pieces, muskets & even their cloaths behind them. As we pursued them we found the road strew'd with arms, cartridges, cloaths, bread, pork, etc. Their confusion was so great, their panic so violent, that they left orderly books & papers, which for their own credit shou'd not have been left. Look whatsoever way one wou'd, he saw men flying & loaden carts driving full speed.... The Surprise & Martin sail'd up the river to destroy the enemy's craft.[7]

Lieutenant Patrick Daly provided a detailed tactical alignment for Carleton's army as it maneuvered through the two gates:

> We came to the ground where the British army fought the 28th April, 1760 expecting all the way that the rebels would advance and give us battle as we saw them assembling at their headquarters from all sides; but it seems they had no stomach to it, for after we had remained above an hour, there was none of them to be seen. We then sent advanced parties who found they had retreated in the utmost hurry and confusion, leaving all their provisions, artillery and ammunition.... Our little army consisted of the fusileers and emigrants on the right, British militia and sailors on the left, with the newcomers [29th Foot and Royal Marines from the three ships] in the center, and Major Nairne with the ... French [militia] were formed as a corps de reserve in the rear, and all, without exception, behaved in the coolest manner.[8]

Colonel McLean was second in command, and presumably commanded the right column with his emigrants, and Colonel Caldwell commanded the British Militia on the left flank.[9]

Colonel Elisha Porter, whose Massachusetts Militia regiment had just arrived at Quebec, attempted to organize a defense:

> The enemy made their appearance upon the heights with their field pieces, and began to fire upon our guards. An alarm was made ... went to headquarters with what men I had and formed. When the enemy were within about 80 rods of us we had orders to retreat slowly and in good order which we did, until we could find a convenient place to defend ourselves.[10]

It should be noted that 80 rods measures 1,280 feet or 426 yards, far beyond musket range. Clearly, the Americans had little interest in presenting a resolute defense. Porter continued:

> We formed in the first wood we came to and remained till the rear had got up with us. We then had orders to retreat again. We retreated about 15 miles that night and

halted — at 8 o'clock had orders to march again at 12. Were called up at 10 by a false alarm, and at 11 to prepare for our march. Set out a little before 12.[11]

The British advance was inexorable. Seemingly in an instant, as American historian Justin Smith has described it, "the shell of a siege collapsed, like a paper balloon in a thunder-shower."[12]

Uriah Cross' experience on the retreat serves as the single most depressing example of the Americans' utter disintegration and demoralization:

> I ... found Adjutant Green setting by the side of the road having hobbled along three fourth of a mile from where the French men left him. He was unable to travel & entirely out of my power to assist him. He begged my assistance & shed tears. I could no way to be of any benefit to him. Traveled on. Left him to the mercy of the French men.[13]

As if the defeat outside of Quebec wasn't demoralizing enough, the Royal Navy's vessels also proceeded past the city to engage the American shipping that had been operating on the St. Lawrence River since that spring. The American boats were two gondolas, constructed by Philip Schuyler at Ticonderoga in 1775 christened *Hancock* and *Schuyler*, and the ship *Gaspé*. The *Gaspé* had been captured from the British during the winter and scuttled to avoid being destroyed by the ice on the river, a common technique in northern climates where the ice could not be kept away from the vessels during the long, cruel winters. Now the *Gaspé* would return to its original owners.

Schuyler described the *Hancock* and *Schuyler*: "I have two flat-bottomed vessels amongst those we have built they are sixty feet long and capable of carrying five twelve-pounders each, but I can unfortunately mount only one, as I have no carriages."[14] These two gondolas had been successfully brought up the rapids between Chamblee and St. Jean in the spring of 1776, able to negotiate the rapids because of their flat bottoms and narrow draughts, running downstream and in high water. Charles Carroll noted, "Flat bottomed boats may go down these rapids in the spring of the year, when the water is high — even a large gondola passed down them this spring."[15] It was intended that they would operate on the Richelieu and St. Lawrence Rivers to carry supplies between Chamblee, Montreal and Quebec. Aside from the single 12-pounder mentioned by Schuyler, these gondolas were unarmed, as their ability to carry baggage was predominate.[16]

Senter reported of the fate of the American shipping on the St. Lawrence:

> Two of their frigates proceeded immediately up the river, not only to annoy us in marching, but in quest of several vessels of the fleet which General Montgomery brought from Montreal. Wind and tide favoring the enemy's frigates, they were very nigh within cannon shot of ours before they could get under way. They hauled upon our shipping so rapidly, as obliged the captains to run them ashore, and put fire to them. They still kept in chase of us up the river both by land and water, and in the most disorderly manner we were obliged to escape as we could.[17]

One of the Royal Navy vessels participating in this assault was the HMS *Surprise*, commanded by Captain Robert Linzee. The journal of May 7 described yet another American debacle:

> At 6 A.M. weigh'd and proceeded up the river with the [sloop HMS] *Martin*.... At 8 saw a Brig & 2 small schooners in shore fir'd a number of guns at them, but finding

the shot to fall short, sent the arm'd schooner to destroy them, as we proceeded up the river saw a great number of the rebel army, marching towards Montreal. Fir'd round & grape shot at them to annoy them whenever we saw them assemble in large parties.... At 3 P.M. the Schooner returned and inform'd us that the Brig was fitted for a fire vessel, but the Rebels fearing she should fall into our hands had run her on shore, and her so leaky that she could not be possibly got off.[18]

One of these gondolas was subsequently salvaged by the British and became the *Loyal Convert*. It was equipped with seven 9-pounders and six swivel guns, and would be operated by the British army for the remainder of the war on Lake Champlain once it was carried back up the rapids.[19]

The young soldier Daniel Kimball of New Hampshire was aboard one of these boats, and provides a first hand impression of being pursued by the British warcraft:

> I ... lost my all my baggage but I went on bard [board] and we had not got far before we saw the ships come in site [sight] we made all spead [speed] & she son [soon] came near and the boat that I was in was forst [forced] to land and they took our skooner [schooner] at the same time and soon after Capt Seebye boat was forst [forced] to land.

The British also captured, or forced to be burned, a number of bateaux that the American army was operating on the St. Lawrence River. Since bateaux were the major transportation on the waterways of Canada, the loss of these bateaux were particularly serious to the fortunes of the American army.

Bateaux were the 18th century equivalent of cargo trucks. Large, flat-bottomed, double-ended boats, they could be easily rowed, sailed under satisfactory wind conditions, and could carry considerable supplies. If particularly shallow water, these boats could also be poled. Because of their flat bottoms and wide frames, they were all but impossible to sink. Their flat bottoms enabled them to operate in very low draughts of water, and they could readily be pulled ashore on any type of beach. They were simple to build — any competent carpenter could fabricate one in a day or two — and the services of the scarcer, more expensive shipwrights were not needed. Given their robust construction, the bateaux could tolerate considerable abuse, and required almost no maintenance except regular caulking. During his journey north, congressional commissioner Charles Carroll of Carrollton had considerable opportunities to become acquainted with bateaux:

> The longest of the boats, made for the transportation of the troops over Lakes George and Champlain, are thirty-six feet in length and eight feet wide; they draw about a foot water when loaded, and carry between thirty and forty men, and are rowed by the soldiers. They have a mast fixed in them to which a square sail, or a blanket is fastened, but these sails are of no use unless with the wind abaft or nearly so.[20]

Phillip Schuyler had expended considerable efforts constructing large number of bateaux, for without them the army in Canada would not only starve, but also have to abandon the campaign for lack of reinforcements, supplies, and ammunition. Schuyler was well experienced with the operation of bateaux, not only on the various military campaigns in which he served in the British Army in the Seven Years' War, but also as a private businessman for two decades on the Hudson River. However, notwithstanding

Schuyler's efforts, lack of supplies even constrained the completion of these critical boats. Schuyler lamented to the Continental Congress on March 19: "The whole of the bateaux I was ordered to build will be finished in eight days as far as they can be for want of pitch of oakum, which is not yet arrived from New York — I have however a sufficiency to transport the troops now here."[21] Because of the importance of these boats, Schuyler continuously kept his superiors informed of their status, writing Washington on April 27:

> Being restricted by Congress to build no more than one hundred bateaux, and eight of these being occupied by the troops above mentioned, General John Thomas, The Commissioners [of Congress], the Artillery and Stores, provisions & Captain Stevens's Company with the Mortars & Shells, I have only twenty new ones left, and thirty seven of those built last year — the whole of which will carry no more then fifteen hundred — I have however ventured to construct an additional number, and such a number of carpenters are now employed as will daily build for the conveyance of fifty men; hence, I hope no considerable delay will be experienced.... The vessels on Lake Champlain are sufficient to convey five hundred men to St. John's, but no sailors are yet arrived.[22]

Schuyler formally notified the Continental Congress on May 3 that he had been forced to construct additional boats:

> I have found myself under the necessity of building a number of bateaux far exceeding what Congress ordered. One hundred and thirty are now built and I propose to complete them to two hundred, but if more troops should be sent even that number will be insufficient.[23]

A large number of American soldiers transited by bateaux up Lake George and Lake Champlain to Canada. The rate of their travel varied considerably based upon weather and wind. Surgeon Lewis Beebe recorded traveling in a "hard snow storm" between Ticonderoga and Crown Point, during which it took him twelve hours to travel about 13 miles. The day previously, he had rowed up Lake George in about fifteen hours, traveling slightly more than 2 miles per hour. The next day, he rowed from Crown Point to the Ausable River, 38.5 miles in about nine hours. The day after that, when he had "fair wind hoist sail" the bateaux covered the 100 miles to St. John in only eighteen hours.[24]

Lt. Benjamin Beal of Colonel Greaton's 24th Continental Regiment (Massachusetts) also traveled up Lake Champlain by bateaux in early May. He noted on March 2: "We went 40 men in a boat with the wind fair around to Ticonderoga about 3 o'clock." Thus, they traveled about 36 miles in about nine hours, averaging four miles per hour. On May 3 they traveled between Ticonderoga and Crown Point, and on May 4 they rowed 22 hours to Split Rock (about two miles per hour). They were delayed by weather several days on Lake Champlain, but then covered fifty miles in a day with a "fair wind."[25]

During the retreat from Quebec, Colonel Elisha Porter of Massachusetts recorded the futility of attempting to row bateaux against adverse winds:

> [May] 11th. Set out in the morning and rowed till we got into Lake St. Francis. It being calm we attempted to cross the middle of the lake. About noon the south wind began to blow and soon grew very hard which obliged us to make the shore as soon as possible. My batteau made the shore without losing much way, others were drove back 8 or 10 miles, some more.[26]

Sergeant Timothy Tuttle with the 1st New Jersey recorded a typical attempt to travel up Lake Champlain in late May. He spent three days essentially halted in place, rowing only a couple of miles each day before they abandoned the attempt due to adverse winds, then making eighty miles in a single day with a favorable wind:

> 28th Sailed down the lake from Crown Point, fair wind. But so hard we were obliged to go ashore where stayed about 1 hours and ½ then put out rowed a few miles & put up for encampment with 2 other regiments. A cold night.
>
> 29th Sailed as far as Willosborough [*sic*] about 5 miles. The wind was so a head we were obliged to encamp about 10 or 12 O'clock where stayed all day & night.
>
> 30th Rowed 4 miles the wind so head were obliged to put up soon in the day & encamped that night.
>
> 31st Got under way at sun half hour high, sailed and rowed as far as Saint Johns, called 80 miles.[27]

Thus, he traveled about one hundred miles in four days, averaging 25 miles (or about 2.5 miles per hour assuming a ten hour day). The author's living history unit has operated bateaux on Lake Champlain, and also averaged about 2.5 miles per hour, confirming these rates using the modern living history technique of experimental archaeology. On June 4, Tuttle recorded rowing 30 miles in a single day on the Richelieu River, presumably averaging about three miles per hour. These journals suggest that the soldiers could row the bateaux about two to three miles per hour, but if they had good winds and could sail the bateaux they could easily achieve five to eight miles per hour.

Research by the New York State Museum, the only professional study performed on these bateaux, suggests that the boats could carry between two or three tons of supplies or men. The bateaux that Schuyler built are consistently noted to have carried "thirty to forty men." Assuming that thirty men with all of their military equipment including muskets and knapsacks would weigh approximately two hundred pounds each, this supports a payload capacity of around three tons or six thousand pounds for the 32-foot bateaux that Schuyler had constructed for Lake Champlain and Lake George.[28]

It should be noted, however, that rowing bateaux did involve certain hazards for both the rower and the passenger. These risks might not be readily apparent. When Chaplain Ammi Robbins traveled upon a bateaux on May 7 during the American retreat from Quebec, he recalled:

> The boatmen sing a very pretty air to "row the boat row" which ran in my head when half asleep, nor could I put it entirely out of mind amid all our gloom and terror, with the water up to my knees as I lay in the boat. My difficulty was, one passage I could not get.[29]

Now, having lost their bateaux on the St. Lawrence, the Americans could not even maintain an army along that river had they been so inclined, for without the bateaux they could not feed their soldiers. But it scarcely mattered. They were not so inclined. Thomas' retreat was, in the vernacular, a debacle. He claimed to have considered a stand at several points along the St. Lawrence River. However, without artillery or gunboats to obstruct the river, the British Royal Navy commanded the St. Lawrence, and could readily interdict or bypass any conceivable American defensive position. Thomas realized his gross inadequacies to resist along the St. Lawrence. He lamented to the commissioners that, "The ships of war were hastening forward with all possible dispatch ... we had no cannon to prevent their passing ... and if cannon could have been procured, we had no ball, and not more provision than would subsist the army for two or three days." By May 7, the van of the American army, if the starving, ragged, terrified, fleeing, smallpox-infested rabble could be called that, had begun to reach Sorel and Chambly. The withdrawal down the St. Lawrence River valley was a miserable experience for the fleeing American soldiers. Lieutenant Colonel Israel Shreve, whose New Jersey Regiment had reached Quebec just in time to turn around and join in the retreat, recorded of the rout:

> I was ordered on board a bateau ... with 10 sick officers and soldiers at point dishambo [Deschambault] in sight of 3 [British] men of war with a little pork and no flour, about half a loaf of bread. In this situation we set off against a strong current for Sorel, about a 100 miles. In our way a wide lake. We had bad weather, headwinds, and often obliged to put to shore where for hard money I bought bread, milk and some eggs at a very dear rate. No other person but myself [had] a copper of hard money. In this manner we came in five days up to Sorel. The 10 sick is all getting better. But two of my oarsmen was taken as soon as we arrived and both died in a few days.[30]

Colonel Porter also described the challenges of this forlorn movement:

> [May] 7th. Got to Point au Tremble a little after sunrise. Stopt and bought 2 loaves of bread for about 70 men I had with me, which was all that could be had.

It should be noted that the strength of Colonel Porter's regiment on May 11, after it had been reorganized, was 496 men.[31] Thus, when the alarm was given in front of Quebec, Porter had been able to organize only one-eighth of his men for the defense. This is another clear portrayal of the fact that the American position in front of Quebec was poorly organized and commanded. Porter continued with his tale of the woeful rout:

> Divided it [the 2 loaves of bread] amongst them. We made this day 30 miles to Point du Chambeau, our men excessively fatigued.... Expected to make a stand here, but want of provisions and everything else except cannon obliged the Gen'l to order a retreat to Sorrell.[32]

Here Thomas intended to make a stand at the "falls of the Richelieu."[33]

Although he had spent less than two weeks in Canada, Benjamin Franklin was sick, and exhausted from the long journey up the lakes. He was also extremely astute, and almost immediately perceived that American fortunes in the fledgling fourteenth colony were doomed to failure. On May 11 Franklin determined to return home to Philadelphia. Charles Carroll recorded in his journal:

> Dr. Franklin left Montreal today to go to St. John's, and from thence to Congress. The Doctor's declining state of health, and the bad prospect of our affairs in Canada, made him take this resolution.[34]

Franklin was accompanied by Father Carroll, whose every effort in Montreal had been rebuffed. Apparently, Father Carroll very rapidly and very easily was convinced that his mission was a failure. Still, it was propitious for Franklin that he was accompanied by the younger and healthier man, for Father Carroll saw to Franklin's physical needs, and nursed him back to health. The fact that Franklin was saved to make further contributions to America must be largely credited to Father Carroll's care and efforts. Franklin would write, in gratitude, "I find I grow daily more feeble, and I think I could hardly have got along so far but for Mr. Carroll's friendly assistance and tender care of me."[35]

Even with the American defeat at Quebec, Haskell and his compatriots continued their march home. The young musketman finally arrived at his home at Newburyport, Massachusetts, on May 30. He had been gone from home for nearly a year, had survived all the privations and starvation of the march up the Kennebec to Quebec, lived through the horrific disease of smallpox, and had suffered through four months of exhausting duty outside of Quebec without adequate food, clothing, or equipment. Halkett did not record his emotions, but he must have been absolutely ecstatic upon his arrival back home. Indeed, we suspect that the young soldier must have kissed the dunes of Newburyport.

Daniel Kimball also departed Canada at this point, noting that on May 12 his company had observed the Sabbath at Sorel when they "stayed 'til sunset to get a pass and then pushed off for Chamblee." Kimball wasted little time in departing Canada, reaching his home on the Connecticut River in New Hampshire on May 27. He had served for less than a month at Quebec, and had never fired a single shot at a British soldier. Kimball and his comrades, apparently with permission for they had received a pass, continued their retreat from Quebec all the way to their homes.

Lieutenant Beal clearly experienced all of the sordid confusion and desperation that the American Army was in by this point. When he reached Chambly on May 8 he reported: "The French are close & will not take paper money & we cannot get no rum." On May 8 things only grew darker for the Americans, as more British reinforcements arrived when three transports and the HMS *Niger* safely landed at Quebec with the entirety of the 47th Regiment of Foot.[36] Meanwhile the American army's fortunes failed to improve. Poor Lieutenant Beal's Canadian experience continued to deteriorate miserably and daily, as extracts from his journal attest:

12 — Col. Bond's regiment arrived here; they brought no provisions with them. We have nothing to eat but pork & bread

13 — I am not well, & nothing to take but salt pork & bread.

14 — Nothing to eat but pork & bread. We cannot buy nothing of the French for want of silver money. I went 3 miles to buy some butter, but could not get any. Nothing but pork & bread & water porridge.

15 — Nothing to eat but pork & bread.

16 — I mounted the guards & nothing to drink but water. Lt. Wiles returned with some of our men with him who have been gone 5 days & they have been where the small pox is.

17 — I went in a boat with Capt. Vose to get some fish. Gen. Thomas arrived here with 100 men inoculated with the small pox. Our men are uneasy because they cannot have the first chance to inoculate.

18 — We had pork & peas today for dinner.

19 — Capt. Cushing & myself inoculated for the small pox. Pork & peas today.

25 — We have not half provision for our men. They draw but half a pound of flower

& ½ pound of meat. The cry is "I can't stand it." We expect to retreat every hour & expect to break out with the small pox every day.[37]

When Colonel Porter arrived at Three Rivers on May 10, during the retreat, he found "no provisions there." Porter, who apparently still had a little bit of money remaining from his journey to Canada, was able to purchase a single sack of flour for his men. When he finally did arrive at Sorel, Porter recalled that on May 18, "We received but ½ allowance of meat this day."[38]

Arnold wrote to Washington on May 8, sadly enough, as he clearly saw the abandonment of the campaign in Canada that he had worked so tirelessly to achieve for a full year:

> Our Army consists of few more than two thousand effective men & twelve hundred sick & unfit for duty chiefly with the small pox which is universal in this country. We have very little provisions, no cash & less credit & until the arrival of the heavy cannon & two mortars from Cambridge our artillery has been trifling ... the want of cash has greatly retarded our operations in this Country.... I set off for the Army with no very agreeable prospects before me. Should the enemy receive any considerable reinforcement soon, I make no doubt, we shall have our hands full, at any rate we will do all that can be expected from raw troops, badly clothed and fed & worse paid & without discipline & trust the event to Providence.[39]

Unknown to Arnold, as he was writing that very letter, the 47th Regiment of Foot was marching through the streets of Quebec, heading for points west. The "considerable reinforcement" that he feared so much had already arrived.

Governor Guy Carleton had the final word of the siege of Quebec, when he issued a formal proclamation from Quebec on May 10. This powerful and magnanimous document generously proclaimed:

> Whereas I am informed, that many of his Majesty's deluded subjects of the neighboring provinces laboring under wounds and diverse disorders are dispersed in the adjacent woods and parishes, and in great danger of perishing for want of proper assistance; all Captains and other Officers of the militia are hereby commanded to make diligent search for all distressed persons, and afford them all necessary relief, and convey them to the General Hospital, where proper care shall be taken of them: All reasonable expenses which may be incurred in complying with this order shall be paid by the Receiver General.
>
> And lest a consciousness of past offences should deter such miserable wretches from receiving that assistance which their distressed situation may require, I hereby make known to them, that as soon as their health is restored, they shall have free Liberty to return to their respective provinces.[40]

It was a brilliant maneuver. In it, Carleton clearly claimed the moral high ground. He convincingly demonstrated His Majesty's clemency and charity, while he turned around the entire Continental invasion of Canada to his own purposes by in turn offering "free Liberty" to those rebels who had previously turned against king and country. Quite certainly, any patriots who took advantage of Carleton's generosity were unlikely to rejoin the Continental Army, and they may well have become Loyalists. When they got home, they were certain to praise the care and treatment that they had received at

British hands, thereby weakening patriot resolve for the cause of independence. With a succinct, two-page parchment Carleton had proven British arms to be forgiving and merciful, reduced the rolls of the Continental army, and introduced an element of doubt into their course of action on behalf of the united American Colonies.

Unbeknownst to Carleton, actions were underway to the west of Montreal that would shortly throw more element of doubt into the American army.

4

"Enough to Make Anybody's Blood Crawl"
Failure of American Leadership at the Affair at the Cedars, May 18 to 30, 1776

The Saint Lawrence River, before the construction of the Saint Lawrence Seaway and other improvements throughout the 19th and 20th centuries, was a treacherous passage to navigate. Numerous sets of wild, dangerous rapids interrupted the flow of the river, and had to be cautiously negotiated, usually by portage. The most precipitous of these rapids was located at a small settlement known as the Cedars, approximately 43 miles west of Montreal. These rapids had caused the British and Provincial army of General Jeffery Amherst great difficulties as it ascended the Saint Lawrence for Montreal in 1760. Amherst recorded in his journal:

> [September] 4th. I marched a little after day break in one Column by the right as the greatest part of the Rapids I had to pass could be only passed with one boat abreast. The Pilots assured me it was very unusual to find so much water in the River yet we found it very bad & difficult to pass tho' the boats were made lighter by putting most of the men on Shore who marched by Land from the Cedars to the end of the cascades. The weather favoured but the Rapids cost us dear, notwithstanding every Corps had a pilot. Several had two & the Pilots sent back as fast as the batteaus passed. We lost 84 men, 20 batteaus of Regts, 17 of Artillery, 17 whaleboats, one Row Galley, a quantity of Artillery Stores & some Guns that I hope may be recovered.[1]

The sweeping American advances of 1775 had cleared the Saint Lawrence and Richelieu River valleys of British forces, but a number of comparatively strong British commands remained isolated in frontier posts to the west including Forts Oswegatchie, Niagara, Detroit, and Michilimackinac. Recognizing the threat that these detachments posed to the American strategic left flank and rear, upon his arrival at Montreal in mid–April Brigadier General Benedict Arnold deployed a reinforced American regiment from Montreal to the Cedars to guard against such a British advance.[2] A post at the Cedars, located at a protrusion into the river immediately north of the rapids, could provide effective observation across the breadth of the river "so that not even a canoe could pass unnoticed."[3]

The American garrison at the Cedars was commanded by Colonel Timothy Bedel of New Hampshire, and consisted of approximately four hundred soldiers, predominantly from Bedel's own regiment of New Hampshire Rangers that he had raised earlier that year. Two 4-pounder cannon supported Bedel, and he constructed a small stockaded fort.[4] This was a substantial allotment of manpower given the weakness of the American

Early nineteenth century view of the Rapids at the Cedars. The swirling rapids were the most dangerous on the St. Lawrence River. During his advance on Montreal in the late summer of 1760, General Jeffery Amherst lost scores of boats, scores of men, and several valuable artillery pieces attempting to pass these rapids. In 1775 they were one of the most formidable obstacles on the St. Lawrence River and were the natural site for an American defensive position. The rapids were essentially removed with the construction of the St. Lawrence Seaway (G.P. Browne, *The St. Lawrence River, Historical, Legendary, Picturesque* [New York and London: G.P. Putnam's Sons, Knickerbocker, 1905]).

army in Canada, and demonstrated the importance that Arnold assigned to guarding his vulnerable flank and rear.

Bedel had previously served as an officer with New Hampshire provincial forces during the Seven Years' War, and had rendered useful services during the American advance northward from Lake Champlain in 1775. Additionally, Bedel was also conversant with Native Americans, and Arnold hoped that he could be of service in maintaining neutrality with several Indian tribes and villages located in the vicinity. Bedel subsequently complained of this assignment:

> It was my miss fortune and a very general one too, that it fell to my lot to be ordered immediately on my arrival in Canada to take the Command of this unlucky post.... The Command was equally as undesired as Difficult & Disagreeable, more especially when considered how ill provided I was with every necessary means of Defence in that quarters, or even to secure a Retreat if that last resource became necessary — in vain did I frequently apply to Genl Arnold ... for the most necessary supplys of ammunition provisions, Intrenching tools and Batteaus.... We were frequently living on less

than half allowance of provisions the natural Consequences of all which was the greatest discontent & dissatisfaction of the officers and very little short of a mutiny amongst the soldiers.[5]

Given the American situation in Canada throughout the winter of 1775 and 1776, Bedel's complaints were unfounded, as the entire American Army in Canada was short of ammunition, provisions, and other necessary military equipage. Additionally, the surviving accounts from Bedel's soldiers, and their subsequent efforts at the Cedars, fail to demonstrate such "discontent and dissatisfaction." Rather the soldiers' accounts suggest a committed determination and resolve to defend the post.

Arnold's concerns were well founded. British Captain George Forster of the 8th Regiment of Foot, commander of the post at Oswegatchie, began gathering a detachment in the spring of 1776 to attack the American strategic rear and left flank at Montreal by way of the Saint Lawrence River.[6] His first significant obstacle would be Bedel's post at the Cedars.

Forster left Oswegatchie on May 12, 1776, with a force consisting of "one captain, two lieutenants, two sergeants, two corporals, one drummer, and thirty-three private soldiers, of his Majesty's eighth regiment; and eleven English and Canadian gentlemen volunteers, and one hundred and sixty savages of different nations. On the 14th we got to St. Regis, and were there joined by fifty-four savages of that village." The Native warriors from St. Regis were acting under the direction of Claude-Nicolas-Guillaume de Lorimier, a member of the French Canadian gentry who had fought with the French in the Seven Years' War but subsequently transferred his allegiance to the British crown forces and had fought with accomplishment at Fort Saint Jean on the Richelieu River in 1775.[7] On the morning of May 18 Forster neared the Cedars with a total force of 41 British regulars, eleven Canadian and English volunteers, and 214 Native American warriors. On that same date reinforcements were assigned to the Cedars, including Private Benjamin Stevens of Colonel Charles Burrall's Connecticut Regiment. "In the afternoon landed at the Cedars by the fort and here we have taken up our adobe for I know not how long."[8] Sadly enough for the young soldier, his stay at the Cedars was to be curtailed.

De Lorimier in his *Memoirs* noted that the Americans had placed soldiers in outposts around their fortification, to include stationing a Sergeant and six soldiers at the home of Curé Deneau at the Cedars. Additionally, Bedel received intelligence from some of the local French Canadian inhabitants regarding Forster's advance. Inexplicably Bedel abandoned his post upon receipt of this information, turned over command to his subordinate, Major Isaac Butterfield, and fled to Montreal.[9]

As he approached the American post, Forster ordered De Lorimier's natives to first invest Butterfield's fortifications:

> We didn't waste any more time talking but legged it towards the enemy positions. When we got near the farm of a man named Lalonde ... a Mohawk called William Johnson ... a natural son of the late William Johnson ... and I saw two Americans taking aim at a distance of about sixty yards, with their muskets resting on a fence. My companion just had time to cry "Look out!" and we flung ourselves into a ditch as the musket balls sang over our heads. Then we rose up and went for them before they could reload. They went leaping away down a steep hill and we were close enough on

their heels to use the same fence from which they had fired as a support for our muskets. William gasped, "Take the one on the right" and we let fly; he winged his in the thigh and I got mine in the shoulder.... All the Indians had followed hard on our heels and now we succeeded in cutting the American line of communications in a skirmish in which we killed one man and wounded four others. A party of twenty Americans had come up from the Cascades in order to regain the line of trenches and when they saw us blocking their path they seized a house near the fort and defended themselves vigorously. The [reverse] slope of the hill protected us from the fire of the trenches, but when Bonneur, one of my Indians, was killed, the Indians became enraged and shouted to each other to storm the house and revenge his death. We burst into the house, but since the enemy had taken refuge in the attic to which there was no access save by a ladder, I gave the order to set the place on fire. While this was going on, two balls from a two-pounder came ripping through the one wall and out the other, to my great astonishment. What had happened was that the defenders, under cover of the racket we were making, had ripped out the gable-end of the roof and had scampered off to their trenches.... A body of 180 Americans then made a sortie. This alarmed me a good deal, because my party of Indians did not number more than 80 or 90 at this point, but all my fears were for nought. The Americans were not after us, but had sortied merely to burn a superb barn belonging to the Chevalier de Longueuil.[10]

De Lorimier's account describes determined opposition by the New Hampshire men. Private Stevens recalled that on the 15th of May "our scouts came back and brought news the enemy was within six miles of this place. We immediately were drawn out to take our posts ... we soon got at breastworks prepared by the pickets, and every man knows his own place."[11] The presence of entrenched works, and the two four-pounder cannon, provided the Americans with substantive military advantages. Although abandoned by their commander, his soldiers knew that Colonel Bedel had gone to Montreal, and presumably reinforcements would soon be heading their way. The evidence is that, with a single exception, the Americans fought with valor and determination. Unfortunately, that single exception was their new commanding officer, Major Butterfield.

Forster constructed "a breastwork out of fence posts" and surrounded the Cedars. He then "summoned the enemy to surrender, while it was yet in his power to save their lives. "Fearing that should [the Americans] not do it [surrender] immediately, the savages could not be restrained by the small numbers of his troops, from committing acts of cruelty." Butterfield contemplated surrendering his command, but his soldiers would not permit him to do so. His summons were "refused, and hostilities again commenced." The next morning, May 19, Forster "advanced, under the cover of some houses, to within one hundred and fifty yards of the enemy's breast-work, where, having no cannon, we kept up a fire of musquetry, whenever there appeared any object for its direction. About ten o'clock we were joined by a Canadian gentleman Monsieur de Montigny, with thirty Canadians."[12]

Bedel's hasty flight to Montreal had not been without benefit. Arnold had dispatched a force under the command of Rhode Island Major Henry Sherburne with 140 men to march to the relief of the Cedars. One of Sherburne's soldiers would relate of this officer, "a braver man never was made, and he was a strict disciplinarian."[13] Forster had received word of Sherburne's approach from de Montigny. Without any cannon of his own, with a larger force well entrenched with artillery to his front, and a relief force of equal strength marching upon his rear, Forster's prospects were not favorable. At this critical juncture, "a flag appeared from the enemy, offering to surrender, if their lives could be secured from the savages." This surrender offer was apparently Butterfield's own idea, for his soldiers would later represent that it was with "great grief and surprise" that they had learned of the capitulation.[14]

Butterfield appears to have been terrified by the threat posed by the Native American warriors fighting with the British, and his fears could only have been heightened by the wily response of Forster:

> I have by entreaty, overcome the resolution formed by the savages, of allowing no quarters, on your refusing my offer to you; and am happy to assure you and your garrison personal safety: as the disposition of savages is not very certain, I would fain take the advantage of their present favourable turn, and grant you the following terms; I. That the fort shall surrender at discretion in half an hour, securing to you your lives and the cloaths which you have on."

Butterfield hastened to accept the terms, and shortly Forster's command occupied the post. Stevens recorded in his diary in verbiage that suggests that Butterfield readily surrendered the fort on his own volition, and not because it was in any danger, "Our officers surrendered up the fort and now we are prisoners. The Lord protect us and keep us from harm." Forster subsequently recorded capturing 390 officers and enlisted men.[15] There is strong evidence that Butterfield was panicked, for the two cannon were not spiked (rendered inoperative), and would be employed against American forces less than a week later.

The Americans had attempted to depart the fort carrying their knapsacks, presumably stuffed with everything that they could possibly contain, which enraged the Indians that had been looking forward to looting the fort, and felt that they were being cheated of their just rewards. De Lorimier reported, "All of our prisoners were stripped of everything they had by the Indians despite whatever protests we were able to make; so much so, in fact, that I had to give Major Butterfield ... some of my old togs to keep him from going naked."[16] Lieutenant Parke would similarly recall:

> Notwithstanding the garrison had only been promised the cloaths on their backs, each person had made up a pack to carry off with them, which Captain Forster observed, might discontent the savages, and be the cause of insults, which he could not prevent, at the same time, two Indian chiefs did say, without consulting the rest, they might take them, and thereupon they did take them. The other savages dissatisfied, did that evening, before the prisoners were lodged in the barracks, strip them of some watches and money, and perhaps of a laced hat or two.[17]

Stevens recorded, "I was stripped of all but one shirt, my great coat, straight bodied coat, pair of shoes, two pair of stockings, and my breeches. I gave my straight bodied coat to Captain Stevens, who was stripped naked to his shirt." An American officer who marched to the relief of the Cedars recalled of the condition of the prisoners when they reached American lines: "They were stripped almost naked by the Indians, and of everything valuable about them."[18] The American prisoners later petitioned:

> We surrendered ourselves as prisoners of war and was to deliver up our arms which accordingly we did, and we was to have our packs and baggage — and Capt Foster

Engaged not to suffer the savages to plunder or abuse us, nor suffer the British troops to do so. But contrary to the Rules of War, they inhumanly without regard to their promise, suffered the savages to rob and plunder us of our packs and baggage, and strip us of our clothes off our backs and left us entirely naked.[19]

With the post at the Cedars disposed of, Forster turned his attention to Sherburne's approaching relief force. The morning of May 20 he dispatched de Lorimier with eighty Native American warriors and eighteen Canadian volunteers under the command of Monsieur Maurer to intercept Sherburne. About four miles east of the Cedars, at a place known as Quinze-chenes (Fifteen Oaks) Sherburne was successfully ambushed. De Lorimier recorded: "As soon as the Americans came opposite to the place where the Indians were concealed the latter rose up and poured upon them a tremendous fire, making at the same time a most hideous noise called the war-whoop." A brisk skirmish ensued, during which Sherburne's force inflicted some casualties upon the Natives, in particular killing a prominent Seneca warrior.[20] Eventually outflanked, outfought and surrounded, Sherburne was forced to yield. Although Sherburne was apparently a respected and capable officer, he had still permitted his command to be first surprised, and then surrounded, by an inferior force.

Enraged by their losses, the Indians carried off a few of the Americans as captives, and the survivors were stripped of their clothes and possessions. De Lorimier describes the treatment of the American commander, Sherburne:

One of the Indians was holding Major Sherburne by the hand and pretending to make off with him. I objected but he said that he had touched Sherburne before I did. I denied this and said that he must not make off with the prisoner.... Hearing this, the Indian remained thoughtful for a moment and then exclaimed, "Keep the bird and I will take his plumes." Immediately he flung himself upon Sherburne and took his uniform, his hat, and his vest and then said "I will get the rest later when we reach camp." In fact he did just that: I later saw him strip Sherburne even of his breeches and shirt.[21]

De Lorimier had taken 97 prisoners in this fight. These prisoners were carried back to join those seized by Forster at the Cedars. American casualties were estimated at 28 killed and wounded. The record is contradictory, but it appears that the Indians subsequently killed at least a few of the wounded. Native and Canadian casualties are imperfectly related, but all sources are in agreement that they were considerably less. Forster's forty British regulars now had a total of 487 American prisoners under their charge.[22]

Arnold, commanding at Montreal, was alarmed at the twin victories achieved by British arms. If Montreal fell to Forster, the American line of supplies and communications running up the Richelieu River from New York could be easily severed, and the American defensive position in Canada lost. Arnold began to hastily fortify a long stone structure at Lachine, west of Montreal, but he had less than 500 men available for the defense of the American rear.[23] Forster's command began a cautious advance upon Montreal, constrained by the need to safeguard the large number of American prisoners, and still with only a small number of regulars. Forster closed to within three miles of Lachine, some light skirmishing ensued and two Americans were taken prisoner by de Lorimier's Indian scouts. However, on May 25 the 1st Pennsylvania Battalion, commanded by Colonel Joseph DeHaas, arrived to the succor of Arnold's defense of Montreal. DeHaas brought with him a total of 549 effectives, providing Arnold with a force strong enough to not only to assure the sanctity of Montreal, but also to enable Arnold to contemplate the resumption of offensive operations.[24] De Lorimier's scouts accurately reported to Forster that "the rebels had six hundred men, with six pieces of cannon, entrenched at Le Chine." Receiving additional information that more American reinforcements were expected, and probably suspecting that Arnold was made of sterner stuff than Butterfield, Forster realized that he lacked sufficient combat power to force the gates of Montreal. In fact, Forster's force was being reduced, as his Canadian partisans were departing, and the Natives "wandered as their fancy led them." Forster called a council of war at which the British officers decided to "repass the river to the Cedars."[25] Forster's advance on the American strategic left flank and rear at Montreal was at an end.

Now strengthened, Arnold initiated a movement forward. By the afternoon of May 26 Arnold had reached St. Anne, at the western end of Montreal Island, just across the St. Lawrence River from Forster's camp now returned to the small French Canadian town of Vaudreuil. Arnold's force, in fifteen bateaux and three canoes, began to probe across the St. Lawrence River in the late afternoon. A brisk firefight ensued, in which Forster placed into action the two four-pounder cannon captured at the Cedars.[26] John Greenwood, a Rhode Island soldier posted with a blunderbuss in the bow of one of Arnold's boats, recalled, "Behind every tree were three or four Indians who poured or showered

Modern view of Cedars battlefield. Today a quiet Canadian farm field, this was the site of the American post at the Cedars in May, 1776 and was the site of desperate struggles. Only a single roadside marker commemorates the engagement (author collection).

their bullets upon us as thick as hailstones. As it was now sundown, General Arnold thought proper to give the signal of retreat to the other side of their river, so back we went. The English had drawn down their two field-pieces to the shore and now began to play amongst us with them." Arnold contemplated a night attack but was dissuaded by his subordinate officers. At this juncture Forster "sent an envoy along with an American captain (actually Major Sherburne) to suggest an exchange of prisoners to General Arnold."[27]

Forster was apparently having troubles controlling his Natives, and feared that a massacre of the American prisoners that he was charged with would ensue. Following negotiations that were at times heated, Arnold and Forster agreed to a mutual exchange of prisoners which was affected on May 27, and the next day Arnold withdrew to Montreal. Forster similarly withdrew to Oswegatchie, after the American prisoners were all repatriated by May 30.[28] With Forster's withdrawal to Oswegatchie the affair of the Cedars was over.

Forster had launched an aggressive and confident attack upon the American strategic left flank and rear. His gambit had initially succeeded and precipitated two stinging defeats upon the American defenders, predominantly because of poor leadership on the part of Bedel, Butterfield and Sherburne.[29] What must have been particularly alarming to Arnold and other American leaders was that Forster with only forty regular soldiers, augmented by an ad hoc assemblage of irregulars, had captured ten times their number of American soldiers, and threatened the entire American effort in Canada. Captain Edward Williams of Massachusetts would relate to his uncle, a veteran of the French and Indian Wars back in Boston:

> The men that were in the fort [at the Cedars were] wanting ... to go out & drive the enemy away. But the major would not let them but gave up the fort to the enemy, when at the same time he now had a reinforcement a coming to help him. Major Sherburn was there within nine miles of the fort, pushing on with all his might to help him with about one hundred & twenty men. But night coming on he was obliged to make a halt. Next morning set out but it was too late, the Damned Coward had give up the fort, he got within about three miles of the fort. The Indians & some Canadians which had joined them by this time ambushed Sherburn & fired upon him, he fought for near two hours like a hero, but having no relief from the fort the enemy cut off his retreat, he was obliged resign [sic] & was treated cruelly by them. Several of his men was killed & tomahawked after they were taken. I need not enlarge upon this subject as you have the points. I am afraid sir I shall tired your patience, but you must excuse me, it being the first I have wrote you. Colonel Beattle [sic] & Major Butterfield was both arrested as soon as they got back, they were both broke cashiered & sent home. Not worthy to wear commission in the Continental Army. Dear Sir, such men & such conduct is enough to make any body's blood crawl.[30]

However demoralizing the affair at the Cedars may have been to the Americans, this action had little real impact upon the 1776 Northern Theater Campaign. Forster lacked adequate strength to press his advantage, and Arnold had rapidly responded to the threat and secured Montreal against further British advances.[31] Still, it revealed grave faults in the American military leadership in Canada. These and similar weaknesses were shortly to prove catastrophic to the success of American arms in their endeavors in the 14th colony during the early summer of 1776.

5

"Founded in Rashness and Executed with Timidity"

The American Attack on Three Rivers, June 7 to 11, 1776

The American retreat, or what more properly should be referred to as the American panicked route, eventually ended up at Sorel, located at the intersection of the Richelieu River and St. Lawrence River and Fort Chambly, located at the modern community of Chambly, Quebec Province, Canada. When the congressional commissioners arrived at Sorel to meet with Thomas they "found the discipline of our camp very remiss, and everything in confusion." When they proceeded to Chambly, they found things to be even more deplorable:

> We got early this morning to Chambly, where we found all things in much confusion, extreme disorder and negligence, our credit sunk, and no money to retrieve it with. We were obliged to pay three silver dollars for the carriage of three barrels of gunpowder from Little Chambly River to Longueil, the officer who commanded the guard not having a single shilling.

The commissioners then proceeded to St. Jean's on May 31, where they again found "all things there in confusion."[1]

Dr. Lewis Beebe, a Massachusetts surgeon recently arrived with the columns of American reinforcements at Sorel on May 11, described the village:

> The Country is exceeding Level & pleasant[,] greatly populated upon the river, scarce 40 rods upon either side of the river, but that there is a French settlement, and many places are considerable populous, their houses in general make no great appearance, yet their churches & nunneries are somewhat elegant.[2]

As Surgeon Beebe noted, Sorel is flat and featureless, and offered no advantages from a military standpoint. Sorel's importance was primarily geographic, because of its location at the intersection of the St. Lawrence and Richelieu rivers. However, nothing had been done to strengthen the position, and no existing military fortifications were located there. Most importantly, from a tactical standpoint, once past Sorel the St. Lawrence River turned sharply south until it had passed Montreal. Only a few miles of land, well traversed with roads, separated the St. Lawrence River from nearly any point upon the Richelieu River. The British navy controlled the St. Lawrence River, and the American army lacked adequate artillery and fortifications to prevent the Royal Navy from passing Sorel. Once past Sorel, the navy could put the British infantry and field artillery ashore at any of a dozen different locations from where they could easily isolate an American army anywhere between Sorel and St. Jean.

And, quite frankly, the Americans at Sorel were in no condition to present a determined opposition to any British assault. Beebe had regarded the American force that plodded into the community, "those who come safe to Sorrell were obliged to leave all their baggage and bring nothing away but the cloaths upon their backs. No person can conceive the distress our people endured the winter past, nor was it much less at the time of their retreat." With Sorel indefensible, the next post south on the Richelieu River was the old French Fort Chambly.

The French originally constructed Fort Chambly in 1711, and by 1776 it comprised a small, four bastioned stone fortification with numerous interior barracks and storehouses. Its configuration had been inspired by the formal European military fortifications of Vauban and Coehorn, but its thin, high stone walls lacked sufficient strength to repel

Fort Chambly. Captured by the Americans in 1775, military stores seized here facilitated American success at the Siege of Fort St. John. Fort Chambly then served as an American supply depot until the American retreat in May 1776 made it briefly the focus of the American defensive position. Major General Thomas died here in early June 1776 and the Americans shortly retreated (author's collection).

cannonballs. Against Indian raids it was an imposing and effective deterrent, but it was hopelessly outmatched when faced by European armies and artillery. During the British invasion of 1760 it was abandoned without offering any resistance, and it had easily fallen in the fall of 1775 to a small American force detached from Montgomery's army. It was constructed on a small protrusion of land that extended from the western bank into the Richelieu River, and it was located on the northern terminus of the rapids that extended between Chambly and St. Jean. Its location controlled the northern end of the rapids, but the Royal Navy could easily reach Chambly from the north by the Richelieu River, and the Americans lacked adequate cannon to effectively defend against the British frigates. Additionally, Fort Chambly was commanded by high ground within easy artillery range to the west, and it could be readily bypassed both tactically and strategically. A British force operating from either the St. Lawrence River Valley or Montreal could easily move to the south of Chambly and cut off any American force there. Neither Sorel nor Chambly offered any defensive advantages to Thomas and the disorganized rabble that comprised his army.

At Sorel and Chambly, Thomas attempted to reorganize his army. Considerably closer to his logistical base at Fort Ticonderoga than he had been at Quebec, he could attempt to establish magazines of provisions and ammunition at Chambly and St. Jean. Thomas ordered Arnold to continue to garrison Montreal, so that the Americans could at least state that one of the great cities in Canada was still retained by them. Thomas also hoped that the efforts of the congressional committee would yield some results. If reinforcements of specie, men and material reached Thomas rapidly enough, Chambly offered him one considerable advantage in that he could easily move north on the Richelieu River and renew a movement on Quebec from there.

The supply situation was desperate. The commissioners from Congress wrote to Schuyler on May 6: "We are informed by General Arnold that the army before Quebec is only victualed up to the 15th or 20th instant at farthest. We need not point out to you the necessity of keeping our forces in this country well supplied with provisions, as, excepting flour, none can be procured here, and that not without hard money."[3] In fact, the precipitous withdrawal from Quebec had resulted in the abandonment of considerable stores, and only made the situation worse. Arnold informed Thomas from Sorel on May 14:

> It was thought most advisable by the Honorable the Commission of Congress, to abandon your post at Deschambes, as it was impossible to support you with Provisions, very little having lately come over the Lake & none expected soon, Men indeed we have, but almost every other requisite for war is wanting. I have brought to this place three hundred barrels flour & now send you in two batteaux thirty barrels flour & six barrels pork, the last articles all I could procure in Montreal.[4]

Benjamin Franklin, as he departed Canada on May 12, mustered the energy to urgently write Schuyler, "You will see the absolute necessity ... of forwarding provisions hither, or the Army must starve, plunder or surrender."[5]

Even Simeon Bloodgood, a young man not yet a teenager who had spent the winter driving supplies on a sleigh to the Continental army, recognized how desperate the situation was: "We were impressed with the necessity of doing everything in our power to keep [our army] in supplies."⁶ Arnold estimated his force at Sorel on that date to be between 2,000 and 3,000 men. Thus, Arnold's six barrels of pork was adequate for full rations for a single day only. However, the three hundred barrels of flour were sufficient to feed the force with full rations for a month (assuming some small amount of inevitable wastage).

Pork or beef was extremely difficult to obtain in Canada by this time. The commissioners of Congress stated to Schuyler, "It is impossible to procure any pork in this Colony, there is none but what came over the Lakes." Recognizing the limited quantity of provisions then in Canada, the commissioners wisely advised Schuyler not to dispatch any more men down the lakes unless they could carry pork with them, as "our soldiers must perish or feed on each other. Even plunder, the last resource of strong necessity, will not relieve their wants." They continued, "We are unable to express our apprehensions of the distress our Army must soon be reduced from the want of provisions, and the small pox."⁷ When the soldiers were issued provisions, quite frequently they were of an extremely poor quality. Pennsylvanian Captain John Lacy was a miller by profession, and was accordingly quite familiar with the preparation of flour and grains. He was aghast at the quality of rations that he received in Canada:

> Our supplies ... were not only bad in quality, but scant and limited in quantity. The meal, I cannot call it flour, for it was hardly ground, it was what at my father's mill in Bucks County we called chopped for horses and cattle. Many a bushel I had ground there for hogs of far better quality that the meal we drew here to eat, none of which had been bolted. We eat it bran and all, some of it very musty. As to meat, we had none but rusty pork, the pickle, if any had ever been on it, had long since leaked from the barrels, such as did not stink was so rusty it could not be eaten; but used in this manner, as I saw and had it done myself. The meat was cut in slices, stewed over the fire in a pan or other vessel, until the lard was extracted, when the meat was thrown away, making the meal & bran into a batter with water, pouring it over the hot lard, holding over the fire a short time, we had a very rich and eatable cake, which served both for meat and bread — a small portion of tea or chocolate sweetened with maple sugar satisfied our repast. This would have done very well could we but procured enough of it — we seldom drew more than half the ration and often not one third. As for fresh meat, I don't recollect seeing any.... I discovered plenty of milk and good rye bread in the houses of the inhabitants, which they were very willing to sell for hard money, but refused our paper.⁸

Thomas also intended to place a great iron chain across the Richelieu River at Chambly to prevent the British from proceeding south on the river. The use of iron chains to obstruct navigable rivers was not a new concept. Such devices had been use in antiquity, at such strategic locations as Istanbul, Cyprus, and Vienna; and a chain had played an important role in defending the island fortress of Malta against a siege by a Turkish army in 1565. In North America, log and chain booms had been used successfully by the French during the Seven Years' War at Fort Carillon at Ticonderoga; across the St. Charles River at Quebec; and astride both channels of the Richelieu River at the Isle Aux Noix.

Although documentary evidence for this chain is limited, at least some portions of this chain were completed by American ironworkers and shipped to Canada in the middle of May 1776, but because of the precipitous American retreat it was never installed.⁹ During the subsequent American withdrawal this chain was evacuated from Canada, and would eventually be placed at Fort Montgomery on the Hudson River. On July 21, 1776, Robert Yates, chairman of the Committee of the State of New York for the defense of the Hudson River, wrote Major General Horatio Gates, then commanding the American field army at Fort Ticonderoga:

> As the chain intended to obstruct the navigation of the river Sorel cannot now be applied to that use, and will serve to prevent the enemy's ships from going beyond the forts on Hudson's River, we must beg the favor of you to send the whole, or such parts of it as may expeditiously be had, to Poughkeepsie ... with the utmost dispatch. We shall by this opportunity request of the Committee of Albany immediately to furnish us with one hundred and fifty sawed logs of the largest size, to support the chain.

Major General Philip Schuyler, commander of the Northern Theater of Operations, forwarded this request to Gates on July 25, 1776, with his own comments:

> If the chain can be spared, I wish you would send it without delay, under the care of a careful officer to attend it to Poughkeepsie.

Gates responded on July 29:

> I send you, under the care of the bearer, the chain requested by General Schuyler's letter to me of the 25th instant, and have enclosed Colonel Baldwin's [the Chief-Engineer's] invoice of the pieces and links that the whole consists of. It will be all in the boats, on the other side of the camping place, this evening, and will not, I hope, be delayed in its passage to you. I must desire you to assist the bearer in getting it forward to Poughkeepsie, as the Committee seems so anxious to have it there.[10]

This chain actually became the first to be placed across the Hudson River. It would successfully obstruct the Hudson against any British advance for over a year, and in turn it would subsequently be succeeded by several more famous and formidable chains at West Point. This great chain was to play no appreciable role in the 1776 Northern Theater campaign, but the fates would dictate that it would play an important part in the next year's operations on the Hudson River.

Before Thomas could implement his plans regarding this chain at either Sorel or Chambly, he came down with the smallpox. Thomas had surprisingly never had the smallpox previously, even though he had been a practicing physician for many years in New England. Thomas had certainly been warned of the hazards that he was running, for the commissioners of Congress had directly written him on May 15, "We submit to you the propriety of immediately inoculating all our troops. We cannot but concur with General Arnold that by such measures, our army in a few weeks would be stronger and more effective than at present. We are, Sir, greatly concerned for your health, it will be almost impossible for you to escape catching the small pox & therefore we [missing word] you would immediately inoculate."[11] Having denied inoculation to his soldiers, Thomas would not let himself be personally inoculated. On May 24 General Wooster received a terse note that must have made his blood run cold.

> Head Quarters Sorrell 24 May 1776
>
> Dear General
>
> I am at this critical period unfortunately seized with the small pox. The safety of the Army makes it necessary that I should be removed from camp & shall be for some

5. "Founded in Rashness and Executed with Timidity"

time unable to discharge the duties of my office. The Command in consequence devolves on you as the main body of the army is here. You will immediately think it necessary repair to this place as soon as possible.

I Am Sir, With Much esteem, Your Most Obedient & Humble Servant;

John Thomas.[12]

It would be the last letter that Thomas would ever write. The General would be incapacitated almost immediately, blind shortly thereafter, and dead at the Fort at Chambly on June 2.

Still, American reinforcements were flowing towards Canada. Although the melting ice delayed their passage over Lakes George and Champlain, by mid–May they had begun to reach Sorel and Chambly. The American reinforcements, particularly the Pennsylvanians, made a spectacular appearance on Lake Champlain and the Richelieu River as they moved north.[13] Captain Persifor Frazer of the 4th Pennsylvania Battalion had written regarding his uniform:

Memorial to General Thomas, Fort Chambly. Although dedicated to Major General John Thomas, who is buried nearby in an unmarked grave, this memorial serves to commemorate the services of several thousand Continental Army soldiers who died in Canada, a few of them killed in battle, but mostly killed by disease and starvation, and who lie today in unmarked, uncommemorated graves throughout Quebec province (author's collection).

> I have used more industry to cloathe my men than any of the other Captains, their regiments were made in Philadelphia by the tailors there, mine at Darby by my own men ... under my own direction and of cloth that I had procured myself. Our regimental coats were deep blue faced with white, white vests and overalls edged with blue cloth. A very beautiful uniform, but on experience was found much better adopted for parade than utility in the hardships of a camp, as they too easily became soiled and hard to keep clean.... Our men without flattery exceed all the other troops both in appearance and subordination. The blue cloth at Darby if it is good and looks well wou'd advise you not to dispose of it and it is likely I shall want a suit of it for my own use.[14]

Captain John Lacey of the same regiment likewise recorded:

> The boats were soon under way. From the best calculation I could make, there were about two Hundred Vessels, Tents were hoisted for Sails. Colonel Wayne's division leading the Van, the whole made a most formidable and beautiful appearance — I presume, something like the Gretion [Grecian] Fleet going to the Siege of Troy.[15]

The Pennsylvania reinforcements might have appeared to their officers to be a spectacular sight, but they made a considerably different impression on the young Simeon Bloodgood, who shared a campground with them as they moved north upon the frozen Lake Champlain in early spring:

> A regiment of Pennsylvania troops overtook us, having traveled in sleighs. They were the most quarrelsome, and I regret to say, profligate set of men I had ever seen together. They had plenty of money with them and spent it profusely. The vices of insubordination, gambling and rioting marked their battalion, and we ourselves had great trouble with them.

To avoid any further contact with these obviously wicked and sinful soldiers, Bloodgood and his father made haste and "proceeded these turbulent Pennsylvanians, to keep out of their way, traveling late and early."[16]

The first reinforcement to arrive was the Connecticut Regiment of Colonel Charles Burrall, which was well along on its movement to Quebec when it ran into the retreating force at Deschambault on May 7. Following closely behind was the brigade commanded by Brigadier General William Thompson of Pennsylvania consisting of:

- The 8th Continental Infantry commanded by Colonel Enoch Poor of New Hampshire;
- The 15th Continental Infantry commanded by Colonel John Paterson of Massachusetts;
- The 24th Continental Infantry commanded by Colonel John Greaton of Massachusetts; and
- The 25th Continental Infantry commanded by Colonel William Bond of Massachusetts.

Brigadier General William Thompson of Cumberland County, Pennsylvania, had been born in Ireland in 1736, and as a Pennsylvania Provincial Captain he had commanded a Troop of Light Horse, although without particular distinction, during the Forbes Campaign on Fort Duquesne in 1758. Thompson had been active on the Pennsylvania frontier as a land speculator, businessman and surveyor in the years before the American Revolution, and as a Colonel had commanded a Pennsylvania rifle battalion in Washington's army before his promotion. An energetic and aggressive man, Thompson had little actual field experience, and had seen practically no combat.

Greaton's Massachusetts Regiment in the van reached Sorel on May 9, but shortly received "strict orders not to go forward." On May 12 "Colonel Bond's Regiment arrived here" at Chambly, but ominously it was noted that "they brought no provisions with them." Lieutenant Benjamin Beal with Greaton's Regiment at Chambly noted on that day, "We have nothing to eat but pork & bread."[17]

Lt. Colonel Joseph Vose of that regiment recorded that "Colonel Stark with Colonel Read arrive here from St. Johns" at Montreal on May 29. At this time Colonel John Stark commanded the 5th Continental Infantry, from New Hampshire. The Connecticut regiment of Colonel Charles Burrall arrived at Chambly on May 28. The 1st New Jersey Regiment reached St. Jean on May 31. Encamping the next day, Sergeant Timothy Tuttle of that regiment would ominously record, "Rainy day & night. The 1st storm we had."[18] There would be many more storms shortly, of both the natural and the manmade variety.

The 1st Pennsylvania Battalion, commanded by Colonel John Philip De Haas, arrived at Montreal on the evening of May 24. Almost immediately, they were ordered by Arnold to march to assist with attempting to reverse the Cedars fiasco, then well underway. Their movement forward was not without difficulty, as the congressional commissioners noted:

> [May] 25th. In the evening of this day Colonel De Haas's detachment marched out of Montreal to join General Arnold at la Chine: they were detained from want of many necessaries, which we were obliged to procure for them, General Wooster being without money, or pretending to be so.[19]

The 2nd Pennsylvania Battalion, commanded by Colonel Arthur St. Clair, arrived at Chambly on May 30.[20] Colonel Anthony Wayne's 4th Pennsylvania Battalion reached Sorel on June 5, 1776.

Thirty-six-year old Brigadier General John Sullivan assumed command of the American army in Canada, succeeding to the command by date of rank and completely accidentally upon the death of Thomas, and the elopement of Wooster. A prominent New Hampshire attorney, Sullivan had been appointed as a Brigade Commander in the Continental army more because he was the senior officer from the colony of New Hampshire than for any demonstrated military acumen. Sullivan had no previous military or leadership experience. Sullivan was an aggressive, fiery, hot-headed Irishman, and he was known to be both audacious and wildly ambitious. Ambition, aggressiveness and inexperience are a poor combination in any military leader, and Sullivan would prove unequal to the challenge of leadership in Canada, a task that could only have been successfully accomplished by a highly skilled and experienced commander. Sullivan was neither.[21] Besides his lack of military training and experience, Sullivan was a poor selection to lead a force into Canada because of his inclinations towards the colony. In 1774 he had authored a strongly worded letter that vigorously denounced "the cursed religion" of the Catholics of Canada as "dangerous to the state and favorable to despotism."[22] It is difficult to imagine that Sullivan's sentiments had changed in the succeeding two years, and given the tone and tenor of his beliefs he would be unlikely to foster much good will among the Canadian habitants.

The senior regimental commander was Colonel Anthony Wayne, who commanded the 4th Pennsylvania Battalion. Thirty-one-year old Wayne was a wealthy businessman and surveyor from eastern Pennsylvania who was also an ardent patriot. Wayne had no previous military service or experience, but he rapidly proved himself to be a competent and skilled regimental commander. His aggressive demeanor shortly earned him the unfortunate sobriquet of "Mad Anthony." In truth, Wayne was not mad, either by temperament or conduct. Rather, he expended considerable effort in learning the military profession, and would become one of the most accomplished and skilled military commanders in the history of the nation. Wayne was recognized as a strict disciplinarian, dedicated to meticulous drill and training of his regiment, and paid careful attention to detail in matters of equipment and clothing of his soldiers. He had a well-deserved reputation among other officers as being exhaustively committed to fulfilling his command responsibilities. In 1776 Wayne's greatest days were ahead of him, but he was already far along in establishing his reputation as one of the Continental army's finest commanders and leaders.

When these reinforcements reached Canada they must have been shocked at the utter pandemonium that had resulted in Canada, caused by the precipitous retreat from in front of Quebec and the lack of adequate commanders. When Colonel Porter assumed command of the garrison and post at St. Jean's on May 26 he "found things in much confusion."[23] The Reverend Ammi Robbins, assigned as the chaplain to Colonel Buel's Connecticut Regiment, documented considerable dissension between Buel, Colonel Hazen of Canada, and General Arnold at Chambly in early May. The Chaplain recorded, "Oh how easy it is, if God suffer it, to have the country destroyed by internal broils and divisions."[24]

The other piece of good news for the American army was that General Wooster had departed, unlamented, for points south, on or about June 1.[25] He would scarcely be missed, by the Canadians, by Arnold, or by the American army as a whole.

With these reinforcements, by May 11, there were no less than 8,048 American soldiers in Canada. Of these, 6,082 men were present and fit for duty, and about 2,000 were sick.[26] The army in Canada at this juncture consisted of the following regiments and commanders:

- 2nd Continental Infantry (New Hampshire) — Colonel James Reed;
- 5th Continental Infantry (New Hampshire) — Colonel John Stark;
- 8th Continental Infantry (New Hampshire) — Colonel Enoch Poor;
- 15th Continental Infantry (Massachusetts) — Colonel John Paterson;
- 24th Continental Infantry (Massachusetts) — Colonel John Greaton;
- 25th Continental Infantry (Massachusetts) — Colonel William Bond;
- 1st Pennsylvania Battalion — Colonel John Philip De Haas;
- 2nd Pennsylvania Battalion — Colonel Arthur St. Clair;
- 4th Pennsylvania Battalion — Colonel Anthony Wayne;
- 6th Pennsylvania Battalion — Colonel William Irvine;

- 1st New Jersey Infantry — Colonel William Winds;
- 2nd New Jersey Infantry — Colonel William Maxwell;
- 3rd New Jersey Infantry — Colonel Elias Dayton;
- Burrall's Connecticut Infantry Regiment — Colonel Charles Burrall;
- Bedel's New Hampshire Infantry Regiment — Colonel Timothy Bedel; and
- Porter's Massachusetts Infantry Regiment — Colonel Elisha Porter.[27]

Of this force, the 4th Pennsylvania Battalion was still moving up Lake Champlain, and was not present in its entirety. Bedel's New Hampshire Regiment was stationed at the Cedars, where it would shortly be destroyed by Forster's expedition from Oswegatchie. The remainder of these battalions was at Montreal, Sorel, Chambly or St. Jean. They were all readily available for offensive action. Additionally, sufficient general officers were now present in Canada to provide effective command and control. Brigadier General John Sullivan was in nominal command following the death of Thomas and departure of Wooster. Brigadier Generals Benedict Arnold and William Thompson supported him. Congress had also dispatched a Prussian officer that they had appointed a Brigadier General, the Baron Frederick William de Woedtke, to provide professional assistance.

The Baron de Woedtke was typical of many European officers who offered their services to the fledgling United Colonies. Only 26 in 1776, Woedtke had seen service as an officer with Frederick the Great of Prussia, although he almost certainly significantly exaggerated his military experience, promoting himself to be a Knight of the Order of Jerusalem and a general officer in the Prussian Army. The Continental Congress, recognizing that the American army desperately needed professional military advice, was prone to offer nearly any European officer that applied with senior military rank in the Continental army, and de Woedtke was no exception. Presenting himself in Philadelphia, Congress appointed de Woedtke a Brigadier General on March 16, 1776, and dispatched him to Canada as a integral component of the reinforcements that they were then pouring into the 14th colony. The congressional commissioners met de Woedtke on the way to Canada and were not particularly impressed with him. Father Carroll wrote to his mother, "Though I had frequently seen him before, yet he was so disguised in furs that I scarce knew him, and never beheld a more laughable object in my life. Like other Prussian officers, he appears to me as a man who knows little of polite life, and yet has picked up as much of it in his passage through France as to make a most awkward appearance."[28] Still, he still provided the American army in Canada with a third Brigadier General to direct operations, and he doubtless possessed at least some previous military experience that was sorely lacking. Yet, de Woedtke did not speak English, and his capability to disseminate whatever rudimentary knowledge he may have possessed must have been distinctly limited.

For the first time this year in Canada, Thomas (until his death), Wooster (until his relief and withdrawal) and finally their successor Sullivan commanded a numerically formidable army in Canada. The Americans were finally organized and had sufficient combat power to resume the offensive. With their newfound strength there was a definite probability that if properly commanded and planned that they could not only inflict a stinging loss on the British army as it moved piecemeal up the river, but quite conceivably reverse American fortunes in the 14th colony.

As these reinforcements poured into Canada, the beleaguered congressional commissioners quietly departed the colony from St. Jean's on June 2.[29] The situation of the American army in Canada would now either fail or succeed, depending upon the fighting abilities of the recently arrived American soldiers, and the skill of their commanding officers. The commissioners recognized that without a war chest, they could do little to affect the action, and that their presence contributed little. Thus, they determined to return to Congress, to report in person on the desperate shortages that constrained every effort of the Americans in the 14th colony.

By early June the vanguard of the British advance under the command of Lieutenant Colonel Simon Fraser of the 24th Foot, temporarily promoted to the local rank of Brigadier General, occupied the small city of Three Rivers. Fraser had at least four regiments available to him: his own 24th, and the 29th, 47th, and 62nd Regiments of Foot.[30] These regiments were at nearly full strength, so his strength was approximately 3,000 men. Three Rivers was located northwest of a prominent river junction, where the St. Maurice River flowed into the St. Lawrence River from the north, and the Rivière Bécancour joined the St. Lawrence River to the south. The town, located approximately halfway between Montreal and Quebec, had originally played a role in the fur trade but that commerce had long since passed to Montreal, and now it existed primarily by supporting river traffic. Thomas Anburey, a young British volunteer who visited the town later in the year, remarked:

> The country is pleasant, and there are several good houses about the town, but they were greatly damaged by the Americans upon abandoning it, after their defeat this summer. There are several churches, and two convents, the nuns of which are reckoned the most ingenious of any city in Canada, in all kinds of fancy ornaments, needle work, and curious toys.[31]

Francis Grant, a English gentleman traveling from New York to Canada in 1767 observed:

> Three Rivers is a small town on the North West bank of the River St. Lawrence, containing in all about 100 houses, most of which are small and mean. There is a battery to the River, but the guns are now dismounted. There is also a Chatteau or barrack of four pavilions, made for containing 200 or 300 men, stockaded round, but of no force. Half a mile to the NW is the River Des Chenaw [St. Maurice River] which falls into the River St. Lawrence. Just at the confluence it is divided into two by an island, which with the St. Lawrence has the appearance of three rivers, from which this place takes its name. The River Chenaux is at its mouth about a mile broad, and runs from a Lake at a great distance to the northwest. Up this river about 3 leagues are some iron mines and a forger, formerly worked by the French King, but now the property of some English merchants.[32]

Thompson, eager to use his command and earn laurels on a northern battlefield, believed that Fraser's detachment was isolated and vulnerable at Three Rivers, and he estimated that it consisted of not more than eight hundred men. Thompson, obtaining Sullivan's concurrence, determined to launch a surprise night attack to capture the garrison.[33] The Americans intended to land four miles upstream of Three Rivers under cover of darkness, march through the ground to the north of the river employing the services of a Canadian guide, and launch a dawn attack on the presumably unsuspecting British at the village. Thompson's plan was to attack in four columns. Colonel William Maxwell commanding the 2nd New Jersey Regiment of 390 men in one column, Colonel William Irvine of the 6th Pennsylvania Battalion the second column, Colonel Arthur St. Clair of the 2nd Pennsylvania Battalion commanding the third column containing 700 men, and Colonel Anthony Wayne with three companies of his 4th Pennsylvania Battalion counting 150 muskets comprising the fourth column. Lieutenant Colonel Thomas Hartley of the 6th Pennsylvania Battalion was designated to command a reserve. Thus, although Thompson had approximately 2,000 men available to him, he immediately segmented his force into five separate commands that would have to execute a difficult night march and then launch a coordinated attack at daybreak. It was almost a certainty that Thompson's attack would be made piecemeal. It was an extremely ambitious plan, but the American soldiers were too inexperienced to perform such a difficult maneuver in darkness, and the entire plan depended upon the reliability and accuracy of a single Canadian guide. Unfortunately, the Canadian guide proved to be either a Loyalist, incompetent, or both. The guide was a Point du Loc farmer, Antoine Gautier.[34] Following the engagement, numerous American officers stated that they believed Gautier to be a Loyalist who had deliberately led them astray. Local Three Rivers and Quebec provincial residents consistently praise Gautier as being loyal to the British, and award him credit for deliberately deceiving the stupid American invaders. They still relate tales about him, and he is today a glorious figure. Yet the truth, simpler and less romantic, may be that Gautier was used to traveling only on the roads, and once he left the familiar paths in the darkness he simply became mis-oriented. Across so many years the truth can no longer be divined.

Thompson issued written instructions to his subordinates. His orders to St. Clair are apparently the only written orders to survive from the engagement:

> You are immediately to proceed with the detachment under your command to Three Rivers, where you will endeavor to surprise the enemy posted there, making prisoners of as many as possible and cutting off all who oppose you. At the same time you will be careful to secure yourself a retreat.... Artillery, ammunition, arms & public stores must be brought off if possible, but should that be found impractible they will be destroyed.
>
> I need not point out to you the necessity of your business being executed with vigor, and that the most proper time for it is before day. I wish you success and honor.[35]

Four American and one British accounts describe the battle, which will be presented in their entirety, and then an analysis of the action will follow. Colonel William Irvine of the 6th Pennsylvania Battalion recorded his personal experiences in his journal:

> [June] 7th 1776. Colonel Irvine's Reg't and three companies of Col. Wayne's, embarked in batteaux at Sorrell, under the command of General Thompson, and proceeded to Nicollet, where we found and were joined by Col. St. Clair, who had about seven hundred men under his command. The 8th crossed the river to Point de Lac; the pilot deceived us, for his orders were to steer to within four miles of Trois Riviere. Point de Lac is nine miles. Notwithstanding this disappointment, we marched with all possible expedition for Trois Riviere; but here our misfortunes began, our guide led us quite out of the way into a swamp, which sufficient to engulph a thousand men. Before we got disintangled from this dreadful place, daylight appeared, so that instead of attacking the town of Trois Riviere before day (as was designed) we found ourselves

three or four miles from it. Here we were at a loss what to do; had no intelligence of the strength of the garrison; to attack was hazardous, and to retreat without knowing the enemy's strength we could not think of, therefore marched on. The river, now on our right about fifty yards, we were soon discovered and were saluted by the men-of-war. They fired incessantly, while we marched about three quarters of a mile; here we inclined to a wood on our left, in order to avoid the fire from the shipping, but avoiding one evil we fell into a greater; for we now entered into a swamp, which I suppose to be four miles over. Nature, perhaps, never formed a place better calculated for the destruction of an army. It was impossible to preserve any order of march, nay, it became at last so difficult, and the men so fatigued, that their only aim was how to get extricated; many of the men had lost their shoes, and some their boots. At length, about seven o'clock, some officers reached one extreme of the swamp; a few went forward to reconnoitre; brought account back that they saw clear ground and horses at a little more than a quarter of a mile. Then Col. St. Clair, Lieut. Col. Allen, and myself, with a few other officers, strove to draw the men up in some order, which we found impracticable, not yet being clear of the swamp or woods. The general then got up with us, and ordered as many as could be collected to move forward to the cleared ground, there to form, which was accordingly done with as much expedition as could be expected from men worn down with fatigue, and who were exquisitely thirsty and faint. A few moments after we were formed, the general ordered the whole body to move on, in order to join Col. Maxwell's division, of whom we had no account of, from our first entry into the swamp, but from a soldier who said he saw some men about a half mile in front. A brisk firing then began, which we took to be Maxwell's party. General Thompson then ran towards the front; the firing increased, and seemed very hot. The general sent word to me to send forward the riflemen of my regiment, but they being chiefly in the rear could not get up as soon as he or I wished. Those of them belonging to the companies then in front, I ordered to turn out and march in Indian file, passing the word for the rear to follow in the same order. I then advanced in front, and joined the general, but by this time Maxwell's division was entirely broken, and retreating in such disorder, that there was no possibility of rallying them. General Thompson then ordered us to retreat fifty paces into the woods, where he and I used every argument we were masters of to collect and engage the men to make a stand; but our utmost efforts were in vain, not more than about forty men could be got together, and before this was done a minute, the communication between us and our main body was entirely cut off. The General, Lieut. Bird and myself, were the only officers now together. When we were consulting what was best to be done with our small party, we were fired on from all quarters by the Canadians, who were in ambush and skulking in the bushes. We then retreated, in hopes to fall in with some of our own people, but the further we marched, instead of our numbers increasing, they decreased, for in less than ten minutes we mustered but seven in all. The whole day we marched through swamps and thickets alternately, without any kind of refreshment, except stagnant water, of which we drank freely....

In short we waded and wandered here till near daylight, our strength and spirits being now nearly exhausted, we made a fire, lay down, and slept about an hour. In the mean time a soldier of our party was dispatched to endeavour to discover the strength and situation of the enemy, at daylight he returned with the disagreeable intelligence that we were quite surrounded, and no way left to get out; to confirm what he stated, we soon saw small parties of soldiers and Canadians dispatched on all sides, who began to fire on stragglers. General Thompson, Bird, and I then concluded it would be better to deliver ourselves up to British officers, than to run the risk of being murdered in the woods by the Canadians. Indeed, we were so exhausted as to be unable to march further; accordingly, we went up to a house where we saw a guard and surrendered ourselves.[36]

Pennsylvania Captain Charles Lacey was not in the attack on Three Rivers, but was on the southern side of the St. Lawrence River and observed the embarkation of the force, and its fate:

June 8th. Last night General Sullivan received a letter from General Thompson advising him, that he proposed to attack the Enemy at the three Rivers by surprise, with his whole body this Morning. The river at this place was very wide, called Lake Saint Peters. The Army was to cross over in Batteaus, land above the three Rivers, and attack the Enemy at Daylight — Early in the morning we heard firing down the River, which we supposed to be the attack on the Enemy according to General Thompson's letter. It was however broken and at intervals not like a General charge. We waited all this day in suspense without a word of intelligence from the Army. On the morning of the 9th we again heard the report of Cannon, tho singly & soon discontinued. About 10 O'clock A.M. the Batteaus of the Army came in sight. In great anxiety we all hastened to the edge of the River to meet the Battaus, but was sadly mortified to find our Army had been defeated. That the Batteaux which transported over the Army being cut off by the Enemy from the Troops[,] who lost their way came up by detachment to the Enemies batteries, were driven back. Finding the Enemy in possession of the place where the Batteaux were left, took to the Woods and Swamps. Major Woods who was left in Command of the Batteaux and Baggage, found himself cut off from the American Army and discovering two of the enemy's Frigates under way ordered the Batteaus to push up the River. Having proceeded some distance & night coming on he halted with an expectation to meet with our Army, on their retreat where he remained till morning. The Ships of War Major Wood discovered under way the Day before, had entered Lake St. Peters, nearly abreast of the Batteaus. Finding himself in this precarious situation he ordered those in the Batteaus to provide directly them to the Mouth of the Sorrell ... thus abandoning the Army to make the best of their way, through horrid swamps, up the North side of the River.

On the 10th by Order of General Sullivan crossed the River St. Lawrence to the North side with a Scout of Ten Riflemen and Lieutenant Read, to proceed down the St. Lawrence until we met the Retreating Army. Proceeded through most horrid swamps, were almost devoured by Muskeetoes of a Monsterous size and innumerable numbers, came into a very indifferent and swampy road, not meeting with a single habitation, which we followed until after Dark, when we lucky fell in with the leading detachment under Captain Smith of the 6th Pennsylvania Regiment, with whom we returned leaving two of our men to direct those in the Rear [of] the Rout to the mouth of the Sorrell. The troops being so scattered, they did not arrive until the latter part or evening of the next Day.[37]

Colonel Anthony Wayne, commander of the 4th Pennsylvania Battalion, wrote a lengthy, detailed letter to Benjamin Franklin immediately after his return to camp:

On the 7th it was agreed in a council on war to attack the enemy at Three Rivers ... whose strength was estimated at 3 or 4 hundred. Gen'l Thompson was appointed for this Command, the Disposition was as follows 4 attacks to be made at the same time viz Col Maxwell to conduct the first, myself the second, Col St. Clair the third & Col. Irvine the 4th. Lieut Col Hartley the Reserves.

On the same evening we Embarked and arrived at Col. St. Clairs Encampment about midnight — it was intended that the Attack shou'd be made at the dawn of day — this we found to be Impracticable therefore we Remained where we were until the 8th when we took to the number of 1450 Men all Pennsylvanians except Maxwells Battalion took boats.

About 2 in the morning we landed nine Miles above the town, and after an Hour's march day began to appear. Our Guides had mistook the road, the Enemy Discovered and Cannonaded us from their ships, a surprise was out of the question — We therefore put our best face on it and continued our line of march thro' a thick deep swamp three miles wide, and after four Hours Arrived at a more open piece of ground — amidst the thickest firing of the shipping when all of a sudden a large Body of Regulars marched down in good order immediately in front of me to prevent our forming — in consequence of which I ordered my Light Infantry together with Captain Hays Company of Riflemen to advance and amuse them whilst I was forming; they began and continued the attack with great spirit until I advanced to support them when I ordered them to wheel to the right & left and flank the Enemy at the same time we poured in a well aimed and heavy fire in front. They attempted to retreat in good order at first but in a few minutes broke and ran in the utmost confusion. About this time the other divisions began to Emerge from the swamp except Maxwell who with his was advanced in a thicket a considerable distance to the left — our rear now becoming our front, etc. At this instant we rec'd a heavy fire in flank from musketry, field pieces, howitzers, etc., etc. which threw us into some confusion, but was instantly remedied. We advanced in column up to their breast works which till them we had not discovered — at this time Gen'l Thompson with Colonels St. Clair, Irvine & Hartley were marching in full view to our support.

Col Maxwell now began to Engage on the left of me, the fire was so hot he could not maintain his post — the other troops had also filed off to the left — my small Battalion composed of my own & two companies of Jersey men under Major Ray amounting in the whole to about 200 were left exposed to the whole fire of their shipping in flank and full three thousand men in front with all their Artillery under the command of Gen'l Burgoyne. Our people taking example by others give way. Indeed, it was impossible for them to stand it longer. Whilst Col Allen and myself were employed in rallying the troops Lt. Col. Hartly had advanced with the Reserves and bravely attacked the enemy from a thicket in a swamp to the left, this hardiness of his was of the utmost consequence to us — we having rallied about 800 men from the different Regiments — we now sent to find the Gen'l and other field officers. At the same time the rifle men of mine and Irvine's kept up a galling fire on the enemy. The swamp was so deep and thick with timber and underwood that a man 10 yards in front or rear wou'd not see the men drawn up — this was the cause of the Gen'l, Col St. Clair, Maxwell & Irvine missing us — or perhaps they had taken for granted that we were all cut off. Col. Hartley who lay near by retreated without a discovery on either side, until he crossed our line near the left, which caused our people to follow him. Allen and myself were now left on the field with only twenty men & five Officers, the Enemy still continuing their whole fire from great and small guns upon us — but afraid to venture from their lines, we thought it prudent to keep them in play by keeping up a small fire in order to gain time for our people to make good their retreat in consequence of which we continued about an hour longer in the field, and then retreated back into the woods which brought us to a road on the far side of the swamp. We followed this road about two miles when we cut loose from our small party & reached the place where our people had enter'd the swamp by which means we soon collected

6 or 700 men with whom we retreated in good order but without nourishment of any kind. The enemy who were strong in number had detached in two or three bodies about 1500 men to cut off our retreat. They way laid & engaged us again about 9 miles from the field of battle, they did us little damage. We continued our march, and the third day almost worn out with fatigue, hunger & difficulties, scarcely to be paralleled we arrived here with 1100 men, but Gen'l Thompson, Col Irvine, Doc'r McCalla and several Officers are prisoners at Three Rivers. Col. St. Clair arrived alone last night.

I believe it will be universally allowed that Col Allen & myself have saved the Army in Canada.... Out of 150 of my own I have lost more than the quarter part-together with a slight touch in my right leg.[38]

Colonel Hartly also left an account of the debacle:

The guide proved faithless, and the Gen. was misinformed as to the number of the enemy as well as to the situation in the town. Our men had lost their sleep for 2 nights, yet were in pretty good spirits. Daylight appeared, and showed us to the enemy. Our guides (perhaps traitors) had led us through several windings, and were rather carrying us off from the post. The Gen. was outraged at their conduct. There were mutual firings. Our people killed some in a barge. Our scheme was no longer an enterprise, it might have been, perhaps, prudent, to have retreated, but no one would propose it. We endeavored to penetrate through a swamp to the town, and avoid the shipping. We had no idea of the difficulties we were to surmount in the mire, otherwise the way by the shipping would have been preferred. We waded 3 hours through the muck, about mid-deep in general, the men fasting. We every minute expected to get through and find some good ground to form on, but were deceived. The great body of the enemy, which we knew nothing of, consisting of 2 or 3,000 men, covered with intrenchments, and assisted with the cannon of the shipping and several field pieces, began a furious fire, and continued it upon our troops in the front. It was so heavy that the Division gave way, and from the badness of the ground could not form suddenly again. Col. St. Clair's Division advanced, but the fire was too heavy. Part of Col. Irvine's division, especially the riflemen, went up towards the enemy. I understand the army was in confusion. I consulted some friends, and led the reserve within a short distance of the enemy ... under the disadvantages, our men would fight; but we had no covering, no artillery, and no prospect of succeeding, as the number of the enemy was so much superior to ours. Cols. Wayne and Allen rallied part of our men, and kept up a fire against the English from the swamp. The enemy, in the meantime, dispatched a strong body to cut off our retreat to the boats, when it was thought expedient to retreat. Our General and Col. Irvine were not to be found, they had both gone up in a very hot fire. This gave us great uneasiness, but a retreat was necessary. This could not be done regularly, as we could not regain the road, on account of the enemy's shipping and artillery, and we went off in small parties through the swamp. Cols. Wayne & Allen gathered some hundreds together, and I have got as many in my division as I could, with several others, amounting to upwards of 200.[39]

Lieutenant John Enys with the 29th Foot fought in the engagement, and left behind a particularly detailed account from the British perspective:

On the 8th of June a boat belonging to our fleet which had been up the [St. Lawrence] River was fired upon by the Rebels. About 2 Oclock in the Morning, and about day light Captain Harvey of the Morten ordered our ship to drop a stern Clear of the reach of his Guns as he was going to fire on Shore. On looking on Shore we could see a large body of Men near the Edge of the wood. A good deal of firing took place from the Mortin Sloop and an Armed transport named the British Queen but believe it had no effect except making the Rebels just enter the Skirts of the Wood that they might not be Seen. The Signal for our party to land was very Soon made which we accordingly did together with two Six pounders which came from England on board one of our transports under the command of Lieuts. Smith and York of the artillery. As soon as we were all on Shore we Marched and took post in there rear in order to cut off their retreat. A very Short time after we had taken up our Ground, a Scattering fire began with the pickets of the Army near the town which was soon succeeded by a very Smart one from the 62d and some other Regts which lasted about ten or twelve minutes when the Rebels retreated into the Wood. About this time we were joined by 4 Companies of the 24th Regt and a field piece from Three Rivers, so that when the Rebels had retreated as far as our post, finding us too strong they never attempted to fire upon us but tried to go round us by Striking deeper into the Wood in order to gain their Boats which they had left at a place called Machiech [Yamachiche] about 15 miles further. This occasioned us another march in order to get possession of the Boats before them, and as we had taken a good Many Prisoners very good Intelligence was got of the place where they were. But unfortunately on our way we saw 5 other boats full of men just as we came to the Banks of Lake St. Peter at a place named Point au Lac at whom we fired a few shot from our cannon which alarmed those we were in pursuit of and gave them time to get off which they did before we reached Macheich. Balked in our hopes and being now 18 miles from our ships and the day pretty far advanced we were ordered to take post, which was accordingly done, on the banks of the River Machieche we found convenient for the purpose. Here we lay all night very quiet. In the morning some of the Rebels showed themselves at the shore of the wood but on seeing us retired. About 7 or 8 in the morning great numbers began to come in to us and give themselves up as prisoners, among whom was General Thomson who commanded.[40]

As the Americans had approached the north shore of the St. Lawrence River, through an error by the pilot the bateaux landed considerably farther away than they had intended. Colonel Irvine estimated the distance to be nine miles. Thompson landed his men, formed them into their columns, and ordered them forward. Inexplicably, he failed to leave any men behind to protect the valuable bateaux.[41] The Americans initially marched along a road paralleling the river, but they were exposed on this road, and they determined to take a course slightly inland to maintain their surprise. Monsieur Gautier, the Canadian guide, whether he himself was lost or was acting with guile to mislead the Americans, led them into a swamp, through which they floundered all night. Daylight found them still three to four miles from the town (approximately the location where they were in fact to have originally landed), but it at least revealed to them the river road. The Americans gratefully returned to it, only to be observed by the British Sloop of War *Martin* and other British vessels on the river. Under close range and accurate artillery fire, they were forced to return to the "most horrid swamp that man ever set foot in."

On June 8, 1776, the moon rose at 12:05 A.M. The moon had just entered the last quarter, and it provided about 40 percent illumination without obscuration. The moon would not set until mid-morning. Thus, the Americans had moon illumination for the entirety of their march, although how much light actually filtered through the tree cover cannot, of course, be ascertained. This relatively good illumination explains why the British ships were able to spot the Americans once they stepped out on the road to Three Rivers. Sunrise was at 4:06 A.M. Since the Americans actually landed only at midnight, they had four hours to traverse the distance to Three Rivers. Given the original plan that called for them to land four miles from the city, this was achievable. However, there was no possibility of the Americans marching nine miles in darkness within four hours (considering that some time for scouting the British and deploying their forces would be required) and launching an attack at dawn.

Obviously, once the booming reverberations of the artillery pieces echoed down the St. Lawrence River valley any possibility of surprise was lost, but against all reason Thompson pushed his force forward. This made uncommonly poor tactical sense. The British controlled the river, and with every foot that Thompson pressed to the front he exposed his withdrawal route to being cut off by the British, and he presented his right flank to naval gunfire to which he could not reply, having no artillery pieces of his own.

Once the Americans were lost in the swamps in the darkness, it is doubtful that they were going to be able to sneak up on anybody. In fact, the British probably heard them coming from miles away. But just in case the British were asleep, local lore is that Gautier's wife made a frantic run to the village, by the straight line of the river road, spreading her cry that the Americans were coming. It is a fascinating and wonderful Quebec tale, and totally unverifiable. But it is one of those fabulous local legends that if not true, it certainly should be.

The British naval vessels and Gautier's wife ensured that Fraser received the alarm. Two bronze 6-pounder cannon were hastily landed from the British ships in time to participate in Fraser's defense. The two 6-pounders, commanded by 2nd Lieutenant William P. Smith and 2nd Lieutenant John H. York, both from the 1st Battalion of the Royal Artillery, went into battery to reinforce Fraser.

Eventually, after struggling through the swamp again, the Americans viewed a clearing to their front. Believing that they had finally reached dry ground at Three Rivers they were sadly disabused of their belief, for although the ground had marginally cleared they were still in a swamp that precluded their ability to form. Additionally, Maxwell's column that was apparently on the left of the American force had to traverse the greatest distance through the swamp, and was accordingly well to the rear of the other columns. Wayne ordered his light infantrymen and riflemen forward to cover his front, and then advanced. Surprisingly, the other columns managed to attack with Wayne.

Here, the American failure to perform adequate reconnaissance of the British position at Three Rivers proved catastrophic. The American force advanced, only to find a British force that outnumbered their own, entrenched behind strong breastworks, reinforced by two 6-pounder cannon, and with several naval vessels sweeping the field across which the Americans had to assault with heavy, accurate cannon fire that enfiladed their lines. It was called a battle but it was really no such thing. The Americans advanced with resolution, but were in short order swept from the field, and forced to retreat into the swamp. Maxwell's column reached the field of strife in time to be engaged but were no more successful than the Pennsylvanians had been.

And now the Americans had to retreat nine miles back through the dreadful swamps to their bateaux, with British gunfire continuing to tear up their southern flank. The American soldiers were already exhausted from their night's struggle to reach Three Rivers and were now further disordered by their failed advance and having to carry some of their wounded with them. The withdrawal was absolutely dreadful. The British themselves caused further distress when they landed a force to the American rear, to cut off their retreat route, and also captured the undefended bateaux.[42] The integrity of Thompson's force vanished. With some success, Colonels Wayne and Hadley formed a crude rear guard to cover the retreat of Thompson's sadly shattered command. The British dispatched Canadians and Native Americans into the swamps to harry the Americans in their retreat.

The biographer of General Thompson reported:

> While listening to the distant battle sounds, Sullivan still was the optimist. He interpreted every cannon shot, every rattle of musketry, as evidence "that our men are in possession of the Ground." He was going to set off immediately, he wrote Washington, to join the victorious Thompson, "but by some strange kind of conduct in General Arnold directly contrary to repeated orders, Arnold had failed to send along DeHaas' detachment from Montreal." Thompson's and DeHaas' troops, Sullivan averred, "constituted the flower of our Army at present."[43]

Arnold, who had considerably more experience in fighting the British, and considerably more experience with conditions in Canada than Sullivan possessed, doubtless knew a shipwreck when he saw one. Arnold observed an opportunity to save at least a portion of "the flower of our army" from being doomed by Thompson at Three Rivers, and he took it.

Both the attack, and the retreat that inevitably followed, were fiascos. Thompson and Irvine were captured, along with 236 of the American soldiers that they commanded. When killed and wounded, and those just plain lost in the swamps and never to be seen again, are added to the total the Americans probably lost about four hundred officers and soldiers. British casualties were reputed to be about one dozen.[44] One-fifth of Thompson's force had become casualties, at almost no cost to the British. Most importantly, Thompson's force, the only regiments capable of taking the offensive in the American Northern Theater Army, had been wrecked.

Thompson's night attack scheme had been exceedingly ill advised. Night attacks were not unknown at the time of the American Revolution but frequently went awry, particularly without detailed intelligence on the opposing force. The great military theorist General Carl Von Clausewitz would shortly thereafter write regarding night attacks, of which he most thoroughly disapproved:

> At first glance it looks highly effective: supposedly the defender is taken unawares, while the attacker, of course, is well prepared for what is about to happen. What an uneven contest! One imagines complete confusion on one side, and on the other an attacker concerned merely to profit by it. This image explains the many schemes for night attacks put forward by those who have neither to lead them nor accept responsibility for them. In practice they are very rare. All such ideas assume that the attacker knows the complete layout of the defense, which have been previously planned and carried out, could not escape his reconnaissance and intelligence. On the other hand,

the attacker's dispositions, made only at the moment of execution, must remain unknown to the other side. But even the latter does not always happen, and the former is even less common.... It is possible to have a perfect view of the area in which a division is encamped ... and still not be able to form a clear picture of its layout.... In a night operation the attacker seldom if ever knows enough about the defense to make up for his lack of visual observation. The defender has another slight advantage; the ground he occupies is better known to him than it is to the attacker, in the same way as a man can find his way around his own room in the dark more easily than can a stranger. He can find and round up all the component parts of his forces more quickly than can his assailants. It follows from all this that the attacker needs his eyes in night operations just as much as the defense. Therefore special reasons are needed to justify a night attack.... Night operations are not merely risky, they are also difficult to execute.[45]

Thompson's attack had been both risky, and difficult. Clearly, Thompson had no idea regarding the condition of the British defenses at Three Rivers, the strength of Fraser's command, or any other details regarding the town that he was attacking. A night march, even over only three or four miles as it was initially planned, depending upon a Canadian guide of dubious reliability, was a dreadfully unrealistic plan. When the landing had to be altered to nine miles away from Three Rivers, it was utterly impossible, and Thompson should immediately have jettisoned the plan. Once his columns either lost their way or were misled by the guide (probably a combination), Thompson again should immediately have stopped the march, waited for daylight to reorganize his battalions, and withdrawn in good order. Finally, once Thompson's advance was detected by the British naval vessels and taken under fire, there was no longer any possibility that Three Rivers could be attacked successfully. Yet, inexplicably, Thompson proceeded with his plans.

It had been a dreadfully botched affair, bungled in concept, bungled in planning, and bungled in execution. In a letter to his friend General Henry Clinton early in July Burgoyne described the attack: "Their attempt upon Three Rivers was founded in rashness and executed with timidity, two principles which compounded make a consummation of preposterous conduct."[46] It is hard to argue with Burgoyne's analysis of this, yet another American debacle in Canada.

6

"I Can Scarcely Imagine Any More Disastrous Scene"

The Destruction and Death of an American Army, June 1776

The Pennsylvanians had climbed aboard their bateaux on June 7 with great ambitions and high morale, glorious in their blue and white regimentals. After days floundering through muddy black Canadian swamps, they must have presented a badly bedraggled and miserable appearance upon their exhausted return to the camp at Sorel. On June 11, barely upon their return, the Orderly Book of the 4th Pennsylvania Battalion decreed:

> Every Non Commissioned or soldier who shall come to the Parade dirty or his breeches knees open, shall be mulcted of a days allowance of provision and do a double tour of duty. For the Colonel lays it down as a position, that every soldier who neglects to appear as decent as the nature of his situation will admit, is unfit for Gentlemens company and is a coward.[1]

Their discipline, morale and fighting ability, sadly enough, reflected their appearance.

As early as May 31, Benedict Arnold saw the writing on the wall, and knew that the great invasion of Canada in which he had expended so much blood, sweat and tears was at an end. On that date, although it must have nearly broken his heart to put his sentiments into writing, Arnold addressed Major General Horatio Gates, then visiting the Continental Congress in Philadelphia:

> I must doubt if affairs go as ill with you as here. Neglected by Congress below, pinched with every want here, distressed with the small pox, want of Generals and discipline in our Army, which may rather be called a great rabble, our late unhappy retreat from Quebec, and loss of the Cedars, our credit and reputation lost, and great part of the country, and a powerful foreign enemy advancing upon us, are so many difficulties we cannot surmount them. My whole thoughts are now bent on making a safe retreat out of this country, however, I hope we shall not be obliged to leave it until we have had one bout more for the honor of America. I think we can make a stand at Isle-Aux-Noix, and keep the lake this summer from an invasion that way ... I am heartily chagrined to think we have lost in one month all the immortal Montgomery was a whole campaign in gaining, together with our credit, and many men, and an amazing sum of money. The Commissioners this day leave us, as our good fortune has long since; but as Miss, like most other Misses, is fickle, and often changes, I still hope for her favors again.[2]

Arnold would be disappointed, for misfortune would not depart the American Army whilst it remained in Canada. Pennsylvania Captain Lacey recalled, "On the night of the 13th a Council of War was held at General Sullivan's Head Quarters, at which it was decided it was advisable for the whole of the American Army to evacuate Canada, and to concentrate and make a stand at Ticonderoga. On the morning of the Fourteenth orders were given to retreat."[3] There really was no decision to be made by the Council of War on June 13. Sorel was not defensible. The flat terrain offered no possibility of a successful defense being made there, and they lacked adequate artillery to secure a post at that point, particularly since the Royal Navy could directly attack the town from the river. Chambly was also not defensible. As previously discussed, the fort was not adequate to defend against artillery, it was commanded by immediately adjacent higher ground, could be directly attacked by the Royal Navy operating on the Richelieu River, and was easily outflanked.

The French had constructed a fort at St. Jean in 1665 to guard the fertile Richelieu River settlements of New France. The fort had been reconstructed as recently as 1748 and was also likely improved during the French withdrawal from Lake Champlain in 1759. It was a small square fort with four bastions, constructed close to the river, consisting of wooden palisaded walls with a handful of interior stone buildings. During the French retreat in 1760, following the fall of their major defensive position at Isle Aux Noix approximately ten miles to the south, they had partially burned this fortification. The British army had then occupied the fort, and maintained a small garrison there through 1775, constructing more substantial barracks at the same time. Upon the American approach in the fall of 1775 they had apparently strengthened the remnants of the French fort with hurriedly constructed earthworks and redoubts. During the extended siege by Montgomery of the fort in 1775, these hasty defensive works were heavily damaged by concentrated American artillery fire. There is no evidence that the British works had been repaired or improved by the American army during its subsequent six-month stay at St. Jean.

St. Jean also offered the American army few advantages as a defensive position. The rapids to the north did prevent the Royal Navy from reaching St. Jean, and the ground was generally flat around the fort, offering few advantages to an attacking force. However, an army maneuvering on the numerous roads that traversed the long settled and relatively heavily inhabited country between the Richelieu River valley and Montreal could easily outflank the post. In short, it offered the Americans no real possibilities as a location to halt or delay the inexorable British advance.[4]

Any defensive position on the Richelieu River possessed one great disadvantage, in that it was at the end of the American supply line from Albany, Ticonderoga and Crown Point, which was already stretched beyond the breaking point. Only until the American army retreated closer to its source of supplies could its badly battered regiments be reorganized and refitted to resume the offensive.

As determined at the Council of War, the Americans evacuated Sorel on June 14, Montreal on June 15, Chambly on June 17, and St. Jean on June 18. Sullivan burned Chambly when evacuating it on June 17, and St. Jean was similarly destroyed during the evacuation on June 18. The British occupied Chambly on June 18.[5] Throughout the withdrawal, Arnold and Sullivan in particular had been indefatigable, ensuring that every soldier and every article that belonged to the American army was withdrawn from Canada, and that anything of military value was removed by the American army. Arnold even carried away the bridges. Sullivan would write with pride that the army had retreated, "taking with us every article, even to a spade."[6] Only three obsolete cannon were abandoned in the Richelieu River during the withdrawal.

During the retreat from Montreal, the Americans burned Fort Senneville, which guarded the western end of Montreal Island, facing the Ottawa River. The French had originally built this fort between 1696 and 1704, primarily to defend against Iroquois Indian raids, as active and intense warfare was at the time underway between New France and the Iroquois nation. It was a simple square stone fort, with four small corner bastions. The fort would have been imposing to the Natives, but offered no real defensive value against a European army equipped with heavy artillery. It had been occupied by the American army in 1775, and served as a minor defensive position to defend Montreal against any possible British advance down the St. Lawrence River, as Forster had actually done at the affairs of the Cedars. Anticipating the withdrawal from Montreal, Arnold ordered it abandoned and burned on May 27, 1776. Throughout the retreat from Canada, it was Arnold's approach to leave nothing that the British could utilize militarily or nautically, and that included the gift of a fort, even an archaic and indefensible one. Archaeological investigations have revealed the intriguing manner in which this was executed. Specifically, exploded hand grenade fragments were located in the cellars of two buildings in the fort. Apparently, the Americans had piled combustibles such as dried straw around these hand grenades and then lit the fuses, as an impromptu but apparently successful demolition and incendiary technique.[7]

Arnold in large measure set the tone and tempo for the retreat. When departing Montreal, the inhabitants were recalcitrant in fulfilling his needs for transportation. In response, "General Arnold gathered together the priests and the friars and told them that if they did not immediately procure all the carts and wagons around the town, to carry the sick and what stores we had, he would set the place on fire. These conveyances were quickly brought."[8] Of greatest import, Arnold collected every boat, ship and canoe that he came across, denying the British the future use of these vessels.

During the retreat from Chambly to St. Jean, the bateaux heavily laden with the sick, stores and artillery had to be drawn through the several miles of rapids with ropes. An anonymous officer of the American army later recalled: "All our baggage, stores and artillery had to be removed, officers as well as men all employed in hauling cannon, etc. Our bateaux loaded were all moved up the rapids six miles: one hundred of them were towed by our wearied men, up to their armpits in water. This was performed in one day and a half."[9] Pennsylvanian Officer John Lacy recorded the retreat:

> On the morning of the Fourteenth orders were given to retreat. The Baggage and stores of the Army were hurried into the batteaux, and the whole proceeded up the river towards Chambly. The wind light or contrary we did not reach the place until the 16th although no halt was made by day or night.... The baggage and many of the batteaux were hauled up ... where the boats were unloaded, and again launched into their proper element. Some of the batteaus were drawn up the rapids with long ropes,

the men drawing on the shore, some in the vessel with long poles to keep it in deep water, the men often up to their armpits in water.¹⁰

Captain Ebenezer Stevens, responsible for evacuating the American artillery, recounted a similar story: "In transporting the cannon and stores the men were up to their waists, and obliged to drag the bateaux by bodily strength up the rapids."¹¹

Captain Charles Cushing with the 24th Continental Infantry recorded the retreat of June 18 in his journal, which graphically depicts the horrible condition that Sullivan's army now found itself in:

> This day our army all retreated from St. Johns, about 2000 had been carried to the Isle of Noise [Isle Aux Noix] the most of them sick with small pox. We kept out scouting parties, and a guard of 6 or 700 men, while the remainder were getting the baggage on board the battoes. We brought all off from St. Johns, burnt the buildings, and set the fort on fire. The confusion the army was in was beyond description, not withstanding Gen. Sullivan exerted himself to the utmost to support order. I was on the second guard with 60 men out of the Regt. As soon as the guard was called in they were ordered to get on board where they could use, there being no care taken for us or boats provided for us. 60 men were ordered on board each battoe, besides cannon and other stores and baggage but the boats continued coming down till there was enough to carry the men. I tarried till I saw my Company on board and then went on board myself, had orders to put off about 7 o'clock. As we came along by the shore about 50 or 60 of our Regiment had been wading along the shore, in the swamp. I came up to one and ordered the men ashore to take the men on board, they told me it was the General's order to go to St. Johns and that they would not stop. I took my gun and told them if they did not put on shore that instant, I would fire upon them. They then went on shore, damning their eyes, and swearing very much. I came to the Isle of Noix about 1 o'clock at night, pitched my tent, and lay down to sleep after being much fatigued and wet with rain in the afternoon.¹²

Clearly, all was not well with the American army. Captain Cushing articulated the disorder in the retreat. Putting sixty men with stores or artillery into each bateau would have drastically overloaded the boats. Captain Cushing actually had to threaten the crew of the bateaux with his musket before they would provide rides to all of his soldiers.

Ensign Bayze Wells of Burrall's Regiment related:

> Our men passed safe by Chamblee on the 17th after they had burnt the fort and arrived to St. Johns in the same condition and retreated to Isle Anon [Isle Aux Noix] with all their baggage cannon and all the stores that they had at that place on the 20th day all the sick was ordered to go over the Lake to Crown Point we imbarked about 10 o Clock and was four days in our passage.¹³

Captain Stevens noted that the withdrawal was a closely run thing, the British entering Chambly just as the rear guard of the Americans departed.¹⁴ During the retreat from Montreal, the young musician John Greenwood recalled, "The road ran alongside of the river opposite the city of Montreal, and we could plainly see the red-coated British soldiers on the other shore, so close were they upon us that, if we had not retreated as we did, all would have been prisoners, for they were in numbers as six to our one, and we moreover half dead with sickness and fatigue and lack of clothing."¹⁵

Arnold, indefatigable to the very end, abandoned St. Jean and Canada only with deep regret. With the entire army continuing south for the island of Isle Aux Noix, and the fortifications burned and abandoned, Arnold still refused to depart until he was absolutely certain that the British would provide him with no other option. Arnold "after the last boat but Arnold's had put off" mounted his horse and rode two miles towards Chambly. Here with his own eyes he finally confirmed the advance of the British army under Burgoyne, and Arnold could personally confirm that the invasion of Canada was finally, inexorably, and permanently at an end. Arnold rode back to St. Jean. Determined that he would leave the British nothing of any possible value, he first stripped his horse of the saddle and tack, loaded them into the waiting bateaux, and then shot his own horse. Finally, in the words of his young and singularly incompetent aide, Lieutenant James Wilkinson:

> The sun was now down, and the enemy's front in view ... General Arnold then ordered all hands on board, and ... pushed off the boat with his own hands, and thus indulged the vanity of being the last man who embarked from the shores of the enemy.[16]

Surgeon Samuel Merrick described the retreat in a letter to his friend John Trumbull:

> On the 20th of June we marched to St. John's, and about sunset we went on board boats for the Isle aux Noix. Orders were peremptory not to stop a moment. There were but two rowers to a boat, they rowed till I thought they would fall from their seats. I, who was not obliged to go on fatigue duty [as a surgeon, Merrick was exempt so that he could care for the sick], could not see the men so worried, took an oar myself, and rowed half the night. We arrived at the Isle aux Noix about two hours before the day, the sick were thrown on shore, and in five minutes the boats were on their return. I was left with the sick. I had tents, but I could not pitch them in the night. I covered the sick up as well as I could, and waited for day.... As soon as it was light I sprang up, examined my sick — found them asleep. I left them and walked around the island, and found the sick of the whole army in the same situation, amounting to thousands, some dead, other dying. Great numbers could not stand, calling on us the physicians for help, and we had nothing to give them. It broke my heart, and I wept till I had no more power to weep. I wiped my eyes, pitched my tents, and others did the same, so that in about an hour the sick were all out of sight.[17]

Ensign Bayze Wells of Burrell's Regiment was at St. Jean, recovering from the infamous small pox, when on June 16

> about 1500 sick men were ordered to this place [Isle Aux Noix]. Oh the groans of the sick. What they undergo I can't express, neither is it in the power of man to give any idea of the distresses of them laying on the ground nothing to cover them but the heavens and wet cool weather.[18]

Captain Cushing described the miserable circumstances that the American army found themselves in once they had arrived at Isle Aux Noix, to include the occasional piece of army gossip:

> Wednesday 19th [June]. The army all encamped on the Isle of Noix. Some of the sick sent forward — here many very bad with the Small pox, and some die for want of attendance, having no friends or acquaintances.
> Thursday 20th. Those unfit for duty all sent up to Crown Point. Lieut. Beal, and Ensign Lincoln gone, with all the company but 32. Many die every day with Small

pox, not having the advantage of inoculation, nothing comfortable, and necessary to take. Last night a Captain of the Southern Forces went to impose on one of the sentries, he shot him through the heart and killed him.

Friday 21st. The men have now nothing but pork to eat, there being no flour to be had on the island.

Saturday 22nd. About 40 men with a number of boats gone up to the Isle of Mott to carry off flour.

Sunday 23rd. Mounted main guard. I was very unwell, and we had nothing to cover us. In the night it rained very hard, and wet us, and made it uncomfortable. There came in 30 or 40 battoes today. The Officers of the Regt had the pleasure to dine with Colonel Greaton, at his marque on roasted and boiled beef, which was a part of an ox sent the General, a very great rarity to us in this country.

Monday 24th. I am something better. We sent off some of the sick, and what stores we could, in the boats that came in last night.[19]

As a sorry example of the disintegration in the American army, it should be noted that at a time of extreme privation and shortages of provisions, the officers of Colonel Greaton's regiment gorged themselves on fresh beef, rather than sharing it with their own soldiers. Discipline and selfless service in the Continental army had crumbled and vaporized.

Contributing to the general misery at Isle Aux Noix, the medical department of Sullivan's army had entirely collapsed by this time. Dr. John Morgan, the Continental army's Surgeon General, would record that "everything in the medical department in Canada displays one scene of confusion and anarchy."[20] In the first place, the number of surgeons was woefully inadequate for the size of the American army. As early as May 6, the congressional commissioners had noted, "The army is entirely without surgeons."[21] A related critical shortage that manifested itself at Isle Aux Noix was medicines for the few surgeons that were with the army.

At the onset of the Revolutionary War, the majority of pharmaceutical medicines were procured from England. Obviously, with the onset of war, this conduit of supplies was cut off. The Continental Congress attempted to remedy the situation by contracting with the largest pharmacists in the colonies to make up the shortages, and by purchasing medicines from ships arriving from Jamaica, Bermuda, Antigua and Barbados. Even this effort was not sufficient. By April 1776, about the time that most of the reinforcements were marching from New York City to Canada, the pharmacists were running out of medicines, and could not completely fill the medicine chests of the surgeons. Many of the regiments marched for Canada with empty medicine chests, and even the well equipped among them marched missing necessary medicine. And, by now, supplies were also running out in Canada after many months with swollen sick rosters.[22] Dr. Samuel Stringer, Medical Director of the Northern Theater for Schuyler, alerted Washington of the situation from St. Jean on May 10:

> The majority of Regimental Surgeons gone up, have neither medicines nor instruments, and the army likely to be overpowered with smallpox, and no possibility of getting supplies in Canada.[23]

Massachusetts Commissary Constant Freeman recorded that at Isle Aux Noix "his friend, the surgeon, was, like the rest, without medicine."[24]

A modern historian, George B. Griffenhagen, has analyzed the situation in considerable detail. He discovered that the Marshall Brothers of New York City furnished twenty medical chests to the Continental army at New York City from February to June 1776. Of these, six battalions were among those that shortly thereafter traveled to reinforce the army in Canada (the four Pennsylvania battalions and the 1st and 3rd New Jersey). Griffenhagen found:

> Congress intended that all chests be substantially the same, but the amount of medicines demanded exceeded the stocks of even the largest druggists. The first several chests were complete as ordered, but as early as April the Marshalls [Brothers] were running out of certain drugs. Gun opium and nitre "found by Congress" was included in the chest for the Pennsylvania 4th Battalion [Wayne's], and by May 11th the Marshalls were out of Peruvian bark, ipecac, cream of tartar, gum camphor, and red precipitate of mercury. The chests outfitted after June 1 also failed to include Epsom Salts, and the last chest lacked jalap as well. Thus the majority of the battalions travelling north were already without some of the most necessary drugs in their chests. Blithely their medical officers thought they could obtain the missing drugs when they arrived at the general hospital.[25]

As noted, upon arrival in Canada, these battalions discovered that it was simply impossible to procure any medicines, as none were available whatsoever. Some medicines of the time were, of course, of limited utility. And none of the remedies could do anything for those stricken with smallpox. Yet, Peruvian or Jesuit's Bark was highly effective against fever (it is actually the raw material from which quinine is extracted). Opium was an extremely effective treatment against diarrhea or dysentery. And of perhaps the greatest importance, the reader can easily imagine the plight of a surgeon having to tell his patient that he possessed no medicines, and could do nothing for his illness. Simply the psychological factor that the doctor couldn't do anything to help must have been a devastating piece of news to a young, ill, homesick, already weakened, and fearful soldier.[26]

Isle Aux Noix, under the best of circumstances, was not a hospitable or charming location. Isle Aux Noix means, in French, Island of Nuts. If there ever had been any nuts, or anything else to eat on the island, they had long since vanished by the arrival of the American army in June of 1776. The Isle Aux Noix is a low-lying island in the middle of the Richelieu River, eleven miles south of St. Jean. It is only 210 acres in size. Its solitary advantage is that it occupies a militarily effective position, for it entirely commands the river, and being an island it is extremely difficult to storm or capture by siege. For this reason, the French had fortified it in 1759, and it had resolutely withstood a conventional siege from a considerably larger and much more powerful British army before it had been finally forced to yield in 1760. In 1776, a single subsistence farm occupied the island. It was entirely unfortified upon the arrival of Sullivan's army.

In June of 1776, given the extreme shortages of provisions, tentage, surgeons, medicines, and medical instruments, Isle Aux Noix transformed to become a veritable hellhole direct from Dante's inferno. In summer great swarms of mosquitoes, flies, gnats, and in fact every species of flying, biting insect known to the Adirondacks (and there are a considerable quantity and variety counted within the region) infest the place. The arrival of an entire army must have seemed like nothing so much as a grand buffet to the bugs.

The island's ground is perpetually moist, with pools of stagnant water and thickened mud appearing with every rain. Thick, clinging morning fogs are almost a daily occurrence. Shade is at a premium on the island. By midday the early mists are replaced by a blazing, relentless sun that reflects without mercy off the waves of the river. And yet it is still damp. Potable water is at a premium, although any quantity of warm, brown, muddy, filthy water can be readily obtained from the river. Drinking of such water is a certain recipe for gastrointestinal distress, but the American soldiers had no alternative. Given the strength of the American army of approximately 5,000 soldiers, they were seriously jammed into the relatively tiny 210 acres that the Isle Aux Noix possessed. Simply excavating adequate numbers of vaults, necessary houses or houses of office (as latrines were then variously known), and maintaining some distance of separation between them, was simply impossible. The American soldiers were quite literally living in their own filth.

Still, Isle Aux Noix at least offered the American soldiers a few choices. On the Island of Nuts they could die of malaria, dysentery, diarrhea, simple dehydration, malnutrition, a diverse range of various types of fevers, or, of course, smallpox.

Surgeon Lewis Beebe provided a hideously graphic surgeon's view of the scene:

> This morning had Colonel Poor's orders to repair to Isle Aux Naux [*sic*] to take care of the sick there, accordingly sailed in a batteau, and arrived there about 3 P.M. was struck with amazement upon my arrival, to see the vast crowds of poor distressed creatures. Language cannot describe nor imagination paint, the scenes of misery and distress the soldiery endure. Scarcely a tent upon this Isle but what contains one or more in distress and continually groaning & calling for relief, but in vain! Requests of this nature are as little regarded, as the singing of crickets in a summers evening. The most shocking of all spectacles was to see a large barn crowded full of men with this disorder [smallpox], many of which could not see, speak or walk — one nay two had large maggots, an inch long, crawl out of their ears, were on almost every party of the body. No mortal will ever believe what these suffered unless they were eye witnesses.[27]

Captain John Lacey of Pennsylvania, who so far had seen little action in Canada except as an observer, found himself in similar circumstances on the island. Bored and "having nothing to do, curiosity led me to visit the New England camp." It was a trip that the youthful Captain was almost immediately to regret ever embarking upon:

> Here my feelings were indescribable, some in and some out tents sick on the bare ground — infected with fluxes, fevers, Small Pox and over run with legions of lice, and none but sick to wait on one another. My eyes never before beheld such a scene, nor do I ever desire to see such another — the lice and maggots seemed to vie with each other, were creeping in millions over the victims, the Doctors themselves sick or out of medicine. The estimation in both camps was that 15 or 20 die daily. I examined the burying ground of each camp, found two large holes dug in the earth, one for each camp. While I there I saw several corpses brought, carried by four soldiers in a blanket, one holt of each corner. On their arriving at the pit or grave, those next to it let go of the blanket, the other two giving a hoist rolled the dead body into the pit, where lay several bodies already deposited in the same way, with no other covering but the rags in which they died, heads and points as they happened to come to the place. In this manner the burial continued all day, as soon as the breath had left the unfortunate victim, the body was thus laid on a dirty blanket and toted off to the

silent tomb, without a sigh from a friend or relative, or a single mourner to follow it. In the evening the dirt in front of this general grave, or deposit of the dead, was thrown over the dead bodies leaving a new space open for the next day. This scene of human retchedness and misery engrossed my ... visit. The New England and New York camp was the most infected with the smallpox, scarcely a single one of whom survived. The whole army was computed to be about five thousand of which it could not be said more than one third was fit for duty.[28]

These brutally descriptive recollections are stunning as they elucidate life at Isle Aux Noix in June 1776, and are so horrific that they can scarcely be credited today. Yet every single primary source is in agreement. Sullivan even recognized this at the time, telling the Continental Congress, "to give you a particular account of the miserable state of our troops there & the numbers which daily kept dropping into their beds and graves would rather seem like the effect of imagination than a history of facts."[29]

It was obvious to all that although the Isle Aux Noix provided Sullivan with a last post in Canada, it could not be defended in summer without the extinction of the entire American army. Sullivan acted promptly to remove the sick to Fort Crown Point, while maintaining his army on the island and waiting for the bateaux to complete the movement and return before he continued the retreat of the main body, for he lacked sufficient bateaux to move his entire army at one time. Sullivan wrote to General Schuyler from the island on June 22, as he contemplated the inevitable further withdrawal:

> The want of discipline & that infernal disorder the Small Pox has ruined our Army. Believe me, Dear General, that when I ordered the sick people from hence to Crown Point many regiments were obliged to apply for men to be draughted from other regiments to row them away they not having well men enough for that purpose. Those that remain here owing to their fatigue & want of fresh provisions are daily dropping off like the Israelites before the destroying Angel. The officers to a man are calling aloud to go on to Crown Point to fortify there & recruit the Army. I am for my own part now convinced that this step must be taken or the army will be lost not by the enemy but by sickness.

Sullivan also wrote to General George Washington on June 24 in a similar vein, as he continued to wait for the boats to return from Crown Point:

> It is with the greatest pain I inform you ... that I find myself under an absolute necessity of quitting this island for a place more healthy. Otherwise the army will never be able to return. As one fortnight longer in this place will not leave us well men enough to carry off the sick, exclusive of the public stores which I preserv'd thus far. The raging of the Small Pox deprives us of whole Regiments in the course of a few days, by their being taken down with that cruel disorder. But that is not all, the camp disorder rages to such a degree that of the regiments remaining from twenty to sixty in each are taken down in a day, and we have nothing to give them but salt pork, flour & the poisonous water of this Lake.[30]

The first transfer of sick from Isle Aux Noix took place on June 20, using bateaux that had been evacuated down the Richelieu River rapids. Finally, beginning on the evening of June 23, additional bateaux arrived from Crown Point. While the exhausted rowers rested, the bateaux were laden with "baggage, stores, sick and invalids." On the next morning, the retreat to Crown Point began. Captain Lacy of Pennsylvania was ecstatic to be leaving "so hateful a place where the scenes of horror were so prevalent."³¹ So desperate were the Americans to depart Isle Aux Noix that the bateaux were seriously overloaded, even with a ninety-mile voyage to Crown Point ahead of them. Colonel Frye Bailey remembered that his instructions were that "every boat to take 30 barrels of pork and 30 men each aboard. My boat being small was much too heavily laden." He also noted, "Many of the men very sick."³²

The movement from Isle Aux Noix was not executed under any British pressure, and was uneventful. That is, it was uneventful to a historian. To an already sick, underfed soldier clad in filthy rags, rowing and bailing an overloaded and overworked, leaky wooden bateaux approximately ninety miles one way, under a merciless summer sun, filled with desperately ill men barely hanging on to life, was almost certainly not uneventful. During the entire withdrawal, Captain Lacy recorded that "the men ... still continued to die from 8 to 10 every day." Lacy reported that the vanguard of the bateaux did not reach Crown Point "until the first day of July, very much wearied by rowing, so many of the men being sick, and the head or contrary winds, very little or no use could be made of the sails."³³

Rations were desperately short on the rowing route between Crown Point and Isle Aux Noix. John Greenwood, a young American musician, recalled of his diet on the journey:

> The rations, served out to us each day, consisted of a pint of flour and a quarter pound of pork for every man, and to cook this we were allowed to land at noon. We were without camp kettles or any utensils whatever to make bread in, and pretty kind of stuff was the preparation dignified by the latter term — mixed up with water from the lake, by fellows as lousy, itchy and nasty as hogs. I have seen it, when made and baked upon a piece of bark, so black with dirt and smoke I do not think a dog could eat it. But with us it went down, lice, itch, and all, without grumbling, while the pork was broiled on a wooden fork and the drippings caught by the beautiful flour cakes. Such was the life of our Continental soldiers who went to Canada, and the sick among them fared not otherwise.³⁴

Crown Point, where the American Northern Theater Army now found itself, had been initially occupied by the French in 1741 and named Fort St. Frederic. They had constructed a stone fort with an impressive stone citadel on the western shore of Lake Champlain, at a point where the lake narrows to a few hundred yards, the narrowest point of Lake Champlain north of Ticonderoga. The fort actually occupied a large peninsula that extended out and into Lake Champlain. To the east, a similar although smaller peninsula was known as Chimney Point. The French had also established a small settlement, complete with at least one fortified windmill, along Lake Champlain in the vicinity of Fort St. Frederic. The French fort was a relatively small structure, and in 1755 upon the initiation of the Seven Years' War the French transferred their primary defensive position to the newly constructed Fort Carillon at Ticonderoga. Following the fall of Fort Carillon to the British advance in the summer of 1759, the French had destroyed and abandoned Fort St. Frederic without a fight.

British General Jeffery Amherst had selected Crown Point to be the location of the major defensive post for New York colony, to defend the Lake Champlain corridor from another advance by the French from Canada. Throughout 1759 and 1760 a British army had labored mightily to construct what would become the largest military fortification in North America. It was a massive pentagonal fortification, constructed of heavy timber casemates reinforced with thick parapets of sod covered earth. To waterproof the fort to prevent the wood from annually rotting, the timber casemates were regularly coated with thick layers of tar. Formidable ditches were carved out of the limestone, with the resultant stones used to face the bottom of the parapets and sides of the ditches. Large limestone barracks, storehouses, and guard houses were constructed inside the fort. Three strong stone and earth redoubts were constructed as outer fortifications, and beyond that three blockhouses were built to provide long range observation and warning of any possible attacking force.

Crown Point, although a formidable fortification when it had been constructed by Amherst, had already deteriorated when Francis Grant, a young Englishman, made an extended tour from New York City into Canada in 1767:

> Crown Point Fort is situated on a point of land running due south, formed by Lake Champlain to the eastward, and a creek which runs a considerable way between the point and the west shore of the lake to the westward, so that the point is a sort of peninsula.... The fort ... is a very extensive place and cost the Government an immense sum of money. It is a regular pentagon, built of logs, and its ramparts very high. Its foundation and such part of the ditch as is finished, is cut out of the rock, none of the outerworks were begun, and the barracks on the inside are not finished. It is now going fast to decay, and it is said will be abandoned.[35]

Grant's information was not correct, and the British had continued to occupy Crown Point until 1773. In that spring, however, disaster struck at Crown Point. On April 21 a soldier's wife, one Mrs. Ross, was cooking a traditional army meal of salt pork and dried peas in one of the fireplaces in the soldier's barracks. Soot in the chimney accumulated over the winter caught aflame, and rapidly set fire to the wooden clapboards of the barracks roof. The barracks were soon completely engulfed in flames, which in turn spread to the tar coated timbers of the fort. In minutes, the entire fortress was ablaze. The fort was evacuated in haste when the conflagration reached the fort's powder magazine, exploding over one hundred barrels of black gunpowder in a spectacular detonation. Within a few hours, the strongest fortification in North America had been reduced to "an amazing useless mass of earth" as British engineer John Montressor assessed it.[36] Captain Edward Williams of Massachusetts, passing through Crown Point in early May, noted, "The fort & barracks at Crown Point chiefly down & blowed up & burnt down."[37] The British garrison subsequently abandoned Fort Crown Point, and transferred to Fort Ticonderoga. The Americans had occupied Crown Point without resistance in May 1775 following the capture of Ticonderoga, and had used it as a base for operations on Lake Champlain for a full year. However, the American army had unaccountably made no efforts to construct any additional fortifications of any kind at Crown Point. The fort remained as they had found it, a great rent torn in it by the gunpowder explosion, the casemates and earthen walls collapsed as a result of the fire, the buildings burned out and destroyed, not one single cannon mounted upon the ramparts, the whole ruined and defenseless.[38]

Commissary Freeman of Massachusetts was typical of the shattered soldiers of the army that arrived at Crown Point following the retreat from Canada. Unlike so many of his comrades in arms, Freeman was relatively fortunate in that he did not have the smallpox. Rather, "he had the dysentery, diarrhea, ague, and fever, etc. all in succession."[39] It is doubtful that he noticed the absence of smallpox, given all of his other afflictions. Dr. Lewis Beebe accompanied the first shipment of sick to Crown Point, arriving there on Sunday, June 23. On Wednesday, June 26, the young surgeon lamented, "The Regiment is in a most deplorable situation, between 4 and 500 now in the height of the small pox. Death is now become a daily visitant in the camp. But as little regarded as the singing of birds." And the next day, Beebe mourned, "The hot weather proves very unfriendly to those who have the small pox." Beebe reported that forty or fifty bateaux were dispatched from Crown Point on June 26 to retrieve the remainder of the American Army from Isle Aux Noix.[40]

One July 2, Surgeon Samuel F. Merrick at Crown Point recorded in his journal, "Last night about twelve o'clock the army arrived from the Isle Aux Noyx [sic] & this morning they encamped."[41] Beebe also reported on the same day, "Last evening about midnight, the army arrived at this place." To obtain some separation between those with smallpox and what passed for healthy soldiers, the sick were sent to Chimney Point, and the well soldiers to Fort Crown Point proper.[42]

The American army, for all practical purposes, no longer existed when it landed at Crown Point. Pennsylvania Quartermaster John Harper saw them arrive "in the most distressing condition that I ever saw. Troops fatigued all most to death."[43] Continental Congress member John Adams would describe its sordid condition, in what effectively served as the epitaph for the army:

> Our Army at Crown-Point is an object of wretchedness enough to fill a humane mind with horror; disgraced, defeated, discontented, dispirited, defeated, diseased, naked, undisciplined, eaten up with vermin; no clothes, beds, blankets; no medicines; no victuals but salt pork and flour.[44]

Captain William Scudder with the 4th New York Regiment similarly recorded of Crown Point:

> Such a scene of mortality as was exhibited at that place, I never had beheld. The hospital ... on the lower floor in two ranges on each side lay the poor sick and distressed soldiers. Their disorders was chiefly the small pox. Some groaning and begging for water; some dying, and others dead and sewed up in their blankets; let it suffice to say, that by the middle of the afternoon, they would begin to carry the dead from the hospital; I counted twenty-one carried out at one time.[45]

When John Trumbull, son of the governor of Connecticut, arrived at Ticonderoga he wrote his father:

> I arrived at this place the fourth day, and from hence went on to Crown Point soon after. At that place I found not an army, but a mob, the shattered remains of twelve or fifteen very fine battalions, ruined by sickness, fatigue and desertions and void of every idea of discipline or subordination. Last spring the army was upwards of ten thousand strong. We have now three thousand sick and about the same number well. This leaves near five thousand men to be accounted for. Of them the enemy have cost

us perhaps one, sickness another thousand, and the others God alone knows in what manner they are disposed of. Among the few we have remaining, there is neither order, subordination, or harmony, the officers, as well as men, of one colony insulting and quarreling with those of another.[46]

Trumbull further went on in his autobiography to describe the wreck that he found:

Thus the wretched remnant of the army reached Crown Point in safety, but it is difficult to conceive a state of much deeper misery. The boats were leaky and without awnings; the sick being laid upon their bottoms without straw, were soon drenched in the filthy water of that peculiarly stagnant muddy lake, exposed to the burning sun of the month of July, with no sustenance but raw salt pork, which was often rancid, and hard biscuit or unbaked flour; no drink but the vile water of the lake, modified perhaps, not corrected, by bad rum and scarcely any medicine.

My first duty, upon my arrival at Crown Point, was to procure a return of the number and condition of the troops. I found them dispersed, some few in tents, some in sheds, and more under the shelter of miserable brush huts, so totally disorganized by the death or sickness of officers, that the distinction of regiments and corps was in a great degree lost; so that I was driven to the necessity of great personal examination, and I can truly say that I did not look into tent or hut in which I did not find either a dead or dying. I can scarcely imagine any more disastrous scene.[47]

Another anonymous soldier wrote of the retreat in mid July:

I never, never knew the fatigue of a campaign until I arrived at Canada. The most shocking scenes that ever appeared in a camp were constantly exhibited to view.... The army was torn in pieces by sickness and other unaccountable occurrences. A whole regiment was not to be found together.... No person who was not present can conceive a tenth part of the difficulties attending it; the enemy at our heels, 3,000 of our men sick with the small pox, those who were most healthy like so many walking apparitions.[48]

In addition to the all encompassing health problems, the Army constituted little more than a mob. Surgeon Beebe recorded, in absolute disgust, on July 4:

The army have been here for several days, and notwithstanding they are under great apprehensions of an attack from the enemy soon ... not the least preparation for fortifying the garrison, which has tumbled to ruin & decay. The Generals have their hands full in riding about their camp, prancing their gay horses. The Field Officers set much of their time upon Court Martials. The Captains & Subalterns may generally be found at the grog shops. The soldiers either sleeping, swimming, fishing, or cursing and swearing most generally the latter.[49]

In perhaps the single most significant action that they would take as regards the Northern Theater, the Continental Congress upon hearing of the death of John Thomas had designated another commander for the army in Canada. Major General Horatio Gates was notified of his appointment by Congressman John Adams of Massachusetts with this endorsement, dated June 18:

We have ordered you to the Post of Honor, and made you Dictator in Canada for six months, or at least until the first of October. We do not choose to trust you Generals with too much power for too long.[50]

When the first bateaux reached Crown Point late on July 1, they found Generals Schuyler and Gates awaiting them. It was the first glimpse that the Canadian army would have of Horatio Gates, and the first glimpse that Horatio Gates would have of the American Northern Theater Army.

Major General Horatio Gates is one of the most intriguing, and controversial, characters of the War for American Independence. Horatio Gates had been born in England in 1727, to decidedly lower class parents. His father was a boater and servant by profession but a smuggler at heart, and his mother was a household servant. However, through a fortuitous set of circumstances, his godfather was the powerful Horace Walpole. Intimations abounded throughout his entire life that Gates' was somebody's illegitimate son, but precisely whose was never specified, and the rumors were never proven. Gates had purchased a commission in the British army, and by 1755 he was a Captain commanding an independent company in New York City. He participated in Braddock's Campaign against Fort Duquesne, and at the desperate fight in the wilderness along the banks of the Monongahela River Gates was severely wounded. One of his soldiers dragged the desperately stricken Captain Gates safely from the battlefield. Some historians have suggested that ever after this battle Gates had an aversion to gunfire, and there is evidence in his later behavior to validate such suggestions. Quite probably, given the horrors of that day in the Western Pennsylvania woods, Gates suffered from what would today be diagnosed as Post Traumatic Stress Disorder (PTSD). He had an aversion to loud noises throughout the rest of his life. Gates served as a Captain throughout the Seven Years' War, in both North America and the West Indies, without again seeing combat or gaining any particular distinction. He did serve as Brigade Major for two separate Generals over two campaigns, earning considerable experience in Army administration and bureaucracy. He ended the war as a Major, but lacked sufficient patronage to avoid being placed on half pay when the army was reduced in strength at war's end. Gates spent approximately a decade on the half pay rolls without accomplishment in England, and in 1773 he returned to North America. Gates purchased a modest western Virginia plantation which he named Traveler's Rest. Gates immediately settled comfortably into his new life as a gentleman planter, and began to participate in American colonial politics. He was a fervent Whig, and had been a strong advocate for American liberties and rights even when he lived in England. His experience as a planter in Virginia only strengthened his political convictions.[51]

Gates was not an imposing physical specimen such as George Washington or Benedict Arnold. In 1776 he was 49 years old, of average height, with stooped shoulders, poor muscle tone, and a weak posture. His features were flabby, his hair was white, and he was shortsighted enough to have to wear spectacles. His portraits suggest a shrewdly calculating personality, with a sense of humor, confident and sly. He was apparently a good drinking companion, and was genial, outgoing, and friendly. He clearly relished his creature comforts.[52] For example, shortly after he arrived at Fort Ticonderoga, Gates found time to have his Aide De Camp order the "Conductor of Military Stores" to: "deliver, for the use of the General, a Coffee Mill now in your Stores."[53] On August 16 at Ticonderoga, General Orders noted that "strayed yesterday from Head Quarters a fat sheep belonging to the General" and that "The General has that opinion of the soldiers under his command that they will return him his sheep whenever they find it."[54] Given the propensities of hungry and mischievous soldiers, it is doubtful that Gates ever saw his "fat sheep" again.

Upon the beginning of the War for American Independence, Gates had quickly offered his services to the fledgling Continental army, and Washington eagerly employed him as his Adjutant General during the Siege of Boston. Gates certainly made his reputation at Boston in 1775 and 1776. He was a highly skilled, extremely efficient administrator. He was meticulously well organized, and rapidly made sense and order of the scattered correspondence of the young army. Gates possessed a companionable personality that enabled him to work in cooperation with a wide range of officers from different colonies. Gates' radical Whig politics earned him strong friendships with the equally strident New Englanders. Gates prepared for Washington the first set of U.S. Army Regulations, and he played a critical role in establishing procedures for recruitment and training. He had a reputation as a strict disciplinarian, a trait that was desperately needed in the American army, and one that Washington greatly respected. Washington sincerely admired Gates' skills as an administrator and organizer, and greatly valued Gates' contributions as Adjutant General.

Gates had another skill, one perhaps not so honorable as a soldier, but one that was highly valuable to any general officer. Specifically, he was quite expert at negotiating with and impressing members of the Continental Congress. Gates, in particular, would shortly form a strong friendship with prominent Massachusetts congressman John Adams that would serve him in very good stead.[55] This trait and this relationship, more than any other factors, were to rapidly gain Gates promotion to Major General, and then the post in Canada. For Gates was also wildly ambitious, and had a burning desire to gain as much power and prestige through his service to the new nation and army as he could possibly garner for himself.

Although he had served in the British Army from 1749 to 1763, and throughout the entire Seven Years' War, Gates possessed almost no tactical or strategic experience, had never operated independently, and had no command experience above the company level. Tactically and strategically, Gates preferred a cautious, safe approach.[56] He believed that bureaucracy, administration, and careful management secured victories — not sweeping maneuvers on the battlefield. Gates was not a man for rash or reckless behavior, rather he believed in a careful, deliberate approach to problem solving and leadership. He apparently rather enjoyed writing regulations and procedures for an army, and found logistics to be an endearing field of study. In short, Gates was a Headquarters General.

Still, by the first of July 1776 the American Northern Theater Army was totally and completely disorganized, without regulations, procedures, provisions, arms, ammunition, uniforms, equipment, medicines, surgeons, discipline, leadership or good order. Because of the extensive correspondence and personal reports of the congressional committee, the Continental Congress was well aware of these circumstances. Given the conditions that existed in this army, the Continental Congress would have been hard pressed to find a more perfect man for the assignment than Horatio Gates.

The first major decision to be made at Crown Point was to determine the site of the American main defensive position astride Lake Champlain. Two legitimate locations were available: Fort Crown Point on the Crown Point Peninsula with Chimney Point across the narrows of Lake Champlain; and the old French Fort Carillon at Ticonderoga Point at another narrows of Lake Champlain. These were the only extant military fortifications.

Major General Philip Schuyler convened a council of war at Crown Point on July 7, consisting of all five General Officers then assigned to the American Northern Theater Army. It was chaired by Schuyler, and attended by Major General Horatio Gates in his first major decision with the Northern Theater Army. The other attendees were Brigadier General Benedict Arnold, Brigadier General John Sullivan, and Brigadier General Baron de Woedtke. Following discussions, the council of war reached the following conclusions:

> Resolved, that under our present Circumstances, the post of Crown Point is not tenable & that with our present force, or one greatly superior to what we may reasonably expect, it is not capable of being made so, this summer.
>
> Resolved therefore, that it is prudent to retire immediately to the strong ground, on the east side of the lake opposite to Ticonderoga, with all the healthy & uninfected troops & that the sick & infected with the small pox be removed to Fort George. It appearing clearly to the Council, that the post opposite to Ticonderoga, will the most effectually secure the country & removing the infected with the small pox, obviate every objection that may at present retard the Militia (ordered by Congress) from joining the Army.
>
> Resolved, that the most effectual measures be taken to secure our superiority on Lake Champlain, by a naval armament of gondolas, row galleys, armed bateaux.
>
> Resolved, that one or more surveyors be immediately employed, to trace out a road, between the high ground opposite to Ticonderoga & the road leading from Skenesboro to the Northern Settlements.[57]

Gates noted in a letter written on July 12, "This miserable situation of our affairs ... induced the council of war, which General Schuyler held a few days ago, unanimously to resolve that the Army should immediately retire from Crown Point to Ticonderoga."[58]

The decision made to move the American army and main defensive position to Ticonderoga, rather than remain at Crown Point, may well have been the most important decision made during the campaign. This simple selection determined not only the course of the 1776 campaign, but also the course of the 1777 Saratoga campaign in the future.

In the end, the decision came down to the conditions at Crown Point, versus the conditions at Ticonderoga. Both locations would require considerable efforts to make them defensible. Both locations had existing fortifications. The fire of 1773 had totally gutted and destroyed the great fortress of Crown Point, but the three exterior English redoubts and an earlier exterior French redoubt were in good repair, and by simply adopting the previous defensive configuration of 1759 and 1760 a large American army could be accommodated. Chimney Point, on the other side of Lake Champlain, would also have to be fortified. A strong fortification at Crown Point would certainly obstruct Lake Champlain.

The original French fort at Ticonderoga had only been partially repaired following its destruction by the French in 1759. However, the French had constructed two additional redoubts as outer works to the main fort in 1755 and 1758, and these remained in relatively viable condition in 1776. These redoubts, and the defensive lines constructed on the Heights of Carillon by the French Commander the Marquis de Montcalm in 1758, if improved and repaired could similarly accommodate a large army. Additional fortifications would be required to secure both the eastern and western flanks of Ticonderoga. A fortification at Ticonderoga would also obstruct Lake Champlain.

Both locations were constructed at places where Lake Champlain considerably narrowed, and navigation by a British navy from the north could easily be constrained by their presence. Both positions, once properly entrenched and garrisoned, could not be easily outflanked. Ticonderoga was only 13 miles south of Crown Point, an easy half a day's rowing, so that logistical distances were not a factor.

Crown Point had one definite disadvantage, and it was a big one. It had already been contaminated by smallpox. Ticonderoga had not been so contaminated. Quartermaster John Harper of the 4th Pennsylvania Battalion arrived at Crown Point from the south on June 28, by which time most of the sick had already been evacuated from Isle Aux Noix. He remembered that "I pitched my tent in the cleanest place that I could find on the Point for the stink, the sick and their nastiness was enough to infect the air."[59] Gates himself would write to Washington on the 29th of July, "Everything about this army is infected with the pestilence, the clothes, the blankets, the air, and the ground they walk upon."[60]

The sick, by being evacuated directly to Fort George and bypassing Ticonderoga, would not contaminate that site with smallpox. In the end, that simple fact was the deciding measure behind the resolution of the Council of War.

And the importance of this determining factor should not be overlooked. Smallpox had just destroyed the American army in Canada. At the time, even for inoculation to be effective, isolation and quarantine were critical to preventing the epidemic spread of the disease. These conditions had already been violated at Crown Point, and thus the American army could not be maintained at that garrison. All other considerations were subordinate to the realities imposed by that horrible, dreaded and terribly infectious disease.

It was a source of great controversy, almost immediately. In fact, the New England Colonels in the army took the unprecedented step of complaining to Washington and the Continental Congress in writing regarding the decision. A military road constructed during the Seven Years' War existed between Crown Point (actually Chimney Point on the east side of Lake Champlain) and Fort No. 4 on the Connecticut River in New Hampshire Colony, which eventually led into Massachusetts Colony. An invading British Army could easily utilize this road as a gateway into New England. Unlike Ticonderoga, Crown Point had specifically been sited, designed and constructed to defend against an attack from the north. Accordingly, the New England Colonels viewed establishing Ticonderoga as the main defensive position, and abandoning Crown Point, as exposing New England to potential attack, and they vehemently contested the final decision.

Crown Point was farther to the north, and provided a better defense in depth than Ticonderoga. As mentioned, Crown Point's occupation would prevent possible British use of the road to Fort No. 4. Additionally, if forced to withdraw from Crown Point, Ticonderoga offered a second extremely strong defensive position. The next defensive position to the south from Ticonderoga was not found until the ends of the lakes, at Skenesboro on Lake Champlain, and at Fort George at the southern end of Lake George. And if Ticonderoga fell, the British could follow either Lake George or Lake Champlain to the south, thus splitting the American defense, which could not possibly be re-united until Fort Edwards on the Hudson River. From a purely tactical perspective, Crown Point was clearly the most advantageous post.

But the smallpox consideration outweighed all others. It is instructive that all five General Officers on the scene voted unanimously to send the sick to Fort George and withdraw the army to Ticonderoga.

Washington duly entered the fray, writing to both Schuyler and Gates to roundly condemn the decision. However, Washington was not on the scene, lacked the information that was available to Schuyler and Gates, and clearly had no comprehension of the severity of the smallpox outbreak that had devastated the army. After a few acrimonious letters, the entire inconsequential and insignificant affair was forgotten, and it had absolutely no effect upon the campaign.[61] Its only possible significance was correctly identified by the young Lieutenant Wilkinson, who noted, "an occurrence took place, which is a worthy note, because it will convey to the reader a distinct idea of the state of the discipline and subordination which prevailed in the American army at that time."[62] Gates, a strict disciplinarian, clearly had his work cut out for him in this army.

Having participated in this council of war, his solitary contribution to the American campaign in Canada, Brigadier General de Woedtke was immediately confined to a sickbed at Crown Point. Rumors abounded that he was an alcoholic and had quite literally drunk himself to death. He would die in late July at Fort George, apparently unlamented and unmissed.

Yet, before he passed away, the Baron de Woedtke wrote two letters to Benjamin Franklin, who had sponsored him upon his arrival in America. Woedtke wrote the letters in French, which was not his native language. De Woedtke did not speak English, and his French was also extremely limited (the transcribers of his letters noted that de Woedtke wrote in what would effectively today be second grade French). The natural question is how effective de Woedtke was in an English speaking army serving in a French and English speaking country, when he was all but illiterate in both languages. One suspects that he was, for all practical purposes, useless. Although the good Baron had an interesting view of several of the recent operations that was not entirely accurate, these two letters are revealing in that he clearly observed many of the problems in the American army. These letters, never previously translated, are provided as Benjamin Franklin perused them:

Camp at Crown Point, July 3d 1776

Sir,

I hope that you will have received my two letters from Sorel and L'Ile des Noix. I would have been honoured to write to you more often if I could only give you good news. You know, Sir, that after our troops ran without turning around or having dead or wounded, under the orders of General Thomas [they] camped for some time at de Chambo [Chambly] and from there arrived at Sorel to join the rest of our troops. We camped on both sides of the river and, at the risk of tiring our troops we made excellent retrenchments and from this position we still, for the most part, commanded the countryside. But, instead of thinking of the importance of this position, General Arnold proposed a shameful expedition to the Cedars, having under him Colonel de Haas, the biggest Tory in the army.

At the same time, the good General Thomson, a respectable man, undertook an expedition to the Three Rivers; a badly conducted expedition.

The two detachments, that from the Cedars and that from Three Rivers returned to the camp at Sorel where it was almost unanimously resolved to immediately leave the camp at Sorel and Canada, despite all of the opposition and remonstrance that I made to the council, we left our camp without doing the least bit of ruin to our batteries as General Sullivan took fright at a false alarm. Colonel Haas advocated immediately, in order to hasten our march, to throw two cannon into the water, which I happily stopped [from happening]. At the camp at Chambli [Chambly], we held a war council where we decided to go immediately to St. Jean. I was of an opposing sentiment since we knew neither if the enemy had taken possession of the position at Sorel nor the size of her force. At St. Jean we again held a war council where it was decided to pass through Lake Champlain despite all my protestations of not knowing if the enemy had taken the position at Chambli. Before leaving we burned some houses instead of demolishing the fortifications at St. Jean. Before passing through the lakes, we stopped at L'île des Noix [Isle Aux Noix] where we finally learned that there were several hundred men at St. Jean. We left an iron chain at L'île des Noix which could well impede the English vessels from coming from St. Jean to us.[63] The English had until present very few boats, but unfortunately we gave them time to construct vessels at St. Jean. We thus arrived at Crown Point, camped and arranged ourselves like a horde of Tartars, although Tartars had an advantage over us because they placed guards and sent scouts to reconnoiter. There is, Sir, a complete disunity between the New Englanders and the others. I fear with certainty what comes next. We have many Tory officers that need to be sent away. There is here a Colonel Antel [Antill] from the Canadian Hazen regiment, which barely exists anymore, an ignorant young man who unfortunately works as the General's aide-de-camp and who meddles in engineering matters. We inoculated our troops from smallpox, and the food that they are eating is salted pork etc. etc. Our lazarets, our hospitals, are neglected to the last. Myself, I have a number of enemies but my enemies are our Tories. I always [perhaps, given his less than stellar French, he means "every day"] begin and end [with the hope] that the respectable Congress will confiscate their goods and cut off their heads in Philadelphia. I cannot say anymore, Sir, than that I desire to do honor to your recommendation and do honor to my service but I cannot as I do not have any power in this regard. I have our soldiers supporting me, but how can it end? I fear, I fear that we will not hold onto this position. If my letter interests you, Sir, and you cannot read it, Mr. Paul Fooks the interpreter will read it to you immediately. I ask you, Sir, my humble regards to President Hancock and to Mr. Adams. I have the honor of writing to you and to communicate to you everything that has happened in particular, nevertheless desiring to have the honor and the pleasure of having news from you. 1,500 men from Pennsylvania directly under my command with a brevet to be their commander would be a pleasure and perhaps the respectable Congress would be happy with their services? I finish since Colonel Alen [Allen] is leaving at the moment.

I have the honor to say with the most distinguished consideration, Sir, Your most humble and obedient servant.

WOEDTKE.[64]

6. "I Can Scarcely Imagine Any More Disastrous Scene"

And the second letter, missing some passages through the ravages of time:

Crown Point the 4th July 1776

Sir,

I hope that Colonel Allen has given you my letter, through which you could only note too much the thorny situation of our troops, as ... than having ... by ... judge ... us ... experienced and that General Sullivan ... governor ... of our troops, nevertheless we have a new General here who leads everyone — Colonel Antheil [is the General's aide-de-camp?], two years ago he ... lacked theory and practical experience as the protégé of the good General ... who is an intimate friend of Antheil's wife. Captain Marquesi, who is carrying this letter, will tell you a lot more. General Sullivan was made to think that he knew nothing of his profession although I've seen his work, which disgusted him so much that he left for Philadelphia. He had the misfortune to lose, without it being his fault, all of his ... I had the misfortune to lose his horses ... trip from Philadelphia to Sorrel, I am very ... I cannot ... in the new ... of more than 20 leagues as much as I ... for the well being of our troops everything which there ... puts on us every imaginable evil in the Chambly camp I've learned from several Canadians attached to Congress that the English have put 500 Guineas for my capture. I can't deny that this flatters me very much. I strongly wish, Sir, to have a word of response to my letters, and recommend as a citizen just like a General and a man of honor to give the position of (aide-de-camp to the general?) to an experienced man. If I had to propose someone, it would be Colonel St. Clair. The disharmony between our troops continues. The 4 warships that we have on the lake are in very bad shape. They hardly have any bullets even though we have lead. I write to you without disguise, and I have the honor to call myself with the highest consideration, Sir, your very humble and very obedient servant.

WOEDTKE.[65]

Sullivan also departed the scene, apparently miffed because he had been passed over for command. He complained in a petulant letter to Schuyler on July 6:

By Congress having thought proper to supercede me, by appointing General Gates (who had not by the rank they were pleased formerly to confer on us the same pretensions as myself), I can construe this in no other light, but by supposing Congress were apprehensive that I was not equal to the trust, they were pleased to repose in me. If this be the case, I am bound in justice to my country to relinquish a command to which I am not equal. If this was not the foundation & they had not such an opinion of me, surely my Honor calls upon me to leave the service, after a person is put in over me without any impeachment of my conduct.[66]

The letter is more than a trifle self-serving. Gates as a Major General outranked Sullivan, as did Thomas before him, and would naturally assume the command by virtue of seniority. Sullivan was never selected by Congress to be the Canadian army commander. He inherited the position only through circumstances of death by smallpox, and capture by foolhardiness. Sullivan, as Congress well recognized, lacked the rank, military maturity, or military experience to be entrusted with such an important command. Schuyler, probably without regret and thus without argument, let him retire. Sullivan had contributed little to the army in Canada except supervising a retreat from Sorel to Crown Point, a retreat which was inevitable, and like the Baron de

Woedtke he would be unlamented and unmissed by the army that he had so briefly commanded.

Gates, who controversy seemed to naturally follow, was immediately embroiled in another dispute. Specifically, Gates' assignment had been to command the "Army in Canada." That was fine when the Continental Congress issued the order, for the army was, in fact, in Canada. But, by the time that Gates had made it to Crown Point, the army was now out of Canada. Legally, Gates no longer had a command. And as with the council of war decision to transfer the American main effort from Crown Point to Ticonderoga, another series of acrimonious letters blazed forth from Schuyler and Gates at Crown Point. Both Schuyler and Gates attempted to determine who was really in charge, who really had a command and who didn't, and precisely what command that just might happen to be. For quite possibly the only time in its existence, the Continental Congress reacted swiftly and decisively, and issued definitive orders nearly immediately, on July 12:

> Resolved, that Major General Gates be informed that it was the intention of Congress to give him the command of the troops whilst in Canada, but that they had no design to vest him with a superior command to General Schuyler whilst the troops should be on this side of Canada, and that the President [of Congress] write to Major General Schuyler and Major General Gates, stating this matter, and recommending to them to carry on the military operations with harmony, and in such a manner as shall best promote the public service.[67]

To both Schuyler's and Gates' credit, they immediately established a sound working relationship. Gates would command the American main army at Ticonderoga, including an advanced post to be retained at Crown Point, and the American fleet on Lake Champlain. Schuyler would remain in overall command of the Northern Theater, with his headquarters at Albany. One significant factor was that Schuyler's habitual poor health constrained him from remaining at the relatively isolated and primitive Ticonderoga. In any event, without the logistical support that Schuyler could best provide, and that Schuyler needed to be in Albany to manage, the American army could not be maintained even at Ticonderoga. In addition to logistical considerations, and although the situation with the American main army at Ticonderoga was certainly critical, Schuyler also still needed to maintain peaceful relations with the Native American tribes of New York colony, and to manage the Mohawk Valley that had dangerous British leanings. Without a secure rear, and without supplies and provisions, Gates would be hard pressed to reorganize the army and hold his ground at Ticonderoga. There was more than enough work necessary if the British advance was to be stopped for the summer on Lake Champlain to keep both men gainfully employed.

The only confusion that this affair caused was in the matter of duplicate appointments, for Gates and Schuyler had designated different individuals to the same staff positions. Although this obviously caused consternation for the individuals involved, it had no lasting detrimental effects upon the American army. As Schuyler and Gates were well aware, there was more than sufficient work to be done in strengthening American affairs in both the Northern Theater Army and at Ticonderoga, for every officer to play a vital role. There was some initial confusion, and a smattering of bitter letters, but the situation in short order resolved itself, and all effected officers found gainful employment either under Gates or Schuyler.[68]

By the middle of July, Schuyler had returned to Albany to superintend the logistical and theater aspects of the campaign, and Gates supervised the transfer of the army to Ticonderoga. Gates found a partially repaired and poorly maintained British fort, with two older French redoubts, and some distinctly limited American logistical infrastructure. Ticonderoga had once been one of the greatest fortresses in North America, but those days were long behind it when Gates arrived. In 1767, returning through Ticonderoga, the young Englishman Francis Grant described the post:

> Ticonderoga, called by the French Carillon, is a point formed by the Lake on the east, and a river running from Lake George on the west. There is here the remains of the French fort, which was a square, defended by two ravelins to the land side. The fort is reckoned too small for the place, and from the westward it is commanded by a rising ground the greatest height of which is ¼ of a mile from the fort. It is distant from the point about 300 yards, ascending all the way. At the point there is a strong redoubt for the defence of the shipping.... At the top of the rising ground to the westward of the fort are Mr. Montcalm's breast works or lines, at which General Abercromby was defeated in 1757. These lines still remain entire, and are very strong. They extend all the way from the river to the lake, about 2 miles in length, flanked at every place, they are built of large round logs of wood, and are about 8 feet thick at bottom, narrowing to the breadth of one log at top. These logs are very large, and at the angles are morticed into one another; the lines are about man height. At the top of the hill there was a battery piquetted and trenched, and the whole lines were defended by fallen trees, with their branches sharpened. Upon the whole nothing could be stronger of the sort. About a mile beyond the breast work is a saw mill, to which place the river is navigable. Here is a slanting fall of water of about 40 feet, and between this and Lake George there is about a mile of a carriage.[69]

The "remains of the French Fort" had not improved in the interim. After almost two decades of disinterest by the British army, Ticonderoga failed to present itself as much of a fortress for the American army to base their defense around. The young man, Simeon Bloodgood, had driven a sleigh for his father under contract to the Continental army earlier that winter. He had passed through the fortress:

> We arrived at Ticonderoga, which presented but a sorry sight. The glories of Ti were rather on the wane.... Its ditches were nearly filled with rubbish, and its ramparts were dismantled and ruinous.[70]

Captain Williams of Massachusetts found "the fort old & a tumbling down."[71]

Fort Ticonderoga was no longer the formidable fortress that the French had constructed, but it was still located on a piece of absolutely key terrain. With careful design and hard work, it could be readily converted to an imposing defensive position. Most importantly, it was smallpox free.

As the General Council of War had decided, those soldiers sick with smallpox were to be sent to a new General Hospital to be established at Fort George, on the southern end of Lake George. This would enable healthy soldiers and reinforcements to proceed through Skenesboro and north on the South Bay of Lake Champlain directly to Ticonderoga, and avoid the smallpox. At the same time, supplies could readily be sent from

Fort Edward on the Hudson River on a good road to Fort George, only a two-day journey. Thus, those sick with smallpox would be isolated, but still closer to supplies than they would have been at Crown Point or Ticonderoga.

Efforts were also being made to recruit additional surgeons to assist the badly strained medical staff of the Northern Theater Army. One great asset thus obtained was that of Dr. Jonathan Potts, a 29-year-old physician from Pennsylvania. Potts had studied at the prestigious University of Edinburgh (Scotland) Medical School, the premier medical college in England, and quite possibly the world, at the time. He had been the valedictorian of the first graduating class of the first school of medicine in America, the College of Philadelphia (now the University of Pennsylvania), in 1768. Potts was a close friend of the famous and renowned Dr. Benjamin Franklin of Philadelphia. Dr. Potts was initially selected by Gates to be his Chief Surgeon, but as a result of the reorganization of the army following the Gates-Schuyler command situation, Potts was directed to assume command of the Fort George General Hospital. Potts was one of the finest physicians in North America, and would make considerable contributions to the Northern Theater Army.[72]

Surgeon John Morgan, medical director of the Continental army, wrote regarding Potts' transfer to Fort George to John Adams on June 25:

> The state of the Army in Canada ... for a supply of medicines is truly deplorable. General Gates sets out tomorrow to take command of the Army in Canada. Dr. Potts will accompany him. I have therefore given orders to supply him from the General Hospital with a large chest of such medicines as I can best spare, and which can be got ready tomorrow before his departure.[73]

Dr. Samuel Stringer, Schuyler's Chief Surgeon for the Northern Theater, issued Potts the following orders on July 7 from Crown Point:

> As the whole of the sick will be removed from this post to Fort George as quick as possible, and are very numerous, beg you will, with all dispatch, have the sheds on the lake shore fitted up with cribs or berths for their reception. Hurry those that are to be built where the old fort stood, as fast as possible. A convenient shop and a kitchen for the cook, contiguous to the principal departments, will be necessary.... A quantity of hemlock tops, if procured, will be no bad bedding, and immediately wanted. They may be gathered along the lake shore and brought in battoes.[74]

The sick were dispatched from Crown Point to Fort George beginning on July 10. Surgeon Merrick with Colonel Porter's Massachusetts Militia Regiment described the journey:

> [July] 10. Wednesday. In the morning received orders from Colonel Porter to be in readiness to go to Fort George with the sick ... about two o'clock PM we sat out. We were forbid to land on the east side of the lake or at Ticonderoga.[75]

As previously noted, during the movement of those soldiers stricken with smallpox it was imperative that they not be landed at Ticonderoga, or the eastern bank of Lake Champlain that was already proposed for a second American encampment. This was ordered so that the future American fortress and encampment at Ticonderoga would not be contaminated with smallpox.

The movement was miserable, the weather was pouring rain, the winds were contrary and slowed the movement of the bateaux to a veritable crawl, and the army was still short on provisions such that there were no fresh rations available for the sick. Dr. Merrick recalled that "we have nothing to eat but flour nor to drink but lake water." As any smoker can sympathize, in an even greater calamity, he also had "nothing to smoke but oak leaves." The sick finally arrived at Fort George on July 13. Merrick's problems were not concluded:

> With difficulty found an empty barrack where we put the sick and delivered them to the Hospital surgeon, then drunk some refreshment, eat supper, pitched our tent, and lay down for sleep. Ordered to set out for Crown Point tomorrow morning.

Surgeon Merrick later provided another description of his journey:

> On the 10th [of July] I was ordered, forward again, with the sick, to Fort George. We took as much pork and flour as we thought we should want; but the pork was bad and we were obliged to throw it overboard, so that we had nothing but flour wet with lake water, and baked on flat stones. We expected to be but two days in going, but the wind was against us, and we were four days. It looked as if we should all starve. I thought I could eat a ten penny nail, but we got in and were supplied.[76]

Given the limited rations that the Northern Theater Army had been under for some time, the condition of the pork must have truly been horrific, otherwise Surgeon Merrick would never have tossed it aside.

The Fort George that Surgeon Merrick discharged his cargo of smallpox and sick at was indeed a sorry sight. The young man, Simeon DeWitt Bloodgood, had passed through Fort George earlier that winter:

> The garrison ... were downright oddities. Their blue coats with white facings were tarnished by the smoke of the pine knots, which it was the fashion in Fort George to use in the double capacity of fire and candle. A more somber family I think I never saw.[77]

Francis Grant described Fort George in 1767: "There is no fortification except a redoubt mounting 12 guns, about 200 yards from the shore, and some barracks. A large fort was intended here but it never was executed."[78] Lieutenant James Hadden of the British Royal Artillery would pass through Fort George during the Saratoga Campaign the next year, and noted: "Fort George, which stands near the water at the end of the Lake, is a small square Fort faced with Masonry and contains Barracks for about a hundred Men secured from Cannon Shot."[79] The redoubt or fort that Grant and Lieutenant Hadden described was actually a stone bastion of a formidable fort that British General Jeffery Amherst had planned in 1759, and which was the only portion of the fort actually constructed following his victories over the French further north. The gorge of the bastion had been closed off to form a classic pentagonal redoubt, and the interior of the bastion become a redoubt had been filled with barracks for a small garrison.

The location around Fort George is a rising, generally flat plateau immediately south of the southern end of Lake George. The site had been used by William Johnson in 1755 as his encampment, and was the location where he had successfully repulsed a French attack in September of that year. In 1757, the British army had constructed a large entrenched position here to supplement Fort William Henry, and this entrenched camp had not been directly attacked by the French during the famous siege in August of that year. In both 1758 and 1759 the massive British armies marching against Fort Carillon at Ticonderoga had camped on this ground. British General Jeffery Amherst, concerned with the health of his soldiers, had burned over the campsite and spread clean sand over it before he would permit his soldiers to encamp. The camp was elevated, relatively flat, well drained, and generally healthy, possibly as a result of Amherst's earlier precautions. Good water was readily available. Adequate building materials and firewood were available, although most of the local wood was pine and thus not preferred for fires. Given these advantages, it was an excellent potential site for a general hospital, but until the site was considerably improved it remained a primitive hospital indeed. Archaeologists have attempted to locate and define the hospital site more precisely, but have not been successful to date. Given the large number of sick, it must have extended over quite a large area. However, the simple wooden sheds constructed would not have left much of an archaeological footprint, doubtless complicating the modern archaeologist's efforts.

Establishing an effective general hospital at Fort George was a monumental task. Nearly three thousand men were to be admitted to the hospital (if, indeed, being unceremoniously dumped ashore from a soaked bateaux could be called admitting). These men were so ill that they could do little to help themselves. In 1776, few towns in North America contained 3,000 people. Suddenly, Fort George became one of the largest communities in New York colony (shortly to become a state), and it was a community composed nearly entirely of sick men. John Potts had a huge responsibility, and he shortly realized that almost no preparations had been made at Fort George for the reception and treatment of the ill. This is not surprising, since no decision was made to even establish a hospital at Fort George until the July 7 council of war. Thus, there was less than one week's organizational and set-up time available before this tidal wave of sick descended.

Dr. Stringer, as Medical Director of the Northern Theater, apparently stayed at Fort George to assist Potts. Late in July Stringer wrote Gates an impassioned letter regarding conditions at the general hospital:

> What we are to do, under these shocking circumstances, I know not; I say shocking, because nothing can appear more so than our present situation — men dying for want of assistance that we are not empowered to give. Besides a want of Surgeons, I am not furnished with clerks or stewards; one clerk, that I took upon myself to appoint, with General Schuyler's concurrence, is not now capable of going through the business he is obliged to take charge of. As our men's lives are thus wasted, would it be improper that I should leave the care of the sick to Dr. Potts, and go to York [New York City] myself, and see the medicines forthwith forwarded by land, until they can be safely conveyed by water, and from thence wait on Congress in person, lay our situation before them, and endeavor to have my powers enlarged, or at least get their consent to provide the number of assistants that are requisite.

Stringer concluded in despair:

> Just now ... acquaints us that a large number of sick are coming, in addition to what we already have.... In the name of God, what shall we do with them all, my dear General?[80]

Surgeon Potts must have felt forlorn and abandoned more than a few times in July and August, as he attempted to organize a functional hospital under great difficulties. He maintained an extensive correspondence as he strove to obtain critical supplies and sufficient staff to respond to the needs of the sick and injured. Typical of his letters is one written on August 1 to Morgan, as Potts related the "distressing situation of the sick" at the southern end of Lake George. He remonstrated how the ill were:

> Without clothing, without bedding or a shelter sufficient to screen them from the weather, I am sure your known humanity will be affected when I tell you we have at present upwards of one thousand sick & wounded in the sheds & laboring under the various disorders of dysenteries, bilious, putrid fevers & the effects of confluent small pox. To attend this large number, we have four seniors [Surgeons] & four [Surgeon] Mates, exclusive of myself.[81]

From the 12th to the 26th of July alone, 1,497 soldiers were admitted to the hospital, and this in only a two week period. Of this number, 51 soldiers died. Surgeon Beebe visited the hospital on August 28, passing through on the way from Albany. Beebe:

> visited the hospital[.] Found the number of sick to be about 700, viewed the burying place counted upwards of 300 graves, which had been opened in about 5 weeks, the appearance of which was melancholy indeed, to see such desolation made in our army.[82]

The situation of the sick was bleak indeed. Colonel Samuel Wigglesworth wrote to the Committee of Safety for New Hampshire on September 22 from Ticonderoga:

> Near half this regiment is entirely incapable of any service, some dying almost every day. Colonel Wyman's Regiment is in the same unhappy situation. There are no medicines of any available in the Continental Chest. Such as there are, are in their native state, unprepared: no emetics, no cathartics, no mercurials or antimonial remedies, no opiate or elixir, tincture, or any capital remedy. It would make a heart of stone melt to hear the moans and see the distress of the dead and dying. I can scarce pass a tent but I hear men solemnly declaring that they will never engage another campaign without being assured of a better supply of medicines.[83]

Surgeon Beebe described a grim event on the night of July19:

> Last evening we had one of the most severe showers of rain, ever known; it continued almost the whole night, with un-remitted violence; many of their tents were ankle deep in water, many of the sick lay their whole lengths in the water, with one blanket only to cover them. One man having the small pox bad & unable to help himself, and being in a tent alone, which was on ground descending; the current of water, came thro his tent in such plenty, that it covered his head, by which means he drowned. Buried two yesterday, and two more today.[84]

One artillery company succinctly stated the case: "Medicine and surgeons, none. Instruments none. Assistance none."[85]

Gates must have truly been in despair as he contemplated the task that he was charged with, for he had only had a single General Officer remaining to assist him. The Baron de Woedtke had accomplished little in Canada, he was now desperately ill and on his way to Fort George, and he would be dead within the month. The painfully inexperienced

Sullivan would depart in a huff from the army nearly immediately. Only the indomitable Arnold stayed. Gates was more than pleased to have an officer with the abilities, experience, and energy of Benedict Arnold to serve as his subordinate. Gates would write of him: "How happy must every good officer be to find himself seconded by so capable and brave a sprit as that possess'd by Arnold." Regarding the controversies that often accompanied Arnold, Gates would observe, "but men of little merit, are ever jealous of those who have a great deal."[86] Still, Arnold was only one man, and Gates would have to carefully choose where he was to assign him.

The efficient young staff officer John Trumbull reported to Gates the strength of the army:

> I found the whole number of officers and men to be five thousand two hundred, and the sick who required the attentions of an hospital were two thousand eight hundred, so that when they were sent off, with the number of men necessary to row them to the hospital ... there would remain but the shadow of an army. Crown Point was not tenable by such a wreck, and we were ordered to fall back upon Ticonderoga immediately.[87]

The army was in such a state of disorganization that it was not until August 24 that Gates could actually obtain an accurate return of his command. The best estimate of Trumbull's was that Gates had only 2,400 men available to him early in July. Even many of those soldiers were sick, although not ill enough to be evacuated to Fort George.

The shattered remnants of the American Northern Theater Army were absolutely, completely and woefully combat ineffective. The men's exertions to save themselves in the blazing heat of summer, continuously rowing the clumsy, heavy bateaux in unceasing retreat for three weeks, had simply exhausted them. Rations were limited to salted pork, most of it ruined or spoiled, and unbaked flour. Fresh provisions were entirely absent. Even those men present for duty were famished, and lacked strength due to their poor diet. Some regiments had nearly no effectives remaining in their ranks. All of them were badly disorganized. Officers, NCOs, soldiers had simply vanished, dead and rolled into the burial pits of Isle Aux Noix, sick, or deserted. Only a handful had been killed by enemy action during the retreat, in a couple of inconsequential Indian ambushes. Nearly every company and regiment was disordered to some extent. The chain of command was shattered, with officers and NCOs absent or missing. Regimental and company records had been abandoned, if they had ever existed. Uniforms were little more than rags, sweat soaked, mud smeared, torn, rent, worn and ragged. Shoes were wet and rotted from constant immersion, their soles broken, or long since sucked off into the clinging Lake Champlain mud. Muskets were lost, broken, or rusted in the haste of the cross water withdrawal. Critical equipment of every description was similarly lost, broken, worn out, or simply gone. Nobody even knew how much ammunition was available. The war chest was bereft of all funds, which had been expended in Canada.

Morale had vanished. The army had been defeated in its assault at Quebec; routed when the British arrived at Quebec in early May; surrendered and disgraced at the Cedars, the relief force surrounded and captured; the best battalions in the army crushed and ruined at Three Rivers; and then the whole driven in disgrace from Canada. Every time that the army had fought in the previous six months it had been embarrassed and bested.

The army had not retreated so much as it had fled in panic before the British. Spiritual behavior had been abandoned. The chaplains were not preaching or ministering to the soldiers' religious needs. Surgeon Beebe reported with disapproving gloom on July 19, "Cursing and damning to be heard, and idleness to be seen throughout the army."[88]

Discipline had also vanished. The New England colonels would soon see fit to question the judgment of the General Officers of the army following a council of war at Crown Point, and the lower ranks followed their example. At Isle Aux Noix as their soldiers starved, the Colonel and Officers of Greaton's 24th Continental Regiment had feasted on roast beef.

Among the myriad problems were disagreements among the New England, New Jersey, and Pennsylvania soldiers. America was still a collection of thirteen individual colonies, and although the Continental Congress was striving to mold them into a United States there was little feeling of unity among the working class from which the soldiers were drawn. The Pennsylvanians called the New England soldiers Yankees, while the New Englanders responded with the epithet of Buckskins. Nobody liked the New Jersey soldiers. Captain Persifor Frazer with Wayne's 4th Pennsylvania wrote to his wife on July 15, complaining, "There is not that dependence on the New England men that I expected. They make a most wretched appearance away from home as they are not able to endure hardships equal to the other American troops. Above three fourths of them are now unfit for service by what I can learn." He repeated similar sentiments in another letter written September 21: "Two or 3 of the Yankee Colonels have died lately more of them are sick, indeed the most of them look like spectres, miserable creatures they are, the more I am acquainted with them the worse I like them."[89] On July 25, he penned another missive in which he articulated his objections to the New England soldiers: "The miserable appearance and whit is worse the miserable behavior of the Yankees is sufficient enough to make one sick of the service. They are by no means fit to endure hardships; among them there is the strangest mixture of Negroes, Indians, and Whites with old men and children which together with a nasty, lousy appearance makes a most shocking spectacle. No man was ever more disappointed than I have been in respect to them." On August 16 he elaborated on his by now familiar theme: "No man was ever more disappointed in his expectations respecting New Englanders in general than I have been. They are a set of low, dirty, griping, cowardly, lying rascals."[90] Lt. Benjamin Beal, with a Massachusetts regiment, described a near mutiny of the New Jersey Regiment:

> [July] 3 — There was a quarrel with the Jersey men. They were put in the guard house. The Jersey men were a-going to rise & take them out. We turned out the whole army to still them. We put a whole company under guard for their abuse to the officers."[91]

Clearly the New Englanders and Jersey men had the same impressions as the Pennsylvania soldiers possessed.

Gates, succinctly, commanded nothing even vaguely resembling an army. He had simply inherited a mob, a gathering of walking dead, hungry, exhausted and ill, lacking the means to feed themselves, much less construct and defend a garrison to block the advance of one of the mightiest armies and navies in the world.

The army had been brought to this sorry stage by a variety of factors. Leadership in

Canada had been entirely lacking, only Arnold's exemplary valor setting a positive example. Wooster had begun the debacle by failing to come forward to Quebec until four months after the crisis. Rather, he had spent the first months of the year effectively alienating the friendly population of Montreal upon which the army desperately relied. Wooster's first action upon arrival at Quebec had then been to antagonize Arnold and drive him from his post. He had accomplished nothing in a month of command at Quebec, except constructing a visually impressive but ineffective fireship. John Thomas, an apparently able officer with a good reputation, had succeeded Wooster. But Thomas had vacillated upon the arrival of the British on May 6, when only decisive and vigorous actions could have saved the day. Thomas had then made the fateful decision to proscribe inoculation against smallpox, thus signing not only his own personal fate, but also that of the army. Colonel Timothy Bedel had fled from his post upon an impending attack, leaving his command to its own fate. His subordinate, Major Butterfield, had surrendered a strong garrison, well entrenched, successfully defending itself, and with high morale, to a vastly inferior force without artillery. So panicked had Butterfield been that he even failed to spike his cannon, and within days they were being used against their own men. Brigadier General William Thompson was inexperienced and aggressive, and his assault on Three Rivers was rash, poorly considered and woefully executed. His successor, John Sullivan was inexperienced, and apparently uninspiring. Arnold had been the only commander who had consistently demonstrated positive leadership, showing immense fortitude in resisting an anticipated British advance following the failed attack on Quebec, even though he himself was grievously wounded. He had maintained, practically without assistance, the blockade of Quebec for four months in the midst of a horrible Canadian winter. He had aggressively acted at Montreal after the collapse of Bedel and Butterfield at the Cedars, and secured the American strategic rear and left flank. He had taken every possible action to delay the British during the withdrawal from Canada. Arnold had been the last man to leave Canada. His actions in removing all the navigable boats from the Richelieu River valley would frustrate any further British advance for critical months. But even one man, no matter how indefatigable, could not turn the inexorable tide in Canada.

The American army had been dreadfully poorly supported in Canada. Provisions were never sufficient. Transportation was never adequate, both wagons and carts to carry goods by land, or the critical bateaux to provide water mobility. There was not enough artillery, and the heavy siege guns necessary to pursue a siege of Quebec were never available. Clothing was insufficient to turn the cutting winter winds and frigid temperatures of a Canadian winter. Their quarters were congested and crowded, the soldiers dirty and lousy. Soap was a distant memory. Critical equipment, accouterments, and tools of every sort were absent. Ammunition was lacking. There was only a single surgeon at Quebec, the desperately overworked Dr. Senter, and great shortages of bandages, medical instruments and medicines. The supply of every critical article was exhausted far too early in the year.

Many of these shortages could be traced directly to the lack of hard currency, to the absence of the precious coins of silver and gold. The Canadians would not accept paper money under any circumstances, and the Continental army's credit was an unknown entity and had in short order been expended. Without receiving silver and gold the Canadian citizens refused to provide the food, the clothing, the blankets, the firewood, the wagons and carts, the horses, and the oxen so desperately needed, much less provide their own invaluable services as guides and scouts. Once the Canadians' good will had vanished, the American army had found itself in a hostile country, far from home and for all practical purposes abandoned by the Continental Congress.

Once smallpox had broken out in front of Quebec and then viciously multiplied, the American army faced a simple choice. The army either needed to immediately initiate wholesale inoculation, or else abandon Canada to escape the ravages of the *variola* virus. No other viable options were available. The decision was John Thomas' to make, and he fumbled it, choosing to remain in place with thousands of vulnerable soldiers exposed to the ravages of the disease. Smallpox was a horribly cruel disease, nearly perfect at spreading itself through infection, and then ruthlessly efficient at killing, maiming and disfiguring. It was greatly to be feared, and the American soldiers were absolutely terrified of it, and rightfully so. John Adams would lament from the Continental Congress in Philadelphia: "The smallpox is ten times more terrible than Britons, Canadians and Indians together."[92] In the final pronouncement, smallpox had concluded the work that all of the other factors combined had started.

What Horatio Gates observed when the purple rays of the Champlain Valley sun rose above the Vermont hills on the morning of July 2 at Crown Point must have been a depressing, demoralizing, distressing sight. Covering the ramparts and knolls in front of him, as far as the eye could see, were human beings in distress. Soldiers that he was now responsible for were lying dead, dying, sick, and exhausted all around him. They filled the landscape. Even the very air was alive with the sickeningly sweet aroma of the smallpox's pustules. The banks of Lake Champlain were covered with the hulls of dark brown, sodden bateaux, drawn up scant hours ago with water still sloshing in their bottoms, reeking from foul bandages and rotten food accumulating within them. The ramparts of the fort, and the mounds of Chimney Point across the narrow blue lake, were covered with ragged scarecrows wrapped in blankets, a lucky few protected from the evening's dews and noon's blazing rays within streaked gray canvas tents. Horatio Gates was observing a sight seen by very few men in the 250 years of American history. He certainly did not count it as a privilege. Horatio Gates was observing the death of an American army.

As Horatio Gates contemplated the shattered vestiges of the army in front on him in the early morning hours of July 2, he must have quailed at the prospect. And he must have realized that an American army had been catastrophically destroyed in Canada. It would be his fate to build a new one upon the foundations of its ruins.

7

"General Gates Is Putting the Most Disordered Army That Ever Bore the Name Into a State of Regularity and Defense"

Reconstitution at Ticonderoga, July to October 1776

Gates tackled the immense task in front of him immediately. Gates would later write Governor Jonathan Trumbull, the steadfast patriotic governor of Connecticut, regarding his comprehension of the American army that he had just inherited, and his initial actions:

> Upon my first joining the troops, or rather the hospital, at Crown Point all was in the utmost disorder, the pestilence raging[,] not a cannon mounted, the vessels lumber'd with stores, the men dispirited with defeat & fatigue & in short the whole a scene varigated with every distress & disappointment that could conspire to ruin an Army. In this miserable state the first thing to be done was, if possible, to remove the pestilence. Accordingly, the General Officers unanimously resolved to send all the sick & infected to the General Hospital at the South End of Lake George; to remove the main body of the Army to the important pass of Tyconderoga; to send the vessels with the utmost dispatch to be refitted at Skenesborough & to begin to erect strong works upon the ground described in the inclosed plan. These measures, thank the Giver of all Victory, the enemy either have not the means, or the wisdom to prevent.[1]

Sullivan reported the strength of the Northern Theater Army to be 4,290 officers and soldiers "present for duty" on June 12, before the retreat from Sorel and the disastrous stay at Isle Aux Noix. Another 2,500 soldiers were reported as sick or "on command" conducting the attack on Three Rivers.[2] When Gates assumed command of the army at Ticonderoga, it is doubtful that he had even 2,400 effectives, and many of these men were so ill and sick that they could provide little useful duty. Another 2,800 sick men, predominately with smallpox either acquired the natural way or through inoculation, had been dispatched to the hospital at Fort George. Gates had a pitifully small force with which to work at Ticonderoga. Still, even with the desperate circumstances at Ticonderoga and Crown Point, significant and multiple efforts were already underway to reconstruct the American Northern Theater Army. Additional reinforcements shortly began to appear, and at least some of the men down with smallpox at Fort George could be expected to recover and rejoin the army.

Gates had numerous actions to perform, and every one of them was both challenging and difficult. Gates, foremost among everything, had to instill discipline in the army. Military discipline, best defined as organizational cohesion and efficiency, was sadly lacking in the vestiges of an army that had landed at Crown Point in early July 1776.

Gates needed to re-build the regiments, and re-establish the chain of command. Leaders who had died or failed, or simply vanished, had to be replaced with effective officers and NCOs. A system of functional military discipline had to be organized, and then enforced.

Gates' earliest step in that direction was necessarily to implement a routine simply to ensure that his orders were accurately recorded, transmitted, understood, and complied with. As a component of this effort, Gates directed the establishment and maintenance of what were called orderly books. Every brigade, regiment, and major detachment (such as an Artillery Company) was mandated to maintain an orderly book. Each and every morning, rain or shine, at a duly designated hour, the Regimental Adjutant and Orderly Sergeants of each company had to report to the Adjutant General of the army. Here, the Adjutant General issued the daily orders, to include the Password and Countersign for the day. The results of courts-martial were also published. Necessary details were assigned. The Regimental Adjutant and Orderly Sergeants then had to copy all of these orders into their orderly books. Once that task was fulfilled, the Regimental Adjutant would return with them to the Regimental Commander, who in turn would issue appropriate regimental orders. If necessary, the Brigade and Division Commander issued their own orders. Each company would then be called to formation, and the Company Orderly Sergeant would read the published orders to his soldiers. The regiment would then be called to formation, and the Regimental Adjutant would amplify these orders with any regimental, brigade or division orders. Then the regiment's day would begin. Although frequently repetitive, for many of the orders issued such as guard and fatigue details rarely varied, these orderly books provide an effective record of what was occurring within the daily routine of the Northern Theater Army. Many of these books have survived, and it is instructive that considerable numbers were initiated in July or August at Ticonderoga. These orderly books serve as permanent, written records of Gates' efforts to instill discipline and administration into his army.

Although Gates had taken great strides to insure that orders were smoothly disseminated, they also had to be obeyed. Gates, with his long experience in the British army, well knew how to handle situations like the absence of good order and discipline in the American army, and he wasted little time in announcing to the army through his actions that rigid discipline was going to be enforced. Lieutenant Beal noted for July 6, "There was 3 of the Jersey whipped for abuse to the officers. They had 78 stripes apiece and drummed through the Camps with a halter on their necks." On July 11 Captain Charles Cushing and the remainder of the 24th Continental Infantry received a vivid demonstration of Gates' determination to establish order within the American camp:

> At 6 o'clock the Regiment paraded and went to see some prisoners whipped. One received 150 lashes for mutiny. Two received 39 for stealing. Five more received 39 each; one of which was for sleeping on sentry.[3]

The punishment of 39 lashes was a common one in the American army. Gates established this as a standard number of lashes, based upon biblical tradition. The actual Old Testament reference to this proscription is in Deuteronomy 25:2–3: "Then it shall be, if the wicked man deserve to be beaten, that the judge shall cause him to lie down, and to be beaten before his face, according to the measure of his wickedness, by number. Forty stripes he may give him, he shall not exceed; lest, if he should exceed, and beat him above these with many stripes, then thy brother should be dishonored before thine eyes." Forty was a number in heavy use in the Hebrew Bible. Some commentators believe that the ancient Hebrews stopped at 39 in order to make sure they didn't pass 40 and thus violate the Mosaic Law. Other commentators suggest that the ancients believed that the 40th lash was to put the person to death, hence any punishment would have to cease at 39. Given the strong Old Testament beliefs espoused by many American soldiers, particularly those from New England, Gates' incorporation of biblical values into the army's judicial system was viewed as being well founded and entirely appropriate.

Quite rapidly, the sight of malcreants receiving 39 lashes in front of their regiments became common. On August 26, no less than six men were ordered to receive punishment for desertion, along with one Corporal punished for "neglect of duty." Other men were punished for a range of miscellaneous offenses such as "mutinous conduct" and "leaving his post when placed as sentry before he was relieved."[4] And this day was typical. It didn't take long for the Continental soldiers at Ticonderoga to discover that the failure to perform one's duties, or to simply adhere to orders, in an army commanded by Horatio Gates was a recipe for a relatively poorly decorated back.

Horatio Gates discovered in this process that even routine orders were not adhered to in this rudimentary American army, and he had to rigorously enforce the standards of the army at regular and frequent intervals. Gates ordered on August 15 that fatigue parties were "to eat their breakfasts before they come over and bring their dinners with them." This was duly ordered so that the working parties wouldn't waste daylight while they marched to and from their camps for dinner. However, even such a simple order had to be reinforced the next day, August 16: "120 Men 1 Capt. 2 Sub's 4 Serjeants 4 Corporal's from Col. Reed for fatigue tomorrow to be paraded at 7 o'clock in the morning, they positively ordered to bring their dinners with them."[5] Similar problems arose when such a mundane issue as regiments returning spare tentage had to be forced to happen. On October 17 Gates required that spare tents be turned in, probably to insure that additional tentage was available for field hospitals in the event of a British assault. He accordingly issued orders in his orderly book: "The Quarter Master of each regiment to deliver the spare tents belonging to their respective Corps to Col. Morgan Lewis D. Q.M. G. at 4 Oclock this Afternoon. Col. Lewis will give his receipt for the same." On October 18, Gates had to formally issue a reprimand to nearly the entire army: "The Genl expect an exact obedience to the Order of yesterday respecting the delivery of all the spare tents to the QM Genl only two Regiments have yet done their duty according to that order. St. Clairs & late Bedels."[6] One has to almost imagine Gates holding his head in his hands at night, bemoaning his fate to command such a young, inexperienced army.

Sadly enough, at times the discipline problem was more severe than just forgetting their dinners. On August 21 Gates noted:

> Marauding is become so frequent that the General expects that every officer will in a spirited manner exert himself to prevent it and bring the perpetrators to exemplary

punishment. Last night a poor inhabitant was robbed of all he himself and his distressed family had to depend upon for their winter supply by certain villains who said they belonged to the Jersey Regiment. There are more villains that wear blue than those suspected in the Jersey Regiments. The General recommends it to the commanding officer of the Fourth Brigade to endeavour by every means in his power to discover and bring to justice all persons suspected of pillaging and marauding. This army is paid to protect, and not to pilfer the inhabitants.[7]

Still, as a result of Gates' attention to instilling good order and discipline throughout the army, soldiers rapidly began to stand straighter, pay closer attention to orders, and to be more attentive in their duties. And this precisely was Gates' intention. Nearly every day throughout the long summer and fall, courts-martial were conducted at Ticonderoga. It was a long and painful process, but the army learned. By as early as August 26 the Reverend Emerson wrote his wife: "We have here ... five fine regiments from the Southern Colonies, Pennsylvania & the Jerseys, dressed in uniform, that appear as well disciplined as the best of the British troops."[8] And this was not idle speculation, for Emerson had seen much of the British troops from the doorstep of his Concord, Massachusetts, rectory on April 19, 1775.

Gates also had to restore the physical and spiritual health of his soldiers, and improve their morale. He had to identify precisely what uniforms, equipment, military accouterments, weapons, ammunition, and rations were required for each regiment. He had to then request these items from Schuyler in Albany, transport them on Lake Champlain, receive them, inventory them to ensure that they had not been rifled along the way, and then issue them to the proper units. To restore physical health he needed clothing, tents, blankets, wholesome rations, fresh food, and liquors and beer for the men to drink rather than the putrid Lake Champlain water.

Besides the infantrymen and artillerymen that Gates would depend upon to construct his fortifications and do the fighting, he also needed a wide and diverse range of specialists. He required surgeons and surgeon mates to care for his sick and injured, and medicines, instruments and bandages for them to employ. He demanded spades, shovels, axes, picks, and specialized engineering tools to construct new fortifications. He needed engineers with their specialized drafting and surveying equipment to direct the construction of those fortifications. He needed carpenters and tools to construct carriages for the cannon, blacksmiths and their tools to manufacture the hardware for the gun carriages, and to repair and maintain the critical bateaux. Tinsmiths (or whitesmiths as they were also known) and their tools were needed to repair mess kettles, canteens, cups, and other tin objects. Farriers and their tools were needed to shoe the oxen and horses that provided the raw muscle power for the army. Harness makers and their tools were needed to manufacture and repair the harnesses for these animals, the leather cartridge boxes to protect the soldiers' precious gunpowder, and the leather harnesses that the artillerymen used to move the guns by hand.

To recruit these men, Gates first turned to his own soldiers. Orders were frequently issued instructing commanders to identify men with specific trades or skills:

> August 12, 1776. Inquiry to be made if there are any Block makers in any of the corps their names Regiments and Companies to be reported to the Deputy Adjutant General this evening.

Block makers manufactured block and tackle out of wood and iron, an indispensable piece of equipment if heavy weights such as cannon or ships' sails were to be moved. On July 27, Arnold's Brigade produced 25 shingle makers, who were ordered to begin producing wooden shingles on a full time basis on Mount Independence.[9] On August 24 Colonel Ephraim Wheelock's Regiment of Massachusetts Militia provided fourteen brickmakers to the various construction endeavors then underway:

> The General orders Lt. Hoit with fourteen men that understands brickmaking to parade tomorrow morning at six O'clock at the General's Quarters, there to receive instructions.[10]

On August 12 a call was sent out for blacksmiths: "An inquiry to be made if there are any Blacksmakers [i.e. Blacksmiths] in any of the corps their names Regt & Companies to be reported to the Deputy Adjutant General this Evening."[11]

The appointment of Gates was, of course, a substantial contribution in its own right. But without being provided the raw materials to work with, even his best efforts would be ineffective. Given the staggering quantity and diversity of men and materials that Gates urgently needed and Schuyler had to procure, it is questionable which man had the more challenging job.

Schuyler had to enlist reinforcements for the Northern Theater Army; appoint effective leaders to command them; organize, arm and equip them; and then forward them to Ticonderoga. Schuyler also had to ensure that adequate resources were available to Gates. The regiments at Ticonderoga had no uniforms, no equipment, their weapons were in deplorable condition, and they were low on ammunition. Gates also had no war chest to make local purchases. Schuyler had to provide Gates with money, while at the same time raising substantial quantities of sufficient money at Albany to fund his own not inconsiderable efforts. Schuyler had to acquire and move black gunpowder to the army, obtain lead and manufacture musket balls, and issue numerous contracts with the relatively small local iron foundries to cast cannonballs.

For every single item of equipment, a reputable vendor had to be located. Then, a contract had to be negotiated. In some cases, an advanced payment to tide over the manufacturer had to be furnished, requiring ready cash or currency. The contractor then had to manufacture a prototype or prototypes of the required items, and an authorized and competent inspector had to validate that the piece of equipment satisfied the needs of the Continental army. Once a sample had been approved, then the contractor fulfilled the terms of the contract. The completed items then had to be selectively inspected and accepted, safely packaged for transportation, and of course the contractor paid to satisfy the public credit. Finally, whatever the finished objects were had to be shipped by land or water to where they were needed, whether that might be Fort George, Skenesboro, Ticonderoga or Crown Point. Invariably, there was some amount of wastage. This had to be estimated at the beginning, and then precisely calculated and accounted for at the end.

Even with all the challenges that they faced, some of Schuyler's and Gates' problems could be solved relatively easily. Gates made no effort at attempting to reconcile the hotheaded Pennsylvanians and stubborn New Englanders, and the New Jersey regiments were in any case a lost cause. Gates simply kept them apart. The New England regiments were all dispatched to Mount Independence. The Pennsylvanians were assigned to the abandoned French lines on the Heights of Carillon. The New Jersey regiments were exiled to the sandy flats of Ticonderoga. A quarter mile of water thus separated the New England regiments from the Pennsylvanians. Steep and nearly inaccessible slopes separated the Pennsylvanians from the New Jerseys. And there was marginally less animosity between the men from the two adjacent colonies. Gates also ensured that soldiers' days were filled with frequent drill and guard duty, and if the men had any free time after that he put them under Baldwin's firm hand constructing fortifications. As an example of the regular drill that Gates' men performed, on September 19 Colonel Anthony Wayne ordered his 4th Pennsylvania Battalion in regimental orders:

> They will also every morning & evening in place of manning the lines, be training their people in the manual exercise, wheeling and firing by grand and sub divisions and forming the line of impression. The officers will be careful in turning out all the soldiers as well as servants and others morning and evening.[12]

Gates clearly subscribed to the George Washington school of military leadership, that a weary, physically exhausted, dead-tired soldier is a soldier that lacks the energy to get into much trouble, and is therefore a good soldier. The men from the different colonies

Fort Ticonderoga from Mount Independence. This photograph, looking northwest from the site of the large star fort at Mount Independence, depicts how close that fort was to Mount Independence (within easy cannon shot), how narrow Lake Champlain is at this point, and how Fort Ticonderoga and Mount Independence entirely commanded Lake Champlain (author's collection).

might not get along without a common foe to occupy them. But Gates made sure that they were functionally separated and that excessive energies were productively expended, and the result was a relative absence of hostilities, the occasional recreational skirmish between Pennsylvania and New Jersey notwithstanding.

Gates instituted close controls over the soldier's appearance, issued them soap, and even dictated how the soldiers were supposed to cook their food. He instituted strict instructions regarding where the vaults or houses of office were to be constructed. All of these actions were intended to improve the health of the soldiers.

A typical example is that Colonel Anthony Wayne on July 18 appointed a barber for each company, to keep the men shaved, and their hair "plaited and powdered." Gates instructed on July 22 that "The Commissary will deliver all the soap he has in store" to every regiment. Shortly another, larger supply of soap arrived, and Gates further ordered that the Commissary issue eight pounds per every one hundred men on July 28, and no less than sixteen pounds of soap per every one hundred men in the camp for the week of August 3. He also specified that "afterwards he [the Commissary] is to issue the usual Continental allowance until further orders."

It was stressed to the soldiers that food was to be boiled in stews and soups, rather than being broiled. In fact, typically soldiers had only mess kettles issued to them, thus forcing them to this single manner of food preparation.[13] The prevailing belief was that food prepared in this manner was considerably healthier for the soldiers. This was, in fact, absolutely true, although the medical officers of the time did not comprehend the actual reason. Modern health practitioners known that when raw meat is broiled over a fire by less than skillful cooks it is often under cooked. The result is that many soldiers were eating food that had not been sufficiently prepared to remove the various types of bacteria that can directly cause food poisoning, which was likely the source of much of the diarrhea and dysentery that was rampant in any military camp of the era. However, if meat was prepared in a soup or stew, the food was boiled, and thus sterilized. Gates' General Orders of August 12 dictated that officers "be particularly careful that the persons who officiate as cooks makes soup."[14] Gates reiterated on September 4, as the Orderly Book of Wheelock's Regiment of Massachusetts Militia attested, "The general insists that no broiling, frying ... be done within the camp."[15]

Gates issued the following orders regarding "necessaries":

> July 15th 1776. The General anxious to preserve the new encampment clean and free from infection recommends in the strongest manner to the Commanding officers of Regiments to have their Necessaries fixed upon the brink of precipices or such places where they are least obnoxious. If there is a necessity off having any dug in the front of the Regiments care must be taken to have them frequently cover'd and no person suffer'd to ease himself in any other part of the incamp'mt.[16]

Nearly every surviving Orderly Book has similar regimental, brigade or divisional orders regarding these overlooked historically, but functionally very important facilities. On August 16 the Regimental Orderly Book for Colonel Mott's Connecticut Regiment, then stationed at Skenesboro, mentioned, "It is likewise desired that the commanding officers of Regiments see that the quartermasters see that the vaults are dug that the camp may be kept clean."[17]

Gates regularly consulted with the surgeons at Ticonderoga to attempt to formulate approaches to enhance the soldiers' health, which was always a problem at the fort. Dr. Samuel Kennedy, with Wayne's 4th Pennsylvania Battalion, reported to his wife on September 2 documenting one of Gates' initiatives to alleviate this problem:

> Two days since all the surgeons on the ground were called together by order of the General, who required a true statement of the sick, the quantum of medicines, the necessary comforts required, and the most salutary measures for the preservation of the army, etc. He also required that an examination might take place relative to the mode of practice in each department. Your Dr. Friend was honored with the Presidency. We met conformably to order, went through the business ... and made report accordingly, which the General accepted very politely and gave out in General Orders.[18]

An ultimately successful attempt to improve the health of the soldiers involved the brewing of the previously discussed spruce beer. The soldiers were well aware that "the lake air and water was very unhealthy." William Chamberlin of Stark's 5th Continental Regiment from New Hampshire described how he conducted a spruce beer brewing operation at Ticonderoga:

> Some time in the latter part of August ... while lingering under the effects of the climate and bad water, Sergeant Seth Spring and myself made an excursion across the lake, and procured some boughs of spruce with a view to make some spruce beer. We gathered a quantity of spicknard or Indian root, and with two quarts of molasses made a barrel of beer, which proved to be very good, but before we had drank up and given away the first barrel, we made another, and we sold the second barrel by the mug, as every one who had drank of it was calling for more. Finding it to be in demand, we concluded to pursue the business. Spring was dispatched to Fort George and bought two barrels of molasses. I hired the soldiers to bring water to my hut, procured spruce and spicknard, and with a kettle which held about 4 or 5 gallons, I boiled my spruce and roots, filled my barrels with cold water, and mixing this warm liquid with the molasses, we produced a barrel of excellent beer, which we sold as fast as we could make for three dollars a barrel. This not only recruited my own health, but the health of almost all who used it.... In this way the army was generally supplied with beer, instead of bad water, which greatly recruited the emaciated army, and tended to set them on their legs.[19]

Chamberlin recalled that "at the end of six or seven weeks Spring and myself divided 300 dollars, which we had cleared by the business. By this time many others had engaged in the brewing." The American army eventually regulated the price of spruce beer because so many brewers such as Chamberlin and Spring had engaged in the profitable business at Ticonderoga.

The "spicknard" that Chamberlin mentions is actually American Spikenard, also known as Indian root. Its scientific name is Aralia racemosa, and it belongs to the family Araliaceae (ginseng). Spikenard grows widely in the Adirondacks, and Chamberlin would not have had any difficulty finding it in the woods near Ticonderoga. When the Chaplain Ammi Robbins had the "camp disorder" on Mount Independence in early October he noted in his journal, "Spikenard is of special service in this disorder."[20] Widely used in the 18th and 19th centuries as an herb or tonic alleged to treat many disorders, it has a taste much like sarsaparilla, and it would have imparted a flavor somewhat like modern root beer to the finished beverage.

Indeed, the entrepreneurial spirit was alive and well within the American army, and did much to encourage its health. Most likely, neither the spruce tips or the spikenard actually helped the soldiers, but by consuming beer that had been boiled in its production, they were drinking sterilized water rather than infected or contaminated water. Naturally, their health immediately improved, suggesting that sobriety may not always be a friend to a soldier.

Perhaps the most critical aspect of health care for the soldiers, and at the same time a potential source of manpower for the army, was obviously the huge general hospital recently established at Fort George. If these soldiers could be healed and returned to duty, they would represent a significant reinforcement to the army. Thus, establishing an effective and efficient general hospital at Fort George was critical to increasing Gates' force at Ticonderoga. To comprehend the magnitude of Potts' assignment, by mid–July he was operating the largest single hospital on the North American continent, and most likely in the history of the colonies.[21] And he was doing this on the southern end of Lake George, an entirely remote site barely settled by a veritable handful of inhabitants, and three day's transit from Albany (the nearest city) with good weather. It was a daunting prospect.

Potts did the best that he could under the circumstances. He had wooden barracks or sheds constructed around the single Fort George redoubt. A committee of Congress inspecting Fort George at the conclusion of the campaign in November found "that there is a range of buildings erected, convenient for the purpose."[22] However, the committee also found that there had been limits to what Potts had been able to achieve: "The sick suffered much from want of good female nurses, and comfortable bedding, many of those poor creatures being obliged to lie upon the bare boards." No architectural description of these sheds has been located. Most likely, they were three-sided, simple wooden structures with initially bark or brush roofs that were converted to wooden shingles as time and resources permitted, with dirt floors, that contained harsh bunks constructed of unadorned wooden boards. Even these crude structures were prone to vandalism, as a Fort George Garrison Orderly Book entry on July 26 noted:

> Regimental Orders Fort George July 26th 1776
>
> Parole London.
>
> One Corporal and 3 privates to be detached from the Main Guard tomorrow morning as a guard at the hospital. They are to take care of the boards and to suffer none to be taken away by the carpenters without order Dr. Stringer or Colonel Buel. Guard to be mounted to morrow as usual[.] Officers for tomorrow Captain Wright[.]
>
> Petter Gansevoort, Lt. Coll.[23]

In the early days of the hospital's operation, these sheds were clearly less than optimal. Reverend Ebenezer David, a Rhode Island chaplain, passed through Fort George on his way to Ticonderoga with his regiment in late August:

> Pass on to Fort George in a wagon box and baggage, here I found near 2,000 sick between 20 & 30 dying in twenty four hours. Colonel Read now Brigadier laying very low. But when I came to where the large sheds called Hospitals were erected, I stood

still & beheld with admiration & sympathetic anguish what neither tongue nor pen can describe.[24]

Efforts were made to ensure that adequate number of nurses were available at the smallpox hospital at Fort George. The following orders were issued to the Pennsylvania regiments from Army Headquarters at Fort Ticonderoga on June 13:

> One woman from each company of each of the Pennsylvania Battalions now at this post to be drafted as soon as possible and sent to the General Hospital at Fort George to nurse the sick. They will have the customary allowance of provisions from Dr. Stringer, director of the Hospital there.[25]

Besides the women, it is documented that a number of soldiers, presumably those who had survived smallpox and were thus immune to the disease, were detailed as male nurses to the sick. In late July no less than 106 soldiers were serving in this capacity.[26]

Almost immediately upon the establishment of the general hospital, orders were given to ensure that quarantine was maintained between the smallpox patients, and those healthy soldiers or at least those without smallpox. Garrison orders were issued on July 16:

> Regimental Orders Fort George July the 16th 1776
>
> Parole Washington
>
> All officers and soldiers are forbid to go among the small pox[,] and by no manner enoculate or sufer them selves to be encocualted on pain to be punished without the benefit of a Court Martial[.] Guards to be mounted as usual[.] Officers for tomorrow Captain Wright[.] By order of the Commanding Officer[.]
>
> Petter B Tiars Adjutant.[27]

To maintain this quarantine throughout the army, inoculation was strictly forbidden, and every soldier detected to be stricken with smallpox was immediately sent to Fort George. Gates issued peremptory orders to the entire army mandating this on August 19. Gates was adamant that any man stricken with smallpox "be immediately removed to Lake George."[28] He issued stringent instructions on August 19 that:

> Every Officer, Non Commissioned & Soldier who shall hereafter be infected with the Small Pox be immediately sent to the General Hospital at Lake George but previous to their being sent they are to make oath as follows: 'I Swear solemnly by the Ever Living God that I have not received the infection of the small pox by inoculation or any other operation internal or external. But have taken the same in a manner unknown to me & I firmly by the Oath I now take in the Natural Way and no other. So help me God.' In case any man refused to take the above oath his conscience accusing him that it would be perjury to do so he is to declare the name of the person who inoculated him & the place where it was done that the perpetrator of so villainous an act may be instantly brought to punishment.[29]

The concern was that the soldiers, still fearing smallpox, would again begin to inoculate themselves. Without proper precautions such as total quarantine of those being inoculated, another outbreak of smallpox was certain to follow.

Thus, Gates was ensuring that self-inoculation without quarantine, as had swept the army in Canada, would not recur. As another example of the care and attention which

Gates paid to the extermination of smallpox, he ensured that only soldiers that had been properly inoculated and therefore were safe from the disease were routed through Fort George where they would almost certainly be exposed to it. On September 6 Gates informed Schuyler:

> The enclosed letter from Lieutenant Colonel Gansevoort, obliges me to send Colonel Phinney's New Hampshire Regiment to Fort George, to bateau the flour from thence. This regiment came lately from Boston, where they were all inoculated and cleansed from the small pox.[30]

During the late summer, when the Continental army was engaged in a frantic, furious ship building effort at Skenesboro, the need to maintain the army free from smallpox still retained priority. Carpenters and militiamen who were detected to have inoculated themselves were quarantined by absolutely rigidly enforced orders before they could even reach Skenesboro. Desperate as Gates's army was for carpenters and workers, the army's leadership and officers were even more desperate to maintain its health.[31]

Potts faced a mighty struggle to first establish, and then operate, an effective hospital.[32] His correspondence provides evidence of the trials and tribulations that he had to overcome. On August 8 he wrote Gates:

> The return of the sick remaining in the General Hospital, which you were pleased to order to be made weekly, will be delivered you by Captain Craig. I hope you will not attribute its late appearance at this time to any neglect of my part, as I can with truth assure your Honor nothing is left undone in my power to reduce every matter relative to the Hospital into order. The number of the sick being very great, they employ our whole time; and having but one clerk, who has to enter the names of every person admitted, discharged, died or deserted, as well as to superintend the issuing of provisions, makes it almost impossible to comply with your order so punctually as I could wish.[33]

Potts described the magnitude of his problem to surgeon John Morgan, the chief physician of the Continental army, in a letter written from Fort George on August 1:

> The distressed situation of the sick here is not to be described. Without clothing, without comforts, or a shelter sufficient to screen them from the weather, I am sure your known humanity will be effected when I tell you upwards of one thousand sick and wounded in the sheds & labouring under the various disorders of dysentery, bilious putrid fever, and the effects of confluent smallpox. To attend the large number we have four seniors [surgeons] and four mates, exclusive of myself & our little shop doth not afford a grain of jalap, ipecac, bark, salts, opium & sundry other capital articles & nothing of the kind to be had in this quarter. In this dilemma our inventions are exhausted for succedaneums [substitutes] but we shall go on doing the best we can in the hopes of a speedy supply.[34]

One of the great problems, as it had been for the army in Canada, was a habitual shortage of medicines for the surgeons. Until July 24 the only medicines at Fort George were "the few that Dr. Potts brought with him" in the large medical chest that Morgan had initially issued to Potts at New York City. Finally, in desperation, Gates had dispatched Medical Director Dr. Stringer on July 29 to New York City to personally procure medicines. General Gates recognized the drastic shortages of supplies, and assured his soldiers in an unprecedented order issued from his headquarters and read to every man in the Army on August 31:

> The Officers & Soldiers may be satisfied that the Genl has left no means in his power untried to procure medicines and every comfort for the sick of this army which the station and circumstances of this place will admit. The Director of the Genl Hospital in this department Dr. Stringer was sent to New York 33 days ago with positive orders to return the instant he had provided the drugs and medicines [sic] so much wanted. Since this repeated letters have been wrote to N York and Philadelphia, setting forth in the strongest terms the pressing necessity of an immediate supply of those articles. The General is credibly informed that Principle Surgeon from the General Hospital at N York has been Dispatch'd from there above a fortnight ago with a supply of medicines and apprehends that the badness of the weather and road has alone prevented his arrival. As the soldiers duty to maintain the post he is orders to defend, the same climate and season that affects us affects our enemies and the favour [sic] of the Almighty to whom we have appeal'd will if we trust in him preserve us from slavery and death. The Genl recommends to the Surgeons of the Different Regiments to communicate to each other the state of the sick in their respective corps their various diseases the remedies principally wanted, and the comforts which are most in requests, for he will leave nothing unattempted in his power to provide for what he can command for their recovery. The General also desires the Medical Gentlemen will consult and adopt the most proper measures for obtaining these salutary purposes.[35]

In the meantime, Dr. Morgan had dispatched a young and aggressive physician, Dr. James McHenry, to scour Philadelphia for drugs; and dispatched a promising pharmacist, Andrew Craigie, to Fort George "to act as an apothecary." What Craigie, or any other pharmacist, was supposed to do without medicines was not specified by Morgan. It appears that the Continental army's Medical Director must have hoped that Craigie would be able to locate suitable wild herbs in the Adirondacks woods around Lake George and the Hudson River for the succor of the ill.

Dr. Stringer helped the situation but little, wandering around Philadelphia and New York City without obtaining any meaningful of supply of drugs, and apparently confusing all ongoing efforts in the process. It was not until September 7 that Stringer was able to dispatch Potts a small supply of medicines, and he then transferred his feeble and confused efforts to New England "to ransack that country of those articles we want." Stringer then wandered about New England for several months without returning to the army or shipping any additional medicines to Potts, and he was eventually dismissed.

Gates was absolutely furious regarding Stringer's failure and extended absence, and the insufficiency of essential medicines. He addressed a blistering letter to the Continental Congress and Dr. Morgan on August 22:

> The troops here are suffering inexpressible distress for want of medicines ... instantly lay this letter before General Washington, and receive his commands for sending a supply of medicines to Doctor Potts, at Lake George. Not one of the ten chests of medicines, which you told me at New York were sent to the ten regiments that marched in the spring from thence, have ever been received by either of those regiments.... Many of the Regimental Surgeons here have not any medicines, nor do I believe there is a pound of bark in the whole camp. I cannot be long answerable for the consequences of the shameful neglect of the Army in this department.[36]

When conditions at Ticonderoga had been sufficiently organized that a comprehensive inventory of medicines could be made, the true gravity of the duress that the army had been under was revealed. Two of the regiments and a number of the independent companies reported "no medicines exclusive of private property." One regiment at Mount Independence had only two ounces of bark and less than that of opium. Surgeon Benjamin Alison of the 1st Pennsylvania Battalion reported, "I have no amputating instruments, no lancet, nor probe, or any kind of instruments. No lint, or bandages, but a few simple rollers."[37] The 6th Pennsylvania Battalion, occupying an advance post at Crown Point, was among the better off of the individual regiments. Their medical chest contained half a pound of bark, and two ounces of opium. This was still an order of magnitude below the recommended minimum for a battalion medical chest of twenty pounds of bark and two pounds of opium.[38] John Trumbull wrote to Potts at Gates' direction from Ticonderoga on August 31:

> Have your medicines arrived? Have Stringer and McHenry made their appearance yet? Our people fall sick by dozens, and not a penny worth of medicine have we for them, even in the most virulent disorders. The moment you receive any supply share it for God's sake with us. We need it almost more than you.... You know 'tis no matter whether the people die for real want of medicine, or because they think they want it —'tis death in either case.[39]

Potts was aggressive in requesting aid and assistance.[40] In mid–August he wrote the Albany Committee of Correspondence, the Salisbury [New Hampshire] Committee of Correspondence, and others throughout the immediate locale:

> As the General Hospital at Fort George which is at present crowded and in great want of old linen for lint and bandages, etc. we therefore entreat all lovers of their country and humanity to send all the old shirts, sheets, aprons, etc. they can spare ... as soon as possible, as well as the thanks of the public, they should receive a good price for every article.

Potts also requested "the good women to dry and cure as many herbs for the use of said Hospital as they can procure. Sage, Balms, Mallows, and Wormwood." The response was rapid, and gratifying. Salisbury sent linen to Potts, which he forwarded to Ticonderoga in response to Trumbull's pleas. The Albany Committee also responded rapidly, on August 23:

> Thereupon Resolved. That copies be made of the said advertisement, and that [Doctor] Jacob Roseboom Junior in the City of Albany and the Chairman of the respective District Committees receive the linen and herbs that may be brought to them and give a certificate to the persons that bring it.[41]

With this and other assistance, Potts and his overworked staff slowly but surely worked miracles. By mid–September, medicines finally began to arrive at Fort George.[42] On August 28 Gates could formally state in writing to Washington, with what must have been considerable gratitude to Potts and a huge sense of relief, "the small pox is now perfectly removed from the Army."[43] Of course, this was achieved not through any single miracle or even through any set of miracles. Potts and his staff had persevered through simple hard, exhausting, unrelenting labor at the southern end of Lake George throughout two months. Much considerable and unremitting work remained to be done. Sick, injured and wounded were always pouring into the American hospitals. There were never enough surgeons, nurses, and medical instruments. Medicines, facilities, and bandages were always to be found only in short supply. Yet, the crisis in health care of the Northern Theater Army had been passed. By mid–October, the general hospital had excess capacity, and was returning soldiers to service with the army.

In addition to the physical well-being of the army, Gates did not forget the spiritual health of the soldiers. The chaplains were directed to resume their duties, and begin regular sermons to the army, both of which had been sorely neglected during the precipitous retreat from Canada. From this point forward, the chaplains of the army began to punctually celebrate every Sabbath, and present weekly sermons to every regiment. Religion was extremely important to the predominately New England soldiers, and most of the soldiers routinely noted the Lord's Day in their journals. Many of these American soldiers believed that they had lost God's protection and assistance in Canada, and that they had to achieve redemption through a return to worship if they were to defeat the British at Ticonderoga. Typical is the account of Joseph Hewes, describing the American retreat:

> Our Northern Army has left Canada and retreated to Ticonderoga and Crown Point. The Smallpox has made great havoc among them. Several Regiments have not enough well men to row all their sick over the Lake and men were drafted from other Regiments to do that service. In short the Army has melted away in a little time as if the Destroying Angle had been sent on purpose to demolish them as he did the children of Israel.[44]

The Orderly Book for Colonel Ephraim Wheelock's Regiment of Massachusetts Militia at Fort Ticonderoga issued brigade orders on Friday, August 23, that mandated attendance at religious services: "The drummers to beat the church call for prayers at sunrise at which time the Regiments are to turn out and attend in order."[45] On Friday, August 30 the necessity of the soldiers to attend prayer services was strictly enforced in Brigade Orders:

> It [is or was] observed that one whole Regt was absent last night at prayer time and a considerable part of some of the others. The practice which by no means is to be approved of is therefore expected that every officer as well as soldier for the future will pay the strictest attention to prayer orders issued from superiors as they may depend upon every neglect of duty being properly noticed.

Colonel Elisha Porter recalled attending a sermon by Chaplain Breck on July 7, "from James 4:10, a good one."[46] Chaplain Breck's selection of this sermon directly supports the perceived need for the American army to achieve redemption with the Lord, and again grant his blessings over the army's endeavors, for James 4:10 states, "Humble yourselves before the Lord and he will lift you up." Dr. Lewis Beebe recorded on Sunday, July 7, being "entertained with a sermon, by Mr. Spring, from Second of Timothy, Chapter 3rd & 16 verse" and the next Sabbath by "the Reverend Mr. Robbins, from Isaiah, 8–9 & 10, delivered in the presence of two Regiments."[47] Chaplain Spring's selection from Timothy was probably not particularly inspiring for the soldiers, for it is a simple call to read and practice "the truth and divinity of the scriptures" as surgeon Beebe described it. However, the selection of Chaplain Robbins from Isaiah was particularly appropriate for soldiers who had recently been driven in defeat from Canada. The Isaiah text begins with a resounding and inspiring exultation to "raise your war cry you nations and be shattered. Prepare for battle and be shattered." The prophet Isaiah warns the enemies of Judah and Jerusalem (most notably in this case the Assyrian empire), that despite their apparent superiority they will be defeated because "God is with us." The King James version of the Holy Bible, which would have seen most frequent use in 1776, renders Isaiah 8:9–10 this way:

> Associate yourselves, O ye people, and ye shall be broken in pieces; and give ear, all ye of far countries: gird yourselves, and ye shall be broken in pieces; gird yourselves, and ye shall be broken in pieces.
> Take counsel together, and it shall come to nought; speak the word, and it shall not stand: for God is with us.

Chaplain Robbins was thus trying to strengthen the soldiers' spirits in a time of apparent defeat. His message was simple, and particularly appropriate for the situation that the Northern Theater Army regiments found themselves in at Crown Point: "We'll win in the end because God is with us. The evil, powerful empire is going to be shattered." Chaplain Robbins himself recalled seeing "a vast concourse of people, the General and great numbers of the principal officers attended."[48]

From this time forth, Gates would ensure that the spiritual well-being of his army received careful attention, and was not neglected. The Reverend William Emerson, a distinguished minister from Concord, Massachusetts, remarked in a letter to his wife:

> I spent the last evening very agreeably at General Gates, and supped upon venison; the General is extremely affable and courteous ... though he does not pretend to a great deal of religion himself, yet he looks upon it, that a Chaplain is a very necessary officer in the Army, and treats them with more respect than many of his Officers under him.[49]

His New England soldiers, in particular, deeply appreciated Gates' ministrations in this vein.

Another challenge that Gates faced was a problem throughout the history of the Continental army, and was a particular difficulty that would plague General George Washington throughout the entire war. Gates was regularly bedeviled by animosity, jealousy, and conflict within the officers' ranks. Fort Ticonderoga seemed to have experienced more than its fair share of dissension of this ilk, which had the potential to seriously erode the morale, discipline, and combat effectiveness of Gates' army. Given the nature of the retreat from Canada, and the numerous reverses that American fortunes had sustained in that country, it is not surprising that such disorders echoed throughout the officer corps. A typical outbreak occurred within Colonel Anthony Wayne's 4th Pennsylvania Battalion, when on August 20 the Quartermaster of the Regiment, John Harper, noted:

> A duel happened between Major Hausagger and Adjutant Ryan, wherein the Major had his ear split and wounded in the side. The Adjutant received a slight wound in his cheek and some cuts on his head and arms. The Major arrested the Adjutant in consequence of which a General Court Martial was called.

The incident was concluded when the Brigade Commander admonished Ryan at the head of the Brigade.[50] The single worst case, although it is merely representative of numerous such incidents, occurred between Brigadier General Benedict Arnold and several other officers just as Arnold was preparing to take charge of the fleet. Early in August a court-martial was convened at Fort Ticonderoga, to review charges against a Canadian officer loyal to the American patriot cause, Colonel Moses Hazen. Arnold maintained that during the retreat from Canada Hazen had refused to accept stores procured for the army by Arnold at Fort Chambly, had failed to secure said Continental army stores, and had permitted them to be subsequently abandoned and plundered (presumably by Hazen's Canadian friends, since he lived nearby to Chambly). During the process of this court-martial, the court refused to accept the testimony of a Major Scott, Arnold's preeminent witness, as "being prejudiced" in Arnold's favor. Without this critical piece of testimony, there was no legitimate basis for any meaningful charge to be sustained against Hazen, and he was accordingly "found not guilty" on August 7.[51] Arnold was absolutely livid, and he hurled invectives against the members of the court. In effect, Arnold had preferred charges against its members. Acrimonious recriminations from the members of the aggrieved court almost immediately followed. Colonel Poor, president of the Court Martial and apparently a close friend of Hazen, recommended Arnold's own arrest for behavior that he alternately referred to as "illegal, illiberal, un-gentlemanlike" and "contemptuous, disorderly, profane."[52] It is now impossible to determine precisely what the truth was, but since Hazen joined the members of the court-martial for a celebratory (and absolutely inappropriate) dinner on August 10, it appears that Arnold had a legitimate grievance.[53]

Gates, whose plate was already overflowing with the multitudes of tasks necessary to rebuild his army, construct fortifications around Ticonderoga, and build a fleet, was not amused. Gates in a communiqué to Congress regarding the occurrence acknowledged that "the warmth of General Arnold's temper" had possibly driven him to exceed "the precise line of decorum to be observed before and toward a court martial." However, Gates then went on to report that Arnold had not been at fault in the exchange, that "too much acrimony" had driven the court's actions, and "the United States must not be deprived of that excellent officer's service at this important moment." Gates peremptorily negated the entire situation by dissolving the court-martial. In doing so, however, he neglected to issue the thanks and appreciation, and congratulatory acknowledgement of their services that was customarily tendered to the members of the court. Gates also did not issue the order himself, delegating it to his Deputy Adjutant General. The Colonels got the point.

Probably historians have made too much of this particular event, since Gates rapidly squelched it.[54] However, when Gates' senior regimental commanders and most accomplished battlefield commander were openly arguing, it was not surprising that similar conduct worked its way down to the junior ranks, and the Ticonderoga garrison was regularly disrupted by acrimonious and sometimes violent arguments among its officers. Gates handled individual cases as they occurred, but he never entirely succeeded in eradicating this "poisonous fountain" from the army. In this he wasn't alone. George Washington never succeeded either.

Although it might appear that Gates faced nearly an insurmountable task, he had one great advantage. All the weak soldiers in the Northern Theater Army had already died, and all the uncommitted soldiers had already deserted. The survivors were strong, absolutely committed to the patriot cause, and were determined to conquer the British and achieve independence. Gates had very good material to work with, and the American (and a few Canadian) soldiers responded rapidly and magnificently to his ministrations.

To supplement the various policies and procedures that Gates instituted at Ticonderoga, more physical manifestations were required. The first was, of course, money. The American army had been crippled by its lack of money in Canada, and Schuyler initiated immediate efforts to ensure that this problem never reared its ugly head again.

Additional supplies of both hard money and paper currency had been dispatched to the army in the spring but had never reached it in Canada. On May 24 the Continental Congress sent General Schuyler "the sum of sixteen hundred and sixty two pounds, one shilling, and three pence in hard money, which was all that was in the treasury."[55] This represented a great sacrifice, and an even more considerable risk, on the part of the Continental Congress, for with this gesture the financial chests of that fabled body were rendered bereft of specie. Large quantities of Continental paper currency were also dispatched to Schuyler. On May 10 Schuyler had requested that Jonathan Trumbull, Jr., Paymaster General to the Forces of the United Colonies in the Northern Department, send him 150,000 dollars. This money did not reach the American army in Canada, but it was available at Ticonderoga by early July. On July 1, Schuyler requested another $100,000 in paper currency from Trumbull.[56] Various amounts of paper money, augmented by an occasional delivery of specie, began to regularly flow to Albany and Ticonderoga. Dr. Lewis Beebe recorded traveling from Albany to Fort George on August 25 with a "Mr. Burrall who had 100,000 Continental Dollars for the Northern Department."[57] By September 1 Schuyler could inform Gates in triumph, and with what must have been considerable relief: "The gentlemen ... have brought half a million of dollars to our military chest. Let us know what part of it you will want. The troops can now be regularly paid off."[58] Currency regularly flowed to Schuyler, as on October 15 when Gates was shipped a "bag of specie from Colonel Trumbull for you."[59] As this various money arrived, Schuyler and through him Gates finally had a meaningful purse to support their beleaguered army.

Once Gates and Schuyler possessed a viable purse, they could begin to obtain many of the other desperately needed supplies for the army. At the top of both of their priorities was to obtain sufficient uniforms for their soldiers. Initially, Montgomery had captured a considerable quantity of British army uniforms that had been stored in Canada, and had been able to adequately equip the American army with this clothing throughout the fall of 1775. However, given weeks and months of hard service this windfall was rapidly exhausted, and the Canadian army shortly found itself in desperate straits. The Canadian citizens had clothing, but it was the all too familiar story that they would not part with it unless they received payment in hard cash. The inevitable result was that upon arrival at Crown Point, some soldiers were almost naked, and the best-dressed soldiers among them were adorned in rags.

Almost immediately upon their embarkation at Crown Point, clothing and other necessary military supplies began to pour into camp. Colonel Porter, commanding a regiment of Massachusetts Militia, recorded as early as July 13 that "this day clothing was divided to the several regiments."[60] As with the rations, the sudden influx of clothing was a result of efforts implemented by Schuyler in the spring of 1776, as soon as he had realized the serious shortages that the forces in Canada were suffering from. However, there were initial delays in locating and manufacturing the clothing, totally understandable since this was the first time in history that the American colonies found themselves having to equip entire armies. Several months later the clothing had finally been organized, and was ready for issue to the army. Unfortunately, because of the transportation shortage, there was insufficient shipping to move the bulky, heavy bales of clothing and cloth to the army in Canada. Upon return to Ticonderoga, however, the army was close enough to its logistical hub of Albany that Schuyler could now adequately supply it.

By July 30 large supplies of clothing began to arrive at Ticonderoga. On this date no less than 1,008 shirts, 454 pair of shoes, and 177 pairs of moccasins were received. On August 5, it was noted that the Commissary had received a further 500 shirts from Albany, "ready to be delivered."[61] Another 489 shirts arrived on August 23.

By modern military standards, the clothing situation at Ticonderoga was always constrained. However, by late summer the regiments had been re-equipped with adequate quantities of serviceable clothing. Soldiers, in fact, were even issued with some limited amount of spare clothes, a luxury unheard of in Canada. When Private Anthony Mash of Colonel Edmond Phinney's 18th Continental Infantry (Massachusetts) Regiment died at Mount Independence on September 7, his conscientious captain had a careful inventory made of his effects:

- 1 pair Leather Breeches
- 3 Shirts
- 3 Pair Stockings
- 1 Pair Shoe Buckles
- 2 Coats
- 1 pair Shoes
- Jacket
- Hat
- Spaterdashes [sic. actually spatter-dashers, or "half gaiters"]
- 1 Black Handkerchief
- 1 pair knee buckles.[62]

Certainly this is not an extensive wardrobe, but considering that Private Mash had to either wear or carry all his possessions in his "napsack" it was a more than adequate wardrobe, and probably was all that any soldier actually desired.

The Quartermaster Records of Colonel Anthony Wayne's 4th Pennsylvania Battalion for the year 1776 fortuitously survive.[63] These provide a detailed record of the quantity of clothing being received, and issued to the soldiers, within this regiment. This battalion numbered 603 officers and men at Fort Ticonderoga in August.[64] The following clothing issues were made from the army storekeeper to Wayne's Quartermaster John Harper, which indicates that immediately upon arrival at Ticonderoga the supply system began to function again.

Crown Point	July 9, 1776	Received 4 blankets (1 point), 9 blankets (1½ points), 6 blankets (2 points), 12 blankets (2½ points), 2 blankets (3 points), 40 hats, 30 pair shoes;
Ticonderoga	July 14, 1776	Received 54 pairs shoes;
Ticonderoga	August 1st	Received 64 "Rushia" [Russia Linen, a coarse, sturdy linen] Shirts, 32 "Ozbrigs" [Osnaburg Linen, a finer quality of linen] Shirts;
Ticonderoga	August 3rd	Received 54 pair shoes, delivered to the Quartermaster of the 2nd Pennsylvania Battalion (St. Clair's);
Ticonderoga	August 6th	Received 10 Ozbrig Shirts, 2 Russian Shirts;
Ticonderoga	August 6th	Received 44 pair Russian Shirts, 10 Ozbrig Shirts;
Ticonderoga	August 20th	Received 23 Russhia Shirts 7 Ozbrig Shirts;
Ticonderoga	August 27th	Received from Continental Stores, 30 Russia Shirts, 30 Oznaburg Shirts, a long list of cloth (Brown, Green, Red, Purple, "drab") for a total of 190 yards.

The cloth was being issued because, at the time, every Company and Regiment had tailors who could easily and rapidly manufacture the raw cloth into finished clothing. Local tailors could also be contracted to manufacture clothing. For example, Quartermaster Harper "paid Mr. Larabe 60 shirts at 12/0 & making 50 pair shirts at 5/0 shirt" on September 21.

Ticonderoga	August 28th	Received from Continental Stores, 19 Watch Coats;
Ticonderoga	August 29th	Received from Major Hay, long list of cloth (Brown, Red, Black, "light color," "drab"), total of 181¾ yards;
Ticonderoga	September 2nd	Received of Major Hay 32 pairs leather breeches, 7 yards Camblet Tw. [twill] Striped.

Camleteen (often called camlet) is a plain weave, fine fabric. It could be made of goat's hair, camel's hair, cotton, silk or linen, but was most typically wool. Often camlet was originally woven from a finer material, and was then mixed with the more common and inexpensive wool. The "striped" is a description of the pattern. This type of fine wool would have been intended for an officer's coat.[65]

As an indication of how much the supply situation in the army had improved, by September 14 Quartermaster Harper actually had excess clothing in his regimental stores, consisting of fifty pairs shoes, 31 hats, 150 Russian Shirts, 89 Oznaburg Shirts, 17 pairs of leather breeches, and four watch coats. Still, clothing supplies continued to pour into the army, as the next day Harper recorded, "Ticonderoga, September 15th Received from Colonel Lewis, DQMG, 294 pair leather breeches." On September 17 the Northern Theater Army Orderly Book stated:

Whereas a quantity of Rushia Sheeting and Oznabrig Shirts are come to the Continental Stores, also a number of pair of linnen Trowsers, such Regiments as are in immediate want thereof, will send tomorrow morning, at eleven o'clock, an orders sign'd by the Commanding Officer of each Corps for the quantity of each sort of goods they demand.[66]

A careful examination of Quartermaster Harper's records for clothing issues in August and September suggests that adequate numbers of all articles except stockings were available by this time. Stockings, however, were being issued in equal numbers to all companies within a day or two of any supply being received by Harper. This is a clear indication that inadequate numbers of stockings were being received, and that they were being issued as soon as received, and in an even number to each company since actual shortages could not be filled. Still, by September 25 Colonel Wayne could order his Pennsylvania battalion:

The 4th Battalion all to be under arms on Sunday next ... as soap is now plenty, and new shirts ready to be delivered to such companies as are in want, no excuse can be admitted for appearing dirty or indecent. All officers and soldiers will take care to appear on parade as neat as possible. Officers will see that the men have their hair well powdered and neatly plaited and tied.[67]

Upon the retreat of the American army from Canada, among one of the many shortages was black gunpowder, lead to cast musket and rifle balls, flints to fire the small arms, and iron cannon shot. Gates took immediate actions to preserve the gunpowder that he did have available. One of his earliest orders was to "The Commanding Officer at Fort George" on July 7, 1776. At this early stage in his command, the leadership structure of the American Northern Theater Army was so disorganized that apparently not only Gates, but nobody else at Ticonderoga for that matter, had any idea who was actually in command at Fort George. Still, Gates had learned that the garrison at Fort George was regularly firing sunrise and sunset cannon. Gates' letter was blistering, and straightforward:

I understand that there is a wanton waste of powder, at your post, in firing a morning & evening gun, & in unnecessary salutes. It is my *positive Order* [highlighted in original letter] that this practice be immediately discontinued, & no ammunition expended on any account whatsoever, except in opposition to the attacks of the enemy.[68]

In 1775, there was but a single gunpowder mill operational in any of the American colonies, the Frankford Mill north of Philadelphia.[69] The only militarily viable supply of gunpowder in the colonies was that stored in public magazines, the majority of which had been immediately confiscated by the Patriots upon the outbreak of hostilities. It is estimated that the Continental army secured approximately 80,000 pounds in this manner. Almost from the very beginning, the Continental army in front of Boston was dreadfully short of gunpowder. Domestic manufacture was initiated, but soon stalled due to a lack of potassium nitrate (saltpeter). Production of saltpeter, which could readily be created from stable and barn floors, was thereafter initiated, and continued throughout the war. Apparently in 1776 sufficient quantities of gunpowder were manufactured, principally in Pennsylvania, but long-term, high quantity and consistent quality production could not be sustained due to habitual shortages of materials, both saltpeter and sulfur. Imports of both gunpowder and saltpeter had to be depended upon, principally from the West Indies islands of St. Eustasia and Martinique.[70] American privateers also captured some relatively inconsequential quantities. It is estimated that 115,000 pounds of gunpowder were manufactured prior to 1777 in America from domestic saltpeter. An additional 2,152,000 pounds of gunpowder was imported, captured, or manufactured from imported saltpeter.[71] Although this sounds like an impressive amount, gunpowder was to remain in comparatively short supply at Ticonderoga throughout 1776. It was not until the French entry into the war in 1778, that an adequate quantity of high quality gunpowder was available to the Continental army. Thus, Gates' proscription of ceremonial cannon firing was well considered. Unfortunately, attempts to trace the source and weight of gunpowder shipped to Gates' army at Ticonderoga have proven fruitless.[72] It is documented that fifteen tons of gunpowder were dispatched by Schuyler to Gates in early October from Philadelphia, in response to a plea by Gates on September 5: "As the fleet is large and mounts a great number of cannon, and the body of troops here very considerable, it is immediately necessary that fifteen tons of powder, ten of lead, with flints and cartridge paper in proportion, should be sent to this post."[73] Three tons of lead had also arrived at Ticonderoga by October 15. Following a six-week transit time, this large quantity of gunpowder and lead arrived just in time to be of service opposing the British advance.[74]

Other necessary items in short supply were flints, and lead musket balls. The patriots had also seized large numbers of gunflints at Crown Point and Ticonderoga, although many of these had been conveyed to Boston or Canada earlier in the war. Still, Gates was concerned that flints not be wasted by the soldiers, and issued specific orders intended to preserve his supply of flints for battle: "The Adjutants will see the Men Equip't with flints immediately[,] which flints are not to be worn out by foolishly snapping the Firelocks."[75] Fortuitously, natural flint was discovered at Mount Independence. On November 10, 1776, General Orders were published:

> A vein of prodigious fine black flint stone being discovered upon Mt. Independence the General desires the Commanding Officers of Regiments will make enquiry if there are any old Countrymen in any of their Corps who understand hammering of gun flints upon such a person or persons being found he or they are to be sent to the General at Head Quarters.[76]

Apparently this request had been successfully answered, for on November 11 Colonel Baldwin noted, "Employed 2 men to Cut flints, getting tools for that purpose."[77]

There was only a single operative lead mine in the North American colonies that was capable of large quantity production when war broke out in 1775. This was in southwestern Virginia, near modern Austinville.[78] This mine would end up providing nearly all of the Continental army's needs, but it was only beginning to turn out the necessary quantity in 1776. Jubilant New York City patriots dismembered the lead statue of King George III in celebration of the Declaration of Independence, and it is likely that at least some of this lead made its way up the Hudson River to Ticonderoga. Large quantities of lead were captured at Ticonderoga and Crown Point in 1775. However, by the summer of 1776 all of this lead had been expended in the Canada campaign to date or shipped to the main American army of George Washington over the previous year, with what remained accompanying Henry Knox to Boston in the dead of winter. In response to Schuyler's pleas on May 17, Washington had shipped him five tons of lead gathered from throughout the colonies to support the war effort.[79] This was apparently sufficient to supply Gates' army throughout nearly the remainder of the year.

Fortunately, one industry that was thriving in America was that of iron manufacture. There were numerous iron works in the colonies, particularly in Maryland, Pennsylvania, New Jersey and the Hudson River valley of New York. Casting of iron shot for cannon was relatively simple, as they were simply solid spheres of set sizes, and required no special skills or techniques. Schuyler entered into agreements with numerous foundries in New York State to have cannonballs cast. A typical contract was let by Schuyler's aide, Captain Richard Varick, with "Colonel Livingston's Furnace" on August 6, 1776:

A Return of Cannon Shot wanted for the Public Serve to be immediately cast at Colonel Livingston's Furnace, Albany, August 6, 1776 —

Size of cannon	Round Shot	Double Headed or Chain Shot
For 32 Pounders	-	50
For 24 Pounders	20	50
For 18 Pounders	-	300
For 14 Pounders	500	600
For 9 Pounders	-	600
For 6 Pounders	600	600
For 4 Pounders	600	400
For 3 Pounders	50	-

Four Ton of Grape Shot, One Ton 18 Pounders, 3 Ton of Smaller Sizes.[80]

Although this might seem a great quantity, it must be remembered that Schuyler was not only outfitting an entire fleet, but was also responsible for scores of cannon at Ticonderoga and Crown Point. In fact, this was a comparatively modest order. Varick let numerous contracts of this size in 1776, to a number of different furnaces.[81] Still, this was one industry that had sufficiently matured to adequately equip the fledgling American army.

Supplies were intermittently noted as arriving at Ticonderoga. On October 16 Colonel Baldwin recorded, "We had 15 tons of powder come into camp this Day and a Quantity of Lead."[82] Gates and Schuyler were never satisfied with the quantity of ordnance supplies that were available to them, but the army was adequately supplied with ammunition by the time that the British actually moved against it.

Thirty-eight-year-old Udny Hay, an experienced merchant from the Hudson River town of Poughkeepsie, was appointed to be Quartermaster General.[83] The young Simeon Bloodgood, who had carried supplies under Hay's direction that winter, recalled that he was "well known as an active and efficient Quartermaster General."[84] Twenty-one-year-old Elisha Avery was appointed as Commissary at Ticonderoga. These youthful, energetic officers provided superlative service to both Gates and the army, and under their tutelage formalized staff procedures were established that considerably enhanced the efficiency of the supply operations of the Northern Theater Army.

As with clothing, Schuyler had initiated early efforts to obtain adequate provisions.

However, he faced grave challenges, as the United Colonies were totally unprepared and unequipped to address provisioning thousands of men, hundreds of miles away. Considering meat, flour, a quart of spruce beer, and other foodstuffs, along with attendant packaging, no less than five pounds of provisions per man per day had to be purchased and transported. And this does not include any ammunition expended (one .72 soft lead musket ball weighs one ounce alone), or any necessary clothing or other equipment. The crisis in Canada had occurred because the American retreat happened at the worst possible time, during the inevitable spring interruption of supplies caused by melting ice on the lakes. Immediately afterwards, all of the available bateaux were pressed into service to evacuate the sick and then the main army to Crown Point. And it should be noted that the army never actually starved during the retreat, although it was on desperately short rations, often had nothing available to eat except salt pork and raw flour, and the salt pork was regularly found to be rancid.

Once the army reached Ticonderoga, and became relatively stable, the Northern Theater army's supply situation improved considerably. The army was in the first place considerably closer to the main American depot of Albany. Additionally, massive quantities of supplies ordered by Joseph Trumbull, the Commissary General of the Continental army, in the spring of 1776 finally began to arrive. Trumbull, hand-picked by Washington, had proven to be an excellent selection as Commissary. The Colony of Connecticut was literally the breadbasket for the cities of New York and Boston. Trumbull's father was governor of Connecticut, and Trumbull himself was a native son of the state. His connections would prove to be invaluable.

When Trumbull eventually resigned over congressional interference and meddling in his operation in 1777, the commissary system for the army in short order collapsed. Under Trumbull's leadership, the Commissary Department was probably run more efficiently than it was at any other time during the Revolutionary War. In June 1776 Washington would state regarding Trumbull's contributions as Commissary General: "Few Armies, if any, have been better and more plentifully supplied than the Troops under Mr. Trumbull's care."[85] Joseph Trumbull is one of the great unsung heroes of American history, and when he turned his attention north to Ticonderoga, the shortages of food that the army had consistently suffered for months slowly vanished.[86]

Trumbull had to overcome considerable challenges in establishing his Commissariat department. He suddenly found himself feeding thousands of men, scattered over hundreds of miles, with inadequate funding, no American experience in logistics of this magnitude, no trained subordinates, and no previously established system in place. The Commissary was under great duress, problems of every conceivable type continuously manifested themselves, and the Commissary Department struggled through almost daily calamities that prevented it from ever operating completely smoothly. But, still, slowly but steadily, day after day, week after week, delivery after delivery, Ticonderoga's worn stone and hastily constructed wooden storehouses became filled with food, and Gates' soldiers no longer resembled human scarecrows. Colonel Anthony Wayne wrote home to Pennsylvania in late August:

> Fresh provision is become more plenty than salt & our people have recovered health and spirits.... I begin to get me in flesh; wine, punch, porter, venison, mutton, beef,

potatoes, peas, bean, butter & cheese begin to make their appearance in camp. Of these good creatures I the more freely partake — as man can not live by bread alone.[87]

The supplies on hand and shipped to the army were dutifully recorded by Schuyler's Commissary Walter Livingston, at Albany.[88] On May 21 219 barrels of pork arrived at Albany; on May 23 370 more barrels of pork were landed. Livingston noted on June 2, "I sent up last week 1,186 barrels of pork, 200 of flour, 125 of corn [meal], 100 sheep and some fat cattle which was upwards of 215 pounds per diem." On June 7 he noted, "I sent lately 150 fat sheep and 7 beaves to Fort George. There is about 500 barrels of flour gone to Fort George from different meals up the country." This suggests that for the army of 5,000 men there was sufficient flour to issue a pound per man daily for over two weeks, meaning that the Continental army was finally beginning to get ahead.

By August 4, Livingston could report to Trumbull:

> About 2,000 barrels of flour were lodged at Fort Edward for the want of carriages.... The flour was under cover. He has ordered proper sheds to be built at each post. Mr. Avery has informed a person of my acquaintance that there was 800 barrels of pork at Ticonderoga, the 26th July. Since which I have purchased 90 barrels. Cattle go forward constantly.... The person who I employ to purchase flour returned and informed me that he has engaged 2,000 barrels ... I now have about 2,000 barrels [of flour] in town. When the above 2,000 barrels arrives I shall have flour sufficient to maintain 8,000 men till the 31st of Dec. at 1 pound per day.

There were, of course, shortages. With the fledgling Continental army, there were *always* shortages. Trumbull alerted Livingston on August 7:

> I have also ordered a quantity of molasses & peas to you, which was in danger when the ships went up. Indian meal, soap & molasses are much wanted at Ticonderoga. I wish you to procure those articles, as fast as possible. The water there is bad, spruce is health & if they had molasses, they might have plenty of beer, which will be healthful.

By September 21, Avery could write from Ticonderoga:

> We have at present a pretty good supply of cattle & flour. What pork remains, is reserved for extraordinary cases (there being about 300 barrels).

This was by no means an inconsequential supply, for it comprised over 100,000 individual daily rations of pork. Avery continued:

> We are somewhat deficient in the small supplies, but having a plenty [sic] of the main articles, we make it do tolerable well. Chocolate and soap are much wanted, which Mr. Livingston says are not to be had in Albany. The latter I shall endeavor to make as much of as I can, but can by no means furnish the Army for want of materials & proper conveniences. Indian Meal I have requested Mr. Livingston repeatedly to furnish but for some reason he finds corn in lieu of it, which cannot be ground here. I have thus far worried through, and surmounted many obstacles, & will continue in my endeavors to serve the Army as long as my presence is required.

Avery concluded, with words that must have made Trumbull proud and pleased:

> This place is now so well secured, that there is but little apprehension of our being routed from Ti.

Gates also encouraged local farmers to bring in provisions that they had raised in their vegetable gardens and farm fields to sell to the soldiers. To facilitate this, Gates established regulated markets on both the Ticonderoga and Mount Independence sides of the lake, carefully monitored and controlled prices, and ensured that counterfeited money did not enter the economy. On September 25 Gates mandated:

> Various Frauds, abuses, and impositions being Every day Committed by Traders and Hucksters coming to this Camp. The Q. M. Gen'l and his Assistants are Immediately to regulate the prices to be paid for the Several Commodities brought to sell Especially Garden Stuff, Venison, Butter, Cheese, & all manner of Eatables; for the Future any person bringing any of the above articles immediately for Sale are to Carry them to the foot of the Glasis of the old Fort where the Market is Constantly to be kept. Should any person or persons be detected in monopolizing or Forestalling the market they will be punished by a Court martial and have all their Goods Siez'd for the sick of the Hospital, the Market is to be observed Every morning at 8 o'clock and to be allowed to Continue till Sunsett.[89]

Further regulations for the market place were established at various dates.

> September 29, 1776. The 200 Bushells of Onions just brought to the Carrying place at Lake George are to be one half of them sold at the Market Port on the Glacis of the old Fort and the other half at the Market places in the front of Col. Peterson's Reg't. upon Mt. Independance.
>
> September 30, 1776. It appearing upon a candid examination that the Onions brought from Weatherfield in Connecticut have cost Mr. Sedgwick upwards of Ninety Five Pounds lawful Money transporting from thence, he is therefore permitted to sell the said onions at twenty shillings York currency per bushel and no more.

When Gates assumed command at Crown Point, the situation that he faced was truly precarious from a manpower standpoint. The army was weak. However, some additional battalions were dispatched to his relief. Two new Continental Regiments raised in Massachusetts arrived, commanded by Colonels Samuel Brewer and Aaron Willard. As a result of Potts' efforts, some recovered sick also began to rejoin the army. By August 24, Gates recorded nearly 8,000 men present and fit for duty at Ticonderoga, Skenesboro and Crown Point. The principal regiments were organized into four brigades. The First Brigade consisted of Greaton's 24th Continental (Massachusetts), Bond's 25th Continental (Massachusetts), Burrall's Connecticut Regiment, and Porter's Regiment of Massachusetts Militia. Stationed on Mount Independence, this brigade was ostensibly commanded by Brigadier General Arnold. He had little to do with this brigade in fact, as Arnold was fully occupied at Skenesboro throughout most of July and August supervising construction of the fleet; and was then detached commanding the fleet on Lake Champlain for nearly all of the remainder of August, and the entirety of September and October. In his absence Colonel John Greaton actually commanded the brigade. The Second Brigade was comprised of Reed's 2nd Continental (New Hampshire), Paterson's 15th Continental (Massachusetts), and Lieutenant Colonel Joseph Wait's Regiment of New Hampshire Rangers. Colonel James Reed, as the senior Colonel with the brigade, served as Brigade Commander. This brigade was also camped at Mount Independence. The Third Brigade consisted of Stark's 5th Continental (New Hampshire), Poor's 8th Continental (New

Hampshire), Maxwell's 2nd New Jersey, Wingate's New Hampshire Regiment, and Wyman's New Hampshire Regiment. Colonel John Stark, a highly experienced officer with long service throughout the Seven Years' War with the famous and renowned Rogers Rangers, was Brigade Commander. The Third Brigade was also encamped on Mount Independence. The Fourth Brigade was organized from St. Clair's 2nd Pennsylvania, De Haas' 1st Pennsylvania, Wayne's 4th Pennsylvania, and an Independent Company of Pennsylvania Riflemen commanded by Captain John Nelson. This brigade was commanded by Colonel Arthur St. Clair, and it was positioned on the Ticonderoga side of the fortifications, encamped directly behind the old French lines on the Heights of Carillon. According to Sergeant Timothy Tuttle of the 1st New Jersey, this was informally referred to as Liberty Hill, although this name was apparently not in common use and has not been preserved for posterity.[90] An informal fifth brigade entirely composed of Massachusetts Militia Regiments was also organized for service at Ticonderoga. The 6th Pennsylvania Battalion was on detached service at Crown Point, under the independent command of its Lieutenant Colonel. Several other regiments also had independent assignments at Ticonderoga and Mount Independence. These were generally under-strength or small organizations. There were the inevitable reorganizations, attachments, and detachments, but Gates maintained this basic configuration throughout the summer and fall.

The Brigade Commanders were generally promoted once they had proved themselves competent. Arthur St. Clair and Reed formally became Brigadier Generals on August 9, 1776. William Maxwell would eventually take over Arnold's Brigade, and also became a Brigadier General on October 23, 1776.[91]

Additional organizational steps were implemented. Major Ebenezer Stevens was appointed on September 15 "to take command of all the artillery on the west side of the Lake, and to encamp on the French lines with General St. Clair's Brigade."[92] Stevens was one of the aggressive young American officers who commanded the Continental army's individual organizations and who held together the army under any and all circumstances. Stevens was a 26-year-old pre-war member of the Massachusetts Militia's Ancient and Honorable Train of Artillery, a fervent Boston patriot, a close friend of Henry Knox, and a participant in the famous Boston Tea Party. He had joined the besieging army outside Boston at the first notice, and he had commanded artillery that had covered the American withdrawal from the Battle of Bunker Hill. Stevens commanded an artillery company that had been transferred to Canada in the spring of 1776, and he was as well trained an artillery officer as Gates' army had available.

Among the most colorful and distinctive of the reinforcements that arrived at Ticonderoga was a company of Stockbridge Mohican Indians. The Mohican Indians were originally known as the River Indians, for they inhabited both sides of the Hudson River from New York City to above Albany. However, a disastrous war with the Mohawk Nation of the Iroquois Confederation in the 1620s had driven them to the eastern bank of the Hudson River, and the Mohican nation would eventually establish a large community at Stockbridge, Massachusetts. During the Seven Years' War, substantial numbers of Mohicans had fought with Rogers Rangers, and a large part of the Rangers' success was because of the woods fighting skills that the Mohicans had taught them. Fighting under Rogers' direction with their own officers, the Mohican Indians had made major contributions to the British war effort throughout the Seven Years' War in the Lake Champlain Valley. With the outbreak of the War of American Independence, the Mohican Indians had chosen to actively support the American patriots. In 1776, one of the Stockbridge missionaries wrote to the Continental Congress:

> Far from desiring to remain neuter in the dispute between Great Britain and America, they have made themselves acquainted with the merits of the controversy, and have taken an active part in our favor, inlisting their young men in our Army, while their counsellors and sachems have carefully sent belts of wampum by their messengers to the Six Nations, to the Canadian Indians, and to the Shawnees on the Ohio, addressing them in such terms as they judged would have the greatest tendency to attach them to the interests of the United States.[93]

With the onset of hostilities, it was only natural that the Mohicans would again return to their old war trails in Lake Champlain. On September 13, 1776, Orderly Books at Ticonderoga contained some variation of the following orders, announcing their arrival with Gates' army:

> The Independent Company of Indians from Stockbridge under the command of Capt Ezra Whittlesey are posted with Regts at the Saw Mills under the command of Col. Brewer, the Col will give proper orders respecting them and they are severally to wear a blue and red cap, as a distinguishing mark from the Enemy's Indians, of this all Officers & Soldiers in the Army are to take particular notice to the end that we might not by mistake kill our Friends instead of our Enemies.[94]

Their location "at the Saw Mills under the command of Col. Brewer" refers to the fortified camp at Mount Hope. Additional orders were posted on September 20:

> The centrys [sic] at the bridge and on the west side of the French lines are not to suffer any of the Stockbridge Indians of Capt Whitlesey's corps to pass into this encampment without a written pass from Col Brewer.

The company of Stockbridge Mohicans was placed under Colonel Brewer's Massachusetts Militia Regiment, which made perfect sense as the majority of the Indians were from the colony. Little information is available on their precise activities, presumably because most of the Indians were illiterate, and thus left no written record. Apparently the Stockbridge Mohicans were skilled and energetic fighters, but they were not well suited to mundane camp life. Captain Whittlesey would write: "It is with the utmost difficulty I have kept them in any order until now."[95] Sergeant Timothy Tuttle of the 1st New Jersey recorded in his journal for September 25, "an alarm supposed to be Indians, but they got drunk & made the Indians Hallos [sic] that alarmed the camps. I mean the Indians that belong to the camp."[96] Corporal Ebenzer Wild of Brewer's Regiment similarly noted, although for September 26: "About 10 o'clock this evening our camp was alarmed. The occasion was by some drunken Indians firing guns."[97] To provide an outlet for their energies, they performed scouting and patrolling duties, and launched small raids and ambushes against the British at St. Jean. When Arnold sailed the Lake Champlain Fleet north, the Mohicans accompanied him as scouts. Under the aggressive Arnold, the Mohicans would provide valuable service to the American fleet, and they were a welcome reinforcement to Gates' army.

Sickness still continued to be a problem, but the sick no longer constituted half the strength of the army. By this time, Gates reported approximately one thousand sick at Fort George, and about two thousand sick at Ticonderoga and Mount Independence but not ill enough to be evacuated to Fort George.[98] And, most importantly, they did not have the smallpox.

It was recorded that the camp at Mount Independence was a particularly unhealthy location. Surgeons blamed the recent clearance of the ground, which they believed had released "ill humors" or "bad vapors" from the soil, in accordance with contemporary medical beliefs. Gates accordingly ordered that:

> As nothing is more necessary to purge the air than fire, the best physician allows large fires to be made in new ground or damp situations. The General therefore desires the Commanding Officers of the regiments upon Mount Independence to order a small fatigue party every morning and evening to burn up heaps of brush around their several encampments.[99]

Not every action that Gates implemented was a logistical or administrative effort. Although his tactical operations were limited, Gates did launch a few scouts to the north. Ostensibly these scouts were just that, patrols to gain information on precisely how the British were spending their summer in Canada. However, several aggressive Americans turned these relatively benign scouts into active combat operations intended to inflict casualties upon the British, and carry the fight to them. One of these men was Lieutenant Benjamin Whitcomb of New Hampshire. As a young man barely of age, Whitcomb had fought with the Provincials and British throughout most of the Seven Years' War in the Lake George–Lake Champlain valley.[100] An ardent patriot, Whitcomb proved himself to be adept at leading what would today be known as deep penetration patrols into the heart of the enemy's country.

Whitcomb launched his first patrol into the Richelieu River Valley as early as July 14, when he set out from Crown Point with four companions, two Americans and two French Canadians.[101] The French Canadians were most likely members of what was intended to be a full company of Canadian Rangers to be enlisted by a Monsieur Jeremiah Dugan, a barber from Quebec. Dugan should have stuck to his shears, for he had almost no success in recruiting his ranger company, and a roster in January 1777 listed only eight men in his whole company. Dugan's company would eventually be formally disbanded for what amounted to lack of interest.[102] Upon Whitcomb's arrival at St. Jean he noted, "The 2 Frenchmen being uneasy and not willing to go near St. John's, I told them to take a Frenchmen and examine him and return home, upon which we left them and went towards St. John's" and that was the last seen of these particular Dugan's Rangers. The Canadians apparently took Whitcomb's instructions to return home literally, and vanished eternally from the rolls of the American army.

Whitcomb and his fellow New Hampshire comrades in arms, however, were made of sterner stuff, and scouted along the Richelieu River between St. Jean and Chambly, counting ships and soldiers for a week. Eventually they laid an ambush between St. Jean and Chambly, intending to capture a British officer for interrogation. Their ambush went awry, and Whitcomb noted that he had "fired on an officer." Whitcomb's officer was actually Brigadier General Patrick Gordon, Lieutenant Colonel of the 29th Foot and appointed a Brigadier General commanding a Brigade of British Regulars during service in Canada.[103] Whitcomb was apparently a good shot, for he "dangerously wounded" Gordon, who rode into St. Jean and collapsed. He died of his wounds on August 2. Whitcomb returned to Ticonderoga on August 6 with considerable intelligence information on the British in the Richelieu River Valley, but much to his chagrin, no prisoners.

The British obtained a good description of Whitcomb, noting of his appearance:

> He is between 30 and 40 years of age [Whitcomb was actually 39 years old], to appearance near 6 feet high ... light brown hair tied behind, rough face ... he wears a kind of under jacket without sleeves, slash pockets, leather breeches, gray woolen or yard stockings, and shoes. Hat flapped, a gold cord tied round it. He had a firelock, blanket, pouch and powder horn.

The British complained bitterly about Whitcomb having the audacity to actually shoot one of their Generals in the midst of a war. Carlton would launch an impassioned verbal tirade, declaring: "The Rebel Runaways not having dared to show their faces as soldiers, have now taken the part of the vilest assassins, and are lurking in small parties to murder, if any single or unarmed officer or soldier may be passing the roads, near the wood side. Brigadier General Gordon was dangerously wounded yesterday by one of these infamous skulkers ... should he, or any of his party, of the same nature, come within reach of our men, it is hoped that they will not honor them with soldiers' deaths if they can possibly avoid it, but reserve them for due punishment, which can only be effected by the Hangman." Carlton conveniently ignored the fact that he had been the first to employ Native American warriors, and that parties of Indians fighting for the British had stripped and plundered American prisoners at the Cedars, and regularly ambushed and slaughtered American soldiers throughout the summer. However, these were inconvenient facts to Carleton. What is instructive is that Whitcomb and his two compatriots had absolutely panicked the British, indicating that their simple patrol had been entirely successful in its objectives.

Whitcomb is documented to have returned to the Richelieu River Valley on numerous occasions, scouts being recorded between July 31 and August 8, between August 20 and August 28, and between September 5 and 17. On September 13 Whitcomb finally succeeded in capturing two British soldiers. They attempted to bribe Whitcomb, "offered me sums of money to let them go" but Whitcomb responded, "I would not for all the money King George was worth." Whitcomb returned, with his prisoners, to Ticonderoga on September 21. By the end of the campaign Whitcomb would be promoted to Captain as a reward for his efforts, and in recognition of his skills and audacity. Besides Whitcomb's frequent sessions between St. Jean and Chambly, Lieutenant Colonel Hartley is also known to have regularly dispatched patrols, both mounted on boats and dismounted, from his forward post at Crown Point throughout the summer and fall. On these raids the American allies of the Stockbridge Mohican Nation played their full part.

Tactically and operationally, these raids were meaningless. The casualties that they inflicted upon the British were trifling, and the intelligence that they gathered was minimal. But they were critically important to the American army's morale and esprit de corps. Whitcomb was the symbol that carried the fight to the British, instead of simply spending the summer and fall waiting for the British to move against them. Whitcomb was willing to take the dare that the British could not impede him on their home ground, and he became a minor, but important, American hero of Fort Ticonderoga in 1776.

Taken together, these efforts considerably strengthened and healed the army. Already by mid–August, Gates had gone far in reorganizing and reconstructing the army. As early as July 26 Lieutenant Colonel Matthew Ogden, the acting commander of the 1st New Jersey Regiment, told a correspondent, "The army are beginning to recruit fast, from the effects of a little fresh meat, and some rum, when on fatigue. Ten days ago there were not in our regiment eighty men fit for duty. We have now upwards of two hundred and thirty; and, in a few days, they will be all as rugged as New-Jersey is firm."[104]

Ogden was not alone in his opinion. A fellow New Jersey officer, Lieutenant Colonel Israel Shreve, wrote to his wife in late August:

> We have got strongly fortified here, upwards of ten thousand troops in high spirits, I think fully sufficient to stand all the force the enemy can bring this campaign. Burgoyne would be welcome here with his Regulars, Canadians, and savage crew [Native Americans]. But I do not expect him this summer. We now live well on a high hill overlooking part of the lake. [105]

Colonel Nathan Hale would write his wife on August 12, with what appeared to be a consistent theme from the army:

> I have had a very fortegooging [fatiguing] time of it in this Northern Department Likewise the whole of owre [our] army as every thing seemed to work a gainst us. Things seem to have a turn now as owre army is a giting beter ... I think we shall be very well prepared for the British army in a short time.[106]

8

"I Think We Shall Be Very Well Prepared for the British Army"

Gates Establishes a Fortified Position at Ticonderoga

Gates and Schuyler, while reconstructing the Northern Theater Army at Ticonderoga, also had to concern themselves with the relatively minor inconvenience of the near certainty that a powerful, well-supplied, extraordinarily disciplined and trained British army and Royal Navy, commanded by exemplary officers, would soon come sweeping down from Canada upon them. Gates, to resist the onslaught that was inevitable, established a layered defensive scenario. Gates' intent was to delay the British advance through a network of defenses, and then construct a formidable set of fortifications around the French Fort Carillon, at Ticonderoga, that the British would have to lay formal siege to in order to capture the position. Thus, Gates' strategy was to sufficiently delay the British on Lake Champlain so that they would not have adequate time in the campaign season to implement an effective siege at Ticonderoga. With winter coming relatively early to Lake Champlain, military operations past November 1 were not feasible. Thus, Gates only had to delay the British for the three months of active campaign season that still remained from early July until early October, and Carleton would not have sufficient time to initiate a siege at Ticonderoga.

Gates' defensive strategy to gain this delay was comprised of the following segments:

- A strong advance guard on Lake Champlain itself, consisting of the American fleet, positioned to challenge and delay the British fleet's progress;
- A small combat outpost at Fort Crown Point, to observe the British, and prevent them from launching a surprise attack directly upon Ticonderoga;
- A major defensive position at Ticonderoga itself;
- A new major defensive position across Lake Champlain, on the eastern bank of Lake Champlain at Ticonderoga;
- An entrenched camp to defend the vulnerable American left (west) flank from an outflanking maneuver by the British; and
- Maintaining a detached, isolated general hospital at Fort George.

Gates had already fixed upon this plan as early as July 12, as correspondence of this date documents:

8. "I Think We Shall Be Very Well Prepared for the British Army"

> The Army should immediately retire from Crown Point to Ticonderoga, where, upon the strong ground on the eastern side of the lake, directly opposite to the east point of Ticonderoga, an encampment is marked out for the Army. The sick and infected are removing to the fort at the south end of Lake George, where the General Hospital is fixed. Our naval force upon the lake is, in the mean time, refitting with the utmost diligence.... Brigadier General Arnold is at Crown Point, forwarding the troops, artillery, stores and provisions to Ticonderoga[.] As fast as these arrive, I shall endeavor to place them in a situation to maintain their post.[1]

Carleton has been roundly criticized by some historians for not aggressively sweeping down Lake Champlain to conquer the Americans while they were still ravaged by smallpox, totally disorganized, and before they had time to construct fortifications at the narrows of Ticonderoga. Although this sounds like a relatively simple matter and painfully obvious strategy, this hypothesis fails to take into account two salient facts. First, there were no roads between St. Jean and Crown Point. There were, of course, some Native American paths, but these were scarcely adequate for artillery and military trains, and were totally inadequate to supply an entire army. If the British army wanted to traverse between St. Jean and Crown Point, it would have to be done by Lake Champlain. And the second fact is that the Americans controlled Lake Champlain. When they evacuated Canada, Benedict Arnold had ensured that they had removed every ship, bateaux, whaleboat, canoe and anything else that could be floated from the Richelieu River valley. Arnold had even removed one ship under construction at St. Jean that could *not* be floated. Until the British constructed bateaux, they could not utilize Lake Champlain. The series of deceptive and dangerous rapids between Chambly and St. Jean prevented bateaux from moving south on the Richelieu River. They had to be built anew at St. Jean, or broken down into pieces and transported by land to St. Jean, where they could then be reassembled. But without warships to protect these bateaux, they would be terribly vulnerable to the American Lake Champlain fleet.

The American Lake Champlain fleet consisted of only four vessels. The largest vessel was the *Royal Savage*, captured at St. Jean by Richard Montgomery during his 1775 invasion. It was a two-masted schooner, and mounted six 6-pounder cannon, four 4-pounder cannon, and twelve swivel guns. Montgomery had also captured the *Revenge* at St. Jean. The *Revenge* was a small two-masted schooner that mounted eight 4-pounder cannon and ten swivel guns. The *Liberty* was another small two-masted schooner that had been captured at the start of hostilities from Philip Skene at Skenesborough. Skene had constructed this schooner in the spring and summer of 1771 and launched it in August of that year. Skene constructed the schooner of red cedar, as that wood was extremely durable.[2] The *Liberty* mounted tiny cannon, two 4-pounders, six 2-pounders, and six swivel guns. Finally, there was the sloop *Enterprise*, captured by Benedict Arnold in an audacious raid on St. Jean in May 1775:

> My last was on the 14th instant by Mr. Romans via New Haven. I then acquainted you of the occasion of delay in not carrying your orders into execution. The afternoon of the same day being joined by Capts. Brown and Oswald with 50 men enlisted on the road they having taken possession of a small schooner at Skenesborough, we immediately proceeded on our way to St. Johns and at 8 O'clock P.M. on the 17th instant arrived within 30 miles of St. Johns. The weather proving calm, we manned

out two small batteau with 35 men and the next morning at 7 O'clock arrived at St. Johns, surprised and took a sergeant and his party of 12 men, the King's sloop of about 70 tons with 2 brass 6 pounders and 7 men without any loss on either side.... We took such stores on board as were valuable and the wind proving favorable in two hours after our arrival weighed anchor for this place with the sloop and 4 of the King's batteau having destroyed 5 others, so that there is not left a single batteau for the King's troops, Canadians or Indians to cross the Lake if they have any such intention.... We are masters of the Lake and of that I make no doubt as I am determined to arm the sloop and schooner immediately.

Arnold had subsequently armed the *Enterprise* with ten 4-pounder cannon, and twelve swivel guns.[3]

The size of the cannon aboard these ships was laughable, but still they were cannon. It wasn't much of a fleet, and the vessels were neither particularly imposing or powerful. But, still, it was a fleet. And it was the only fleet afloat on Lake Champlain, and that meant that the Americans controlled Lake Champlain. And until a British fleet could be constructed, manned, trained, and succeed in removing the American fleet from Lake Champlain, their transport boats, be they bateaux, whaleboats or canoes, could not move south. Carleton was stopped at St. Jean, just as General Jeffery Amherst had been stopped at Crown Point in 1759 until he had also constructed a fleet. And until those circumstances were altered, neither Carleton nor any other British officer was going to move south down Lake Champlain.

Gates' advance guard consisted of the American fleet on Lake Champlain. This was intended to be an especially strong advance guard that could readily contest the waters of Lake Champlain with the British vessels. Gates established a strong combat outpost at Crown Point, a regimental position to be maintained by the 6th Pennsylvania Battalion under the command of Lieutenant Colonel Thomas Hartley, specifically to preclude any type of surprise attack upon Fort Ticonderoga or Mount Independence. Centered around the French fort at Ticonderoga, Gates intended to construct a ring of earthworks and redoubts on the high ground, and along the banks of Lake Champlain, to defend the west bank of Lake Champlain. Gates then intended to construct another strong set of entrenchments on what was known as Rattlesnake Hill or East Point, a promontory directly east of Fort Ticonderoga on the eastern bank of Lake Champlain. Once Ticonderoga and East Point could be fortified, this would serve as his main defensive position astride Lake Champlain. To prevent Fort Ticonderoga from being outflanked on its left (western) flank, Gates also planned to construct fortifications on what would become known as Mount Hope. This was a prominent knoll located on a commanding piece of terrain above the portage to Lake George and the bateaux landing place at the Falls on the Chute River. At the same time, the American general hospital would be maintained at Lake George, thereby safely isolating the smallpox from the army.

Writing a relatively few years after American independence had been won, the brilliant Prussian General Carl Von Clausewitz wrote regarding the employment of a strong advance guard:

> In cases where our dispositions require a lot of time, it can put up a stronger degree of resistance, and so impose greater caution on the advancing enemy, in this way, it augments the effect of an ordinary vanguard.[4]

James Hunter, *A View of Ticonderoga from the Middle of the Channel in Lake Champlain* (1777). In this drawing, the Jersey Redoubt and other fortifications are prominent in the background, depicting the strength of the American entrenchments as seen by the British on Lake Champlain (Library and Archives Canada, Acc. No. 1989-246-2).

This was certainly the case that the American Northern Theater Army found itself in. It would require considerable time to place the American main defensive positions at Ticonderoga and East Point into condition that they could resist the British advance. Carleton, who would command the British advance, was certainly an officer who could easily be imbued with greater caution. Accordingly, a strong advance guard was mandated. Gates intended that the American fleet should fill this role, under the known leadership of the aggressive, resolute Brigadier General Benedict Arnold. Gates revealed his intentions in his instructions to Arnold, dated as early as August 7:

> Should the Enemy come up the Lake, and attempt to force their way through the pass you are stationed to defend in that case you will act with such cool determined valor, as will give them reason to repent their temerity. But if, contrary to my hope and expectation, their fleet should have so increased, as to force an entrance into the upper part of the Lake then after you shall have discovered the insufficiency of every effort to retard their progress, you will, in the best manner you can, retire with your Squadron to Ticonderoga.[5]

James Hunter, *A View of Ticonderoga from a Point on the North Shore of Lake Champlain* (1777). British gunboats, a royal artillery officer, and various members of the British Army in the foreground. The American fortifications are in the background, and Fort Ticonderoga is prominent upon the knoll in the center along with other fortifications. (Library and Archives Canada, Acc. No. 1989-246-2).

The establishment of the American advance guard, Arnold's Lake Champlain fleet, will be discussed in detail in the subsequent chapter.

Gates established his strong combat outpost at Crown Point, providing a shield between him and any potential British advance. Gates issued Hartley detailed orders on July 20 regarding his assignment:

> Upon your arrival at Crown Point, you will post the detachment under your command in the most secure manner, taking care to preserve a communication with your batteaux and the vessels stationed at the Point. You will constantly report all extraordinaries, and by every means in your power procure intelligence of the motions of the enemy. Such as you think of consequence must, without delay, be sent by an express boat to Ticonderoga.... As the detachment under your command is meant more as an advanced guard than a post to be defended to the last extremity, you are carefully to keep your retreat open to your batteaus, and when the enemy appear with a force to which, from all circumstances, you are convinced you and your detachment are

unequal, and with whom it would be rashness to contend, you are then to make as secure a retreat as possible to Tyonderoga.[6]

Hartley and his men took station at Crown Point on July 21, reporting to Gates: "I have laid out my encampment near the Grenadier Redoubt. The sick I will keep in the long storehouse. From the numerous detachments and sickness, I have not two hundred men now here fit for duty. Part of these are daily employed in the boats."[7] Although not mentioned in his orders, an important aspect of his command was to manufacture oars for the fleet, and he regularly shipped oars back to Gates at Ticonderoga. Nearly all of the scores of oars required by the American Lake Champlain fleet were constructed by the Crown Point oar makers, working under Hartley's protection and supervision.

Lieutenant Colonel Hartley was a youthful 28-year-old attorney from York, Pennsylvania. Although he possessed no prior military experience, he was a competent and conscientious officer, and excelled at this independent assignment. His vigilance at keeping Gates informed, particularly as regards the operations of the fleet and the various scouting forays dispatched down the Lake, was particularly noteworthy. Hartley, naturally nervous as he commanded the most forward element of the army, told Gates:

> I mount a guard of a subaltern, two sergeants, three corporals, forty-two privates; and a picket of a subaltern, one sergeant, three corporals, and thirty men, daily. One of the Captains acts as Officer of the Day. I have at least twenty-five sentries every night. I believe I shall not be surprised. I send out parties daily. The men here are recovering in their health fast, notwithstanding their duty.[8]

This is an exceptionally heavy security detail, and validates Hartley's skills as a military commander.

Hartley and the 6th Pennsylvania Battalion constructed a set of new fortifications at Crown Point. His position was intended to be nothing more than a fortified outpost, to support the advance guard of the fleet, and to serve as a base for scouting parties up Lake Champlain. Hartley was intended to serve as a screen for the main American position at Ticonderoga, so that Gates would not be surprised by a stealthy attack. Hartley had his men construct these new fortifications at what is known as Coffin Point, a few hundred yards south of Grenadier Point.[9] The major British fort at Crown Point was far too large to be defended by a single regiment, and in any case was in such disrepair that a single regiment (or even a thousand men) could not hope to repair it in a summer's labor. Why Hartley did not utilize either an older French redoubt located immediately to the west of the fort, or one of the three British redoubts surrounding the fort, is not documented. Quite likely, these extant redoubts were so contaminated by the sick and ill of the Northern Theater Army during its passage through Crown Point in early July that Hartley felt that a new encampment was essential to protect his men's health. Possibly, Hartley also felt that a new set of earthworks at a new location would surprise the British, and offer him a more defensible position in case of attack.

The Coffin Point earthworks were a simple irregular lineal line of works constructed in a roughly triangular shape to enclose the small point of land, with one minor salient angle to the north, and a major salient angle that was designed as a small bastion to the south. The works were constructed on high ground, and were essentially a redoubt. Given the cleared nature of the area following two decades of military occupation and settlement, the Coffin Point earthworks provided excellent fields of observation and fire towards Fort Crown Point and the peninsula itself. It was easily defensible. From these works, Hartley would dispatch regular patrols down Lake Champlain, using both bateaux and canoes by water, and land scouts. Hartley mentioned that it was under construction on August 14: "I am forming an intrenchment round my camp, which will effectually serve us against any attempt of the savages, Canadians, or the light troops of the enemy. We have made a considerable progress in it."[10] Hartley further described his work in a letter to Gates on August 25: "I have nearly completed a good intrenchment round my camp, and am forming an interior work which will further add to our security." He continued on September 6, "In my works here I can fight one thousand or fifteen hundred men conveniently."[11] Colonel Hartley appeared to be proud of the large redoubt that he had constructed, telling Arnold late in September from "Mount Hartley" that: "Our little Battery looks formidable. I have got my colours flying."[12]

Hartley apparently built at least rudimentary barracks inside his works. He told Gates on October 10:

> I understood from you and General St. Clair that it was intended two or three companies should be stationed here this winter. You were pleased to approve of some small essays of buildings I was making. I have, with a few carpenters and other tradesmen, erected a sufficient number of convenient barracks (when finished) for the men proposed to be stationed here. This you will find more proper than attempting to repair the barracks in the old fort, which could not be effected without many hands and much labor, and the party stationed in the old fort would not have been secure, with the works in their present ruin.[13]

At the same time Hartley complained about the quality of axes that had been provided to him:

> Had the last axes sent me been worth a farthing, I should not have desired my Ensign yesterday to call for more. Colonel Lewis some time since sent eighteen. I got them helved. They flinch at the first attack. Nothing can be done with them.

Small level pads for several huts also remain visible today, carefully cut into the reverse slopes of the point, protected by the earthworks but close by the fortifications for convenience.

Hartley mentioned in late August that he was searching the ruins of Fort Crown Point for artillery to reinforce his works, and had located "two good small guns" for which he required carriages.[14] Apparently Hartley kept searching, for on August 30 he reported having "three rusty cannon from the ruins of the works near here."[15] Gates noted that "the artillery stores which you have wrote for shall be sent immediately" on August 31.[16] These guns were mounted with carriages that Gates provided at Hartley's request. Hartley noted on September 6, "I shall fire three four-pounders, within a short space of time from each other, in case the enemy approach before I can send or hear from you."[17] Hartley also mentioned that he had an 18-pounder on this date, but that it needed a carriage. Hartley specifically requested in late September that canister rounds for the four-pounders be sent to him.

During the summer and fall, Doctor Johnston stayed with Hartley's Regiment at Crown Point. Hartley complained that the location was sickly and that many of his men suffered from agues and fevers. The situation was apparently particularly serious in October, for on October 10 Gates specifically ordered Doctor Potts to supply Johnston with "his wants."[18]

Upon the eventual defeat of the American fleet and approach of the victorious British, Hartley followed Gates' instructions and evacuated his Coffin Point fortifications, thus ending their brief history. Hartley and his 6th Pennsylvania Battalion had faithfully served as Gates' listening post at Crown Point for the entire summer and most of the fall, and had fulfilled all of Gates' expectations.

A Massachusetts officer, 44-year-old Colonel Jeduthan Baldwin, would design the main defensive position at Ticonderoga and Mount Independence. Baldwin was assigned as the Chief American Military Engineer of the Northern Theater Army. Although Baldwin had never received any formal military engineering training, he had served under renowned British engineer Captain William Eyre at the construction of Fort William Henry in 1755 and 1756.[19] Eyre was one of the finest British military engineers alive, and Baldwin had studied carefully under his tutelage as Fort William Henry was created.

By 1775 Baldwin was a prosperous farmer in Brookfield, Massachusetts, with a wife and four children. Without hesitation, he had joined the Patriots outside of Boston at the onset of the conflict, and had fought the British at Bunker Hill as early as June 1775. He had been dispatched to the Northern Theater in early 1776. How close a relationship Baldwin might have had with Gates is not known. He definitely met with Gates at the siege works of Boston on at least two occasions (January 22 and February 17, 1776) during the winter's activities there.[20]

Baldwin had moved north from New York City up the Hudson River to Canada, arriving at Fort Chambly on May 14. Within three days of his arrival he had chosen to be inoculated for smallpox, and had started suffering from the onset of the disease as early as May 23. Thus, he had contributed just over a week's worth of his engineering expertise to the Canadian army before he became incapacitated. Baldwin's inoculation derived case of smallpox was extremely severe, and he was doubtless fortunate that he had not contracted it in the natural way, for it would probably have proven fatal. Baldwin suffered severely, with a high fever, sore throat, and problems seeing. He noted that on June 5, "I broke out all over as thick as possible which caused severe itching." The next day he complained, "Had a high fever last night, my body being covered with the pox and an extreme fire & itching made me very uncomfortable." He joined in the retreat from Canada on June 11, although he was "very weak and unfit for travel." Baldwin reached Crown Point on June 24, having been sent ahead on "orders from Genl Sullivan to be ready with my baggage & intenching tools on board my battoe to go with him up the Lake to look out a convenient place to fortify or to proceed to Crown Point." It was not until he finally landed at Crown Point that it appears that Colonel Baldwin had sufficiently recovered from smallpox to render full service.

Baldwin's stay at Crown Point was short, for on July 7 he "received orders to go to Ticonderoga with some carpenters & to carry all my baggage, I collected all the intrenching tools together." Baldwin arrived at Ticonderoga on July 8 with Schuyler and Gates, and immediately began to survey the surrounding area. The day of his arrival, with the two Generals he examined "the grounds on the east side the Lake."

Baldwin, over the course of the summer, would direct an exhaustive construction project on both sides of Lake Champlain at Ticonderoga. Baldwin's final design would be meticulously considered, and it created an imposing citadel. As Von Clausewitz discussed, what Baldwin created was properly referred to as a fortified position. That is, a position "which nature and skill have made so strong that it must be considered unassailable. Fortified positions are not easily created by simple entrenchment.... Still less are they created by exploiting natural obstacles. Nature and skill usually work hand in hand in their creation."[21]

At Ticonderoga, Baldwin was concerned with two potential British avenues of approach. The first, which the British had used in both 1758 and 1759, was the promontory referred to as the Heights of Carillon. This prominent ridge ran from the Chute River roughly due north, with a width at its relatively flat top of 1,500 feet. It was along this ridge that the French commander the Marquis de Montcalm had constructed a strong line of log breastworks, which had inflicted a stunning and costly defeat on the British army in 1758. The British had again advanced against these works in 1759, initially capturing them, and then incorporating the works into their siege lines against the fort itself. The remnants of these breastworks were still discernable, but as they had been constructed entirely of logs and earth, and were never intended to be anything more than temporary features, after the passage of twenty years they were no longer defensible. Baldwin determined to exploit the trace of these breastworks. Accordingly, he constructed a formidable series of heavy earthworks along Montcalm's old lines, interspersed with new artillery batteries, several sally ports through which infantry could sortie to launch counterattacks, and massive new camps directly behind the earthworks so that they could be instantaneously manned. Baldwin incorporated one large new redoubt into the center of Montcalm's lines, and constructed three new square redoubts to protect the rear and flanks of the new lines. The smaller square redoubts were to be defended by one hundred men apiece, and mounted no artillery.

To the north, the Heights dropped off precipitously to a flat, level, sandy plain that extended approximately 1,800 feet to the west shoreline of Lake Champlain. This plateau, geologically a portion of the sandy floor and beaches of a once larger Lake Champlain, was extremely vulnerable. It was so flat that it offered no militarily dominant terrain upon which to base a defense, and it would be favored as an avenue of advance for any army coming from the North, as the British were certain to. In order to command not only this plain, but also Lake Champlain, Baldwin constructed a number of redoubts, several directly on the lake shore from which embedded batteries of artillery could command the lake. Baldwin cleverly constructed these redoubts to provide interlocking fields of fire, and backed them up with another formidable line of earthworks drawn across the plain and literally directly underneath the guns of Fort Ticonderoga, with a number of redoubts also integrated into them. It is obvious from the defensive configuration of Ticonderoga that Baldwin favored the construction of redoubts, particularly preferred to integrate redoubts into defensive lines, and located artillery batteries safely within the redoubts.

8. "I Think We Shall Be Very Well Prepared for the British Army"

A redoubt, as military engineering manuals of the time clearly stated, was a well-recognized and frequently utilized piece of military fortifications:

> The Redoubt is a work generally enclosed on all sides. It served to secure a post, a grand guard, or communications; to defend a defile, a bridge, a ford, etc. and is of various dimensions, that is, of different plans and profiles. The extent of it is proportioned to the number of men who are to defend it, and the parapet is generally of sufficient height to cover them. The redoubt has no precise or common form ... the form, indeed, is determined by the spot of ground on which it is raised, and the purposes for which it is constructed.... By redoubt ... is understood a work enclosed on all sides, and formed wholly of salient angles.[22]

Redoubts have a number of significant advantages. First, they are relatively simple structures, and can be readily built by soldiers with a minimum of professional engineering oversight. Since the number of trained engineers at Ticonderoga was strictly limited, this was an important consideration. Second, by definition any redoubt must be an enclosed work, and thus cannot be easily outflanked or turned. Third, they were specifically sized to the number of soldiers and artillery pieces that could reasonably be assumed to be available for their defense. A frequent mistake of the American army was to construct extensive lineal earthworks that required many soldiers to defend, often many more than would ever be available. Redoubts were not liable to this error. The expeditious use of redoubts sited to provide flanking and coordinated fields of fire permitted considerable ground to be guarded, with a minimum expenditure of labor and minimum numbers of soldiers. When they were integrated with external defensive lines, and contained artillery batteries, a redoubt was a considerably difficult work to be assaulted and seized. They were perfectly adapted to the utilization of the American army at Ticonderoga.[23]

Their construction must have been extremely challenging. The soil at this location, being predominantly sand, would have required considerable efforts to be used for construction. Timber would have to be obtained from another location either up or down the lake, as twenty years of occupation of the fort would have long since removed any construction sized timber from the area. Stone would have had to be first quarried and then carried down from the actual fort location, where limestone is readily available. Sod might have been cut and used to face the redoubts.

The major redoubt was referred to as the Jersey Redoubt for the soldiers of the 1st New Jersey Regiment that constructed the redoubt. It was located the farthest to the northeast, directly on the shores of Lake Champlain. The Jersey Redoubt was the largest of the numerous redoubts at Fort Ticonderoga. The redoubt was constructed of sand and timber, with a defensive dry ditch. Sergeant Timothy Tuttle of the 1st New Jersey first recorded "our party is at work at the Redout [redoubts] down by the side of Lake" on August 8, 1776.[24] Two days later he first noted its name: "Same day on fatigue at the Jersey Redoubt, 3 hours on and & 3 off fatigue." Lieutenant Colonel Matthew Ogden actually commanded the 1st New Jersey during the construction of this redoubt, as its Colonel William Winds was not then with the army. On August 11 Ogden wrote to his friend Aaron Burr, "I shall have the honor to command the New-Jersey redoubt, which I am now building with the regiment alone. It is situated on the right of the whole, by the water's edge. It is to mount two eighteen-pounders, two twelve, and four nine-pounders.

In this I expect to do honor to New-Jersey."²⁵ On September 12 Sergeant Tuttle stated, "Our Battalion has now don [done] the Jersey Redoubt," although his diary recorded various work continuing through late October. Regrettably, Tuttle provides only one account of the actual construction of the Jersey Redoubt, on October 22: "Pa. Battalion at work [on] the blind [on] the inside of Jersey Redoubt." By blind Tuttle was referring to a traverse, a heavy parapet constructed perpendicular to the main work to protect it from enfilading fire. A map from the Collections of the New York Historical Society noted that the Jersey Redoubt was designed for 300 men, and Lieutenant Ebenzer Elmer of Colonel Dayton's Third New Jersey Regiment recorded on November 20, 1776, that the Jersey Redoubt mounted one 32-pounder, two 18-pounder, one 9-pounder, and one 6-pounder cannon.²⁶ The Jersey Redoubt was intended to be the defensive strongpoint of the line of redoubts on the flat plateau immediately north of Lake Champlain, and also to provide artillery fire to control the lake. The particularly large cannon, among the heaviest at Fort Ticonderoga, were capable of inflicting considerable damage upon any British shipping in the lake's channel.

From a design standpoint, these redoubts were quite distinctive. The Jersey Redoubt was a particularly odd shape, consisting of three sharp salient angles to the north, east and south, with a square protrusion and entrance to the west. No reasons for this relatively odd configuration have been located. In accordance with military engineering treatises of the time, redoubts were to be specifically designed to fit the terrain that they were defending. The great instructor of military engineering at Woolwich Academy, Lewis Lochee, who exhaustively addressed how different redoubt shapes could be laid out and utilized, specified: "The redoubt has no precise or common form, but may be a square, a rhombus, a trapezium, a trapezoid, a pentagon either regular or irregular, a circle, or any other form. The form, indeed, is determined by the spot of ground on which it is raised, and the purposes for which it is constructed. When there is no essential reason to the contrary, the form is commonly a square."²⁷ Another highly experienced British engineering officer, Lieutenant J.C. Pleydell, who devoted nearly an entire work to an examination of how the shape of a redoubt could be adapted to the terrain, dictated: "It is not at all necessary redoubts should be traced exactly square, they are full as serviceable made in the figure of a rhomb, or with one side longer than another. This method, so far from being defective, becomes absolutely necessary when the ground neither allows, nor indeed requires, works to be exactly regular. Generally speaking, it is the spot redoubts are to be constructed on, as well as the lying of the ground near them, which should determine their figure."²⁸ Still, given the flat conditions alongside Lake Champlain, a regular square or rectangular configuration would have been entirely appropriate, and such an odd configuration as the Jersey Redoubt displayed was simply not warranted. The three particularly extreme salient angles resulted in a vulnerable configuration, and the design received a strong rebuke from Baldwin's assistant engineer that fall.

Christopher Pelissier, a French operator of a foundry at Three Rivers, had cast his lot with the Americans. Forced to flee Canada one step ahead of an arrest warrant issued by Governor Carleton, he had accepted a position as Engineer Lieutenant Colonel on July 29, 1776, and served as Baldwin's subordinate at Ticonderoga. He apparently did not arrive at Ticonderoga until September 18, as Baldwin noted on that date, "Dined at

General Gates with Mrs. Hay, Colonel de Haas, Lieutenant Colonel Pallicer and others. Colonel Pallicer is a Lieutenant Colonel, a Frenchman. Lieutenant Colonel Pallacer is come up as an Assistant Engineer."[29] In October 1776 Colonel Pelessier carefully evaluated the Jersey Redoubt:

> It is highly probable that the enemy will attack that redoubt at the salient angle on the north side, for the following reasons:
> Firstly, their column cannot be enfiladed from that angle.
> Secondly, their left, bearing on the water side, cannot be galled on that quarter.
> Thirdly, that angle is not at all defended.
> It is true the next redoubt may fire a little on the right of the column of the enemy, but nothing stops a column which is not enfiladed.
> It is evident that a column cannot be enfiladed from that acute angle, and that, therefore, the column will succeed. The enemy may then form a lodgement in the ditch without being seen either by the guard in the redoubt, the flanks of which are not defended, or by the next redoubt. And even through they should be seen from that redoubt, we could not fire upon them from that without running an imminent danger of firing upon ourselves. In this case the enemy have two ways left of carrying the redoubt. 1st, They can blow up that angle by opening a gallery under it. 2dly, By storming it, in which last case every thing will be in their favour. 1st. They may, unseen, destroy the fraises. 2nd, The interior epaulment, which is now making within the redoubt, is an insuperable obstacle to the continual fire which might be made for preventing its being carried, for now there is no sufficient room left between that epaulment and the banquette of the parapet. But even though there should be no epaulment, there is not room enough between the banquette and the platform of those guns which fire on the water, so that the troops within cannot perform their manoeuveres.
> I judge, therefore, that if the redoubt be attacked it will be at that acute angle, and that if attacked it must be carried, unless another redoubts should be made to cover it. And this last redoubt ought to be strong enough not to be carried by the enemy, for it cannot be too much remarked that the Jersey Redoubt on account of its too acute angle, cannot defend it.[30]

Four hundred feet to the left flank (or west) of the Jersey Redoubt, Baldwin designed a semi-circular redoubt, or as he referred to it "a half circular redoubt."[31] The Circular Redoubt was to be defended by one hundred men, and contained one 9-pounder and three 4-pounder cannon. As with the Jersey Redoubt, there is no reason for this configuration. The only contemporary military engineering manual that suggested such a design was Sir James Young's *An Essay on the Command of Small Detachments*, which proposed the use of a semi-circular shaped redoubt when defending the point of a hill.[32] This circumstance certainly did not occur at Fort Ticonderoga. The author suspects that Baldwin, by the time that he designed this redoubt, had designed numerous square or rectangular redoubts, and simply wanted to try something different. This circular design might have been clever on Baldwin's part, but it resulted in relatively limited enfilading fires to cover the front of the Jersey Redoubt, as previously discussed.

Four hundred feet to the left (or west) flank of the Circular Redoubt, Baldwin designed a more traditional rectangular redoubt. Although the evidence is sketchy, this redoubt was most likely referred to as The Sandy Redoubt. It was designed for one hun-

Fort Ticonderoga, seen from due north, from the position of the Half Circular Redoubt on the Lake Champlain Plains (author's collection).

dred men, and mounted one 12-pounder, one 9-pounder, and two 4-pounder cannon. This redoubt was located such that another four hundred feet to its left (west) flank was the precipitous slopes of the Heights of Carillon. Thus, all three of the redoubts that guarded this potential avenue of British attack were separated by four hundred feet, which provided for mutually supporting fires by both muskets and artillery.

To the rear of the Jersey Redoubt, another redoubt was constructed to cover the Lake Champlain flank (and rear) of the Jersey Redoubt. The British capability of performing effective amphibious assaults was well known and had been frequently demonstrated on other fields of strife, and Baldwin must have been concerned that the British could make such a landing from Lake Champlain. This irregular shaped redoubt was a very rough pentagon, facing to the north, in the direction of Lake Champlain. It contained a distinctive and large inside traverse, apparently to prevent artillery fire from sweeping its interior. Again, it was located about four hundred feet to the right rear of the Jersey Redoubt. The Oblong Redoubt as it was known, had been laid out by Colonel Baldwin on August 16, was to be defended by 250 men, and contained three 4-pounder cannon.[33]

Baldwin, utilizing a tactical version of Gates' operational layered defense, constructed a short segment of fortifications well to the rear of the main line of four redoubts. Thus, even if the British overwhelmed the main line of the Jersey, Half Circular, Sandy and Oblong Redoubts, they would still have to overcome another layer of defenses before they could strike at Fort Ticonderoga directly. This line was anchored on another Baldwin designed large, strong redoubt on the northern (right) flank. This was a roughly square redoubt that guarded the flank of a lineal section of earthworks, approximately four hundred feet long, that ran roughly southwest and terminated in a reconstructed French redoubt. The French had built this redoubt of dry stacked stone in 1758 to guard the left flank of Montcalm's earthworks on the Heights of Carillon. Formally known as The Germain Redoubt it was designed to contain two hundred men, but no artillery.

Finally, to safeguard Fort Ticonderoga itself from a direct amphibious assault from

Lake Champlain, Baldwin reconstructed another original French redoubt on Ticonderoga point, approximately seven hundred feet to the southeast of Fort Ticonderoga. The French had originally constructed this redoubt in 1756 to serve a traditional fortifications role to secure the eastern end of Fort Carillon. Known as the Grenadier Redoubt, this was a five faced work, connected to the main fort by a covered way. The Grenadier Redoubt was a substantial fortification of cut limestone laid with mortar, then filled with earth and rock rubble. It was to be defended with 250 men, and was known by the Americans as the Stone Redoubt. Baldwin maintained his quarters in this redoubt, as it was equidistant to both Ticonderoga and Mount Independence. Lieutenant Ebenezer Elmer of Colonel Dayton's Third New Jersey Regiment recorded on November 20, 1776, that the Stone Redoubt mounted one 24-pounder, one 9-pouner, two 6-pounder, three 4-pounder, and one 3-pounder cannon.[34] Thus, this redoubt was a formidable defensive position in its own right.

Baldwin apparently performed limited improvements or repairs to Fort Ticonderoga itself. The main Fort Ticonderoga, consistently referred to as The Old French Fort, served as the administrative headquarters for Gates and his army, as a secure warehouse for important supplies and as the guardhouse for the garrison. Some barracks space was also maintained within the fort. When he arrived at the army in late August, the Reverend Emerson wrote home to his wife in Concord:

> There are a number of very fine Barracks in the Fort, built of stone, that makes as good an appearance at a distance, as Harvard College, though not equal in height, yet of much greater length. In one of these I am at present stationed, where I want nothing to complete my satisfaction but my Friend's Company.[35]

A dungeon was also maintained underneath one of the demi-lunes (or ravelins) of the old French fort, which served as a jail for particularly hardened criminals of the army. Colonel Baldwin gleefully recorded in his journal on August 5, after a thief who had plundered him was apprehended:

> This afternoon I found in a thief's pack, who was discharged & going home, my Surtout, silk breeches & 2 pair of stockings. The thief is now confined in Irons in the dungeon (Great Demi-Lune).

Major Stevens supervised mounting and emplacing numerous artillery pieces throughout the French lines, the newly constructed redoubts, and the old French fort itself. In addition to the artillery pieces that were already present at Ticonderoga, and those few field pieces successfully evacuated from Canada, Stevens and his artillery artificers were responsible for constructing no less than forty-seven new cannon carriages and installing dismounted artillery barrels into them.[36]

The second component of the Ticonderoga Entrenched Position was a matching set of fortifications across Lake Champlain, on the eastern bank of Lake Champlain. These entrenchments and structures on what was initially known as Rattlesnake Hill or East Point were planned to accomplish two primary goals. First, fortifications at this point would be integrated with batteries on the Ticonderoga (west) side of Lake Champlain to obstruct naval traffic on Lake Champlain. Second, East Point was intended to serve as a major logistical support base for Ticonderoga.

Very early in its life, East Point or Rattlesnake Hill received a new christening. The thirteen United Colonies had signed a Declaration of Independence from England on July 4, 1776. By July 23 a copy of the Declaration of Independence had reached Ticonderoga. Brigadier General Arthur St. Clair of Pennsylvania publicly read it for the first time at Sabbath worship on July 28. From that point forward, every soldier suddenly began referring to the location exclusively as Mount Independence. No military orders have been located formally designating this name, but it was unquestionably in common usage. Because this title was hereafter exclusively used, Mount Independence will be subsequently employed throughout this study.

Mount Independence is located on a high, rocky peninsula of approximately three hundred acres size that extends into Lake Champlain. Lake Champlain bounds it upon its western side. It is bounded on its northern and eastern sides by East Creek. This creek, which empties into Lake Champlain at Mount Independence, is too deep to be forded. Rather, it must be formally bridged. East Creek is also lined with swamps and marshes, and thus comprises a highly effective defensive obstacle against any potential British approach. Only to the southeast is Mount Independence readily accessible by land, along with good landing spots on Lake Champlain to the southwest. To take advantage of this land access, the American army in 1776 constructed a road from Vermont settlements to the Mount. Because of the vagaries of topography, Mount Independence was an extremely secure installation.

Colonel John Trumbull, who assisted Baldwin with evaluating the site in early July, described it as such:

> The ground was finely adapted for a military post. At the northern point, it ran low into the lake, offering a good landing place; from thence the land rose to an almost level plateau, elevated from fifty to seventy-five feet above the lake, and surrounded, on three sides, by a natural wall of rock, every where steep, and sometimes an absolute precipice sinking to the lake. On the fourth and eastern side of the position ran a morass and deep creek at the foot of the rock, which strengthened that front, leaving room only, by an easy descent, for a road to the east, and to the landing from the southern end of the lake. We found plentiful springs of good water, at the foot of the rock. The whole was covered with primeval forest.[37]

Construction at Mount Independence began immediately in July, and continued until the onset of winter. By the termination of the construction season in late fall of 1776, Baldwin had supervised an immense number of construction projects on Mount Independence. The mount now featured a road leading from the southern landing into the interior of the fortifications. The whole was surrounded by a line of stout earthworks, rendering it impervious from infantry assault when combined with East Creek. A formidable battery had been erected on the northern point, sighted to fire directly up Lake Champlain. A large fort was constructed at the center of the works, with another battery known as the Horseshoe Battery located between the two. Ancillary structures included two guardhouses, a hospital, a wharf, a giant gin-tripod, a magazine, a munitions laboratory, and numerous soldiers' huts. The fortifications on Mount Independence were well-sited. Lieutenant Ebenezer Elmer would visit on November 5: "went over and viewed the works on Mount Independent [sic], which are very strong both by nature and art."[38]

Colonel Baldwin described the various engineering projects that he had underway on Mount Independence, in a litany that reveals the frenetic building pace that the American army under Gates sustained.

> [July] 9. Found water by digging on the top of the Hill.
> [July] 10. Went over & marked out a road from the North Point to the top of hill....
> [July] 11. Went over to the Point with 200 men to clear a road, dig well, etc.
> [July] 23. Laid out the park for the artillery on Rattlesnake Hill.
> [July] 25. General Gates and several other officers went over to the point with me & highly approved of the works that I had laid out there & ordered that 200 men should work daily at least & as many more as could be employed.
> [August] 3. Laid out the ground for the Laboratory & Store near the park on Mount Independence, drawing timber together for those buildings.
> [August] 17. Laid out a wharf at the South side of Independent Point & ordered a large Store House to be built & also 2 guard houses....
> [August] 22. Ordered the setting of the Great Store House....
> [September] 26. I went across Independent Point to ... see the Store & Wharf & other works going on there.
> [September] 27. Went over to Independent Point with General Gates, General St. Clair & Colonel Trumbull to view the ground for a fort to the built.
> [October] 1. Went over to the [Independent] Point with Colonel Pallicer to lay out the Fort. We run round the work but did not finish.
> [October] 2. Went with Colonel Pallicer, Captain Newland & Lieutenant Dallas over to Independent Hill, laying out the Fort agreeable to a New Plan I had drawn.
> [October] 11. Went over to Independent Point. Began to set up the pickets.
> [October] 17. Began to make a log across the Lake or chain to prevent shipping coming past the Jersey Redoubt.
> [October] 20. Proposed making a bridge across to Independent Point. It was approved of by the General.
> [October] 25. Finish the boom across & building a Bridge.
> [October] 29. Finished the bridge across the Lake to Independent Point, so that men could pass.
> [November] 7. Raised a barrack on Independent Point.
> [November] 16. Raised 2 barracks on Independent Point.

In addition to the fortifications and logistical structures, the Continental Army constructed numerous wooden huts for living on Mount Independence. Captain Cushing of Greaton's 24th Regiment noted as early as July 31: "Lieutenant [Nathaniel] Niles and myself employed in Building an house." By August 29, Cushing was already improving his hut, "built a chimney on the house."[39] Henry Sewall of Massachusetts was also involved in hut building endeavors on Mount Independence. Almost immediately upon his regiment's arrival there he noted, "The regt. employ'd building wooden tents and without tools too." Sewall dedicated numerous entries to the engineering of his hut, on September 20 and 21 he added a chimney to his residence, and on October 10 and 11 he made shingles and "finish'd shingling our house."[40]

Baldwin would record in his journal on July 28 on the frantic activity that he was supervising:

> I paid Esquire Gilliland 212 Dollars for Carpenters tools as there is no Quartermaster general at present with this army, I have that duty to do in part & I have the entire direction of all the House & Ship Carpenters, the Smiths, Armorers, Rope Makers,

the Wheel & Carriage makers, Miners, Turners, Coalyers, Sawyers & Shingle makers, which are all together 286, besides the direction of all the fatiguing parties, so that I have my hands & mind constantly employed night & day, except when I am asleep and then sometimes I dream.[41]

This intense amount of labor continued throughout the summer and fall at Mount Independence. As late as October 5, the Orderly Book for Colonel Mott's Connecticut State Regiment stipulated from "Mount Independant":

> The former work on Mount Independant now completed, the three brigades on the mount, hundred men, in following to proportion, viz.: The first brigade, 56 men; 2 brigade, 102 men; 3 brigade, 154 men — two hundred are to be imployed in cutting pickets; one hundred in digging a trencht & foundation for a magazine for powder. This party to be furnished dayly.[42]

Gates' army also constructed a new road running southeast from Mount Independence, to link the Ticonderoga fortress with communities in Vermont. Previously, the road between Crown Point and Fort No. 4 on the Connecticut River had provided a land route between New England and Lake Champlain. However, with the abandonment in early July of Crown Point, this road was vulnerable to being interdicted by British action, thus leaving the American army on Lake Champlain without land linkage to the east. Accordingly, the Continental Army determined to construct a new road, from the replacement Mount Independence on Lake Champlain. General Schuyler had previously contemplated not only fortifications at Mount Independence, but also a road to connect it to New England, but lack of resources had prevented him from completing the project, as he had described to Washington in mid–June:

> The spot where Ticonderoga now stands was, I conceive, very judiciously occupied by the French, because it commanded both the passes by water into these Colonies, and afforded an easy access to any reinforcements they might choose to send up, as well as a safe retreat whenever they might be under the necessity of making one. But although it equally commands, now in our possession, the waters which lead to this part of the country, yet it is so situated that, if invested by an army, the intercourse with the fort by Lake George is immediately cut off.... If a fortress was erected on the east side of Lake Champlain, nearly opposite to Ticonderoga, it would equally command both communications, with this advantage, that the militia of the Northern Colonies are more at hand for immediate succor, may all march by land to the fort, and attempt to raise a siege, while their provisions may be conveyed by Wood Creek, the waters of which are navigable to within thirteen miles of Fort Edward. But, as I have already observed in mine of the 15th, we have no men, and I may add, no implements, even to put Ticonderoga in a state of defense.[43]

Gates, finding himself with sufficient men and implements, shortly began to construct just such a line of communications. On September 8, 1776, Gates' army Orderly Book maintained by the stalwart John Trumbull, his Deputy Adjutant General:

> One Captain, two Sub[altern]s, two Serjeants, one Drum & Fifty Rank and File to parade at Sunrise tomorrow morning to begin to cut the road from the East side of Mt. Independence toward the Bridge, now building cross Otter creek, Mr. Hecock & Mr. David Remington who have marked the road will constantly attend to direct the party. The party to be taken from Col. Wyngate's N. Hampshire Regts and to

take their Arms, ammunition & packs with them. The captain to attend at Hd Quarters at 6 o'clock this afternoon.[44]

Construction is recorded to have continued on this road through at least November 1776.[45] Thus, it had little impact on the 1776 campaign, but it would play a critical role in the 1777 Saratoga campaign.

In early September, Baldwin also laid out fortifications on the large, flat knoll north of the sawmill and bateaux landing on La Chute River:

> [September] 8. In the afternoon I went out to Colonel Brewer's and Willard's Encampments & laid out a fort on the Top of the Mount, North of Mills.[46]

Baldwin, assisted by Colonels Wayne and St. Clair, had actually picked out the site on August 24, when Gates ordered:

> The Chief Engineer with Colonel St. Clair and Colonel Wayne will tomorrow morning at 10 o'clock take a review of the ground near the saw mill, fix upon the proper spot for the incampment of two Continental Regiments and the best situation for throwing up a redoubt for to command the pass.[47]

This set of relatively simple fortifications would come to be known as Mount Hope. They were located about 1,500 feet northwest of the sawmill, on top of a steep and prominent hill. It consisted of a simple entrenched camp, with several sally ports, and a triangular redoubt on the western face. It also contained a guard house.[48] The small, relatively tight earthworks were built around a precipitous cliff to the north that was entirely impossible to ascend. These fortifications constituted a strong post that would have required a deliberate attack to overrun; and were perfectly sized for two regiments reinforced by the company of Mohican Indians. Contrary to popular interpretation established at the Mount Hope site several years ago, there was never a formal blockhouse at Mount Hope.[49] Mount Hope was garrisoned by two regiments of Massachusetts Militia that had been raised that summer specifically for service at Ticonderoga, under the command of Colonels Samuel Brewer and Aaron Willard. In September these regiments mustered just over eight hundred healthy militiamen between them.[50]

The fortified camp at Mount Hope was not significant because of its military engineering design, but simply because of its location. It commanded the high ground above the La Chute River and Ticonderoga Portage. So long as the Americans occupied Mount Hope, the British could not outflank the works at Fort Ticonderoga and the Heights of Carillon to the west. Mount Hope thus prevented a British force from swinging around to the southeast side of the La Chute River, and occupying a prominent hill then popularly known as Sugar Loaf Hill.[51] Sugar Loaf completely dominated both Fort Ticonderoga and Mount Independence, and artillery emplaced here could easily command both the La Chute River and the South Bay of Lake Champlain, preventing any American force from retreating to the south. It was absolutely key terrain, although some American officers considered the height to be inaccessible. Colonel Trumbull did not believe them, and sometime during the late summer he performed an experiment in which he had conclusively determined the military significance of Sugar Loaf:

> Our entire position formed an extensive crescent, of which the center was a lofty eminence [later] called Mount Defiance, the termination of that mountain ridge which

> separates Lake George from Lake Champlain, and which rises precipitously from the waters of the latter to a height of six hundred feet. This important position had hitherto been neglected by the engineers of all parties, French, English and American. I had for some time, regarded this eminence as completely overruling our entire position. It was said, indeed, to be at too great a distance to be dangerous; but by repeated observation I had satisfied my mind that the distance was by no means so great as was generally supposed, and at length ... I ventured to advance the new and heretical opinion, that our position was bad and untenable, as being overlooked in all parts by this hill. I was ridiculed for advancing such an extravagant idea. I persisted, however, and ... I requested and obtained the general's [General Gates'] permission to ascertain it by experiment. Major Stevens [Ebenezer Stevens, Commanding Officer of Artillery in the Northern Department] was busy at the north point of Mount Independence in examining and proving cannon; I went over to him on the following morning and selected a long double fortified French brass gun, a twelve pounder, which was loaded with the proof charge of best powder and double shotted. When I desired him to elevate this gun so that it should point at the summit of Mount Defiance, he looked surprised, and gave his opinion that the shot would not cross the lake. "That is what I wish to ascertain, Major" was my answer, "I believe they will, and you will direct your men to look sharp, and we too will keep a good look-out; if the shot drop in the lake their splash will easily be seen; if, as I expect, they reach the hill, we shall know it by the dust of the impression which they will make upon its rocky face." The gun was fired, and the shot were plainly seen to strike at more than half the height of the hill. I returned to head-quarters and made my triumphant report, and after dinner requested the general and officers who were with him to walk out upon the glacis of the old French fort, where I had ordered a common six pound field gun to be placed in readiness. This was, in their presence, loaded with the ordinary charge, pointed at the top of the hill, and when fired, it was seen that the shot struck near the summit. Thus the truth of the new doctrine was demonstrated, but still it was insisted upon, that this summit was inaccessible to an enemy. This also I denied, and again resorted to experiment. Gen. Arnold, Col. Wayne, and several other active officers, accompanied me in the general's barge, which landed us at the foot of the hill, where it was most precipitous and rocky, and we clambered to the summit in a short time. The ascent was difficult and laborious, but not impracticable, and when we looked down upon the outlet of Lake George, it was obvious to all, that there could be no difficulty in driving up a loaded carriage ... the summit of Mount Defiance looked down upon, and completely commanded the narrow parts of both the lakes.[52]

Still, although Trumbull's experiment had revealed the importance of Sugar Loaf, the promontory was neither occupied nor guarded. It remained vacant and vulnerable.

There is no evidence in his meticulous and detailed journals that Baldwin ever visited Sugar Loaf Hill. There is similarly no evidence in Gates' lengthy papers that he ever personally ascended or inspected Sugar Loaf. Although the entrenchments on Mount Hope screened Sugar Loaf from a direct occupation by the British, a small scouting party could certainly have circumnavigated the American posts, and reached the slopes of Sugar Loaf. It was common knowledge that Sugar Loaf afforded an excellent observation site of Fort Ticonderoga. Throughout the Seven Years' War, the famous Robert Rogers of New Hampshire and his almost exclusively Provincial Rangers had regularly used the location to spy on the French Carillon. Previous to the 1758 attack on Fort Ticonderoga, British Chief Engineer Lieutenant Matthew Clerk, guarded by a party of the Rangers, twice evaluated the

French fortifications on the Heights of Carillon from Sugar Loaf.[53] During the British assault on July 8, Sir William Johnston and his Native American force watched the attack from Sugar Loaf. On March 6, 1759, Rogers with a large party of his Provincial Rangers escorted British Military Engineer Lieutenant Diederick Brehm to the top of what he called "Sugar Bush Mountain " to enable Brehm to prepare a detailed map of the French defenses.[54]

Given the fact that Sugar Loaf was absolutely a piece of key terrain, and offered an incredible overlook of the American fortified position at Ticonderoga, it should never have been left unsecured regardless of the fact that, so long as Mount Hope was defended, a major British force could never reach the slopes of Sugar Loaf. The Americans certainly had sufficient time and resources available to have established a solitary blockhouse, garrisoned by a company of infantry, on top of the mountain. It could thus have been secured from any potential British utilization.[55] In the event, in 1776 no British soldier or Indian scout ever climbed Sugar Loaf. But the next year, the Year of the Hangman, the failure of the Americans to defend Sugar Loaf Mountain would be dramatically revealed as a catastrophic flaw in their defensive configuration, and would compromise the entire American position at Ticonderoga and Mount Independence.

Baldwin recorded his progress on these various new fortifications:

> [July] 30. At Ticonderoga & lodged in the Redoubt east of the Garrison in the point of Rocks.
> [August] 8. I laid out a redoubt on the North end of the French Lines by the Lake.
> [August] 15. Laid out & began 2 Redoubts on the North end of the old French lines in the afternoon.
> [August] 16. Laid out a Redoubt on the North side of the point with Colonel St. Clair & Captain Newland.
> [August] 20. Went with General Brickett to the Redoubts. Laid out a ½ Circular one.
> [August] 24. Laid out a Redoubt on the North West side on the plain at the old French lines.
> [September] 17. Began to repair my Redoubt.
> [October] 12. Laying platforms in my Redoubt.

Two colored drawings exist of these redoubts, both completed by British Lieutenant James Hunter in 1777, looking south down Lake Champlain from the British landings further down the lake. The Jersey redoubt and its attendant flanking redoubts occupy only the backgrounds of these two pieces of artwork. Hunter's primary interest was the British army and navy that he portrayed in the foreground. Few military engineering or architectural details are discernable. But what is distinctive is just how imposing and formidable these earthworks appeared. They clearly controlled Lake Champlain, and their frowning presence certainly made an impression on Hunter. In the short months between July and October 1776 the Americans had created a true fortress at Ticonderoga. It was not a neat process, as it involved the excavation of multitudes of damp, muddy earth. But through a summer and fall of arduous work, the American Northern Theater Army at Ticonderoga actually became an army, and it was an army that now occupied a formidable defensive position.

9

"We Build a Thing Called a Gondola"
Creation of the American Advanced Guard, Skenesboro, July to September 1776

Colonel John Trumbull described the condition of the American Northern Theater Army as it wrested to gain domination of Lake Champlain, and the seemingly overwhelming challenges that it faced, in a letter to his father on July 12:

> It is true that we build a thing called a gondola, perhaps as much as one in a week, but where is our rigging for them, where our guns? We have to be sure a great train of artillery, but very few of them are mounted on carriages, and materials or conveniences for making them are very slender. We have carpenters, shipbuilders, and blacksmith, in plenty, but neither places for them to work in, nor materials in that plenty we ought to have. To oppose the enemy on the lake, we have now a schooner of twelve carriage guns, a sloop of eight, two small schooners to carry four or six each, and three gondolas. The large schooner will be in good sailing order in two or three days, the sloop [*Royal Savage*] is a most unmanageable thing; it is not possible to beat up against a head wind in her, the two small schooner are not armed, the gondolas are not armed, and even the carriages of the guns are yet to be made.[1]

The augmentation to the small American Lake Champlain fleet was to be created at Skenesboro (now Whitehall), on the southern end of what is known as the South Bay of Lake Champlain. Skenesboro was named for its founder, Philip Skene, a former Major in the British Army.[2]

Born in London in 1725, Skene had joined the Royal Regiment of Foot, also known as the Royal Scots, when he was only eleven years old. He served in his first campaign in 1739 in the West Indies. He fought on the European Continent in the War of Austrian Succession; and then for King George II at the Battle of Culloden on April 16, 1746, where he was severely wounded. Now a Lieutenant, Skene sailed for North America in 1756. He served at the unsuccessful assault on Fort Carillon in July 1758, and the successful British siege of the French Fort in 1759. Promoted to Brigade Major for gallantry at Ticonderoga in 1759, he spent the remainder of the war in the construction of Fort Crown Point. Upon termination of hostilities, he transferred to the West Indies and participated in the Storming of Havana in 1762. Returning to North America, Skene sold his commission in 1769, and settled at the southern bay of Lake Champlain.

Skene had acquired a large tract of 45,000 acres of land at the falls of Wood Creek in 1763, and he had obtained another 1,000 acres in 1765. Skene rapidly organized a settlement of 25 families, and began to establish what was known as Skene's Patent. Within only ten years, Skene had constructed a large industrial complex, supported by the largest and most prosperous settlement on the southern end of Lake Champlain. Only St. Jean at the northern end of Lake Champlain rivaled Skenesboro in size and facilities.

The first facility established by Skene was a sawmill at the east side of the falls of Wood Creek. A dam was constructed to support the sawmill, and also supported a stone gristmill at the same location. To the west was an iron foundry and iron forge, as Skene described it "a most complete bloomery for constructing bar iron of four fires and two hammers with its implements" housed in a 46-foot square building, with an adjacent coal house. Skene also constructed a large barn and stables, no less than 134 feet long and 35 feet wide. Rounding out the industrial complex were a shipyard and carpentry, cooper and furrier shops.[3] Skene operated a two-masted schooner, which eventually became the *Liberty* of the American Lake Champlain fleet.

He also constructed a prominent limestone mansion, worthy of his position as a long-serving English officer gentleman and the squire of his manor. Surrounding the industrial complex were the houses of the 24 families that had settled with him, and numerous slaves.

Skene, having fought for the House of Hanover in no less than four wars, remained loyal to the Crown. He had been arrested at the onset of hostilities, and remained in arrest through the 1776 campaign. However, the valuable and complete industrial complex that he had constructed at the terminus of Wood Creek was immediately taken over by the American patriots, and would shortly become the hub of the American fleet building efforts.

When Captain Edward P. Williams of Massachusetts passed through Skenesboro in late April on his way to join the northern army, he noted of the hamlet, "This Skenesborough the whole township belongs to Major Skene ... he has a fine saw mill & grist mill, forges to make iron. A fine stream called Wood Creek empties here into the South Bay."[4] Captain Williams would shortly have occasion to become much more intimately acquainted with Major Skene's small settlement, as he commanded a company of carpenters here during the fleet's construction, arriving there in early July. Henry Sewall, a soldier with a Massachusetts regiment who was passing through Skenesborough en route to Ticonderoga, provided a divergent opinion on September 1. Sewall found the encampment to be "a low unwholsom country."[5] Given the fact that many of the ship's carpenters assigned to Skenesboro would eventually become ill with various fevers, Sewall was correct in his assessment of the low, swampy ground around Skene's little community in the wilderness.

The shipyard was established directly at the southern end of Lake Champlain, on the west side of Wood Creek, on deep water to simplify launching the ships, and immediately adjacent to Skene's iron works and sawmill, thus eliminating the requirement for transportation of lumber and iron. Directly to the west was a storehouse that Skene had previously established for his plantation, and which was presumably commandeered by the Americans to serve a similar purpose for the fleet. Again, this insured that necessary supplies and equipment for construction of the fleet were instantly available, without having to be moved to the site.

For the Americans to maintain control of Lake Champlain, a considerable augmentation of the tiny, under-armed fleet on the lake was necessary. Most likely it was General Philip Schuyler that personally selected Skenesboro as the location to expand the American fleet, as he would have been well familiar with the industrial resources that Skene had previously constructed there (after all, Skene was a competitor in business with Schuyler). To prevent congestion at Skenesboro, and since all of the cannon were already located at Ticonderoga and Crown Point, once the ships were afloat in the muddy brown waters of Lake Champlain, they were sent up the South Bay to Mount Independence and Ticonderoga, where they were armed, rigged and outfitted for action.

Schuyler anticipated the need for naval power on Lake Champlain. As early as April 20 Schuyler had sent his Assistant Deputy Quartermaster, Harmanus Schuyler (no relation) to Skenesboro. Harmanus Schuyler started by constructing bateaux for use on Lake Champlain, but by June 12 he had transitioned to building gondolas. On that date, Harmanus Schuyler reported that he had two gondolas under construction.[6] Quartermaster Schuyler reported that one gondola was launched on June 27, and the second launched on June 30, while the American army was still ensconced in Canada. He described these gondolas as being "50 foot long and 15 foot beem and 4½ deep."

Gates, early in July, dispatched a large contingent of his army to Skenesboro to augment Quartermaster Schuyler's team of carpenters at work. By this date, Schuyler's industrious workers had already placed another three gondolas on the stocks under construction. Considerable numbers of artisans and carpenters, drawn from throughout his army and augmented from various colonies, were in the greatest demand. All of Skene's facilities were inspected, and put back into operation. Logs were cut from the surrounding countryside, and drawn by oxen and horses to Skene's mills to be cut into lumber. A shipyard sprung into existence, almost overnight, for a fleet had to be constructed at Skenesboro, and not a moment could be wasted.

The Continental Army fleet that already existed, and which was to be considerably strengthened by the fledgling shipyard at Skenesboro, would eventually consist of three general classes of vessels. The first were the sailing ships, schooners and sloops. These were ships propelled entirely by wind power and sailing skill, were without oars, and could not be rowed. A schooner is a type of ship with sails on two or more masts, usually a fore and aft mast. A sloop has a single mast. The four previously existing ships of Arnold's fleet, the *Liberty, Enterprise, Revenge* and *Royal Savage*, were all sailing ships. Although these vessels were all armed with cannon, they were generally small in poundage, and these ships possessed limited combat capabilities. In fact, the *Liberty*'s fighting capacity was so marginal that Arnold employed it as a messenger vessel; and the *Enterprise* was utilized as a hospital vessel rather than being employed in combat. On September 6 Surgeon McCrea provided a list of the sick and wounded "on board the fleet to be sent to the General Hospital" from "on board Sloop Enterprise."[7] The *Royal Savage* was the largest ship of the fleet, apparently possessed an actual cabin, and was thus used as the flagship. However, to its detriment, the *Royal Savage* had sailing problems in unstable or irregular winds. On October 3 Bayze Wells, aboard the gondola *Providence*, recorded: "This day the wind continued southerly and very strong we ware oblig'd to pay out the whole length of our cables to keep out of the way of the Royall Savage."[8]

All of the newer vessels constructed by the Americans were capable of being rowed. The second class was the gondolas. Essentially, a gondola was a gigantic, oversized bateaux complete with flat bottom, pointed ends, and a large rear rudder. All of the eight gondolas constructed at Skenesboro were generally similar. Based upon the dimensions of the gondola *Philadelphia*, recovered in 1935 from the floor of Valcour Bay, the gondolas were 54 feet in length, and mounted three cannon. The largest cannon was mounted on the bow on a sliding carriage, and two smaller cannon were mounted on field carriages on the left and right broadside. Two of the gondolas had platforms installed for firing mortars on their sterns, but this feature was quickly deleted when the available mortars all self-destructed during test firings. The gondolas were equipped with oars, and possessed a single mast with two square sails (a mainsail and topsail). Because the gondolas lacked a keel and had flat bottoms, they were notoriously poor sailors, and any contrary wind would send them skipping wildly across the surface of Lake Champlain. Horatio Gates, when he espied his first gondolas at Ticonderoga, was singularly unimpressed. He complained, "They seem to be vessels very unwieldy to move & very indifferent for the purpose intended."[9] Their sails were generally useful only when the wind was blowing dead astern. The gondolas were apparently constructed because they were simple to build, could be assembled relatively rapidly, and required less cordage than the other ships. When launched they would be easier to operate than the row galleys. Apparently these factors influenced their early construction, although it should be noted that the four row galleys that were subsequently constructed were the preeminent vessels of the Lake Champlain fleet. In truth, because of their odd gun configuration and poor sailing qualities, the gondolas contributed little to the American cause, except through numerically augmenting the fleet's size.

The third class of vessels constructed was a distinctive hybrid, known as row galleys. They were based upon the Moorish row galleys that American sailors had seen used to great advantage in the Mediterranean Ocean. They contained two masts, which were rigged with a lateen or triangular sail that was highly adaptable to the shifting wind conditions that are endemic to Lake Champlain. The row galleys possessed a well-defined keel and graceful lines that when combined with the lateen sails made them quite maneuverable. When they could not be sailed, or as an augmentation when speed was mandated, the row galleys were also equipped with a suite of oars, creating a highly adaptable vessel. They could be operated in comparatively shallow waters, another great advantage on Lake Champlain. Row galleys were also used with considerable success to defend both the Hudson and Delaware rivers during the War for American Independence. Once Arnold arrived at Skenesboro, he transferred all of his efforts from constructing gondolas to row galleys, as Quartermaster Schuyler reported on July 24:

> General Arnold arrived here yesterday and thinks ten [gondolas] in number will be sufficient. Capt. Winslow has arriv'd from Connecticut and General Arnold thinks proper for him to go immediately to work at building a Spanish Galley. Her length is to be 63 feet Long 18 feet beam 5 foot hold 14 inches waist.[10]

The *Lee*, constructed from the frame of a vessel wisely evacuated from Canada by Arnold, was a somewhat contrived, field expedient row galley, best defined as a cutter.

The most capable vessels in the American fleet were the four specifically designed row galleys — the *Congress, Trumbull, Washington*, and *Gates*. The *Gates* would be completed too late in the season to join the fleet in 1776. These four vessels were relatively large, being 72 feet in length, and mounted between eight to ten large cannon. They also had larger crews than the smaller gondolas, consisting of:

> A Captain, Lieutenant, Master, Mate, Gunner, Boatswain, Carpenter & Knotter & twenty-eight seamen; for the Marines, Captain, 2 Lieutenants, 2 Sergeants, 2 Corporals, 1 Drum & 32 privates — in all 76.[11]

Given their sailing qualities, rowing versatility, and weight of metal they comprised the most effective and powerful vessels in the American fleet. The first of the four row galleys was launched at Skenesboro on August 3.

The first class of vessels worked on was the eight flat-bottomed gondolas. Quartermaster Schuyler already had several gondolas completed by the end of July, reporting on the 24th of that month, "There is four Gundolas sent of to Ticonderoga the last of which was sent off yesterday about 4 Oclock in the afternoon. There is two more almost completed and will be ready in a few days."[12] The last gondola was completed by August 15, and Quartermaster Schuyler announced: "I can inform yr Excellency that we are to build no more gundelos by the Generals Arnold and Waterbury orders."[13]

The first row galley to be worked on was the small cutter *Lee*, which was already partially completed when it was evacuated from Canada. The rapidity and ease with which the gondolas could be constructed was proven when the first five vessels launched at Skenesboro were all ships of this class, followed by the *Lee*. The row galleys came last, predominantly because they were more complex designs, and also required considerably larger quantities of cordage than the relatively simplistic gondolas.

To construct this fleet at Skenesboro, Schuyler had to locate every single piece of nautical equipment. He first had to find the personnel including experienced shipwrights and carpenters, to the sawyers and sailors and marines. Then he had to supply a veritable avalanche of requirements including cordage, nails, iron, cannon, shot, gunpowder, sails, rigging, anchors, cookware, navigational equipment, literally everything that would be required to be tossed into a sailing vessel before it would be deemed to be seaworthy. It all had to be located, then purchased. One of the great unsung heroes of this massive logistical effort was Captain Richard Varick, who was Schuyler's Aide de Camp. Varick, 23, had been born in New Jersey, but had joined a New York regiment as early as 1775. Varick was a practicing New York City attorney before the war, and his legal training clearly facilitated his issuing contracts and making arrangements with contractors. Varick had a reputation as an energetic, active, vigorous and enthusiastic young officer whose administrative and organizational skills were particularly valued. Varick would serve first Philip Schuyler, then Benedict Arnold and finally George Washington as a principal staff officer throughout the entire American Revolution.[14]

Varick appears to have coordinated this supply system, with Schuyler providing the contacts, and Varick actually issuing the orders for the equipment. Schuyler and Varick expended exhaustive efforts on obtaining the supplies for the fleet, which they eventually obtained from practically every conduit that can be imagined. A letter from Varick to

Gates written from Albany on August 4 essentially described the convoluted supply system that Schuyler and Varick had to establish and depend upon:

> I have procured about twenty-five hundred weight [of rope], from two-and-a-half-inch downwards, which was ... sent up two days since from Schenectady. I have also procured four new cables of four inch by sixty fathoms, at that place; and we have still here seven or eight good anchors and cables, to be forwarded as soon as wagons can be procured.... The sail cloth and cordage is sent for to Connecticut; and an invoice of such other articles as are not to be had here is sent to his Excellency General Washington. The blocks will be finished in about ten days. By the General's orders I have sent an officer with two bateaux to Poughkeepsie for such of them as are finished, and for sixty coils of slow match, and one hundred pounds of twine, which are to be had there. An express is sent to Governor Trumbull and the Salisbury Iron Works for the swivels, and to Colonel Robert Livingston for the different kinds of cannon and grape shot, as also for the anchors and cables which are wanting. A skipper is sent down the river to purchase all the anchors, cables, sails, and rigging, that are to be procured from the proprietors of vessels between this place and Poughkeepsie. The six anchors and cables lately sent from New York, I hope, will arrive by the first southerly wind.[15]

On those rare occasions that some few necessary items could actually be located with the army, they were dispatched to either Skenesboro or Ticonderoga, depending upon whether or not they were needed to construct the fleet, or to outfit the ships once launched. On August 2 Varick ordered Lieutenant Colonel Peter Gansevoort, Commanding Officer of Fort George:

> I am directed by General Schuyler to desire you to forward to General Gates with all possible dispatch, all the junk & oakum from your post & all the pitch, except one barrel, together with all the steel & iron & that you will immediately send me a return of what has been forwarded from your post to Ticonderoga & that hereafter you will send me a return every three days of what articles you forward to General Gates. All the anchors, cables, rigging, cordage, military & naval stores, axes & intrenching tools which are or shall arrive at your post are immediately to be forwarded without the least delay.[16]

Schuyler wrote to Washington from Albany on August 3, "I have procured from the proprietors of vessels and the merchants of this place and Schenectady all the anchors, cables, and cordage that was to be had from them."[17] Whatever could be obtained from the well-established Albany nautical community was purchased, and Schuyler's experience in operating commercial sailing vessels on the Hudson and Mohawk rivers doubtless provided him with valuable connections.

Varick regularly forwarded Gates supplies that had been purchased or manufactured in Albany or on the Hudson River. On July 27:

> I send you this morning about twelve hundred weight of spikes, of different sizes, and four hundred weight of twenty-four penny nails, for the carpenters at Skenesborough, as also some axes, in addition to the twelve hundred heretofore sent, and some spades and pickaxes.[18]

Varick followed up, writing Assistant Commissary General Harmanus Schuyler from Albany on August 3:

> I have some days since sent a bellows & a set of blacksmiths tools, one ton of iron, 1 hogshead of oakum & a quantity of junk to Ticonderoga, to be forwarded to you & have sent orders to have it pushed on with dispatch. By the General's directions I have ordered the pitch & tar & steel to be sent to you from Fort George. I shall however, by the very first waggons, send to Mr. Yates ... for your use 500 [hundredweight] iron, 200 [hundredweight] steel, 3 grindstones, some more oakum & spades & axes.[19]

When General Waterbury ran short of "deck nails" at Ticonderoga and Skenesboro, he did not hesitate to "send this moment an express to Albany to have them forwarded with all speed."[20] This suggests that the blacksmiths in Albany were also working long hours and days to satisfy the voracious appetite of the fleet for supplies of every ilk.

Varick wrote to His Excellency General George Washington on August 5, describing the supplies that were still available at or around Albany:

> Of the many articles wanted, handspikes, round shot, rammers, sponges, worms, priming horns, priming wires, and tube boxes are the only ones that can possibly be procured or made at or near this place; and no copper, lead, or tin is to be had between this place and New York. In mine of the 3d, by express, I forgot to inform your Excellency that I had sent for the anchors to Colonel Robert Livingston.[21]

The Continental Army maintained a major shipyard at Poughkeepsie on the eastern bank of the Hudson River, from which they were endeavoring to construct a sufficient fleet to obstruct the passage of the Hudson River. They had created and amassed considerable shipbuilding stores at this shipyard, which Schuyler was able to requisition for the Skenesboro fleet. The Continental Shipyard at Poughkeepsie would be Schuyler's major source for the Lake Champlain fleet.[22] Varick regularly dispatched officers and bateaux from Albany to Poughkeepsie to summon and retrieve necessary supplies for the Skenesboro fleet. The first such effort was launched on August 3, when Varick ordered Lieutenant Timothy Hughes:

> You, with the party of men under your command, will immediately embark in three large batteaus & proceed from this place with all possible dispatch to Poughkeepsie, where you will deliver the letter directed to Mr. [Jacobus] Van Zandt, or in his absence, to the gentlemen having the direction of building the frigates there & will there receive from him or them six coils slow match, six dozen large sail, bolt rope & marline needles, one hundred weight of twine & as many blocks are already finished for the Northern Army & a quantity of oakum & other articles, which you will take on board & immediately re-embark & return with your charge to this place. Captain Peter Dop of this place is to embark with you on board one of your bateaux, he has orders to purchase anchors & cables & other articles from the proprietors of sloops between this place & Poughkeepsie, you will order one bateau to attend him & stop at such places as he shall choose to land it, for the purpose of fulfilling his orders.[23]

Another party was dispatched by Varick to Poughkeepsie on August 18 for "such blocks, slow match, cordage & rigging" as could be obtained from the Continental Shipyard there.[24]

Completion of the four row galleys was considerably delayed for lack of cordage for their rigging. Gates would write Schuyler in mid–September, "The General [Arnold] makes no doubt the enemy will soon pay him a visit; I hope not before we get the Row

Gallies to his assistance — then succeed or fail, we have done our best. It is a lamentable case that our gallies must wait for cordage and for gun carriages to be completed."[25] General Schuyler was significantly concerned, and urgently dispatched Captain John Hunn to Poughkeepsie on September 17 with a personal letter to "The Committee for Building the Continental Frigates at Poughkeepsie." Schuyler pleaded, "I have this moment received a line by express from Gen Gates he is in the greatest distress for the cordage mentioned in the inclosed list not a fathom of it is to be had in place."[26]

Varick dispatched Sergeant David Ensign to Poughkeepsie on September 23 specifically to receive "two cables."[27] Varick sent Captain Hunn back to Poughkeepsie on September 25 for more cables and cordage.[28] The Poughkeepsie Continental Shipyard supplied so much cordage and rigging to the Lake Champlain fleet that by the end of September the agents for the Continental Congress at Poughkeepsie raised concerns that their stocks were running perilously low, and in fact they had to remove the rigging intended for one of their own ships and send it to Schuyler to fulfill his requisitions for the row galleys.[29] As a testimony to the contributions of the Poughkeepsie shipyard, its considerable efforts and industry alone were responsible for Arnold having the row galleys *Washington* and *Congress* with him at Valcour Island. Schuyler notified the Continental Congress on October 3, "The cables are by this time arrived at Ticonderoga. They were made at Poughkeepsie with dispatch and forwarded without a moment's delay."[30]

Connecticut would also prove to be a significant source of supplies for the fleet. This was due predominantly to three reasons. First, Benedict Arnold had operated a significant commercial shipping operation from the state for many years, and he had considerable business and mercantile contacts that he drew upon. On August 3 Varick noted: "General Arnold informs me that the sail cloth may be had of Mr. Thomas Mumford of New London & Cordage of Mr. Mortimer of Middletown, to which places & persons you are pleased to go & endeavour to procure these articles."[31] Second, Governor Jonathan Trumbull of Connecticut was an ardent patriot, and he had several sons enlisted in the Continental army, to include Colonel John Trumbull then serving directly for Gates at Ticonderoga. Third, Connecticut had well-established marine and iron industries, which although not sufficiently developed to be solely capable of equipping an entire fleet, were fully adequate of making a significant contribution to such an effort. Varick specified the colony as a source of supply in a missive to Captain Leonard Van Buren, as early as August 3: "I do herewith deliver you an invoice of sail cloth & cordage wanted for the public service, on Lake Champlain. Which you are to purchase for the United States, at the cheapest rate they can be procured, in the colony of Connecticut or elsewhere."[32]

Captain Leonard Van Beuren initiated purchases in the colony shortly thereafter, reporting: "Inclosed is Robert Knights receipt for some cordage & sail cloth, which is intended for the vessels fitting on the Lake & must be immediately sent for Albany to the care of Philip Van Renslear Store Keeper."[33] Trumbull reported of his efforts to the Continental Congress on August 22:

> Upon General Schuyler's request, three Sea Captains are appointed here, to raise crews of seamen, and proceed to Lake Champlain, and take command of some of the armed vessels on the lake.... A quantity of cordage and rigging, upon General Schuyler's application, have been purchased in this state and at his request, two hundred

swivels will be cast with all expedition for the use of the armed vessels on Lake Champlain.[34]

Another conduit for supplies for the fleet was the main Continental Army commanded by George Washington, then in New York City. Washington had supply problems of his own, but he carefully scrutinized the lengthy lists that Varick sent him, and had his principal staff officers dispatch whatever they could supply north. Washington informed Varick on August 10:

> I now send you a list from the Colonel of Artillery and Quarter Master General of what is and will be forwarded from this place, which is all that can be procured. There was some Duck arrived at Providence out of which I have requested Governor Cooke to supply the Northern Army, provided its not other ways disposed of. The water communication being yet stopped make it exceedingly difficult to transport these articles to Albany.[35]

The first documented augmentation of carpenters arrived on July 25, when Quartermaster Schuyler reported, "Fifty two carpenters arrived last night from Philadelphia which is immediately to go to work at another galley."[36] Another supplement reached Skenesboro on August 3, when Varick reported to Hermanus Schuyler, "A Captain Bernard Eddy from Rhode Island is on his way to Skenesborough with fifty ship carpenters under his command, these persons are to be employed in constructing such vessels as you shall direct.[37] The demand for carpenters and blacksmiths was so extreme that even the Continental army regiments at Skenesboro were solicited for soldiers with these talents. The Orderly Book for Colonel Mott's Connecticut State Regiment on August 21, from "Skeensborough" announced: "If any solgiers in either Col. Mott's or Col. Swift's [Connecticut State] Regiments wanted either by Smiths or Carpenters, the Solgiers has a wright [right] to engage if he sees fit to forward the work."[38]

By the middle of August substantial numbers of carpenters were at work at Skenesboro. Harmanus Schuyler, the indefatigable bateaux builder over the winter, was now hard at labor on the fleet. He reported to Schuyler on August 10, "I have 159 Carpenters from Philadelphia and Connecticut. Eleven more have arrived here last night from Rhode Island which I have divided among the carpenters that work at the galleys."[39]

The construction of the fleet was pushed as rapidly as circumstances would possibly permit. All of Skene's facilities at his little community were operated to their maximum speed. As one example of the urgency with which affairs were carried on this summer and fall at Skenesboro, Nathaniel Dodge, a Massachusetts soldier stationed at Mount Independence, recorded in his journal for September 22, a Sunday:

> The 22 Day which is the Sabbath it was the Jenerals orders that no labour should be done but the black smiths [and] carpenters that make the Carridges for the gundelos.[40]

Gates himself would document these efforts to Schuyler.

> 23d September 1776. It is the blacksmiths work that has delay'd us much, notwithstanding we have got more forges, and although with different gangs of men, they are work'd night & day.
>
> September 30th 1776. I am informed the fourth row galley is ready to be launched.

The whole of the different gangs of ship carpenters being consolidated into one body to finish her.[41]

Surprisingly, one shortage that apparently did not hinder the fledgling American fleet was that of cannon, although the quality of these cannon was of particular concern. Certainly although the best and most modern of the cannon had been transported by Henry Knox to the main American Continental army in Boston the previous winter, numerous cannon still remained at both Crown Point and Ticonderoga. All of these cannon had been brought to America by the Royal Navy or Royal Artillery during the Seven Years' War, and had been carried to Lake Champlain in 1759 or 1760. Following the end of that war, the British garrisons at these two posts had been significantly reduced, and these cannon received minimal (if, indeed, any) maintenance. Many of the cannon were mounted at Fort Crown Point, had been burned over by the catastrophic 1773 fire, and when that conflagration had destroyed the fort's casemates they had been partially buried in the ground and for three years exposed to constant moisture and corrosion. Upon Benedict Arnold's capture of Crown Point in 1775 he had excavated many cannon. Some of the more valuable guns had been rescued and carried to Ticonderoga, but Knox had presumably carted away most of these higher quality cannon to Boston that winter. Even with Arnold's exertions, Colonel Hartley recorded unearthing additional cannon in the fall of 1776 to assist him with defending his new post at Coffin Point. These cast iron cannon, relics of the Seven Years' War, abandoned in place for twenty years and buried for three years, were the only cannon available to the American fleet, and they were not good guns.[42]

All of the American vessels were equipped with varying numbers of small swivels, relatively small cannon (typically less than 1-pounders) that were principally employed to defend ships against enemy boarding parties or from enemy infantry on shore. They were so named because they were mounted on a pintle mount that could be easily swiveled to engage their target. A single soldier could effectively serve a swivel. They had a relatively limited range and little penetration power against obstacles, but could be devastating against infantry or dismounted targets, and Native Americans generally feared them. Swivels were not as difficult to cast as the larger and heavier cannon, and a number of the American swivels were cast at the iron furnaces of both Salisbury, Connecticut and Livingston Manor. Varick informed Arnold on September 12 that swivels were being sent forward from being cast. One swivel gun was recovered from the *Philadelphia*, a cast-iron ¾-pounder swivel bearing a prominent broad arrow, meaning that it was a British Board of Ordnance weapon and not an American manufactured piece.[43] It could have been obtained from a number of sources, captured at forts St. Jean or Chambly in the fall of 1775, been captured at Ticonderoga, or recovered from the ruins of Crown Point. Arnold reported capturing nineteen swivels at Ticonderoga in 1775, and at least two more swivels were documented to have been located at Crown Point.[44] Again, this documents the different venues that had to be employed by the Americans to equip the fleet.

As previously noted, the Continental Army's artisans on Mount Independence manufactured new carriages for the cannon for all the gondolas and row galleys. Gates noted to Schuyler, "We were necessitated to make all the Carriages upon the spot."[45] Baldwin recorded of his contribution to these efforts on August 29, "We double manned our Smiths' fires & worked in all the shops both night & day to get the shipping rigged &

the artillery mounted."[46] The twenty carpenters working on the gun carriages at Mount Independence were under the direction of Lt. Moah Nichols, detached from Burrall's Connecticut Regiment. A petition on Nichols' behalf sent to Schuyler at the end of the campaign documented his contributions to the Continental fleet:

> Mr. Moah Nichols, who listed a Soldier in Col. Burralls Regiment last winter and went into Canada was drafted out at Chambly to work at gun carriages who served as foreman at that place and since he came to Ticonderoga has served and received the pay of a Lieut. of the works, has had constantly above 20 men under his direction in making carriages for the fleet & other works. He having the direction of that branch has given good satisfaction to all ... I judge him to be a faithful workman.[47]

The urgency of outfitting the fleet was documented by Lieutenant Benjamin Beal of Greaton's 24th Massachusetts Regiment, who was responsible for a party of carpenters engaged in raising new buildings on Mount Independence. On September 10 his orders were changed, and Beal reported, "I had orders from the General to take all my men off the carpenters work & go to making carriages for cannons."[48]

Once mounted on their new carriages, many of these cast iron cannon were not only old and obsolete, but they were also in fact extremely dangerous. During early August, in test firings from the fleet, two 13-inch mortars had split apart in thrilling and terrifying accidents.[49] Captain Cushing on Mount Independence reported these incidents, as did nearly every other soldier present in the army, for the explosions must have been particularly loud and spectacular.[50] Colonel Baldwin recorded of these debacles:

> [August 1] At sunset, one howitzer was fired on board a large gondola by way of experiment, the shell broke in the air, one 13 inch bomb was also thrown from the same gondola on board of which were about 20 men, when the bomb went off, the mortar split & the upper part went above 20 feet high in the air over the men's heads into the water & hurt no man. The piece that blowed off weighed near a ton, I was nigh [near] & saw the men fall when the mortar burst & it was a great wonder no man was killed. August 2 This morning I went early to Independent Point where we charged the other 13 inch mortar, by way of trial, when she was fired, she burst, just in the same manner only this was on the land & the other was upon the water, that the other did near about the middle of the whole length, so that we have no large mortar here now.[51]

Four cannon are positively documented to have come from the American Lake Champlain fleet, and one from Mount Independence. Three cannon were recovered when the gondola *Philadelphia* was raised in 1935; and the Lake Champlain Maritime Museum has recovered one 6-pounder cannon that burst aboard the gondola *New York* during the Battle of Valcour Island. The Lake Champlain Maritime Museum recovered another cannon from the bottom of Lake Champlain near Mount Independence, where it was abandoned during the British retreat from Ticonderoga in November 1777.

The cannon recovered with the *Philadelphia* were woefully obsolete by the time of the American Revolution.[52] The bow cast iron 12-pounder has the letter "F" inscribed on one of its trunnions, believed to represent Finspong, Sweden, where it was cast, and these guns are today referred to as finbankers after their home city. According to naval historian John Bratten, this cannon was likely cast in Sweden in the late 17th century, then sold to the Danish navy, and eventually ended up with the American Lake Champlain fleet. The other two 9-pounders are also cast iron and of Swedish origin. Most likely, these three cannon were brought to Fort Crown Point or Ticonderoga during the Seven Years' War and had been recovered from one of those posts and added to the Continental army inventory.

A catastrophic explosion had fragmented the cast iron 6-pounder, found at the bottom of Valcour Bay. Six sundered pieces have been located archaeologically. This cannon is also believed to have been Swedish in origin, and contemporary with the *Philadelphia*'s cannon. The only definitive marking located was a "No. XIII" chiseled into the end of the muzzle. The origin of this marking is unknown, but was most likely not original to the casting, as the Swedish used the abbreviation "Nr." for number. Research by the Lake Champlain Maritime Museum has documented that the gondola *New York* had a 6-pounder explode onboard during the Battle of Valcour Island, killing Lt. Thomas Rodgers, and wounding Sergeant Jonas Holden.[53]

In 1992 and 1993 archaeologists from the Lake Champlain Maritime Museum discovered a cast iron 12-pounder cannon near Mount Independence in Lake Champlain, with its left trunnion completely knocked off. This cannon was almost certainly rendered useless by British Royal Artillerymen during the withdrawal from Mount Independence and Ticonderoga in November 1777. This particular cannon was probably not utilized aboard the American Lake Champlain fleet due to its particularly heavy weight (3,124 pounds), and had subsequently been abandoned by the Americans during their retreat in July 1777. This cannon had served with the Royal Navy since at least 1696 (and possibly since 1679), and was transferred from the Royal Navy to the Royal Artillery in the colonies during the Seven Years' War.[54] Again, this is typical of the obsolete and badly dated nature of many of the cast iron cannon available for use aboard the American fleet.

It is also documented that at least one cannon had previously had a firing accident aboard the gondola *Providence*. Lieutenant Bayze Wells, a Connecticut officer, had been "the 27th [July] 1776 moved over the lake in order to work on Board Gundelow Providence under the command a Cpt Simmons." Wells recorded that on August 4, 1776, the *Providence* had sailed from Three Mile Point south to Ticonderoga, and then performed a practice firing of their cannon as a salute to the fortress. Wells documented what happened next:

> By the command of Cpt Simmons we ware ordered to fire five cannon we fird our bow and labboard midships guns and ware ordered to lode them again they sponged the bow gun and put in the cartrich one Solomon Dyer who servd the spung went to ram down the cartrich there being fire in the gun it went of while he was standing before the mouth of the cannon which blew boath his hands & one nee almost off and likewise the spung rod part or all of it went through the left part of his body at the root of his arm blew him overboard we could not find him until 7th he rose and floted we took him up and buried him decently.[55]

Colonel Baldwin also documented for August 5, "In clearing the guns on board of one of the gondolas, one of the cannon went off as they were charging it & killed the gunner's mate. He was blown into many pieces and scattered on the water."[56] Sponging the gun should have rendered it entirely safe, but an ancient cast iron cannon that had probably received little if any maintenance during its twenty year stay at the posts on Lake Champlain was liable to have pits or deterioration inside the bore, which could easily have contained a residual spark that ignited the cartridge as it was being rammed down the bore.

Cast iron cannon of the time, even if relatively new and well maintained, were prone to shattering or breaking during firing. For example, at the Siege of Fort William Henry on Lake George in August 1757 every single piece of the large caliber cast iron cannons and mortars within the fort had fractured, rendering the British defenders incapable of further resistance.[57]

Another concern has been revealed by the three cannon recovered from the *Philadelphia* and available for professional study. Naval historian John Bratten discovered that the 12-pounder cannon has a bore of five inches, considerably greater than the English Board of Ordnance standard of 4.623 inches. This excessive bore size may be reflective of its century of previous use. The two 9-pounder cannon similarly had oversized bores at 4.5 inches, again much greater than the 4.2 inch standard.[58] This considerable amount of windage means that ballistically the American cannon had considerably reduced muzzle velocity (and thus penetration power and potential to cause damage), and extremely reduced accuracy. The American fleet obviously had no other cannon available with which to outfit the fleet, but the quality of their guns was decidedly inferior to the British Royal Artillery, which had a magnificent artillery train of modern bronze guns, many of them cast as recently as the first few months of 1776.[59]

On September 26, 1776, the row galley *Trumbull*, under the command of a Captain Warner, was armed with munitions at Mount Independence. A comprehensive listing of these ordnance materials was compiled.[60] Interestingly enough, this list contains small but distinctive "X" marks randomly placed at the bottom within each column, suggesting that this list was actually used to issue these items to the Captain, and that items were crossed off as they were provided, identically as a modern military hand receipt or business inventory would be completed today. This also intimates that this list was previously completed, and suggests that each vessel's requirements were ascertained while the ship was under construction at Skenesboro, and then the materials for each ship pre-positioned at Mount Independence waiting for each vessel to be launched and then make its way forward. Obviously, this would save considerable time in outfitting each vessel, as the necessary ordnance materials would already be collected and waiting, and would thus only have to be loaded aboard at Mount Independence, and then the vessel would be ready to join the fleet. This is the first time that such a comprehensive listing of the ordnance material positively aboard one of Arnold's vessels has been presented, and it also provides a glimpse into the significant organization and planning that went into the construction and arming of the American Lake Champlain fleet.

	Size of Cannon: 18	Size of Cannon: 12	Size of Cannon: 9	Size of Cannon: 6	Size of Cannon: 4	Swivels
No. of Cannon	1	1	2	2	2	10
Paper Cartridges Filled	40	30	80	60	84	100
Flannel Cartridges Unfilled	"	10	"	20	"	"

	Size of Cannon: 18	Size of Cannon: 12	Size of Cannon: 9	Size of Cannon: 6	Size of Cannon: 4	Swivels
Round Shot	80	80	60	80	60	72
Canister Shot	10	10	"	32	20	"
Rammers & Sponges	1	1	2	2	2	"
Worms	1	1	2	2	2	"
Double Head Shott	8	"	16	16	16	"
Ladles	1	1	1	1	1	"
Coils Slow Match	-	-	4	2	-	-
Powder Horns	1	1	2	2	2	"
Portfires	"	"	"	"	"	6
Tubes	"	20	"	40	"	"
Aprons	1	1	2	2	2	"
Linstocks	1	1	2	2	2	"
Musquets [sic]	15	"	"	"	"	"
Cartrouch Boxes [sic]	15	"	"	"	"	"
Flints	-	-	-	-	-	-
Handspikes	3	3	6	6	6	"
Musquet Cartridges [sic]	"	"	"	"	"	3200
Priming Wires	1	1	2	2	2	"
Loose Powder	500	"	"	"	"	"

Note: Deliverd to Capt. Warner on September 26.

Similar lists have also been located for the row galley *Washington*, commanded by Captain John Thrasher, and row galley *Congress*, commanded by a Captain Arnold (no relationship to General Arnold). Unlike the ordnance list for the row galley *Trumbull*, these lists do not contain the distinctive marks, but they are recorded as "military stores delivered." Once the row galleys arrived at the fleet General Arnold transferred his flag to the *Congress*, rather than the *Royal Savage*. Apparently, once he saw the row galleys in action, Arnold preferred the more capable and maneuverable *Congress* to command from than the less than stable *Royal Savage*.

Row Galley *Washington*

	Size of Cannon: 18	Size of Cannon: 12	Size of Cannon: 9	Size of Cannon: 4	Size of Cannon: 2	Swivels	Total
No. of cannon	1	1	2	4	2	8	18
Round Shott	30	30	60	114	80	200	514
Canister Shot	10	10	20	40	-	-	80
Double headed Shot	10	10	10	0	-	-	30

Row Galley *Washington* (ctd.)

	Size of Cannon: 18	Size of Cannon: 12	Size of Cannon: 9	Size of Cannon: 4	Size of Cannon: 2	Swivels	Total
Paper Cartridges Filled	40	30	80	106	80	200	590
Flannel Cartridges Unfilled	-	10	-	-	-	-	10
Rammers & Sponges	1	1	2	4	2	8	18
Ladles	1	1	1	2	1	2	8
Worms	1	1	2	4	2	2	12
Handspikes	3	3	6	12	-	-	24
Linstocks	1	1	2	4	-	-	8
Priming Horns	1	1	2	3	1	-	8
Priming Wires	1	1	2	4	2	-	10
Lead Aprons	1	1	2	4	-	-	8
Coil Slow Match	-	-	-	-	-	-	3
Portfires	-	-	-	-	-	-	6
Tubes	-	12	-	-	-	-	12
Musquets [sic]	-	-	-	-	-	-	7
Rifel Guns [sic]	-	-	-	-	-	-	1
Priming Wires & Brushes	-	-	-	-	-	-	32
Cartridges Boxes [sic]	-	-	-	-	-	-	10
Bayonets	-	-	-	-	-	-	7
Bayonet Belts	-	-	-	-	-	-	6
Blunderbusses	-	-	-	-	-	-	1
Musquet cartridges [sic]	-	-	-	-	-	-	3200
Flints	-	-	-	-	-	-	200
Common Cartridge Papers	-	-	-	-	-	-	4 quire
Cannon Cartridges fill'd with Damag'd Powder [sic]	1	1	2	4	2	-	10
Barrels Powder	-	-	-	-	-	-	1
Pounds Powder	-	-	-	-	-	-	100

Row Galley *Congress*

	Size of Cannon: 18	Size of Cannon: 12	Size of Cannon: 26	Size of Cannon: 22	22 Swivels	22 Total
No. of cannon	2	2	4	2	8	18
No. of Round Shott	50	50	120	80	200	500

Row Galley *Congress* (ctd.)

	Size of Cannon: 18	Size of Cannon: 12	Size of Cannon: 26	Size of Cannon: 22	22 Swivels	22 Total
Canister Shot	20	20	40	-	-	80
Doubleheaded Shot	10	10	20	-	-	40
Paper Cartridges Filled	80	60	120	80	200	540
Flannel Cartridges Unfilled	0	20	40	-	-	60
Rammers & Sponges	2	2	4	2	8	18
Ladles	1	1	1	1	3	7
Worms	2	2	4	2	2	12
Handspikes	6	6	12	-	-	24
Linstocks	2	2	4	2	-	10
Priming Horns	2	2	4	2	-	10
Priming Wires	2	2	4	2	-	10
Lead Aprons	2	2	4	2	-	10
Coil Slow Match	-	-	-	-	-	6
Portfires	-	-	-	-	-	6
Tubes	-	25	45	-	-	70
Musquits [sic]	12	-	-	-	-	12
Cartridges Boxes	12	-	-	-	-	12
Bayonets	11	-	-	-	-	11
Musquat Cartidges [sic]	2500	-	-	-	-	2500
Musquit Balls [sic]	300	-	-	-	-	300
Flints	200	-	-	-	-	200
Powder Barrels	4	-	-	-	-	4
Powder-Pounds	400	-	-	-	-	400
Musqt Cartridge Papers [sic]	-	-	-	-	-	4 quires
Cannon Cartadge Paper [sic]	-	-	-	-	-	4 quires
Cartridge Fill'd with Damaged Powder [sic]	2	2	4	2	-	10
Sheep skins	1	-	-	-	-	1

Henry Sewall, during his visit through Skenesboro on September 1, recalled seeing "A row galley lanch'd into the lake there."[61] Viewing a ship being launched must have been a particularly noteworthy spectacle, nearly as good as watching a 13-inch mortar explode. Finally, at considerable effort, Arnold would have a fleet and Gates would have an advance guard.

Numerous shortages plagued the entirety of the ship building effort, and similar shortages hindered outfitting the ships once they were completed. As a simple example, the fleet was equipped with heavy cast iron cookware, not something that an army would ever have been issued because of its weight and bulk. But cast iron cookware could be easily manufactured, and readily obtained, from the same iron furnaces and foundries that created cannonballs and grapeshot. John Rees, a modern historian who has performed exhaustive research and written extensively on provisions and cooking during the War for American Independence, has recounted:

> Soldiers serving with Brigadier General Benedict Arnold's Lake Champlain fleet were in a situation similar to garrison duty, where more cumbersome cookware was suitable. A 3 August 1776 list of stores: "Wanting on ... [the] Gundola *Providence*" included "two Camp Kettles." The kettles on the *Providence* were undoubtedly of cast iron, like those found on her sister ship, the *Philadelphia*, when she was raised from the lake in 1935. The recovered utensils included two cast iron pots (one 9¾ inches wide, 5³⁄₁₆ deep; and a larger pot, 10¾ inches wide, 14¾ inches deep), a large skillet (13 inches wide, with an 18½ inch long handle), and a three-legged skillet (with a 14¾ Inch wide pan, 14¾ inch long handle, and standing 8½ inches high). As far as the author knows, the iron pots found on the *Philadelphia* are the only intact examples known to have been used by Continental soldiers.[62]

Where possible, additional weapons and equipment were obtained from the army. Orderly books stipulated on August 16 that "all the brass blunderbusses in camp, belonging to the public, or taken from the enemy, are to be delivered in immediately to Mr. Lame, Conductor of Naval Stores."[63] Another problem was that the soldiers, not surprisingly interested in enhancing their creature comforts, had absconded with both oars and sails to either build or modify their shelters. Shortly, the Orderly Books were replete with instructions that these items be returned to stores for issue to the fleet.

> August 10th 1776. The Batteau Master is immediately to send to the different Incampments and collect all the oars — Neither officer or soldier is for the future to use any of the oars for any other purpose than that they were design'd for. Proper poles must be cut to carry provisions and baggage.
>
> 14th Aug 1776. The Commanding Officers of the Corps are desired to see that all the sails belonging to the publick, which have been used as tents, be immediately delivered to Mr Lame Conductor of the Naval Stores.
>
> Aug 28th 1776. The Batteau Master is ordered to take a fatigue party and proceed immediately to collect all the oars from the different incampments, and places where they are scattered.[64]

As an indication of the magnitude of the effort necessary to equip the fleet once the raw floating platforms had been constructed, Arnold's fleet required no less than 2,500 oars alone. All of these oars were of domestic manufacture, created by Hartley's oar makers based out of the 6th Pennsylvania's post at Crown Point.[65]

When Arnold joined the fleet at Crown Point in early August it was comprised of only the original four small, under-gunned sailing ships; and four gondolas that had already been completed by the frantic American ship building effort at Skenesboro. On August 5 the fleet was recorded as follows.[66]

Names of Vessels	Names of Captains	No. of Guns	Size of Guns	No. of Swivels	No. Men
Schooner Royal Savage	Wynkoop	12	4 lbs.	10	50
Sloop Enterprise	Dickson	12	4 lbs.	10	50
Schooner Revenge	Seaman	8	4 lbs. & 2 lbs.	10	35
Schooner Liberty	Primmer	8	2 lbs. & 1 lbs.	8	35
Gundola New Haven	Mansfield	3	12 Pdr. & 9 Pdr.	8	45
Gundola Providence	Simmonds	3	9 lbs.	8	45
Gundola Boston	Summer	3	12 Pdr. & 9 Pdr.	8	45
Gundola Spitfire	Ulmer	3	9 lbs.	8	45
A Gundola Not Rigged*	-	-	-	-	-
A Spanish built Row Galley, not Rigged†	-	-	-	-	-

*The Philadelphia, which joined the fleet on August 20.
†Probably the Lee.

Rather than waiting for all of the ships in the fleet to be constructed, Arnold began exercising the fleet immediately, and additional vessels were dispatched individually as they were fit for service. Lieutenant Bayze Wells on board the *Providence* recorded, "Tuesday [August] 20th. Gundelo Philadelphia Captain Rue arrived which made nine sail of the line."[67] The row galley *Washington*, under the direct command of General Waterbury, and row galley *Congress* both reached the fleet on October 6. However, it was the arrival of the *Washington* that occasioned great rejoicing amongst the sailors, "General Waterbury arrived came in Washington and joined our fleet they brought a barrel of rum for each gondola."

Having assembled the fleet, Arnold now began the monumental task of teaching his hastily drafted sailors to actually be sailors; learning the lake; ascertaining the capabilities, strengths and weaknesses of his newly constructed vessels; acquainting his individual vessels to sail together as a flotilla; and selecting his battlefield. Initially, Schuyler had placed the small vessels under New York Commodore Jacob Wynkoop, 52 years of age. Wynkoop claimed considerable military experience in the Seven Years' War:

> I have served in the last two wars both by sea and by land, and have been in many engagements. I have a commission from General Shirley as Captain of a Company of batteaumen; and in consequence of an action under Col. Broadstreet, in which we lost forty-nine men the first fire, I was honored, with the command of His Excellency General Gage, to be called by the name of his company, to whom his baggage was always entrusted; and had likewise the offer of a commission in the "Royal Americans." I have a good deal of experience of cannon as well as small arms.[68]

A member of a Dutch family long established in New York colony, he had previously served as an infantry captain in the 4th New York until Schuyler assigned him to Lake Champlain in 1776. Wynkoop, whose limited surviving correspondence suggests that he was pompous, bombastic and argumentative, was entirely undistinguished in this assignment. However, it is apparent that Schuyler and Gates selected Wynkoop to command the small flotilla so that Arnold could be free to concentrate on designing, constructing and outfitting the new fleet at Skenesboro. Schuyler would later note of Wynkoop's assignment, "When I recommended him to the command of the vessels on Lake Champlain, they were few and the Army in Canada, and although I believe him brave, yet I do not think him equal to the command of such a fleet as we now have there."[69] Once this new fleet was established, Arnold would supersede Wynkoop, and Arnold would fight the fleet with Wynkoop's assistance. Unfortunately, Schuyler and Gates had obviously failed to notify Wynkoop of this arrangement in terms that he could comprehend, and Wynkoop managed to scuttle this plan through his incompetence and arrogance before it could ever be implemented.

Before he assumed command Arnold conferred with Gates at length at his headquarters inside the old French Fort Ticonderoga. Gates then confirmed his oral instructions with comprehensive written orders.

> Upon your arrival at Crown Point you will proceed with the Fleet of the United States under your command, down Lake Champlain ... preventing the enemy's invasion of our country, is the ultimate end of the important command, with which you are now intrusted. It is a defensive war we are carrying on, therefore ... should the enemy come up the Lake, and attempt to force their way through the pass you are stationed to defend in that case you will act with such cool determined valor, as will give them reason to repent their temerity. But if, contrary to my hope and expectation, their fleet should have so encreased, as to force an entrance into the upper part of the Lake then after you shall have discovered the insufficiency of every effort to retard their progress, you will, in the best manner you can, retire with your squadron to Ticonderoga.[70]

Now that he understood Gates' intent, Arnold joined the fleet to assume command of it at Crown Point on August 15. Two days later he observed a large signal smoke lit by Lieutenant Colonel Hartley's oar makers to inform the main post at Crown Point that they feared an attack. Arnold immediately ordered Colonel Hartley with one hundred of his Pennsylvanians in bateaux, supported by two of his fleet's schooners (the *Revenge* and *Liberty*), to get underway and move to the relief of the isolated oar makers, who lacked sufficient numbers to make much of a defense against any British raid.

Astoundingly, as Arnold immediately informed Gates, "They were no soon under way than Commodore Wynkoop fired a shot and brought them to." Needless to say, Arnold "went on board" Wynkoop's vessel (the *Royal Savage*), and discovered to his astonishment that "he refuses to be commanded by any one, and imagines his appointment, which is by General Schuyler, cannot be superseded."[71] Wynkoop, attempting to defend himself, would later claim that he had only fired two comparatively small swivel guns, with the implication that they were fired as a signal rather than as a threat.[72] Regardless of what had actually been fired and with what intentions, shots had definitely been fired and the damage had been done. Arnold, in what must have been a fiery interview with Wynkoop doubtless interspersed with a full volley of invectives, finally "brought him so far to reason" and immediately informed Gates of the incident.

Horatio Gates, who probably in his entire military career never imagined that one of his commanding officers would actually fire upon his own men and vessels, reacted like lightning. In unmistakable terms he ordered Arnold:

> I have this moment received your letter from Crown Point of yesterday evening. It is my Orders you instantly put Commodore Wynkoop in Arrest and send him prisoner

to Head Quarters at Tyconderoga. You will at the same time acquaint the Officers of the Fleet that such of them as do not pay an Implicit Obedience to your Commands, are instantly to be confined & sent to me for Trial.[73]

Gates was absolutely livid at Wynkoop's conduct. It appears that the Commanding General entertained certain preconceived notions regarding proper military discipline and deportment. Firing at friendly ships and other officers was clearly not to be found on Gates' list. Wynkoop had violated every single one of Gates' expectations, and brought down Gates' wrath upon himself. Gates followed up with a blistering letter to Schuyler:

I shall send Mr. Wynkoop to Albany immediately on his arrival here, and I dare say you will without scruple, forthwith dismiss him the Service — he ought, upon no account, to be again employed. Many officers of rank in this department say, he is totally unfit to command a single vessel, at this important hour of business.[74]

Astute observers will note that Gates had summarily demoted Wynkoop to "Mr. Wynkoop," having apparently already stripped him of his military rank. Wynkoop attempted to justify his actions, writing long, rambling, bombastic proclamations and letters to both Gates and Schuyler, but he had already well and truly exterminated his career. He was never heard from or seen by the Northern Theater Army again. From this moment forward, the fleet was absolutely commanded by Benedict Arnold, just as Gates had always intended.

Once the fleet was well underway, and Arnold's leadership of it clearly established, one his most important and frustrating tasks was simply manning the fleet with adequate officers and sufficient numbers of sailors and marines. The first order of business was to identify a second in command for the fleet. Following the events of August 17 Wynkoop was no longer available to fulfill this (or any other) role in the Northern Theater Army. Wynkoop would be replaced by two superlative officers who would provide Arnold with a strong corps of leadership for his fleet. These two men were Brigadier General David Waterbury, who would be assigned as Arnold's second-in-command, and Colonel Edward Wigglesworth, who would assume the role of Arnold's third-in command.

Waterbury, at the age of 54 a relatively senior officer, was a lifelong resident of Connecticut. He possessed considerable military experience. A veteran of the Seven Years' War, he served in the Connecticut Provincials under then Colonel William Johnson in the initial Lake George Campaign of 1755, and returned to Lake George and Champlain with Abercrombie's army in 1758. In this campaign, his first experience at Ticonderoga was not an enjoyable or successful one. An ardent and serious patriot, he joined the American cause early, and accompanied Montgomery in his campaign on the Richelieu River in 1775 as Lieutenant Colonel of the 9th Connecticut regiment. Waterbury was appointed a Brigadier General by Connecticut on June 3, 1776, and his first assignment as a general officer was to assist Arnold with the construction of the fleet at Skenesboro. Gates would note on two separate occasions regarding Waterbury, "He is an able Seaman and a brave Officer ... as Genl Arnold and he are upon the best terms, I am satisfied no Dispute about command, or want of Confidence in each other, will retard the public service"; and "The Colonel is a good seaman, appears to be much of a gentleman, and has, as far as I can learn, an unimpeached good character."[75]

A Massachusetts man, Wigglesworth was 34 years of age, and already Colonel of his own regiment of Massachusetts militia. His Massachusetts coastal connections apparently provided Wigglesworth with some nautical experience, and he was shortly assigned to service on Lake Champlain. Gates issued Wigglesworth extremely involved instructions when he was detailed to Arnold's fleet, which were particularly complimentary to the Colonel. Gates would write:

> The character which I have constantly heard of you as an experienced, active, and determined officer, has induced me to intrust the important post of third in command on this lake to you, in preference to any other person. I have not a doubt that your conduct will justify the idea I have formed. The Honorable Brigadier General Arnold has the first command of the fleet. General Waterbury has the second. Your conduct is to be governed by the orders you may receive from them ... if by any misfortune your two superiors shall be taken off, the command of the whole by that devolves on you.[76]

Arnold would write Gates regarding Wigglesworth: "I am extremely glad you have sent Colonel Wigglesworth. He is a gentleman of whom I have a good opinion."[77] Arnold was well pleased with both Waterbury and Wigglesworth, telling Gates, "I shall do nothing of consequence without consulting both General Waterbury and Colonel Wigglesworth, both of whom I esteem judicious, honest men, and good soldiers."[78]

Sailors and marines were drafted from the various regiments of the army. The hope, or perhaps dream would be more appropriate, was that sufficient soldiers with nautical skills or experience would be found within the army to fulfill all of Arnold's requirements. In fact, there were not nearly sufficient men with such skills available. Arnold's vessels would be primarily manned by sailors and marines whose solitary qualification to the titles was to have not been adept enough to avoid being drafted into the fleet. Arnold complained to Gates that "the drafts from the Regiments at Ticonderoga are a miserable set, indeed, the men on board the fleet in general, are not equal to half their number of good men."[79] Arnold would bitterly complain to Gates following the Battle of Valcour Island, "We suffered much for want of seamen and gunners."[80] Eventually, Arnold would have 547 sailors and marines on board his fleet.[81]

This effort at drafting began in August and continued into September. The Orderly Book of St. Clair's Pennsylvania Battalion specified as early as August 10:

> [Colonel Joshua] Wingate's [New Hampshire Regiment] & Colonel [Anthony] Wayne's [4th Pennsylvania Battalion] Regiment to furnish 12 Subs 12 Sergts 12 Corpls 3 Drummers & 239 Privates to assist in among the fleet they must be sent to General Arnold's Head Quarters this evening at 6 Oclock and will have the same extra pay serving the fleet. The General desires that as many seamen as those Corps can furnish may be sent with this command.[82]

On August 17, the Army's Orderly Book stipulated: "Forty seamen from the same Brigade commanded by General Brickett to be draughted & parade at Head Quarters tomorrow morning at 7 o'clock, to go on board the fleet a Crown Point."[83] The drafting effort had to be expanded as the fleet grew, and on September 4 the Orderly Book of Brigadier General James Brickett's brigade again required that:

> Thirty-three men of Col. Whitcomb's Regiment to Parade tomorrow morning at 6 o'clock at Head Quarters to serve as Marines on board the Fleet. The same number

of seamen from Col. Brewer's Regiment will parade the same time & place to serve on board the same fleet they will proceed directly and Join Gen. Arnold under the command of Lieut. Col. Underwood of Marines.[84]

As was typical when soldiers were drafted out of one regiment for another service, the regiment's commanding officers were loath to part with reliable, hard working, sober, and industrious soldiers. Instead, they normally viewed any draft as a heavensent opportunity to purge their ranks of troublemakers, scoundrels, slackards, rogues, and artful dodgers who avoided hard work and discipline. This is an old army tradition, which was probably well established in Roman times. Arnold regularly complained about the quality of sailors and marines that he was provided through these various drafts. He grumbled to Gates on September 18: "I beg that at least one hundred good seamen may be sent me as soon as possible. We have a wretched motley crew in the fleet; the Marines, the refuse of every Regiment, and the Seamen, few of them, ever wet with salt water. We are upwards of one hundred men short of our complement."[85] New Hampshire Officer Frye Bailey, commanding the guard at Fort Ticonderoga, discovered the quality of Arnold's sailors:

> It was all confusion, they were manning Arnold's fleet. They had drafted 20 mechanicks belonging to the fort, the most of whom were from the south [Pennsylvania or New Jersey], a very profane and drunken set. In about two hours I had them all in the guard house.[86]

To augment the less than exemplary results of the forced nomination of soldiers as marines and seamen, sailors were also recruited wherever they could be located. Governor Jonathan Trumbull was particularly active in the port cities of Connecticut. On August 13 he reported to his friend, General Schuyler:

> Captain Seth Warner, one of the Sea Captains you mention came to me, and hath consented to undertake and raise a Company of seamen for the lake service—he informs me that he can soon procure twenty seamen here and as many out of the Companies in Colonel [Samuel] Mott's Regiment which went from his neighborhood, and are at or on their march to Skenesborough.[87]

Warner was apparently as good as his word, for he would eventually command the row galley *Trumbull* (appropriately enough) in the fleet.

Surprisingly, men from different regiments were intermingled aboard ships, rather than assigning all of the men from one specific regiment to a single ship. When diver Lorenzo Hagglund salvaged the remnants of the *Royal Savage* in 1934 from Valcour Island, he located distinctive, numbered buttons from the following four regiments on board:

- 1st Pennsylvania Battalion;
- 2nd Pennsylvania Battalion;
- 10th Regiment of Continental Infantry (Connecticut);
- 25th Regiment of Continental Infantry (Massachusetts).[88]

The reason for this promiscuous mixing of regiments, from various states, is unknown. Certainly, it appears that maintaining men from the same regiment together would maintain previously existing morale and esprit de corps, and would simplify discipline and command. As documented earlier, men from different states in Gates' Continental army had a reputation of not playing particularly well together. Most likely, it appears that only a few men were drafted from each regiment at a time, so as not to decimate a single organization. Thus, there were not sufficient men from a single regiment to man a single ship, and soldiers had to be mixed onboard to fill out a crew. There are no surviving accounts of discord or disunity aboard any of Arnold's vessels, even with the extremely crowded conditions on board the ships. The author suspects that there was so much physically demanding work to do, and the officers were experienced enough seamen to enforce acceptable discipline, that problems never arose. Certainly this was the case aboard Captain Simmons' *Providence*, as one of his officers, Bayze Wells, noted on two occasions; first, on September 20, "Ansel Fox was caned twelve strokes on his naked buttocks for sleeping on his watch." Apparently the lesson did not take, for on September 22 it had to be repeated: "This morning at Eight A.M. Ananius Tubbs was caned twelve strokes on his naked buttocks for sleeping on his watch."[89]

Among the most valuable of Arnold's men were the Stockbridge Indians, as either most or all of them were dispatched from Mount Hope to join the fleet to provide Arnold with an active and aggressive scouting capability. Jahiel Stewart, a soldier with Brewer's Regiment of Massachusetts Militia stationed at Mount Hope, recorded in his journal for October 2:

> This day Capt Ferguson went aboard of one of the rogalleys [the row galley *Washington*] with 17 white men and about 10 Indians to go down to the fleet and then to go a shore in order to scout. Capt Ferguson had the command of the scout, and the most of us went without any brakefast [breakfast] and we went about 12 a Clock and hoisted sails put out all the oars and they fired all the guns aboard and we drew one days allowance we drew flower instead of bread and we was fort [forced] to make some do boys and boiled them with some meat and we eat about sun down. And our rogalle [row galley] ran a ground and we had bad work to git [get] off and after we got off we went down against the Crown Point, but we come by the other row galley a ground. We come to crown Point about twelve a Clock and cast ankr [anchor].[90]

Even such a relatively simple act as staffing the fleet with a naval surgeon, medical instruments, and medicines proved challenging.[91] Assuming command of the fleet at Crown Point in mid–August, Arnold wrote to Gates upon his arrival:

> I have applied to Doctor Sparham who (I believe) cannot be persuaded to go with the fleet — I don't think it prudent to go without a Surgeon, Lieutenant Dunn acquaints me, that the Surgeons Mates of Colonel St. Clair's Regiment has a good box medicines & will incline to go with the fleet, I wish he could be sent here ... I can procure a case of capital instruments for him here — nothing but the Surgeon & some few articles I have sent a boat for prevents our proceeding.[92]

It took Gates a full week to locate a surgeon who was willing to sail with Arnold's Lake Champlain Fleet, as Gates responded on August 23:

> This will be deliver'd to you by Doctor [Stephen] McCrea, whom at the recommendation of Doctor Potts, I have appointed First Surgeon to the Fleet under your command. He has instruments & medicines, two things much in request with you. Mr. Francis Hagan accompanies Mr. McCrea, as his Assistant Surgeon. I cannot procure

any instruments for him here, but wish you could hire Doctor Speram's for the voyage. You are I am told acquainted with Doctor McCrea. I am assured his abilities are their own recommendations.[93]

Once Arnold had assembled and manned his fleet, his early efforts were expended in locating a preferred battlefield. Arnold understood that his fleet would have to fight on the defensive, as his boats were not nearly as maneuverable as the British vessels, and his sailors were far less skilled than the highly experienced British sailors drawn directly from the Royal Navy vessels in the St. Lawrence River. Additionally, the British were certainly going to have to assume the offensive. If they did not, Arnold, Gates and Schuyler were more than happy to have the British stay in Canada and do nothing, for thus they would have won the fall's campaign. But that was unlikely, and as soon as Carleton was satisfied with his fleet and had favorable weather, he would be certain to attack from the north. The British fleet was almost certainly going to be both numerically, and in weight of metal, heavier than the American fleet. But Arnold would have the advantage of choosing his ground (or, rather, his water).

Arnold expended considerable time and efforts in scouting Lake Champlain. This scouting effort provided his vessels and sailors with valuable experience in operating together, and in maneuvering their vessels. Arnold had two concerns. The first, obviously, was where he would meet the British. The second shortly revealed itself, as soon as Arnold sailed the flat bottomed gondolas on the lake. He shortly discovered that they were not particularly navigable. Living historians and highly experienced sailors of the Lake Champlain Maritime Museum have recounted that sailing the historically authentic full-scale replica *Philadelphia II* on Lake Champlain is extremely challenging, as the gondola tends to literally skip and bounce across the surface of the lake in whatever direction the wind is blowing. This was precisely the difficulty that Arnold had, and he realized that locating a safe and protected anchorage for the gondolas was critical to simply preserving his fleet, for it was already too small for the job ahead of it. Lieutenant Bayze Wells, on board the gondola *Providence*, recorded just such a problem on August 27 during a severe storm on the lake, "At 11 A.M. I was informd that the [gondola] Spitfire was ashore the storm continued all day and night following." Wells recorded a similar experience on a traditionally unlucky day, Friday the 13th of September, "this day the wind south very stronge four of our Gondolas were obligd to move for a better harbour." Arnold noted to Gates on September 9 from Isle La Motte: "Now I think we are very safe from gales of wind & this anchorage good. Several small harbors in the vicinity where the gundolas will ride safe any wind that blows."[94]

Wells also recorded Arnold's search for acceptable anchorages on Lake Champlain, "thirsday 29th August ... we tried the water in fall Bay found four fathom and an Half Sande Bottom."[95] By early September Arnold was very aggressive, Wells noting of his visit to Schuyler Island, "Tuesday 3rd Sept this Day ... about Sun half an houre in the morning orders ware given that some men out of all the vessals in the fleet to go on Shore on Shilers Island to make Discovering."

By the middle of September, Arnold had fixed upon Valcour Bay, a narrow body of water located to the west of Valcour Island, and to the east of the west shore of Lake Champlain, as his preferred defensive position. Valcour Island is today and was in 1776 heavily wooded with high stone cliffs, and shoals to the north prevented larger ships from entering the bay from that direction. Accordingly, this position offered Arnold a huge advantage. The British, who could advance only when the wind was at their backs, from the north, would not be able to ascertain Arnold's fleet until they had sailed past him, as the tall pine trees and high elevation of Valcour Island completely obstructs any views of Valcour Bay from the primary Lake Champlain channel. In any event, larger vessels can only enter Valcour Bay from the south. In order to engage Arnold, the British fleet would thus have to turn around once past Valcour Island and sail into the wind to enter the bay, a difficult proposition that would likely cause the British fleet to have to attack in a piecemeal or segmented manner, thus negating many of the British advantages. On September 18 Arnold announced this decision to Gates:

> I make no doubt of their [the British] soon paying us a visit, and intend first fair wind to come up as high as Isle Valcour, where tis a good harbour, and where we shall have the advantage over the enemy, and if they are too many for us, we can retire.[96]

Arnold reached the anchorage at Valcour Bay on September 23, informing Gates, "an excellent harbor, we are moored in a small bay, on the west side the island, as near together as possible & in such a form that few vessels can attack us at the same time & those will be exposed to the fire of the whole fleet."[97] All dispatches written by Arnold subsequent to September 23 are headed from Valcour Island.[98]

Conditions aboard the fleet must have been absolutely brutal, particularly by mid–October when the Lake Champlain weather is already beginning to turn toward winter. For example, the gondola *Philadelphia* contained a crew of 44 officers and men.[99] The gondola contained two principal decks, a main deck, and a smaller poop (or rear) deck. The poop deck was kept clear of everybody except officers on duty, so that they had a relatively unobstructed view of their vessel, and could navigate and manage the gondola without interference. The main deck contained only 700 square feet of space, or less than sixteen square feet per man, and even this is exaggerated for clear space would have to be maintained around the three cannon, several swivels, and brick fireplace. A canvas awning was apparently stretched above this deck, but there was no other covering from rain, snow, sleet or sun; and a horizontal awning did little to impede weather or wind from blowing across the deck. At night, the men were crowded and jammed together, although by October they probably valued the body heat. Sanitary facilities were non-existent, except for ready access to Lake Champlain (which, of course, also provided the gondola's drinking water). Living conditions were crowded and primitive, privacy was unknown, and the food was poor. Jahiel Stewart, then on board the row galley *Washington*, recalled of his fare on October 3:

> We draw no bread yet. Sergeant Campbell was put shore [ashore] for refuson [refusing] to take flower [flour] but he got free in about an houre & we forced to boil do [dough] boys as yet and drink lake worter [water]. We draw salt pork and pees [peas] to day.[100]

Arnold complained to Gates on October 1, "Great part of my seamen and marines are almost naked. The weather has been very severe for some time. I don't expect to be able to keep my station above a fortnight longer. We have continual gales of wind, and the duty very severe."[101]

To assist with breaking the frigid fall north wind that must have absolutely scoured the decks of his fleet, and also with the defense of the vessels against boarding during battle, Arnold insisted that fascines were to be cut on the shore of the lake, and then fastened vertically around the exterior of each ship. Bayze Wells, on the *Providence*, recorded, "thirsday 5th Septr 1776 ... about twelve oclock our Boat Was ordered on shore after fasheens for our Gondolas round the fore castle."[102] Fascines are bundles of wood, from small sticks up to about wrist thickness, tightly bound together. Fascines were intended to have a diameter, once completed, of about nine inches. They were easily manufactured entirely from brush or cut wood, and when properly constructed were proof against musketry.

By the first week in October the American army's Lake Champlain fleet lacked only a single vessel (the row galley *Gates*). As the fleet was finally organized at Valcour Bay, Arnold had sixteen vessels available to him. Four of the vessels were the three schooners and single sloop that had comprised the original Lake Champlain fleet. Of these, the *Liberty* and *Enterprise* were so small and under-armed that Arnold chose not to utilize them as fighting vessels. The *Liberty* was employed as a messenger vessel, carrying rations, supplies, and letters between Arnold and Gates. Several of its small cannon were actually removed by Arnold to the *Trumbull* row galley to permit the *Liberty* to carry a greater quantity of baggage.[103] In fact, it was not present at Valcour Island when the British finally appeared in mid–October. The *Enterprise* was used as a hospital ship, as recorded by American soldier Jahiel Stewart who served aboard her during the engagement.[104] The *Royal Savage* was a poor sailor as previously documented, and it was of limited service to Arnold. Thus, of the four sailing ships only the *Revenge* could be depended upon as a core fighting vessel, and its armament consisted of eight 4-pounder cannon, for a total broadside weight of a pitiful sixteen pounds (little more than the single ball that a modern professional bowler throws down a bowling alley).

Half of Arnold's entire fleet strength was comprised of the relatively small, ungainly gondolas. The gondolas were abysmal sailors because of their flat bottoms, and under a heavy wind were literally at the complete mercy of the gale. Each gondola mounted three cannon, a large single cannon in the bow, and two smaller cannon amidships. Thus, the gondolas could only engage a single cannon at one time. Although the larger cannon in the bow meant that the gondolas would present a smaller head-on target, the sliding carriage could not be adjusted for deflection, and the entire gondola thus had to be aimed, considerably slowing the rate of fire and complicating the entire aiming process. Assuming that these eight gondolas employed their heaviest cannon, in total all eight could still only employ a broadside weight of a dismal eighty-seven pounds. It is not surprising that Arnold stopped production at eight gondolas.

It was only the four row-galleys that comprised effective fighting vessels, and it was upon these four ships that Arnold primarily depended. The *Lee* was a small ship and rather an improvised row galley properly classified as a cutter, but it could still be rowed or sailed effectively, and it carried two large cannon (a 12-pounder and a 9-pounder) augmented by four smaller 4-pounders. The *Washington*, *Congress* and *Trumbull* carried numerous large cannon, and were highly versatile fighting vessels. Unfortunately, because of the demands of their relative complexity of construction (particularly as compared to the easily fabricated gondolas), and their need for considerably more rigging, only these four row galleys could be completed by mid–October. A fifth one, the *Gates*, never left Mount Independence.

Thus, although Arnold had an impressive sixteen vessels on paper, and to the American soldiers at Ticonderoga and Mount Independence the fleet appeared to be formidable as their numerous sails filled the entirety of Lake Champlain, he actually only had four major combat vessels which were substantial and effective enough to legitimately challenge the British fleet. And the extremely poor cast iron cannon with which they were armed distinctly limited their capabilities. Further complicating his command was that the three different classes of vessels had such disparate nautical capabilities. The four tiny sailing ships could only be sailed, did not have oars, and could not be operated in shallow water. The eight gondolas depended almost exclusively upon oars, for they sailed so poorly, but they could be operated in shallow waters. Only the four row galleys could be both sailed and rowed, and operated in relatively shallow waters. Arnold had been provided with a woefully ineffective combat instrument.

Arnold desperately wanted a larger fleet and he particularly wanted more row galleys, but more than anything else two factors constrained its size. As previously noted, the construction of the Lake Champlain fleet, when combined with the demands of constructing a second defensive fleet on the Hudson River, had exceeded the capacity of the Poughkeepsie Shipyard. There simply were not enough materials in New York and Connecticut to outfit two fleets. The second problem is that Skenesboro, being located on low, swampy ground, was not a healthy location. Within one month of their arrival, most of the carpenters were ill. Harmanus Schuyler complained on August 25:

> We have had 55 blacksmiths they are the greater part of them sick so that they are not able to make the iron work as fast as the carpenters want it[.] It is with great reluctance that I must inform your Excellency that the carpenters begin also a great many to get sick. Capt. Pitering[?] has but 10 men at work today out of fifty. Capt Winslow and Capt Cardish[?] has also a great many sick.[105]

By September 2 the situation was dire, Schuyler reporting:

> The carpenters most all sick. Capt Winslow and Tipcom are gone back in the country to get these helt [healed]. Day [They] have but eight men at work out of the two companies this morning. Derick & my self has the feaver.

General Waterbury, supervising construction at Skenesboro, was brief but articulate: "I never saw so much fever and ague in my life as there is at this post."[106] Gates complained the "natural unwholsomeness of the place alone is the cause of all the fever and ague there."[107] Even had Arnold had adequate materials, and of course he did not, it is doubtful that he had sufficient healthy carpenters to build any more of a fleet than he finally possessed.

Ascertaining the actual broadside weight of Arnold's American fleet is problematic. Assuming that the Americans positioned their ships to permit their largest guns to be employed (the fact that the *Philadelphia*'s fatal shot was lodged directly in her bow lends credence to this scenario), and deducting the guns of the *Royal Savage* which was such a poor sailor that it ran aground early in the Valcour Island engagement, Arnold's fleet had a maximum estimated broadside of 264 pounds (excluding the smaller and much less capable swivel guns), nearly two-thirds of this weight being provided exclusively by the four row galleys. This was a less than imposing weight of metal.

Still, the chain of command was well established with Arnold, Waterbury and Wigglesworth working smoothly together. The fleet was fully manned, and after nine weeks on Lake Champlain the crews were as proficient as they were likely to become. Given the shortfalls in materials and carpenters, the fleet was as large as the American Northern Theater could feasibly produce. Once Valcour Bay had been selected as Arnold's battleground, and the vessels protected with their breastworks of fascines, the American advanced guard was ready to delay the British advance.

The American army had performed a major accomplishment in constructing a large enough fleet on Lake Champlain to contest the British Royal Navy's obvious superiority. By mid–October, even through Carleton had by now constructed a formidable fleet, augmented by numerous Royal Artillery gunboats, and with several hundred bateaux to transport Burgoyne's army, he still had not advanced. This was the strength of the American fleet — not numbers of vessels, superiority of construction or design, or weight or quality of cannon, but mere presence. The months of July, August, September and most of October had passed for the British in fleet construction at St. Jean. That is, the heart of the campaign season had been expended while their army rested quietly in quarters and performed repetitive, incessant drills. The American Lake Champlain fleet had provided Gates the months necessary to reconstruct the American army and fortify a new integrated defensive position at Ticonderoga, Mount Hope and Mount Independence. It was time and labor well spent.

When the British navy and army finally moved south on Lake Champlain, it was already the second week in October, and they still had to move aside the American fleet before they could reach Ticonderoga. Thanks to the great efforts of Schuyler, Arnold, Varick and scores of individual officers and soldiers and carpenters, this would not be an easy task. And of greatest import, as Horatio Gates stressed to the soldiers at Fort Ticonderoga, Mount Independence and Mount Hope on September 6, "Our fleet is only our advanced guard; that defeated, the defense of the United States and the support of American freedom falls upon this army."[108] Gates was under no illusion that the small American fleet could defeat the considerably larger and spectacularly equipped British fleet in open battle upon Lake Champlain. But simply by existing the crude, unpainted American vessels had already achieved victory.

10

"The Enemys Fleet Attacked Ours with Great Fury"

Destruction of the American Advanced Guard on Lake Champlain, October 1776[1]

The British, like the Americans, had spent the late summer and fall of 1776 constructing a naval force on Lake Champlain. In their case, they had chosen St. Jean as their shipyard, located directly on the Richelieu River, and with immediate access to deep water. The British possessed three considerable advantages over the Americans, but one significant constraint. The British had almost unlimited resources available to construct their fleet. They had arrived in Canada on board a substantial fleet from England, which contained great quantities of naval materials readily available to hand. The same ships also carried hundreds of trained, experienced sailors who were ordered to join the fleet, thus providing an instant cadre of seasoned seamen not available to the Americans. As mentioned, the British also were outfitted with a superb train of modern bronze artillery. Not only was there an impressive quantity of land-based guns owned and operated by the Royal Artillery, but these were augmented by the hundreds of well-maintained, effective cannon stationed aboard the Royal Navy vessels. Considerable and daunting efforts were still required to construct a fleet on Lake Champlain, but the British only had to concentrate on building ships, not locating the means to create a fleet as did Schuyler and Arnold. Their single largest constraint was one of geography, specifically the series of rapids between Chambly and St. Jean that had previously caused the Americans so many difficulties during their withdrawal up the Richelieu River earlier that summer. These rapids now worked to the Americans' advantage, as they substantially delayed the British boat construction at St. Jean, since everything had to be hauled by hand or cart around the rapids, a time consuming and exhausting task. Although the British eventually constructed a formidable fleet, it would have been larger, and assembled considerably more rapidly, without the presence of the rapids.

From the beginning, the British had known that naval supremacy on Lake Champlain would be integral to a successful invasion into New York colony. The British were well familiar with the experience of 1759, when General Jeffery Amherst's advance had been stopped for the summer at Crown Point due to the absence of a Lake Champlain navy in the presence of a small French flotilla. Carleton's fate in the summer of 1776 was the same as Amherst's had been nearly two decades previously, and he could not advance until an armed force was constructed to wrest control of Lake Champlain from the American fleet, and until he fabricated sufficient bateaux to transport his soldiers and their supplies. The British high command in England had predicted this contingency, and had shipped the components for fourteen flat-bottomed artillery gunboats designed to carry a single cannon from England, such that they could be rapidly re-assembled upon their arrival in Canada.[2] These gunboats were transported by land from Chambly to St. Jean and launched at the shipyard there, and a number of new gunboats were also constructed to an identical pattern.

Unlike the conventional sailing vessels that would be commanded by Royal Navy officers and manned by Royal Navy seamen, the gunboats were to be commanded by Royal Artillery and Hesse-Hanau officers, and the cannon that they mounted were to be fired by Royal Artillerymen and Hessian Artillerymen. When Carleton finally moved south in October 1776 these artillery gunboats comprised an important contingent of his naval force, and once Carleton began land operations against the Americans the cannon and artillerymen would be disembarked and become the British army's train of artillery.

The precise number of these gunboats has proven a perplexing question to historians, for the simple reason that the participants from both fleets were less than definitive regarding these gunboats. Captain Charles Douglas, the senior Royal Navy Officer present in Canada, reported "20 gunboats each having a brass field piece, some 24s to 9s, some with howitzers."[3] Lieutenant John Enys, whose 29th Foot provided infantrymen to augment the crews of the gunboats, noted "about 20 gun boats with one gun in each."[4] An anonymous officer of the 47th Foot, who observed the gunboats from his post aboard a bateau carrying the British infantry down Lake Champlain, listed no less than 29 gunboats.[5] Lieutenant James Hadden of the Royal Artillery, commanding one of the gunboats, recorded a definitive 22 gunboats.[6] Captain George Pausch of the Hesse Hanau Artillery, similarly commanding one of the artillery gunboats, reported a divergent number, "27 bateaux armed with 24, 12 and 6 pound cannon and a few howitzers."[7] From the American perspective, Arnold, whose knowledge of the gunboats was limited to a single day's contest in Valcour Bay, would recall facing: "28 gondolas with one gun each 12 18 & 24 pounders and one 8 Inch Howitzer, 2 gondolas 3 guns each 12 pounders."[8]

Confounded by such contradictory evidence, scholars have variously estimated the number of gunboats at between twenty and twenty-eight.[9] Historian James Nelson, the most recent author to tackle the Battle of Valcour Island, found the problem too challenging to unravel and simply chose to employ the safe but vague: "twenty or so gunboats."[10]

The Orderly Book of the Royal Regiment of Artillery, May 8, 1776, to June 29, 1777 from the Lloyd W. Smith Collection at Morristown National Historical Park, Morristown, New Jersey, provides a definitive record of these artillery gunboats, to include their ordnance, commanding officers, deployment, and even the names of the gunboats.

> Octr. 2ᵈ, [1776]Morning Brigade Orders
>
> The armed Boats to move so soon as they are Complete. Those which are now ready to go this day the Disposition in the order of the Battle will be given. The Officers and Non Commiss'd Officers are appointed to the Armed Boats as follows — Captain Borthwick with Lᵗ. Duvernett to be in a Boat Armed with a Royal Howitzer [5½-

Inch Howitzer] and will command the Right—Captain Mitchelson with L[t]. Reade to be also in a Boat Arm'd with a Royal Howitzer [5½-Inch Howitzer] and will command the Left—Captain Peauch [sic] of the Hessian Artillery in a Boat Arm'd with a light Six Pounder & will Command the Hessian Brigade in the center.—

Lieu[t]. Barnes   L[t], 24 P[r].
Lieu[t]. Smith   ditto
Lieu[t]. Dysart   Howitzer 8 Inch
Lieu[t]. Remington   ditto

Lieu[ts]. York, Collier, Cox and Hadden to have each a Medium 12 P[rs].

Four Non Commissioned Officers to 4 Medium 12 P[rs].

Four Non Commissioned Officers to 4 Light 6 P[rs].

The Non Commissioned Officers to be chosen from Cap[t]. Borthwick's Company and from the Detachments of Williams's & Carters—Four Artillery Men to be in each Arm'd boat and two Additionals from the 29th Regiment. Captain Borthwick with the rest of the Officers will immediately take charge and Command, of the Arm'd Boats.

Oc[t]. 3d [1776] Brigade Orders by M.G. [Major General] Phillips

...The armed Boats are to have in each, six Private[s] in a proportion of four of the Artillery & two Additionals. Those Boats which are Commanded by Non Commissioned Officers to be from the Best and most experienced of that station. The Commanding Officers of Companies to be made answerable for this and Captain Carter to see it Performed. The Howitzer & 24 P[r]. Boats to have each a Carefull Non Commiss[d]. Officer to assist the Officer on that Particular Service.—

Return of Gun Boats Mann'd by the R.R. [Royal Regiment] of Artillery

[# of boat—added by author]	Nature of Ordnance	By whom Commanded	Names of Boats	Remarks
[1]	5½ Inch Howitzer [Royal Howitzer]	Captain Borthwick	Carcass	Right Division
[2]	24 Pounder	Lieut. Barnes	Invincible	Right Division
[3]	8 Inch Howitzer	Lieut. Dysart	Firebrand	Right Division
[4]	12 Pounder	Serjt. Sipple	Renown	Right Division
[5]	12 Pr.	Serjt. Hayter	Desperate	Right Division
[6]	6 Pr.	Corpl. Mennans	Revenge	Right Division
[7]	6 Pr.	Corpl. Batton	Dreadful	Right Division
[8]	12 Pr.	Lieut. Yorke	Resolution	Left of the Right Division
[9]	12 Pr.	Lieut. Cox	Terrible	Left of the Right Division
[10]	6 Pr.	[Captain Pausch] Hessian Artillery	[Not Given or Not Named]	Center
[11]	6 Pr.	[Lieutenant Dufais] Hessian Artillery	[Not Given or Not Named]	Center [Author's Note: Sunk at Valcour Island]

[# of boat — added by author]	Nature of Ordnance	By whom Commanded	Names of Boats	Remarks
[12]	6 Pr.	[Lieutenant Spangenburg] Hessian Artillery	[Not Given or Not Named]	Center
[13]	12 Pr.	Major Blomefield	Pluto	Rear of the Center
[14]	5½ Inch Howr. [Royal Howitzer]	Captain Mitchelson	Blast	Left Division
[15]	24 Pounder	Lieutenant Smith	Infernal	Left Division
[16]	8 Inch Howr.	Lieut. Rimington	Tartar	Left Division
[17]	12 Pr.	Sergeant Turner	Destruction	Left Division
[18]	12 Pr.	Sergeant Somerville	Vesuvius	Left Division
[19]	6 Pr.	Corporal Hawkins	Thunderbolt	Left Division
[20]	6 Pr.	Corporal Innes	Aetna	Left Division
[21]	12 Pr.	Lieutenant Hadden	Furious	Right of the Left Division
[22]	12 Pr.	Lieutenant Collier	Repulse	Right of the Left Division

This accounts for twenty-two armed British and Hessian gunboats present at the commencement of the Battle of Valcour Island, with twenty-one of these gunboats surviving that battle to participate in future maneuvers. The two gunboats that raised the total from the October 2, 1776, Orderly Book entry are the two additional German gunboats (referred to as gunboats #11 and #12, since the German gunboats were apparently not named). Captain Pausch noted that Lieutenant Dufais and Lieutenant Spangenburg of the Hanau Artillery commanded these two gunboats. Not surprisingly, since he commanded the *Furious* in the fight at Valcour Island, this Orderly Book entry also reveals that Lieutenant Hadden's count of 22 gunboats was absolutely correct.

These Royal Artillery gunboats were essentially the equivalent of Arnold's eight gondolas. The American gondolas were actually twice as large (54 feet in length, versus the gunboats' 27 feet), but both craft could fire only a single cannon at the time, and both were intended to be fought bow-on rather than in the traditional broadside manner. Both mounted their bow cannon in a sliding carriage, which meant that the entire boat had to aimed, rather than just the cannon. Both craft could be rowed, were flat bottomed so that they could operate in shallow water, and could be sailed when the wind was favorable (dead astern). The larger size of the American gondolas offered no real tactical advantages, and the Americans would have been better off building more single gun gunboats similar to the British model, rather than fewer numbers of the larger *Philadelphia* class gondola.

At St. Jean, Carleton also supervised the construction of considerably larger and more capable vessels than Arnold had been able to manufacture given his limitations at Skenesboro. By the time that Carleton's fleet finally departed St. Jean during the first days of October, he could employ five major sailing vessels. The first, the gondola *Loyal Convert*, had been captured by the British Royal Navy from the Americans on the St. Lawrence River in early May. It was formerly known as the gondola *Hancock* or *Schuyler*, and with what must have been prodigious efforts the British were able to successfully carry this gondola around the rapids of the Richelieu River by brute hand and animal strength. It had been outfitted with seven 9-pounders and a number of swivels, turning it into a capable vessel the equal of anything the Americans had on the lake. Her commander was Lieutenant Edward Longcroft, of the Royal Navy.

The largest British vessel was the *Inflexible*, a formidably large ship that mounted no less than eighteen 12-pounder cannon. A single broadside from the *Inflexible* alone nearly equaled half the weight that the entire American fleet could throw, and its 12-pounder shot were significantly larger and capable of causing more damage than the miniscule 4-pounders and 6-pounders that many of the American craft mounted. It fought under the command of Lieutenant John Schank, Royal Navy.

The British fleet counted two schooners, the *Carleton* directed by Lieutenant John Starke of the Royal Navy, and the *Maria* under the guidance of Lieutenant James Dacres, Royal Navy. The *Maria*, named for Carleton's wife, served as the flagship of the fleet and Carleton sailed aboard this vessel. Both ships were heavily armed, the *Carleton* mounting twelve 6-pounders, and the *Maria* carrying an impressive fourteen 6-pounders.

The fifth British ship was a distinctive class of vessel, specifically designed for military use on interior waters in North America, the radeau *Thunderer*. A radeau was a large, seven-sided, floating gun battery. It was named radeau for the French word for a raft. This was an extremely accurate moniker, as essentially the radeau was a gigantic floating raft, with a flat bottom, no keel, and a distinctive, almost turtle shape. The only surviving example of this class is the radeau *Land Tortoise*, which is believed to be representative of this type of vessel, and which has been discovered intact in deep water at the bottom of the southern end of Lake George. The *Land Tortoise* was constructed on Lake George in 1758 by British and Colonial soldiers. The British had constructed a number of radeaux on both Lake George and Lake Champlain during the Seven Years' War, and they had given good service in support of army operations. The length of the radeau *Land Tortoise* was 52 feet long, and eighteen feet across at its widest point. The flat-bottomed vessel was propelled by 26 oars, and was rigged with two simple masts so that it could perform at least rudimentary sailing under favorable winds to rest the oarsmen. The *Land Tortoise* has seven cannon ports in her sides and was constructed with angular lines and sloping bulwarks to protect her crew from enemy fire. The radeau *Thunderer* that was used by the British Royal Artillery on Lake Champlain in 1776 was considerably larger than the *Land Tortoise*, as the *Thunderer* carried no less than fourteen massive cannon (an intimidating six 24-pounder cannon, six 12-pounder cannon, and two 8-inch howitzers), suggesting that it may have been up to three times larger than its predecessor. Its large size enabled it to serve as the Royal Artillery Headquarters, and carry numerous sailors and artillerymen, along with staggering quantities of ordnance stores and spare ammunition. But it also meant that the *Thunderer* handled very poorly indeed in any type of rough or unfavorable weather. A single broadside from the *Thunderer* propelled nearly two-thirds the weight of metal of the entire American fleet across the waves, and its cannon were considerably larger.[11] The *Thunderer* was, for all practical purposes, a nautical fortress.

When augmented by the twenty-two Royal Artillery gunboats, the British fleet considerably outmatched Arnold's ragtag assemblage of floating rafts. The five major vessels were larger, carried more and heavier cannon, were highly maneuverable, and even the smallest of them (the *Loyal Convert*) was equal to the most capable four American row galleys. The British gunboats were in fighting capacity fully the equal of the American gondolas, and they employed twenty-two of them versus the eight American craft. The American gondolas were crewed by sailors who six weeks previously had been soldiers who had never served on board anything larger than a bateau, while the British gunboats were manned by experienced, seasoned Royal Navy sailors and professional, highly trained artillerymen. Additionally, the entire British fleet was crewed by the Royal Navy and commanded by veteran Royal Navy officers with numerous years of service. The Royal Navy would eventually provide no less than 670 sailors, eight officers, and nineteen petty officers for the Lake Champlain fleet.[12] Captain Thomas Pringle of the Royal Navy, a long serving officer of distinguished Scottish descent, was Commodore of the overall British flotilla.

The composition and nature of Arnold's fleet had in large measure dictated the selection of his battleground in Valcour Bay, which he had first identified as early as mid–September, and had occupied continuously since October 1. Arnold's fleet was comprised of four ships that could be sailed, but not be rowed. And of those four, Arnold's ostensible flagship, the *Royal Savage,* was a very poor sailor indeed. But still, it sailed immeasurably better than the eight gondolas, which could maneuver well only when the wind was perfectly dead astern, but could be rowed with considerable efficiency. Only the four row galleys could be both sailed and rowed with skill and aplomb. The result was that Arnold in effect commanded three different fleets which were nautically incapable of fighting a unified action on the water. The British fleet outmatched Arnold in size and number of ships, capability and size of cannon, number of cannon, quality of crews, and sailing capabilities on the water. In fact, Arnold possessed not a single advantage over the British fleet. Thus, Arnold had to find an anchorage in which he could fight his fleet without maneuvering it, and which would provide him with a tactical advantage that his fleet could never hope to provide. Valcour Bay perfectly fit the bill.

In the early days of October Guy Carleton finally felt that his naval strength was adequate to wrest control of Lake Champlain from the Americans, and he assembled his fleet, boarded his army commanded by Lieutenant General Jonathan Burgoyne onto their bateaux, organized his flotilla into divisions, and moved south. The movement down Lake Champlain was slow, methodical, well-disciplined and uneventful. This was just the way that Guy Carleton liked his military campaigns.

Carleton organized his fleet into a series of columns. In the lead were the five major vessels, with the *Maria* on the right (western) flank, the *Thunderer* next, the *Inflexible* in the center, then the *Loyal Convert*, and finally the *Carleton* on the left (eastern) flank. To their rear was the line of twenty-two gunboats stretching across the lake, which maintained the tactical alignment previously described. Following them came the bateaux with Brigadier General Simon Fraser's Advanced Corps; then the bateaux containing the British Regular Brigade, the bateaux containing the Brunswick and Hesse Hanau Brigade commanded by the superb Brunswick officer Major General Frederick Von Riedesel, and finally the numerous bateaux containing provisions, stores, and similar baggage. Surrounding all were the canoes with Native American warriors from a range of tribes. Carleton would write, "We have likewise a considerable body of Indians serving with the Army of which no exact return is made out."[13] Brunswick Brigadier General Von Gall reported of the numbers of these Natives on September 12: "About 800 Indians, who are divided into two corps, have gone on in advance with two English officers."[14]

Carleton, who was meticulous in his combat preparations, and additionally a stickler for good order, ensured that the flotilla maintained this precise configuration during the movement. The craft required to transport the soldiers and supplies amounted to no less than four hundred bateaux and thirty longboats.[15] It had been a busy summer and fall indeed for the British carpenters and laborers on the Richelieu River. The British flotilla must have been a tremendous and imposing sight as over 450 floating vessels of various configurations and sizes filled the lake in neat geometric patterns.

From the shipyard at St. Jean where the fleet had assembled the nautical cavalcade progressed down the broad channel of the Richelieu River, passing the low, swampy ground of Isle Aux Noix where a small British garrison was now established, and paying little if any heed to the bones of the numerous American dead that remained just below the surface. Not far to the south the river opened up onto the expanse of Lake Champlain. The first landmark is Point au Fer, Point of Iron, protruding into the lake from the west. Here on the west shore is the shelter of King Bay, and the British fleet spent the night ashore at this location. By the sunset of October 10 the fleet had continued south, passing the wooded bulk of Isle La Motte to the west, and sweeping past Point Au Roche, the aptly named Point of Rocks for here a host of dangerous rocks and stone shoals tumble into the lake from the shore, requiring vessels to swing wide to avoid their danger. Once past Point Au Roche the large protrusion of Cumberland Head to the west is encountered, which in turn shields the open waters of Cumberland Bay. The fleet and army camped on the night of October 10 at various points between Point au Fer and Cumberland Head. At dawn on Friday, October 11, the weather was clear and the wind was strong from the north, perfect conditions to facilitate a British advance upon Crown Point and Ticonderoga.

At the Ticonderoga and Mount Independence garrison, October 11 was busily occupied as every other day that summer and fall had been. Horatio Gates was holding a host of courts-martial.[16] To his north, at the secluded position within Valcour Bay, Benedict Arnold was occupied in a slightly more martial manner. He was in the fight for his life with the entirety of the British fleet.

The weather was crisp and clear, and Lieutenant Bayze Wells reported from on board the gondola *Providence* that snow could be seen on the green mountains to the east and west.[17] The British soldiers re-boarded their craft, and rowed and sailed past the broad expanse of Cumberland Bay, slowly leaving the small green intrusion of the Island of Saint Michael (known today as Crab Island) in the distance off to their west behind their right shoulders. The wind was extremely favorable, and the radeau, gunboats, and bateaux could all be sailed rapidly and easily down the lake.

Arnold, anticipating the British advance (indeed, he had expected it for some time now), had posted his Stockbridge Mohican Native Americans and other trusted scouts in the tall trees on the high ground of Valcour Island, and they afforded him ample notice that the British fleet was approaching. Jahiel Stewart, with this scouting party, reported being sent "to the loer [lower] part of the island" meaning the northern portion of Valcour Island.[18] In any event, 450 vessels with sails raised and filling the entire lake's surface were highly unlikely to slip past anybody. But just to make sure, Arnold also had a guard boat (probably one of the bateau that was attached to each of his vessels, armed with a swivel gun) out on the lake. Lieutenant Wells reported, "About eight A.M. the guard boat came in and fired an alarm and brought news of the near approach of our enemy."[19]

At approximately 10:00 A.M. the British fleet pounded proudly down the lake, swept past Valcour Island, and were then stunned to discover Valcour Bay filled with the American naval force behind them, and with four of those ships headed out of the protected waters of the bay apparently with the intent of engaging their vulnerable bateaux and longboats to the rear. The neat, precise, confident British accounts that survive to this day scarcely document the panic that must have swept the British naval commanders at that moment. The British fleet had sailed entirely past the American fleet, failed to detect their presence, and were now well beyond Valcour Island and approaching the mouth of the Ausable River. This was a critical error, of the greatest magnitude. The British five sailing vessels now had to turn about and work against a brisk northern wind to be able to engage Arnold's force.

To compound their mistake, Arnold had dispatched the row galleys *Congress*, *Washington* and *Trumbull* and the schooner *Royal Savage* out of Valcour Bay. If these ships could reach the British transport bateaux, they could wreak deadly havoc. Signals were urgently dispatched to the twenty-two artillery gunboats, following in the rear of the five major sailing vessels, to turn and engage the aggressive Americans. Presumably, the gunboats immediately dropped their sails, shook out their oars, and began to hurriedly row against the wind around the southern point of Valcour Island. Their job was made slightly easier because the prevailing current in Lake Champlain consistently flows to the north, but the strong wind would have cancelled out any marginal advantage that this provided. They also had to be careful to swing wide to the south, for approximately five hundred to one thousand meters to the south of Valcour Island is the small Little Island and attendant shoals that must be avoided (named by the French as Petit Isle but anglicized as Little Island, today known as Garden Island and Garden Ledge), along with a shallow shelf that extends out from the southwestern corner of Valcour Island itself. In fact, there was sufficient water for the gunboats to traverse these obstacles, but the British did not know that fact until Lake Champlain was effectively surveyed in 1779.[20]

When the Americans saw the gunboats maneuvering against his four ships, Arnold determined to withdraw them to join the main American force in Valcour Bay. At this moment, Arnold's single tactical flaw of the engagement occurred. Specifically, he had erred in his selection of the *Royal Savage* to sortie out against the British. The *Royal Savage* had proven itself to not be a particularly adept sailor, and as it returned to Valcour Bay sailing against the wind, it missed stays and was blown onto the shallow southwestern shelf of Valcour Island.[21] Missing stays is a nautical expression that means that the

British gunboat view of Valcour Island. The *Royal Savage* wreck spot is on the right foreground. This view is looking northeast on Valcour Bay (author's collection).

schooner failed to change tack properly into the wind, losing the ability of the ship to maneuver, and leaving it entirely at the mercy of the wind. In this particular case, the wind was utterly without mercy, and it drove the *Royal Savage* violently ashore.

Without order due to the wind and individual proficiency in rowing, the artillery gunboats began moving towards the entrance to Valcour Bay. At the same time, the five major British ships wallowed to the south, buffeted by the wind and unable to make headway north, just as much out of the fight as the grounded *Royal Savage* was. Lieutenant Hadden, commanding one of the gunboats, described their movement to begin the fight:

> About 11 o'clock this morning one of the enemies vessels was discovered, and immediately pursued into a bay on the eastern [actually the western] shore of the lake, where the rest of their fleet was found at an anchor in the form of a crescent, between Valcour Island and the Continent. The pursuit of this vessel was without order or regularity.... The vessel which proved to be the *Royal Savage* ... was run on shore and most of the men escaped on to Valcour Island, in effecting which they were fired upon by the Gun Boats, this firing at one object drew us all in a cluster and four of the Enemies vessels getting under way to support the *Royal Savage* fired upon the boats with success. An order was therefore given by the Commanding Officer for the Boats to form across the bay; this was soon effected though under the Enemies whole fire and unsupported, all the King's vessels having dropped too far to leeward.[22]

10. "The Enemys Fleet Attacked Ours with Great Fury" 237

American retreat route down Lake Champlain. Looking South on Valcour Bay (author's collection).

The artillery gunboats, for the first two hours of the engagement, were the only British ships in the fight. Finally, the *Carleton* was able to work its way into the bay, having taken advantage of a fortuitous bit of wind, and demonstrating considerable sailing skill in the bargain. Lieutenant Hadden again reported:

> This unequal combat was maintained for two hours without any aid, when the *Carlton* schooner of 14 guns 6 pounders got into the bay and immediately received the Enemies whole fire which was continued without intermission for about an hour, when the boats of the fleet towed her off, and left the Gun Boats to maintain the conflict, this was done until the Boats had expended their ammunition when they were withdrawn, having sunk one of the Enemies Gondolas, and considerably damaged others. Being small objects the loss in the Gun Boats was inconsiderable, 20 men (a German Gun Boat blown up). Each Gun Boat carried 1 gun in the bow (or howitzer), 7 artillery men, and 11 seamen, the whole under an Artillery officer. It was found that the Boat's advantage was not to come nearer than about 700 yards, as whenever they approached nearer, they were greatly annoyed by grape shot, although their case could do little mischief. Each Boat had 80 rounds of ammunition, 30 of which were case shot & could not be used with effect.[23]

The British officers engaged universally noted the predominant, and nearly exclusive, role of the artillery gunboats at Valcour Island. General Jonathan Burgoyne, commanding the army brigades to the rear of the fleet, reported, "The *Carleton* with one division of artillery boats engaged, the rest of the ships could not get into action, the wind being strong at Northeast."[24] Carleton noted in two different letters written on October 14, "Our attack, that day, was only with a part of our force, the *Carleton* and the gun boats" and, "I cannot omit taking notice to your Lordship of the good service done, in the first action, by the spirited conduct of a number of officers and men of the Corps of Artillery, sustained for many hours the whole fire of the enemy's fleet, the rest of our vessels not being able to work up near enough to join effectually in the engagement."[25] Captain Charles Pringle, commander of the British flotilla, echoed: "The wind was so unfavorable that for a considerable time nothing could be brought into action with them, but the gun boats. The *Carleton* Schooner ... by much perseverance at last got up to their assistance, but as none of the other vessels of the fleet could then get up."[26] Lieutenant Enys, whose 29th Foot provided a number of men to support the artillerymen on the gunboats, echoed: "The gunboats bore the brunt of their whole fire the greatest part of that day."[27]

The *Carleton* had performed quite credibly by working its way into the fight, but it didn't remain in Valcour Bay for long. The American gunners were having considerable difficulties aiming their cannon at the small British gunboats, which presented extremely low and difficult targets. However, when the *Carleton* swung into the bay and settled in broadside to fight, she presented an object that the American gunners could scarcely miss, and they absolutely pounded the schooner. Jahiel Stewart, on board the American hospital sloop *Enterprise*, recorded in his journal: "The battle was very hot on both sides & one of the regular skooners came up very bold & the battle was very hot. We cut her rigen [rigging] most all away & bored her threw and threw [through and through] & she was forst to toss off of us [i.e. forced to retreat]."[28] The American cannon were too small in size to sink the *Carleton*, but they raked her with devastating gunfire, and shortly an artillery gunboat had to rescue the *Carleton* to prevent it from sinking. In fact, the *Carleton* was so badly battered during its short visit to Valcour Bay that it could no longer be sailed, and a pair of artillery gunboats had to be eventually withdrawn from the firing line to draw her wrecked, shattered hulk out of the bay. An 1835 account, written with the assistance of Admiral Sir Edward Pellew, 1st Viscount Exmouth, who had served as a 19-year-old Midshipman on board the *Carleton*, recounts the pummeling that the schooner absorbed at the hands of the Americans that day:

> She was suffering most severely. Very early in the action [Midshipman] Mr. Brown lost an arm; and soon after Lieutenant Dacres fell, severely wounded and senseless. He would have been thrown overboard as dead, but for the interference of Mr. Pellew, who now succeeded to the command. He maintained the unequal contest until Captain Pringle ... made the signal of recall; which the *Carleton*, with two feet water in her hold, and half her crew killed and wounded, was not in a condition to obey. In attempting to go about, being at the time near the shore, which was covered with the enemy's marksmen, she hung in stays, and Mr. Pellew, not regarding the danger of making himself so conspicuous, sprang out on the bow spirit to push the jib over. The artillery boats now took her in tow, while the enemy maintained a very heavy fire, being enabled to bear their guns upon her with more effect, as she increased her distance. A shot cut the tow-rope, and Mr. Pellew ordered some one to go and secure

it; but seeing all hesitate, for indeed it appeared a death-service, he ran forward and did it himself. The *Carleton* was then towed out of gun-shot.[29]

Pellew would earn a richly deserved promotion to Lieutenant for his gallantry this day.

The fighting in Valcour Bay that Friday was a veritable artillery hell. There was little maneuvering, and aside from the *Carleton*'s brief foray into and just as rapid exit out of the engagement, no real naval tactics were exercised. The American fleet and the British artillery gunboats formed two parallel lines across the bay, both battle lines stretching across from island to mainland, and did their energetic best to blast their opponents' vessels into toothpicks. They generally succeeded, although by the end of the day it was apparent that the British artillery gunboats had the best of the struggle. Arnold wrote to Gates in his official report of the action:

> The *Congress* & *Washington* have suffered greatly, the latter lost her First Lieutenant killed & Captain & Master wounded, the *New York* lost all her officers except her Captain, the *Philadelphia* was hulled in so many places that she sank about one hour after the engagement was over, the whole killed & wounded amounts to about sixty. The *Congress* received seven shot between wind & water, was hulled a dozen times, had her main mast wounded in two places & her yard in one, the *Washington* was hulled a number of times, her main mast shot through & must have a new one, both vessels are very leaky & want repairing.[30]

The fight was brutal and ugly, and both sides suffered. One of the British gunboats, manned by the Hesse Hanau Artillery and located in the center of the British gunboat line, was sunk in the midst of the contest. Captain Pausch, whose gunners were onboard the gunboat, described the debacle:

> The 11th of October. We had very good winds and early in the morning we raised anchor and set sail.... Already at about ten-thirty a cannon fire was heard and shortly thereafter, with very good winds, all the batteaux came upon the enemy ships in a bay lying behind an island.... Our attack with the small batteaux armed with 24 12 and 6-pound cannons and several howitzers was furious and after all had come together very lively.... During the affair, it could have been a bit after one o'clock, the naval battle became very serious. Lieutenant Dufais had the misfortune to run aground with all of his troops because his ammunition exploded when hit by an enemy cannonball. He stopped at a great distance off to the right, and the sergeant major who I had with me in my batteau, first became aware of the fire. He called this to my attention as I was just in the process of directing my cannon. I could not immediately recognize the men until shortly thereafter a case [the exploding ammunition chest] flew into the air, and after the smoke had cleared. I then recognized my troops by cords on their caps. This batteau came back burning furiously and I hurried in order to save the lieutenant and his crew, if possible, as by the now the batteau was completely filled with water. Those who could, jumped into another batteau, which was also about to sink from being overcrowded. Finally a lieutenant of artillery by the name of Schmidt [Lieutenant Smith with the gunboat *Infernal* mounting a 24-pounder cannon, which would have been stationed to the left of the Hessian gunboats] came and took the lieutenant, Bombadier Engelhard, and one cannoneer into this batteau. I had taken the other nine cannoneers and nine sailors into my boat, together with my ten cannoneers, one drummer, one sergeant, one servant, and nine sailors, altogether 42 people in this small batteau, so that I was now overloaded and was no longer in condition

to move away from the spot where I had embarked these half lost individuals, and taken them on board. Here I had each moment to fear suddenly drowning both myself and all those with me. As it would soon be evening, the batteau pulled back. The radeau now arrived, but not until dusk ... it tested its 24-pound cannons against the enemy frigates, but the distance was too great so that no cannonball could have effect.[31]

Jahiel Stewart, onboard the American hospital sloop, observed at first hand the horrific results of the devastating British cannon fire: "The cannon balls & grape shot flew very thick & I believe we had a great many cilld [killed] and I was abord [on board] of the hospital sloop and they brought the wounded aboard of us the Dockters cut off great many legs and arm and see seven men threw overboard that died with their wounds while I was aboard."[32] American sailor Pascal De Angelis recorded the engagement succinctly: "The enemys fleet attacked ours with great fury and we returned the fire with as great spirit and vigor."[33] Colonel Wigglesworth was even more brief, noting "there ensued a most terrible fire without the least intermission till half past five P.M. when the enemy drew off."[34] Lieutenant Bayze Wells echoed: "The battle lasted eight hours very hot."[35]

To compound the Americans' difficulties, Carleton's Native Americans landed on Valcour Island and the main body of land, and poured small arms fire into the American vessels. This gunfire was probably more of an annoyance than anything, as the fascines that the Americans had placed around their ships would have been proof against musketry, but certainly this was one more thorn in the side of Arnold's men.[36] However, Lieutenant Pellew's account suggests that the Americans also landed marksmen and their own Natives on the shores to similarly harass the artillery gunboats. Valcour Bay must have been a very uncomfortable location to loiter that October afternoon.

Just at sunset, the fates finally claimed the *Royal Savage*. Aground since late morning, it had played little role in the action of the long afternoon. The *Royal Savage* had been driven hard onto Valcour Island, and since "one of her masts was wounded and rigging shot away" she was totally helpless.[37] Under duress from heavy cannon fire from the gunboats and the *Carleton*, and with her tilted decks being further swept by musketry from the Native American allies of the British that had landed on the island, the American crew abandoned ship and swam to safety. About dusk the British boarded the *Royal Savage* and set her on fire, which shortly spread to her magazines. The ensuing explosion destroyed the schooner, and along with it Arnold's papers that had remained onboard when he had transferred his flag to the Congress. The British would later salvage some of these papers for their intelligence value.[38]

The total broadside weight of the British and German artillery gunboats was 312 pounds.[39] Arnold's fleet was slightly outgunned by the gunboats, as his entire fleet could throw only 264 pounds at one broadside. Moreover, the British gunboats had the advantage of generally larger cannon, to include two 24-pounders, no less than nine 12-pounder cannon, two 8" howitzers, and two Royal (5½") howitzers. These larger guns were more powerful, packed considerably greater penetration power and caused more damage when they struck their target. As a testimony to this fact, the American gondola *Philadelphia* was sunk by a single 24-pounder that struck her in the bow, while the *Carleton* was impacted by numerous balls but still remained afloat. The American cannon were cast-iron relics of the previous century. The tragic explosion of a cast iron 6-pounder broadside on the gondola *New York* in the midst of the battle graphically demonstrated the obsolete nature of their ordnance. The British cannon were modern bronze pieces, none older than the Seven Years' War, and meticulously maintained by the Royal Artillery in the intervening period. Most likely, the American cannon simply could not produce the muzzle velocities or accuracy that the British cannon were capable of. The lack of skilled gunners, and constraints imposed by limited stockpiles of gunpowder and shot, also inhibited Arnold's fleet. Arnold himself noted, "We suffered much for want of seaman & gunners, I was obliged myself to point most of the guns on board the *Congress*."[40] The British had no such limitations, and they had drilled and performed live fire training relentlessly throughout the summer and fall. Finally, the British armed bateaux, fighting with their bows forward, could not have presented very large targets to the Americans. Charles Terrot, an assistant engineer serving with the Royal Artillery, wrote following the battle that: "The G. [Gun] Boats being low in the Water made the Shot go over their heads."[41]

It was an ugly and vicious fight, at relatively close range, and it ended only when the British artillery gunboats had expended all of their ammunition and had to withdraw to the radeau *Thunderer* to re-arm. During the engagement, the gunboats had fired a minimum of 1,100 rounds of ammunition, and almost certainly more depending upon how many rounds of case shot were employed, and how many shells from the howitzers were fired (both these types of ammunition would have had reduced effectiveness, but that does not mean that they were not fired; in fact a number of 8" howitzer shells have been recovered from Valcour Bay). One of the great mysteries of the Battle of Valcour Island has always been why the gunboats were withdrawn from Valcour Bay, and not reformed across the entirety of the bay in such a manner as to interdict Arnold's retreat route. The answer is simple, it was entirely dictated by logistical considerations. Sir Francis Clerke, Aide-de-Camp to General John Burgoyne, accurately reported: "the gun boats being obliged to repair to the ships to take in fresh ammunition."[42]

One of the artillery gunboats was sunk, compared to the *Philadelphia* and *Royal Savage* lost from Arnold's fleet. Arnold estimated his casualties at about 60, or 10 percent of his total force. British casualties are difficult to ascertain, but are believed to have been lighter.[43] Yet it had certainly not been a one-sided contest, Captain Pausch recording the effects of the cannonball that sunk Lieutenant Dufais' gunboat: "During this affair Lieutenant Dufais lost Cannoneer Rossmer, who was killed; Drummer Billand and the helmsman were burned to death; and a sailor, when the cannoneer was killed, had his leg shot off by the cannonball, which had bored through the bow under the cannon support, three inches above the water."[44] Surgeon J.F. Wasmus of the Brunswick Dragoon Regiment, stationed in the rear of the British army at Isle-Aux-Noix, was called upon to treat a number of the British wounded on October 12: "A bateau arrived on which there were an English officer, 8 English soldiers and one Hesse-Hanau Artillerymen. They had all been wounded in an action on Lake Champlain. They were [operated on] in the field hospital here; one arm and 2 legs were amputated."[45]

The spare ammunition for the gunboats was carried aboard the radeau *Thunderer*. One gunboat could pull up on either side of the *Thunderer* at a time, and then the ammunition would have to be hand carried from the hold of the *Thunderer*, taken across deck, handed across the side to the gunboat while both the radeau and the gunboat bobbed independently of each other, and then stowed aboard the gunboat's ammunition chests. Certainly the Royal Artillerymen and Hesse Hanau gunners were well versed in handling ammunition, and would have been adept at this process. However, the gunners were also exhausted, having just fought an intense all day battle. It is impossible, without involved and expensive experimental archaeology, to ascertain just how quickly one round of ammunition could have been safely loaded aboard each gunboat. However, slightly less than sixty seconds per round of ammunition (including both the charge of gunpowder and projectile) per gunboat does not seem excessive, and in fact this timing probably represents the absolute fastest that the exercise could have possibly been executed. This operation would also have had to be performed in nearly complete darkness, the sun having set at 5:15 P.M., and because gunpowder was being transferred and the Americans remained a threat, prudence dictated that no open lights be allowed on deck (the Royal Artillery stores contained so-called dark lanterns that provided some limited light in safety). Since two gunboats at a time could be re-loaded, one hour to re-supply two gunboats would have been required, including the necessary time to maneuver the gunboats and secure them to the radeau. Thus, simply re-arming the twenty-one surviving gunboats would have filled no less than eleven hours, removing them from position to the south of Valcour Bay at precisely the time when Arnold effected his escape.

Until the gunboats were re-supplied with ammunition, they were combat ineffective, and attempting to position them piecemeal in the darkness, after having fought an exhausting engagement, and while the necessary ammunition resupply was in process was probably deemed too challenging of a task. Given the rigors of the day's contest, the task might simply have been beyond the physical and mental capabilities of either the sailors or the gunners to execute. Thus, the gunboats did not secure the southern channel of Valcour Bay, being involved in another operation. The result of this ongoing process was that once the sun dipped beneath the peaks of the Adirondack Mountains to the west and plunged the waters of Lake Champlain into darkness, Arnold's retreat route lay wide open.

And the night was certain to be dark. In 1776, the new moon was to occur on October 12 at 9:54 A.M., and thus there was only 1 percent of the available moon's illumination visible when the moon was out. But in any event the moon set at 5:18 P.M. on October 11, and did not return until 5:51 A.M. on October 12. Essentially, sunset and sunrise coincided on this date with moonset and moonrise. The night of October 11 had no moon illumination whatsoever, and this does not take into account the fact that Lake Champlain during fall evenings and nights is renowned for heavy fogs and mists which would have further served to obscure the stars. Finally, Valcour Bay is topographically in a bowl, with the high ground of Valcour Island to the east and north, and the continuously rising high ground of the Lake Champlain shore to the west and north. There were no settlers in the vicinity in 1776, and thus there was no artificial illumination of any kind. Given the rising ground, particularly to the west, the American ships would have blended into the dark natural background nearly perfectly.

Arnold, upon the cessation of combat, consulted with General Waterbury and Colonel Wigglesworth regarding the future of the American fleet. Arnold would note that "every vessels ammunition was nearly three fourths spent." With most of their ammunition expended, the American officers really had little choice in the matter. Arnold's fleet could not maintain its position in Valcour Bay for another day. The three commanders were unanimous: "It was thought prudent to retire to Crown Point."[46]

The recovery of the gondola *Philadelphia* provided interesting archaeological confirmation of the great expenditure of the American ammunition. Although the smaller, broadside 9-pounder cannon were recovered with fifty-five solid shot and one bar shot onboard, the larger, bow mounted 12-pounder cannon had but three shot available. Only two spare 12-pounder solid shot remained, and a bar shot was loaded in the cannon when it was discovered.[47] This reflects two significant facts: first, that the *Philadelphia* was deliberately employing its larger cannon as its primary weapons system, and secondly, that most of the 12-pounder ammunition on board had been fired away by the time the *Philadelphia* sank at sunset. It should also be noted that bar shot was effectively employed against the rigging and sails of enemy ships only at close range, as this type of artillery projectile was quite inaccurate because the round spun once it had been fired. Attempting to hit the relatively small target area of an artillery gunboat with such a round would have been problematic, and in any event a bar shot was intended to chop up ropes and canvas, not penetrate the thick wooden sides of a fighting vessel. Using this type of projectile reflected desperation on the part of the *Philadelphia*'s crew.

Arnold's plan was audacious and bold. His fleet would raise anchor, form a column of single ships, and then slip past the British fleet en route for Crown Point. He was helped immeasurably by the lack of security by the British. Their gunboats and the radeau *Thunderer* were completely absorbed with re-loading the gunboats' ammunition chests with gunpowder and solid shot, an exercise that would occupy most of the night. The other four British capital ships' precise locations are unknown, but clearly none of them were in a position to observe or monitor the southern end of Valcour Bay. The British believed that they had Arnold's fleet surrounded, and it would be captured in the morning. Numerous written accounts all confirm their gross overconfidence.

American journals describe what must have been a hair-raising escape. Jahiel Stewart remembered, "About sun down the firen [firing] ceased and we had orders to set sail when it was dark and try to get thre [through] the regulars fleet for they was betwick [between] us and home so we histed [hoisted] sails & put out our oars & maid all the speed we could and they did not give us one gun nor we did not fire one at them ... so we got threw the fleet very safe ... and we sailed all night and rowed so we thought we was safe."[48] Colonel Wigglesworth recalled, "Upon consultation with Generals Arnold and Waterbury, I was ordered to get underway as soon as it was dark and show a light astern for the gondolas, in order to retreat up the lake as fast as possible. It being calm, we rode out clear of the enemy, without being discovered."[49] Arnold's official report stated, "At 7 o'clock Colonel Wiggilsworth [sic] in the *Trumbull* got under way, the gondolas & small vessels followed & the *Congress* & *Washington* brought up the rear, the enemy did not attempt to molest us, most of the fleet is this minute came to an anchor."[50] It is interesting that Arnold used his most valuable and capable combat vessels in the most exposed and important locations of this retreat—leading the column (a mistake on Colonel Wigglesworth's part could easily have led the entire column aground), and forming the rear guard.

The greatest danger during the withdrawal was the shoals of the Ausable River, for where it empties into Lake Champlain sand and dirt is deposited. This is exacerbated because, over geological time, this deposition became Ausable Point, which extends east into Lake Champlain. The Americans would have had to be alert for this shallow water to prevent running aground, but they had spent nearly three full weeks at Valcour Island, and Arnold almost certainly would have required his ships to have taken careful soundings of the surrounding waters well before the British arrived for battle.

By the next morning, Saturday, October 12, Arnold's battered flotilla reached the prominent bulk of Schuyler Island, a distinctive landmark of this portion of Lake Champlain. Ominously, as Lieutenant Bayze Wells recorded, "the wind being hard against us ... this day the wind at south."[51] Arnold spent the entire morning and a good portion of the afternoon attempting to repair his shot up vessels. Arnold reported, "The *Washington* galley was in such a shattered condition" and also noted that the *Washington*'s sails had to be mended at the anchorage at Schuyler Island.

During the retreat the American fleet had became somewhat disorganized. The majority of the ships apparently reached Schuyler Island, but at least the *Enterprise*, *Trumbull*, and two of the gondolas (the *New Jersey* and the *Spitfire*) had reached the cluster of the Four Brothers Islands further to the southeast. Here the two gondolas' damage proved fatal and they sank, the *New Jersey* in such shallow water that the British would eventually salvage her, and the *Spitfire* in extremely deep water. Colonel Wigglesworth reported that he had to anchor in the *Trumbull* to "stop our leaks, and secure our mainmast, which was split in two."[52]

Still, as bad as things must have appeared to the Americans, things were even worse in the British fleet. Carleton and his sailors and soldiers anticipated bagging the entire lot of the Americans in the morning, and were shocked and appalled to find Valcour Bay entirely empty except for a few pieces of flotsam from the previous day's engagement. Furious, Carleton ordered his fleet in immediate pursuit. His ships began to pound down the lake when he suddenly realized that, in his anger, he had forgotten to issue instructions to anybody else in his force, such as the entire army. The British fleet bashfully turned about, returned to Valcour Island, and finally got underway, stymied through inefficiency not once but twice.

Arnold's fleet, having performed their critical repairs, resumed their retreat at 2:00 P.M. However, the wind was not favorable for the American retreat. Arnold recalled they

> weighed anchor with a fresh breeze to the southward ... our gondolas made very little way a head. In the evening the wind moderated and we made such progress that at 6 o'clock next morning we were about off Willsborough 28 miles from Crown Point.

Arnold's rather terse recounting rather skips over the minor fact that the Americans had just spent a second straight night without sleep, performing back breaking labor to row their wallowing, damaged ships to the south. Sadly, at this moment, good luck entirely deserted the American patriots. Mrs. Sally Markham, a patriotic settler who lived with her family "north of Crown Point" recalled, "Quite early in the morning the 12th of October we saw the shipping a-coming in shattered condition."[53] Actually, it was almost certainly the morning of Sunday, October 13, and it was a Sunday the 13th that would prove less than fortuitous for the Continental army's Lake Champlain fleet. Arnold described the debacle in a matter of fact manner, which fails to capture the heartbreaking disappointment that he must have experienced:

> The enemy's fleet were very little way above Schuyler Island, the wind breezed up to the southward so that we gained very little by beating or rowing, at the same time the enemy took a fresh breeze from the Northeast and by the time we had reached Split Rock were along side of us.

Lieutenant Colonel Hartley at Crown Point, by now well aware of the contest that was underway, echoed in discouragement at "October 13, 1776 half after 11 o'clock A.M.":

> The alarm of yesterday proves to be a true one. The enemy are approaching. The wind is very favorable to them. They have been firing, for two hours past, a few heavy guns. I know not whether our fleet will be able to effect a retreat to this place or not. The enemy, I presume, will be soon on the neighboring banks.[54]

Arnold reported the ensuing naval contest on Lake Champlain:

> The *Washington* and *Congress* were in the rear, the rest of our fleet were a head except two gondolas sunk at Schuylers Island ... they kept up an incessant fire on us for about five glasses with round and grape shot, which we returned as briskly.

Five glasses aboard ship meant that the contest was carried on for 2½ hours, a duration which is confirmed by Dr. Robert Knox, a British surgeon serving on board the *Maria*.[55]

Early in the engagement the *Washington* was surrounded, and forced to surrender to the British. Waterbury reported that "my vessel was so torn to pieces that it was almost impossible to keep her above water" and that his sail was split from "foot to head."[56] Once surrounded by the three larger vessels of the British fleet, the *Washington* was in no condition to sustain a pitched fight, and Waterbury had no choice but to yield. Eighteen men from the already sunk *Philadelphia* had joined the *Washington*, as its crew had sustained particularly heavy casualties, and they now found themselves both sunken and surrendered within two days.[57] None of them probably gambled for years afterwards, if ever again.

With the *Washington* forced to yield, the British now turned their attention to the *Congress*. From the British side, their major sailing vessels were finally able to get into the fight. The *Inflexible*, *Maria* and *Carleton* starred in this contest. The radeau *Thunderer*, a notoriously hideous sailor, and the gondola *Loyal Convert* that doubtless sailed just as well as any of the American gondolas, which is to say quite poorly, never came up, and they are not mentioned in any of the accounts of the engagement.[58] The British sailing abilities and size and number of cannon finally were able to demonstrate their great superiority, and the American flotilla would shortly find itself in duress. Although the Americans had believed that they had severely damaged the *Carleton*, it is obvious that the British sailors had performed an incredible feat in repairing her such that she could fully participate in the pursuit and ensuing naval battle. By this time the young Midshipman Pellew had been elevated to command of the schooner, and he would eventually become one of the most remarkable and accomplished officers in the long and heralded history of the Royal Navy. Clearly he proved his worth and skills by his accomplishment in returning the *Carleton* to service in so short a time.

Finally, Arnold realized that escape for the *Congress* and the four gondolas with him

(*Providence, New Haven, Boston* and *Connecticut*) was simply no longer an option. By this time the American vessels' conditions were critical:

> The sails rigging and hull of the *Congress* was shattered and torn in pieces, the first Lieutenant and 8 men killed ... on board of the *Congress* we had twenty odd men killed and wounded. Our whole loss amounted to eighty odd.

Arnold, having gained intimate knowledge of the lake from his previous explorations, suddenly turned the fleet ashore onto Ferris Bay "ten miles from Crown Point on the east side." Here, at the dwelling place of Squire Ferris, Arnold beached his shattered craft, set them on fire, drew up his Marines on the high bank to cover his withdrawal, and headed cross country for Crown Point and the protection of the 6th Pennsylvania. James Wilkinson, at the time a junior Lieutenant and not present at Valcour Island, received a full recounting of the events from a participant and later related the scene:

> [Arnold] set them on fire, but ordered the colours not to be struck; and as they grounded, the marines were directed to jump overboard, with their arms and accoutrements, to ascend a bank about twenty-five feet elevation, and form a line for the defense of their vessels and flags against the enemy, Arnold being the last man who debarked. The enemy did not venture into the cove, but kept up a distant cannonade, until our vessels were burnt to the water's edge, after which Arnold commenced his march for Crown Point, about fifteen miles distant, by a bridle way through an unsettled wilderness.[59]

Squire Ferris recalled, "The British fleet arrived at the mouth of the bay before the explosion of Arnold's vessels and fired upon his men on the shore, and upon the house of Mr. Ferris, which stood near the shore."[60]

This one-sided exchange of cannon fire is confirmed by archaeological explorations directed by historic archaeologist David R. Starbuck at what is now known as Arnold's Bay in 1988. During this archaeological investigation no less than eight grapeshot were discovered, which suggests that the British were indeed firing on targets of men fleeing from their boats, rather than the ships which were doubtless already aground and ablaze.[61] These grapeshot were of the following categories of sizes:

- Three grapeshot for 1-pounder cannon (swivel guns) of 0.87" diameter (.actual measurements of 861", .844" and .860");
- Two grapeshot for 1½-pounder cannon (swivel gun) of 0.96" diameter (actual measurements of .987" and 1.053");
- Two grapeshot for 3-pounder cannon of 1.21" diameter (actual measurements of 1.156" and 1.122"): and
- One grapeshot for 4-pounder cannon of 1.38" diameter (actual measurement of 1.378."[62]

These sizes do not equate particularly well to the calibers of cannon known to be on board the British vessels, suggesting that they might not have been firing grapeshot that confirmed rigidly to British Board of Ordnance standards.

Arnold's vessels were beached and evacuated under heavy British artillery fire, and clearly the process was harried and hasty. One unfortunate officer, Lieutenant Goldsmith of the *Congress*, badly wounded by a grapeshot and helpless, lay on the deck and was forgotten in the confusion:

> Arnold had ordered him to be removed on shore, but by some oversight he was neglected, and was on the deck of the galley when the gunner set fire to the match. He then begged to be thrown overboard, and the gunner, on returning from the galley, told him he would be dead before she blew up. He remained on deck at the explosion, and his body as seen when blown up into the air. His remains were taken up and buried on the shore of the lake. To his credit Arnold showed the greatest feeling upon the subject, and threatened to run the gunner through on the spot.[63]

Arnold's small army, the crews of the *Congress* and four gondolas, marched overland to Crown Point. This 15-mile march took Arnold until four o'clock in the morning, the General and his men by this point having been without sleep for a third straight night. Arnold and his men were utterly spent, Arnold himself complaining, "I reached this place exceedingly fatigued and unwell having been without sleep or refreshment for near three days."[64] General Gates would state, clearly in awe, "It has pleased providence to preserve General Arnold. Few men ever met with so many hair breadth scrapes in so short a space of time."[65]

From onboard the *Trumbull*, Pascal De Angelis and Colonel Wigglesworth watched the final chapter being played out. De Angelis recorded:

> This morning at day light we espied several sail, and as it grew light we saw the enemies ship and 2 schooners but a little astern of our fleet, and about 9 o'clock came up with our fleet and fired at the *Washington* galley and *Congress* galley. And after four or five shot the *Washington* galley strike without firing one gun. General Waterbury being on board ... but the galley *Congress* sustained the fire of the two schooner, ship, etc. till about half an hour after twelve, when she and four of the gundolas thrust into a small crick on the east side of the lake, and we saw a great expultion [explosion] and supposed, as General Arnold was aboard the galley, that he ordered them blow up.[66]

Colonel Wigglesworth recounted a relatively similar account:

> On Sunday 13th ... at ten A.M. the enemy began to fire upon the two galleys in the rear. I soon discovered that the *Washington* galley, in which was General Waterbury, had struck, and that General Arnold was engaged with the ship and two schooners, and that he could not get clear. I thought it my duty to make sail and endeavor to save the *Trumbull* galley if possible. About one o'clock General Arnold run his galley ashore, with four other gondolas, and blew them all up.[67]

De Angelis was aboard the *Trumbull*, and he recalled "we were closely persued [pursued], but by rowing and heaving out our ballace [ballast] and making all the sail we could, we arrived at Crown Point about half after one o'clock. The end of the fight." Colonel Wigglesworth's account is nearly identical: "We double manned our oars and made all the sail we could, and by throwing over our ballast got off clear."

The American Lake Champlain fleet had been defeated. The cutter *Lee* was also missing; it was grounded ashore during the retreat and would be subsequently captured by the British, her crew having made it safely to Crown Point. Only a few ships would return safely to Crown Point and then Ticonderoga, the schooner *Revenge*, the sloops *Liberty* and *Enterprise*, the row galley *Trumbull*, and the gondola *New York*.[68] And, of course, the row galley *Gates* had remained at Mount Independence as it was still being outfitted while the engagement was being fought.

As regards the actions on Lake Champlain the second week of October 1776 the leadership and decision making skills of the British command were abysmal, and most of the failures must be laid at the feet of Carleton and fleet commander Captain Thomas Pringle. Their first error was one of inadequate reconnaissance. They had numerous Native Americans, the adept Company of Select Marksmen under Captain Alexander Fraser, and an entire corps of Light Infantry under the Earl of Balcarres as a component of the British Advanced Corps commanded by Brigadier General Simon Fraser. Numerous canoes were available from the Indians. They also had the relatively nimble *Maria* and *Carleton* to support any scouting patrols that found themselves in trouble. Inadequate reconnaissance was performed, and the location of the American fleet at Valcour Island was a complete surprise to the British on the morning of October 11. To compound this error, the British failed to maintain adequate security during their nautical movement down the lake. The American vessels were not spotted until the British main fleet had already passed them and were nearly to the mouth of the Ausable River. This offered the Americans a great tactical advantage, which only the swift action of the gunboats prevented them from exploiting. This failure of security meant that the artillery gunboats would have to fight the engagement of October 11 nearly by themselves, with only the assistance of the *Carleton*, which proved to be of dubious utility. Their next error, again in the realm of security, was the failure to provide adequate protection across the southern end of Valcour Bay on the night of October 11 and 12. Certainly the artillery gunboats had expended all of their ammunition, but proper ammunition discipline and leadership could have prevented this from occurring in the first place. Just as certainly a proper tactical disposition would have maintained a patrol of gunboats along the shoreline, replacing gunboats as they were resupplied with ammunition. A rotation of crews from the relatively well rested *Thunderer* and *Loyal Convert* could have made this possible by relieving the exhausted gunboat crews.

Alternately, the three available sailing vessels (the *Maria*, *Inflexible* and *Loyal Convert*) should have been positioned to provide adequate observation and security. This was not done, and Arnold was able to successfully escape the trap. The next great error occurred on the morning of October 12, when Carleton permitted his "great mortification" at discovering the Americans gone to color his judgment and launch an immediate, and poorly prepared, pursuit of Arnold. So precipitous was Carleton's departure from Valcour Island that he actually had to return to adequately organize and issue appropriate commands to execute a disciplined, integrated pursuit. The time lost should have provided Arnold with more than enough time to escape. Only the fickle Lake Champlain gusts, which provided the British fleet with a propitious wind and the American fleet simultaneously with an adverse wind; and the severe battering that the Americans had received at Valcour Island at the hands of the artillery gunboats, enabled the British flotilla to catch Arnold's command. Succinctly, Carleton and Pringle had fought a miserable campaign on Lake Champlain. Once returned to Canada, the result was angry recriminations among the naval officers involved.[69] Carleton himself would pay a significant professional price for his mismanagement, as will be discussed in comprehensive detail later in this narrative.

Only Phillips' artillery gunboats had served adequately during the destruction of the

American advanced guard on Lake Champlain. Phillips would report to Lord George Germain in England on November 9:

> The late expedition upon the Lake has fully made to appear the great utility of Gun Boats when they are served by the Royal Artillery. That it is an armament peculiarly adapted to the service of the lakes in almost every case that can happen, and possessing singular advantages in light wind, and calms, by covering our own vessels, or attacking those of the enemy, of which the instance in the action of the 11th October strongly evinces the truth.[70]

Arnold must have been pleased with the time that the Advanced Guard had bought for Gates' main defensive position at Ticonderoga and Crown Point. Merely by being a force in being, the tiny American fleet had delayed the inevitable British advance from July until October. And Arnold had bought a portion of another week through his skillful engagements on Lake Champlain.

He could not have been particularly pleased with the fighting performance of his navy. Arnold certainly hoped to have inflicted more losses upon the British flotilla, and preserve more of his fleet than he was able to. Only a single British artillery gunboat had been sunk, that of Lieutenant Dufais at Valcour Bay. Although the *Carleton* had been severely damaged in the same engagement, it was back in action two days later. Captain Pausch of the Hesse Hanau Artillery documented that the Americans had inflicted punishment on the British fleet, observing, "The rebels directed their cannon none too badly, because our frigates, as I later saw, were patched with boards and caulking."[71] Pausch was a highly experienced artillery officer who had seen considerable service on the European Continent, and he was quick to criticize poor artillery performance or techniques. Coming from the veteran German gunner, the simple statement that "the rebels directed their cannon none too badly" was indeed high praise.

Yet, Arnold's fleet had lost no less than ten vessels while only inflicting minimal casualties upon the British flotilla. Included among Arnold's losses were the row galleys *Washington* and *Congress*, and the cutter *Lee*, which Arnold considered the most capable of his vessels and the ones that he could most ill afford to lose. Certainly Arnold wanted to save these three ships, if no others, for future service on the lake. Of the five ships that had survived, three were small, weakly armed sailing ships; and the fourth was a relatively ineffectual gondola. Only one truly valuable ship had been saved, the row galley *Trumbull*. Bad luck, particularly with the wind during the retreat, had played a role. The poor sailing capabilities of the American gondolas, when combined with the dismal quality of the American cannon and inexperience of the gunners, and the battering that the entire fleet had absorbed at the hands of the artillery gunboats at Valcour Island, had resulted in the catastrophic casualties of the fleet.

Still, the single finest assessment of Arnold's advanced guard action is provided by renowned naval historian and officer Alfred Thayer Mahan, arguably the greatest strategist in the history of the U.S. Navy, and one of the single most influential international scholars in the art and science of naval warfare. In an 1898 magazine article Mahan concluded:

> The little American navy on Lake Champlain was wiped out, but never had any force, big or small, lived to better purpose or died more gloriously, for it had saved the lake for that year.[72]

11

"Our Appearance Was Indeed So Formidable"

British Advance and Withdrawal Before Ticonderoga, October 1776

Lieutenant Colonel Israel Shreve of New Jersey expressed what was nearly the universal opinion of Gates' reborn Continental army, standing strong and proud behind their newly constructed fortifications at Ticonderoga and Mount Independence, noting that his regiment was "in good order waiting impatiently to see them [the British enemy], not in the least doubting that we shall defeat them."[1] With the demise of Arnold's flotilla, the American main defensive position would have the opportunity to see the British soon enough.

On October 14, Major General Horatio Gates issued the following orders, which announced to the army in no uncertain manner that the British were, indeed, coming:

> As every Regiment & Corps are well acquainted with their alarm post, the General expects the troops will be alert in marching to support the works they are severally appointed to defend. He has the utmost dependance upon the bravery & fidelity of the whole army & believes when they are called to action, they will show themselves worthy of the noble cause they are engaged to defend. He returns his thanks to General Arnold and the Officers, Seamen & Marines of the Fleet for the gallant defense they made against the great superiority of the enemy force. Such magnanimous behavior will establish the fame of American arms throughout the globe.[2]

As previously discussed, the American defensive configuration extended from Mount Hope to the west, to the major defensive position outside of Fort Ticonderoga, to Mount Independence across Lake Champlain. Two regiments of Massachusetts Militia garrisoned Mount Hope with about eight hundred muskets, reinforced by the company of Stockbridge Mohican warriors.[3] Given the withdrawal of Hartley's 6th Pennsylvania from Crown Point, there were four regiments of Pennsylvanians at the reconstructed French Lines position on the Heights of Carillon. These four battalions mustered approximately one thousand muskets on November 9, under the command of Brigadier General Arthur St. Clair of Pennsylvania. Three New Jersey Regiments and one Massachusetts regiment garrisoned the four new redoubts on the sandy plain to the north of Fort Ticonderoga and immediately to the west of Lake Champlain. These battalions mustered approximately nine hundred muskets under the command of Colonel William Maxwell of New

Jersey. These soldiers were subsequently placed under the command of Arnold upon his arrival from Crown Point:

> Brigadier General Arnold is to take the Command of all the Troops of Ridoubts on the Flatt Ground North of Ticonderoga and of the Vessels which Guard the Boom, the Stone Ridoubt upon the Point included.[4]

Three brigades of Continentals were stationed at Mount Independence, the majority of the Ticonderoga garrison, comprising approximately 2,100 muskets present for duty. These men were predominantly from the states of Massachusetts and New Hampshire, with a few battalions of Connecticut troopers. Finally, when the fleet was defeated a number of Massachusetts Militia regiments were present at Ticonderoga, guarding the three new redoubts to the rear of the Pennsylvanians, the entrenched line tied into one new redoubt and two older French redoubts behind the New Jersey Brigade, and stationed at the old French redoubt at the point of Ticonderoga to the east of the French stone fort. This militia mustered about nine hundred muskets. When it arrived later in October the 3rd New Jersey regiment commanded by Colonel Elias Dayton was specifically assigned "to occupy the Old Fort."[5] Brigadier James Brickett was assigned the responsibility of commanding the defense of the old French Fort and its covered way, ditch and associated outerworks. A small force of artillerymen were scattered wherever artillery pieces were emplaced, and Colonel Baldwin commanded several hundred skilled artisans predominantly on Mount Independence. The five surviving vessels of Arnold's fleet, augmented by the newly completed row galley *Gates*, were also stationed between Ticonderoga and Mount Independence on Lake Champlain. On the morning of October 11th Gates mustered a total strength of about 7,700 officers and men, and approximately 5,700 muskets. Once the alarm was raised, additional militia regiments began pouring into Ticonderoga, to the number of at least eight hundred muskets, although this number appears to be low as it does not include militia from New York. By November 9 Gates had increased his total strength to 8,900 officers and men, fielding about 6,500 muskets.

The fortifications at Mount Hope, the Heights of Carillon, the sandy plain adjacent to Lake Champlain, the inner defenses centered on the historic stone Fort Ticonderoga, and Mount Independence were more than sufficient, and were without obvious weak points. One significant weakness was the absence of a garrison or any defenses upon Sugar Loaf (the modern Mount Defiance) overlooking Ticonderoga and Mount Independence, but so long as Mount Hope was secured this position was safe, and it would not be threatened in 1776. The only true vulnerability in the American defensive configuration was Lake Champlain itself. The British fleet had graphically demonstrated its strength and power, and the surviving six ships clearly lacked adequate strength to prevent the British fleet from sundering the two major components of the American defensive position, and then penetrating up Lake Champlain to establish control of Ticonderoga's logistical rear through which all supplies had to flow to the fortress. Accordingly, Gates acted to quickly blockade the narrow point at Ticonderoga.

During the 1759 British advance, the French had constructed a log barricade across this point to prevent the British and Provincial army from outflanking their fortifications by water. This could not have been of particularly substantial construction, for on July

26, 1759, General Jeffery Amherst dispatched the renowned Rogers Rangers in boats with saws to sever the boom. Amherst noted in his journal for that date, "I had ordered Major Roberts to go tonight and cut the boom."[6] Major Robert Rogers, commanding his Rangers, would similarly record in his own journal:

> I this day received orders from the General to attempt to cut away a boom which the French had thrown across the lake opposite the fort, which prevented our boats from passing by, and cutting off their retreat. Rangers in one English flat-bottomed boat, and two whale-boats, in which, after night came on, I embarked, and passed over to the other side of Lake Champlain, opposite to the Rangers encampment, and from that intended to steer my course along the east-shore, and privately saw off their boom, for which end I had taken saws with me, the boom being made with logs of timber.[7]

This boom is displayed on one map of the 1759 Ticonderoga as "a work made to prevent our cutting off the enemy's retreat."[8] Fort Carillon being evacuated and destroyed by the French the night of Rogers' expedition against the boom, he never actually reached the log obstacle, and no additional records of this defensive measure have been located. The fact that simple saws were to be used to cut this boom suggests that it cannot have constituted much of an obstacle.

Gates determined to construct a considerably more formidable obstacle across Lake Champlain than the French log boom had been, and for this he turned to his chief engineer, Colonel Baldwin, who had already served him so well. Baldwin began work on Thursday, October 17: "Begun to make a log across the Lake or chain to prevent shipping coming past the Jersey Redoubt." Baldwin, energetic, skilled, and naturally imaginative, shortly determined to improve this simple boom into an actual bridge. Baldwin proposed such a project to Gates over supper on October 20. Gates must have approved of the concept, for Baldwin noted in his journal for October 25, "finish the boom across & building a bridge." Baldwin perceived the urgency of the situation and must have pushed his workers quite hard. Convincing the laborers to focus upon their work was probably not very challenging, for clearly the prospect of the heavily armed *Thunderer* and *Inflexible* sailing down Lake Champlain at leisure, with guns blazing, was less than a pleasant vision. By October 29 Baldwin could record, "Finished the bridge across the Lake to Independent Point, so that men could pass." Baldwin had reason to be proud, for he had designed and executed a major construction project of considerable tactical importance in record-breaking time. After this date, the British flotilla no longer had freedom of action on Lake Champlain. It is an insight into Baldwin's character that he was not satisfied with his effort, and that winter he would substantially improve both the bridge and boom across the lake.[9]

On the morning of October 14 the British fleet, having disposed of Arnold's small force, moved on Crown Point. Upon the British approach, and following positive orders that Gates had issued months ago when Hartley first assumed his post, Colonel Hartley and Arnold determined that Crown Point was not tenable against the entire force of the British army, and with their combined forces in good order, evacuated the post. Colonel Baldwin noted on October 13 [apparently mis-dated and should have been October 14]:

> We had this day frequent information that our fleet was in a shattered condition. About three o'clock our Schooner came in sight. Soon after a Sloop & then another

Schooner & then the Row Galley & after a gondola & they were followed by the inhabitants of Crown Point and from Panton, they were followed by Colonel Hartley's Regiment, part by water & part by land, bringing all the Horses, Cattle & So Forth. All the buildings at & about Crown Point were burned by our people.[10]

By the evening of October 14 the British had seized whatever Hartley left at Crown Point, which wasn't much. When the British occupied Hartley's works, they described them as follows:

> was fortified by the Rebels in a circular manner having various curtains and angles with a battery of five guns in the middle rais'd so high as to command the whole plain before it; they had huts built within the works for their officers, but they destroy'd both them and works when they left it.[11]

Doctor Knox with the *Maria* recalled "the Rebels had burned all the houses before they left it."[12] By October 16 Baldwin recorded that the British had occupied Crown Point in strength: "One of our Spies came in from Crown Point & says that the enemy were all encamped in Colonel Hartley's fort & on Chimney Point, about 100 tents in all."[13]

Shortly thereafter the American army was surprised to discover that Carleton had paroled General Waterbury and all of the sailors captured on board the row galley *Washington*. As he had earlier that spring when he had pardoned and released all of the American soldiers captured after his victory at Quebec on May 6, Carleton would score another significant information operations victory over the American patriots by this action. Colonel John Trumbull would relate Carleton's coup on this occasion:

> As soon as the action was over, Sir Guy gave orders to the surgeons of his own troops, to treat the wounded prisoners with the same care as they did his own men. He then ordered that all the other prisoners should be immediately brought on board his own ship, the Royal Charlotte [actually the *Maria*], where he first treated them to a drink of grog, and then spoke kindly to them, praised the bravery of their conduct, regretted that it had not been displayed in the service of their lawful sovereign, and offered to send them home to their friends, on their giving their parole that they would not again bear arms against Great Britain until they should be exchanged. He then invited Gen. Waterbury to go below with him to his cabin, and requested to see his commission, the moment he saw that it was signed by the Governor of Connecticut (my father) he held out his hand, and said, "General Waterbury, I am happy to take you by the hand, now that I see that you are not serving under a commission and orders of the rebel Congress, but of Governor Trumbull. You are acting under a legitimate and acknowledged authority. He is responsible for the abuse he has made of that authority. That which is a high crime in him, is but an error in you; it was your duty to obey him, your legitimate superior." A few days after this defeat, a number of row boats approached our advanced post, and there lay upon their oars with a flag of truce. I was ordered to go down and learn their object. I found Capt. [James Henry] Craig [47th Foot], with Gen. Waterbury and the other prisoners who had been taken in the recent action; dismissed, as Sir Guy had promised, upon parole. The usual civilities passed between Sir James and me, and I received the prisoners; all were warm in their acknowledgment of the kindness with which they had been treated, and which appeared to me to have made a very dangerous impression. I therefore placed the boats containing the prisoners under the guns of a battery, and gave orders that no one should be permitted to land, and no intercourse take place with the troops on shore

until orders should be received from Gen. Gates. I hurried to make my report to him, and suggested the danger of permitting these men to have any intercourse with our troops; accordingly they were ordered to proceed immediately to Skeensborough, on their way home, and they went forward that night, without being permitted to land.[14]

These 97 prisoners, who had been surrendered by Waterbury on board the *Washington*, represented the survivors of the original crew of the *Washington* and eighteen soldiers from the *Philadelphia* who had apparently filled out the *Washington*'s crew to account for losses at the Battle of Valcour Island.[15] It appears that by unexpected courtesy and good treatment that Carleton had well and truly turned these men into British sympathizers, and it was in the best interests of the Continental army for Gates to send them home forthwith, on October 16 according to Baldwin, without stopping to contaminate or subvert the Ticonderoga garrison. By demonstrating simple clemency, Carleton had effectively eliminated one hundred men from Gates' army without having to fire a single shot.

Gates had fully apprised Schuyler of the American fleet's defeat on Lake Champlain, and Schuyler immediately called out the New York and Massachusetts Militia to march for Ticonderoga. Their response was rapid, and significant. However, it should be noted that the Albany Committee of Correspondence had learned their lesson regarding the Continental army. This time, they specified upon receiving Schuyler's request:

> This Board being informed that there is a small Chest of medicine in the Custody of Mrs. Rachel Van Deusen and the same being much wanted on this present Call for the Militia. Resolved that Mrs. Van Deusen be and she is hereby requested to deliver the said Chest to Dr. Wilhelmus Mancious, and that this Committee will indemnify the said Mrs. Van Deusen of & from all Damages which she may be brought to for and on Account of Said Chest of Medicine. Resolved that Dr. Macious take an inventory of the Medicine contained in said Chest and make a return of the same to this Board. Resolved that Mr. Jillis Winne procure a Waggon to Convey Dr. Mancious with his Medicine etc. to Fort Edward.[16]

Schuyler also dispatched what few reinforcements he had immediately available to Ticonderoga. The 3rd New Jersey Regiment had been stationed in the Mohawk Valley, to garrison that important location against British raids, and to monitor the numerous Loyalists that infested the valley. Captain Joseph Bloomfield of the regiment (acting as Major) recorded in his journal for October 19:

> By an express to Colonel Dayton we are informed General Arnold our Admiral on Lake Champlain has been severely handled by the British fleet & obliged to retreat with great loss, and that our regiment is ordered immediately to Ticonderoga & all the militia of this & the lower countys to Saratoga. Lt. Colonel Bellinger with whom we lodge & the militia in this placed marched at 12.[17]

Other measures were also taken to ensure that Ticonderoga did not fall. Mr. James Yancey, deputy commissary at Ticonderoga, immediately initiated efforts to dramatically increase the quantity of provisions at the fortress, in case the British lingered to besiege the works. On October 20 Yancey noted that Ticonderoga had only enough flour for sixteen days worth of bread. Since it was late fall, just at the time that the harvest was being brought into the barns by the farmers, ample provisions were available. Unfortunately, since the militia was called out for the defense of Fort Ticonderoga, the normal quantity of manpower was not available to move the provisions forward. Yancey directed that supplies were to be sent by way of Bennington and Skenesboro. Still, even with manpower reserves serving with the militia, one thousand bushels of flour (or approximately 60,000 pounds, enough flour for 72,000 pounds of bread) were hastened to the fort in response to Yancey's pleas.[18] Schuyler continued to forward flour to Ticonderoga, sending it by two routes in case the British had closed off one avenue of communications to Gates, and also to avoid overwhelming the transportation capabilities on any single route at one time. He informed Gates "flour is now on its way to you in great quantities partly by way of Skenesborough partly by Fort George."[19]

Other supplies also poured into the post, hurried on by Schuyler. The arrival of fifteen tons of gunpowder and three tons of lead was extremely timely. This provided enough lead for approximately 100,000 musket rounds, which augmentation should have been more than sufficient to repulse any British infantry assault on the works. On the Plains of Abraham outside Quebec in 1759, the majority of the British regiments engaged had fired only two volleys of two musket balls each to shatter the French. When 2nd Lieutenant Ebenezer Elmer of the 3rd New Jersey arrived at Fort Ticonderoga on November 2, he noted that "the men were supplied with 24 rounds of cartridges each" which suggests that this was the amount of ready ammunition available per man.[20] Again, this represented a full cartridge box per each American soldier, more than sufficient ammunition to repel the British invaders.

Gates dispatched his men who were too ill to man the earthworks back to Fort George, so that they did not burden the regimental surgeons and hospital at Mount Independence, who would presumably be busy with wounded in the event of a British assault.[21] At the same time Gates sent for Dr. Potts still with the general hospital at Fort George, and ordered him to forthwith repair to Ticonderoga to ensure that immediate medical care was available in the event of a British assault. Gates informed Potts on October 14:

> The advantage the Enemy have obtained by the very great superiority of their fleet, gives reason to believe we are going immediately to be attacked here, therefore, the General orders you or Dr. Stringer to come immediately to this camp and bring such articles with you as you may judge most necessary under the present circumstances.[22]

Gates issued positive orders for the stationing of his army's medical officers, and for the treatment of the wounded, in the event of a British assault:

> The following arrangements of the surgeons of the Army is to take place in case of action, viz: Dr. Kennedy, Barnet, Taylor, Thaching [Thacher] & Silsby & Packer to attend at the Old Fort with their mates. Dr. Johnson, Holmes, Allison, Harvey & Stuart to attend at the place appointed near Col. Wayne's marquee with all their instruments. All the surgeons & mates on Mount Independence to attend Dr. Potts at the General Hospital on the mount.... Whenever an action happens on the Ticonderoga side, the wounded, after being dressed at the places appointed ... are to be carried to Dr. Potts at the General Hospital on Mount Independence. Boats will be kept in the cove near the Carpenter Shop for that purpose.[23]

In further expectation of casualties, and routinely concerned with the spiritual as well as the physical health of his soldiers, Gates ordered the Reverend Ammi Robbins, a chaplain from Connecticut, on October 15 to "go to Fort George with the sick and wounded of the fleet."[24]

Gates, as he had previously demonstrated during the long and tedious process of reconstructing the army, did not neglect the spiritual preparations for combat. On Sunday, October 20, Lieutenant Rufus Wheeler of Rowley, Massachusetts, recorded the stirring church services that Gates ordered:

> Six battalions of Bostoners, Pennsylvanians and Jersey blues drawn up and a priest from the Southerd [southward, meaning Pennsylvania or New Jersey to Lieutenant Wheeler] made a fine prayer and gave them an exhortation pronouncing all the blessings on those that would fight boldly for their country and likewise that these blessing might be turned into curses upon all those that were cowards and turned their backs upon their enemies which was the finest discourse ever I heard. After exercise was over the whole body gave three cheers which made a beautiful show.[25]

The address, delivered to "countrymen, fellow-soldiers and friends" survives today. The stirring and lengthy rendition is both evangelistic and Old Testament in tone. But to the New England soldiers, it was entirely appropriate, highly motivating and inspirational. For Lieutenant Wheeler, a Massachusetts soldier, to record that a Pennsylvania or New Jersey minister had given "the finest discourse ever I heard" witnesses the power and impact that this church service had upon the garrison. Horatio Gates knew his principally New England soldiers well, and he was readying them for battle in a manner that proved to be extremely effective.

The morale of the American army appeared high, and one example was provided when Dr. Potts arrived at Ticonderoga from Fort George, for he did not arrive alone. Colonel Anthony Wayne of Pennsylvania related on October 18:

> I can't in justice omit mentioning one hundred Pennsylvanians who arrived here last evening from Lake George — where they were lately sent for the recovery of their health to the General Hospital — on hearing of the defeat of our fleet they immediately returned to this place determined to conquer or die, with their country men — these poor emaciated worthy fellows are entitled to more merit than I have time or ability to describe.[26]

Gates also initiated a set of tactical responses, intended to prepare his garrison for the impending assault. Doctor James Thacher, surgeon's mate to Colonel Asa Whitcomb's 6th Continental (Massachusetts) Regiment, had been stationed at Ticonderoga since September. Thacher recalled of Gates' preparations to meet the enemy:

> Each regiment has its alarm post assigned, and they are ordered to repair to it and to man the lines at day light every morning. Among our defensive weapons are poles, about twelve feet long, armed with sharp iron point, which each soldier is to employ against the assailants when mounting the breastworks ... every morning, our continental colors are advantageously displayed on the ramparts, and our cannon and spears are in readiness for action ... our soldiery express a strong desire to have an opportunity of displaying their courage and prowess; both officers and men are full of activity and vigilance.[27]

Interestingly, Gates issued buckshot to his men, probably because he anticipated that they were less likely to miss with ammunition of this type, and also that buckshot could be universally loaded into any weapon, thus simplifying the logistics of his ammunition. On October 24 General Orders from Gates specified: "The Commanding Officers of Regiments are directly to draw ¼ pound Buck Shott for Every Man fit for duty in their respective Corps."[28] This order was almost certainly carried out, for Pascal de Angelis recorded for October 26, "We drew some more buck shot."[29] Repeat orders were issued on October 27: "The Corps who have not drawn the Buck Shott agreeable to order of the 24th are to send in their returns immediately & receive the Same."[30]

Gates issued various orders daily:

> October 18, 1776. The Commissary to supply all the empty casks he has in store that will hold water to such regiment as have not got water convenient to their alarming posts. These to be kept filled with pure water that the troops may have a supply ready when wanted.[31]
>
> October 19, 1776. All the spears that can be spared from the vessels to be delivered for the defense of the French lines and redoubts. The commanding officer of the artillery will prove and scale such guns as want it.

Scaling of the cast iron artillery pieces of the time entailed loading a particularly heavy gunpowder charge into the cannon and firing it, presumably loosening and discharging any rust that had formed in the barrel. This was considered to be a preliminary and necessary maintenance that was required to be performed prior to any sustained firing of the cannon.

> October 27, 1776. As the enemy's attack will most probably be rash & sudden, the General earnestly recommends to each commanding officer of a Regiment, party, post or detachment to be deliberate & cool in suffering their men to fire, never allowing them to throw away their fire in an un-soldierlike manner. One close, well-directed fire at the distance of eight or ten rods, will do more towards defeating the enemy than all the scattered, random shot, fired in a whole day. The good effects of a due observance of this order will, with the favour of Heaven, secure the victory.[32]

Brigadier General Arthur St. Clair, carefully monitoring the British movements from the Pennsylvania earthworks on the Heights of Carillon, described his assessment of the situation:

> Mr. Carleton has not yet made us a visit which surprises me very much. His passing the Lake defeating our fleet was to very little purpose if he rests there, at any rate he gives the time to be prepared, and we shall be well reinforced as some of the militia are already come in and great numbers on the way ... this however I am certain of, General Winter cannot be very far off, though the weather is uncommonly fine at present, and has been so for some time. When Mr. Carleton does come on we expect his march will be both by land and water. To guard against his penetrating with his vessels, part of boom was laid last night across the river [i.e. Lake Champlain] and will be completed today, and is defended by two batteries and the remains of the fleet. I scarce expect that it will resist the shock of a heavy vessel, should they have a brisk gale, but it will retard them, and as the channel is not very wide, the vessels are still be subdued when the boom is broken, but I expect a better effect from it yet, for I have no doubt of the enemies being acquainted that a boom is laid, I think as they will not know exactly its strength, they will not attempt it [at] all. After all, I don't know but we may turn the tables, and attempt to send them back. I am satisfied they

are not in readiness, but are waiting for part of their army, or their apparatus from Canada [i.e. siege equipment]. We have parties constantly out reconnoitering them and this night I think we shall have a pretty certain account of their strength. If it is not considerable, we may probably attack them before they are reinforced.[33]

The British had arrived at Crown Point on October 14, embarked from their bateaux, and occupied the remnants of the burned over fort and Hartley's newer earthworks. They set up shop inside the shattered barracks, which had been destroyed for the first time in 1773, and then burned again by Hartley before his retreat. They could not have comprised particularly enticing quarters; and compared quite unfavorably with the comfortable, spacious Canadian barns that the British had spent all winter and fall quartered in. A number of artillery pieces were unloaded to facilitate the defense of the encampment. Four light 3-pounders were embarked from bateaux on October 20, where they had been carried disassembled (apparently these cannon were deemed too light for naval combat on the lake), and two 6-pounder cannon were landed from two of the artillery gunboats on October 19.[34] The army commander, Lieutenant General Jonathan Burgoyne, also landed, along with his artillery commander Major General William Phillips. The army's strength was 4,666 English muskets as of October 1, 1776, with a total British army strength of over 5,000 including officers, increased by the Brunswick Brigade of Von Riedesel.[35]

The British had a formidable train of artillery, twenty-one heavy guns from 6-pounders to 8" howitzers and 24-pounders aboard their surviving artillery gunboats, along with the fourteen massive cannon placed on the *Thunderer* (an intimidating six 24-pounder cannon, six 12-pounder cannon, and two 8-inch howitzers). Alone, these thirty-five cannon comprised an effective artillery train fully capable of initiating a formal siege against the American works. With the exception of the four tiny 3-pounders and two 6-pounders, these guns were never landed. Without them, the British could never aspire to capture Ticonderoga.

Once ashore, the British actions were, in two words, lethargic and inactive. They failed to initiate any aggressive action. Several of the British officers complained that the Americans failed to sortie out of their strong fortifications, so that the British could presumably annihilate them in the open field.[36] This was not an entirely unreasonable expectation, as the Americans had done just that at Three Rivers. However, Gates was made of considerably more circumspect material than Thompson and Sullivan. He had no intention of leaving the strong redoubts and batteries that he had just spent all summer and fall designing and constructing, to expose his regiments to the well-drilled British regulars. Gates knew that the calendar was his friend, and with every date ticked off, the British position became more precarious. Carleton and Burgoyne, if they were going to initiate offensive action against Ticonderoga, had to do it immediately. A regular siege was certain to require at least several weeks. If the British expended too much time on such a siege, the weather could change, and they could conceivably be trapped between a strong American garrison and Lake Champlain. If they delayed until Lake Champlain started to ice over, their return to Canada by water would be nearly impossible, and there was no land route. The British vacillated in this conundrum, and lost whatever small, fleeting opportunity they might have possessed for offensive action against Ticonderoga.

During their stay north of Ticonderoga, the British launched several minor scouting forays against the Americans. Most of these were ineffectual, and no combat actions are documented to have resulted from these patrols. They were predominantly conducted by Native American allies of the British, and a ranging company commanded by Captain Alexander Fraser, cousin of Brigadier General Simon Fraser, an experienced officer from the 34th Foot with a reputation for daring and initiative. Fraser's Company of Select Marksmen, as it was known, and the Native Americans found their activities curtailed by the presence of the Stockbridge Mohicans stationed at Mount Hope. However, one successful raid was performed. This was executed utilizing a local loyalist sympathizer who had recently immigrated from Scotland to establish a homestead near Crown Point, John McAlpine, as a guide.[37] Their target was not the American defenders of Fortress Ticonderoga, but a large quantity of live beef cattle that McAlpine was aware of that were grazed near Ticonderoga, and that the patriots were using as rations. McAlpine described the great British beef expedition of October 22, 1776:

> A party ... consisting of two hundred & sixty brave fellows under the command of the gallant officers, Captain Frazer of the Rangers, and Captain Monie [Monet] of the Canadians; I going as confident conductor of the expedition.... We agreed to divide our whole force into three parties acting distinct or separately under those two Captains and me in allotted numbers, and thus making some bold, even desperate push, with mutual exertions, for obtaining some prizes ... thus we proceeded cheerfully and resolutely in three separate bodies, and after each party had closed to our enemy's sentries, surrounded & captured some parcels of straggling cattle, we severally marched away, undisturbed & unmolested, with our separately collected prizes, to our appointed ground of rendezvous, and there joined again in one collected body, without a single man missing. The number of cattle we had collected by no means gratifying my avidity, I requested the commanding officers to grant me a party of chosen men who would re-adventure with me to scour the woods and grounds again for more cattle. My proposal being accepted ... thirty-two brave volunteers instantly turned out to obey my orders; with whom I proceeded on the route I thought to be most eligible, where we discovered and carried away thence above thirty very fine bullocks ... thus proceeding in one collected cheerful column, with imminent danger & the utmost expedition reasonable, for Crown Point, we arrived in safety and high spirits that afternoon, possessed of one hundred & seven head of excellent beef cattle, ten of which number happened to be part of my own stock that were formerly plundered by, and now recovered from, the rapacious Rebels.

In conjunction with this raid, several Native American warriors successfully ambushed a small American party apparently carrying a sick or wounded soldier on a stretcher near the landing at the La Chute River. The incapacitated man was killed, and two other Americans were taken prisoner. Lieutenant Digby reported: "Our Indians who with Captain Frazier [Fraser] were advanced nearer their lines, took a prisoner and before they brought him to us painted the poor devil in a most curious manner, which almost frightened him out of his wits."[38] Baldwin recorded, "One man killed & 2 taken by the Indians between the Mills & the landing."[39] Pascal de Angelis recounted the gory details: "They say he was found with a tomahawk sticking in his head."[40] This was probably army gossip, for it is doubtful that any Native American warrior would have left behind anything as valuable as a steel tomahawk. These were the only casualties inflicted upon the Americans by the British during their almost three week stay at Crown Point.

The cattle were turned over to Carleton for the use of the British army, who welcomed the fresh beef, having been subsisting on salt pork for the greater part of the month. Carleton ordered the cattle picked up from McAlpine on October 28, instructing the Grenadier Battalion from Fraser's Advanced Corps:

> Brigade Evening Orders. One Sub One Serjt One Corpl One Drumr and Twenty men to parade tomorrow morning at seven o'clock with arms, they are to go along the road leading to Ticonderoga 'till they arrive at Mr. Kalpins [Mr. McAlpine's] house who will deliver a number of bullocks to the party; which they are to drive to this place to deliver them over to the guard — within the fort.[41]

Although this comprised a fairly audacious raid, the operation had been executed with skill and daring, and obtaining fresh provisions was important to both British morale and the health of the soldiers, stealing a few score head of undefended cattle was a less than inspirational feat of arms.

At the same time, the American demonstrated more aggressive combat actions than the British. For example, on Friday, October 18, Gates launched a strong party from Ticonderoga towards Crown Point to destroy bridges on the roads between those two communities. This patrol was confirmed by Jahiel Stewart, by now a hardened combat veteran: "This day is a wet day, and this morning there was a party sent off to cut down all the bridges between Ty and Crown Point so the enemies may not get along there artillery by land."[42] This party successfully obstructed the roads from Crown Point that the British required to move their artillery, when and if they ever determined to embark it, forward. The fact that this party succeeded also casts doubt upon the effectiveness of the British security detachments, and attests that the British forward patrols to monitor the American lines were not particularly adept. On October 23 Quartermaster John Harper of Wayne's 4th Pennsylvania Battalion recorded in his journal other successful American scout and patrol activities:

> We have had several out reconnoitering, amongst which was that noble Partisan Lieutenant Whitcomb, who says that he discovered a number of the enemy encamped on Crown Point and that he was so near their Quarter Guard as to hear one of our spies describe our camp. Lieutenant Butler, who went with another party, saw ten fires at Putnams Creek, around which he saw numbers of Canadians and Indians.[43]

On Monday, October 28, the British finally initiated a reconnaissance up Lake Champlain. A number of artillery gunboats, variously reported, moved south. This reconnaissance was performed by one or two divisions of gunboats, between nine and eighteen gunboats. The artillery gunboats were carefully observed by Carleton and Phillips, as recorded by Lieutenant William Digby of the 53rd Foot: "General Carleton and General Phillips who command the artillery, went up towards their lines to reconnoiter their strength, situation, etc. and which by them were thought of great extent & force."[44] The lead gunboat rowed down Lake Champlain, and the American gunners at the Jersey Redoubt sent their first shot, an 18-pounder, directly through the middle of the gunboat.[45] Splinters flew, and the gunboat hastily and awkwardly withdrew, obviously having numerous casualties aboard. Surgeon Lewis Beebe observed, "One of their boats received a few merry shot from our batteries for coming too near us."[46]

Gates ordered the three regiments commanded by Colonels Greaton, Reed and Poor to immediately move from Mount Independence to Ticonderoga to reinforce the point where the British apparently intended to assault. The American regiments, six hundred muskets in strength, swiftly poured down from the heights of Mount Independence, and their carefully ordered ranks flowed over Baldwin's new bridge to the western shore of Lake Champlain, where they in short order filled the plains to the rear of the American fortifications. The British were doubtless alarmed at the rapidity and smoothness with which this tactical maneuver was conducted. At the same time, the two American row galleys (*Trumbull* and *Gates*) moved up the lake to engage the remainder of the gunboats. By now the British artillery gunboats had apparently gotten close enough to perceive Baldwin's new boom across the lake.

Stunned by the accuracy of the American artillery fire, the strength of the defenses, and the aggressive American response to their advance, the remainder of the gunboats rapidly withdrew down the lake. For the rest of the day they hovered about ineffectually outside of the American artillery range, and withdrew at sunset without taking further action. In truth, they had received all the answers that a reconnaissance was likely to reveal. The American gunners were alert, Lake Champlain was controlled by heavy artillery and now obstructed by a log boom of indeterminate but probably formidable strength covered by the surviving armed vessels, and the Americans had responded immediately by tactically repositioning entire regiments. What was even worse, the American gunners knew how to shoot straight. The lake was well and truly obstructed, and a naval advance was out of the question. The preferred British avenue of approach was no longer feasible.

Nearly every American soldier within sight recorded the British advance. The Americans paid close attention to these maneuvers, as they expected that this was the first movement in the long-anticipated British advance. Micah Hildreth, a soldier from Massachusetts, recorded the abortive British scout up the lake:

> Ticonderoga Oct ye 28 1776 on Sunday [actually Monday]. Then we Was a Larmed and Every man to his arms and marched to his alarm Post for the Enemy appeared in Sight upon the lake and a Number of Boats began to land abought 3 miles of and then 1 boat board won [went] towards us and come within 3 quarters of a mile of our Batries and We Fired 2 Cannon from ye Sandy Redout and 3 Cannon ye Jarze [Jersey] Redoubt at the Boat and we understand that the Last Shot struck the Boat and kild 3 men. Then the Enemy Retreated Back to Putnams Point and some to Crown Point.[47]

Bayze Wells, the experienced officer on board the *Providence* and now a hardened combat veteran, recalled of the British probe:

> Monday 28th Oct. This day the wind at north. Early in the morning our enemies appeared at the Three Mile Point three boats with a carriage gun in each bow, one of which came within cannon shot of our North East Battery and of our Row Galleys which gave them several shots and we are of the opinion killed some men but that I cannot tell at this time. Fifteen other boats of a smaller size appeared also but at sun set they all disappeared and as we supposed returned to Crown Point.[48]

Colonel Baldwin similarly reported:

> About 9 o'clock, 4 boats hove in sight at Three Mile Point. One of the boats of the enemy sounded the Channel within a Mile of our Battery. At 11 o'clock, we gave them a few shot. Made them haul off again. About 17 boats rowed about in sight till sun an hour high & then they all went off. [49]

The actual number of artillery gunboats available was nineteen, the twenty-one boats that had survived Valcour Island, less the two that had already embarked their 6-pounders at Crown Point.

On October 19 an officer of the 47th Foot, whose name is now permanently separated from his journal, recorded the British army's minor scouting forays:

> This little Army, which had encamped within a few miles of the Rebel lines can only say, that they dared show themselves by sending out frequent Detachments within sight of them, particularly one, consisting of four companies of Light Infantry, a few Indians and some Canadians, part of which went so near shore that several shots were fired at them from the Rebel batteries.[50]

This appears to be the sum total of the British military accomplishments once ensconced in front of Ticonderoga, and there is no evidence that they even crossed to the east bank of Lake Champlain to reconnoiter Mount Independence. They sent out a handful of scouting parties, only one of which actually got close enough to be fired upon by the Americans. This hardly demonstrates a determined, committed focus upon attacking the American fortress. Rather, it demonstrates a determined, committed focus upon not getting shot at. Clearly, the British leadership had no interest in actually pressing the American garrison. The British subordinates perceived this and acted accordingly. In short, Carleton had no resolution to do much of anything except clear Lake Champlain of the American fleet, and return to winter quarters in Quebec.

Doubtless, the snow that began falling in early November was all the inducement that Carleton needed to order a full withdrawal to Canada for the winter. Benjamin Beal, with Greaton's 24th Continental Regiment (Massachusetts) on Mount Independence, recorded in his journal for November 2, "squally & snow & cold."[51] Jahiel Stewart recounted on November 3, "Some of the scout that has come in they say the snow is over shoes at Crown Point."[52] Pascal de Angelis echoed the weather report for early November, noting, "Nov. 2 this morning the snow was very hard, it has not been so hard for the season."[53]

As early as October 26 a portion of the Royal Artillery was already withdrawn from Crown Point to return artillery stores to St. Jeans for the winter. Over the next several days additional boats and stores continued to be returned to Canada. Carleton issued General Orders on October 31 for the retreat of the army:

> The severity of the approaching season rendering it impossible to pursue the rebels any further this year without endangering the health of the troops, the part of the army on this side the Lake, will hold itself in readiness to begin its return into Canada on the 2nd November, the General to beat at 8 O'Clock in the morning and the Assembly of the First Brigade an hour after when they will embark and proceed immediately.[54]

The British army departed Crown Point *en masse* on Saturday November 2, 1776. Schuyler would write Congress on November 11: "The enemy will give us no further trouble, until another campaign takes place, as on Tuesday, the 4th instant, not the sign of any was to be seen on Lake Champlain, forty miles below Crown Point."[55] Brigadier General Arthur St. Clair documented the British withdrawal on that date:

> Mr. Carleton after lying three weeks at Crown Point ... has thought proper to retire back to Canada. A party was sent out the night before last to beat up his advanced guards at yesterday morning at break of day, but they found their posts evacuated, and from the information of the country people they left them the morning before. Major Delap who commanded the party on the Crown Point side of the Lake (for as the enemies army lay on both sides of the river it was intended to attack the advanced posts on both sides at the same time) sent and reconnoitered the grounds at Crown Point, and to all appearance they have actually gone off, as no tents were to be seen on either side and only one vessel in the basin, which a few Canadians seemed to be busy in charging with baggage.[56]

In fact, what the American scouts had seen were not Canadians but the remaining Loyalist inhabitants of Crown Point loading what few possessions the Americans had not looted or plundered on board bateaux for a move to Canada. Carleton had issued specific orders to facilitate the evacuation of the inhabitants on October 31, the date when the withdrawal from Crown Point was announced:

> One sub two Serjeants, two Corporals, and twenty-one men, to parade tomorrow morning at 7 o'clock in front of the Grenadiers Battalion, three bateaux to be shown the officer by the major of Brigade in which with this party he will proceed to Captain Frasers post — he will give them directions to take in the boats the family and household furniture of Richardson, Smith, Camble [Campbell], Macalpin and Patterson and with them to return to this place there to be received in six long boats for that purpose.[57]

Phillips was bitterly disappointed at Carleton's decision to abandon the advanced position at Crown Point. Clearly he had anticipated that Carleton was going to withdraw, for his lethargic actions indicated that no other course was to be followed, but he desired that an advanced post be established and maintained at Crown Point throughout the winter to facilitate an advance upon Ticonderoga the next spring. Phillips would write his close friend Burgoyne from Fort Crown Point on October 23, 1776:

> My Dear Sir —
>
> I have passed a very unpleasant time since here and lament your absence most sincerely. I stand alone unable to bear up against the sloth and changes of this atmosphere. You will scarcely suppose that there is neither reconnoitering post nor scout sent forward, but as the whim of a drunken Indian prevails. I have endeavored in vain to form a small detachment to feel the pulse of the enemy; the answer is that it is wrong to teach these rebels *war*. There are deserters who are daily accounts of the panic of these people.... The post of Crown Point, when we leave it, which is this day determined after bringing away all the artificers from Isle Aux Noix and St. John.... I must be of opinion that, notwithstanding the success upon the lake, we terminate the campaign ill. It was upon the positive declaration that a post was to be established here, at all events, that I proposed sending the troops back into Winter Quarters for

the power of more easily supplying the corps here, and to be left for the winter with provisions; for I do protest that otherwise I think the army should have moved forward and a trial made at Ticonderoga. Had we failed in a strong feint we could but have retired, and I must think there were good chances of success from the very strong panic which has taken the rebels. But it is the humor here to suppose that it is no disgrace to retire if it is not done in the face of the enemy. I have been uniform in my ideas of the manner this army was to have proceeded upon the lake. One brigade to attend the fleet, the rest to move at the moment of success. Had it been so, the army might have been at Crown Point the 15th, and the fleet and armed vessels going up the lake towards Ticonderoga with a show of attacking with the army and strong parties towards Lake George and Skenesborough we should have destroyed their communications if we had not frightened them out of Ticonderoga. I never was of opinion to attach the entrenchments seriously, but I am and shall ever be of opinion that every art of war should be practiced upon these people, whose ignorance renders stratagem and surprise so easy to succeed. I am tardy in saying all this as it has been our joint opinion, and it is a flattering, most flattering, most satisfactory reflection to me that we have agreed, I think, almost in every proposal and plan for this campaign.... As an officer, I wish this Army might have been allowed the share in the war which it should, in my opinion, have had. I write my mind freely to you and repose my griefs in the bosom of a friend, such I believe you, such I respect and regard you for at my heart. I do not talk to the folks here thus, my pride of soldiership forbids it. The army seems distressed and hurt at the langor which governs every movement. I still fear a dreadful winter, but still I shall be myself, nor let chagrin prey upon me, nor will I grow languid in the public service. I promise you to do my utmost to preserve the army for an early opening of the campaign, and I do most sincerely hope you will come out to us. The next year must divide this army, and we will go together, if it be possible. Take care of our cause in England, I rely on your goodness and regard for me to represent me favorably to the King if you think I deserve it.... Yours Sincerely, W. Phillips.[58]

Burgoyne was appalled to learn from Phillips that Carleton had determined not to leave a garrison at Crown Point for the winter, to control the lake and harass the Americans, and to force the Americans to maintain a similarly large force at Ticonderoga for the winter. Burgoyne would write his friend General Henry Clinton:

You will have heard of the compleat [sic] victory obtained over the enemy's fleet — I joined the General with two brigades of the army at Crown Point; He held the attack of Ticonderoga at so advanced a season of the year, inexpedient — It was too strong for a coup de main. The blow could not be followed. The lake was secured without it, & the place must necessarily fall with small loss & in short time by a regular attack next spring. In these reasons Philips & I acquiesced upon the idea that Crown Point was to be maintained; but I could have wished to throw a corps of Indians & light troops round the enemy's post, to have felt their pulse & attempted their convoys from Lake George & Fort Edward — Finding nothing of that sort or any other operation was in contemplation, I thought myself at liberty to withdraw on my way to England & left the General consulting the speediest & properest [sic] means to make Crown Point (all the buildings of which were burnt) tenable for one brigade for the winter. The greatest difficulty therein appeared to be the supply of provisions. This task I undertook & in my passage down established a conveyance & arrangement of posts that ensured success before the Lake should become impracticable. I cannot express my surprise nor concern at hearing since that the post has been judged untenable for want of season to cover the troops & fortify them, & that the whole is coming back. I think this step puts us in danger, besides conveying a bad impression to the publick, of losing the fruits of our summer's labour & certain victory — It may perhaps be a race which shall build fastest for a new naval dispute next spring, the Lake which was positively & effectually [sic] secured by possessing Crown Point being again entirely open. I must honour Carleton's abilities & judgement, I have lived with him upon the best terms & bear him real friendship — I am therefore doubly hurt that he has taken a step in which I can be no otherwise serviceable to him than by silence; for I cannot bring myself to think that he might not have held the post if he had ordered the troops to cover themselves, to construct huts instead of barracks & called in his own good sense to direct the fortification without being guided by the drawings & technical reasonings [sic] of dull, formal, methodical, fat, engineers.[59]

The British were gone from Crown Point. The work of the entire year's campaign would all have to be done over again next year.

Whether or not a garrison could effectively be maintained at Crown Point throughout the winter of 1776 and 1777 is speculation. Certainly, Carleton was adamant that a garrison could not be safely established for the winter at this isolated post, and once established it certainly could not be sustained throughout the winter. Carleton would definitively state, "The Corps left there must have been inevitably lost."[60] Canadian historian R. Arthur Bowler, whose specialty is British army logistics during the War for American Independence, has also noted that Carleton's logistical resources were severely strained in the fall of 1776, and concurs that Carleton could not have successfully sustained a forward post at Crown Point.[61]

Still, Carleton had been timid, almost cowardly, in front of Ticonderoga in late October 1776. Carleton failed to push forward his scouts and Native Americans, and it is obvious that he neglected to perform an adequate reconnaissance of Ticonderoga, and apparently never even made an effort to scout either Mount Hope or Mount Independence. He failed to make a vigorous push upon the American defensive positions, even though he had a formidable fleet and substantial army available at Crown Point from October 14 to November 2. If a substantial weakness in the American defensive configuration existed, Carleton made no effort to locate or identify it. The Lake Champlain corridor was clearly the most fragile segment of the American works, but when Carleton did attempt to probe this chink in Gates' armor, his effort was weak for the gunboats were unsupported, and even if he had succeeded in accidentally making a lodgment, he did not have adequate strength in place to sustain it, much less exploit it. Certainly Carleton lacked sufficient time, given the lateness of the season, to initiate the formal siege that would have been necessary to conquer Ticonderoga. But, as Phillips suggested, Carleton certainly could have launched an aggressive thrust to test the temper of the American defenses. Instead, he never adequately tested the strength of Gates' defenses or army. Carleton's actions before Ticonderoga were, in a word, anemic.

Carleton's utterly lackluster performance in the fall of 1776 earned him censure from political opponents in both Canada, and of considerably greater significance, in England.

Over the winter Carleton would remain in Quebec, while Burgoyne would return to Great Britain, ostensibly to take care of the affairs of the estate of his wife, who had died while he was on campaign in Canada. The exact machinations of Burgoyne with the British high command over the winter properly belong in a recitation of the Saratoga Campaign of 1777, the Year of the Hangman. However, when Burgoyne returned to Canada early in May 1777, he carried orders restricting Carleton to serving as governor of Canada, while giving Burgoyne the exclusive command of the major expedition of the year into New York colony. Thus, in June 1777 Lieutenant General Jonathan Burgoyne would lead a magnificent army down from Canada again, this time with the intention of reaching Albany. However, because of Carleton's failure to retain a garrison at Crown Point, Burgoyne would again have to begin his expedition from St. Jean. Burgoyne expended a full month simply in transporting his army from St. Jean to Crown Point, a month that Carleton had first earned, and then given away, in the fall of 1776. By the ending stages of the campaign, in late September and early October 1777, Burgoyne desperately missed that month. In fact, had Burgoyne had that single month available to him, the course of the campaign, and the war, could have easily turned.

The British had come to see Ticonderoga, and in a modification of the famous saying, "They Came, They Saw, They Retreated." When taken as a whole, the new redoubts on Lake Champlain, the works at Mount Independence, the additional outer defensive works at Mount Hope, the reconstruction of the abandoned French defensive breastworks, and the old French fort itself, Ticonderoga was an imposing fortification. Colonel John Trumbull describes the impression that Ticonderoga made upon the British army as it advanced in late October 1776:

> Ticonderoga must have had a very imposing aspect that day, when viewed from the lake. The whole summit of cleared land, on both sides of the lake, was crowned with redoubt and batteries, all manned, with a splendid show of artillery and flags.... Our appearance was indeed so formidable, and the season so far advanced, that the enemy withdrew without making any attack.[62]

12

"As Great Consequence as if They Had Been Defeated"

The Campaign Ends; Analysis and Conclusions

On November 4, 1776, Brigadier General Arthur St. Clair wrote to a correspondent, noting the British retreat, and declaring: "I may be able to assure you of the retreat an event which I look upon as of as great Consequence as if they had been defeated."[1]

With the British gone and winter beginning to settle in, there was no longer a requirement for a large force at Ticonderoga. In any event, once Lake Champlain and Lake George began to freeze over, which could be anticipated at any time in November or December, it would be impossible to supply a substantial force so far to the north. Gates reported on November 27 that Lake Champlain had already frozen over "as low as Three Mile Point." There was also another consideration. The American main Continental army under General George Washington was, at this very moment, being crushed at Fort Washington in New York and Fort Lee in New Jersey, and being driven in defeat through New Jersey towards the Delaware River. Washington desperately needed reinforcements, and the force at Ticonderoga was one of the only reservoirs of trained, disciplined, dependable soldiers available to him.

Schuyler thus took action to reduce the size of the American garrison at Ticonderoga. First, all of the militia were discharged and sent home. For militia, they had proven remarkably dependable and efficient throughout the summer and fall. Horatio Gates had managed the militia quite well, and was able to obtain effective use from them. Second, on November 12, he ordered all of the "New Jersey and Pennsylvania battalions whose term of enlistment is expired" to the south to the succor of Washington.[2] Gates identified six regiments as being in this category. Third, all of the regiments whose time had expired, or was close to expiring, were similarly discharged. The anonymous clerk who maintained the Orderly Book for Brigadier General James Brickett's Massachusetts Brigade on Mount Independence gleefully wrote in huge letters that occupied an entire page, "November 17th Going To Winter Quarters." Later that day, the ecstatic young soldier had the pleasure to formally issue the orders: "Col. Greatons, /late Col. Bonds/, & Col. Porters Regiments are to march tomorrow morning to Fort George, where Boats will be provided for their immediate Embarkation."[3] As the men boarded their boats it must have been an occasion for great merriment and festivity.

Colonel Anthony Wayne was appointed to be winter commandant of the small garrison that was to be retained at Ticonderoga and Mount Independence. Gates justified his decision, "I have fixed Colonel Wayne in the command at Ticonderoga. He is a capable, good officer, and has health and strength fit to encounter the inclemency of that cold inhospitable region."[4] Wayne was less than thrilled with this rather dubious honor. He complained of Ticonderoga on several occasions:

> It appears to be the last part of the world that God made, and I have some ground to believe that it was finished in the dark: that it was never intended that man should live in it is clear, for the people who attempted to make any stay have, for the most part, perished by pestilence or the sword. I believe it to be the ancient Golgotha, or place of skulls; they are so plenty here that our people for want of other vessels, drink out of them, while the soldiers make tent pins of the shin and thigh bones of Abercrombie's men.

And on December 15:

> Last night has frozen Lake Champlain to the center — it is all one solid mass of ice — our poor fellows severely felt the effect of it — for my own part I was so congeal'd that after turning before the fire for three hours by Shrewsbury Clock — I was not half thawed until I put one bottle of wine under my sword belt at dinner. I have been toasting you all but can't toast myself — for by the time that one side is warm the other is froze.[5]

Gates left Colonel Wayne the following articles at Fort Ticonderoga for his use, which doubtless did little to improve his humor:
- 1 dozen new pewter plates
- 4 pewter dishes of sorts
- near 3 dozen knives & 3 dozen forks
- about 5 dozen worn plates & 6 or 7 oval dishes
- 2 table clothes
- a dozen pewter spoons
- 3 iron pots
- kettle
- 2 tea kettles, copper
- 1 sauce pan, copper
- grid iron
- frying pan & other kitchen furniture.[6]

By late November the militia had departed, and Gates was well in the process of releasing the Continental army regiments. First, however, one of Gates' regiments had reached the expiration of their term of service, and against Gates' remonstrations they determined to depart Ticonderoga, which they did on November 6. At the time of their departure, the British had just left Crown Point, and Gates was absolutely furious that they would even consider evacuating his garrison when a British attack was still a possibility. The regiment was the 1st New Jersey commanded by Colonel William Winds. Sergeant Timothy Tuttle of the regiment recorded in his journal of the sentiments of the regiment:

> [November] 4th At the camp, our men wants to go home; good weather to march, we hear the enemy has gone down the Lake & we are uneasy about staying at this place.
>
> 5th At the camp, same morning our men seemed to insist to go home & orders comes out from the General that Colonel Winds & what men is a mind to follow him to be off to morning at 8 O'clock, some of officers say we go away with scandal but Colonel Winds says we go with honor.
>
> Nov. 6th We left Ticonderoga about 105 men of our Battalion. Left that place & is said with a great deal of scandal.[7]

Actually, a number of men from the regiment remained at Ticonderoga, under the command of Major William DeHart. Still, the Jersey men were entirely within their rights, as their enlistments had expired, and they were thus free men. In spite of this, Gates in a pique of anger "upbraided" Colonel Winds "for a coward, called him a rascal, with everything that was bad, and finally he [Winds] was escorted off the ground with the drums and fifes playing the Rogues March after him and his men." This less than magnanimous gesture was noted by many soldiers, and it was a gesture that earned Gates few friends among the remaining men from New Jersey, who thought that their friends had served with honor, and had justly and completely fulfilled the terms of their contract with the Army.[8] Second Lt. Ebenezer Elmer of the companion 2nd New Jersey Regiment felt that Gates' conduct was outrageous: "Must not the blood of every Jersey man boil at such treachery."[9] And still, even after the *Rogue's March*, Gates could not resist having the last word, and issued General Orders on November 7:

> The General returns his thanks to the officers & soldiers of the 1st Jersey Regiment who remain with the army for the honor & public spirit they showed in disdaining to follow the infamous example of their Colonel & the deluded soldiers who accompanied him yesterday. The General would inform them that the drums were beat by his order in derision of the few who had the baseness to quit the post in this time of danger.[10]

The initial two regiments destined for Washington's army that still had time remaining in their enlistments, unlike the 1st New Jersey, had departed in early November, and the rest soon followed, accompanied by Gates himself, who was ordered to join Washington in New Jersey. Arnold returned home to Connecticut for the first time in two years. Gates would note regarding Arnold: "General Arnold, who is now here, is anxious, after his very long absence, to see his family, and settle his public accounts." The first of the Ticonderoga Regiments would reach Washington on the western shores of the Delaware River following a long and difficult mid-winter march on December 21, just in time to participate in the assault on Trenton on Christmas.[11]

The winter garrison of Ticonderoga would consist of six regiments, all under the command of Colonel Anthony Wayne as the equivalent of a joint garrison and brigade commander. Now Major Persifer Frazer of Wayne's own 4th Pennsylvania Battalion noted of the post's garrison:

> Three of the Pennsylvania Regiments, one of the Jerseys and as many New England troops as will make about 2,500 are to form a garrison for this place until fresh troops are sent to relieve them.[12]

Major Frazer was entirely accurate in his description of the force's winter strength. Colonel Charles Burrall's Connecticut Regiment and Colonel Asa Whitcomb's 6th Continental Regimental (Massachusetts) with about three hundred effectives would stay at Mount Independence. Colonel Elias Dayton's 3rd New Jersey with about 450 effectives would stay to garrison the Jersey Redoubt and surrounding redoubts. The four hundred men of Colonel Joseph Wood's 2nd Pennsylvania Battalion and Lieutenant Colonel Hartley's 6th Pennsylvania would remain stationed in a large hut camp to the rear of the old French Lines on the Heights of Carillon. Wayne's own 4th Pennsylvania Battalion provided a headquarters detachment of just over three hundred soldiers at the old French Fort Carillon. The total garrison, including sick detached at the general hospital, was 2,783 officers and soldiers.[13] Wayne actually commanded a fairly robust winter garrison, which contained more than sufficient strength to repulse any British winter raid.

Dr. Samuel Adams, a surgeon who had spent the fall at the hospital at Fort George and then been transferred to Mount Independence upon the British approach, provided the epitaph for the post's transformation that summer and fall:

> Mount Independence which 3 months agone [sic] was a doleful wilderness & a haven for wild beasts and rattlesnakes; is now become a pleasant city, and it renders our soldiers way of life less disagreeable than was at our first coming here. What we then thought hardships was often but inconveniences & what we then thought inconvenience we have learned patiently to put up with; many things which we then seemed to suffer for, we now contentedly do without.[14]

With the departure of the majority of Gates' Ticonderoga army, with Lake Champlain having turned into a gigantic sheet of smooth ice, and with the ground being slowly covered by a mantle of thick white snow, winter had taken over the Adirondacks for another year. The urgent hurry of the summer's campaign gave way to the quiet routine of garrison life, soldiers and officers alike primarily occupied by trying to stay warm and fed. Calm and monotony returned to Ticonderoga until the seasons changed once again; 1776, the Year Before the Hangman, had ended in the Northern Theater.

Analysis of the Campaign

The Year Before the Hangman had begun in front of Quebec. The Americans had just launched a vigorous attack on Quebec. This attack was absolutely reckless and desperate, yet it almost succeeded. It had been a very, very closely run thing. All that long, frigid winter the American army blockaded Carleton's garrison in the citadel city. It was never a really effective blockade. It certainly was never a siege.

The Americans possessed no conceivable advantages, and their position was without strength, yet Colonel Benedict Arnold determined to maintain the tiny army outside of Quebec, if for no other reason than he just simply refused to be beaten. Although Arnold was indefatigable, he received little meaningful support from the Continental Congress far to the south in comparatively balmy Philadelphia. The Continental army in front of Quebec had been provided with far too few men, and no real train of artillery, for the mission at hand. The soldiers suffered from inadequate clothing, short rations, no pay, a limited medical staff without medicines, restricted quantities of ammunition, and the army's empty war chest contained not a shilling of hard currency to purchase any of these articles for their use. Their immediate commander, Brigadier General David Wooster, was an old, paranoid man who may well have had overmuch fondness for the liberal consumption of rum. Wooster remained ensconced in comfortable quarters in Montreal, and given his activities in that city which antagonized and angered the citizens whose support was absolutely critical to facilitate support, his absence might in fact have been better for Continental army fortunes before Quebec. It appears that Benedict Arnold, wounded, bedridden, weakened and in pain was still more effective a combat commander than Wooster was healthy.

When the weather improved and Wooster finally stirred from his warm headquarters in Montreal, his solitary actions in front of Quebec were to antagonize and insult Arnold and drive him away from the city, and to construct a single fire ship. When it was eventually employed on the St. Lawrence River Wooster's fire ship burned in a magnificent pyrotechnic display that turned out to be all light and spectacle, bereft of any real accomplishment. The fire ship could just as well have described Wooster's command performance in Canada.

The American response to reinforce the army before Quebec was too little and too slow. When John Thomas arrived at Quebec he discovered an army only in name, an army that had entirely disintegrated. What little discipline it possessed had departed with Arnold, and the circumstances in which the American army found itself were custom made to result in its own destruction. Living conditions that were crowded and filthy, with poor rations, inadequate clothing, frigid cold temperatures that prevented proper hygiene, privations of every kind, an utter lack of anything vaguely resembling pay, miserable leadership, and long hours of arduous and exhausting duties all marked the American experience in Canada. These horrific circumstances caused an outbreak of smallpox, and once the disease erupted in December it swept through the Americans with devastating, and utterly terrifying, consequences. The men that arrived with Thomas, and their commanding general, all succumbed to the smallpox within days of their arrival. The ensuing catastrophe was, for all practical purposes, a medical panic.

The British response to relieve the citadel city was aggressive and overwhelming. Launched from as far away as Cork, Ireland, the British relief convoy had traversed the North Atlantic in winter, and penetrated up the St. Lawrence River dodging ice in a masterful piece of seamanship. Unlike the Americans, the British relief column that sailed up the St. Lawrence in early May had every conceivable advantage. It possessed numerous large vessels of the Royal Navy, hundreds and eventually thousands of well armed, splendidly equipped and heavily armed soldiers, well fed, with a plentitude of provisions, and magnificently outfitted with a modern, massive artillery train. When the British reinforcements arrived in Quebec, Thomas' response was dilatory and indecisive, and when Carleton sortied from the city within hours (instead of days as Thomas gambled on) he simply scattered the American army all the way back to Sorel.

In short order, and with little effort and against no real organized opposition, this Britannic host then proceeded to sweep the American army from Canada like a giant scarlet broom.

John Thomas contracted the smallpox and died the first week in June. By that time, the only thing that the American army had in adequate supply was the *variola* virus. Rations were all but non-existent, "scarcely anything to sustain nature," and what little food existed was half rotten salt pork and uncooked flour. The Americans had no artillery, no gunpowder even if they did have guns, no clothing, and no equipment. They lacked land and water transport. There were few doctors available and these crippled for absence of medicines and instruments. Their pay chests remained bankrupt, and they had already exhausted their credit. All of these shortages could perhaps have been overcome with firm, positive, decisive leadership. Sadly enough, the one thing that the American army absolutely required had also disintegrated. Colonel Timothy Bedel fled his post at The Cedars in panic upon the simple approach of a numerically tiny British force, lacking artillery or any siege equipment or storming capability (in fact, the British force consisted principally of Native Americans and loyal French Canadians, and only a handful of British regulars). His subordinate, Major Isaac Butterfield, surrendered his post upon the mere appearance of this miniscule British column. Butterfield was so eager to capitulate that he failed to even render his own cannon inoperable, and the British would employ them to slaughter American soldiers within days. An American counterattack upon The Cedars was bungled because of inept tactical leadership, suffering heavy casualties in the process. Another American counterattack on Three Rivers was inadequately planned and organized, and was shattered with catastrophic losses. The least important of those casualties was the capture of Brigadier General William Thompson, whose incompetent preparations and leadership had doomed the assault from its inception.

The American army now found itself commanded by a youthful, ambitious, and woefully inexperienced Brigadier General John Sullivan, who had assumed the reins simply because everybody senior to him was dead, captured, or in the case of Wooster had fled from Canada. Sullivan was determined and aggressive, but he lacked the skills, military knowledge, and maturity necessary for the post. Benedict Arnold implored Sullivan to remove the semblance of an American army from Canada, while it still retained the ability to do so.

Sullivan pondered Arnold's advice in indecision while his soldiers were consumed in great numbers on the Isle Aux Noix midstream in the Richelieu River. The Island of Nuts for all practical purposes became the American "Île de la mort," the calvary of the American Northern Theater Army. As American soldiers suffered and died on Isle Aux Noix, their officers gorged on roast beef. When Sullivan finally concurred with Arnold and the American Northern Theater Army staggered ashore at Crown Point on the evening of July 1, thousands of men were dead, simply missing from the rolls, vanished from the face of the earth without a single trace or record, and the few men still on their feet were sick, debilitated, exhausted, and fevered. Thousands of the survivors were afflicted with varying stages of the devastating scourge of smallpox. Some regiments had so few healthy men available that soldiers had to be drafted from other states to row their bateaux.

Within less than two months of the arrival of the British fleet, the American army had been driven from the citadel city to Crown Point, a retreat of approximately 275 miles. Over two hundred years later, this still constitutes one of the single most remarkable routes in military history. And, in the process, the American army was utterly and completely destroyed. The force that staggered ashore at Crown Point the first day of July was a shadow of an army, without strength, without morale, without arms, food, equipment, or artillery. The only item that it had in plentitude was smallpox.

An American army died in Canada in May and June 1776.

But the British advance was brought to a cessation in St. Jean on the Richelieu River, in large part because of the foresight of Benedict Arnold in evacuating all nautical transportation from the Richelieu River Valley, and due to the presence of a tiny American fleet on Lake Champlain, a force in being that effectively barred Carleton's further progress south. Carleton would be forced to spend the entire summer and fall of 1776 in constructing a fleet of his own, and he would not move south until very late in the season, in early October. And, this time, he would face an entirely new American army. To the British, who had easily driven the first American Northern Theater Army before them, this powerful, confident, and determined new army must have seemed to have risen like the phoenix from the ashes of the first army, atop the stone promontory of Ticonderoga.

Major General Horatio Gates, no battlefield general but an administrator of the first order, supported by Major General Philip Schuyler, also no battlefield general but an unsurpassed theater commander and logistician, had been responsible for the reconstruction of this army.

Gates stationed himself at Ticonderoga with the main army, while Schuyler remained at Albany pushing the supplies and assets forward without which Gates could not hope to rebuild the army. Their first decisions, mandated by the infectious smallpox, was to send the sick to Fort George where a new general hospital was established, and to evacuate Crown Point, already contaminated by the disease. Ticonderoga would be the center of the new defensive position. Great pains were taken to avoid infesting the Fort Ticonderoga vicinity with the disease during this movement. Once the smallpox army had been transferred, Gates moved what little of his force remained to Ticonderoga. In a summer and fall of intense and unremitted activity, Gates and Schuyler reconstructed an American army at Ticonderoga and Mount Independence, while at the same time outfitting a strong advanced guard in the guise of a fleet on Lake Champlain. They placed this forward flotilla under the command of Brigadier General Benedict Arnold, who had already proven to be a magnificent leader of soldiers; and a valiant, dauntless battlefield commander. The success of Schuyler, Gates and Arnold in simultaneously reconstituting and training an army, constructing a formidable defensive position at Ticonderoga, and creating an effective nautical advanced guard, all within the span of three short months between early July and early October, and in the very face of the enemy, remains one of the single most impressive accomplishments in American military history, a success which has never been adequately acknowledged by historians.

Gates certainly had a full plate that summer and fall at Ticonderoga, reestablishing discipline, implementing training efforts, improving the health of his army, and reorganizing it administratively, all the while building a defensive position of considerable strength. But the accomplishments of Schuyler were, if anything, even more impressive. Schuyler fixed the tangled logistical muddle of the Northern Theater Army, all while supervising the construction of a fleet at Skenesboro, and implementing the establishment and operation of an efficient and effective general hospital at Fort George. At the same time, although not within the purview of this study, Schuyler also retained the loyalty of the Mohawk Valley to the American patriot cause, and maintained the neutrality of the powerful six nations of the Iroquois Confederation. Surgeon Jonathan Potts' medical accomplishments at Fort George are monumental, for he not only saved the lives of literally thousands of men who would otherwise have succumbed to smallpox and a range of other debilitating diseases, but he returned hundreds of these men to the rolls of the Northern Theater Army in time for them to participate in the successful defense of Ticonderoga in October. The fifth most significant officer was Colonel Baldwin, the indomitable engineer who designed the Ticonderoga defenses. Although his creative energies were sometimes excessive (as with his propensity for constructing redoubts to various shapes), he designed a superlative fortress perfectly well adapted to the topography and the force that would be available to defend it, and oversaw its construction such that the British were so impressed that they were hesitant to even probe its strength, much less launch any serious assault against it, in late October. The American army, by then, had already won the campaign.

The 1777 Campaign, The Year of the Hangman

That next spring, once the ice had again departed the North Atlantic and Upper St. Lawrence River, His Majesty's Frigate *Ariadne* docked at Quebec. Lieutenant General Jonathan Burgoyne then regally disembarked, returning to Canada with a packet of dispatches direct from London. These letters, although signed by Lord George Germain, secretary of state, were fully authorized and approved by King George III himself. Their contents informed Carleton that he would remain in Canada as governor in 1777, while Burgoyne again led the British army and Royal Navy south, with the objective of penetrating down the familiar Lake Champlain route and then the Hudson River, to seize Albany. It was certainly a blow, and a stunning royal rebuke, to Carleton.

Burgoyne would be obliged to spend nearly the entire month of June transporting his large army and mound of critical supplies and miscellaneous military paraphernalia from St. Jean to Crown Point, thus duplicating Carleton's effort the previous October. This time, the American fleet did not endeavor to obstruct the Royal Navy. The Saratoga or Burgoyne Campaign, as it came to be known, started ostentatiously enough for the British, but soon bogged down. It would not be until September that Burgoyne could finally begin his ultimate movement upon Albany, and he would be first halted at the Battle of Freeman's Farm on September 17, then repulsed at Barber's Wheatfield on October 7, and the same afternoon he would be driven back north. His retreat would be initially stymied by heavy rain, giving the Amerians enough time to surround him, and Burgoyne would be forced to surrender his entire army on the banks of the Hudson on October 17 of the Year of the Hangman. This stunning defeat, the capture of an entire British army complete with a modern, state-of-the-art artillery train of nearly fifty pieces of cannon, propelled the French to formally sign a treaty of alliance with the fledgling United States of America. Much work remained to be done, and a multitude of challenges had to be overcome, but once this alliance was cemented American independence was for all practical purposes preordained.

The American Northern Theater Army of 1777 that achieved this momentous victory was a completely different army than that of 1776, for the Americans were then adhering to a distressing approach of only enlisting their regiments for a single year's service. Still, the leadership of the American Northern Theater Army was essentially the same. Philip Schuyler and then Horatio Gates commanded the army. Benedict Arnold played a key role on the battlefield. Arthur St. Clair retained a major command. Colonel Baldwin continued his engineering duties, and Doctor Potts still looked after the hospital. Richard Varick first served as Schuyler's aide and then performed the same task for Arnold.

And many of the subordinate soldiers and officers also reenlisted, many into the Continental army. These men were indeed the heart of the army that defeated Burgoyne.

As Burgoyne's army penetrated farther south, more and more of the veterans of 1776 re-joined the American Northern Theater Army. This time, many of them served with militia units. The presence of the experienced, seasoned veterans made a major contribution to the numerous militia regiments that joined Gates. These militia regiments had a reputation of being both unreliable and untrustworthy, and rarely contributed to any battlefield. Indeed, their sole propensity was at absorbing and expending military supplies, particularly rations, at a prodigious rate. However, with a leavening of tough, well-trained, formidable veterans of the Canada campaign, the militia regiments achieved a level of consistency and performance rarely seen throughout the war.

The model 1777 American Northern Theater Army would experience crushing defeats and demoralizing retreats, and absorb staggering battlefield blows, but it never disintegrated. This army knew that it had seen, and survived, far worse. It was an army that was resilient and strong, and both leaders and soldiers knew how to overcome defeat and wrest victory against the greatest odds. Officers and enlisted men now knew how to reconstruct an army, even in the very face of a confident, powerful enemy, and they knew how to do it successfully.

Horatio Gates felt confident that he had discovered a working concept to defeat the British. In 1777, he constructed another formidable series of earthworks behind which a badly shaken army could be successfully rebuilt. In 1777, he even duplicated the presence of a powerful, capable advanced guard to safeguard his defense against a surprise British assault. Benedict Arnold again commanded this new model advanced guard. It consisted of the formidable Morgan's Riflemen and Dearborn's Light Infantrymen, who again controlled the ground to the front of the American army, and who would have to be defeated before the British advance could continue. The concept worked again, this time on Bemis Heights instead of Ticonderoga. Later in the war, George Washington would again adopt a similar strategy, at a place known as West Point.

Conclusions

The single most important factor behind the successful reconstruction of the American army was leadership. The logistical expertise, and supply efforts provided by Schuyler from Albany were absolutely integral to the army. Without the necessary supplies, rations, clothing, armament, and equipment the Continental army could never have been reconstructed. The administrative and organizational leadership provided by Gates at Ticonderoga was similarly critical. Arnold provided the decisive, energetic battlefield leadership that was necessary to guide the admittedly unsuccessful advanced guard fight that his fleet performed in October. Without the efforts of these three general officers, the Continental army would never have successfully delayed the British advance from July to October, and then repulsed it once it finally did develop.

Other superlative leaders that contributed more than their fair share to the success of the Continental army were Dr. Jonathan Potts at the general hospital at Fort George, and engineer Colonel Baldwin supervising the positioning, design and physical construction of the American fortress at Ticonderoga. Lieutenant Colonel Hartley's command of the Advanced Post at Crown Point was flawlessly performed. Captain Whitcomb's Scouts carried the fight to the British throughout the summer and fall. American Commissary General Joseph Trumbull managed to provide adequate provisions to the American Northern Theater Army for the first time in its existence. Captain Richard Varick was indomitable in requisitioning and coordinating the flow of supplies, particularly to the nascent American fleet at Skenesboro.

These men, collectively, proved that there is no substitute for dynamic military leadership at every level, from theater level strategic command as exercised by Schuyler, down to a Captain such as Whitcomb commanding tactical scouts and raiding parties. The American Northern Theater Army clearly enjoyed just such leadership. In 1777, the Year of the Hangman, the American army would again prove its mettle, and win the victory at Saratoga that more than any single victory would lead to American independence. This same leadership would then go on to contribute more than their full share to Washington's Continental army and a new nation.

In February 1783, at the conclusion of the war, George Washington would write to his good friend and fellow army commander, Nathaniel Greene:

> If historiographers should be hardy enough to fill the page of history with the advantages that have been gained with unequal numbers (on the part of America) in the course of this contest, and attempt to relate the distressing circumstances under which they have been obtained, it is more than probable that posterity will bestow on their labors the epithet of fiction.[15]

But the Year Before the Hangman was not fiction. In the pages written in the history of this year, the American soldier had suffered as severely as he would at any time in our nation's history. But his trials and tribulations, as horrible as they would be, were not in vain. In 1776, the British never passed beyond Ticonderoga.

Chapter Notes

Preface

1. A lively account of the assault on Quebec was recorded by George Morison, "An Account of Assault on Quebec, 1775" *Pennsylvania Magazine of History and Biography* 14 (1890), 434–439.
2. Kenneth Roberts, *Rabble In Arms: A Chronicle of Arundel and the Burgoyne Invasion* (Garden City, NY: Doubleday, Doran, 1935).

Chapter 1

1. Barbara W. Tuchman, *The March of Folly, From Troy to Vietnam* (1984; paperback edition New York: Ballantine Books, 1985), 198.
2. Paul Langston, "Tyrant and Oppressor, Colonial Press Reaction to the Quebec Act," *The Historical Journal of Massachusetts* 34, no. 1 (2006), 1–17.
3. John Jenks, "Diary, 1775–1776." Massachusetts Historical Society, Boston.
4. Captain Samuel Jenks, "Journal of Captain Jenks," *Proceedings of Massachusetts Historical Society* (March 1890), 388.
5. John C. Miller, *Origins of the American Revolution* (Boston: Little, Brown, 1943), 374–375.
6. Colonel Thatcher T.P. Luquer, ed., "Journal from New York to Canada 1767," *New York State Historical Association Proceedings* 30 (1932), 311–312.
7. Arnold to George Washington, letter dated "Camp Before Quebec" January 14, 1776, in William Bell Clark and William J. Morgan, eds., *Naval Documents of the American Revolution* (Washington, DC: U.S. Government Printing Office, 1964–2006), 3:781. Hereinafter cited as *NDAR*.
8. Dr. Isaac Senter, "Journal of Dr. Isaac Senter" in Kenneth Roberts, ed., *March to Quebec: Journals of the Members of Arnold's Expedition* (New York: Doubleday, Doran, 1938), 234–235.
9. There have been numerous biographies of Arnold. Although dated, Willard W. Wallace, *Traitorous Hero, The Life and Fortunes of Benedict Arnold* (New York: Harper & Brothers, 1954) remains the best of the older biographies. The two finest contemporary biographies of Arnold are Willard S. Randall, *Benedict Arnold: Patriot and Traitor* (New York: Morrow, 1990); and James Kirby Martin, *Benedict Arnold, Revolutionary Hero: An American Warrior Reconsidered* (New York: New York University Press, 1997). A fine succinct biography is Willard W. Wallace, "Benedict Arnold: Traitorous Patriot" in George A. Billias, ed., *George Washington's Generals* (New York: Morrow, 1964), 163–192. An interesting Canadian perspective is provided by Barry K. Wilson, *Benedict Arnold, A Traitor in our Midst* (Montreal and Kingston, Canada: McGill-Queen's University Press, 2001),
10. Different historians have suggested that Arnold served in the 1758 and 1759 campaigns, but the evidence is limited, and historian James Kirby Martin believes that his only military service was a brief tenure during the 1757 campaign. Martin, *Benedict Arnold, Revolutionary Hero*, 28–29.
11. Congressman Charles Carroll of Carrollton, *Dear Papa, Dear Charley: The Peregrinations of a Revolutionary Aristocrat, As Told by Charles Carroll of Carrollton and his father, Charles Carroll of Annapolis, with Sundry Observations on Bastardy, child-rearing, romance, matrimony, commerce, tobacco, slavery and the politics of Revolutionary America* (Chapel Hill, North Carolina: University of North Carolina Press, 2001): 902–903.
12. Eric Manders, "Notes on Troop Units in the Northern Army, 1775–1776." *Military Collector and Historian* 23 (Winter 1971): 119.
13. Arnold probably never really knew how many soldiers precisely he had available. For this, see Allen MacLean, "Arnold's Strength at Quebec." *Military Collector and Historian* 29 (Fall 1977): 139.
14. Quoted in Lt. Col. Louis C. Duncan, *Medical Men in the American Revolution, 1775–1783* (Carlisle Barracks, PA: Medical Field Service School, 1931), 94.
15. Musketman Caleb Haskell, "Caleb Haskell, Diary at the Siege of Boston and on the March to Quebec," in Roberts, *March to Quebec*, 485.
16. James Knowles, Letter to "Dear Wife" from Quebec, January 15, 1776, Sol Feinstone Collection of the American Revolution, David Library of the American Revolution, Washington's Crossing, PA.
17. There are a large number of excellent biographies of Carleton. Succinct biographies are available at G. P. Browne, "Guy Carleton, 1st Baron of Dorchester," in *Dictionary of Canadian Biography* (Toronto: University of Toronto Press, 1966–1994), 5: 141–155; and Paul H. Smith, "Sir Guy Carleton: Soldier Statesman" in George A. Billias, ed., *George Washington's Opponents: British Generals and Admirals in the American Revolution* (New York: Morrow, 1969), 103–141. Full-length biographies are A.G. Bradley, *Sir Guy Carleton (Lord Dorchester)* (Toronto: University of Toronto Press, 1966); Perry E. Leroy, *Sir Guy Carleton as a Military Leader During the American Invasion and Repulse in Canada, 1775–1776* (Ph.D. diss., Ohio State University, 1960); Paul. D. Nelson, *General Sir Guy Carleton, Lord Dorchester: Soldier-Statesman of Early British Canada* (Madison, NJ, and London: Fairleigh Dickin-

son University Press, 2000); and Paul R. Reynolds, *Guy Carleton: A Biography* (Toronto: Gage, 1980). Carleton's greatest detractor is Canadian historian A.L. Burt, *Guy Carleton, Lord Dorchester, 1724–1804* (Ottawa: Canadian Historical Association, 1955).

18. Michel Brisebois, "Books from General Wolfe's Library at the National Library of Canada" *National Library News* 28, no. 2 (February 1996), accessed December 5, 2007, at http://epe.lac-bac.gc.ca/100/202/301/nl-news/nlnews-h/1996/02/2802e-15.htm.

19. Lieutenant Patrick Daly, Colonel Allen MacLean's Royal Highland Emigrant Regiment, "Journal of the Siege and Blockade of Quebec by the American Rebels in Autumn of 1775 and Winter of 1776," in Literary and Historical Society of Quebec, *4th Series of Historical Documents* (Quebec: 1875), 9.

20. Christopher Ward, *The War of the Revolution in Two Volumes* (New York: Macmillan: 1952), Vol. 1, 183.

21. Victor Coffin, *The Province of Quebec and the Early American Revolution: A Study in English-American Colonial History* (1896; reprint edition Port Washington, NY: Kennikat Press, 1970), 495–509.

22. Major Henry Caldwell, *The Invasion of Canada in 1775* (Quebec: 1866), 8, 16.

23. "Anonymous British Artillery Officer" [Captain Thomas Jones], "Journal of the Siege [of Quebec] from 1st December, 1775," Frederick Christian Wurtele, ed., *Blockade of Quebec in 1775–1776 by the American Revolutionists* in *Literary and Historical Society of Quebec, Historical Documents*, 7th and 8th ser. (Quebec: The Daily Telegraph Job Printing House, 1905–1906).

24. Arnold to Wooster, Quebec, January 2, 1776, in *NDAR*, 3:570.

25. Randall, *Benedict Arnold: Patriot and Traitor*, 58–60, 82–83; and Wallace, *Traitorous Hero*, 36.

26. Wallace, *Traitorous Hero*, 87.

27. General David Wooster, "Public Letters of General David Wooster, from April 1775 to 1777, the date of his death." Accessed September 19, 2003, at http://web.cortland.edu/woosterk/rev_ltrs.html.

28. Quoted in Justin H. Smith, *Our Struggle for the Fourteenth Colony* 2 Volumes (1907; reprint edition, Cranbury, NJ: Scholar's Bookshelf, 2005), Vol. 2, 229.

29. Martin, *Benedict Arnold, Revolutionary Hero*, 215–16; and Kate Mason Rowland, *The Life of Charles Carroll of Carrollton, 1737–1823 With His Correspondence and Public Papers*. 2 volumes (New York: The Knickerbocker Press, 1897), Vol. 1, 169.

30. For Canadian perspectives on Wooster, refer to Wilson, *Benedict Arnold, A Traitor in our Midst*, 118; and Michal P. Gabriel, ed., and S. Pascale Vergereau-Dewey, trans., *Quebec During the American Invasion, 1775–1776, The Journal of Francois Baby, Gabriel Taschereau, & Jenkin Williams* (East Lansing: Michigan State University Press, 2005), xxxix.

31. Smith, *Our Struggle for the Fourteenth Colony*, Vol. 2, 233.

32. Wooster, "Public Letters of General David Wooster."

33. General David Wooster, "Letter from Colonel David Wooster, from Quebec, dated April 23, 1776" Boston Public Library, Boston.

34. Carroll, *Dear Papa, Dear Charley*, Vol. 2, 910.

35. Arnold to Wooster, January 2, 1776. *NDAR*, 3:571.

36. Regarding the use and shortage of species in the colonies, refer to Douglas R. Cubbison, "The Coins of the British Private Soldier in the American Revolution" accessed on-line at http://www.csmid.com.

37. Francois Micheloud, "Canada's Playing Card Money" accessed January 5, 2004, at http://www.micheloud.com/FXM/MH/canada.htm; and P.N. Breton, *Illustrated History of Coins and Tokens Relating to Canada* (Montreal: Breton, 1894), 10–20.

38. Gabriel and Vergereau-Dewey, *Quebec During the American Invasion*, xxxviii–xxxix, 30.

39. For British Army counterfeiting operations in New York City, refer to Kenneth Scott, "A British Counterfeiting Press in New York Harbor, 1776." *New York Historical Society Quarterly* 39, nos. 2–3 (April–July 1955), 117–120; and Kenneth Scott, "New Hampshire Tory Counterfeiters Operating from New York City." *New York Historical Society Quarterly* 34, no. 1 (January 1950), 31–57.

40. Gustave Lanctot, *Canada & The American Revolution, 1774–1783*, translated by Margaret M. Cameron. (Cambridge, MA: Harvard University Press, 1967), 9.

41. Jenks, Diary.

42. Simeon DeWitt Bloodgood. *The Sexagenary; or Reminiscences of the American Revolution* (Albany, NY: Joel Munsell and Sons, 1866), 46.

43. Albany Committee of Correspondence, *Minutes of the Albany Committee of Correspondence, 1775–1778, Prepared for Publication by the Division of Archives and History*. 2 vols. (Albany: University of the State of New York, 1923–1925), Vol. 1, 450.

44. Massachusetts Laws & Statutes, 1776, Massachusetts Historical Society, Boston.

45. Peter Force, *American Archives: Consisting of a collection of authentick records, state papers, debates, and letters and other notices of publick affairs, the whole forming a documentary history of the origin and progress of the North American colonies; of the causes and accomplishment of the American revolution; and of the Constitution of government for the United States, to the final ratification thereof* 4th Series (M. St. Clair Clarke and Peter Force, 1837–46), 3:1964.

46. The finest succinct biography of Schuyler is John H.G. Pell, "Philip Schuyler, The General As Aristocrat" in George A. Billias, ed., *George Washington's Generals* (New York: Morrow, 1964), 54–78. The best full-length biography of Schuyler is Don R. Gerlach, *Proud Patriot: Philip Schuyler and the War of Independence, 1775–1783* (Syracuse, NY: Syracuse University Press, 1987). Schuyler's earlier biographies have been superceded by Gerlach's exemplary study.

47. Simeon DeWitt Bloodgood, *The Sexagenary; or Reminiscences of the American Revolution*. (Albany: Joel Munsell and Sons, 1866), 20.

48. Major General Philip Schuyler, "Letter to Lieutenant Colonel Israel Shreve, 2nd New Jersey Regiment" dated from Albany. April 5, 1776. Israel Shreve Revolutionary War Letters, Special Collections, University of Houston.

49. Colonel Rudolphus Ritzema, 1st New York, "Journal," *Magazine of American History* 1 (1877), 105. Ritzema succeeded in never returning to Canada; rather he transferred to New York City where he assumed command of another New York regiment closer to home and in a warmer climate. His less than illustrious military career would then be terminated by a court-martial, followed by his subsequent defection to the British army.

50. Alexander Graydon, *Memoirs of His Own Time*

With Reminiscences of the Men and Events of the Revolution (Philadelphia: Lindsay & Blakiston, 1846), 138–145.

51. John Williamson, *A Treatise on Military Finance* (London: T. Egerton, 1782), 57–59.

52. Joseph Lee Boyle, ed., *From Redcoat to Rebel: The Thomas Sullivan Journal* (Bowie, MD: Heritage Books, 1997), 23.

53. James. A. Huston, *The Sinews of War, Army Logistics, 1775–1953* (Washington, DC: Center of Military History, United States Army, 1997), 26–27; and Erna Risch, *Supplying Washington's Army* (Washington, DC: Center of Military History, United States Army, 1981), 190.

54. The only professional research on spruce beer has been performed by Virginia M. Westbrook, "Spruce Beer," *Bulletin of the Fort Ticonderoga Museum* 15, no. 6 (1994): 509–515. The author regularly brews spruce beer for his living history organization, and the members of that august organization have deemed it to be eminently drinkable.

55. Fred Anderson, *A People's Army: Massachusetts Soldiers and Society in the Seven Years' War* (Chapel Hill, N.C., 1984), 83–90; and John Rees, " 'The foundation of an army is the belly': North American Soldiers' Food, 1756–1945" accessed at *http://www.revwar75.com/library/rees/*.

56. Katherine E. Manchester, "General Washington and the Patriot Soldiers: They Won A War With Little Food," *Journal of the American Dietetic Association* 68 (1976), 424.

57. "Proceedings of a General Court Martial for the Trial of Major General St. Clair, August 25, 1778" (Philadelphia: Hall and Sellers, 1778; in *Collections of the New York Historical Society for the Year 1880*, New York: 1881), 108, 162.

58. Mark A. Lender and James Kirby Martin, *Citizen Soldier: The Revolutionary Journal of Joseph Bloomfield* (Newark: New Jersey Historical Society, 1982), 113.

59. "Expense Book of John Halsted, Commissary Under Benedict Arnold Before Quebec, 1776" Massachusetts Historical Society, Boston. Several of these weights are recorded in old English hundredweight units, such that the first weight is 112 pounds, the second weight is a quarterweight of 28 pounds, and the last or third weight is individual pounds.

60. Charles H. Lesser, *The Sinews of Independence: Monthly Strength Reports of the Continental Army* (Chicago: 1976), 18.

61. Jonathan Hill, "Diary Kept on the Expedition from New York to Quebec, April and May 1776," Massachusetts Historical Society, Boston.

62. John Thomas Papers.

63. Rowland, *The Life of Charles Carroll of Carrollton*, Vol. 1, 169.

Chapter 2

1. Title adopted from Ward, *War of the American Revolution*, Vol. 1, p. 196; and Kenneth Roberts, *Arundel* (Garden City, NY: Doubleday, 1929; revised edition, 1933), 369.

2. All entries for this Orderly Book from "Orderly Book, 3d (J. Clinton's) New York Regiment, Canada, January 1, 1776 – March 10, 1776," Early American Orderly Books, New York State Historical Society. Microfilm Copy, U.S. Military Academy Library, West Point, NY.

3. Arnold to Wooster, January 4, 1776. *NDAR*, 3:596.

4. Arnold to Wooster, January 5, 1776. Ibid., 3:624.

5. "Colonel Arnold's Letters Written During the Expedition to Quebec," in Roberts, *March to Quebec*, 108–109.

6. Ibid., 109–112.

7. Arnold to Continental Congress, January 12, 1776. *NDAR*, 3:741; and "Colonel Arnold's Letters Written During the Expedition to Quebec" in Roberts, *March to Quebec*, 113.

8. For a comprehensive discussion of the effect of smallpox in Canada, refer to Ann M. Becker, "Smallpox in Washington's Army," *The Journal of Military History* 68 (April 2004): 431–469.

9. Vernon A. Ives, ed., "Narrative of Uriah Cross in the Revolutionary War" *New York History* 63, no. 3 (July 1982): 289–290.

10. Centers for Disease Control and Prevention, "Smallpox," accessed November 27, 2007; at *http://www.bt.cdc.gov/agent/smallpox/*.

11. Information on early inoculation in Boston is discussed in John B. Blake, "The Inoculation Controversy in Boston, 1721–1722," *The New England Quarterly* 25, no. 4 (December 1952): 489–506.

12. Quoted in Richard L. Blanco, "Military Medicine in Northern New York, 1776–1777," *New York History* 63, no. 1 (January 1982): 48.

13. Ibid.

14. Quoted in Risch, *Supplying Washington's Army*, 379.

15. Wooster to Schuyler, January 13, 1776, in "Public Letters of General David Wooster."

16. "Colonel Arnold's Letters Written During the Expedition to Quebec" in Roberts, *March to Quebec*, 113–115.

17. Ibid., 116.

18. Ibid., 117–119.

19. Anonymous Artillery Officer [Jones], "Journal of the Siege," 22.

20. "Colonel Arnold's Letters Written During the Expedition to Quebec" in Roberts, *March to Quebec*, 119–120.

21. John Spafford, soldier with Captain Walker's Company, Colonel Bellow's Regiment, "Journal, February 8, 1776 – May 27, 1776," Revolutionary War Pension File, M804, Roll 2249, Pages 545–549, National Archives and Records Administration, Washington D.C., Microfilm Copy at David Library of the American Revolution, Washington's Crossing, PA.

22. Schuyler to Continental Congress, February 7, 1776. *NDAR*, 3: 1160.

23. Anonymous, "Journal of the Most Remarkable Occurrences in Quebec Since Arnold Appeared Before the Town on the 14th November 1775," in Frederick Christian Wurtele, ed., *Blockade of Quebec in 1775–1776 by the American Revolutionists* in *Literary and Historical Society of Quebec, Historical Documents*, 7th and 8th ser. (Quebec: The Daily Telegraph Job Printing House, 1905–1906), 114.

24. Daly, "Journal of the Siege and Blockade of Quebec by the American Rebels in Autumn of 1775 and Winter of 1776," 13.

25. Anonymous British Artillery Officer [Jones],

"Journal of the Siege [of Quebec] from 1st December, 1775," 24.

26. Anonymous, "Journal of the Most Remarkable Occurrences in Quebec Since Arnold Appeared Before the Town on the 14th November 1775," 115.

27. Arnold to Continental Congress, February 12, 1776. *NDAR*, 3:1221; and "Colonel Arnold's Letters Written During the Expedition to Quebec," in Roberts, *March to Quebec*, 120–121.

28. Wooster to Schuyler, February 13, 1776, in "Public Letters of General David Wooster."

29. Wooster to Schuyler, February 19, 1776. *NDAR*, 4:2.

30. Wooster to Continental Congress, February 21, 1776, in "Public Letters of General David Wooster."

31. "Colonel Arnold's Letters Written During the Expedition to Quebec," in Roberts, *March to Quebec*, 121–123.

32. Schuyler to Continental Congress, February 27, 1776. *NDAR*, 4: 96–97.

33. Lesser, *Sinews of Independence*, 17.

34. Anonymous artillery officer, "Journal of the Siege," 29.

35. Schuyler to Continental Congress, March 6, 1776. *NDAR*, 3: 193.

36. Adjutant Russell Dewey, "Military Journal, January to April 1776," In A.M. and L.M. Dewey, *Life of George Dewey* (Westfield, MA: Dewey, 1898), 266–571.

37. Senter, "Journal," in Roberts, *March to Quebec*, 237.

38. Gabriel and Vergereau-Dewey, *Quebec During the American Invasion*, 68, 95, 96.

39. Ibid., xxxvi-xxxvii, 68; and Smith, *Our Struggle for the Fourteenth Colony*, 241–243

40. Quoted in Wilson, *Benedict Arnold, A Traitor in Our Midst*, 100.

41. Schuyler to George Washington, *NDAR*, 4: 540.

42. Interpretation of this and other sermons generously provided by my brother, the Rev. Robert "Bob" Kaylor, an elder in the United Methodist Church.

43. Jenks, Diary.

44. Lesser, *Sinews of Independence*, 18.

45. Thomas has, unfortunately, been the subject of only one single biography, which is badly dated. Charles Coffin, *The Life and Services of Major General John Thomas* (New York: Egbert, Hovey & King, 1844).

46. Schuyler to Thomas, letter dated March 29, 1776. General John Thomas papers, Massachusetts Historical Society, Boston.

47. Ward, *War of the Revolution*, Vol. 1, 196.

48. Quoted in William Y. Thompson, *Israel Shreve, Revolutionary War Officer* (Ruston, LA: McGinty Trust Fund Publications, 1979), 10.

49. Smith, *Our Struggle for the Fourteenth Colony*, Vol. 2, p. 299–300.

50. Coffin, *John Thomas*, 30.

51. Schuyler to Continental Congress, April 2, 1776. *NDAR*, 4: 626.

52. Daniel Kimball, "Journal, February 8, 1776 – May 27, 1776," Revolutionary War Pension File, M804, Roll 1483, 543–559, National Archives and Records Administration, Washington DC, Microfilm Copy at David Library of the American Revolution, Washington's Crossing, PA.

53. Schuyler to Continental Congress, April 12, 1776. *NDAR*, 4: 786–787.

54. Carroll, *Dear Papa, Dear Charley*, Vol. 2, 888.

55. Wilson, *Benedict Arnold, A Traitor In Our Midst*, 119.

56. Quoted in Ellen Hart Smith, *Charles Carroll of Carrollton* (Cambridge, MA: Harvard University Press, 1942), 137–138.

57. Kate Mason Rowland, *The Life of Charles Carroll of Carrollton, 1737–1823 With His Correspondence and Public Papers*. 2 volumes (New York: Knickerbocker Press, 1897), Vol. 1, 145.

58. Quoted in Annabelle M. Melville, *John Carroll of Baltimore, Founder of the American Catholic Hierarchy* (New York: Charles Scribner's Sons, 1955), 44.

59. Quoted in Randall, *Benedict Arnold*, 228.

60. Jenks, Diary.

61. Rowland, *The Life of Charles Carroll of Carrollton*, Vol. 1, 392–393.

62. Wilson, *Benedict Arnold, A Traitor In Our Midst*, 119–120.

63. Coffin, *John Thomas*, 25.

64. Senter, "Journal," in Roberts, *March to Quebec*, 238.

65. Commissioners to Congress, May 1, 1776. *NDAR*, 4: 1354–1355.

66. Becker, "Smallpox in Washington's Army," 415–416.

67. Jones, *The Campaign for the Conquest of Canada*, 41.

68. "Journal of HM Sloop Hunter, Captain Thomas Mackenzie," *NDAR*, 4:744.

69. Caldwell, *The Invasion of Canada*, 16.

70. Ainslee, *Journal of the Most Remarkable Occurrences*, 81–82.

71. Lieutenant John Shreve, 2nd Continental Regiment, "Personal Narrative of the Services of Lieutenant John Shreve of the New Jersey Line of the Continental Army," *Magazine of American History* III (1879), 566.

72. "Journal of Henry Dearborn," *NDAR*, 4: 1402.

73. Senter, "Journal," in Roberts, *March to Quebec*, 238.

74. Anonymous, *Journal of the Most Remarkable Occurrences*, 153.

75. Anonymous artillery officer [Jones], *Journal of the Siege*, 50.

76. Quoted in Thompson, *Israel Shreve*, 13.

77. Samuel Hodginkson, "Before Quebec, 1776, Letter of Samuel Hodginkson to his Parents, Camp Before Quebec, April 27, 1776." *Pennsylvania Magazine of History and Biography* 10 (1886), 160–161.

78. Thomas to Commissioners in Canada, May 7, 1776. *NDAR*, 4: 1433.

79. Ward, *The War of the Revolution*, Vol. 1, p. 196.

80. Smith, *Our Struggle for the Fourteenth Colony*, Vol. 2, 317.

Chapter 3

1. Commissioners to Congress, May 6, 1776, *NDAR*, 4: 1417.

2. Senter, "Journal," in Roberts, *March to Quebec*, 238.

3. *NDAR*, 4:1413.

4. Anonymous, "Public Diary, April to May 1776," in *Literary and Historical Society of Quebec Transactions* 22 (1898): 49.

5. Thomas to Commissioners, May 7, 1776, *NDAR*, 4: 1435.

6. Artillery Officer (Jones), "Journal of the Siege," 99.
7. Ainslee, "Journal of the Most Remarkable Occurrences," 82–83.
8. Patrick Daly, "Journal of the Siege and Blockade of Quebec," 25.
9. Anonymous, "Public Diary," 49.
10. Morgan Appleton, ed., "The Diary of Colonel Elisha Porter of Hadley, Massachusetts: Touching His March to the Relief of the Continental Forces Before Quebec, 1776," *Magazine of American History* 30 (1893): 192–193.
11. Ibid., 193.
12. Smith, *Our Struggle for the Fourteenth Colony*, 2: 320.
13. Ives, "Uriah Cross," 291.
14. Quoted in Bellico, *Sails and Steam in the Mountains*, 121.
15. Rowland, *The Life of Charles Carroll*, 1: 393.
16. For confirmation, refer to Arnold to Washington, May 8, 1776, *NDAR*, 4: 1456.
17. Senter, "Journal," in Roberts, *March to Quebec*, 238–239.
18. "Journal of HMS *Surprise*," *NDAR*, 4: 1432–1433.
19. Cohn, Valcour Bay Research Project, 22.
20. Rowland, *The Life of Charles Carroll of Carrollton*, 1: 375.
21. Schuyler to Continental Congress, March 19, 1776, *NDAR*, 4: 409.
22. Schuyler to Washington, April 27, 1776, *NDAR*, 4: 1284–1285.
23. Schuyler to Continental Congress, May 3, 1776, *NDAR*, 4: 1392.
24. Frederic R. Kirkland, ed., "Journal of Dr. Lewis Beebe, A Physician on the Expedition Against Canada, 1776," *The Pennsylvania Magazine of History and Biography* 59, no. 4 (October 1935): 325–326.
25. Lieutenant Benjamin Beal, Greaton's 24th Continental Regiment (Massachusetts), "Journal, July- October 1776," American Antiquarian Society, Worcester, MA.
26. "Diary of Colonel Elisha Porter," 193–194.
27. Sergeant Timothy Tuttle, 1st New Jersey Continental Regiment, "Diary, December 21, 1775 — November 5, 1776," New Jersey Historical Society, Newark, NJ.
28. Dr. Joseph F. Meany, "Batteaux and Battoe Men: An American Colonial Response to the Problems of Logistics in Mountain Warfare," Accessed December 15, 2000, at http://www.dmna.state.ny.us/historic/bateau.html.
29. Reverend Ammi. R. Robbins, *Journal of the Rev. Ammi R. Robbins, A Chaplain in the American Army, in the Northern Campaign of 1776* (New Haven, CT: B.L. Hamlen, 1850), 18.
30. Quoted in Thompson, *Israel Shreve*, 14.
31. Lesser, *The Sinews of Independence*, 22.
32. "Diary of Colonel Elisha Porter," 193.
33. Thomas to Commissioners, *NDAR*, 4: 1435.
34. Rowland, *Life of Charles Carroll of Carrollton*, 1: 393.
35. William B. Willcox, ed., *The Papers of Benjamin Franklin* (New Haven, CT: Yale University Press, 1982), 22: 440.
36. Artillery Officer (Jones), "Journal of the Siege," 99.
37. Beal, "Journal."
38. "Diary of Colonel Elisha Porter," 193, 194.
39. Arnold to Washington, *NDAR*, 4: 1455–1456.
40. General Sir Guy Carleton, " Proclamation, Quebec, May 10, 1776," Frederick Mackenzie Papers, William L. Clements Library, University of Michigan, Ann Arbor, MI.

Chapter 4

1. J. Clarence Webster, *The Journal of Jeffery Amherst, Recording the Military Career of General Amherst in America from 1758 to 1763* (Chicago: University of Chicago Press, 1931), 244.
2. There has been no recent scholarship on the engagement at the Cedars. The most useful secondary sources are Edgar Aldrich, "The Affair of the Cedars and the Service of Colonel Timothy Bedel in the War of the Revolution," *The Proceedings of the New Hampshire Historical Society* 3 (December 1891): 194–231; S.E. Dawson, "The Massacre at the Cedars," *Canadian Monthly* (April 1874): 1–15; and William Kingsford, *The History of Canada* (Toronto: Rowsell & Hutchison, 1893), 6: 46–64.
3. Dawson, "The Massacre at the Cedars," 8; and G.P. Browne, *The St. Lawrence River: Historical, Legendary, Picturesque* (New York and London: G.P. Putnam's Sons, Knickerbocker Press, 1905).
4. James Wilkinson, *Memoirs of My Own Times* (Philadelphia: Abraham Small, 1816), 1: 45.
5. "Colonel Bedel's Defense," in Isaac W. Hammond, ed., *Papers of the State of New Hampshire, Part I, Rolls and Documents Relating to Soldiers in the Revolutionary War*. Vol. 4 of the *War Rolls* (Manchester, New Hampshire: John B. Clarke, Public Printer, 1889), 57–59.
6. Oswegatchie is now Ogdensburg, New York.
7. Lieutenant Andrew Parke, *An Authentic Narrative of Facts Relating to the Exchange of Prisoners Taken at the Cedars* (London: T. Cadell, 1777), 21–22; and Peter Aichinger, ed. and trans., *At War With the Americans: The Journal of Claude-Nicholas-Guillaume de Lorimier* (Victoria, BC: Press Porcepic, n.d.). Parke's narrative is the only British primary source account, and de Lorimier's *Journal* is the only Canadian primary source of this engagement that could be located.
8. Private Benjamin Stevens, Colonel Charles Burrall's Regiment of Connecticut Militia, "Diary of Diary of Benjamin Stevens of Canaan, Connecticut," *Daughters of American Revolution Magazine* 45 (August 1914): 138.
9. "Colonel Bedel's Defense."
10. De Lorimier, *Journal*, 51–52.
11. "Diary of Benjamin Stevens," 138.
12. De Lorimier, *Journal*, 52; Letter from Captain Edward P. Williams to his uncle, Colonel Joseph Williams, Skenesborough, August 27, 1776, Library of the Society of Cincinnatus, Washington, DC; Parke, *An Authentic Narrative*, 24.
13. Dawson, "Massacre at the Cedars," 9; Isaac J. Greenwood, *The Revolutionary Services of John Greenwood of Boston and New York 1775–1783* (New York: De Vinne, 1922), 26.
14. Parke, *An Authentic Narrative*, 24; "Petition from some of the Sufferers by the Surrender at the Cedars, May 19, 1776," in Isaac W. Hammond, ed.,

State of New Hampshire Rolls of the Soldiers in the Revolutionary War, 1775 to May 1777 (Concord, NH: Parsons B. Cogswell, State Printer, 1885), 1: 477.

15. "Diary of Benjamin Stevens," 139; Parke, *An Authentic Narrative*, 25, 28–29.

16. De Lorimier, *Journal*, 53.

17. Parke, *An Authentic Narrative*, 26.

18. William Chamberlin, "Letter of General William Chamberlin," *Proceedings of the Massachusetts Historical Society* 10, 2nd ser. (1896): 497.

19. "Diary of Benjamin Stevens," 139; "Petition from some of the Sufferers by the Surrender at the Cedars, May 19, 1776."

20. Greenwood, *The Revolutionary Services of John Greenwood*, 27; Kingsford, *The History of Canada*, I: 48–49; De Lorimier, *Journal*, 54.

21. Ibid., 54–55.

22. Dawson, "Massacre at the Cedars," 9.; Parke, *An Authentic Narrative*, 28–29.

23. Reported by Wilkinson to be a magazine, most likely a strong stone warehouse or similar structure. Wilkinson, *Memoirs*, 41. Also see Kingsford, *The History of Canada*, 1: 53.

24. Wilkinson, *Memoirs*, 41–42; Parke, *An Authentic Narrative*, 30.; Lesser, *The Sinews of Independence*, 22.

25. Parke, *An Authentic Narrative*, 30–31.

26. Ibid., 36.; De Lorimier, *Journal*, 56.

27. Greenwood, *The Revolutionary Services of John Greenwood*, 31–32.; Wilkinson, *Memoirs*, 45–46; De Lorimier, *Journal*, 57.

28. The terms of this convention, this first use of Native American warriors by the British, and the treatment of the American prisoners would subsequently become a source of controversy. Although not without interest, these arguments are more political than military in nature, and are outside the purview of this treatise.

29. Both Bedel and Butterfield were subsequently court-martialed and cashiered from the Continental army. Sherburne, whose faults were exclusively tactical, continued to serve honorably.

30. Williams, Letter.

31. One Canadian historian has noted: "The event itself is utterly unimportant; it was without significance and led to no result." Kingsford, *The History of Canada*, 1: 64.

Chapter 5

1. Rowland, *The Life of Charles Carroll of Carrollton*, 1: 395–397.

2. Kirkland, ed., "Journal of Dr. Lewis Beebe," 327.

3. *The Papers of Benjamin Franklin*, 22: 420.

4. Thomas Papers.

5. *The Papers of Benjamin Franklin*, 22: 432.

6. Bloodgood, *The Sexagenary*, 37.

7. Commissioners of Congress to Schuyler, May 11, 1776, in *NDAR*, 5:42–43.

8. Lacy, "Memoirs of Brigadier General John Lacy," 345–346.

9. Schuyler to Washington, May 10, 1776, *NDAR*, 5:31.

10. Information on this chain provided by Douglas R. Cubbison, *Historic Structures Report, The Hudson River Defenses at Fortress West Point, 1778–1783* (West Point, NY: Directorate of Housing and Public Works, U.S. Military Academy, January 2005), 20–21.

11. General John Thomas Papers, Reel 3- 1776 Letterbooks, Massachusetts Historical Society, Microfilm copy at David Library of the American Revolution, Washington Crossing, PA.

12. General John Thomas Papers.

13. 14. Peter F. Copeland, "Clothing of the Fourth Pennsylvania Battalion, 1776–1777," *Military Collector and Historian* 28 (Fall 1966): 69–70.

15. Captain John Lacey, "Memoirs of Brigadier General John Lacey of Pennsylvania," *The Pennsylvania Magazine of History and Biography* 25, no. 1 (1901): 194.

16. Bloodgood, *The Sexagenary*, 39–40, 42.

17. Joseph Vose, "A Journal of Lieutenant Colonel Joseph Vose, Written During the Expedition Against Canada, from 26 April to 2 July, 1776," *Publications of the Colonial Society of Massachusetts, Transactions, 1900–1902.* Boston: Published by the Society, 1905). Volume 3, 11; Beal, Journal.

18. Robbins, *Journal of the Reverend Ammi Robbins*, 13; Tuttle, "Diary."

19. Rowland, *The Life of Charles Carroll of Carrollton*, 1: 396–397.

20. *Journal of the Reverend Robbins*, 14.

21. Although Sullivan's 1779 Campaign against the Iroquois Indians in New York State has been widely documented, biographies of Sullivan are limited. A succinct biography is Charles P. Whittemore, "John Sullivan: Luckless Irishman" in Billias, ed., *George Washington's Generals*, 137–162. Other biographies are Thomas C. Amory, *Military Services and Public Life of Major General John Sullivan of the American Revolutionary Army* (Boston: Wiggin and Lunt, 1863; reprint ed., Port Washington, NY: Kennikat Press, 1968); and Charles P. Whittemore, *A General of the Revolution: John Sullivan of New Hampshire* (New York and London: Columbia University Press, 1961).

22. Sullivan, letter dated September 5, 1774, in "Catholics and the American Revolution," *The American Catholic Historical Researches* New Series, Vol. 3 (July 1907), 206.

23. "Diary of Colonel Elisha Porter," 195.

24. *Journal of the Reverend Robbins*, 15–16.

25. Public Letters of General David Wooster.

26. Lesser, *Sinews of Independence*, 22.

27. Ibid.

28. Melville, *John Carroll of Baltimore*, 47.

29. Rowland, *The Life of Charles Carroll of Carrollton*, 1: 397.

30. K.G. Davies, ed., *Documents of the American Revolution, 1770–1783, Colonial Office Series* (Irish University Press, 1976), 12: 145, 152.

31. Thomas Anburey, *Travels Through the Interior Parts of America* (London: 1798), 1: 96–99.

32. Colonel Thatcher T.P. Luquer, ed., "Journal from New York to Canada 1767," *New York State Historical Association Proceedings* 30 (1932): 310.

33. There has never been a published secondary account focused on the Battle of Three Rivers. The most detailed account, although considerably romanticized and embellished, is in Justin H. Smith, *Our Struggle for the Fourteenth Colony* (1907; reprint ed., Cranbury, NJ: The Scholar's Bookshelf, 2005), 2: 402–417.

34. Smith, *Our Struggle for the Fourteenth Colony*, 2: 404.

35. Arthur St. Clair Papers, Ohio Historical Society, Columbus, Ohio.

36. Colonel William Irvine, "General Irvine's Jour-

nal of the Canadian Campaign, 1776," *Historical Magazine* 6 (April 1862), 115–117.
37. Lacey, "Memoirs of Brigadier General John Lacey," 200–201.
38. Charles J. Stille, *Major General Anthony Wayne and the Pennsylvania Line in the Continental Army* (1893; reprint ed., Port Washington, NY: Kennikat Press, 1968), 29–31.
39. Quoted in Allan G. Crist, *William Thompson: A Shooting Star* (Cumberland County Historical Society and Museum, 1976), 31–32.
40. Elizabeth Cornetti, ed., *The American Journals of Lieutenant John Enys* (Syracuse, NY: Syracuse University Press, 1976), 13–14.
41. Lieutenant John Shreve, "Personal Narrative of the Services of Lieutenant John Shreve of the New Jersey Line of the Continental Army," *Magazine of American History* 3 (1879): 565.
42. Shreve, "Personal Narrative of the Services of Lieutenant John Shreve," 565.
43. Crist, *William Thompson*, 34.
44. Ward, *The War of the Revolution*, I: 200.
45. General Carl Von Clausewitz, *On War*, Michael Howard and Peter Paret, eds. and trans. (New York: Alfred P. Knopf, 1973 Everyman's Library Edition), 325–328.
46. Burgoyne to Clinton, July 7, 1776, in Clinton Papers, William L. Clements Library, University of Michigan, Ann Arbor, MI.

Chapter 6

1. Copeland, "Clothing of the 4th Pennsylvania Battalion," 70.
2. Arnold to Gates, May 31, 1776, Major General Horatio Gates Papers (New York Historical Society, New York, NY. Microfilm copy at U.S. Military Academy Library, U.S. Military Academy, West Point, NY).
3. Lacey, "Memoirs of Brigadier General John Lacey," 201–202.
4. E.L. Caldwell, "Fort St. Jean on the Richelieu River," *The Bulletin of the Fort Ticonderoga Museum* 4, no. 7 (July 1938): 5–18; Gisèle Piédalue, "Fort Saint-Jean," Research Bulletin 207 (Quebec, Canada: History and Archaeology, Parks Canada, November 1983).
5. Pierre Nadon, *Fort Chambly: A Narrative History* (Ottawa, Canada: National Historic Sites Service, Department of Indian Affairs and Northern Development, 1965), 34, 67.
6. Sullivan to Schuyler, June 19, 1776, in *NDAR*, 5: 613.
7. Donald B. Webster, "Grenades at Fort Senneville," *Arms Collecting* 32, no. 3 (August 1994): 94–95.
8. Isaac J. Greenwood, *The Revolutionary Services of John Greenwood of Boston and New York 1775–1783* (New York: De Vinne, 1922), 35.
9. Thomas C. Amory, *Military Services and Public Life of Major General John Sullivan of the American Revolutionary Army* (Boston: Wiggin and Lunt, 1863; reprint ed., Port Washington, NY: Kennikat Press, 1968), 300–301.
10. Lacy, "The Memoirs of Brigadier General John Lacy," 202.
11. John Austin Stevens, "Ebenezer Stevens, Lieutenant Colonel of Artillery in the Continental Army," *The Magazine of American History* 1 (1877): 594–595.

12. Captain Charles Cushing, "Journal of the Retreat from Canada under General Sullivan, 1776," manuscript copy by Henry Steven, Jr., 1845 (Library of Congress, Washington, DC).
13. Bayze Wells, "Journal of Bayze Wells," *Connecticut Historical Society Collections* 7 (Hartford: 1899), 267.
14. "Ebenezer Stevens," 595.
15. Greenwood, *The Revolutionary War Services of John Greenwood*, 35–36.
16. *Memoirs by General Wilkinson*, 1: 54–55.
17. John Trumbull, *Autobiography, Reminiscences and Letters of John Trumbull, From 1756 to 1841* (New Haven, CT: B.L. Hamlen, 1841), 299–300.
18. "Journal of Bayze Wells," 266–267.
19. Cushing, "Journal."
20. Quoted in James T. Flexner, *Doctors on Horseback: Pioneers of American Medicine* (New York: Viking Press, 1937), 33.
21. *The Papers of Benjamin Franklin*, 22: 420.
22. Information on the shortages of pharmaceutical medicine is primarily provided through the meticulous research of George Griffenhagen, of the American Pharmaceutical Association. George B. Griffenhagen, *Drug Supplies in the American Revolution* (Washington, DC: Smithsonian Institution, Contributions from the Museum of History and Technology Bulletin 225, Paper 16), 110–133; Griffenhagen, "Medicines in the American Revolution," in George A. Bender and John Parascandola, eds., *American Pharmacy in the Colonial and Revolutionary Periods* (Madison, WI: American Institute of the History of Pharmacy, 1977). 25–36; and Griffenhagen, "The Evolution of the Medical Chest," *The Antiques Dealer* 26 (October 1974): 34.
23. Quoted in Duncan, *Medical Men in the American Revolution*, 97.
24. Reverend James Freeman, "Record of the Services of Constant Freeman, Captain of Artillery in the Continental Army," *The Magazine of American History* 2 (1878): 351.
25. Griffenhagen, *Drug Supplies in the American Revolution*, 112–113.
26. Blanco, "Military Medicine," 44.
27. Kirkland, ed., "Journal of Dr. Lewis Beebe," 335–336.
28. Lacey, "Memoirs of Brigadier General John Lacey of Pennsylvania," 203–204.
29. Hammond, *The Letters and Papers of Major General John Sullivan*, 1: 274.
30. Otis G., Hammond, ed., *Letters and Papers of Major General John Sullivan Continental Army*, (Concord, NH: New Hampshire Historical Society, 1930), 1: 257–258, 261.
31. Lacey, "Memoirs of Brigadier General John Lacey of Pennsylvania," 205–206.
32. Colonel Frye Bailey, "Colonel Frye Bailey's Reminiscences," *Proceedings of the Vermont Historical Society* (1923–1925): 39–40.
33. Lacey, "Memoirs of Brigadier General John Lacey of Pennsylvania," 206.
34. Greenwood, *Revolutionary Services of John Greenwood*, 36–37.
35. Grant, "Journal from New York to Canada, 1767," 319.
36. Quoted in E. Eugene Barker, "The Lost Cannon of Crown Point," *Journal of the Company of Military Historians* 26 (Fall 1974): 159.
37. Williams, Letter.

38. Information on Crown Point provided by two archaeological reports: Paul Huey, "The History and Archaeology of Crown Point," *Fortress* 5 (May 1990): 44–54; and Lois M. Feister, *Archaeological Excavations at the Crown Point Soldiers Barracks, 1976 and 1977* (Peebles Island: New York State Office of Parks, Recreation and Historic Preservation, 1998). The New York State Office Of Parks, Recreation and Historic Preservation, which operates Crown Point as a New York State Historic Site, has performed extensive archaeology at Crown Point and has amassed considerable information on the site.

39. "Record of the Services of Constant Freeman," 351.

40. Kirkland, ed., "Journal of Dr. Lewis Beebe," 336–337.

41. David B. Davis, ed., "Medicine in the Canadian Campaign of the Revolutionary War: The Journal of Doctor Samuel Fisk Merrick," *Bulletin of the History of Medicine* 44 (September–October 1970): 468.

42. Vernon A. Ives, ed., "Narrative of Uriah Cross in the Revolutionary War," *New York History* 63, no. 3 (July 1982): 292.

43. Quartermaster John Harper, Wayne's 4th Pennsylvania Battalion, "Short Account of His Journey from Philadelphia in the Year 1776," (Fort Ticonderoga Museum), 7.

44. Risch, *Supplying Washington's Army*, 379.

45. Quoted in G. William Glidden, "Prelude to Saratoga" (Unpublished Paper, 1991. Fort Ticonderoga Museum, Ticonderoga, NY).

46. Ibid.

47. Theodore Sizer, ed., *The Autobiography of Colonel John Trumbull, Patriot-Artist, 1756–1843* (1841; revised ed., New Haven, CT: Yale University Press, 1953), 27–28.

48. Quoted in Amory, *The Military Services of Major General John Sullivan*, 300–301.

49. Kirkland, ed., "Journal of Dr. Lewis Beebe," 339.

50. John Adams to Gates, June 18, 1776, Gates Papers.

51. Gates biographical information is provided by five principal sources: George A. Billias, "Horatio Gates: Professional Soldier," in Billias, ed., *George Washington's Generals*, 79–108; Max M. Mintz, *The Generals of Saratoga: John Burgoyne & Horatio Gates* (New Haven, CT: Yale University Press, 1990); Samuel W. Patterson, *Horatio Gates: Defender of American Liberties* (New York: Columbia University Press, 1941); Paul D. Nelson, *General Horatio Gates: A Biography* (Baton Rouge: Louisiana State University Press, 1976); and Edward W. Stitt, Jr., "Horatio Gates," *The Bulletin of the Fort Ticonderoga Museum* 9, no. 2 (Winter 1953): 93–115.

52. Ward, *The War of the Revolution*, 2: 500.

53. Isaac Pierce to "Conductor of Military Stores" July 18, 1776, in Gates, Papers.

54. Vernon, "Orderly Book, Captain Frazer's Company, 4th Pennsylvania Battalion."

55. Bernhard Knollenberg, "Correspondence of John Adams and Horatio Gates," *Proceedings of the Massachusetts Historical Society, October 1941– May 1944*, 67 (Boston: Massachusetts Historical Society, 1945), 135–151.

56. Billias, "Horatio Gates," 85.

57. *NDAR*, 5:961.

58. Gates, Letter to Moses More, Ticonderoga, July 12, 1776, Gates Papers.

59. "Diary of John Harper," 7.

60. Gates to Washington, July 29, 1776, Gates Papers.

61. For a discussion of this totally inconsequential affair, refer to Mintz, *The Generals of Saratoga*, 98–100.

62. Wilkinson, *Memoirs by General Wilkinson*, 1: 62.

63. This iron chain mentioned by de Woedtke was in fact evacuated to Fort Ticonderoga, and subsequently transferred to Poughkeepsie to obstruct the southern reaches of the Hudson River.

64. *The Papers of Benjamin Franklin*, 22: 496–499. The translation was generously provided by my good friend, Dr. Walter L. Powell of Gettysburg, PA, and his son, Nathaniel Powell.

65. Ibid., 22: 500–501.

66. Hammond, *Letters and Papers of John Sullivan*, 1: 280–281.

67. Gates Papers.

68. Again, for a discussion of this insignificant affair, refer to Mintz, *The Generals of Saratoga*, 100–101.

69. Grant, "Journal from New York to Canada, 1767," 319–320.

70. Bloodgood, *The Sexagenary*, 36–37.

71. Williams, Letter.

72. Information on Potts is provided by the following sources: Edward D. Neill, "Biographical Sketch of Doctor Jonathan Potts," *The New England Historical and Genealogical Register* 18 (1864): 21–36; Richard L. Blanco, *Physician of the American Revolution, Jonathan Potts* (New York: 1979); Isabella James [Mrs. Thomas Potts James], *Memorial Of Thomas Potts, Junior, Who Settled in Pennsylvania; With An Historic-Genealogical Account of His Descendants to the Eighth Generation* (Cambridge: Privately Printed, 1874, accessed December 29, 2003, at http://www.heritagepursuit.com/Potts/PottsM.htm); and John W. Krueger, *Gentleman of Zeal and Character in the Public Service: Doctor Jonathan Potts and the Northern Medical Department* (master's thesis, University of Vermont, 1974).

73. Quoted in Griffenhagen, *Drug Supplies in the American Revolution*, 118.

74. Quoted in Neill, "Biographical Sketch of Doctor Jonathan Potts," 21–22, 25.

75. Davis, "Medicine in the Canadian Campaign of the Revolutionary War," 468–469.

76. Ibid.

77. Bloodgood, *The Sexagenary*, 25–26.

78. Grant, "Journal from New York to Canada, 1767," 321.

79. Brigadier General Horatio Rogers, ed., *Hadden's Journal and Orderly Books: A Journal Kept in Canada and Upon Burgoyne's Campaign in 1776 and 1777 by Lieutenant James M. Hadden, Royal Artillery* (1884; reprint ed., Boston: Gregg Press, 1972), 107.

80. Stringer to Gates, Fort George, July 24, 1776, in Gates Papers.

81. James, *Memorial of Thomas Potts*.

82. Kirkland, Editor, "Journal of Dr. Lewis Beebe," 345.

83. Quoted in Duncan, "Medical Men in American Revolution," 102.

84. Kirkland, Editor, "Journal of Dr. Lewis Beebe," 344.

85. Blanco, *Physician of the American Revolution*, 102.

86. Knollenberg, "Correspondence of John Adams and Horatio Gates," 143.

87. Sizer, *John Trumbull*, 27–28.

88. Kirkland, ed., "The Journal of Dr. Lewis Beebe," 344.
89. Frazer, "Some Extracts from the Papers of General Persifor Frazer," 313.
90. Frazer, "Letters from Ticonderoga 1776," 388, 390.
91. "Lt. Benjamin Beale Journal," July 5 and 6, 1776.
92. Quoted in Gillett, *The Army Medical Department, 1775–1818*, 60.

Chapter 7

1. Matt B. Jones, ed., "Revolutionary Correspondence of Governor Nicholas Cooke, 1775–1781," in *Proceedings of the American Antiquarian Society at the Annual Meetings Held in Boston, October 20, 1926*. New Series, Vol. 36, Part 2 (Worcester, MA: Published by the Society, 1927), 332–334.
2. Lesser, *The Sinews of Independence*, 25.
3. Cushing, "Journal of the Retreat from Canada under General Sullivan, 1776."
4. Vernon, "Orderly Book, Captain Frazer's Company, 4th Pennsylvania Battalion."
5. "Orderly Book, Brigadier General Brickett's Militia Brigade, Fort Ticonderoga, August 14 1776 – November 17, 1776," New York Public Library.
6. "Orderly Book, Colonel Wigglesworth's Regiment."
7. "Orderly Book, Brigadier General Brickett's Militia Brigade."
8. Amelia Forbes Emerson, ed., *The Diaries and Letters of [Reverend] William Emerson, 1743–1776* (Boston: Thomas Todd, 1972), 109.
9. Sergeant Edward Vernon, "Orderly Book, Captain Frazer's Company, 4th Pennsylvania Battalion, May 30, 1776 – August 26, 1776." Fort Ticonderoga Museum, Ticonderoga, NY.
10. "Orderly Book, Colonel Ephraim Wheelock's Regiment of Massachusetts Militia, Fort Ticonderoga, August 18, 1776 – November 26, 1776." Fort Ticonderoga Museum, Ticonderoga, NY.
11. "Orderly Book, 2d (St.Clair's/Wood's) Pennsylvania Battalion, February 22, 1776 – September 11, 1776." National Archives and Records Administration. Microfilm Copy, USMA Library, West Point, NY.
12. Colonel Anthony Wayne, "The Wayne Orderly Books." *Bulletin of the Fort Ticonderoga Museum* 11 (1963): 182.
13. For an excellent discourse on ration preparation in armies during this timeframe, refer to Gregory Theberge, "To Nourish His Majesty's Troops: The Mess, Kitchens and Provisions for the Common British Soldier During the American War for Independence" *The Brigade Dispatch* 30, no. 1 (Spring 2000): 2–15.
14. Vernon. "Orderly Book, Captain Frazer's Company, 4th Pennsylvania Battalion."
15. "Orderly Book, Colonel Ephraim Wheelock's Regiment of Massachusetts Militia, Fort Ticonderoga, August 18 1776 – November 26 1776." Fort Ticonderoga Museum, Ticonderoga, NY.
16. Vernon. "Orderly Book, Captain Frazer's Company, 4th Pennsylvania Battalion."
17. *Orderly book of Capt. Ichabod Norton of Colonel Mott's regiment of Connecticut troops destined for the northern campaign in 1776 at Skeensborough (now Whitehall), Fort Ann and Ticonderoga, N.Y., and at Mount Independence, Vt.: together with a fac similie of Captain Norton's map of Ticonderoga and Mount Independence, with introduction by Robert O. Bascom* (Fort Edward, NY: Keating & Barnard, 1898), 11.
18. Dr. Samuel Kennedy, surgeon, Wayne's Pennsylvania Battalion, "Letters from Dr. Samuel Kennedy to his Wife in 1776," *The Pennsylvania Magazine of History and Biography* 8 (1884): 116.
19. William Chamberlin, "Letter of General William Chamberlin," *Proceedings of the Massachusetts Historical Society* 10, 2nd Series (1896): 499.
20. Robbins, *Journal of the Reverend Ammi Robbins*, 43.
21. Blanco, *Physician of the American Revolution*, 96.
22. Quoted in Duncan, *Medical Men in the American Revolution*, 110.
23. "Orderly Book, Fort George Garrison Orders, July 10, 1776 – August 19, 1776," New York Historical Society. Published as Appendix in B.F. DeCosta, *Notes on the history of Fort George during the colonial and revolutionary periods, with contemporaneous documents and an appendix* (New York: J. Sabin & Sons, 1871), 66.
24. Jeannette D. Black and William Greene Roelker, eds., *A Rhode Island Chaplain in the Revolution, Letters of Ebenezer David to Nicholas Brown, 1775–1778* (Providence: The Rhode Island Society of Cincinnati, 1949), 26–27.
25. Quoted in Peter F. Copeland, "Clothing of the Fourth Pennsylvania Battalion, 1776–1777," *Military Collector and Historian* 18 (Fall 1966), 70.
26. Mary C. Gillett, *The Army Medical Department, 1775–1818* (Washington, DC: The Center of Military History, United States Army, 2004), 61.
27. "Orderly Book, Fort George Garrison Orders, July 10, 1776 – August 19, 1776," 65.
28. Vernon, "Orderly Book, Captain Frazer's Company, 4th Pennsylvania Battalion."
29. Vernon, "Orderly Book, Captain Frazer's Company, 4th Pennsylvania Battalion"; Salsig, ed., *Parole: Quebec, Countersign: Ticonderoga*, 213.
30. Gates to Schuyler, Ticonderoga, September 6, 1776, in Gates, Papers.
31. Numerous examples are contained within the Gates Papers. For examples, see Reverend Bulkley Olcott to Gates, Fort No. 4, August 26, 1776, and Samuel Hunt, Committee of Safety, Fort No. 4, August 26, 1776, in Gates, Papers.
32. A particularly good account of the Fort George General Hospital can be found in Gillett, *The Army Medical Department, 1775–1818*, 60–65.
33. Potts to Gates, Fort George, August 8, 1776, in Gates Papers.
34. James, *Memorial of Thomas Potts*.
35. "Orderly Book, Colonel Wigglesworth's Regiment of Massachusetts Militia, Fort Ticonderoga and Mount Independence, July 30, 1776 – November 23, 1776," Huntington Library, San Marino, CA.
36. Gates to Congressman Egbert Benson, August 22, 1776, in Gates Papers.
37. Blanco, *Physician of the American Revolution*, 102.
38. Griffenhagen, *Drug Supplies in the American Revolution*, 119–120.
39. Quoted in Neill, "Biographical Sketch of Dr. Potts," 28.
40. Blanco, *Physician of the American Revolution*, 98.
41. Albany Committee of Correspondence, *Minutes of the Albany Committee of Correspondence*, 1: 531.

42. Blanco, "Military Medicine," 51.
43. Gates to Washington, Ticonderoga, August 28, 1776, in Gates, Papers.
44. Quoted in James E. Gibson, *Dr. Bodo Otto and the Medical Background of the American Revolution* (Springfield, IL, and Baltimore, MD: Charles C. Thomas, 1937), 98–99.
45. "Orderly Book, Colonel Ephraim Wheelock's Regiment of Massachusetts Militia, Fort Ticonderoga, August 18, 1776 – November 26, 1776," Fort Ticonderoga Museum, Ticonderoga, NY.
46. Morgan Appleton, ed., "The Diary of Colonel Elisha Porter of Hadley, Massachusetts, Touching His March to the Relief of the Continental Forces Before Quebec, 1776," *Magazine of American History* 30 (1893): 200.
47. Kirkland, ed., "The Journal of Dr. Lewis Beebe," 340–341, 343.
48. Reverend Ammi Robbins, *Journal of the Rev. Ammi R. Robbins, A Chaplain in the American Army, in the Northern Campaign of 1776* (New Haven, CT: B.L. Hamlen, 1850), 30.
49. Emerson, *Diaries and Letters of William Emerson*, 112.
50. Quartermaster John Harper, "Short Account of His Journey from Philadelphia in the Year 1776," Fort Ticonderoga Museum.
51. Salsig, ed., *Parole: Quebec, Countersign: Ticonderoga*, 98.
52. Samuel L. Shober, ed., "Arnold and a General Court Martial." *American Historical Record* 3 (November 1874), 444–448.
53. Martin, *Benedict Arnold, Revolutionary Hero*, 243; "Diary of Colonel Elisha Porter," 204.
54. For discussions of this event, refer to Martin, 238–243; and Randall, *Benedict Arnold, Patriot and Traitor*, 262–264. An early Arnold biographer and still one of the best, Willard M. Wallace, devoted an entire chapter to this court-martial. Wallace, *Traitorous Hero*, 99–109.
55. *The Papers of Benjamin Franklin*, 22: 438–439.
56. Paymaster Jonathan Trumbull, Jr., Papers, Connecticut Historical Society. Microfilm copy at David Library of the American Revolution, Washington Crossing, PA.
57. Kirkland, ed., "Journal of Dr. Lewis Beebe," 345.
58. Schuyler to Gates, Albany, September 1, 1776, in Gates, Papers. The men mentioned were "Philadelphia gentlemen," meaning that they had been dispatched by the Continental Congress.
59. Elisha Avery to Gates, Albany, October 15, 1776, in Gates, Papers.
60. "Diary of Colonel Elisha Porter," 201.
61. Vernon, "Orderly Book, Captain Frazer's Company, 4th Pennsylvania Battalion."
62. John H.G. Pell, "A Few Military Manuscripts in the Fort Ticonderoga Museum Library, Anthony Mash: Account and Inventory of Money, Clothing and Goods, September 7, 1776," *The Bulletin of the Fort Ticonderoga Museum* 9, no. 1 (Winter 1952): 28.
63. Quartermaster John Harper, "Quartermaster Records, Wayne's 4th Pennsylvania Battalion, 1776," Fort Ticonderoga Museum, Ticonderoga, NY.
64. Lesser, *The Sinews of Independence*, 30.
65. Florence M. Montgomery, *Textiles in America, 1650–1870* (1984; revised edition New York and London: W.W. Norton, 2007), 188–190.

66. Trumbull's Orderly Book, 94–95.
67. Quoted in Copeland, "Clothing of the 4th Pennsylvania Battalion," 71.
68. Gates to "Commanding Officer at Fort George," Headquarters at Ticonderoga, July 7, 1776, in Gates, Papers.
69. David L. Salay, "The Production of Gunpowder in Pennsylvania During the American Revolution," *The Pennsylvania Magazine of History and Biography* 99, no. 4 (October 1975): 423.
70. Donald E. Reynolds, "Ammunition Supply in Revolutionary Virginia," *The Virginia Magazine of History and Biography* 73 (January 1965): 62–63.
71. Huston, *The Sinews of War, Army Logistics*, 23–24
72. There has been little professional study of gunpowder and associated ordnance supplies of the Continental army during the War of American Independence. Besides the previously referenced works, see Orlando W. Stephenson, "The Supply of Gunpowder in 1776," *American Historical Review* 30 (1925): 271–81; and Risch, *Supplying Washington's Army*, 310–372.
73. Gates to Schuyler, Ticonderoga, September 3, 1776, in Gates, Papers.
74. Salsig, ed., *Parole: Quebec, Countersign: Ticonderoga*, 267; Schuyler to Gates, Albany, October 11, 1776, in Gates, Papers; and Gates to Schuyler, Ticonderoga, October 15, 1776, in *NDAR*, 6:1277.
75. "Orderly Book, Brigadier General Brickett's Militia Brigade."
76. "Orderly Book, Colonel Wigglesworth's Regiment."
77. Baldwin, Journal, 29.
78. Reynolds, "Ammunition Supply in Revolutionary Virginia," 65.
79. O.W. Stephenson, *The Supplies for the American Revolutionary Army* (University of Michigan: Ph.D. diss., 1919), 121.
80. Richard Varick, "Letter to Henry Beekman Livingston, August 6, 1776," Sol Feinstone Collection of the American Revolution, Microfilm, Moore Wing, U.S. Military Academy Library, West Point, NY.
81. For example, during the 2004 archaeological investigations of the 1787 through 1810 era Queensboro Furnace at West Point, NY, of which the author was the government project manager, a 4-pounder cannonball cast on site was unearthed.
82. Baldwin, Journal, 27.
83. Udny Hay, who rose to the rank of Lieutenant Colonel in the Continental Army and served throughout most of the War for American Independence, has been the subject of no serious studies. His only biography, succinct and badly dated, is Helen Wilkinson Reynolds, "Udny Hay" *Dutchess County Historical Society Yearbook* 4 (1925): 49–59.
84. Bloodgood, *The Sexagenary*, 51.
85. Quoted in Risch, *Quartermaster Support of the Army*, 10.
86. Joseph Trumbull passed away at age 41 on July 23, 1778. His untimely death was a great loss to the young nation.
87. Stille, *Major General Anthony Wayne and the Pennsylvania Line*, 35–36.
88. Commissary General Joseph Trumbull, Papers, Connecticut Historical Society. Microfilm copy at David Library of the American Revolution, Washington Crossing, PA.

89. "Orderly Book, Brigadier General Brickett's Militia Brigade."

90. Sergeant Timothy Tuttle, "Diary, December 21, 1775 – November 5, 1776," New Jersey Historical Society, Newark, NJ.

91. The only discussion of Gates' Table of Organization is in two articles by Eric Manders, "Notes on Troop Units in the Northern Army, 1775–1776," *Military Collector and Historian Journal of the Company of Military Historians* 23 (Winter 1971): 117–120; and "Notes on Troop Units in the Northern Army, 1776," *Military Collector and Historian Journal of the Company of Military Historians* 27 (Spring, Fall 1975): 8–12, 113–117.

92. Stevens, "Ebenezer Stevens," 595.

93. Quoted in Colin G. Calloway, *The American Revolution in Indian Country* (Cambridge University Press, 1995), 95.

94. "Orderly Book, Colonel Wigglesworth's Regiment of Massachusetts Militia, Fort Ticonderoga and Mount Independence, July 30, 1776 – November 23, 1776," Huntington Library, San Marino, CA.

95. The best history of the Stockbridge Mohican Nation is Patrick Frazier, *The Mohicans of Stockbridge* (Lincoln: University of Nebraska Press, 1992), 209–211.

96. Tuttle, "Diary."

97. Corporal Ebenezer Wild, "The Journal of Ebenezer Wild, Who Served as Corporal, Sergeant, Ensign and Lieutenant in the American Army of the Revolution" *Massachusetts Historical Society Proceedings* 2nd Series, Vol. 6 (1891), 84.

98. Lesser, *The Sinews of Independence*, 30.

99. Trumbull Orderly Book, 86.

100. Whitcomb, a colorful but sadly neglected figure in the history of the Champlain Valley, has received little attention from historians. An early, but still relevant biography, is George F. Morris, "Major Whitcomb, Ranger and Partisan Leader in the Revolution" in *Proceedings of the New Hampshire Historical Society* (Concord, New Hampshire) Vol. 4, Part 3, 298–321.

101. Lieutenant Benjamin Whitcomb, "A Journal of a Scout from Crown Point to Saint Johns, Chambly, etc., etc. by Lieutenant Benjamin Whitcomb and Four Men," *The American Historical Record* 1 (1872): 437–440.

102. Dugan's Rangers, at best a minor footnote to this campaign, are addressed in David B. Sweet, "Dugan's Canadian Rangers, 1776," *Military Collector & Historian* 28, no. 1 (Spring 1986): 20.

103. British perspectives on this incident are provided by Rogers, ed., *Hadden's Journal and Orderly Books*, 4–5, 236–237.

104. Matthew L. Davis, *Memoirs of Aaron Burr*, 2 vols. (1836–1837).

105. Quoted in Thompson, *Israel Shreve*, 18–19.

106. Colonel Nathan Hale, Letter to Mrs. Abigail Hale, August 12, 1776, Library of Congress, Washington, DC.

Chapter 8

1. Gates to Moses Morse, Ticonderoga, July 12, 1776, in Gates, Papers.

2. John H.G. Pell, "Philip Skene of Skenesborough" *New York State Historical Association Proceedings* 26 (1928): 32.

3. Arthur B. Cohn, et al., *Valcour Bay Research Project, 1999–2004 Results from the Archaeological Investigation of a Revolutionary War Battlefield in Lake Champlain, Clinton County, New York* (Vergennes, VT: Lake Champlain Maritime Museum, 2007), 12, 17–18.

4. Clausewitz, *On War*, 362.

5. "Major General Horatio Gates's Orders to Brigadier General Benedict Arnold," August 7, 1776, in Gates, Papers.

6. Gates, "Instructions for Lieutenant Colonel Hartley, Going Upon Command to Crown Point, Ticonderoga, July 20, 1776," in Gates, Papers.

7. Hartley to Gates, Crown Point, July 21, 1776, in Gates, Papers.

8. Hartley to Gates, Crown Point, July 28, 1776, in Gates, Papers.

9. The origin of the name Coffin Point cannot now be determined, per personal communication with Paul Huey, archaeologist with the New York State Historic Preservation Office.

10. Hartley to Gates, Crown Point, August 14, 1776, in Gates, Papers.

11. Hartley to Gates, Crown Point, September 6, 1776, in Gates, Papers.

12. Hartley to Arnold, Crown Point, September 23, 1776, in Arnold, "Documents sur l'Invasion Americaine," 927–928. The Coffin Point earthworks survive in excellent preservation condition at Crown Point State Campground, but are not interpreted to the public.

13. Hartley to Gates, Crown Point, October 10, 1776, in Gates, Papers.

14. Hartley to Gates, Crown Point, August 25, 1776, in Gates, Papers.

15. Hartley to Gates, Crown Point, August 30, 1776, in Gates, Papers.

16. Gates to Hartley, Ticonderoga, August 31, 1776, in Gates, Papers.

17. Hartley to Gates, Crown Point, September 6, 1776, in Gates, Papers.

18. Gates to Potts, Ticonderoga, October 10, 1776, in Gates, Papers.

19. Colonel John H. Calef, ed., "Extracts from the Diary of a Revolutionary Patriot," *Journal of the Military Service Institution of the United States* 39 (July-August 1906): 123–130.

20. *Diary of a Revolutionary Patriot*, 259

21. Clausewitz, *On War*, 491.

22. Lewis Lochee, *Elements of Field Fortification* (London: T. Cadell and T. Egerton, 1783), 36.

23. For comprehensive information on the 18th century military use of redoubts, refer to Douglas R. Cubbison, *Historic Structures Report: The Redoubts of West Point* (West Point, NY: Directorate of Housing and Public Works, U.S. Military Academy, January 2004).

24. "Journal of Sergeant Timothy Tuttle, 1st New Jersey Regiment, 1775–1776," New Jersey Historical Society, Newark, NJ.

25. Matthew L. Davis, *Memoirs of Aaron Burr*, 2 vols. (1836–1837).

26. "Proceedings of a General Court Martial for the Trial of Major General St. Clair, August 25, 1778," in Collections of the New York Historical Society for the Year 1880 (New York: n.p., 1881); "Journal Kept During An Expedition to Canada in 1776 by Ebenezer Elmer," *Proceedings of the New Jersey Historical Society* 2, no. 4 (1847): 43–44.

27. Lochee, *Elements of Field Fortification*, 36–37.

28. Lieutenant J. C. Pleydell, *An Essay on Field Fortification: Intended Principally for the use of Officers of*

Infantry, showing how to trace out on the ground and construct in the easiest manner, all sorts of Redoubts and other field works, translated from the original manuscript of an officers of experience in the Prussian Service (London: Printed for J. Nourse, Bookseller to His Majesty, 1768; new edition, London: Printed for F. Wingrave, 1790), 20–21.

29. Baldwin, *Journal*, 24.
30. Force, *American Archives*, 5th Series, 2:1970.
31. Baldwin, *Journal*, 18.
32. Sir James Young, *An Essay on the Command of Small Detachments* (London: n.p., 1766), 20 and Figure 5.
33. Baldwin, *Journal*, 17.
34. "Journal Kept During An Expedition to Canada in 1776 by Ebenezer Elmer," 43–44.
35. Emerson, *Diaries and Letters of William Emerson*, 108.
36. Stevens, "Ebenezer Stevens," 595.
37. Sizer, *Life of John Trumbull*, 29.
38. 2nd Lieutenant Ebenezer Elmer, 2nd New Jersey Continental Regiment, "The Lost Pages of Ebenezer Elmer's Revolutionary Journal," *New Jersey Historical Society Proceedings* 10 (1925), 417.
39. Cushing, *Journal*.
40. Lieutenant Henry Sewall, "The Diary of Henry Sewall," *Bulletin of the Fort Ticonderoga Museum* 9 (1963): 79–80.
41. Baldwin, *Journal*, 13.
42. *Orderly book of Capt. Ichabod Norton of Colonel Mott's regiment of Connecticut troops destined for the northern campaign in 1776 at Skeensborough (now Whitehall), Fort Ann and Ticonderoga, N.Y., and at Mount Independence, Vt.: together with a fac simile of Captain Norton's map of Ticonderoga and Mount Independence, with introduction by Robert O. Bascom* (Fort Edward, NY: Keating & Barnard, 1898), 29.
43. Schuyler to Washington, June 17, 1776, quoted in Thomas B. Furcron, "Mount Independence, 1776–1777," *The Bulletin of the Fort Ticonderoga Museum* 9, no. 4 (Winter 1954), 231.
44. "Orderly Book, Fort Ticonderoga Garrison Orders, July 10, 1776 – November 17, 1776," M-2172, Fort Ticonderoga Museum. Also known as Colonel John Trumbull's Orderly Book. Transcription published as "The Deputy Adjutant General's Orderly Book, Ticonderoga, 1776," *The Bulletin of the Fort Ticonderoga Museum* 3, no. 2 (July 1933): 91.
45. Joseph L. and Mable A. Wheeler, *The Mount Independence-Hubbardton 1776 Military Road* (Benson, VT: J.L. Wheeler, 1968), 195.
46. Baldwin, *Journal*, 23.
47. Vernon, "Orderly Book, Captain Frazer's Company, 4th Pennsylvania Battalion."
48. These earthworks are still quite visible, and are currently owned by the Fort Ticonderoga Museum. They are open for visitation during daylight hours, but visitors should be cautioned that they are today overgrown with the greatest quantity of poison ivy that the author has ever seen at any single location.
49. Donald Wickham, "Was There a Blockhouse at Mount Hope?" Research paper prepared for Fort Ticonderoga Museum, July 1993, Fort Ticonderoga Museum.
50. Lesser, *The Sinews of Independence*, 34. Unfortunately, only one primary source for these two regiments has been located, and it contains almost no information on Ticonderoga. Thomas Greaton, Continental Army Soldier with Brewer's Massachusetts Regiment. Revolutionary War Pension File, M804, Roll 1110, Pages 302–325 (National Archives and Records Administration, Washington D.C., Microfilm Copy at David Library of the American Revolution, Washington's Crossing, PA).
51. Sugar Loaf would later become known as Mount Defiance, although that name was not in use in 1776.
52. Sizer, ed., *The Autobiography of Colonel John Trumbull*, 29–31.
53. This scout has recently been evaluated by Ronald F. Kingsley and Harvey J. Alexander, "The Failure of Abercromby's Attack on Fort Carillon, July 1758, and the Scapegoating of Matthew Clerk," *The Journal of Military History* 72 (January 2008): 43–70.
54. Timothy J. Todish, *The Annotated and Illustrated Journals of Major Robert Rogers* (Fleischmanns, NY: Purple Mountain Press, 2002), 155.
55. Following the British occupation of Ticonderoga in July 1777, they in fact constructed and garrisoned just such a blockhouse on what was now known as Mount Defiance.

Chapter 9

1. Colonel John Trumbull, letter dated Ticonderoga, July 12, 1776, *The Bulletin of the Fort Ticonderoga Museum* 6, no. 4 (July 1942): 144–145.
2. The only biography on Skene is Doris Begor Morton, *Philip Skene of Skenesborough* (Granville, New York: Grastorf Press, 1959).
3. Edward G. Farmer, "Skenesborough: Continental Navy Shipyard," *United States Naval Institute Proceedings* 90 (1964): 160–161.
4. Williams, Letter.
5. "The Diary of Henry Sewall," 78.
6. Deputy Quartermaster Harmanus Schuyler, "Letters to Major General Philip Schuyler," Cornell University Archives, New York.
7. Dr. Stephen McCrea, "List of Sick on Board the Fleet," in Gates, Papers.
8. "The Journal of Bayze Wells," 282.
9. Gates to Continental Congress in *NDAR*, 5:1099–1101.
10. Quartermaster Harmanus Schuyler Letters.
11. Trumbull to Arnold, Ticonderoga, 12 September 1776, in Brigadier General Benedict Arnold, "Documents sur l'Invasion Americaine," *La Revue de l'Universite Laval, Quebec* 2 (1947–1948): 845.
12. Quartermaster Harmanus Schuyler Letters.
13. Ibid.
14. Surprisingly, Varick has never been the subject of a biography. The only scholarship on his life, which was never formally published, is John G. Rommel, *Richard Varick, New York Aristocrat* (Ph.D. diss., Columbia University, 1966).
15. Varick to Gates, Albany, August 4, 1776, in Gates, Papers.
16. Varick to Gansevoort, Albany, August 2, 1776, in *NDAR*, 6: 19.
17. Quoted in Lundeberg, *The Gunboat Philadelphia*, 15–16.
18. Varick to Gates, Albany, July 27, 1776, in Gates, Papers.
19. Varick to Harmanus Schuyler, Albany, August 3, 1776, in *NDAR*, 6: 34.

20. Waterbury to Gates, Skenesboro, August 17, 1776, in *NDAR*, 6: 217.
21. Quoted in Dorothy U. Smith, "Historic War Vessels in Lake Champlain and Lake George," *New York State Museum Bulletin* no. 313 (October 1937): 127.
22. Regrettably, the Poughkeepsie Continental Navy shipyard has never been adequately documented by a professional or comprehensive study.
23. Varick to Hughes, Albany, August 3, 1776, in *NDAR*, 6: 35.
24. Varick to Lieutenant [blank], Albany, August 18, 1776, in *NDAR*, 6: 224.
25. Gates to Schuyler, Ticonderoga, September 23, 1776, in *NDAR*, 6: 961.
26. Schuyler, various letters, Albany, September 17, 1776, in *NDAR*, 6: 872–873.
27. Varick to Ensign, Albany, September 23, 1776, in *NDAR*, 6:962.
28. Varick to Hunn, Albany, September 25, 1776, in *NDAR*, 6: 986.
29. Various Letters, Poughkeepsie, September 27, 1776, in *NDAR*, 6: 1035–1036.
30. Schuyler to Hancock, Albany, October 3, 1776, in *NDAR*, 6:1117,
31. Varick to Captain Leonard Van Buren, Albany, August 3, 1776, in *NDAR*, 6: 36.
32. Ibid.
33. Nathaniel Shaw to Captain Samuel Alcott, New London, Connecticut, August 10, 1776, in *NDAR*, 6: 139.
34. Trumbull to John Hancock, Lebanon, August 22, 1776, in *NDAR*, 6: 265.
35. Library of Congress. "George Washington Papers at the Library of Congress, 1741–1799." Accessed on-line at http://memory.loc.gov/ammem/gwhtml/gwhome.html.
36. Quartermaster Harmanus Schuyler Letters.
37. Varick to Schuyler, Albany, August 3, 1776, in *NDAR*, 6: 34.
38. *Orderly book of Capt. Ichabod Norton of Colonel Mott's regiment*, 13.
39. Harmanus Schuyler to General Philip Schuyler, Skensboro, August 10, 1776, in Harmanus Schuyler, Letters.
40. Nathaniel B. Dodge, "A Letter and Diary of 1776," *Vermont History* 21 (January 1953): 34.
41. *NDAR*, 6: 962, 1062
42. Regrettably, only one professional study of the cannon at Ticonderoga and Crown Point has been performed, that by Barker, "The Lost Cannon of Crown Point," which remains the best source on this neglected topic.
43. Bratten, *The Gondola Philadelphia*, 118–119.
44. Barker, "The Lost Cannon of Crown Point," 161, 163.
45. Gates to Schuyler, Ticonderoga, September 23, 1776, in *NDAR*, 6: 961.
46. Baldwin, *Journal*, 18.
47. Nathaniel Buell, Letter to General Philip Schuyler from Mount Independence, December 3, 1776, Fort Ticonderoga Museum.
48. Benjamin Beal, "Journal, July-December 1776," American Antiquarian Society, Worcester, MA.
49. A portion of one of these mortars remains on display at the Fort Ticonderoga Museum, Ticonderoga, NY.
50. Cushing, Journal.
51. Baldwin, "Diary," 13–14.

52. Cannon information provided by Philip K. Lundeberg, *The Gunboat "Philadelphia" and the Defense of Lake Champlain in 1776* (rev. ed. Basin Harbor, VT: Lake Champlain Maritime Museum, 1995), 57–58; Arthur B. Cohn, et al., *Valcour Bay Research Project, 1999–2004 Results from the Archaeological Investigation of a Revolutionary War Battlefield in Lake Champlain, Clinton County, New York* (Vergennes, VT: Lake Champlain Maritime Museum, May 2007), 63–69; John R. Bratten, *The Gondola Philadelphia and the Battle of Lake Champlain* (College Station: Texas A&M University Press, 2002), 113–120.
53. Cohn, *Valcour Bay Research Project, 1999–2004*, 139–149.
54. Scott A. McLaughlin, *History Told From the Depths of Lake Champlain: 1992–1993 Fort Ticonderoga-Mount Independence Submerged Cultural Resource Survey* (Ferrisburgh, VT: Lake Champlain Maritime Museum, 2000), 241–257.
55. Lieutenant Bayze Wells, "Journal of Bayze Wells." *Connecticut Historical Society Collections* 7 (Hartford: N.p. 1899), 267–268.
56. Baldwin, *Journal*, 14.
57. Ian K. Steele, *Betrayals, Fort William Henry & The "Massacre"* (New York: Oxford University Press, 1990), 100, 102, 104, 105, 109.
58. Bratten, *The Gondola Philadelphia*, 113–114.
59. Refer to the author's previous work, Douglas R. Cubbison, *The Artillery Never Gained More Honour, The British Artillery in the 1776 Valcour Island and 1777 Saratoga Campaigns* (Fleischmans, NY: Purple Mountain Press, 2008).
60. "Stores for Galleys Trumbull, Congress and Washington" War Department Collection of Revolutionary War Records, Volume 120, National Archives and Records Collection, Washington, DC. Microfilm copy at U.S. Military Academy Library, West Point, NY.
61. "The Diary of Henry Sewall," 78.
62. John U. Rees, "'To Subsist an Army Well...' Soldiers' Cooking Equipment, Provisions, and Food Preparation During the American War for Independence" *Military Collector & Historian* 53, no. 1 (Spring 2001), 8.
63. Trumbull's Orderly Book, 48.
64. *NDAR*, 6: 139, 182, 335.
65. Lundeberg, *The Gunboat Philadelphia*, 17.
66. "List of Continental Arm'd Vessels on Lake Champlain, August 5th 1776," in Gates, Papers.
67. "Journal of Bayze Wells," 269, 283.
68. Force, *American Archives*, 4th ser., 3: 140.
69. Schuyler to Gates, Albany, August 29, 1776, in Gates, Papers.
70. "Major General Gates Orders to Brigadier General Benedict Arnold," August 7, 1776, in Gates, Papers.
71. Arnold to Gates, Crown Point, August 17, 1776, in Gates, Papers.
72. Governor George Clinton, *Public Papers of George Clinton* (New York and Albany: Synkoop Hallenbeck Crawford Company, State Printers, 1899). 1: 324.
73. Gates to Arnold, Ticonderoga, August 18, 1776, in *NDAR*, 6: 223.
74. Gates to Schuyler, Ticonderoga, August 18, 1776, in *NDAR*, 6: 223.
75. Gates to Arnold, Ticonderoga, September 5, 1776, in *NDAR*, 6: 708.
76. E. Vale Smith, "Diary of Colonel Edward Wigglesworth." in *History of Newburyport* (Newburyport, MA: E. Vale Smith, 1854), 356–357.

77. Brigadier General Benedict Arnold, "Letter from Brigadier General Benedict Arnold to Major General Horatio Gates, from Isle La Motte, New York, dated September 9, 1776," Boston Public Library, Boston, MA.
78. Arnold to Gates, Valcour Island, October 10, 1776, in Gates, Papers.
79. Arnold to Gates, Bay St. Amont, September 21, 1776, in Gates, Papers.
80. Arnold to Gates, October 11, 1776, *NDAR*, 6:1235.
81. Lundeberg, *The Gondola "Philadelphia,"* 19.
82. "Orderly Book, 2d (St.Clair's/Wood's) Pennsylvania Battalion."
83. Trumbull's Orderly Book, 49.
84. "Orderly Book, Brigadier General Brickett's Militia Brigade, Fort Ticonderoga, August 14, 1776–November 17, 1776," New York Public Library.
85. Arnold to Gates, Isla La Motte, September 18, 1776, in *NDAR*, 6: 884.
86. *Colonel Frye Bailey's Reminiscences*, 41.
87. Trumbull to Schuyler, Lebanon, Connecticut, August 13, 1776, in *NDAR*, 6: 165,
88. Lorenzo F. Hagglund, "Scrapbook from the Recovery of the *Royal Savage.*" c. 1934. Courtesy of the Horse Soldier Relic Shop, Gettysburg, Pennsylvania and Dr. Walter L. Powell, Gettysburg, PA. Correspondence from this scrapbook documents that renowned archaeologist and historian William L. Calver identified these buttons.
89. "Journal of Bayze Wells," 279, 280.
90. Jehiel Stewart, "Journal of Jehiel Stewart, 1775–1776." Revolutionary Pension Files, Reel 2290, W25138, National Archives and Records Administration, Washington, DC.
91. Maurice B. Gordon, "Naval and Wartime Medicine During the Revolution" in *NDAR*, 6:1483–1484.
92. Arnold to Gates, Crown Point, August 16, 1776, in Gates, Papers.
93. Gates to Arnold, Ticonderoga, 23 August 1776, in Gates, Papers.
94. Letter from Brigadier General Benedict Arnold to Major General Horatio Gates, from Isle La Motte, New York, dated September 9, 1776.
95. "Journal of Bayze Wells," 272, 274, 277.
96. Arnold to Gates, Isle La Motte, September 18, 1776, in *NDAR*, 6: 884.
97. Arnold to Gates, Valcour Island, September 28, 1776, in Gates, Papers.
98. *NDAR*, 6: 1084.
99. Lundeberg, *The Gunboat "Philadelphia,"* 46, 55.
100. "Journal of Jehiel Stewart."
101. Arnold to Gates, Valcour Island, October 1, 1776, in Gates, Papers.
102. "Journal of Bayze Wells," 275.
103. Arnold to Gates, Valcour Island, October 10, 1776, in Gates, Papers.
104. "Journal of Jehiel Stewart."
105. Quartermaster Harmanus Schuyler Letters.
106. Waterbury to Gates, Skenesborough, August 30, 1776, in Gates, Papers.
107. Gates to Governor Trumbull, Ticonderoga, Septembere 16, 1776, in Gates, Papers.
108. Quoted in Doyen Salsig, ed., *Parole, Quebec—Countersign, Ticonderoga: Second New Jersey Regimental Orderly Book 1776* (Rutherford, NJ: Farleigh Dickinson Press, 1980), 231.

Chapter 10

1. Some portions of this chapter have previously appeared in considerably different form in Douglas R. Cubbison and Justin Clement, "The Artillery Never Gained More Honour: The British and Hesse-Hanau Artillery Gunboats at the Battle of Valcour Island," *Journal of the Society for Army Historical Research* 85, no. 343 (Autumn 2007): 247–255.
2. Carleton to Lord George Germain, September 28, 1776, in Canadian General Staff, Editor of the Historical Section, *A History of the Organization, Development and Services of the Military and Naval Forces of Canada from the Peace of Paris in 1763 to the Present Time. Volume II: The War of the American Revolution, the Province of Quebec under the Administration of Governor Sir Guy Carleton, 1775–1778* (Ottawa, Canada: 1919–1920), 191.
3. Official report of Douglas, *NDAR*, 6: 1344–1345.
4. Elizabeth Cometti, ed., *The American Journals of Lieutenant John Enys* (Syracuse, NY: Syracuse University Press, 1976), 18.
5. George F. G. Stanley, ed., *For Want of a Horse* (Sackville, New Brunswick, Canada: Tribune Press, 1961), 91–92.
6. Rogers, ed., *Hadden's Journal and Orderly Books,* 16.
7. William L. Stone, ed., *Journal of Captain Pausch Chief of the Hanau Artillery During the Burgoyne Campaign* (Albany, NY: Joel Munsell's Sons, 1886), 82.
8. Arnold to Schuyler, Ticonderoga, October 15, 1776, in *NDAR*, 6:1277.
9. Bellico, *Sails and Steam in the Mountains,* 152, 341; Cohn, et al., *Valcour Bay Research Project: 1999–2002 Survey Results,* 43.
10. James L. Nelson, *Benedict Arnold's Navy* (McGraw Hill, 2006), 292.
11. Bateaux Below, "The Land Tortoise, America's Oldest Intact Warship" accessed on April 4, 2008, at *http://www.thelostradeau.com*.
12. Official report of Douglas, *NDAR*, 6: 1344–1345.
13. Carleton, General Sir Guy. "Military Dispatches, Quebec and Canada, 1776–1780," War Office Records, W.O. 1, Vol. 11, Part 1, Canadian Archives and Library, Ottawa, Canada.
14. Brigadier General Von Gall, "Letters from Brigadier General Van Gall, Hesse Hannau Infantry Regiment, to Sovereign of Hesse Hannau," Morristown National Historic Park, Morristown, New Jersey. Microfilm copy at David Library of the American Revolution, Washington Crossing, PA.
15. Official report of Douglas, *NDAR*, 6:1341.
16. "Orderly Book, Brigadier General Brickett's Militia Brigade, Fort Ticonderoga, August 14, 1776–November 17, 1776." New York Public Library.
17. "Journal of Bayze Wells," 283.
18. "Journal of Jahiel Stewart."
19. "Journal of Bayze Wells," 283.
20. Captain William Chambers, Royal Navy, *Atlas of Lake Champlain, 1779–1780* (Montpelier and Bennington: Vermont Heritage Press and Vermont Historical Society, 1984), viii, xii, 22–23.
21. Charles M. Snyder, ed., "With Benedict Arnold at Valcour Island: The Diary of Pascal De Angelis," *Vermont History* 42 (1974), 198.
22. *Lieutenant Hadden's Journal*, 22–23.
23. Ibid.

24. Burgoyne to Captain Charles Douglas, Camp at River La Cole, October 12, 1776, in *NDAR*, 6: 1230.
25. Carleton to Captain Charles Douglas; Carleton to Lord George German, "On Board the *Maria* off Crown Point," October 14, 1776, in *NDAR*, 6: 1257–1258.
26. Captain Charles Pringle to Philip Stephens, "On Board the Maria off Crown Point," October 15, 1776, in *NDAR*, 6: 1275.
27. *The American Journals of Lieutenant John Enys*, 19.
28. "Journal of Jahiel Stewart."
29. Edward Osler, *The Life of Admiral Viscount Exmouth* (London: Smith, Elder, 1835), 17–18.
30. Arnold to Gates, Schuyler Island, October 12, 1776, in *NDAR*, 6: 1235.
31. Burgoyne, ed., *Journal and Reports of Pausch*, 41–42.
32. "Journal of Jahiel Stewart."
33. "The Diary of Pascal De Angelis," 198.
34. E. Vale. Smith, "Diary of Colonel Edward Wigglesworth," in *History of Newburyport* (Newburyport, MA: E. Vale Smith, 1854), 358.
35. "Journal of Bayze Wells," 284.
36. "Diary of Joshua Pell, Junior, An Officer of the British Army in America, 1776–1777," *The Bulletin of the Fort Ticonderoga Museum* 1, no. 6 (July 1929): 7.
37. Arnold to Gates, Schuyler Island, October 12, 1776, in Gates, Papers.
38. These papers remain at Laval University in Quebec. They have been published as Brigadier General Benedict Arnold, "Documents sur l'Invasion Americaine," *La Revue de l'Universite Laval, Quebec* Vol. 2 (1947–1948), 344–349; 642–648; 742–748; 838–846; 926–934.
39. Weights of howitzer shells provided by Adrian B. Caruana, *British Artillery Ammunition, 1780* (Bloomfield, Ontario: Museum Restoration Service, 1979), 20–21.
40. Arnold to Gates, Schuyler Island, October 12, 1776, in *NDAR*, 6: 1235.
41. Assistant Engineer Charles Terrot, Letter to John Frott, from St. Johns, Canada, November 13, 1776, Fort Ticonderoga Museum.
42. Ronald F. Kingsley, ed., "Letters to Lord Polwath from Sir Francis-Carr Clerke, Aide-de-Camp to General John Burgoyne," *New York History* (October 1998), 414.
43. For a discussion of British casualties, see Bratten, *The Gondola "Philadelphia,"* 65.
44. Burgoyne, ed., *Journal and Reports of Pausch*, 43–44.
45. Helga G. Doblin, trans., *An Eyewitness Account of the American Revolution and New England Life, The Journal of J. F. Wasmus, German Company Surgeon, 1776–1783* (New York: Greenwood Press, 1990), 32.
46. Arnold to Gates, Schuyler Island, October 12, 1776, in Gates, Papers.
47. Bratten, *The Gunboat "Philadelphia,"* 120–121.
48. "Journal of Jahiel Stewart."
49. Smith, "Diary of Colonel Edward Wigglesworth." 358.
50. Arnold to Gates, Schuyler Island, October 12, 1776, in Gates, Papers.
51. "Journal of Bayze Wells," 284.
52. Arnold to Schuyler, Ticonderoga, October 15, 1776, in *NDAR*, 6:1276; Smith, "Diary of Colonel Edward Wigglesworth." 358.
53. Mrs. Sally Markham, Crown Point Refugee, Pension Application, November 1846, Fort Ticonderoga Museum.
54. Hartley to Gates, October 13, 1776, in Gates, Papers.
55. J. Robert, Maguire, ed., "Dr. Robert Knox's Account of the Battle of Valcour, October 11–16, 1776," *Vermont History* 3 (Summer 1978): 148.
56. Quoted in Peter S. Palmer, *Battle of Valcour on Lake Champlain, October 11th 1776* (Plattsburgh, New York: 1876), 19.
57. Bratten, *The Gondola "Philadelphia,"* 141.
58. Report of Captain Douglas, quoted in Palmer, *Battle of Valcour*, 23–24.
59. Wilkinson, *Memoirs of My Own Times*, 91–92.
60. Art Cohn, "An Incident Not Known to History: Squire Ferris and Benedict Arnold at Ferris Bay, October 13, 1776," *Vermont History* 55 (1987): 110.
61. David R. Starbuck, *The Ferris Site on Arnold's Bay, Vermont* (Vergennes, VT: Lake Champlain Maritime Museum, 1989), 38, 41, 46–47, 50.
62. Grapeshot sizes from Caruana, *British Artillery Ammunition, 1780*, 18.
63. Cohn, "An Incident Not Known to History," 109–110.
64. Arnold to Schuyler, Ticonderoga, October 15, 1776, in *NDAR*, 6:1276.
65. Gates to Schuyler, Ticonderoga, October 15, 1776, in *NDAR*, 6:1277.
66. "The Diary of Pascal De Angelis," 199.
67. Smith, "Diary of Colonel Edward Wigglesworth." 358–359.
68. Bellico, *Sails and Steam in the Mountains*, 162.
69. For example, refer to Lieutenants John Schank, John Starke and Edward Longcroft, "An Open Letter to Captain Pringle, Saint Johns Canada, June 8, 1777," *The Bulletin of the Fort Ticonderoga Museum* 1, no. 4 (July 1928): 14–20.
70. Phillips to Germain, St. Johns, November 9, 1776, in Germain Papers, William L. Clements Library, University of Michigan, Ann Arbor.
71. Burgoyne, Editor, *Journal and Reports of Pausch*, 42.
72. Alfred Thayer Mahan, "The Naval Campaign of 1776 on Lake Champlain," *Scribner's Magazine* (1898), 158.

Chapter 11

1. Thompson, *Israel Shreve*, 23.
2. Salsig, ed., *Parole: Quebec; Countersign: Ticonderoga*, 265.
3. All strengths provided by Lesser, *The Sinews of Independence*, 38–39.
4. "Orderly Book, Brigadier General Brickett's Militia Brigade, Fort Ticonderoga, August 14, 1776 – November 17, 1776," New York Public Library.
5. "Orderly Book, Brigadier General Brickett's Militia Brigade."
6. J. Clarence Webster, ed., *The Journal of Jeffery Amherst, Recording the Military Career of General Amherst in America from 1758 to 1763* (Chicago: University of Chicago Press, 1931), 146.
7. Timothy J. Todish, ed., and Gary Z. Zaboly, illus., *The Annotated and Illustrated Journals of Major Robert Rogers* (Fleischmanns, NY: Purple Mountain Press, 2002), 168.

8. Bellico, *Sails and Steam in the Mountains*, 105, 107.
9. Baldwin, "Journal," 27–29.
10. Baldwin, "Journal of Colonel Baldwin," 16–17.
11. "Diary of Joshua Pell," 7.
12. Maguire, ed., "Dr. Robert Knox's Account," 148.
13. Baldwin, "Journal of Colonel Baldwin," 17.
14. Sizer, *John Trumbull*, 33–34.
15. Bratten, *The Gondola "Philadelphia,"* 141–146.
16. Albany Committee of Correspondence, *Minutes of the Albany Committee of Correspondence*, 1: 582.
17. Lender and Martin, *Citizen Soldier*, 111.
18. Deputy Commissary James Yancey, Army of the Northern Department. Letters from Ticonderoga, October 20–December 15, 1776. Accessed November 12, 2003, http://www.geocities.com/Heartland/Acres/7647/jamesy.htm.
19. Quoted in John H.G. Pell, "Philip Schuyler, Esquire, An Unfinished Biography," *The Bulletin of the Fort Ticonderoga Museum* 15, No. 3 (Winter 1991): 31.
20. Elmer, "The Lost Pages of Ebenezer Elmer's Revolutionary Journal," 416.
21. *Journal of Ebenezer Wild*, 85.
22. Morris H. Saffron, ed., "The Northern Medical Department, 1776–1777," *The Bulletin of the Fort Ticonderoga Museum* 14, no. 2 (Winter 1982): 97.
23. Salsig, ed., *Parole: Quebec; Countersign: Ticonderoga*, 271–272.
24. *Journal of the Rev. Ammi R. Robbins*, 44.
25. Anonymous American Minister. "An Address to General St. Clair's Brigade at Ticonderoga, When the Enemy Were Hourly Expected, October 20, 1776," n.p.: n.d., c. 1776. Fort Ticonderoga Museum; also transcription in *Bulletin of the Fort Ticonderoga Museum* 3, no. 2 (July 1933): 82–84.
26. Charles J. Stille, *Major General Anthony Wayne and the Pennsylvania Line in the Continental Army* (1893; reprint edition Port Washington, NY: Kennikat Press, 1968), 41–42.
27. James Thacher, *Military Journal of the American Revolution* (Hartford, CT: Hurlbut, Williams & Co., American Subscription Publishing House, 1862), 62, 64.
28. "Orderly Book, Brigadier General Brickett's Militia Brigade."
29. "The Diary of Pascal De Angelis."
30. "Orderly Book, Brigadier General Brickett's Militia Brigade."
31. *Orderly book of Capt. Ichabod Norton of Colonel Mott's regiment*, 40–41.
32. Salsig, ed., *Parole: Quebec; Countersign: Ticonderoga*, 270, 275.
33. Brigadier General Arthur St. Clair, Letter to Unknown, from Ticonderoga, October 25, 1776. Fort Ticonderoga Museum.
34. Royal Artillery Orderly Book, 66–67.
35. General Returns, British Army in Canada, 1776, WO 17/1494 (Public Records Office, London, England).
36. For example, *Lieutenant Digby's Journal*, 174.
37. John McAlpine, *Genuine Narratives and Concise Memoirs of Some of the Most Interesting Exploits and Singular Adventures of J. McAlpine, a Native Highlander, from the Time of his Emigration from Scotland to America in 1773, during the long period of his faithful attachment to ... the British Armies under the command of the Generals Carleton and Burgoyne... till December 1779* (1780; reprint edition Greenock, Scotland: Black Pennell Press, 1985), 11–15; Stephen G. Strach, "A Memoir of the Exploits of Captain Alexander Fraser and His Company of British Marksmen, 1776–1777," *Journal of the Society for Army Historical Research* 63 (1985): 91–98.
38. *Lieutenant Digby's Journal*, 174.
39. Baldwin, "Journal," 28.
40. "The Diary of Pascal De Angelis."
41. Orderly Book of Major Acland's Grenadier Battalion, October 8, 1776 — March 4, 1777 (Collection of the Society of Cincinnati, Washington, D.C.), 42–43.
42. "Journal of Jahiel Stewart."
43. Harper, "Short Account of His Journey."
44. It should be noted that although Digby noted this occurring on October 29, most likely it actually took place on October 28 in conjunction with the Artillery Gunboat reconnaissance. *Lieutenant Digby's Journal*, 174–175.
45. Harper, "Short Account of His Journey."
46. Kirkland, ed., "Journal of Dr. Lewis Beebe," 357.
47. Lieutenant Micah Hildreth, "Military Journal, August to October 1776," in Silas R. Coburn, *History of Dracut, Massachusetts* (1922), 149–150.
48. "Journal of Bayze Wells," 286.
49. Baldwin, "Journal," 28.
50. Stanley, ed., *For Want of a Horse*, 90.
51. Benjamin Beal, "Journal, July-December 1776."
52. "Journal of Jahiel Stewart."
53. "The Diary of Pascal De Angelis."
54. Orderly Book of Major Acland's Grenadier Battalion, 46–47.
55. General Phillip Schuyler, Miscellaneous Letters, October-November 1776, *The Bulletin of the Fort Ticonderoga Museum* 6, no. 4 (July 1942): 147.
56. Brigadier General Arthur St. Clair, Letter to Unknown, from Fort Ticonderoga, November 4, 1776. Fort Ticonderoga Museum.
57. Orderly Book of Major Acland's Grenadier Battalion, 49.
58. Edward B. DeFonblanque, *Political and military episodes in the latter half of the eighteenth century; Derived from the life and correspondence of the Right Hon. John Burgoyne, general, statesman, dramatist* (London: Macmillan, 1876), 218–221.
59. General John Burgoyne to General Henry Clinton, Letter, Quebec, November 7, 1776, in Sir Henry Clinton Papers. William L. Clements Library, University of Michigan, Ann Arbor.
60. Quoted in R. Arthur Bowler, "Sir Guy Carleton and the Campaign of 1776, in Canada," *The Canadian Historical Review* 55, no. 2 (June 1974): 138.
61. Ibid.
62. Sizer, *The Autobiography of John Trumbull*, 34.

Chapter 12

1. St. Clair, Brigadier General Arthur. Letter to Unknown, from Fort Ticonderoga, November 4, 1776. Fort Ticonderoga Museum.
2. Schuyer to Gates, Letter, Albany, November 12, 1776, in Gates, Papers.
3. "Orderly Book, Brigadier General Brickett's Militia Brigade."
4. Gates to Congress, Albany, November 27, 1776, in Gates, Papers.
5. Stille, *Major General Anthony Wayne*, 45.
6. "Memorandum of Articles left at Ticonderoga

with Gen. Wayne," November 18, 1776, in Gates, Papers.

7. Tuttle, "Diary."

8. Harry M. Ward, *General William Maxwell and the New Jersey Continentals* (Westport, CT: Greenwood Press, 1997), 47. For the American soldiers' perspective on the contracts under which they enlisted, refer to Fred W. Anderson, "Why Did Colonial New Englanders Make Bad Soldiers? Contractual Principles and Military Conduct During the Seven Years' War," *The William and Mary Quarterly* 3rd ser., no. 38, (1981): 395–417.

9. Elmer, "The Lost Pages of Ebenezer Elmer's Revolutionary Journal," 418.

10. Salsig, Editor, *Parole: Quebec; Countersign: Ticonderoga*, 284.

11. Martin, *Benedict Arnold, Revolutionary Hero*, 291.

12. Frazer, Letter to his wife, Mary Worrall Frazer, Ticonderoga, November 18, 1776, in Frazer, "Some Extracts from the Papers of General Persifor Frazer," 318.

13. Lesser, *Sinews of Independence*, 41.

14. Dr. Samuel Adams, Letters, October 5, 1776, through November 16, 1776 (Sol Feinstone Collection of the American Revolution, Moore Wing, U.S. Military Academy Library, West Point, NY).

15. Quoted in Stuart Murray, *Washington's Farewell, To His Officers after Victory in the Revolution* (Bennington, VT: Images from the Past, 1999), 209.

Bibliography

Primary Sources

Adams, Dr. Samuel. Letters. October 5, 1776, through November 16, 1776. Sol Feinstone Collection of the American Revolution, Moore Wing, U.S. Military Academy Library, West Point, NY.

Aichinger, Peter, ed. *At War With the Americans: The Journal of Claude-Nicholas-Guillaume de Lorimier*. Victoria, BC: Press Porcepic, n.d.

Ainslie, Thomas. "Journal of the Most Remarkable Occurrences in the Province of Quebec from the Appearance of the Rebels in September 1775 until their retreat on the Sixth of May." In *Blockade of Quebec in 1775–1776 by the American Revolutionists*, in *Literary and Historical Society of Quebec, Historical Documents*, 7th and 8th ser., edited by Frederick Christian Wurtele. Quebec: The Daily Telegraph Job Printing House, 1905–1906.

Albany Committee of Correspondence. *Minutes of the Albany Committee of Correspondence, 1775–1778, Prepared for Publication by the Division of Archives and History*. 2 vols. Albany: University of the State of New York, 1923–1925.

Ali Isani, Mukhtar, ed. "Phillis Wheatley in London: An Unpublished Letter to David Wooster." *American Literature* 51, no. 2 (May 1979): 255–260.

Anbury, Thomas. *Travels Through the Interior Parts of America*. 2 vols. London: n.p., 1798.

Anonymous American Minister. "An Address to General St. Clair's Brigade at Ticonderoga, When the Enemy Were Hourly Expected, October 20, 1776." n.p.: n.d., c. 1776. Fort Ticonderoga Museum; also transcription in *Bulletin of the Fort Ticonderoga Museum* 3, no. 2 (July 1933): 82–84.

Anonymous American Officer. "Account Book, New York, July 1, 1776, to Albany, September 2, 1776." Society of Cincinnati Library, Washington, DC.

Anonymous British Artillery Officer [probably Captain Thomas Jones]. "Journal of the Siege [of Quebec] from 1st December, 1775." In *Blockade of Quebec in 1775–1776 by the American Revolutionists*, in *Literary and Historical Society of Quebec, Historical Documents*, 7th and 8th ser., edited by Frederick Christian Wurtele. Quebec: The Daily Telegraph Job Printing House, 1905–1906.

Anonymous Officer. *From Cambridge to Champlain, March 18 to May 5 1776, A Manuscript Diary*. Middleboro, MA: Privately printed, 1957. Anonymous diary of an officer with Colonel John Greaton's 24th (Massachusetts) Continental Line.

_____, Colonel Specht's Regiment, Second Division of Ducal Brunswick Mercenaries. "Diary of Voyage From Stade in Hanover to Quebec in America of the Second Division of Ducal Brunswick Mercenaries." *The Quarterly Journal of the New York State Historical Association* 8, no. 4 (October 1927): 323–351. Diary stops with arrival at Quebec, but good description of sea journey to America.

Arnold, Colonel Benedict. "Colonel Arnold's Letters Written During the Expedition to Quebec." In Kenneth Roberts, ed. *March to Quebec: Journals of the Members of Arnold's Expedition*. New York: Doubleday, Doran, 1938.

Arnold, Brigadier General Benedict. Letter from Brigadier General Benedict Arnold to Major General Horatio Gates, from Isle La Motte, New York, dated September 9, 1776 (MSS 363): Boston Public Library, Boston, MA.

Arnold, Brigadier General Benedict. Papers recovered from *Royal Savage*. "Documents sur l'Invasion Americaine." *La Revue de l'Universite Laval*, Quebec Vol. 2 (1947–1948): 344–349; 642–648; 742–748; 838–846; 926–934.

Atkinson, C.T., ed. "Some Evidence for Burgoyne's Expedition." *Journal of the Society for Army Historical Research* 26 (1948): 132–142. Letters to Brigadier General Simon Fraser, 1776 and 1777 campaigns.

Bailey, Colonel Frye. "Colonel Frye Bailey's Reminiscences." *Proceedings of the Vermont Historical Society* (1923–1925): 22–86.

Baldwin, Jeduthan. "Extracts from the Diary of Colonel Jeduthan Baldwin, Chief Engineer of the Northern Army, July 6, 1776, to July 5, 1777." In *Bulletin of the Fort Ticonderoga Museum* 4, no. 6 (January 1938): 10–40.

_____. "The Baldwin Letters." *American Monthly Magazine* 6 (1895): 193–197.

Baldwin, Williams, ed. *Revolutionary Journal of Colonel Jeduthan Baldwin, 1775–1776*. Bangor, ME: n.p., 1906; reprint edition, New York: Arno Press, 1971.

Baxter, James Phinney, ed. *The British Invasion from the North: Digby's Journal of the Campaigns of Generals Carleton and Burgoyne from Canada, 1776–1777*. N.p: n.p., 1887; reprint edition, New York: DaCapo Press, 1970. Lieutenant William Digby was with the Grenadier Company, 53rd Foot.

Beal, Benjamin. Greaton's 24th Continental Regiment (Massachusetts): Journal, July- December 1776. American Antiquarian Society, Worcester, MA.

Bigelow, Major John. "Military Journal, July to August 1776." *American Historical Record* 1 (1872): 438–440.

Black, Jeannette D., and William Greene Roelker, eds. *A Rhode Island Chaplain in the Revolution: Letters of Ebenezer David to Nicholas Brown, 1775–1778*. Prov-

idence: The Rhode Island Society of Cincinnati, 1949.
Blake, Fifer Henry. Journal, April 1–October 7, 1776. American Antiquarian Society, Worcester, MA.
Bliss, Thomas T. Letter to Sister Phebe Emerson, Pennsylvania, June 1776. In *The Diaries and Letters of [Reverend] William Emerson, 1743–1776*, edited by Amelia Forbes Emerson. Boston: Thomas Todd, 1972.
Blood, Josiah. Letter to Wife, Mount Independence, September 4, 1776. Fort Ticonderoga Museum.
Bloodgood, Simeon DeWitt. *The Sexagenary; or Reminiscences of the American Revolution*. Albany, NY: Joel Munsell, 1866.
Bond, Colonel William, 25th Continental Regiment (Massachusetts). Papers. Mandeville Special Collections Library, Geisel Library, University of California, San Diego.
Brimhall, Sylvanus. Pension Deposition, December 1775–December 1776 (Mount Independence, July–December 1776). Fort Ticonderoga Museum. Nothing useful, just a list of Revolutionary War services.
Buell, Nathaniel. Letter to General Philip Schuyler from Mount Independence, December 3, 1776. Fort Ticonderoga Museum.
Burgoyne, Bruce E., ed. *Canada during the American Revolutionary War: Lieutenant Friedrich Julius Von Papet's Journal of the Sea Voyage to North America and the Campaign Conducted There, 15 May 1776 to 10 October 1783*. p.p.: 1998.
_____. *They Also Served: Women with the Hessian Auxiliaries*. p.p. 1999.
Burgoyne, General John. Correspondence. In Sir Henry Clinton Papers. William L. Clements Library, University of Michigan, Ann Arbor, MI.
Burton, Lieutenant Jonathan, New Hampshire Militia. In *Diary and Orderly Book of Lieutenant Jonathan Burton while in the Canada Expedition at Mount Independence, August 1, 1776–November 29, 1776*, edited by Isaac W. Hammond. Concord, NH: n.p., 1885.
Caldwell, Major Henry. "The Invasion of Canada in 1775." Quebec: n.p., 1866.
Calef, Colonel John H., ed. "Extracts from the Diary of a Revolutionary Patriot." *Journal of the Military Service Institution of the United States* 39 (July–August 1906): 257–273.
_____. "Extracts from the Diary of a Revolutionary Patriot, Colonel Jeduthan Baldwin, Engineers, Continental Army 1775–1779." *Journal of the Military Service Institution of the United States* 39 (September–October 1906): 257–273.
Carleton, General Sir Guy. "Military Dispatches, Quebec and Canada, 1776–1780." War Office Records, W.O. 1, Vol. 11, Part 1, Canadian Archives and Library, Ottawa, Canada.
_____. "Proclamation, Quebec, May 10, 1776." Frederick Mackenzie Papers. William L. Clements Library, University of Michigan, Ann Arbor, MI.
Carroll, Charles. *Dear Papa, Dear Charley: The Peregrinations of a Revolutionary Aristocrat, As Told by Charles Carroll of Carrollton and his father, Charles Carroll of Annapolis, with Sundry Observations on Bastardy, child-rearing, romance, matrimony, commerce, tobacco, slavery and the politics of Revolutionary America*. Chapel Hill: University of North Carolina Press, 2001.
Caruana, Adrian B. *British Artillery Ammunition, 1780*. Bloomfield, Ontario: Museum Restoration Service, 1979.
Chambers, Captain William. *Atlas of Lake Champlain, 1779–1780*. Montpelier and Bennington: Vermont Heritage Press and Vermont Historical Society, 1984.
Chamberlin, William. "Letter of General William Chamberlin." *Proceedings of the Massachusetts Historical Society* 10 (2nd ser., 1896): 491–506.
Clark, William Bell, and William J. Morgan, eds. *Naval Documents of the American Revolution*. Washington, DC: Government Printing Office, 1964–1981.
Clinton, Governor George. *Public Papers of George Clinton*. Volume I — Military, 1775–1777. New York and Albany: Synkoop Hallenbeck Crawford Company, State Printers, 1899.
Clinton, Sir Henry. Papers. William L. Clements Library, University of Michigan, Ann Arbor, MI. Miscellaneous correspondence.
Cohen, Sheldon S., ed. *Canada Preserved: The Journal of Captain Thomas Ainslie*. New York: New York University Press, 1968.
Cometti, Elizabeth, ed. *The American Journals of Lieutenant John Enys*. Syracuse, NY: Syracuse University Press, 1976.
Continental Congress Committee Sent to the Northern Department. "Report of the Committee." *Bulletin of the Fort Ticonderoga Museum* 3, no. 5 (January 1935): 205–206.
Cushing, Charles. "Journal of the Retreat from Canada under General Sullivan, 1776." Manuscript Copy by Henry Steven, Jr., 1845. Library of Congress, Washington, DC.
Cumberland, Richard. Letter to Unknown, Plantation Chambers, London, 1776. Sol Feinstone Collection of the American Revolution, Moore Wing, USMA Library. British correspondence discussing 1776 Northern Campaign.
Daly, Lieutenant Patrick, Colonel Allen MacLean's Royal Highland Emigrant Regiment. "Journal of the Siege and Blockade of Quebec by the American Rebels in Autumn of 1775 and Winter of 1776." In Literary and Historical Society of Quebec. *4th Series of Historical Documents*. Quebec: 1875.
Danford, Jacob. "Journal of the Most Remarkable Occurrences in Quebec from 14 November 1775 to May 7, 1776, by an Officer of the Garrison." *New York Historical Society Collections* 13 (1880).
Davies, K.G. *Documents of the American Revolution, 1770–1783 [British] Colonial Office Series*. Vol. 12: "Transcripts, 1776." Dublin: Irish University Press, 1976.
Davis, David B., ed. "Medicine in the Canadian Campaign of the Revolutionary War: The Journal of Doctor Samuel Fisk Merrick." *Bulletin of the History of Medicine* 44 (September–October 1970): 461–473.
Davis, Matthew L. *Memoirs of Aaron Burr*. 2 vols. New York: Harper, 1836–1837.
Dayton, Colonel Elias. Letter to General Philip Schuyler from Fort Ticonderoga, November 5, 1776. Fort Ticonderoga Museum. Simple letter requests leave to depart Fort Ticonderoga.
Dewey, Adjutant Russell. "Military Journal, January to April 1776." In A.M. and L.M. Dewey, *Life of George Dewey*. Westfield, MA: Dewey, 1898, 266–571.
"Diary of Joshua Pell, Junior, An Officer of the British Army in America, 1776–1777. *The Bulletin of the Fort Ticonderoga Museum* 1, no. 6 (July 1929): 1–14.

Dodge, Nathaniel B., "A Letter and Diary of 1776." *Vermont History* 21 (January 1953): 29–35.

_____. "The Fourth of July in 1776 at Crown Point." *New York History* 34 (1936): 75–78.

Doblin, Helga G., trans. "A Brunswick Grenadier With Burgoyne: The Journal of Johann Bense, 1776–1783." *New York History* 66 (October 1985): 421–444.

_____, trans. *An Eyewitness Account of the American Revolution and New England Life: The Journal of J. F. Wasmus, German Company Surgeon, 1776–1783.* New York: Greenwood Press, 1990.

_____, trans. *The American Revolution, Garrison Life in French Canada and New York: Journal of an Officer in the Prinz Friedrich Regiment, 1776–1783.* New York: Greenwood Press, 1993.

_____, trans. *The Specht Journal: A Military Journal of the Burgoyne Campaign.* New York: Greenwood Press, 1995.

Eaton, Isaah. Journal, March–June 1776. Revolutionary War Pension File, M804, Roll 891, Pages 27–32. National Archives and Records Administration, Washington DC, Microfilm Copy at David Library of the American Revolution, Washington's Crossing, Pennsylvania.

Elmer, Ebenezer, 2nd Lieutenant, 2nd New Jersey Continental Regiment. "Diary of His Services in American Revolution." *New Jersey Historical Society Proceedings* 2 (1846–1847): 95–150; 3 (1949): 21–90.

_____. "The Lost Pages of Ebenezer Elmer's Revolutionary Journal." *New Jersey Historical Society Proceedings* 10 (1925): 410–424.

Embarkation Returns, British Army, April 1776. WO 25/1145. Public Records Office, London, England.

Emerson, Amelia Forbes, ed. *The Diaries and Letters of [Reverend] William Emerson, 1743–1776.* Boston: Thomas Todd, 1972.

Emerson, Edward. "Chaplain of the Revolution." *Proceedings of the Massachusetts Historical Society, 1921–1922.* Boston: Massachusetts Historical Society, 1923.

Epping, Charlotte, ed. *The Journal of DuRoi the Elder.* Philadelphia: University of Pennsylvania Press, 1911. Also in *German-American Annals 3* (1911): 40–64, 77–128, and 131–239.

Ewing, Thomas, Jr., ed. *The Military Journal of George Ewing.* Yonkers, NY: n.p., 1928. Accessed on-line at http://www.sandcastles.net/journal.htm on April 27, 2005.

Farnsworth, Corporal Amos, Massachusetts Militia. "Amos Farnsworth's Diary." *Massachusetts Historical Society Proceedings* 12 (1899): 78–102. 2nd ser.

Frazer, Captain Persifor, Wayne's Fourth Pennsylvania Battalion. "Letters from Ticonderoga 1776." *Bulletin of the Fort Ticonderoga Museum* 10, no. 5 (1961): 386–394; 10, no. 6 (1962): 450–459.

Frazer, Captain Persifor. "Some Extracts from the Papers of General Persifor Frazer." *The Pennsylvania Magazine of History and Biography* 31 (1907): 129–144, 311–319, 447–451.

_____. "Quartermaster Records, 4th Pennsylvania Battalion." Fort Ticonderoga Museum.

Freeman, Reverend James. "Record of the Services of Constant Freeman, Captain of Artillery in the Continental Army." *The Magazine of American History* 2 (1878): 349–352.

Freiberg, Malcolm, ed. "The Reverend William Gordon's Autumn 1776 Tour of the Northeast." *The New England Quarterly* 65, no. 3 (September 1992): 469–480.

Gabriel, Michal P., ed., and S. Pascale Vergereau-Dewey, trans. *Quebec During the American Invasion, 1775–1776, The Journal of Francois Baby, Gabriel Taschereau, & Jenkin Williams.* East Lansing: Michigan State University Press, 2005.

Gates, Major General Horatio. Letter to General Artemus Ward, November 9, 1776, from Ticonderoga, New York. Special Collections and Archives, U.S. Military Academy Library, U.S. Military Academy, West Point, NY.

_____. Papers. New York Historical Society. Microfilm copy at U.S. Military Academy Library, U.S. Military Academy, West Point, NY.

General Returns, British Army in Canada, 1776, WO 17/1494. Public Records Office, London, England.

Glen, Henry. Papers. New York Public Library. Deputy quartermaster general at Schenectady, New York, in 1776.

Grant, Francis. "Journal from New York to Canada, 1767." *New York State Historical Association Proceedings* 30 (1932): 181–196, 305–322.

Greaton, Thomas. Continental Army Soldier with Brewer's Massachusetts Regiment. Revolutionary War Pension File, M804, Roll 1110, Pages 302–325. National Archives and Records Administration, Washington DC, Microfilm Copy at David Library of the American Revolution, Washington's Crossing, Pennsylvania.

Graydon, Alexander. *Memoirs of His Own Time With Reminiscences of the Men and Events of the Revolution.* Philadelphia: Lindsay & Blakiston, 1846.

Great Britain Army Records. "Adjutant General's Orderly Book, May 11, 1776, to 1784, of Major R. B. Lernoult." Burton Historical Collection, Detroit Public Library, Detroit, MI.

Green, Samuel A., ed. "Diary Kept by Lieutenant Amos Farnsworth of Groton, Mass., During a Part of the Revolutionary War, April 19, 1775–May 6, 1779" In *Three Military Diaries Kept By Groton Soldiers In Different Wars.* Groton, MA: University Press, 1901.

Greenwood, Isaac J. *The Revolutionary Services of John Greenwood of Boston and New York 1775–1783.* New York: De Vinne, 1922.

Guild, Joseph. Journal, March 29, 1776–December 7, 1776. Dedham Historical Society, Dedham, MA.

Hale, Colonel Nathan. Letters to Mrs. Abigail Hale, August 12, 1776; September 5, 1776; and October 14, 1776. Library of Congress, Washington, D.C.

Hamilton, Sir John. "Journal of the Principal Occurrences During the Siege of Quebec by the American Revolutionists under Generals Montgomery and Arnold in 1775–1776." Edited by W.T. P. Short. London: Simpkin & Company, 1824. In *Blockade of Quebec in 1775–1776 by the American Revolutionists,* in *Literary and Historical Society of Quebec, Historical Documents,* 7th and 8th ser., edited by Frederick Christian Wurtele. Quebec: The Daily Telegraph Job Printing House, 1905–1906.

Hammond, Isaac W., ed. "Diary of Lieutenant Jonathan Burton, While in the Canada Expedition, From August 1, 1776, to November 29, 1776." In *State of New Hampshire Rolls of the Soldiers in the Revolutionary War, 1775 to May 1777.* Vol. 1. Concord, NH: Parsons B. Cogswell, State Printer, 1885.

_____. *Papers of the State of New Hampshire, Part I, Rolls* and Documents Relating to Soldiers in the Revolutionary War. Vol. 4 of the War Rolls. Manchester, NH: John B. Clarke, Public Printer, 1889.

_____. "Petition from some of the Sufferers by the Surrender at the Cedars, May 19, 1776." In State of New Hampshire Rolls of the Soldiers in the Revolutionary War, 1775 to May 1777. Vol. 1. Concord, NH: Parsons B. Cogswell, State Printer, 1885.

Hammond, Otis G., Editor. Letters and Papers of Major General John Sullivan Continental Army. 2 vols. Concord, NH: New Hampshire Historical Society, 1930.

Hanley, Thomas O'Brien. The John Carroll Papers. South Bend, IN: University of Notre Dame Press, 1976.

Harper, Quartermaster John. Wayne's 4th Pennsylvania Battalion. "Short Account of His Journey from Philadelphia in the Year 1776." Fort Ticonderoga Museum.

_____. "Quartermaster Records, 1776." Fort Ticonderoga Museum.

Haskell, Caleb. "Caleb Haskell's Diary 1776." The Magazine of History 22, Extra No. 68, 1912.

_____. "Caleb Haskell, Diary at the Siege of Boston and on the March to Quebec." In March to Quebec: Journals of the Members of Arnold's Expedition, edited by Kenneth Roberts. New York: Doubleday, Doran, 1938.

Hastings, Hugh, ed. Public Papers of George Clinton, First Governor of New York. Vol. 1: Military. New York and Albany: Wynkoop, Hallenbeck, Crawford Company, State Printers, 1899.

Hildreth, Lieutenant Micah. "Military Journal, August to October 1776." In Silas R. Coburn, History of Dracut, Massachusetts (1922): 147–152.

Hill, Jonathan. "Diary Kept on the Expedition from New York to Quebec, April and May 1776." Manuscript in Massachusetts Historical Society, Boston.

Hodginkson, Samuel. "Before Quebec, 1776, Letter of Samuel Hodginkson to his Parents, Camp Before Quebec, April 27, 1776." Pennsylvania Magazine of History and Biography 10 (1886): 158–163.

Houlding, J.A., and G. Kenneth Yates. "Corporal Fox's Memoir of Service, 1766–1783: Quebec, Saratoga, and the Convention Army." Journal of the Society for Army Historical Research 68 (Autumn 1990): 146–168.

Hubbs, V.C., ed., trans. "Journal of the Brunswick Corps in America under General Von Riedesel." In Sources of American Independence: Selected Manuscripts from the Collections of the William L. Clements Library, Vol. 1, edited by Howard H. Peckham. Chicago: University of Chicago Press, 1978: 226–285.

Hughes, Ensign Thomas. A Journal by Thomas Hughes for his Amusement & Designed Only for his Perusal by the Time he attains the Age of Fifty if he lives so Long. Cambridge, MA: University Press, 1947.

Ingalls, Phineas. "Revolutionary War Journal Kept by Phineas Ingalls of Andover, Massachusetts." The Essex Institute Historical Collections 53 (1917): 81–92.

Irvine, Colonel William. "General Irvine's Journal of the Canadian Campaign, 1776." The Historical Magazine 4 (April 1862): 115–117.

_____. Irvine Family Papers. Archives and Special Collections, Dickinson College, Carlisle, PA.

Ives, Vernon A., ed. "Narrative of Uriah Cross in the Revolutionary War." New York History 63, no. 3 (July 1982): 279–294.

Jenks, John. "Diary, 1775–1776." Massachusetts Historical Society, Boston.

Jones, Matt B., ed. "Revolutionary Correspondence of Governor Nicholas Cooke, 1775–1781." Proceedings of the American Antiquarian Society at the Annual Meetings Held in Boston, October 20, 1926. New Series, Vol. 36, Part 2 (Worcester, MA: American Antiquarian Society, 1927).

"A Journal of Carleton's and Burgoyne's Campaigns." The Bulletin of the Fort Ticonderoga Museum 11, no. 5 (December 1964): 235–269; 11, no. 6 (September 1965): 307–335; 12, no. 1 (March 1966): 5–59. Journal probably prepared by a British officer.

"Journal of the Most Remarkable Occurrences in Quebec Since Arnold Appeared Before the Town on the 14th November 1775." In Blockade of Quebec in 1775–1776 by the American Revolutionists, in Literary and Historical Society of Quebec, Historical Documents, 7th and 8th ser., edited by Frederick Christian Wurtele. Quebec: The Daily Telegraph Job Printing House, 1905–1906.

Kennedy, Dr. Samuel. "Letters from Dr. Samuel Kennedy to his Wife in 1776." The Pennsylvania Magazine of History and Biography 8 (1884): 111–116.

Kennedy, Matthew. Letter to Mr. Robert Kennedy from Camp at Mount Independence, October 11, 1776. Proceedings of the Vermont Historical Society New Series, 1, no. 4 (1930): 182.

Kimball, Daniel. Continental Army Soldier, New Hampshire Regiment. Journal, February 8, 1776–May 27, 1776. Revolutionary War Pension File, M804, Roll 1483, Pages 543–559, National Archives and Records Administration, Washington DC, Microfilm Copy at David Library of the American Revolution, Washington's Crossing, PA.

Kingsley, Ronald F., ed. "Letters to Lord Polwath from Sir Francis-Carr Clerke, Aide-de-Camp to General John Burgoyne." New York History (October 1998): 393–424.

Kirkland, Frederic R., ed. "Journal of Dr. Lewis Beebe, A Physician on the Expedition Against Canada, 1776." The Pennsylvania Magazine of History and Biography 59, no. 4 (October 1935): 321–361.

Knollenberg, Bernhard. "Correspondence of John Adams and Horatio Gates." Proceedings of the Massachusetts Historical Society, October 1941–May 1944. Vol. 67. Boston: Massachusetts Historical Society, 1945.

Knowles, James. Letter to "Dear Wife" from Quebec, Canada, January 15, 1776. Sol Feinstone Collection of the American Revolution, David Library of the American Revolution, Washington's Crossing, PA.

Lacey, John. "Memoirs of Brigadier General John Lacey, of Pennsylvania." The Pennsylvania Magazine of History and Biography 25 (1901): 191–207, 341–354, 498–515.

Lamb, R. An Original and Authentic Journal of Occurrences During the Late American War. Dublin: 1809.

Leary, Thomas O. Expense Book of John Halsted, Commissary Under Benedict Arnold Before Quebec, 1776. Montreal: C.A. Marchand, 1913. Copy at Massachusetts Historical Society, Boston.

Lender, Mark A., and James Kirby Martin. Citizen Soldier: The Revolutionary Journal of Joseph Bloomfield. Newark: New Jersey Historical Society, 1982.

Library of Congress. "George Washington Papers at the Library of Congress, 1741–1799." Accessed online at http://memory.loc.gov/ammem/gwhtml/gwhome.html.

Lochee, Lewis. *Elements of Field Fortification*. London: T. Cadell and T. Egerton, 1783.

Luquer, Colonel Thatcher T.P., ed."Journal from New York to Canada 1767." *New York State Historical Association Proceedings* 30 (1932): 181–196, 305–322.

Maguire, J. Robert, ed. "Dr. Robert Knox's Account of the Battle of Valcour, October 11–16, 1776." *Vermont History* 3 (Summer 1978): 141–150.

Markham, Mrs. Sally. Crown Point Refugee. Pension Application, November 1846. Fort Ticonderoga Museum.

Massachusetts Laws & Statutes. House of Representatives, Resolution, February 14, 1776. Massachusetts Historical Society, Boston.

———. House of Representatives, Resolution, June 26, 1776. Massachusetts Historical Society, Boston.

Mayer, Brantz, ed. *Journal of Charles Carroll of Carrollton, During His Visit to Canada in 1776, As One of the Commissioners from Congress, With A Memoir and Notes*. Baltimore: John Murphy, 1876.

McAlpine, John. *Genuine Narratives and Concise Memoirs of Some of the Most Interesting Exploits and Singular Adventures of J. McAlpine, a Native Highlander, from the Time of his Emigration from Scotland to America in 1773, during the long period of his faithful attachment to ... the British Armies under the command of the Generals Carleton and Burgoyne ... till December 1779*. 1780; reprint edition Greenock, Scotland: Black Pennell Press, 1985.

Melsheimer, Reverend Frederick Valintine. "Journal of the Voyage of the Brunswick Auxiliairies from Wolfenbuttel to Quebec." *Transactions of the Literary and Historical Society, no. 20, Sessions of 1889 to 1891*. Quebec: Printed at the Morning Chronicle Office, 1891): 133–178.

Melvin, James. "Journal of the Expedition to Quebec in the Year 1775." Philadelphia: Franklin Club, 1864. Copy at Massachusetts Historical Society, Boston. Taken prisoner during assault, good account of assault.

Meyrick, Doctor Samuel J. "Letter to John Trumbull." *The Bulletin of the Fort Ticonderoga Museum* 6, no. 6 (July 1943): 186–187.

Moore, Augustus. Letter from Mount Hope, Ticonderoga, to Wife, October 3, 1776. In *Ticonderoga: Historic Portage*, edited by Carroll V. Lonergan. Ticonderoga, NY: Fort Mount Hope Society Press, 1959, 180–181.

Morgan, Appleton, ed. "The Diary of Colonel Elisha Porter of Hadley, Massachusetts. Touching His March to the Relief of the Continental Forces Before Quebec, 1776." *Magazine of American History* 30 (1893): 185–206.

Morison, George. "An Account of the Assault on Quebec, 1775." *Pennsylvania Magazine of History and Biography* 14 (1890): 434–439.

———. "Quebec Expedition Under Arnold, July 13, 1775–September 24, 1776." *Magazine of History*, Extra No. 52 (1916): 295–296.

Mott, Colonel. "Service Record Including Manuscript 'Plat Showing Location of Col. Mott's Regiment at Skenesborough, c. 1776.'" Fort Ticonderoga Museum.

Mudge, Simon. "Military Journal, July to November 1776." In Alfred Mudge, "Memorials" (Boston: 1868): 204–205; and *Danvers Historical Society Collections* 27 (1939): 40–43.

Nairne, Colonel John. "The Siege of Quebec in 1775–1776." In *A Canadian Manor and Its Seigneurs*, edited by George N. Wrong. Toronto: Macmillan, 1908): Appendix C, 273–277.

New York Convention and Committee of Safety. "Miscellaneous Correspondence." *The Bulletin of the Fort Ticonderoga Museum* 4, no. 7 (July 1938): 18–56.

Nichols, Francis. "Diary." *Pennsylvania Magazine of History and Biography* 29 (1896). Nichols was taken prisoner during December 31, 1775, assault but his memoirs contain some useful information.

O'Callaghan, E.B., trans. "The Eye Witness of the War of the Americans in Canada in the Years 1775 and 1776, by B.V. Miscel." Section "O." New York Historical Society. Canadian Military Account (British),

O'Leary, Thomas, ed. *Expense Book of John Halsted, Commissary Under Benedict Arnold Before Quebec, 1776*. Montreal: C.A. Marchand, 1913. Copy at Massachusetts Historical Society, Boston.

"Orderly Book, Extracts from the Brigade Orders of Major General Phillips, Royal Artillery, Canada, June 3 1776–September 14 1777." Royal Artillery Institution, Woolwich, London, England.

"Orderly Book, General von Gall, Colonel and Commandant of the Hesse-Hanau Regiment, October 28, 1776–June 18, 1777." Morristown National Historic Park Library, Morristown, New Jersey. In *Hesse-Hanau Order Books, A Diary and Rosters*, edited and translated by Bruce Burgoyne. Bowie, MD: Heritage Books, 2003, 32–77.

"Orderly Book, Major Acland's Grenadier Battalion, October 8, 1776–March 4, 1777." Society of the Cincinnati Library, Washington, DC.

"Orderly Book, Colonel Arnold's Expedition to Quebec, January 1, 1776–February 26, 1776." Library of Congress, Washington, DC.

"Orderly Book, Fort Ticonderoga Garrison Orders, July 10, 1776–November 17, 1776." M-2172, Fort Ticonderoga Museum. Also known as Colonel John Trumbull's Orderly Book. Transcription published "The Deputy Adjutant General's Orderly Book, Ticonderoga, 1776." *The Bulletin of the Fort Ticonderoga Museum* 3 (1933).

"Orderly Book, Fort George Garrison Orders, July 10, 1776–August 19, 1776." New York Historical Society, and published as DeCosta, B.F. *Notes on the history of Fort George during the colonial and revolutionary periods, with contemporaneous documents and an appendix*. New York: J. Sabin & Sons, 1871.

"Orderly Book, Brigadier General Brickett's Militia Brigade, Fort Ticonderoga, August 14, 1776–November 17, 1776." New York Public Library.

Orderly book of Capt. Ichabod Norton of Colonel Mott's regiment of Connecticut troops destined for the northern campaign in 1776 at Skeensborough (now Whitehall): Fort Ann and Ticonderoga, N.Y., and at Mount Independence, Vt.: together with a fac similie of Captain Norton's map of Ticonderoga and Mount Independence / with introduction by Robert O. Bascom. Fort Edward, NY: Keating & Barnard, 1898.

"Orderly Book, Lieutenant Colonel William Worthington, Colonel Mott's Connecticut State Battalion, Fort Ticonderoga, 16 August 1776–19 November 1776." Fort Ticonderoga Museum.

"Orderly Book, 24th (Greaton's Massachusetts) Continental Regiment, Fort Ticonderoga, January 1, 1776–August 7, 1776." Huntington Library, San Marino, CA.

"Orderly Book, 15th (Paterson's Massachusetts) Continental Regiment, Canada and Fort Ticonderoga, June 19, 1776–October 20, 1776." Adjutant William Walker. Fort Ticonderoga Museum, Ticonderoga, New York.

"Orderly Book, Royal Regiment of Artillery (Canadian Department): May 8, 1776–June 29, 1777." Morristown National Historic Park, Morristown, New Jersey.

"Orderly Book, Colonel Wigglesworth's Regiment of Massachusetts Militia, Fort Ticonderoga and Mount Independence, July 30, 1776–November 23, 1776." Huntington Library, San Marino, CA.

"Orderly Book, Colonel Ephraim Wheelock's Regiment of Massachusetts Militia, Fort Ticonderoga, August 18, 1776–November 26, 1776." Fort Ticonderoga Museum, Ticonderoga, NY.

"Orderly Book, Colonel Benjamin Woodbridge's Regiment of Massachusetts Militia, Fort Ticonderoga, August 25, 1776–October 27, 1776." Copy located at Sparks Mss Collection, Houghton Library, Harvard University, Cambridge, MA.

"Orderly Book, 5th (John Stark's New Hampshire) Continental Regiment, April 13, 1776–September 11, 1776." New Hampshire Historical Society, Concord, NH.

"Orderly Book, 3d (Dayton's) New Jersey Regiment, Fort Ticonderoga, November 20, 1776–December 29, 1776." Folder 9, Ebenezer Elmer Papers, New Jersey Historical Society, Newark, NJ.

"Orderly Book, 3d (J. Clinton's) New York Regiment, Canada, January 1, 1776–March 10, 1776." Early American Orderly Books, New York State Historical Society. Microfilm Copy, USMA Library, West Point, NY.

Captain John Wendell. "Orderly Book, 4th (Wynkoop's) New York Regiment, April 20, 1776–August 27, 1776." Fort Ticonderoga Museum.

Captain John Wendell. "Orderly Book, 4th (Wynkoop's) New York Regiment, May 10, 1776–October 4, 1776." Fort Ticonderoga Museum.

"Orderly Book, 2d (St.Clair's/Wood's) Pennsylvania Battalion, February 22, 1776–September 11, 1776." National Archives and Records Administration. Microfilm Copy, USMA Library, West Point, NY.

"Orderly Book, Captain Frazer's Company, 4th Pennsylvania Battalion, May 30, 1776–August 26, 1776." Sergeant Edward Vernon. Fort Ticonderoga Museum.

Papet, First Lieutenant F.J. Von. "The Brunswick Contingent in America, 1776–1783." *The Pennsylvania Magazine of History and* Biography 15 (1891): 218–224. Extracts from his diary.

Parke, Andrew. *An Authentic Narrative of Facts Relating to the Exchange of Prisoners Taken at the Cedars.* London: T. Cadell, 1777.

Pell, John H.G. "A Few Military Manuscripts in the Fort Ticonderoga Museum Library, Anthony Mash: Account and Inventory of Money, Clothing and Goods, September 7, 1776." *The Bulletin of the Fort Ticonderoga Museum* 9, no. 1 (Winter 1952): 25–29.

Pell, Joshua. "Diary of Joshua Pell, Junior, An Officer of the British Army in America, 1776–1777." *The Magazine of American History* 2 (1878): 43–47, 107–112.

Phillips, Major General William. Correspondence in Germain Papers, William L. Clements Library, University of Michigan, Ann Arbor.

Pleydell, Lieutenant J. C. *An Essay on Field Fortification: Intended Principally for the use of Officers of Infantry, showing how to trace out on the ground and construct in the easiest manner, all sorts of Redoubts and other field works, translated from the original manuscript of an officers of experience in the Prussian Service.* London: Printed for J. Nourse, Bookseller to His Majesty, 1768; new edition, London: Printed for F. Wingrave, 1790.

Porter, Colonel Elisha. "Original Manuscript Journal of the American Revolution, An Account of the Expedition from Cambridge to Quebec and the Failure of the Expedition, January 19 to August 25, 1776." *The Bulletin of the Fort Ticonderoga Museum* 10, no. 1 (1957): 34–58.

Potts, Doctor Jonathan. Pay Book, 1776–1781. Morristown National Historical Park, Morristown, New Jersey. Microfilm Copy at Moore Wing, U.S. Military Academy Library, West Point, NY.

Pringle, Captain Thomas. "Letter to John Falconar, Commanding the Brig Polly, August 2, 1776." Sir Guy Carleton Papers, Microfilm copy at Moore Wing, U.S. Army Military Academy Library, West Point, NY.

"Proceedings of a General Court Martial for the Trial of Major General St. Clair, August 25, 1778." Philadelphia: Hall and Sellers, 1778; in *Collections of the New York Historical Society for the Year 1880*, New York: 1881).

"Public Diary, April to May 1776." In *Literary and Historical Society of Quebec Transactions* 22 (1898): 45–40. Notes on the weather and general events during the Siege of Quebec.

Public Records Office. "Embarkation Returns, Cork, Ireland, 1776" and "Returns of the Royal Army in Canada, 1776."

Retzer, Henry J., trans. "Journal of the Hessen-Hanau Erbprinz Infantry Regiment, Kept by 2nd Lieutenant Carl Augustus Sartorius, Regimental Quartermaster." *Journal of the Johannes Schwalm Historical Association* 6, no. 3 (1999): 26–34.

_____. "Journal of the Hessen-Hanau Infantry Regiment Erbprinz, Kept by Judge-Advocate Paul Wilhelm Schaeffer — March 1776 to April 1777, Plus Letters to His Parents." *Journal of the Johannes Schwalm Historical Association* 7, no. 1 (2001): 30–39.

_____. "Philipp Theobold, Hanau Regiment Chaplain." *Journal of the Johannes Schwalm Historical Association* 6, no. 2 (1998): 39–44.

Ritzema, Colonel Rudolphus. "Journal of Colonel Rudolphus Ritzema of the First New York Regiment August 8 to March 30, 1776." *The Magazine of American History* 1 (1877): 98–107.

Robbins Reverend Ammi. R. *Journal of the Rev. Ammi R. Robbins, A Chaplain in the American Army, in the Northern Campaign of 1776.* New Haven: B.L. Hamlen, 1850.

Roche, John F., ed. "Quebec Under Siege, 1775–1776: the 'Memorandums' of Jacob Danford (British Militia)." *Canadian Historical Review* 50, no. 1 (March 1969): 68–85.

Rogers, Horatio, ed. *Hadden's Journal and Orderly Books: A Journal Kept in Canada and Upon Burgoyne's Campaign in 1776 and 1777 by Lieutenant James M. Hadden, Royal Artillery.* 1884; reprint edition Boston: Gregg Press, 1972.

Rowland, Kate Mason. *The Life of Charles Carroll of*

Carrollton, 1737–1823 With His Correspondence and Public Papers. 2 vols. New York: Knickerbocker Press, 1897.

Saffron, Morris H., ed. "The Northern Medical Department, 1776–1777." *The Bulletin of the Fort Ticonderoga Museum* 14, no. 2 (Winter 1982): 81–120. Letters of Dr. Jonathan Potts, Northern Department Surgeon, Continental Army.

St. Clair, Brigadier General Arthur. Papers. Ohio Historical Society; Microfilm copy at U.S. Military Academy Library, West Point, NY.

———. Letter to Unknown, from Ticonderoga, October 25, 1776. Fort Ticonderoga Museum.

———. Letter to Unknown, from Fort Ticonderoga, November 4, 1776. Fort Ticonderoga Museum.

Salsig, Doyen, ed. *Parole, Quebec—Countersign, Ticonderoga: Second New Jersey Regimental Orderly Book 1776*. Rutherford, NJ: Fairleigh Dickinson Press, 1980.

Scammell, Colonel Alexander. Letter to Abigail Bishop, October 29, 1776. Boston Public Library, Boston.

Schefer, Paul Wilhelm. "An Anonymous Diary." In *Hesse-Hanau Order Books, A Diary and Rosters*, edited and translated by Bruce Burgoyne. Bowie, MD: Heritage Books, 2003, 1–31.

Schank, John, John Starke, and Edward Longcroft. "An Open Letter to Captain Pringle, Saint Johns Canada, June 8, 1777." *The Bulletin of the Fort Ticonderoga Museum* 1, no. 4 (July 1928): 14–20.

Schuyler, Assistant Deputy Quartermaster Harmanus. "Letters to Major General Philip Schuyler." Cornell University Archives, New York.

Schuyler, General Philip. Letter to Lieutenant Colonel Israel Shreve, 2nd New Jersey Regiment, from Albany. Apr. 5, 1776. Israel Shreve Revolutionary War Letters, Special Collections, University of Houston.

———. Miscellaneous Letters, October–November 1776. *The Bulletin of the Fort Ticonderoga Museum* 6, no. 4 (July 1942): 146–148.

Schuyler Papers. Manuscript Division, The New York Public Library. Microfilm copy at David Library of the American Revolution, Washington Crossing, PA.

Scott, Kenneth. *Counterfeiting in Colonial America*. New York: Oxford University Press, 1957.

Senter, Doctor Isaac. "Journal of Dr. Isaac Senter." In *March to Quebec: Journals of the Members of Arnold's Expedition*, edited by Kenneth Roberts. New York: Doubleday, Doran, 1938.

———. *Journal*. 1846; reprint edition New York: Arno Press, 1969. Identical version to that provided by Roberts.

Sewall, Lieutenant Henry. "The Diary of Henry Sewall." *Bulletin of the Fort Ticonderoga Museum* 9 (1963): 75–92.

Shaw, Thomas. "Melancholy Shipwreck." In *A Down East Yankee From The District of Maine*, edited by Windsor Daggett. Portland, ME: A. J. Huston, 1920, 66–72.

Shober, Samuel L., ed. "Arnold and a General Court Martial." *American Historical Record* 3 (November 1874): 444–448.

Shreve, Lieutenant Colonel Israel. Papers and Correspondence. Shreve Papers, Coburn Allen Buxton Collection, Louisiana State University, Baton Rouge.

Shreve, Lieutenant John. "Personal Narrative of the Services of Lieutenant John Shreve of the New Jersey Line of the Continental Army." *Magazine of American History* 3 (1879): 564–578.

Shreve, Lieutenant Colonel Israel, 2nd New Jersey Regiment, Letter to Mary Shreve, dated August 28, 1776, from Ticonderoga, New York. Rutgers University.

Sizer, Theodore, ed. *The Autobiography of Colonel John Trumbull, Patriot-Artist, 1756–1843*. New Haven: Yale University Press, 1953.

Smith, E. Vale. "Diary of Colonel Edward Wigglesworth." in *History of Newburyport*. Newburyport, MA: E. Vale Smith, 1854.

Snyder, Charles M., ed. "With Benedict Arnold at Valcour Island: The Diary of Pascal De Angelis." *Vermont History* 42 (1974): 195–200.

Spafford, John. Soldier with Captain Walker's Company, Colonel Bellow's Regiment. Journal, February 8, 1776–May 27, 1776. Revolutionary War Pension File, M804, Roll 2249, Pages 545–549, National Archives and Records Administration, Washington DC, Microfilm Copy at David Library of the American Revolution, Washington's Crossing, PA.

Spaulding, Phineas. "The Diary of Phineas Spaulding: A Pioneer's Life in the Champlain Valley." *Vermont History* (Spring 1971).

Stanley, George F. G., ed. *For Want of a Horse*. Sackville, NB, Canada: Tribune Press: 1961. Journal of anonymous British officer of 47th Foot.

Stevens, Private Benjamin. "Diary of Benjamin Stevens of Canaan, Connecticut." *Daughters of American Revolution Magazine* 45 (August 1914): 137–140.

Stewart, Jehiel. "Journal of Jehiel Stewart, 1775–1776." Revolutionary Pension Files, Reel 2290, W25138, National Archives and Records Administration, Washington, DC.

Stocking, Abner. "Quebec Expedition Under Arnold, September 13, 1775–September 22, 1776." In *Magazine of History* Extra No. 75 (1921).

Stone, William L., ed. *Journal of Captain Pausch Chief of the Hanau Artillery During the Burgoyne Campaign*. Albany, NY: Joel Munsell's Sons, 1886.

———, ed. *Memoirs and Letters and Journals of Major General Riedesel*. 2 vols. Albany: NY: Joel Munsell's Sons, 1861.

———, trans. *Letters of Brunswick and Hessian Officers During the American Revolution*. Albany, NY: Joel Munsell's Sons, Publishers, 1891.

"Stores for Galleys Trumbull, Congress and Washington" War Department Collection of Revolutionary War Records, Vol. 120, National Archives and Records Collection, Washington, DC. Microfilm copy at U.S. Military Academy Library, West Point, NY.

Stringer, Dr. Samuel, to General Philip Schuyler. Letter dated November 5, 1776. Fort Ticonderoga Museum. Short letter discusses transfer of General Hospital from Fort George to Albany.

Sullivan, James, ed. *Minutes of the Albany Committee of Correspondence, 1775–1778*. Albany: University of the State of New York, 1923.

"Supplies for the Galley 'Washington.'" *Bulletin of the Fort Ticonderoga Museum* 4 (1936): 21–22.

Tay, Samuel. Letter to Mr. William Tay, Woburn, Massachusetts, from Ticonderoga, October 28, 1776. Accessed September 21, 2004, at http://cgi.ebay.com/ws/eBayISAPI.dll?ViewItem&category=10951&item=2270535983&rd=1.

Terrot, Assistant Engineer Charles. Letters to John Frott, from St. Johns, Canada, October 17, 1776, and November 13, 1776. Fort Ticonderoga Museum.

Thacher, James. *Military Journal of the American Revolution*. Hartford, CT: Hurlbut, Williams, 1862.
Thomas, John. Papers. Massachusetts Historical Society. Microfilm copy at David Library of the American Revolution. Washington Crossing, PA.
Thompson, Brigadier General William. Papers. Cumberland County Historical Society, Carlisle, PA.
Thorp, Jennifer D. *The Acland Journal, Lady Harriet Acland and the American War*. Winchester, England: Hampshire County Council, 1993.
Tiffany, Consider. "The American Colonies and the Revolution." 1929. Transcript by Clarence Carter, Library of Congress, Washington, DC.
Todish, Timothy J., ed., and Gary Z. Zaboly, illus. *The Annotated and Illustrated Journals of Major Robert Rogers*. Fleischmanns, NY: Purple Mountain Press, 2002.
Trumbull, Governor Jonathan. "Proclamation by the Governor of Connecticut, January 18, 1776." Sol Feinstone Collection of the American Revolution, Microfilm, Moore Wing, U.S. Military Academy Library, West Point, NY.
Trumbull, Commissary General Joseph. Papers. Connecticut Historical Society. Microfilm copy at David Library of the American Revolution, Washington Crossing, PA.
Trumbull, Assistant Paymaster Jonathan. Papers. Connecticut Historical Society. Microfilm copy at David Library of the American Revolution, Washington Crossing, PA.
Trumbull, Colonel John. *Autobiography, Reminiscences and Letters of John Trumbull, from 1756 to 1841*. New Haven: B.L. Hamlen, 1841.
———. Orderly Book, Deputy Adjutant General, Army of the Northern Theater, July 18, 1776–November 18, 1776." Fort Ticonderoga Museum.
———. Letter dated Ticonderoga, July 12, 1776. *The Bulletin of the Fort Ticonderoga Museum* VI, no. 4 (July 1942): 144–145.
———. Letter from Colonel John Trumbull, dated October 6, 1776, regarding Mount Independence, New York (MSS 372): Boston Public Library, Boston.
———. "Revolutionary Letters." *The Historical Magazine* 1, no. 10 (October 1857): 289–292.
Tuder, Samuel. "Letter to Philip Schuyler, September 30, 1776." Sol Feinstone Collection of the American Revolution, Microfilm, Moore Wing, U.S. Military Academy Library, West Point, NY.
Tuttle, Sergeant Timothy. "Diary, December 21, 1775–November 5, 1776." New Jersey Historical Society, Newark.
Van Gall, Brigadier General. "Letters from Brigadier General Van Gall, Hesse Hanau Infantry Regiment, to Sovereign of Hesse Hanau." Morristown National Historic Park, Morristown, New Jersey. Microfilm copy at David Library of the American Revolution, Washington Crossing, PA.
Van Germann, Captain Friedrich. Letters, 1776–1777. In *Most Illustrious Hereditary Prince: Letters from the Hesse-Hanau Military Contingent During the American Revolutionary War*, edited and translated by Bruce Burgoyne. Bowie, MD: Heritage Books, 2003, 1–30.
Van Wyck, Dr. Pierre C. "Autobiography of Philip Van Cortlandt." *The Magazine of American History* 2 (1878): 278–298.
Varick, Richard. "Letter to Henry Beekman Livingston, August 6, 1776." Sol Feinstone Collection of the American Revolution, Microfilm, Moore Wing, U.S. Military Academy Library, West Point, NY.
Vechten, Captain Samuel Van. "Account Book 12 March 1776–13 May 1777." MSS 93.1.129. Society of the Cincinnati Library, Washington, DC.
———. "Receipt Book, 10 May 1776–4 October 1776." Fort Ticonderoga Museum.
Vialar, Captain Anthony, and Captain Robert Lester. "Orderly Book of the British Militia during the Siege of Quebec by Montgomery." In *Blockade of Quebec in 1775–1776 by the American Revolutionists*, in *Literary and Historical Society of Quebec, Historical Documents*, 7th and 8th ser., edited by Frederick Christian Wurtele. Quebec: The Daily Telegraph Job Printing House, 1905–1906.
Von Riedesel, General Baron. Correspondence. Morristown National Historic Park, Morristown, NJ. Microfilm copy at David Library of the American Revolution, Washington Crossing, PA.
Vose, Joseph. "A Journal of Lieutenant Colonel Joseph Vose, Written During the Expedition Against Canada, from 26 April to 2 July, 1776." *Publications of the Colonial Society of Massachusetts, Transactions, 1900–1902*. Vol. 3: 245–263. Boston: Colonial Society of Massachusetts, 1905).
Wasmus, J.F. *An Eyewitness Account of the American Revolution and New England Life: The Journal of J.F. Wasmus, German Company Surgeon, 1776–1783*. Translated by Helga Doblin, edited and with an introduction by Mary C. Lynn. Contributions in Military Studies, no. 106. New York: Greenwood Press, 1990.
Wayne, Anthony. Letter to Anthony Robinson from Ticonderoga, October 14, 1776. Fort Ticonderoga Museum.
———. "Letter to General Schuyler, from Ticonderoga, February 4, 1777, Collection of the Fort Ticonderoga Museum." *Bulletin of the Fort Ticonderoga Museum* 4, no. 1 (January 1936): 22–23.
———. "Miscellaneous Correspondence." Sol Feinstone Collection of the American Revolution, Microfilm, Moore Wing, U.S. Military Academy Library, West Point, NY.
———. Notebooks. Archives and Special Collections, Dickinson College, Carlisle, PA.
———. *Orderly Books of the Northern Army at Ticonderoga and Mount Independence, From October 17, 1776 to January 8, 1777*. Albany: J. Munsell, 1859.
———. Papers. Historical Society of Pennsylvania, Philadelphia, Pennsylvania. Largely published in Stille, *Major General Anthony Wayne and the Pennsylvania Line in the Continental Army*.
———. Papers. New York Public Library, New York, New York.
———. "The Wayne Orderly Books." *Bulletin of the Fort Ticonderoga Museum* 11 (1963): 94–204.
———. "Orderly Book, Fourth Pennsylvania Battalion, Col. Anthony Wayne, 1776." *Pennsylvania Magazine of History and Biography*, 29 (October 1905): 470–478; 30 (January, July 1906): 91–103, 206–219.
Webster, J. Clarence, ed. *The Journal of Jeffery Amherst, Recording the Military Career of General Amherst in American from 1758 to 1763*. Toronto: Ryerson Press, and Chicago: University of Chicago Press, 1931.
Wells, Bayze. "Journal of Bayze Wells." *Connecticut Historical Society Collections* 7 (Hartford: N.p. 1899): 240–296.

Wheeler, Rufus. "Journal of Lieutenant Rufus Wheeler of Rowley." *The Essex Institute Historical Collections* 68 (October 1932): 371–377.

Whitcomb, Benjamin. "A Journal of a Scout from Crown Point to Saint Johns, Chambly, etc., etc. by Lieutenant Benjamin Whitcomb and Four Men." *The American Historical Record* 1 (1872): 437–440.

Wickman, Donald, ed. "A Most Unsettled Time on Lake Champlain: The October 1776 Journal of Jahiel Stewart." *Vermont History* 64 (1996): 89–98.

Winds, Colonel William. Pay Receipts. Fort Ticonderoga Museum.

Wild, Corporal Ebenezer. "The Journal of Ebenezer Wild, Who Served as Corporal, Sergeant, Ensign and Lieutenant in the American Army of the Revolution." *Massachusetts Historical Society Proceedings* 2nd Series, Vol. 6 (1891): 79–160.

Wilkinson, James. Letters, 1776. Miscellaneous Collections, New York Public Library, New York, NY.

_____. *Memoirs of My Own Times.* Philadelphia: Abraham Small, 1816. Volume 1 contains 1776 campaign.

Willcox, William B., ed. *The Papers of Benjamin Franklin.* New Haven: Yale University Press, 1982. Vol. 22, March 23, 1775, through October 27, 1776; and Vol. 23, October 27, 1776, through April 30, 1777.

Williams, Captain Edward P. Letter to uncle from Skenesborough, August 27, 1776. Society of Cincinnatus Library, Washington, DC.

Williamson, John. *A Treatise on Military Finance, Containing the Pay, Subistence, Deductions and Arrears of the Forces on the British and Irish Establishments, And All the Allowances in Camp, Garrison and Quarters, With An Enquiry into the Method of Clothing and Recruiting the Army, And An Extract from the Report of the Commissioners of Public Accounts Relating to the Office of the Pay Master General.* London: T. Egerton, 1782.

Wooster, Major General David. "Letter from Colonel David Wooster, from Quebec, dated April 23, 1776." Boston Public Library, Boston.

_____. "Letter to Colonel Moses Hazen, March 23, 1776." Sol Feinstone Collection of the American Revolution, Microfilm, Moore Wing, U.S. Military Academy Library, West Point, NY.

_____. "Public Letters of General David Wooster, from April 1775 to 1777, the date of his death." Accessed September 19, 2003 at http://web.cortland.edu/woosterk/rev_ltrs.html.

Yancey, Deputy Commissary James. Letters from Ticonderoga, October 20–December 15, 1776. Accessed November 12, 2003, at http://www.geocities.com/Heartland/Acres/7647/jamesy.htm.

Young, Sir James. *An Essay on the Command of Small Detachments.* London: J. Millan, 1766.

Zlatich, Marko. "Extracts from an Account Book of Samuel Van Vechten's Company, 4th New York Regiment, March-October 1776." *Military Collector & Historian* 52, no. 1 (Spring 2000): 25–29.

Secondary Sources

Amory, Thomas C. *Military Services and Public Life of Major General John Sullivan of the American Revolutionary Army.* Boston: Wiggin and Lunt, 1863; reprint edition, Port Washington, NY: Kennikat Press, 1968.

Bateaux Below, Inc. "The Land Tortoise: America's Oldest Intact Warship." Accessed April 4, 2008, at http://www.thelostradeau.com/.

Bellico, Russel P. *Chronicles of Lake Champlain—Journeys In War and Peace.* Fleischmanns, NY: Purple Mountain Press, 1999.

_____. *Sails and Steam in the Mountains- A Maritime and Military History of Lake George and Lake Champlain.* Fleischmanns, NY: Purple Mountain Press, 2001.

Bennett, Clarence E. *Advance and Retreat to Saratoga in the American Revolution.* Schenectady, NY: Robson & Adee, 1927.

Billias, George A. "Horatio Gates: Professional Soldier." In *George Washington's Generals*, edited by George A. Billias. New York: Morrow, 1964, 79–108.

_____. "John Burgoyne: Ambitious General." In *George Washington's Opponents: British Generals and Admirals in the American Revolution*, edited by George A. Billias. New York: Morrow, 1969, 142–192.

Bird, Harrison. *Navies in the Mountains: The Battles on the Waters of Lake Champlain and Lake George, 1609–1814.* New York: Oxford University Press, 1962.

Blanco, Richard L. *Physician of the American Revolution, Jonathan Potts.* New York: Garland STPM Press, 1979.

Bowler, R. Arthur. *The Influence of Logistics on the Operations of the British Army in America, 1775–1782.* Ph.D. diss., University of London, 1971. Expanded into 1975 book.

_____. *Logistics and the Failure of the British Army in America: 1775–1783.* Princeton: Princeton University Press, 1975.

Bradley, A.G. *Sir Guy Carleton (Lord Dorchester).* Toronto: University of Toronto Press, 1966.

Bratten, John R. *The Gondola Philadelphia and the Battle of Lake Champlain.* College Station, Texas: Texas A&M University Press, 2002.

Brown, Gayle K. "The Impact of the Colonial Anti-Catholic Tradition on the Canadian Campaign, 1775–1776." *Journal of Church and State* 35, no. 3 (Summer 1993): 559–575.

Browne, G.P. "Guy Carleton, 1st Baron of Dorchester." In *Dictionary of Canadian Biography*, edited by John English and Real Belanger. Toronto: University of Toronto Press, 1966–1994, 5: 141–155.

_____. *The St. Lawrence River: Historical, Legendary, Picturesque.* New York and London: G.P. Putnam's Sons, The Knickerbocker Press, 1905.

Burt, A.L. *Guy Carleton, Lord Dorchester, 1724–1804.* Ottawa: Canadian Historical Association, 1955.

Bush, Martin H. *Revolutionary Enigma: A Re-Appraisal of General Philip Schuyler of New York.* Port Washington, NY: Ira J. Friedman, 1969.

Calloway, Colin G. *The American Revolution in Indian Country.* New York: Cambridge University Press, 1995.

Canadian General Staff, Editor of the Historical Section. *A History of the Organization, Development and Services of the Military and Naval Forces of Canada from the Peace of Paris in 1763 to the Present Time.* Vol. 2. *The War of the American Revolution, the Province of Quebec under the Administration of Governor Sir Guy Carleton, 1775–1778.* Ottawa, Canada: Department of Militia and Defence, 1919–1920.

Carp, E. Wayne. *To Starve the Army at Pleasure: Continental Army Administration and American Political*

Culture, 1775–1783. Chapel Hill: University of North Carolina Press, 1984.

Chapelle, Howard I. *The History of American Sailing Ships*. New York: W.W. Norton, 1935.

———. *The History of the American Sailing Navy*. New York: Bonanza Books, 1949.

Charbonneau, Andre. *The Fortifications of Isle Aux Noix*. Ottawa: Parks Canada, 1994.

Cincinnati, Society of. *New York in the American Revolution, An Exhibition from the Library and Museum Collections of the Society of Cincinnati, Anderson House, Washington, D.C., September 29, 1998–April 3, 1999*. Washington: DC: Society of Cincinnati, 1998.

Clausewitz, General Carl Von. *On War*. Michael Howard and Peter Paret, editors and translators. New York: Alfred P. Knopf, 1973.

Coffin, Charles. *The Life and Services of Major General John Thomas*. New York: Egbert, Hovey & King, 1844.

Coffin, Victor. *The Province of Quebec and the Early American Revolution: A Study in English-American Colonial History*. 1896; reprint edition, Port Washington, NY: Kennikat Press, 1970.

Cohn, Arthur B. *Galley Congress Inspection Report*. Washington Navy Yard: Naval Historical Center, October 31, 2001.

Cohn, Arthur B., Adam I. Kane, Christopher R. Sabick, and Edwin R. Scollon. *Valcour Bay Research Project: 1999–2002 Results from the Archaeological Investigation of a Revolutionary War Battlefield in Lake Champlain, Clinton County, New York*. Vergennes, VT: Lake Champlain Maritime Museum, June 2003.

Cohn, Arthur B., et. al. *Valcour Bay Research Project: 1999–2004 Results from the Archaeological Investigation of a Revolutionary War Battlefield in Lake Champlain, Clinton County, New York*. Vergennes, VT: Lake Champlain Maritime Museum, May 2007.

Crist, Allan G. *William Thompson: A Shooting Star*. Lancaster, PA: Cumberland County Historical Society and Museum, 1976.

Cubbison, Douglas R. *Historic Structures Report: The Redoubts of West Point*. West Point, New York: Directorate of Housing and Public Works, U.S. Military Academy, January 2004.

———. *Historic Structures Report, The Hudson River Defenses at Fortress West Point, 1778–1783*. West Point, New York: Directorate of Housing and Public Works, U.S. Military Academy, January 2005.

———. *The Artillery Never Gained More Honour: The British Artillery in the 1776 Valcour Island and 1777 Saratoga Campaigns*. Fleischmans, NY: Purple Mountain Press, 2008.

Davis, Robert P. *"Where a Man Can Go": Major General William Phillips, British Royal Artillery, 1731–1781*. Westport, CT, and London: Greenwood Press, 1999.

DeCourcy, Henry. *The Catholic Church in the United States: A Sketch of Its Ecclesiastical History*. New York; Edward Dunigan and Brother, 1856.

De Fonblanque, Edward Barrington. *Political and Military Episodes in the Latter Half of the Eighteenth Century: Derived from the Life and Correspondence of the Right Hon. John Burgoyne, General, Statesman, Dramatist*. London: Macmillan, 1876.

Drake, Samuel. *Burgoyne's Invasion of 1777; with an Outline Sketch of the American Invasion of Canada, 1775–1776*. Boston: Lee and Shephard, 1889.

Desloges, Yvon. "From a Strategic Site to a Fortified Town, The City of Quebec, 1759–1830." In *The Plains of Abraham*, edited by Jacques Mathieu and Eugen Kedl. Chapter 4. Ottawa, Canada: Septentrion, 1993.

Diamant, Lincoln. *Bernard Romans: Forgotten Patriot of the American Revolution, Military Engineer and Cartographer of West Point and the Hudson Valley*. Harrison, NY: Harbor Hill Books, 1985.

Duncan, Lt. Col. Louis C. *Medical Men in the American Revolution, 1775–1783*. Carlisle Barracks, PA: Medical Field Service School, 1931.

Egly, T.W., Jr. *History of the First New York Regiment, 1775–1783*. Hampton, NH: Peter E. Randall, 1981.

Ernst, Joseph A. *Money and Politics in America, 1755–1775*. Chapel Hill: University of North Carolina Press, 1973.

Everest, Allan S. *Moses Hazen and the Canadian Refugees in the American Revolution*. Syracuse, NY: Syracuse University Press, 1970.

Feister, Lois M. *Archaeological Excavations at the Crown Point Soldiers Barracks, 1976 and 1977*. Peebles Island, NY: New York State Office of Parks, Recreation and Historic Preservation, 1998.

Fenn, Elizabeth A. *Pox Americana: The Great Smallpox Epidemic of 1775–82*. New York: Hill and Wang, 2001.

Flexner, James T. *Doctors on Horseback: Pioneers of American Medicine*. New York: Viking Press, 1937.

Fowler, William M. *Rebels Under Sail: The American Navy During the Revolution*. New York: Charles Scribner's Sons, 1976.

Frazier, Patrick. *The Mohicans of Stockbridge*. Lincoln: University of Nebraska Press, 1992.

Gelinas, Cyrille. *The Role of Fort Chambly in the Development of New France, 1665–1760*. Ottawa, Canada: National Historic Parks and Sites Branch, Parks Canada, 1983.

Gerlach, Don R. *Philip Schuyler and the American Revolution in New York, 1733–1777*. Lincoln: University of Nebraska Press, 1964.

———. *Philip Schuyler and the Growth of New York, 1733–1804*. Albany, NY: Office of State History, 1968.

———. *Proud Patriot: Philip Schuyler and the War of Independence, 1775–1783*. Syracuse, NY: Syracuse University Press, 1987.

Gillet, Mary C. *The Army Medical Department, 1775–1818*. Washington, DC: The Center of Military History, United States Army, 2004.

Haggland, Lorenzo F. *"A Page from the Past:" The Story of the Continental Gundelo Philadelphia on Lake Champlain*. Privately printed: 1936.

Hagglund, Lorenzo F. "Scrapbook from the Recovery of the *Royal Savage*." c. 1934. Courtesy of the Horse Soldier Relic Shop, Gettysburg, Pennsylvania, and Dr. Walter L. Powell, Gettysburg, Pennsylvania.

Hamilton, Edward P. *Fort Ticonderoga: Key to a Continent*. 1964; reprint edition, Ticonderoga, NY: Fort Ticonderoga, 1995.

Hatch, Robert McConnell. *Thrust for Canada: The American Attempt on Quebec in 1775–1776*. Boston: Houghton Mifflin, 1979.

Hanley, Thomas O'Brien. *Revolutionary Statesman: Charles Carroll and the War*. Chicago: Loyola University Press, 1983.

Harman, Mieceslaud. *Kosciuszko in the American Revo-

lution. New York: Polish Institute of Arts and Sciences in America, 1943.

Hedin, Bruce. Undergraduate paper, "Faunal Analysis from Mount Independence, 1992." Fort Ticonderoga Museum.

Higginbotham, Don. *The War of American Independence: Military Attitudes, Policies & Practice, 1763–1789*. Boston: Northeastern University Press, 1983.

Howe, Archibald M. *Colonel John Brown of Pittsfield, Massachusetts; The Brave Accuser of Benedict Arnold: An Address Delivered Before the Fort Rensselaer Chapter of the Daughters of the American Revolution and Others., at the Village of Palantine Bridge, New York, September 29, 1908*. Boston: W. B. Clarke, 1908.

Howson, Gerald. *Burgoyne of Saratoga: A Biography*. New York: Times Books, 1979.

Huey, Paul R. *Animal Husbandry and Meat Consumption at Crown Point, New York, in the Colonial Period and Revolutionary War*. Peebles Island, Waterford, NY: New York State Office of Parks and Recreation, Division for Historic Preservation, Bureau of Historic Sites, October 1979.

Huston, James A. *Logistics of Liberty: American Services of Supply in the Revolutionary War and After*. Newark: University of Delaware Press; London ; Cranbury, NJ: Associated University Presses, 1991.

———. *The Sinews of War, Army Logistics, 1775–1953*. Washington, DC: Center of Military History, United States Army, 1997.

Jacobs, James R. *Tarnished Warrior: Major General James Wilkinson*. New York: Macmillan, 1938.

James, Isabella [Mrs. Thomas Potts James]. *Memorial Of Thomas Potts, Junior, Who Settled in Pennsylvania; With An Historic-Genealogical Account of His Descendants to the Eighth Generation*. Cambridge: Privately printed, 1874. Accessed December 29, 2003, at http://www.heritagepursuit.com/Potts/PottsM.htm.

Jones, Henry Charles. *History of the Campaign for the Conquest of Canada in 1776*. Philadelphia: Porter & Coates, 1882; reprint, New York: Research Reprints, 1970.

Kajencki, Francis Casimir. *Thaddeus Kosciuszko: Military Engineer of the American Revolution*. El Paso, Texas: Southwest Polonia Press, 1998.

Korvemaker, E. Frank. *1967 Salvage Excavations at Fort Lennox, Isle-Aux-Noix, Quebec*. Ottawa: National Historic Parks and Sites Branch, Parks Canada, 1968.

———. *Archaeological Excavations at Fort Lennox National Historical Park, 1971, Isle-Aux-Noix, Quebec*. Ottawa: National Historic Parks and Sites Branch, Department of Indian Affairs and Northern Development, 1972–1973.

Krueger, John W. *A Gentleman of Zeal and Character in the Public Service: Doctor Jonathan Potts and the Northern Medical Department*. Master's thesis, University of Vermont, 1974.

———. *Troop Life at the Champlain Valley Forts During the American Revolution*. Ph.D. diss., State University of New York at Albany, 1981.

Lanctot, Gustave. *Canada & the American Revolution, 1774–1783*. Translated by Margaret M. Cameron. Cambridge: Harvard University Press, 1967.

Laws, Lt. Col. M.E.S. *Battery Records of the Royal Artillery, 1716–1859*. Woolwich: Royal Artillery Institute, 1952.

Lee, D. "The Americans on Isle-Aux-Noix, 1775–1776." In D. Lee, et al. *Theme Papers, Isle-Aux-Noix, Manuscript Report Series No. 47*. Ottawa, Canada: Parks Canada, 1967.

Leroy, Perry E. *Sir Guy Carleton as a Military Leader During the American Invasion and Repulse in Canada, 1775–1776*. Ph.D. diss., Ohio State University, 1960.

Lesser, Charles H. *The Sinews of Independence: Monthly Strength Reports of the Continental Army*. Chicago: 1976.

Lewis, Paul. *The Man Who Lost America: A Biography of Gentleman Johnny Burgoyne*. New York: Dial Press, 1973.

Lonergan, Carroll V. *Ticonderoga: Historic Portage*. Ticonderoga, NY: Fort Mount Hope Society Press, 1959.

Lossing, Benson J. *The Life and Times of Philip Schuyler*. 2 vols. New York: Sheldon, 1872–1873.

Lundenberg, Philip K. *The Continental Gunboat "Philadelphia."* Washington DC: Smithsonian Institute, 1966. Updated in 1995 by Lake Champlain Maritime Museum.

———. *The Gunboat "Philadelphia" and the Defense of Lake Champlain in 1776*. Basin Harbor, VT: Lake Champlain Maritime Museum, 1995.

Mahan, A.T. *Types of Naval Officers, Drawn from the History of the British Navy*. Boston: Little, Brown, 1901.

Malcomson, Robert. *Warships of the Great Lakes, 1754–1834*. Rochester, Kent, Great Britain: Chatham, 2001.

Marshall, Douglas W., and Howard H. Peckman. *Campaigns of the American Revolution: An Atlas of Manuscript Maps*. Ann Arbor: The William L. Clements Library of the University of Michigan, 1976.

Martin, James Kirby. *Benedict Arnold, Revolutionary Hero: An American Warrior Reconsidered*. New York: New York University Press, 1997.

McCusker, John J., and Russell E. Menard. *The Economy of British America, 1607–1789*. Chapel Hill and London: University of North Carolina Press, 1985.

McLaughlin, Scott A. *History Told From the Depths of Lake Champlain: 1992–1993 Fort Ticonderoga–Mount Independence Submerged Cultural Resource Survey*. Ferrisburgh, VT: Lake Champlain Maritime Museum, 2000.

Melville, Annabelle M. *John Carroll of Baltimore: Founder of the American Catholic Hierarchy*. New York: Scribner, 1955.

Mintz, Max M. *The Generals of Saratoga: John Burgoyne & Horatio Gates*. New Haven, CT: Yale University Press, 1990.

Montgomery, Florence M. *Textiles in America, 1650–1870*. 1984; revised edition, New York and London: Norton, 2007.

Morton, Doris Begor. *Birth of the United States Navy*. Whitehall, NY: Whitehall Times, 1982.

———. *Philip Skene of Skenesborough*. Granville, NY: Grastorf Press, 1959.

Murray, Joseph Alexander. "Autobiographical Sketch of General William Thompson." Cumberland County Historical Society, Carlisle, PA.

Murray, Stuart. *Washington's Farewell: The Final Parting with His Officers After Victory in the Revolution*. Bennington, VT: Images from the Past, 1999.

Nadon, Pierre. *Fort Chambly: A Narrative History*. Manuscript Report Series no. 17. Ottawa: Parks Canada, 1965.

Nelson, Paul D. *Anthony Wayne, Soldier of the Early Republic*. Bloomington: Indiana University Press, 1985.

_____. *General Horatio Gates: A Biography*. Baton Rouge: Louisiana State University Press, 1976.

_____. *General Sir Guy Carleton, Lord Dorchester: Soldier-Statesman of Early British Canada*. Madison, NJ, and London: Fairleigh Dickinson University Press, 2000.

Osler, Edward. *The Life of Admiral Viscount Exmouth*. London: Smith, Elder, 1835.

Palmer, Peter S. *Battle of Valcour on Lake Champlain, October 11th, 1776*. Plattsburgh, New York: 1876.

Patterson, Samuel W. *Horatio Gates: Defender of American Liberties*. New York: Columbia University Press, 1941.

Peckham, Howard H., ed. *The Toll of Independence: Engagements & Battle Casualties of the American Revolution*. Chicago: University of Chicago Press, 1974.

Pell, John H.G. "Philip Schuyler: The General as Aristocrat." In *George Washington's Generals*, edited by George A. Billias. New York: Morrow, 1964, 54–78.

Piedalue, Gisele. "Research Bulletin no. 207, Archaeology at Fort Saint-Jean, 1980–1982." Ottawa, Canada: Parks Canada, November 1983.

Randall, Willard Sterne. *Benedict Arnold: Patriot and Traitor*. New York: Morrow, 1990.

Rankin, Hugh F. "Anthony Wayne: Military Romanticist." In *George Washington's Generals*, edited by George A. Billias. New York: Morrow, 1964, 260–290.

Reynolds, Paul R. *Guy Carleton: A Biography*. Toronto: Gage Publishing, 1980.

Risch, Erna. *Quartermaster Support of the Army, 1775–1939*. Washington, DC: Center of Military History, United States Army, 1989.

_____. *Supplying Washington's Army*. Washington, DC: Center of Military History, United States Army, 1981.

Roberts, Kenneth. *Arundel*. Garden City, NY: Doubleday, 1929; revised edition, 1933.

_____. *Rabble In Arms, A Chronicle of Arundel and the Burgoyne Invasion*. Garden City, NY: Doubleday, Doran, 1935.

Rommel, John G., Jr. *Richard Varick, New York Aristrocrat*. Ph.D. diss., Columbia University, 1966.

Smith, Charles R. *Marines in the Revolution*. Washington DC: United States Marine Corps, 1975.

Smith, Ellen H. *Charles Carroll of Carrollton*. Cambridge, MA; Harvard University Press, 1942.

Smith, Justin H. *Our Struggle for the Fourteenth Colony, Canada and the American Revolution*. 2 vols. 1907; reprint edition Cranbury, NJ: Scholar's Bookshelf, 2005.

Smith, Paul H. "Sir Guy Carleton: Soldier Statesman." In *George Washington's Opponents: British Generals and Admirals in the American Revolution*, edited by George A. Billias. New York: Morrow, 1969, 103–141.

Spargo, John. *Lieutenant Colonel Joseph Wait of Rogers Rangers and the Continental Army*. Barre, VT: Grand Lodge of Vermont, 1942.

Stanley, George F. G. *Canada Invaded, 1775–1776*. Toronto, Canada: Hakkert, 1973.

Starbuck, David R. *The Ferris Site on Arnold's Bay, Vermont*. Vergennes, VT: Lake Champlain Maritime Museum, 1989.

_____. *Mount Independence and the American Revolution, 1776–1777*. Montpelier, VT: Vermont Division Historic Press, 1991.

Steele, Ian K. *Betrayals, Fort William Henry & The "Massacre."* New York: Oxford University Press, 1990.

Stephenson, O.W. *The Supplies for the American Revolutionary Army*. Ph.D. diss., 1919, University of Michigan.

Stevens, Paul Lawrence. *His Majesty's "Savage" Allies: British Policy and the Northern Indians during the Revolutionary War, The Carleton Years, 1774–1778*. Ph.D. diss., 1984, State University of New York at Buffalo.

Stille, Charles J. *Major General Anthony Wayne and the Pennsylvania Line in the Continental Army*. 1893; reprint edition, Port Washington, NY: Kennikat Press, 1968. Contains numerous letters and extracts from the papers of Wayne.

Strach, Stephen G. *An Episode in the History of the Schuyler Mansion: The Visit of Lieutenant General John Burgoyne, October 18–27, 1777*. Albany, NY: Friends of Schuyler Mansion, 1982 and 2002. Contains list of Burgoyne's staff officers.

Stuart, Isaac W. *Life of Jonathan Trumbull, Governor of Connecticut*. Hartford: Belknap & Warfield, 1859.

Thompson, William Y. *Israel Shreve: Revolutionary War Officer*. Ruston, LA: McGinty Trust Fund Publications, 1979.

Tuchman, Barbara W. *The March of Folly: From Troy to Vietnam*. 1984; paperback edition, New York: Ballantine Books, 1985.

Tucker, Glenn. *Mad Anthony Wayne and the New Nation: The Story of Washington's Front-Line General*. Harrisburg, PA: Stackpole Books, 1973.

Trussell, John B.B. *The Pennsylvania Line: Regimental Organization and Operations, 1775–1783*. Harrisburg: Pennsylvania Historical and Museum Commission, 1993.

Wallace, Willard M. "Benedict Arnold: Traitorous Hero." In *George Washington's Generals*, edited by George A. Billias. New York: Morrow, 1964, 163–192.

_____. *Traitorous Hero: The Life and Fortunes of Benedict Arnold*. New York: Harper & Brothers, 1954.

Walker, Paul K. *Engineers of Independence*. Washington, DC: Office of the Chief of Engineers, U.S. Army Corps of Engineers, 1981.

Ward, Harry M. *General William Maxwell and the New Jersey Continentals*. Westport, CT: Greenwood Press, 1997.

Ward, Christopher. *The War of the Revolution in Two Volumes*. New York: Macmillan, 1952.

Welcome to the Crown Point Forts: A Self-Conducted Post Tour. New York: Crown Point Foundation, 1971.

Wheeler, Joseph L., and Mable A. Wheeler. *The Mount Independence-Hubbardton 1776 Military Road*. Benson, VT: J.L. Wheeler, 1968.

Whittemore, Charles P. *A General of the Revolution: John Sullivan of New Hampshire*. New York and London: Columbia University Press, 1961.

_____. "John Sullivan: Luckless Irishman." In *George Washington's Generals*, edited by George A. Billias. New York: Morrow, 1964, 137–162.

Wickman, Donald H. *Built with Spirit, Deserted in Darkness: The American Occupation of Mount Independence, 1776–1777*. Master's thesis, University of Vermont, 1993.

_____. "Life in Camp: Mount Independence, 1776–1777." Undergraduate paper, University of Vermont, 1992. Fort Ticonderoga Museum.

_____. "Was There a Blockhouse at Mount Hope?" Research paper prepared for Fort Ticonderoga Museum, July 1993. Fort Ticonderoga Museum.

Wildes, Harry E. *Anthony Wayne: Troubleshooter of the American Revolution.* New York: Harcourt, Brace, 1941.

Wilhelmy, J. P. *German Mercenaries in Canada.* Quebec: Maison des Motts, 1985.

Wrong, George M. *Canada and the American Revolution; The Disruption of the First British Empire.* New York: Macmillan, 1935.

Wylly, Colonel H.C. *The Loyal North Lancashire Regiment* (47th Foot). London: The Royal United Service Institution, 1933.

Periodical Articles

Aldrich, Edgar. "The Affair of the Cedars and the Service of Col. Timothy Bedel in the War of the Revolution." *New Hampshire Historical Society Proceedings,* 3 (December 1891): 194–231.

Aimone, Alan C., and Barbara A. Aimone "'Brave Bostonians: New Yorkers' Roles in the Winter Invasion of Canada." *Journal of the Company of Military Historians* 36 (Winter 1984): 134–150.

Aimone, Alan. "New York's 1776 Fighting Minority." Unpublished mss.

Arndt, Karl. "The German Occupation of Quebec in 1776." *Journal of German-American Studies* 14, no. 4 (1978): 107–113.

Barker, E. Eugene. "The Lost Cannon of Crown Point" *Journal of the Company of Military Historians* 26 (Fall 1974): 159–164.

Becker, Ann M. "Smallpox in Washington's Army: Strategic Implications of the Disease During the American Revolutionary War." *The Journal of Military History* 68 (April 2004): 381–430.

Blanco, Richard L. "Military Medicine in Northern New York, 1776–1777." *New York History* LXIII, no. 1 (January 1982): 39–58.

Bolander, L.H. "Arnold's Retreat from Valcour Island." *United States Naval Institute Proceedings* (December 1929): 1060–1062.

Bowler, R. Arthur. "Sir Guy Carleton and the Campaign of 1776 in Canada." *The Canadian Historical Review* 55, no. 2 (June 1974): 131–140.

Bredenberg, Oscar R. "The American Champlain Fleet, 1775–1777." *The Bulletin of the Fort Ticonderoga Museum* 12, no. 4 (September 1968): 249–263.

_____. "The Royal Savage." *The Bulletin of the Fort Ticonderoga Museum* 12, no. 2 (September 1966): 128–149.

Brisebois, Michel. "Books from General Wolfe's Library at the National Library of Canada." *National Library News* 28, no. 2 (February 1996), accessed December 5, 2007, at *http://epe.lac-bac.gc.ca/100/202/301/nl news/nlnews-h/1996/02/2802e-15.htm.*

Brown, Gayle K. "The Impact of Colonial Anti-Catholic Tradition on the Canadian Campaign, 1775–1776." *Journal of Church & State* 35, no. 3 (Summer 1993): 559–575.

Burt, A. L. "The Quarrel Between Germain and Carleton: An Inverted Story." *The Canadian Historical Review* 11, no. 3 (September 1930): 202–222.

Caldwell, Lieutenant Colonel E.L. "Fort Saint Jean on the Richelieu River." *The Bulletin of the Fort Ticonderoga Museum* 4, no. 7 (July 1938): 5–18.

Carlson, Dr. Eric T. "Benjamin Rush on Revolutionary War Hygiene." *The Bulletin of the New York Academy of Medicine.* 55, no. 7 (July-August 1979): 614–635.

Cash, Philip. "The Canadian Military Campaign of 1775–1776: Medical Problems and Effects of Disease." *Journal of the American Medical Association* 236 (1976): 52–56.

Cifaldi, Sue. "Henry Blake, A New Hampshire Fifer in the Revolutionary War." *The Sonneck Society Bulletin* 14, no. 3 (Fall 1988).

Clark, Jane. "The Command of the Canadian Army for the Campaign of 1777." The *Canadian Historical Review* 10, no. 2 (June 1929): 129–135.

Cohn, Art. "An Incident Not Known to History: Squire Ferris and Benedict Arnold at Ferris Bay, October 13, 1776." *Vermont History* 55 (1987): 96–112.

Copeland, Peter F. "Clothing of the Fourth Pennsylvania Battalion, 1776–1777." *Military Collector and Historian* 18 (Fall 1966): 69–74.

Crown Point Foundation. "Welcome to the Crown Point Forts; A Self-Conducted Post Tour." 1971.

Cubbison, Douglas R. "The Coins of the British Private Soldier in the American Revolution." Accessed at *http://www.csmid.com.*

_____, and Justin Clement. "The Artillery Never Gained More Honour: The British and Hesse-Hanau Artillery Gunboats at the Battle of Valcour Island." *Journal of the Society for Army Historical Research* 85, no. 343 (Autumn 2007): 247–255.

Dawson, S.E. "The Massacre at the Cedars." *Canadian Monthly* (April 1874): 1–15.

DeLancey, Edward F. "Chief Justice William Allen." *Pennsylvania Magazine of History and Biography* 1 (1877): 202–211.

Dusablon, L.A. "Pelissier, The Foundry Man of Three Rivers, Canada, Maker of Ammunition for the Americans Attacking Quebec." *The American Catholic Historical Researches* 3, no. 3 (1907): 193–196.

_____. "Miscellaneous Documents, French-Canadians in the 1776 Campaign." *The American Catholic Historical Researches* 3, no. 3 (1907): 206–250.

Farmer, Edward G. "Skenesborough: Continental Navy Shipyard." *United States Naval Institute Proceedings* 90 (1964): 160–162.

Furcron, Thomas B. "Mount Independence, 1776–1777." *The Bulletin of the Fort Ticonderoga Museum* 9, no. 4 (Winter 1954): 230–248.

Glidden, G. William. "Prelude to Saratoga" Unpublished paper, 1991. Fort Ticonderoga Museum.

Gorssline, R.M. "Medical Notes on Burgoyne's Campaigns, 1776–1777." *Canadian Defence Quarterly* (April 1929): 356–363.

Grange, Roger T., Jr. "Early Fortification Ditches at Isle-Aux-Noix, Quebec." *History and Archaeology* 18A and 18B. Ottawa: National Historic Parks and Sites Branch, Parks Canada, Environment Canada, 1982.

_____. "Excavation of the Right Redoubt and Blockhouse, British Fortifications at Isle-Aux-Noix, Quebec." *History and Archaeology* 36. Ottawa: National Historic Parks and Sites Branch, Parks Canada, Environment Canada, 1982, 1–161.

Gradish, Stephen F. "The German Mercenaries in North America During the American Revolution: A Case Study." *Canadian Journal of History* 4, no. 1 (March 1969): 23–46.

Haarmann, Albert W. "Notes on the Brunswick Troops in British Service During the American War of Independence, 1776–1783." *Journal of the Society for Army Historical Research* 48, no. 195 (Autumn 1970): 140–143.

Hagglund, Lorenzo F. "The Continental Gunboat 'Philadelphia.'" *United States Naval Institute Proceedings* 62 (1936): 655–669.

Higginbotham, Don. "The Early American Way of War: Reconnaissance and Appraisal." *The William and Mary Quarterly* Third Series, 44, no. 2 (April 1987): 230–273.

Hoffman, Howard P. "The Gunboat 'Philadelphia': A Continental Gunboat of 1776 and Her Model." *Nautical Research Journal* 30 (1984): 55–67.

Howe, Dennis E., William Murphy, and Marjorie Robbins. "The Southern Battery at Mount Independence." *The Journal of Vermont Archaeology* 1 (1994): 127–140.

Huey, Paul. "The History and Archaeology of Crown Point." *Fortress* 5 (May 1990): 44–54.

Hubbard, Timothy W. "Battle of Valcour Island: Benedict Arnold as Hero." *American Heritage* 17 (October 1966): 8–11, 87–91.

Hunter, Thomas M. "Doctor Samuel Adams, Revolutionary Army Surgeon and Diarist." *United States Armed Forces Journal* 8 (1957): 625–643.

Kingsley, Ronald F. "An Archaeological Survey of the Land Approach to Mount Independence, 1776–1777, Orwell, Addison County, Vermont." *The Journal of Vermont Archaeology* 2 (1997): 57–71.

Kingsley, Ronald F., and Harvey J. Alexander. "The Failure of Abercromby's Attack on Fort Carillon, July 1758, and the Scapegoating of Matthew Clerk." *The Journal of Military History* 72 (January 2008): 43–70.

Kingsley, Ronald F., and John P. Chiamulera. "An Investigation of the South Side Landing Area of Mount Independence, Orwell Township, Addison County, Vermont." *The Journal of Vermont Archaeology* 4 (2003): 19–40.

Kingsley, Ronald F., and James Rowe, Jr. "In Search of the Eighteenth Century Road, Shoreham Township, Addison County, Vermont." *The Journal of Vermont Archaeology* 3 (2003): 61–68.

Krueger, John W. "Troop Life at the Champlain Valley Forts During the American Revolution." *Bulletin of the Fort Ticonderoga Museum* 14, no. 3 (Summer 1982): 158–183; 14, no. 5 (Summer 1984): 277–310.

Langston, Paul. "Tyrant and Oppressor, Colonial Press Reaction to the Quebec Act." *The Historical Journal of Massachusetts* 34, no. 1 (2006): 1–17.

Larter, Harry C. "German Troops With Burgoyne, 1776–1777." *Bulletin of the Fort Ticonderoga Museum* 9, no. 1 (Winter 1952): 13–24.

Lundenberg, Philip K. "Microcosm of Revolution." *Bulletin of the American Society of Arms Collectors* 37 (1977): 43–51.

MacLean, Allen. "Arnold's Strength at Quebec." *Journal of the Company of Military Historans* 29 (Fall 1977): 137–139.

Mahan, Alfred T. "The Naval Campaign of 1776 on Lake Champlain." *Scribner's Magazine* (1898): 147–160.

Manders, Eric I. "Notes on Troop Units in the Northern Army, 1776." *Military Collector and Historian Journal of the Company of Military Historians* 27 (Spring, Fall 1975): 8–12, 113–117.

_____. "Notes on Troop Units in the Northern Army, 1775–1776." *Military Collector and Historian Journal of the Company of Military Historians* 23 (Winter 1971): 117–120.

Martin, James Kirby. "Benedict Arnold's Treason As Political Protest." *Parameters, Journal of the US Army War College* 11, no. 3 (1981): 63–74.

McBarron, H. Charles, and Rene Chartrand. "The Quebec Militia, 1775–1776." *Military Collector and Historian* 23, no. 2 (Summer 1971): 45–47.

Meany, Dr. Joseph F. "Batteaux and Battoe Men: An American Colonial Response to the Problems of Logistics in Mountain Warfare" Accessed December 15, 2000, at http://www.dmna.state.ny.us/historic/bateau.html.

Morris, George F. "Major Whitcomb, Ranger and Partisan Leader in the Revolution." *Proceedings of the New Hampshire Historical Society*, Vol. 4, Part III, 298–321.

Neill, Edward D. "Biographical Sketch of Doctor Jonathan Potts." *The New England Historical and Genealogical Register* 18 (1864): 21–36.

Nelson, Paul D. "Guy Carleton vs. Benedict Arnold: The Campaign of 1776 in Canada on Lake Champlain." *New York History* 57, no. 3 (1976): 339–366.

Pell, John H.G. "Philip Schuyler, Esquire, An Unfinished Biography." *The Bulletin of the Fort Ticonderoga Museum* 15, no. 3 (Winter 1991): 9–56.

_____. "Philip Skene of Skenesborough" *New York State Historical Association Proceedings* 26 (1928): 27–44.

_____. "The Revenge." *The Bulletin of the Fort Ticonderoga Museum* 1, no. 4 (July 1928): 6–13.

Rees, John U. " 'To Subsist an Army Well...' Soldiers' Cooking Equipment, Provisions, and Food Preparation During the American War for Independence." *Military Collector & Historian* 53, no. 1 (Spring 2001): 7–23

Reynolds, Helen Wilkinson. "Udny Hay." *Dutchess County Historical Society Yearbook* 4 (1925): 49–59.

Robbins, Peggy. "The Forgotten Battle of Valcour Island" *Journal of America's Military Past* 23, no. 2 (Summer 1996): 53–64.

Scott, Kenneth. "A British Counterfeiting Press in New York Harbor, 1776." *New York Historical Society Quarterly* 30, nos. 2–3 (April-July 1955): 117–120.

_____. "New Hampshire Tory Counterfeiters Operating from New York City." *New York Historical Society Quarterly* 34, no. 1 (January 1950): 31–57.

Shea, John Gilmary. "Why is Canada Not a Part of the United States?" *United States Catholic Historical Magazine* 3, no. 10 (1890–1891): 113–127.

Skerrett, Robert G. "Lake Champlain Yields Wreck of 'Royal Savage.'" *Compressed Air Magazine* 40, no. 1 (January 1935): 4626–4630.

_____. "Wreck of the 'Royal Savage' Recovered." *United States Naval Institute Proceedings* 61 (1935): 1646–1652.

Smith, Dorothy U. "Historic War Vessels in Lake Champlain and Lake George." *New York State Museum Bulletin* no. 313 (October 1937): 123–136.

Starbuck, David R. "Building Independence on Lake Champlain." *Archaeology* 46, no. 5 (1993): 60–63.

_____, and William Murphy. "Archaeology at Mount Independence: An Introduction" *The Journal of Vermont Archaeology* 1 (1994): 115–126.

Stevens, John Austin. "Ebenezer Stevens, Lieutenant Colonel of Artillery in the Continental Army." *The Magazine of American History* 1 (1877): 588–610.

Stitt, Edward W., Jr. "Horatio Gates." *The Bulletin of the Fort Ticonderoga Museum* 9, no. 2 (Winter 1953): 93–115.

Strach, Stephen G. "A Memoir of the Exploits of Captain Alexander Fraser and His Company of British Marksmen, 1776–1777." *Journal of the Society for Army Historical Research* 63 (1985): 91–98.

Sweet, David B. "Dugan's Canadian Rangers, 1776." *Military Collector & Historian* 28, no. 1 (Spring 1986): 20.

Theberge, Gregory. "To Nourish His Majesty's Troops: The Mess, Kitchens and Provisions for the Common British Soldier During the American War for Independence." *The Brigade Dispatch* 30, no. 1 (Spring 2000): 2–15.

Watson, Winslow C. "Arnold's Retreat After the Battle of Valcour." *Magazine of American History* 6 (June 1881): 414–417. Watson's interpretation of Arnold's Retreat Route from Valcour Island, no longer generally accepted.

_____. "Naval Campaign on Lake Champlain in 1776." *American Historical Record* 3 (November 1874): 438–444, 501–506. Use with caution; some errors noted.

Webster, Donald B. "Grenades at Fort Senneville." *Arms Collecting* 32, no. 3 (August 1994): 94–95.

Westbrook, Virginia M. "Spruce Beer." *Bulletin of the Fort Ticonderoga Museum* 15, no. 6 (1994): 509–515.

Wheeler, Joseph L., and Mabel A. Wheeler. "The Mount Independence–Hubbardton Military Road." *Vermont History* 27, no. 2 (April 1959): 88–122.

Whiteley, W.H. "The British Navy and the Siege of Quebec, 1775–1776." *Canadian Historical Review* 61, no. 1 (1980): 3–27.

Williams, Colonel John A. "Mount Independence In Time Of War, 1776–1783." *Vermont History* 35 (1967): 89–96.

Background Information on the American Army

Anderson, Fred W. *A People's Army: Massachusetts Soldiers and Society in the Seven Years' War*. Chapel Hill: University of North Carolina Press, 1984.

_____. "Why Did Colonial New Englanders Make Bad Soldiers? Contractual Principles and Military Conduct During the Seven Years War." *The William and Mary Quarterly* 3rd series, 38, (1981): 395–417.

Applegate, Howard L. "The Medical Administrators of the American Revolutionary Army." *Military Affairs* 25 (1961): 1–10.

_____. "The American Revolutionary War Hospital Department." *Military Medicine* 126, no. 4 (April 1961): 296–306.

_____. "Preventive Medicine in the American Revolutionary Army." *Military Medicine* 126, no. 5 (May 1961): 379–382.

_____. "Remedial Medicine in the American Revolutionary Army." *Military Medicine* 126, no. 6 (June 1961): 450–453.

_____. "Effect of the American Revolution on American Medicine." *Military Medicine* 126, no. 7 (July 1961): 551–553.

_____. "The Need for Further Study of the Medical History of the American Revolutionary Army." *Military Medicine* 126, no. 8 (August 1961): 616–618.

Beardsley, Dr. Ebenezer. "History of a Dysentery in the 22nd Regiment of the Late Continental Army." *The American Museum* 5 (1789): 245–250.

_____. "Remarks on the Effects of Stagnant Air." *Memoirs of the American Academy of Arts and Sciences* 1 (1785): 542–543.

Becker, Ann M. "Smallpox in Washington's Army: Strategic Implications of the Disease during the American Revolutionary War." *The Journal of Military History* 68, no. 2 (April 2004): 381–430.

Blake, John B. "Diseases and Medical Practice in Colonial America." *International Record of Medicine* 171, no. 6 (June 1958): 350–363.

_____. "The Inoculation Controversy in Boston, 1721–1722." *New England Quarterly* 25 (1952): 489–506.

_____. "Smallpox inoculation in Colonial Boston." *Journal of the History of Medicine and Allied Sciences* 8 (1953): 284–300.

Blanco, Richard L. "Continental Army Hospitals and American Society, 1775–1781." In *Adapting to Conditions, War and Society in the Eighteenth Century*, edited by Maarten Ultee. Tuscaloosa: University of Alabama Press, 150–173.

Breton, Pierre N. *Illustrated History of Coins and Tokens Relating to Canada*. Montreal: Breton, 1894.

Burnett, Edmund C. "The Continental Congress and Agricultural Supplies." *Agricultural History* 2, no. 3 (July 1928): 111–128.

Calomiris, Charles W. "Institutional Failure, Monetary Scarcity, and the Depreciation of the Continental." *Journal of Economic History* 48 (March 1988): 47–68.

Cash, Philip. "Medical Men at the Siege of Boston, April 1775-April 1776: Problems of the Massachusetts and Continental Armies." *Memoirs of the American Philosophical Society* 98 (Philadelphia: 1973).

Centers for Disease Control and Prevention, "smallpox," accessed November 27, 2007, at *http://www.bt.cdc.gov/agent/smallpox/*.

Cowen, David L. *Medicine in Revolutionary New Jersey* (Trenton: New Jersey Historical Commission. 1976).

Cutbush, Edward. *Observations on the Means of Preserving the Health of Soldiers and Sailors: and on the Duties of the Medical Department of the Army and Navy, with Remarks on Hospitals and Their Internal Arrangement*. Philadelphia: Printed for Thomas Dobson, at the Stone House, no. 41, South Second Street, Fry and Kammerer, printers, 1808.

DeForest, Major Henry P. "Benjamin Rush's Directions for Preserving the Health of Soldiers, with a note upon Surgeon Ebenezer Alden." *The Military Surgeon, Journal of the Association of Military Surgeons of the United States* 22 (March 1908): 182–190. Contains copy of Rush's "Directions."

DePauw, Linda Grant. "Women in Combat, The Revolutionary War Experience." *Armed Forces and Society* 7, no. 2 (Winter 1981): 209–226.

Ferguson, James E. "Currency Finance, An Interpretation of Colonial Monetary Practices." *William and Mary Quarterly* 10, no. 2 (April 1953): 153–180.

Frost, Robert I. *The Northern Wars, 1558–1721*. Essex, England: Pearson Education, 2000.

Gibson, James E. *Dr. Bodo Otto and the Medical Background of the American Revolution*. Springfield, IL, and Baltimore, MD: Charles C. Thomas, 1937.

Gibson, James E. "The Role of Disease in the 70,000 Casualties in the American Revolutionary Army." *Transactions and Studies of the College of Physicians in Philadelphia* 4th Series, 17 (1949): 121–127.

Gibson, Dr. Maurice B. "Naval and Maritime Medicine During the Revolution," in *Naval Documents of the*

American Revolution, edited by William James Morgan. Vol. 6. Appendix A, 1483–1489. Washington, D.C.: U.S. Government Printing Office, 1964–1981.

Gilman, Dr. C. Malcolm. "Military Surgery in the American Revolution." *Journal of the Medical Society of New Jersey* 57, no. 8 (August 1960): 491–496.

Godbeer, Richard. *Sexual Revolution in Early America*. Baltimore and London: Johns Hopkins University Press, 2002.

Gordon, Dr. Marice B. "Naval and Maritime Medicine During the Revolution." In *Naval Documents of the American Revolution*, edited by William Bell Clark and William J. Morgan. Vol. 6: Appendix A. Washington, D.C.: U.S. Government Printing Office, 1964–1981.

Griffenhagen, George B. *Drug Supplies in the American Revolution*. Washington, D.C.: Smithsonian Institute, Contributions from the Museum of History and Technology Bulletin 225, Paper 16, 110–133.

———. "Medicines in the American Revolution" In *American Pharmacy in the Colonial and Revolutionary Periods*, edited by George A. Bender and John Parascandola. Madison, WI: American Institute of the History of Pharmacy, 1977, 25–36.

———. "The Evolution of the Medical Chest." *The Antiques Dealer* 26 (October 1974): 32–35; and 26 (November 1974): 37–39.

Harlow, Ralph V. "Aspects of Revolutionary Finance, 1775–1783." *The American Historical Review* 35, no. 1 (October 1929): 46–68.

Hanson, John R. II. "Money in the Colonial American Economy: An Extension" *Economic Inquiry* 17 (April 1979): 281–286.

———. "Small Notes in the American Colonies." *Explorations in Economic History* 17 (1980): 411–420.

Heaton, C.E. "Medicine in New York During the English Colonial Period." *Bulletin of the History of Medicine* 17 (January 1945): 9–37.

Heldman, Donald P. "Coins at Michilimackinac." *Historical Archaeology* 14 (1980): 82–107.

Hume, Ivor Noel. "1972 Excavations at the Colonial Public Hospital Site in Williamsburg, Virginia." *Post-Medieval Archaeology* 7 (1973): 91–92.

Kebler, Lyman F. "Andrew Craigie, The First Apothecary General of the United States." *Journal of the American Philosophical Association* 17 (January 1928): 63–78; and 17 (February 1928): 167–178.

Lender, Mark E. *The Enlisted Line: The Continental Soldiers of New Jersey*. Ph.D. diss., Rutgers University, 1975.

Lender, Mark E. "The Social Structure of the New Jersey Brigade, The Continental Line as an American Standing Army." In *The Military in America, From the Colonial Era to the Present*, edited by Peter Karsten. New York: The Free Press. Revised Edition 1986, 65–78.

Manchester, Katherine E. "General Washington and the Patriot Soldiers, They Won A War With Little Food." *Journal of the American Dietetic Association* 68 (1976): 421–433.

Micheloud, Francois. "Canada's Playing Card Money: A Historical Parabola on Inflation and Deficit Spending." Accessed January 5, 2004, at http://www.micheloud.com/FXM/MH/canada.htm on.

Michener, Ronald. "Comment on Charles W. Calomiris, 'Institutional Failure, Monetary Scarcity, and the Depreciation of the Continental.'" *Journal of Economic History* 48 (September 1988): 682–692.

Morison, Samuel Eliot. *The Ropemakers of Plymouth: A History of the Plymouth Cordage Company, 1824–1949*. Boston: Houghton Mifflin, 1950.

Murphy, Orville T. "The French Professional Soldier's Opinion of the American Militia in the War of the Revolution." *Military Affairs* 33 (1969): 191–198.

Murray, Eleanor M. "The Medical Department of the Revolution." *The Bulletin of the Fort Ticonderoga Museum* 8, no. 3 (January 1949): 83–109.

New York Department of Environmental Conservation. "A Divers' Guide to Lake George: New York's Submerged Heritage Preserves Guide." Albany, NY: n.d.

Norwood, Dr. William F. "Medicine in the Era of the American Revolution." *International Record of Medicine* 171, no. 7 (July 1958): 391–407.

Osborne, George E. "Pharmacy in British Colonial America." In *American Pharmacy in the Colonial and Revolutionary Periods*, edited by George A. Bender and John Parascandola. Madison, WI: American Institute of the History of Pharmacy, 1977, 5–14.

Postell, William D. "Medical Education and Medical Schools in Colonial America." *The International Record of Medicine* 1717 (June 1958): 364–370.

Ravitch, Dr. Mark M. "Surgery in 1776." *Annals of Surgery* 186 (1977): 291–300.

Reynolds, Donald E. "Ammunition Supply in Revolutionary Virginia" *The Virginia Magazine of History and Biography* 73 (January 1965): 56–77.

Riznik, Barnes. *Medicine in New England, 1790–1840*. Sturbridge, MA: Old Sturbridge Village, 1965.

Robertson, John K. "'39 lashes on his naked back...' Military Justice in the Revolutionary War Armies." *The Brigade Dispatch* 33, no. 2 (Summer 2003): 2–7; "Part 2: Articles of War, Continued" *The Brigade Dispatch* 33, no. 3 (Autumn 2003): 23–27.

Salay, David L. "The Production of Gunpowder in Pennsylvania During the American Revolution." *The Pennsylvania Magazine of History and Biography* 99, no. 4 (October 1975): 422–442.

Sellers, John R. "The Common Soldier in the American Revolution" in *Military History of the American Revolution, The Proceedings of the 6th Military History Symposium, United States Air Force Academy, 10–11 October 1974*, edited by Major Stanley J. Underal. Washington: Office of Air Force History, Headquarters U.S. Air Force and United States Air Force Academy, 1976, 151–161.

Shryock, Richard H. "Eighteenth Century Medicine in America." *American Antiquarian Society Proceedings* 59 (1949): 275–292.

———. *Medicine and Society in America, 1660–1860*. Ithaca, NY: Cornell University Press, 1960.

Shy, John. "Logistical Crisis and the American Revolution: A Hypothesis." In *Feeding Mars, Logistics in Western Warfare from the Middle Ages to the Present*, edited by John A. Lynn. Boulder, San Francisco & Oxford: Westview Press, 1993, 161–179.

Snook, George A. "An Eighteenth-Century Hospital at Oswego." *Military Collector & Historian* 38, no. 2 (Summer 1986): 74–75.

Stanley, John Henry. "Preliminary Investigation of Military Manuals of American Imprint Prior to 1800." Master's thesis, Brown University, 1964.

Stephenson, Orlando W. "The Supply of Gunpowder in 1776," *American Historical Review* 30 (1925): 271–81.

Thursfield, Hugh. "Smallpox in the American War of Independence." *Annals of Medical History* 3rd series 4 (1942): 312–318.

Weiss, Roger. "The Issue of Paper Money in the American Colonies, 1720–1774." *Journal of Economic History* 30 (December 1970): 770–784.

West, Roger C. "Money in the Colonial American Economy." *Economic Inquiry* 16 (January 1978): 1–15.

White, John T. "The Truth About Molly Pitcher." In *The American Revolution: Whose Revolution?* edited by James Kirby Martin and Karen R. Stubaus. Huntington, NY: Krieger, 1977, 99–105.

Wicker, Elmus. "Colonial Monetary Standards Contrasted: Evidence from the Seven Years War." *Journal of Economic History* 45 (December 1985): 869–884.

Wilbur, Dr. C. Keith. *Revolutionary Medicine, 1700–1800*. Chester, CT: Globe-Pequot Press, 1980.

Wooden, Allen C. "The Wounds and Weapons of the Revolutionary War From 1775 to 1783." *Delaware Medical Journal* 44, no. 3 (March 1972): 59–65.

Index

Adams, Congressman John 34, 132, 134, 142, 149
Adams, Dr. Samuel 270
Ainslee, Capt. Thomas, British militia 78, 83
Albany 16, 18, 21, 153, 166, 167, 172, 173; logistical base for construction of American fleet on Lake Champlain 200–227
Albany Committee of Correspondence 16, 162, 254
Alison, Surg. Benjamin 162, 255
Amherst, Gen. Jeffery 17, 92, 93, 129, 144, 228, 252
Anbury, Thomas 110
Anderson, Fireship Capt. 77–78
Arnold, Brig. Gen. Benedict 1, 6, 7–8, 9, 10, 12–14, 21, 24, 25–80, 92, 93, 97, 98, 99, 102, 103, 104, 107, 108, 109, 117, 120–149, 154, 165, 174, 176, 181, 182, 183, 184, 186, 198, 251, 270, 271, 272, 273, 275, 276; Battle of Valcour Island 228–250; construction of Lake Champlain fleet 200–227
Arundel 25n
Ausable River 86, 235, 244, 248
Avery, Commissary Elisha 171, 173

Bailey, Col. Frye 129, 221
Bakers 60
Baldwin, Col. Jedutha 104, 170, 187, 193, 194, 195, 196, 209, 210, 211, 251, 252, 259, 262, 274, 275, 276; efforts to fortify Fort Ticonderoga and Mount Independence 180–199
Barber 156
Bateaux 17, 65, 85–87, 98, 122–123, 128–132, 142–143, 148, 160, 172, 182, 187, 202, 205, 208, 216, 233, 234, 241, 267, 272

Beal, Lt. Benjamin 86, 89, 89–90, 107, 124, 147, 151, 210, 262
Bécanour River 110
Bedel, Col. Timothy 92–99, 109, 148, 272
Beebe, Dr. Lewis 86, 100, 101, 127, 131, 132, 145, 147, 163, 164, 166, 261
Beef 20, 23, 125, 173, 259–260, 272
Blacksmith 60, 153, 154, 195, 200, 206, 208, 209, 226, 251
Blake, Merchant John 16
Bloodgood, Simeon 16, 18, 102–103, 106, 141, 143, 171
Bloomfield, Capt. Thomas 21–22, 254
Blunderbuss 216
Bond, Col. William 106, 107, 108
Boom *see* River defenses
Boston 22, 32, 35, 44, 67, 160, 171, 209
Boston Massacre 59–60
Bradstreet, Col. John 17
Bread 88
Breck, Chaplain 163
Brehm, Lt. Diederick, royal engineer 199
Brickett, Brig. Gen. James 220–221, 251, 267
Briggs, Reverend 65–66
British Army 274; advance on Fort Ticonderoga in October 1776 250–266; British Army regiments: 8th Regiment of Foot 92–99; 24th Regiment of Foot 110; 29th Regiment of Foot 82, 110, 115–116, 229; 47th Regiment of Foot 89, 90, 110; 62nd Regiment of Foot 110; uniforms 166
Brown, Maj. John 9, 25–80
Buckshot 256–257
Buel, Col. Nathaniel 108
Burgoyne, Lt. Gen. Jonathan 2, 119, 237–238, 258, 263–264, 264–265, 265–266, 274
Burrall [Burrell], Col. Charles 94, 106, 109

Butterfield, Maj. Isaac 92–99, 148, 272

Caldwell, Maj. Henry, British militia 12, 77
Camleteen 168
Campbell, Lt. Col. 1
Cannon 73–74, 143, 209, 257; 3-pounder 186, 258; 4-pounder 92–99; 6-pounder 82, 117, 198, 211, 240–241, 258; 9-pounder 85, 211, 212, 243; 12-pounder 84, 197–198, 210–211, 211, 212, 243; 18-cannon 186, 260; 24-pounder 239, 240; at Battle of Valcour Island 228–249; carriage 74, 84, 200, 209, 210; explosion 73, 210, 211, 212; premature detonation 73, 211–212; spiked 96; swivel guns 85, 209, 218
Canoes 98, 182, 234, 248
Carleton, Gov. and Gen. Guy 5, 10–11, 13, 78, 82, 90, 178, 181, 227, 270, 274; advance on Fort Ticonderoga and Lake Champlain in October 1776 250–266; Battle of Valcour Island 228–249; proclamation of May 10, 1776 90–91; release of American prisoners on Lake Champlain, October 1776 253–254
Carpenters 153, 154, 160, 195, 200, 202, 205, 208, 209, 226, 251; Connecticut 203, 208, 210; Philadelphia 208; Rhode Island 208
Carroll, Charles, of Carrollton 8, 14, 69, 70, 74, 75, 88
Carroll, Father John 70, 88–89, 109
Catholics 5–6, 14, 70, 107–108, 110
Cedars: Continental Army fort 92–99, 107, 109, 146, 148, 178, 272; rapids 92, 93
Chain *see* River defenses
Chamberlin, Pvt. William 157–158

Chase, Congressman Samuel 69, 70
Chateau Ramezay (Montreal) 75
Chimney Point *see* Fort Crown Point
Chocolate 173
Church services *see* Religious services
Clerke, Sir Francis 241
Clinton, Col. James 9, 10, 30, 62
Clinton, Gen. Sir Henry 119, 264–265
Coffee mill 133
Continental Army artillery 18, 26, 35, 52, 58, 63, 68, 69, 72, 123, 148, 171, 175; Fort Ticonderoga and Mount Independence fortifications 180–199
Continental Army fleet on Lake Champlain 180–184, 217, 251, 252, 253–254, 261; Battle of Valcour Island 228–249; *Boston* 246; *Congress* 176, 180, 204, 207, 213, 214–215, 217, 225–226, 235, 239, 241, 243, 245, 247, 249; *Connecticut* 246; construction at Skenesboro and Ticonderoga 200–227; *Enterprise* 181–182, 202, 225, 238, 247; *Gates* 204, 225, 226, 247, 251, 261; *Lee* 203–204, 225, 247, 249, 261; *Liberty* 181, 201, 202, 218, 225, 247; *New Haven* 246; *New Jersey* 244; *New York* 210, 211, 240–241, 247; *Philadelphia* 203, 209, 210–211, 212, 216, 217, 224, 226–227, 231, 239, 240, 241, 243, 245, 254; *Providence* 211, 216, 217, 222, 223, 225, 234, 246; *Revenge* 181, 202, 218, 225, 247; *Royal Savage* 181, 200, 202, 213, 218, 221, 225, 226, 235, 236, 240, 241; *Spitfire* 244; *Trumbull* 204, 212–213, 221, 225, 225–226, 236, 243, 244, 247, 249, 261; *Washington* 204, 207, 213–214, 217, 224, 225–226, 235, 239, 243, 244, 245, 247, 249, 253–254
Continental Army fleet on St. Lawrence River 84; *Gaspé* 84; *Hancock* 84, 232; *Schuyler* 84, 232
Continental Army regiments 108–109, 147; 1st New Jersey Regiment (Col. William Winds) 87, 107, 109, 175, 179, 189–190, 268–269; 1st Pennsylvania Regiment (Col. John DeHaas) 79, 97–98, 107, 108, 117, 162, 175, 221; 2nd Continental Infantry (Col. James Reed of New Hampshire) 108, 152, 174, 261; 2nd New Jersey Regiment (Col. William Maxwell) 109, 111, 111–115, 175; 2nd Pennsylvania Regiment (Col. Arthur St. Clair) 107, 108, 111, 111–115, 152, 175, 220, 221, 222, 270; 3rd New Jersey Infantry (Col. Elias Dayton) 109, 251, 254, 255, 270; 4th Pennsylvania Regiment (Col. Anthony Wayne) 107, 108, 109, 111, 111–115, 120, 147, 155, 156, 157, 164, 167–169, 175, 220, 260, 269, 270; 5th Continental Infantry (Col. John Stark of New Hampshire) 107, 108, 174; 6th Continental Infantry (Col. Asa Whitcomb) 256, 270; 6th Pennsylvania Regiment (Col. William Irvine) 108, 111, 111–115, 162, 175, 246, 250, 252–253, 270; 8th Continental Infantry (Col. Enoch Poor of New Hampshire) 106, 108, 174–175, 261; 15th Continental Infantry (Col. John Paterson of Massachusetts) 106, 108, 174; 18th Continental Infantry (Col. Edmond Phinney of Massachusetts) 167; 24th Continental Infantry (Col. John Greaton of Massachusetts) 106, 107, 108, 123, 125, 147, 151, 174, 195, 210, 261, 262, 267; 25th Continental Infantry (Col. William Bond of Massachusetts) 106, 107, 108, 174, 221, 267; Col. Brewer's Massachusetts Militia Regiment 176; Col. Charles Burrall's Connecticut Regiment 92–99, 106, 109, 123, 174, 210, 270; Col. Elisha Porter's Regiment of Massachusetts Militia 108, 109, 142, 174, 267; Col. Ephraim Wheelock's Regiment of Massachusetts Militia 154, 156, 163; Col. Mott's Connecticut Regiment 156, 196, 208, 221; Col. Nathaniel Buel's Connecticut Regiment 108; Col. Timothy Bedel's Regiment of New Hampshire Rangers 92–99, 109, 152; Col. Wingate's New Hampshire Regiment 175, 220; Col. Wyman's New Hampshire Regiment, 175; Independent Company of Pennsylvania Riflemen 175; Lt. Col. Joseph Wait's Regiment of New Hampshire Rangers 174
Continental Congress 16–17, 17, 23, 29, 43, 46, 49, 55, 56, 60, 67, 79, 86, 132, 140, 149, 165, 166; Committee on Canada 69–71, 74–75, 76, 81, 87–88, 100, 102, 103, 107, 110, 120
Cooking gear 156, 157–157, 216, 268
Counterfeiting of money 15
Court martial 41, 41–42, 42, 43, 44, 46, 47, 49, 51, 62, 151–153, 165
Crab Island (Island of Saint Michael on Lake Champlain) 234
Craigie, Apothecary Andrew 161
Credit (financial) 15, 148–149
Cross, Uriah 30, 84
Cul-de-Sac Harbor, Quebec 77–79
Cumberland Head (Lake Champlain) 234
Cushing, Capt. Charles 123, 124, 151, 195, 210
Cutter 203–204

Daley, Lt. Patrick 48, 83
David, Rev. Ebenezer 158
Dayton, Col. Elias 109, 251, 254
deAngelis, Pascal 240, 247, 259–260, 262
Dearborne, Capt. Henry 78
DeHaas, Col. Joseph 97–98, 107, 108, 117, 190
DeHart, Maj. William 269
deLorimier, Claude-Nicolas-Guillaume 92–99
Dewey, Adjutant Russel l 63, 65, 68, 72, 73
deWoedtke, Brig. Gen. Baron Frederick 109, 135, 139–140, 145; letters to Benjamin Franklin 137–139
Digby, Lt. William, 53rd foot 259, 260
Dodge, Nathaniel 208
Douglas, Capt. Charles, Royal Navy 229
Dried peas 20, 23
Duel 164
Dufais, Lt., Hesse-Hanau artillery 231, 239, 241, 249
Duggan, Lt. Col. Jeremiah 9, 177; Canadian Rangers 9, 177

East Creek *see* Mount Independence
East Point *see* Mount Independence
Elmer, Lt. Ebenezer 190, 193, 194, 255, 269
Emerson, Rev. William 153, 164
Ensign, Sgt. David 207
Entrenching tools 54, 55, 153, 187
Enys, Lt. James, 29th foot 115, 229, 238
Eyre, Capt. William 187

Fascines 63, 225
Fellows, Col. John 9
Ferris, Squire 246
Ferris Bay (Lake Champlain) 246
Fifteen Oaks (Quinze-chenes) 97
Fireship 77–79, 271
Flour 20, 23, 24, 53, 90, 102, 103, 129, 143, 160, 172, 173, 254–255
Forbes Campaign of 1758 106
Forster, Capt. George, 8th Regiment of Foot 92–99, 109
Fort Anne 21–22
Fort Chambly 23, 67, 84, 88, 89, 100, 101–102, 104, 105, 107, 108, 109, 121, 165, 177, 187, 209, 228
Fort Crown Point 5, 18, 22, 52, 86, 87, 121, 124, 128, 129–130, 139, 170, 171, 172, 175, 181, 182, 209, 211, 228, 243, 244, 247, 272, 274; American Army 128–149; British Army 250–266; Coffin Point (Crown Point) defenses 182, 184–187, 209, 246, 250, 252–253, 276; Grenadier redoubt 185
Fort Detroit 92
Fort DuQuesne 106, 133
Fort Edward 21, 69, 142, 254
Fort Frontenac 17
Fort George 69, 141, 143, 158, 166, 169, 205, 206, 255, 267, 273; American smallpox and general hospital 141–142, 144–145, 146, 150, 158–163, 177, 180, 255–256, 256, 274, 276
Fort Michilimackinac 92
Fort Montgomery 104
Fort Niagara 92
Fort Oswegatchie 92–99, 109
Fort Oswego 17
Fort St. Jean 21, 101, 121, 209
Fort Senneville (near Montreal) 122
Fort Ticonderoga 2, 18, 22, 52, 86, 104, 121, 133, 140, 141, 155, 170, 211, 221, 234, 270, 273, 276; American Army reconstitution 150–179; American decision to establish as main American defensive position 134–137; American defensive position at 180–199; defense against British advance in October 1776 250–266; dungeon 193; Fort Carillon (French Fort) 17, 103, 135, 141, 144, 180; Germain redoubt 135–136, 192; guardhouse 221; half circular redoubt 191, 192; Jersey redoubt 183, 189–190, 191, 192, 199, 260, 261, 270; oblong redoubt 192; old French fort 135–136, 193, 251, 270; old French lines 175, 188, 250, 270; outfitting of American fleet at 200–227; portage 22; sandy redoubt 191–192; Stone Redoubt 135–136, 193, 251
Fort William Henry 7, 144, 187, 212
Franklin, Congressman Benjamin 69–70, 75, 88–89, 102, 142; letters from Brig. Gen. DeWoedtke 137–139
Fraser, Capt. Alexander 248, 259; marksmen commanded by 248, 259–260
Fraser, Lt. Col. Simon 110, 248
Frazer, Capt. Persifor 105–106, 147, 269
Freeman, Commissary Constant 125, 131

Gansevoort, Lt. Col. Peter 205
Gates, Maj. Gen. Horatio 104, 120, 132, 133–134, 234, 267, 268, 269, 273, 275, 276; commander of Northern Theater Army at Fort Ticonderoga 133–276; construction of Lake Champlain fleet 200–227; defense of Fort Ticonderoga and Mount Independence against British Advance in October 1776 250–266; efforts to fortify Fort Ticonderoga and Mount Independence 180–199; efforts to reconstitute American Army at Fort Ticonderoga 150–179
Gautier, Antoine 111–115, 116, 117
Germain, Lord George, British Secretary of State 249, 274
Goldsmith, Lt. 246–247
Gondola 84, 200, 202, 203, 223, 225, 226, 231

Gordon, Brig. Gen. Patrick 177–178
Grant, Mr. Francis 6, 110, 130, 141, 143
Grapeshot 246, 247
Graydson, Capt. Alexander 19
Greaton, Col. John 106, 107, 108, 125, 174, 261
Greenwood, John 98–99, 123, 129
Grenades (hand) 122
Griffinhagen, Historian George B. 126
Gunboats, British Royal artillery 227–249, 260–262
Gunflints 170
Gunpowder 154, 169–170, 171, 255
Guy Fawkes Night 5

Hadden, Lt. James, Royal artillery 143, 229, 231, 236
Hagan, Asst. Surg. Francis 222
Hale, Col. Nathan 179
Halsted, Commissary John 22–23, 36
Harper, QM John 131, 136, 164, 167–169, 260
Hartley, Lt. Col. Thomas 111; Battle of Three Rivers 111–119; commander of Coffin Point Outpost at Crown Point 175, 184–187, 209, 218, 245, 250, 252–253, 276
Haskell, Musketman Caleb 10, 25–80, 89
Hay, Quartermaster Gen. Udny 171, 191
Hazen, Col. Moses 108, 165
Hesse-Hanau artillery at Battle of Valcour Island 228–249
Hewes, Joseph 163
Hildreth, Micah 261
Hill, Jonathan 23
Hodgkinson, Sgt. Samuel 79
Holden, Sgt. Jonas 211
Hospital 7, 9, 10, 26, 27, 28, 3135, 36, 40, 42, 45, 52, 81, 241, 255–256; *see also* Fort George, American smallpox and general hospital
Houses of Office *see* Vaults
Hudson River 18–19, 66, 74, 104, 142, 161, 170, 171, 187, 205, 206, 226, 274
Hughes, Lt. Timothy 206
Hunn, Capt. John 207

Ice, effects on military operations 22, 60, 65, 66, 69, 71, 72, 81, 105, 258, 262, 265, 267, 270, 274
Indian Root *see* Spikenard
Iron furnace 171

Iroquois Confederation 18, 273–274
Irvine, Col. William 108, 111; Battle of Three Rivers 111–119
Isle Aux Noix 103, 150, 234, 241, 272; destruction of American Army 120–149
Isle La Motte (Lake Champlain) 125, 234

Jay, Congressman John 77
Jenks, Merchant John 16, 66, 71
Johnston, Surg. 187
Jones, Capt. Thomas (Royal artillery) 12, 41, 48, 60, 78, 82

Kennedy, Dr. Samuel 157, 255
Kimball, Daniel 68, 74, 76–77, 79, 85, 89
King Bay 234
King George III 5, 274
Knowles, James 10,
Knox, Gen. Henry 18, 22, 171, 209
Knox, Dr. Robert 253

Lacey, Capt. John 103, 106, 121, 122–123, 127–128, 128–129
Lachine 97, 98
Lake Champlain 6, 60, 65, 66, 71, 74, 85, 86, 87, 93, 105, 134, 135, 140, 141, 142, 149, 153, 155, 176, 224, 270, 273, 274; American defense against British Advance in October 1776 250–266; American defensive position at Fort Ticonderoga and Mount Independence 180–199; American fleet 180–183, 200–227; American retreat from Isle Aux Noix 128–129; Battle of Valcour Island and naval engagement 228–249
Lake George 22, 60, 65, 66, 69, 71, 74, 86, 105, 141, 145, 158, 161, 198
Land Tortoise 232
Lantern 242, 244
Latrines *see* Vaults
Lashes *see* Whipping (punishment)
Lead 26, 154, 170–171, 255
Lewis, Col. Morgan 152
Little Island (Petit Isle, Garden Island, Garden Ledge near Valcour Island) 235
Livingston, Col. James 9, 25–80
Livingston, Commissary Walter 173

Mahan, Alfred Thayer 249
Markham, Mrs. Sally 244
Mash, Pvt. Anthony 167

Maxwell, Col. William 19, 23, 79, 109, 111, 175, 250
McAlpine, Loyalist John 259–260, 263
McHenry, Dr. James 161
McLean, Col. 11, 48, 83
McRea, Dr. Stephen 202, 222–223
Medical chests 9, 125, 126, 161, 162, 254
Medicine 9, 125–126, 142, 145, 148, 157, 160–162, 187, 222
Merrick, Surg. Samuel 124, 131, 142
Military chain of command, re-establishment at Fort Ticonderoga 151–153
Military discipline, re-establishment at Fort Ticonderoga 151–153
Military roads: between Crown Point and Fort No. 4 136, 196; between Mount Independence and Vermont 194, 196
Militia at Quebec 11
Moccasins 46, 167
Mohawk Valley 18,
Montcalm, Marquis de 136
Montgomery, Brig. Gen. Richard 1, 6, 19, 27, 29, 43, 75, 102, 166, 181
Montreal 271; American defense at the Cedars 92–99; American withdrawal 120–149; winter of 1775–1776 1–24, 25–80
Morgan, Dr. John 34, 125, 142, 145, 160, 161
Mortars 210
Mount Defiance *see* Sugar Loaf Mountain
Mount Hope 176, 182, 198, 199; defense against British advance in October 1776 250–266; fortifications 197; occupation 197
Mount Independence 155, 157, 174, 175, 177, 194, 196, 208, 209, 210, 211, 226, 234, 270, 273; defense against British advance in October 1776 250–266; fortification 180–199; naming 193; occupation 194

Necessaries *see* Vaults
Nelson, Capt. John 175
New York City 71, 205, 208
Nichols, Lt. Moah 210
Nurses 159

Oars 203, 216, 218, 235
Ogden, Lt. Col. Matthew 46, 179, 189–190

Onions 174
Orderly Book 10, 25–80, 151, 156, 158–159, 163, 168–169, 170, 176, 196, 216, 220–221, 229–230, 231, 257, 260, 262, 263, 267, 269
Orderly sergeant, duties 151–153

Paper money 15–17, 19–20, 23, 50, 72, 148–149, 165
Parke, Lt. Andrew, 8th regiment of foot 92–99
Paterson, Col. John 106, 108
Patrols *see* Raids
Pausch, Capt. George, Hesse-Hanau artillery 229, 231, 239, 241
Pelessier, Christopher 39, 190–191
Pellew, Lt. Edward 238–239, 240
Phillips, Maj. Gen. William, Royal artillery 248–249, 258, 260, 263–264, 265
Playing cards 15
Pleydell, Lt. J.C. 190
Point Au Fer (Point of Iron on Lake Champlain) 234
Point of Rocks (Lake Champlain) 234
Poor, Col. Enoch 106, 108, 127, 165, 261
Porter, Col. Elisha 83, 86, 88, 89, 108, 109, 163
Potts, Dr. Jonathan 142, 144, 145, 158–163, 187, 255–256, 256, 274, 275, 276
Poughkeepsie 104, 171, 205, 207; Continental shipyard 200–227
Pringle, Capt. Thomas 233, 248

Quebec 1–24, 25–80, 81–90, 146, 148, 149, 270, 271, 274; New Years assault 1, 6–7, 8, 270; Palace Gate 39; St. Johns Gate 82; St. Louis Gate 82
Quebec Act 5, 6, 11

Rabble in Arms 1
Radeau 232–233, 234, 240, 245
Raids 177–178, 260, 276
Rations 20–23, 24, 47, 52, 53, 54, 102–103, 129, 146, 156, 172, 172–173, 254–255
Rattlesnake Hill *see* Mount Independence
Red Hot Shot 72
Redoubt 143, 189, 190
Reed, Col. James 108, 152, 158, 174, 175, 261

Regimental adjutants, duties 151–153
Religious services 39–40, 65–66, 147, 163–164, 256
Richelieu River 6, 22, 23, 84, 87, 92, 100, 102, 121, 126, 128, 148, 177, 181, 234
Ritzema, Col. Rudolphus 19
River defenses 103–104; at Fort Ticonderoga across Lake Champlain 251, 251–252, 261
Robbins, Chaplain Ami 87, 108, 157, 163–164, 255–256
Roberts, Kenneth 1, 25n, 36
Rockets (signal) 40
Rodgers, Lt. Thomas 211
Rogers, Maj. Robert 252; see also Rogers Rangers
Rogers Rangers 175–176, 198, 252
Row galley 203–204, 206–207, 215, 225–226
Royal artillery 12, 65, 72, 73–74, 82, 212, 223, 258, 259–260, 262, 274; at Battle of Three Rivers 100–119; at Battle of Valcour Island 228–249
Royal Marines 11, 83
Royal Navy 11, 77, 82–85, 100–101, 211, 223, 227, 271, 274; *Ariadne* 274; *Isis* 82; *Martin* 82, 84, 116; *Niger* 89; *Surprise* 82, 84–85
Royal Navy, Lake Champlain fleet 228–249, 252; *Carleton* 232, 233, 237, 238, 239, 240, 245, 248; *Inflexible* 232, 233, 245, 248, 252; *Loyal Convert* 85, 232, 233, 245; *Maria* 232, 233, 245, 248, 253; *Thunderer* 232–233, 240, 241, 243, 245, 248, 252
Rum 28, 44, 45, 50, 57, 61, 217

St. Anne (near Montreal) 98
St. Clair, Col./Brig. Gen. Arthur 107, 108, 111, 175, 194, 197, 199, 220, 250, 257–258, 263, 267, 275; Battle of Three Rivers 111–119
St. Jean 23, 52, 84, 86, 100, 102, 108, 109, 110, 176, 177, 178, 181, 201; Shipyard at 228–249, 266, 273, 274
St. Lawrence River 1–29, 67, 72, 77–79, 80, 81–91, 92–99, 100–119, 271, 274
St. Lawrence Seaway 93
St. Maurice River 110
St. Regis 94
Salt pork 20, 60, 102, 103, 129, 143, 172, 173
Saratoga 18, 69, 135, 274, 276
Schuyler, QM Harmanus 202; construction of American Fleet at Skenesboro 200–227
Schuyler, Maj. Gen. Phillip 2, 8, 13, 17–18, 19, 21, 34, 46, 50, 52, 53, 56, 60, 65, 69, 84, 85, 86, 102, 103, 133, 135, 137, 139, 153, 154, 166, 171, 180, 187–188, 196, 202, 204, 207, 217, 218, 219, 221, 226, 228, 254, 255, 263, 273, 275, 276
Schuyler Island (Lake Champlain) 244
Scouts see Raids
Scudder, Capt. William 131
Senter, Dr. Isaac 7, 9, 10, 25, 26, 27, 28, 30, 33, 63, 68, 72, 73, 76, 81, 84, 148
Sewall, Henry 195, 201, 215
Sheep 133–134, 173
Sherburne, Maj. Henry 95, 97, 99
Shreve, Lt. Col. Israel 19, 67, 79, 88, 179, 250
Skene, Maj. Philip 200–201
Skenesboro 156, 160, 174, 200–201, 255, 273; construction of American Fleet 200–227, 276
Smallpox 30–34, 38, 48–49, 49, 64, 65, 76, 104, 126–127, 136–137, 141, 142, 145, 149, 150, 158–163, 271, 272, 273; inoculation 32–33, 49, 68, 76, 104, 159–160, 187; vaccination 32
Smith, Historian Justin 84
Smith, 2nd Lt. William P., Royal artillery 1, 17, 231, 239
Snowshoes 26, 28, 48
Soap 156, 173
Sorel 23, 88, 90, 100, 101, 103, 104, 105, 107, 109, 120, 121, 139, 150, 271
Spafford, John 44–45
Spangenburg, Lt., Hesse-Hanau artillery 231
Species (hard silver or gold currency) 14–17, 19–20, 23, 53, 60, 76, 88, 102, 148–149, 165, 166
Spikenard (*Aralia racemosa*) 157–158
Spring, Chaplain 40, 163
Spruce beer 20, 21, 157–158, 172
Stark, Col. John 107, 108, 175
Stevens, Pvt. Benjamin 94, 95, 96
Stevens, Capt. Ebenezer 96, 123, 175, 193, 198
Stewart, Jahiel 224, 235, 238, 240, 260, 262
Stockbridge Mohican Native Americans 175–176, 178, 197, 222, 235, 250, 259
Stringer, Dr. Samuel 125, 142, 144, 160–161
Sugar Loaf Mountain (Mount Defiance) 197–199, 251
Sullivan, Brig. Gen. John 107–108, 109, 110, 117, 120–149, 150, 187, 272
Sullivan, Pvt. Thomas, 49th foot 20

Terrott, Ens. Charles, Royal engineer 241
Thatcher, Dr. James 255, 256
Thomas, Maj. Gen. John 23, 66–67, 74, 75, 76, 79, 81–91, 100, 101, 103, 104, 105, 107, 109, 132, 148, 149, 271
Thompson, Brig. Gen. William 106–107, 109, 110, 111–119, 148, 272
Three Rivers (Trois Rivieres) 66, 71; American attack 100–119, 146, 148, 150, 272; French foundry 39, 190
Trumbull, Col. John 131–132, 146, 162, 166, 173, 194, 196, 197, 200, 207, 253–254, 266
Trumbull, Gov. Jonathan 150, 205, 207, 207–208, 221
Trumbull, Paymaster and Commissary Gen. Joseph 46, 172, 276
Tuttle, Sgt. Timothy 87, 107, 175, 176, 189, 190, 268–269

Valcour Bay/Island 223–224; Arnold's selection of 223–224; naval engagement 228–249
Varick, Capt. Richard 171, 204, 276; obtains supplies for American Lake Champlain fleet 200–227
Variola virus see Smallpox
Vaults 156
Von Clausewitz, Gen. Carl 118–119, 182, 188
Vose, Lt. Col. Joseph 107

Walker, Mr. Thomas (Montreal merchant) 74, 75
Ward, Historian Christopher 25n, 80
Warner, Capt. Seth 221
Warner, Col. Seth 9
Washington, His Excellency Gen. George 8, 18, 33, 35, 65, 67, 128, 133, 134, 155, 164, 165, 171, 172, 204, 205, 206, 208, 267, 269, 275, 276
Wasmus, Surgeon J.F. 241
Watch (timepiece) 53

Waterbury, Brig. Gen. 217, 219, 220, 226, 227, 242, 247, 253
Wayne, Col. Anthony 106, 107, 108, 111, 155, 156, 164, 169, 172, 197, 198, 220, 255, 256; Battle of Three Rivers 111–119; garrison commander at Fort Ticonderoga, winter 1776–1777 268–270
Wells, Ens. Bayze 123, 124, 202, 211, 222, 223, 225, 234, 235, 240, 244, 261
Wesson, Brigade Maj. Frederick 25
West Point, New York 104, 275
Whaleboats 182
Wheeler, Lt. Rufus 256
Whipping (punishment) 42, 151–152
Whitcomb, Lt. Benjamin 177–179, 260, 276
Whittlesey, Capt. Ezra 176
Wigglesworth, Col. Samuel 145, 219, 220, 227, 240, 242, 243, 247
Wilkinson, Lt. (Aide-de-Camp) James 124, 137, 246
Williams, Capt. Edward 99, 130, 141, 201
Winds, Col. William 109, 268–269
Wolfe, Gen. James 10, 12, 255
Wood Creek 21, 201
Wool, Capt. Isaiah 9
Wooster, Brig. Gen. David 9, 12, 13–14, 14, 25–80, 104, 107, 108, 109, 148, 271
Wynkoop, Cdre. Jacob 217–219

Yancey, Deputy Commissary James 254–255
Yates, Robert 104, 206
York, 2nd Lt. John H., Royal artillery 117
Young, Sir James 191

www.ingramcontent.com/pod-product-compliance
Lightning Source LLC
Chambersburg PA
CBHW081539300426
44116CB00015B/2683